OECD EMPLOYMENT OUTLOOK

JUNE 1999

ORGANISATION FOR ECONOMIC CO-OPERATION AND DEVELOPMENT

The OECD Employment Outlook

provides an annual assessment of labour market developments and prospects in Member countries. Each issue contains an overall analysis of the latest market trends and short-term forecasts, and examines key labour market developments. Reference statistics are included.

The **OECD Employment Outlook** *is the joint work of members of the Directorate for Education, Employment, Labour and Social Affairs, and is published on the responsibility of the Secretary-General. The assessments of countries' labour market prospects do not necessarily correspond to those of the national authorities concerned.*

The Organisation for Economic Co-operation and Development (OECD)

was set up under a Convention signed in Paris on 14 December 1960, which provides that the OECD shall promote policies designed:

– *to achieve the highest sustainable economic growth and employment and a rising standard of living in Member countries while maintaining financial stability, and thus to contribute to the development of the world economy;*
– *to contribute to sound economic expansion in Member as well as non-member countries in the process of economic development; and*
– *to contribute to the expansion of world trade on a multilateral, non-discriminatory basis in accordance with international obligations.*

The original Member countries of the OECD are: Austria, Belgium, Canada, Denmark, France, Germany, Greece, Iceland, Ireland, Italy, Luxembourg, the Netherlands, Norway, Portugal, Spain, Sweden, Switzerland, Turkey, the United Kingdom and the United States. The following countries became Members subsequently through accession at the dates indicated hereafter: Japan (28 April 1964), Finland (28 January 1969), Australia (7 June 1971), New Zealand (29 May 1973), Mexico (18 May 1994), the Czech Republic (21 December 1995), Hungary (7 May 1996), Poland (22 November 1996) and Korea (12th December 1996). The Commission of the European Communities takes part in the work of the OECD (Article 13 of the OECD Convention).

Publié en français sous le titre :
PERSPECTIVES DE L'EMPLOI DE L'OCDE
Juin 1999

Photo Credit: Antonio Mio. VCL/Pix

© OECD 1999
Permission to reproduce a portion of this work for non-commercial purposes or classroom use should be obtained through the Centre français d'exploitation du droit de copie (CFC), 20, rue des Grands-Augustins, 75006 Paris, France, Tel. (33-1) 44 07 47 70, Fax (33-1) 46 34 67 19, for every country except the United States. In the United States permission should be obtained through the Copyright Clearance Center, Customer Service, (508)750-8400, 222 Rosewood Drive, Danvers, MA 01923 USA, or CCC Online: http://www.copyright.com/. All other applications for permission to reproduce or translate all or part of this book should be made to OECD Publications. 2. rue André-Pascal. 75775 Paris Cedex 16. France.

TABLE OF CONTENTS

EDITORIAL

Giving Youth a Better Start 7

Chapter 1

RECENT LABOUR MARKET DEVELOPMENTS AND PROSPECTS

Summary 13
INTRODUCTION 15
I. RECENT DEVELOPMENTS AND PROSPECTS ... 15
   A. Economic outlook to the year 2000 15
   B. Employment and unemployment 15
   C. Compensation and unit labour costs 18
II. HOW DO PART-TIME JOBS COMPARE WITH FULL-TIME JOBS? 18
   A. Introduction 18
   B. Main findings 21
   C. Hourly earnings 22
   D. Benefits 25
   E. Training 26
   F. Preferences for part-time and full-time working .. 32
   G. Transitions out of part-time working 34
CONCLUSIONS 35
Annex 1.A: Supplementary Tables 36
Annex 1.B: Data Sources 42
BIBLIOGRAPHY 44

Chapter 2

EMPLOYMENT PROTECTION AND LABOUR MARKET PERFORMANCE

Summary 47
INTRODUCTION 49
MAIN FINDINGS 49
I. EMPLOYMENT PROTECTION REGULATION IN OECD COUNTRIES 50
   A. Definitions and historical context 50
   B. Current standards in employment protection regulation 54
II. EXPLORING THE LINK BETWEEN EPL AND LABOUR MARKET PERFORMANCE 68
   A. Theoretical predictions and prior empirical evidence 68
   B. Effects on employment and unemployment 71
   C. Effects on labour market dynamics 82
CONCLUSIONS 86
Annex 2.A: Detailed Description of Employment Protection Regulation and Practice 90
Annex 2.B: Calculation of Summary Indicators of EPL Strictness 115
Annex 2.C: Summary of the Empirical Literature 119
Annex 2.D: Definitions and Data Sources of the Performance and Control Variables Used for the Analysis in Sections II.B and II.C 126
BIBLIOGRAPHY 129

Chapter 3

TRAINING OF ADULT WORKERS IN OECD COUNTRIES: MEASUREMENT AND ANALYSIS

Summary 133
INTRODUCTION 135
MAIN FINDINGS 135
I. REVIEW OF LITTERATURE 136
II. TRAINING ACROSS COUNTRIES: LESSONS FROM "HARMONISED" SURVEYS ... 138
   A. Sources and definitions 138
   B. The level of training 141
   C. The distribution of training 146
   D. Bivariate analysis of the associates of training ... 154
III. ANALYSES OF TRAINING PROBABILITIES AND EARNINGS OF TRAINEES 160
   A. Main features of the datasets 160
   B. Results of estimation of models of the probability of being trained 162
   C. Results on the relation between training and wages 162
IV. WHAT POLICIES ARE IN PLACE FOR IMPROVING ACCESS TO TRAINING FOR EMPLOYEES? 163
CONCLUSIONS 167

OECD

Annex 3.A: Overview of Findings from Recent Studies of Job-Related Training 168
Annex 3.B: Data Sources, Definitions and Methods for the Analysis in Section III 170
BIBLIOGRAPHY 172

Chapter 4
NEW ENTERPRISE WORK PRACTICES AND THEIR LABOUR MARKET IMPLICATIONS

Summary 177
INTRODUCTION 179
STRUCTURE OF THE CHAPTER 181
MAIN FINDINGS 181

I. HOW COMMON ARE FLEXIBLE WORK ORGANISATION PRACTICES IN OECD COUNTRIES? 183
    A. Indicators of work organisation 183
    B. Comparisons of indicators of work organisation.. 184
    C. Comparisons of change...................... 189
    D. Summary of national patterns................ 189

II. IN WHAT TYPES OF WORKPLACES ARE FLEXIBLE WORK ORGANISATION PRACTICES MOST COMMON? 190
    A. Theory 190
    B. Empirical evidence 193

III. DO FLEXIBLE WORK ORGANISATION PRACTICES TEND TO CLUSTER? 198

IV. WHAT ARE THE LABOUR MARKET CORRELATES OF FLEXIBLE WORK PRACTICES? 200
    A. Theory 201
    B. Empirical evidence 203

CONCLUSIONS 209
Annex 4.A: Sources and Definitions 211
BIBLIOGRAPHY 217

STATISTICAL ANNEX

A Standardised unemployment rates in 25 OECD countries...................... 224
B Employment/population ratios, activity rates and unemployment rates by sex for persons aged 15-64 years......................... 225
C Unemployment, labour force participation rates and employment/population ratios by age and sex........................... 228
D Unemployment, labour force participation rates and employment/population ratios by educational attainment for persons aged 25-64, 1996........ 237
E Incidence and composition of part-time employment, 1990-1998.................... 240
F Average annual hours actually worked per person in employment 241
G Incidence of long-term unemployment from survey-based data in selected OECD countries................... 242
H Public expenditure and participant inflows in labour market programmes in OECD countries........ 245

LIST OF TABLES

1.1 Growth of real GDP in OECD countries 16
1.2 Employment and labour force growth in OECD countries......................... 17
1.3 Unemployment in OECD countries............ 19
1.4 Business sector labour costs in OECD countries . 20
1.5 Median hourly earnings of part-time workers, by gender, 1995 24
1.6 Median part-time hourly earnings, by hours usually worked and gender, 1997 24
1.7 First decile and median part-time hourly earnings, 1995 26
1.8 Distribution of job tenures for part-time and full-time wage earners and salaried employees aged 15 years and older, by gender, 1997 27
1.9 Proportion of temporary jobs within full-time and part-time employment, by gender, 1997 28
1.10 Incidence of training for part-time and full-time workers, by gender, age group and education attainment, 1994................ 30
1.11 Relative incidence of employer-provided training for part-time workers, by gender, 1997......... 31
1.12 Relative likelihood of employer-provided training: hypothetical individuals, 1997................ 31
1.13 Preferences for full-time and part-time employment, 1994 33
1.14 Share of involuntary part-time employment in total part-time employment, by gender, 1997.. 33
1.A.1 Contributions of part-time and full-time employment to overall employment change 1987-97, by gender 36
1.A.2 Median hourly earnings of part-time workers, by gender and sector, 1995 37
1.A.3 Median hourly earnings of part-time workers, by gender and broad occupational group, 1995 .. 38
1.A.4 Incidence and composition of part-time employment of short hours and total part-time employment, by gender, 1997 39
1.A.5 Coefficients from logistic regression model for likelihood of employer-provided training, for men.................................. 40
1.A.6 Coefficients from logistic regression model for likelihood of employer-provided training, for women 41
2.1 Employment protection legislation: illustrative changes since the mid-1980s........ 52
2.2 Indicators of the strictness of employment protection for regular employment 55

2.3	Regulation of temporary employment	62
2.4	Regulation of collective dismissal, late 1990s	65
2.5	Summary indicators of the strictness of employment protection legislation	66
2.6	Comparing EPL indicators in selected studies with new OECD data	67
2.7	Correlation coefficients between EPL indicators and static measures of employment and unemployment	76
2.8	Two-period panel regressions to explain (log) overall unemployment rate	78
2.9	Two-period panel regressions to explain log unemployment rates	79
2.10	Two-period panel regressions to explain employment	80
2.11	Regressions to explain changes in the performance variables, from the late 1980s to the late 1990s	81
2.12	Correlation coefficients between EPL indicators and measures of employment and unemployment dynamics	87
2.13	Two-period panel regressions to explain employment and unemployment dynamics	88
2.A.1	Administrative procedures for individual notice and dismissal	91
2.A.2	Required notice and severance pay for individual dismissal	94
2.A.3	Notice periods and severance pay for individual dismissal at three lengths of service	97
2.A.4	Conditions under which individual dismissals are fair or unfair	98
2.A.5	Compensation and related remedies following unjustified dismissal	101
2.A.6	Compensation pay and related provisions following unjustified dismissal	103
2.A.7	Regulation of fixed-term contracts	104
2.A.8	Regulation of temporary work agency (TWA) employment	107
2.A.9	Procedures and standards for collective dismissal	109
2.B.1	Assignment of numerical strictness scores to first-level EPL indicators	117
2.B.2	EPL summary indicators and weighting scheme	118
2.C.1	Effects of EPL on labour market performance, findings from selected studies	120
3.1	Overview of surveys providing harmonised training statistics	140
3.2	Participation rate in career or job-related training	142
3.3	Volume of career or job-related training	144
3.4	Spearman rank correlations of national measures of the level of career or job-related training across different data sources	147
3.5	Differences in career or job-related training by gender	148
3.6	Differences in career or job-related training by age	150
3.7	Differences in career or job-related training by education	151
3.8	Spearman rank correlations of national measures of the distribution of career or job-related training across different data sources and definitions	152
3.9	Training expectancy given current conditions	157
3.10	Correlations of national measures of training with other measures of human capital and related investments	159
3.11	Correlations of national measures of training with measures of labour market institutions and economic outcomes	161
3.12	Results of estimation of probits of the probability of being trained	164
3.13	Proportional mean wage differences for workers trained	164
3.14	Results of estimation of OLS wage regressions with selection	165
3.A.1	An overview of main findings from recent studies of job-related training	169
3.B.1	Data sources for the analysis in Section III	170
3.B.2	Definitions of variables for the econometric analysis in Section III	171
4.1	Indicators of delegation of responsibility	186
4.2	Percentage of workplace reporting the use of selected work organisation practices, by firm size, 1998	187
4.3	Incidence of selected workplace practices in the United States and Spain	188
4.4	Percentage of workplace in 1996 reporting selected management initiatives over the past three years	188
4.5	Methods of employee involvement, Australia	189
4.6	Flexible work organisation practices by workplace size	193
4.7	Flexible work organisation practices by industry	195
4.8	Correlates of initiatives in flexible work organisation practices	196
4.9	Cross-country differences in the probability of having taken an initiative in flexible work organisation practices	198
4.10	Correlates of initiatives in flexible work organisation practices	199
4.11	Correlates of initiatives in flexible work organisation practices	201
4.12	Percentage distribution of number of flexible work organisation practices	203
4.13	Mean values for labour market outcomes by presence of flexible work organisation practices	204
4.14	Mean values for labour market outcomes by presence of flexible work organisation practices	205
4.15	Mean percentages for labour market outcomes by presence of flexible work organisation practices	206
4.16	Labour market outcomes and initiatives in flexible work organisation practices	208
4.A.1	EPOC survey 1996: gross, actual and weighted samples by country, ranked by weighted share	212
4.A.2	Economic sectors used in the analysis	212

LIST OF CHARTS

1.1	Proportion of women employees working part-time, and of women part-time employees preferring full-time work, 1994	32
2.1	Evolution of the EPL summary indicators, from the late 1980s to the late 1990s	60
2.2	Overall EPL strictness, employment and unemployment	72
2.3	Overall EPL strictness and labour market dynamics	83
2.B.1	Four-step procedure to construct summary indicators of EPL strictness	116
3.1	Alternative definitions of the participation rate in training	141
3.2	Cross-survey indices of the relative level of training: participation rates versus volume	145
3.3	Employers' training costs as a share of total labour costs, 1994	146
3.4	Differences in career or job-related training by literacy level	153
3.5	National differences in the level and concentration of training participation	155
3.6	Participation rate in career or job-related training by labour force status	156
3.7	National differences in training participation and educational attainment	158
4.1	Effect of changes in structural variables on the probability of having taken initiatives in flexible work organisation practices	196
4.2	Effect of changes in characteristics of work on the probability of having taken initiatives in flexible work organisation practices	200
4.3	Effect of changes in compensation variables on the probability of having taken initiatives in flexible work organisation practices	202

EDITORIAL

Giving Youth a Better Start[1]

The situation of young people in OECD countries today and their future prospects is of vital concern to us all. The reasons for concern are obvious: many young people face high unemployment or joblessness and serious difficulties in getting a firm foothold in the labour market; many leave school without the requisite skills or competences needed in today's economy and society; many are also experiencing falling relative (and sometimes real) wages and considerable uncertainty as to whether or not they will be able to settle into good careers. At the same time, with ageing populations in almost all OECD countries, our economies and societies need, more than ever before, to harness the potential of our young people.

Low skills, low pay and poor job prospects for many young people concern societies needing to harness the full potential of this generation.

The stylised facts about youth labour market performance over the past two decades make for sombre reading:

For young people:

- The average employment rate of youth aged 15-24 years in the OECD area has dropped from 53% in 1979 to 45% in 1998, only in part due to rising enrolment rates in education. Worryingly, out-of-school young men have fared particularly badly.

Employment has fallen.

- The average youth unemployment rate in the OECD area stood at 13% in 1998, 3 percentage points higher than in 1979, and is in double-digits in most countries.

Unemployment has risen.

- A hard-core of young people experience prolonged periods of unemployment or joblessness interspersed with spells of low-wage employment. This group exists in most OECD countries and is characterised by multiple disadvantages, *e.g.* they often come from poor families, unstable family backgrounds, live in communities with high overall unemployment, tend to perform poorly in school and often drop-out of school early.

Job problems are concentrated among a core disadvantaged group...

- Inequalities within the youth population, both in terms of employment prospects and earnings, have increased considerably in some countries, especially to the detriment of those with low levels of educational attainment.

... with inequalities rising...

- About one-fifth of all unemployed youths live in households with no one else in employment and that fraction has increased over the past decade.

... and more living in workless households.

However, the picture is not completely bleak. On the positive side of the ledger:

However, more stay on at school, and the number outside both school and work is stable.

- More young people are staying on longer in school and the proportion of dropouts has declined virtually everywhere in the OECD area. For example, the proportion of 18-year-olds in school in 1997 was 67% compared with 50% in 1984.

---

1. This editorial is based partly on the lessons learned at the High-level Conference on "Preparing youth for the 21st century: the policy lessons from the past two decades", jointly organised by the OECD and the US Departments of Labor and Education, 23-24 February 1999, in Washington, D.C. and on the accumulated work on labour market, education and training policies carried out in the Directorate for Education, Employment, Labour and Social Affairs. A follow-up Ministerial-level policy conference is planned for 2000 in co-operation with the United Kingdom authorities.

- The percentage of youths neither in school nor in a job has at least remained relatively stable over the past two decades in the OECD area as a whole.

More jobs need to be created across the economy, but this editorial focuses on specific policies to help young people.

Targeted programmes, on their own, are not *the* answer to giving young people a better start in their careers. As long as overall unemployment remains high, it is unrealistic to expect significant improvement for young people as their employment and unemployment rates are highly responsive to the overall state of the labour market. Hence, there is a premium on designing and implementing policies which will lower overall unemployment on a durable basis. This is one of the main aims of the OECD *Jobs Strategy* which embraces a wide range of macroeconomic and structural policies. The latter include education, training, and targeted labour market programmes which aim to improve young people's prospects in general, and which help disadvantaged youth overcome serious labour market obstacles. The rest of this editorial concentrates on the lessons for the design and implementation of these policies.

Key challenges for policy in the domain of education and training

To reduce upper secondary school non-completion.

- *Preventing failure at school*: The minority of young people who fail to complete upper secondary education nowadays – roughly 25% – find themselves particularly penalised in the labour market in terms of both employment and earnings.

To improve employability, even among those who complete upper secondary schooling.

- *Ensuring that young people, including those who complete upper secondary, are employable, both when they first enter the labour market and over time*: completing upper secondary education is not always a sufficient condition for a stable entry into the labour market as many, perhaps up to 25%, as shown in results from the International Adult Literacy Survey, leave without the occupational qualifications or competences to compete in today's labour market.

Early and sustained interventions, involving everyone dealing with at-risk young people, is needed.

The evidence suggests that, in order to overcome these two challenges, it is vital to intervene *as early as possible* in favour of at-risk youths including education and care prior to the start of compulsory schooling, and *to persist* with these interventions in order to give these young people the best chance to overcome their multiple disadvantages. However, early and sustained interventions must not only focus on the young people in question, but also must involve their families, communities, teachers and social workers. This is the only way to overcome the range of disadvantages they face.

One response is to reform schooling itself, creating new relationships between vocational and general studies...

One *policy response* to these challenges has been to attempt to make schooling diverse, flexible and attractive enough to meet the interests and aspirations of the widest possible range of young people. Various strategies have been adopted to this end:

- *The development and re-appraisal of the vocational stream* within the initial education system: a few examples are Australia, Canada, Spain and the United States.

- The broadening and strengthening of advanced general studies within the vocational stream, thus *further blurring the boundaries between vocational and general or "academic" education,* as in Norway and Sweden.

- The development of *double-qualifying pathways* which provide, in principle, qualifications for both work and tertiary education, offers the opportunity to increase the attractiveness of the vocational stream. In response to such a development, overall participation rates in vocational and technical education have risen in Austria, the Netherlands and Norway.

Another *policy response* seeks to create better linkages between education and employment. This trend, which is underway in many countries, is partly in response to the empirical evidence which shows that the so-called "dual" or traditional apprenticeship systems in Austria, Denmark, Germany and Switzerland have been much more successful in integrating non-college-bound young people into stable employment and jobs, although these systems are also facing challenges and undergoing reforms.

... another is to strengthen linkages between learning and working...

This renewed interest in work-based learning is very welcome, but it is unrealistic to expect many countries to be able to emulate the wide range of specific conditions and institutions that have contributed to the success of the traditional apprenticeship countries. These include: a statutory framework for the definition of and the rights of apprentices; strong links with the educational system; a set of agreed-upon standards of certification of skills which is externally assessed; joint administration of the system by governments, educational authorities, employer organisations and unions; and significant co-financing of the costs via public subsidies and apprentices being paid below the market rates for adult workers. Recognising this, countries attempting to emulate the success of apprenticeship countries have taken many routes:

... but the specific conditions of apprenticeship countries are hard to duplicate, so:

- In countries with a less developed vocational education sector, emphasis has been placed on the development of *unified qualification frameworks*. Such a system of national standards helps employers to both inform training providers and prospective employees of their skill needs and evaluate the skill levels of applicants. It also helps to provide the informational and incentive structures needed to spur pupil achievement, encouraging higher educational aspirations and skill outputs.

some countries use national skill standards and equivalent qualifications to lead change...

- The introduction of *work-based learning* within schools. Many countries are trying to revive or develop their apprenticeship system. Some countries – Australia, Canada, the Netherlands, Norway, Sweden and the United States – have been attempting to reinforce the workplace component within secondary education. But participation in programmes that combine work-based learning with school-based education in Canada and the United States remains low.

... others strengthen work-based learning for students...

- Whatever the type of links between work skills and the content of education, the *involvement of employers or employer organisations in the design of occupational qualifications* is very important in tailoring curricula and programmes to match current and emerging labour market needs. This is done either through advisory committees that assist educational authorities or through tripartite decision-making bodies with strong employer and trade union engagement, as in the apprenticeship countries.

... in all cases strong employer involvement is crucial.

The goals of these policies are both quantitative, *i.e.* to increase enrolment rates at secondary and tertiary levels, and qualitative, *i.e.* to provide young people with the basic skills and competences relevant to the world of work. The available evidence shows that countries that ensure broad pathways with multiple exit points and increase the range of opportunities for young people to cross from one pathway to another have managed to raise the attractiveness of vocational pathways, and thus to increase participation rates. This is a positive development, but more needs to be done to improve the parity of esteem between vocational and "academic" streams. However, the big unanswered question is: What, if any, will be the labour market impacts of these reforms? It will take some time before this question can be answered, but in the meantime it is important that policy reforms are carefully monitored and the requisite data for proper evaluations be gathered and analysed.

In countries with wider options for young people, more are staying in education, but the quality and outcomes of their learning must be carefully monitored.

Key challenges for active labour market policies targeted to disadvantaged youths

Labour market programmes to help disadvantaged young people into jobs have had limited success...

Much optimism was expressed in the past that well-designed and targeted active labour market programmes (ALMPs) could do much to help at-risk youths. Today, we know how difficult it is to develop effective labour market policies for this group. Evaluations of past policies have been fairly discouraging in the sense that few remedial or employment-insertion programmes targeted at disadvantaged young people appear to have resulted in significant gains in employment or earnings after they have participated in the programmes.

... but are more likely to work if:

But this disappointing record does not mean that we should give up on this front. First, some programmes have worked. Second, we are now beginning to know more about what does and what does not work, why and in what circumstances:

... they collaborate with local employers to improve the quality of the jobs...

- *Close contact with the local labour market.* Effective programmes work closely with local employers, doing their utmost to target jobs with relatively high earnings, strong employment growth, and opportunities for individual advancement. Some job programmes do this by assessing the local job market carefully. Tying training to employment in large, stable firms – albeit, in some cases, in relatively low-level jobs – is another path. Programmes that fail to consider adequately the quality of those jobs for which they provide training are more likely to place youths in positions with few prospects for advancement, with inevitable negative effects on their motivation. Programmes that understand the hiring practices of local employers, or to try actively to change these practices through, for example, establishing strong employer support for the programme, are likely to be particularly effective.

... they ensure an appropriate mix and intensity of education and on-the-job learning...

- *An appropriate mix and intensity of education and work-based learning.* Programmes must contain an appropriate mix of academic (or remedial, or basic) education, occupational skills, and work-based learning, in the best cases integrated with one another. These are complementary as they facilitate the development of the full range of competences required in employment. Furthermore, the intensity of both academic and vocational education must be appropriate to the jobs being targeted. Short-term job training lasting 12 weeks on average has, for example, usually been ineffective, and very short 3 to 4-week programmes cannot possibly do better. Short and non-intensive programmes for disadvantaged youths will almost invariably produce disappointing results.

... they ensure that instruction is of high quality...

- *Pay close attention to what is being taught or learned.* Good programmes pay attention to the pedagogy of everything they teach, whether classroom-based or work-based. Poorly-taught basic skills, or occupational education, do not really help individuals master the competences they need for long-run independence. Only well prepared and inspired teachers and trainers will be adequate to the teaching challenges in such programmes, and the lack of attention to teacher training in many programmes is an indication that the quality of instruction is likely to be poor.

... they provide ladders to further learning...

- *Provide opportunities for further education and training.* Effective programmes attempt to provide their students with pathways or "ladders" of further education opportunities, so they can continue their education and training when able. When short training programmes are entirely independent of further education possibilities, the possibilities of such ladders are destroyed.

- *Provide a range of supportive services tailored to individual needs.* Effective programmes also provide a variety of supportive services, tailored to the specific needs of the disadvantaged. This precept has been incorporated in many programmes providing services such as child-care, counselling, and placement services, and caseworkers also act to provide (or find) a variety of services. Of course, there are limits to the range of services a programme can provide. However, a programme that fails to consider the need for supportive services may have low completion rates and be a failure for that reason alone.

... they address related needs of participants such as childcare and counselling...

- *Evaluate programmes rigorously and use the information to improve quality.* Effective programmes collect appropriate information about their results and use these to improve their quality. This precept has been embedded in job training programmes in a few countries, with performance measures required as a way to monitor and enhance effectiveness. While accountability requirements are expanding, they are still often viewed as requirements to be circumvented, rather than mechanisms that might enhance performance. Indeed, rigorous evaluations remain far too few and have not spread to enough countries yet, especially in Europe.

... they use evaluation more constructively than has often been the case...

These are formidable "guidelines" for programmes aimed at helping at-risk young people to meet. In addition, it is likely that they are not the only factors that need to be considered. But the key point is that they are a good starting point in any attempt to design and implement effective programmes.

...none of which is easy...

It is, in this context, important to emphasise that countries are clearly not discouraged by the past disappointing record of targeted labour market programmes for disadvantaged young people. Some new large-scale initiatives have recently started in a number of countries, usually spelling out the rights and obligations of youth, often also targeted at other at-risk groups. Examples include the "New Deal" in the United Kingdom, the social assistance scheme for youth in Denmark, *"Wet Inschakeling Werkzoekenden"* (WIW) in the Netherlands and the programme *"Nouveaux services-emplois jeunes"* in France. It is too early to make any judgement on the effectiveness of such programmes, but it will be crucial to carefully monitor and rigorously assess them.

...but several countries have embarked on ambitious new programmes, which should be watched closely.

Policy imperatives do not, of course, change overnight. They will require *sustained* and *coherent* development involving education, training and labour market authorities, among other actors, working together. To resolve the problems facing disadvantaged and low-paid youth necessitates broad and comprehensive reforms to reduce the large, and in some cases widening, educational and labour market inequalities they face.

Efforts to help disadvantaged young people should above all be co-ordinated and sustained.

3 May 1999

Chapter 1

RECENT LABOUR MARKET DEVELOPMENTS AND PROSPECTS

Special focus on the quality of part-time jobs

Summary

Part-time working has increased over recent years in most OECD countries, sometimes at a rapid rate, and has often made a major contribution to job growth. Along with these developments has come increased concern about the quality of part-time jobs, particularly with respect to remuneration and career prospects. This section takes a new look at this issue by focusing on the hourly earnings and incidence of training of part-time workers in comparison with full-time workers. The analysis of these objective indicators is complemented by an assessment of the preferences expressed by employees for part-time working as against full-time working.

The results highlight the fact that, on average, part-timers tend to receive lower levels of earnings per hour worked, as well as training, compared with their full-time counterparts. They are also less likely to be in stable jobs. To some extent, but by no means completely, these disadvantages reflect the personal characteristics of those working in part-time jobs, including education levels, and the sectors and occupations in which part-time working tends to be found. Part-time working is very heterogeneous, varying significantly across countries and across groups in any given country.

Nevertheless, part-time employment, by comparison with other forms of "non-standard" employment, such as temporary employment and shift-working, tends to be viewed favourably by many employees, both among those who already work part-time and, in many cases, among those who work full-time. Attitudes to part-time working tend to be more favourable, on average, in those countries where it is more strongly developed. As with most international assessments of part-time working, variations in definitions and data limit the conclusions that can be drawn, but these general patterns appear to hold in most of the OECD countries examined.

Chapter 1

RECENT LABOUR MARKET DEVELOPMENTS AND PROSPECTS

Special focus on the quality of part-time jobs

Introduction

While calm and confidence have returned to world financial markets, the performance of the global economy has been mixed. On the positive side, strong non-inflationary growth has continued in the United States; the crisis in Brazil has largely been confined to South America; and the contraction of activity in emerging Asia appears to have come to an end. On the other hand, the European expansion has slowed somewhat; the Japanese economy only now appears to be bottoming out and clear signs of recovery are not yet apparent; there is little prospect of strong growth in emerging markets in the near future; and concerns have been expressed that global deflation could become a problem. Overall, the modest growth that both the OECD area and the world economy have been experiencing since last year is continuing (Table 1.1).[1]

Section I provides an overview of these recent developments and prospects and their labour market implications. Section II contains a special focus on part-time work, which has been one of the major sources of job growth in recent years, in Japan and many European countries. It discusses how the quality of part-time jobs compares with that of full-time jobs, in areas such as hourly earnings and employer-provided training.

I. Recent developments and prospects

A. Economic outlook to the year 2000

During 1999 and 2000 growth in the OECD area is likely to remain sluggish at just over 2 per cent this year and next. This, however, masks significant shifts in regional patterns since last year. The strong momentum of the US economy should start to abate during 1999. In the euro area, consumer spending remains fairly buoyant and should operate to support activity. However, substantial divergences in cyclical conditions across the euro area will persist as the gaps between actual and potential output narrow sharply or close in most countries but remain large in Germany and Italy. In Japan, on the technical assumption that there is no supplementary budget later this year, the contraction in output which occurred last year should come to an end in 1999, but no sustained recovery is on the horizon.

The outlook across the rest of the OECD area is mixed, reflecting a diverse set of cyclical situations. In many countries, prospects are favourable. Australia, Canada, Greece, Hungary, Iceland, Poland and Sweden are likely to continue to enjoy strong, if in some cases moderately slowing, growth. Activity in Korea should rebound, and New Zealand's recovery from last year's recession should gather strength. The United Kingdom, the Czech Republic, Norway and Turkey, on the other hand, will enjoy little or no growth this year and Denmark will slow to below its potential rate. Projected recoveries in these countries in 2000 are fairly weak.

B. Employment and unemployment

Employment growth slowed in the OECD area in 1998, with an annual increase of 1.0 per cent as compared with an increase of 1.5 per cent in 1997 (weighted averages, Table 1.2). Ireland experienced the highest employment growth rate, followed by Mexico, Luxembourg and Spain. Although the rate of employment increase in Mexico was well above average, it nevertheless slowed substantially from the previous year. The rate of employment growth in the United States slowed somewhat, while in OECD Europe on the whole it increased; in both cases it was above average for the OECD as a whole. There was a substantial employment contraction in Korea

---

1. This analysis is taken from OECD *Economic Outlook No. 65*, June 1999.

Table 1.1. Growth of real GDP in OECD countries[a, b]
Annual percentage change

	Share in total OECD GDP 1991	Average 1986-1996	1997	1998	Projections 1999	Projections 2000
Australia	1.7	3.4	3.6	5.1	3.2	3.4
Austria	0.8	2.5	2.5	3.3	2.2	2.6
Belgium	1.0	2.1	3.0	2.9	1.9	2.2
Canada	3.2	2.1	3.8	3.0	2.9	2.8
Czech Republic	0.6	..	1.0	-2.7	-0.5	2.4
Denmark	0.6	1.8	3.1	2.9	1.6	2.0
Finland	0.5	1.5	5.5	4.7	3.3	3.6
France	6.2	2.0	2.3	3.2	2.3	2.6
Germany[c]	8.1	2.6	2.2	2.8	1.7	2.3
Greece	0.6	1.6	3.2	3.5	3.0	3.5
Hungary	0.5	..	4.6	5.1	4.1	3.2
Iceland	0.0	1.8	5.4	5.0	5.1	4.8
Ireland	0.3	5.9	9.8	10.4	7.5	6.7
Italy	5.8	1.8	1.5	1.4	1.4	2.2
Japan	14.1	3.2	1.4	-2.8	-0.9	0.0
Korea	2.2	8.1	5.0	-5.8	4.5	4.3
Luxembourg	0.1	5.5	4.7	5.7	3.3	3.8
Mexico	3.0	2.1	6.8	4.8	3.2	3.7
Netherlands	1.5	2.6	3.6	3.8	2.2	2.4
New Zealand	0.3	1.8	3.0	-0.8	2.6	3.5
Norway	0.5	2.8	4.3	2.1	0.6	2.6
Poland	1.0	..	6.9	4.8	3.5	5.0
Portugal	0.6	3.3	3.7	3.9	3.1	3.2
Spain	3.0	2.8	3.5	3.8	3.3	3.3
Sweden	0.9	1.3	1.8	2.9	2.4	2.8
Switzerland	0.9	1.1	1.7	2.1	1.2	1.8
Turkey	1.6	4.4	7.5	2.8	1.4	3.9
United Kingdom	5.5	2.3	3.5	2.1	0.7	1.6
United States	35.2	2.5	3.9	3.9	3.6	2.0
OECD Europe[d]	**40.2**	**2.2**	**3.0**	**2.8**	**1.9**	**2.6**
EU	**35.2**	**2.3**	**2.7**	**2.8**	**1.9**	**2.4**
Total OECD[d]	**100.0**	**2.6**	**3.3**	**2.3**	**2.2**	**2.1**

.. Data not available.
a) The OECD Secretariat's projection methods and underlying statistical concepts and sources are described in detail in "Sources and Methods: OECD Economic Outlook" which can be downloaded from the OECD Internet site (http://www.oecd.org/eco/out/source.htm).
b) Aggregates are computed on the basis of 1991 GDP weights expressed in 1991 purchasing power parities.
c) The average growth rate has been calculated by chaining on data for the whole of Germany to the corresponding data for western Germany prior to 1992.
d) Average for 1986-1996 excludes the Czech Republic, Hungary and Poland.
Source: OECD Economic Outlook, No. 65, May 1999.

Table 1.2. **Employment and labour force growth in OECD countries**[a]

Annual percentage change

	Employment					Labour force				
	Level 1997 (000s)	Average 1986-1996	1997	1998	Projections 1999	Projections 2000	Level 1997 (000s)	Average 1986-1996	1997	1998	Projections 1999	Projections 2000
Australia	8 451	1.8	0.8	1.9	1.9	1.6	9 251	1.9	0.9	1.3	1.3	1.5
Austria	3 424	0.6	0.3	0.7	0.4	0.5	3 658	0.8	0.3	0.7	0.3	0.3
Belgium	3 773	0.4	0.3	1.4	1.1	0.6	4 314	0.5	0.2	0.4	0.4	0.4
Canada	13 936	1.2	1.9	2.8	2.3	1.7	15 346	1.3	1.3	1.8	1.7	1.6
Czech Republic	4 890	..	–0.6	–1.5	–1.1	–0.5	5 131	..	0.3	0.4	0.2	0.3
Denmark	2 643	–0.2	2.1	2.2	0.6	0.2	2 863	–0.1	1.0	0.7	–0.1	0.2
Finland	2 170	–1.3	2.0	2.4	1.4	1.2	2 484	–0.3	–0.2	1.0	0.5	0.4
France	22 545	0.3	0.4	1.4	1.2	1.3	25 734	0.5	0.5	0.7	0.6	0.6
Germany[b]	33 962	0.2	–1.3	0.0	0.3	0.4	38 347	0.4	–0.1	–0.3	–0.3	–0.3
Greece	3 854	0.7	–0.5	0.2	0.3	0.6	4 294	1.1	–0.6	0.0	0.5	0.5
Hungary	3 567	..	0.3	1.5	1.5	1.3	3 916	..	–1.0	0.4	0.8	1.0
Iceland	131	0.2	2.9	2.1	1.9	1.7	136	0.6	2.1	1.3	1.3	1.2
Ireland	1 380	1.9	4.8	8.4	5.2	3.8	1 539	1.2	3.0	5.4	3.7	3.3
Italy	20 087	–0.3	0.0	0.4	0.4	0.5	22 891	–0.1	0.2	0.3	–0.2	0.3
Japan	65 584	1.0	1.1	–0.6	–1.0	–0.5	67 881	1.1	1.1	0.1	–0.2	–0.1
Korea	21 048	3.0	1.4	–5.3	0.7	2.0	21 604	2.8	2.0	–1.0	1.5	1.9
Luxembourg	227	2.9	3.2	4.4	2.5	2.7	177	1.1	1.4	1.7	1.0	1.0
Mexico	17 557	5.2	13.3	4.9	2.6	2.8	18 237	5.3	11.3	4.3	2.6	2.8
Netherlands	6 400	1.8	3.4	2.9	1.7	1.4	6 775	1.6	2.2	1.4	1.5	1.5
New Zealand	1 736	1.1	0.4	–0.6	0.6	1.9	1 860	1.4	1.0	0.3	0.6	1.3
Norway	2 192	0.2	2.9	2.4	–0.2	–0.1	2 285	0.5	1.0	1.5	0.1	0.4
Poland	15 163	..	1.3	1.2	0.3	1.2	17 100	..	0.1	0.3	0.7	0.9
Portugal	4 297	0.4	1.9	2.4	1.0	0.9	4 609	0.2	1.3	0.5	0.9	0.9
Spain	12 765	0.9	2.9	3.4	2.6	2.4	16 121	1.1	1.1	0.9	0.9	0.9
Sweden	3 921	–0.8	–1.1	1.4	1.7	0.9	4 264	–0.2	–1.1	–0.2	0.7	0.6
Switzerland	3 803	1.1	–0.3	1.2	0.7	0.9	3 991	1.4	0.2	0.0	–0.2	0.6
Turkey	20 505	2.0	–1.9	2.8	0.7	1.6	21 899	1.8	–1.5	2.8	0.9	1.5
United Kingdom	26 885	0.7	1.6	1.4	–0.1	–0.2	28 866	0.3	0.4	0.7	0.4	0.4
United States	129 559	1.5	2.2	1.5	1.9	1.1	136 285	1.3	1.7	1.0	1.6	1.3
OECD Europe[c]	**198 581**	**0.5**	**0.3**	**1.4**	**0.7**	**0.8**	**221 391**	**0.6**	**0.2**	**0.7**	**0.5**	**0.6**
EU	**148 331**	**0.4**	**0.6**	**1.3**	**0.8**	**0.8**	**166 933**	**0.4**	**0.4**	**0.5**	**0.4**	**0.4**
Total OECD[c]	**456 451**	**1.2**	**1.5**	**1.0**	**0.9**	**0.9**	**491 855**	**1.2**	**1.2**	**0.8**	**0.9**	**0.9**

.. Data not available.
a) See note a) to Table 1.1.
b) The average growth rate has been calculated by chaining on data for the whole of Germany to the corresponding data for western Germany prior to 1992.
c) Averages for 1986-1996 exclude the Czech Republic, Hungary and Poland.
Source: OECD *Economic Outlook,* No. 65, May 1999.

while the Czech Republic, Japan and New Zealand experienced more modest declines. Overall, the OECD labour force grew at a slightly slower rate than employment. Ireland and Mexico experienced growth rates well above the other OECD countries, while in Germany, Korea and Sweden, the labour force contracted.

The unemployment rate for the OECD area as a whole declined by one-tenth of one percentage point (Table 1.3). The unemployment rate declined or showed no change in all but four OECD countries in 1998, with Ireland experiencing the largest percentage point decline. On average, the unemployment rate in OECD Europe declined by six-tenths of one percentage point, slightly more than the fall seen in the United States, where the rate remains under half that of OECD Europe. The unemployment rate rose by more than four percentage points in Korea, and by lesser amounts in the Czech Republic, Japan and New Zealand. In November, the seasonally-adjusted standardised unemployment rate for Japan rose above that of the United States for the first time.

Over the next two years, the OECD-wide unemployment rate is expected to remain broadly stable, with only a slight decline in 1999. Within OECD Europe, the unemployment rate is projected to decline by about 0.2 percentage points per year. Ireland and Spain are forecast to have the largest overall percentage point declines. Even with such improvements, unemployment will remain a serious economic and social problem and some countries face particular difficulties. For example, eight OECD countries are projected to have unemployment rates above 10 per cent in the year 2000. Also, although the unemployment rates in the Czech Republic and Japan are below the OECD average, they are expected to continue to increase for 1999 and 2000.

C. Compensation and unit labour costs

In the OECD area as a whole, the rate of growth in compensation per employee in the business sector slowed by about one percentage point in 1998 (Table 1.4). Excluding high inflation countries (Greece, Hungary and Poland), compensation per employee rose by about 2.6 per cent during 1998. The rate of growth remained well below the 4.1 per cent annual growth during the period 1986-1996. The rate of growth in unit labour costs was stable in 1998, despite a slowdown in the growth of productivity. Excluding high inflation countries, unit labour costs grew at a rate of 1.6 per cent, the same as in 1997.

There were signs of tightening in the labour markets of Denmark, Iceland, the Netherlands, Norway, Sweden and the United Kingdom. Those countries experienced below average unemployment rates, accompanied by increases in the rate of growth in compensation per employee and unit labour costs. Ireland, as well, experienced increases in compensation per employee and unit labour costs, although its unemployment rate remained somewhat above the OECD average. In the United States, change in the labour cost indicators remained relatively stable despite the relatively low and declining unemployment rate.

OECD projections indicate a slight increase in the rate of growth in compensation per employee in the business sector for 1999 and 2000. The overall rate of change in unit labour costs is expected to decline slightly in 1999 followed by an increase in 2000. The growth rates for both of these labour cost indicators are expected to decrease substantially in Hungary and Poland, and to a lesser extent in eight other countries. At the same time, in Norway and the United Kingdom an increase in unemployment is expected to offset some of the tightening experienced in 1998.

II. How do part-time jobs compare with full-time jobs?

A. Introduction

In most OECD countries, part-time working has been increasing over recent years, sometimes at a rapid rate. Its contribution to job creation has been important for the OECD area as a whole, for many European countries, and for Japan. Concern is often expressed, however, about the quality of part-time jobs compared with full-time jobs. As yet, there has been no OECD-wide survey of two highly relevant indicators of the quality of part-time jobs – their earnings and training opportunities. This section aims to fill that gap. Despite its possible disadvantages in these areas, part-time working appears to be valued by many workers, for example, as a means for reconciling work and family life. This section thus complements the objective indicators on earnings and training by data illustrating the preferences expressed by employees for part-time as opposed to full-time working.

Since the beginning of the 1970s, most OECD countries have seen a marked growth in the proportion of part-time working in total employment. A particularly rapid rate of growth has been observed in France over the 1990s. The exceptions include the southern European countries, where the incidence of part-time working has remained low, and some of the Nordic countries, where there are some indications of women moving from part-time into full-time working [European Commission

Table 1.3. Unemployment in OECD countries[a]

	Percentage of labour force			Projections			Millions			Projections	
	Average 1986-1996	1997	1998	1999	2000	Average 1986-1996	1997	1998	1999	2000
Australia	8.5	8.6	8.1	7.5	7.4	0.7	0.8	0.8	0.7	0.7
Austria	5.2	6.4	6.4	6.3	6.1	0.2	0.2	0.2	0.2	0.2
Belgium	11.0	12.5	11.7	11.1	10.9	0.5	0.5	0.5	0.5	0.5
Canada	9.5	9.2	8.3	7.8	7.7	1.4	1.4	1.3	1.2	1.2
Czech Republic	..	4.7	6.5	7.7	8.5	..	0.2	0.3	0.4	0.4
Denmark	9.7	7.7	6.3	5.7	5.8	0.3	0.2	0.2	0.2	0.2
Finland	9.3	12.7	11.4	10.6	10.0	0.2	0.3	0.3	0.3	0.3
France	10.6	12.4	11.8	11.3	10.8	2.6	3.2	3.1	2.9	2.8
Germany	8.0	11.4	11.2	10.7	10.0	2.8	4.4	4.3	4.1	3.8
Greece	8.4	10.3	10.1	10.2	10.1	0.3	0.4	0.4	0.4	0.4
Hungary	8.9	8.0	7.3	7.0	..	0.3	0.3	0.3	0.3	..
Iceland	2.6	3.7	2.9	2.4	2.0	0.0	0.0	0.0	0.0	0.0
Ireland	14.8	10.3	7.7	6.4	5.9	0.2	0.2	0.1	0.1	0.1
Italy	10.3	12.3	12.2	12.1	11.9	2.4	2.8	2.8	2.8	2.8
Japan	2.6	3.4	4.1	4.9	5.3	1.7	2.3	2.8	3.3	3.6
Korea	2.6	2.6	6.8	7.6	7.5	0.5	0.6	1.5	1.6	1.7
Luxembourg	2.0	3.3	3.1	3.1	3.0	0.0	0.0	0.0	0.0	0.0
Mexico	3.8	3.7	3.2	3.2	3.2	0.5	0.7	0.6	0.6	0.6
Netherlands	6.9	5.5	4.2	3.9	4.1	0.4	0.4	0.3	0.3	0.3
New Zealand	7.2	6.6	7.5	7.4	6.8	0.1	0.1	0.1	0.1	0.1
Norway	4.5	4.1	3.2	3.5	4.0	0.1	0.1	0.1	0.1	0.1
Poland	..	11.3	10.5	11.0	10.7	..	1.9	1.8	1.9	1.9
Portugal	6.0	6.8	5.0	5.0	5.0	0.3	0.3	0.2	0.2	0.2
Spain	19.7	20.8	18.8	17.4	16.2	3.0	3.4	3.1	2.9	2.7
Sweden	4.5	8.0	6.5	5.6	5.3	0.2	0.3	0.3	0.2	0.2
Switzerland	2.2	5.2	3.9	3.0	2.7	0.1	0.2	0.1	0.1	0.1
Turkey	7.8	6.4	6.3	6.5	6.4	1.6	1.4	1.4	1.5	1.5
United Kingdom	8.8	6.9	6.2	6.7	7.3	2.5	2.0	1.8	2.0	2.1
United States	6.2	4.9	4.5	4.2	4.4	7.8	6.7	6.2	5.9	6.3
OECD Europe[b]	**9.5**	**10.3**	**9.7**	**9.5**	**9.3**	**17.7**	**22.9**	**21.7**	**21.3**	**20.9**
EU	**9.9**	**11.2**	**10.5**	**10.1**	**9.8**	**15.9**	**18.7**	**17.6**	**17.1**	**16.6**
Total OECD[b]	**7.0**	**7.2**	**7.1**	**7.0**	**7.0**	**30.4**	**35.5**	**35.0**	**34.9**	**35.1**

.. Data not available.
a) See note a) to Table 1.1.
b) Averages for 1986-1996 exclude the Czech Republic, Hungary and Poland.
Source: OECD Economic Outlook, No. 65, May 1999.

Table 1.4. **Business sector labour costs in OECD countries**[a, b]

Percentage changes from previous period

	Compensation per employee					Unit labour costs				
	Average 1986-1996	1997	1998	1999	2000	Average 1986-1996	1997	1998	1999	2000
				Projections					Projections	
Australia	4.8	3.7	3.2	3.5	3.6	3.0	0.6	-0.3	2.2	1.6
Austria	4.3	3.0	2.3	2.9	2.8	2.0	1.5	-0.5	1.0	0.5
Belgium	4.0	2.7	2.3	2.5	2.6	2.3	-0.3	0.8	1.6	0.7
Canada	3.9	6.1	1.8	2.7	2.9	2.8	4.1	1.6	2.1	1.9
Czech Republic	..	10.6	9.2	8.8	8.9	..	8.7	10.5	8.0	5.7
Denmark	4.7	3.7	4.8	4.9	5.3	2.4	2.4	3.9	3.2	2.6
Finland	5.6	2.5	4.6	3.1	3.5	1.5	-0.6	2.7	0.6	0.6
France	3.7	2.3	2.0	2.1	2.3	1.5	0.1	0.0	0.8	0.7
Germany[c]	2.9	1.8	1.3	2.6	2.4	1.6	-2.0	-1.4	1.0	0.3
Greece	14.4	10.9	5.9	5.0	4.8	13.2	6.5	2.1	2.0	1.5
Hungary	..	20.4	17.9	9.6	9.8	..	15.4	14.0	6.9	7.7
Iceland	13.5	1.3	8.9	8.4	9.2	11.3	-1.1	5.7	4.8	5.7
Ireland	4.4	5.8	5.9	6.5	6.4	0.0	0.7	4.1	4.1	3.4
Italy	6.6	4.1	-0.1	2.4	2.5	4.1	2.3	-1.4	1.0	0.7
Japan	2.4	1.2	-0.3	-0.7	-0.9	0.0	0.9	2.2	-0.9	-1.5
Korea	13.3	7.5	-1.5	1.7	3.9	7.4	3.5	-1.1	-2.2	1.6
Netherlands	2.5	2.6	3.0	3.8	3.3	1.2	1.6	2.0	3.1	2.0
New Zealand	4.1	2.9	2.4	2.4	2.5	3.4	1.3	2.0	0.2	0.9
Norway	4.8	4.6	5.9	5.2	4.3	2.7	3.0	4.8	4.4	3.8
Poland	..	20.6	14.9	8.6	8.1	..	14.2	11.0	5.1	4.2
Portugal	11.2	5.0	4.5	4.3	4.0	7.5	2.9	2.9	1.9	1.4
Spain	6.1	2.8	1.3	2.2	2.5	3.8	2.0	1.0	1.6	1.6
Sweden	6.6	3.1	5.2	3.7	3.7	4.2	0.3	3.6	2.6	1.4
Switzerland	3.6	2.7	0.9	1.8	1.8	2.9	0.6	0.0	1.5	0.9
United Kingdom	5.8	6.4	6.9	4.9	4.3	4.4	4.4	6.3	4.0	2.3
United States	3.7	3.9	3.9	4.1	4.2	2.9	2.2	2.1	2.1	3.6
OECD Europe[d, e]	**4.9**	**4.2**	**3.2**	**3.3**	**3.2**	**3.0**	**1.7**	**1.5**	**2.0**	**1.4**
EU[e]	**4.9**	**3.4**	**2.6**	**3.0**	**2.9**	**3.0**	**1.1**	**0.9**	**1.7**	**1.1**
Total OECD less high inflation countries[e, f]	**4.1**	**3.5**	**2.6**	**2.8**	**2.9**	**2.5**	**1.6**	**1.6**	**1.4**	**1.7**
Total OECD[d, e]	**4.2**	**3.8**	**2.8**	**3.0**	**3.0**	**2.6**	**1.9**	**1.7**	**1.5**	**1.8**

.. Data not available.
a) See note a) to Table 1.1.
b) Aggregates are computed on the basis of 1991 GDP weights expressed in 1991 purchasing power parities.
c) The average growth rate has been calculated by chaining on data for the whole of Germany to the corresponding data for western Germany prior to 1992.
d) Averages for 1986-1996 exclude the Czech Republic, Hungary and Poland.
e) Countries shown.
f) High inflation countries are defined as countries which have had 10 per cent or more inflation in terms of GDP deflator on average during the 1990s on the basis of historical data. Consequently, Greece, Hungary and Poland are excluded from the aggregate.

Source: OECD Economic Outlook, No. 65, May 1999.

(1994); Smith *et al.* (1998)]. On the OECD definition (see below), the highest figures can now be observed in the Netherlands (just under 30 per cent of total employment), Australia, Switzerland and the United Kingdom (Statistical Annex Table E).

Between 1987 and 1997, the contribution of part-time working to the growth of total employment in Europe was equally as important as full-time employment. For the EU 12 countries (the 12 countries of the former European Community), the average annual growth rate of total employment over this period was the same for the two types of employment, at just over 0.4 per cent (Annex 1.A, Table 1.A.1).[2] Part-time employment growth was particularly important in a number of countries where total employment growth was comparatively slow, such as France and Germany, and often of less relative importance where total employment growth was rapid (such as Ireland and the Netherlands). It was also responsible for the bulk of the average 1.1 per cent employment growth in Japan. However, in the United States, the share in part-time employment fell slightly.

There are few theoretical reasons to expect the productivity per hour of a part-time worker to be lower than the productivity of a full-time worker, other things being equal.[3] However, in practice, things tend not to be equal. It is well-documented that part-time workers have lower levels of education, on average, than full-time workers, and do different types of jobs, in terms of both occupation and sector [EUROSTAT (1997)]. In addition, a number of factors may tend to reduce the level of training employers provided to part-time workers by comparison with full-time workers. For example, part-time workers take as long to train as full-time workers, leaving a shorter time for the training to bear fruit for their employers. In addition, where part-time workers have relatively high job turnover, this is also likely to lead to lower incentives for employers to provide job-related training.

Another important aspect of part-time working is where part-time workers come from and where they go when they leave it. These transitions are an important part of the role played by part-time working in the different national labour markets. For example, in some countries, part-time employment may be mainly a temporary source of employment during periods of unemployment or absence from the labour force, in others it may often be used as the basis for an employment career.

The main objective of this section is, thus, to answer the following questions:

- How do the hourly earnings of part-time workers compare with those of full-time workers, and how does this vary according to the industry and occupation of workers?
- How much training do part-time workers receive compared with full-timers, and can this be explained by factors such as the different ages and education levels of part-time workers and the different levels of experience that they have?
- To what extent do part-time workers say they would prefer to work full-time?
- What is known about the patterns of transition out of part-time jobs into other forms of employment?

The structure of this section is as follows. Sub-section B presents the main findings. Sub-section C provides information on the earnings of part-time workers relative to those of full-time workers. This draws on the recently-released information from the EUROSTAT Structure of Earnings Survey, as well as complementary information for a number of other countries. It includes information on job tenure, known to be an important influence on the level of earnings, as well as data on the relative earnings of part- and full-time workers in a number of occupations and industries. Sub-section D briefly describes the benefit experience of part-time and full-time workers. Sub-section E, on training, refers to a number of factors which can account for part of the observed differences between the training received by part- and full-time workers. Sub-section F contains data on preferences. Sub-section G then presents the limited amount of information available on transitions out of part-time working. Box 1 discusses the definitions of part-time working for statistical purposes.

B. Main findings

The main findings of this section are as follows:

- For the countries for which data are available, the median hourly earnings of part-time workers are lower than those of full-time workers. Without taking account of the differences in the characteristics of part- and full-time jobs, median hourly earnings of part-time workers range between 90 and 55 per cent of full-time earnings, depending on the country. The figures are lower for men than for women. At

---

2. When employment growth is expressed in terms of hours of work, as opposed to the numbers of people employed, the contribution of part-time working to total employment growth for the EU 12 countries falls to between one-third and one-half of that of full-time employment, depending on the country.
3. If a task requires set-up time, this will represent a proportionately greater handicap for the performance of a part-time worker. On the other hand, the performance of a full-time worker may tend to drop off towards the end of the working period, owing to fatigue.

> **Box 1. Definitions of part-time working**
>
> Defining part-time working for statistical purposes is not straightforward. The standard ILO definition refers to work which is significantly lower than the normal hours for the job concerned [Hussmans *et al.* (1990)]. This is the definition used for administrative purposes in some countries. However, such definitions are inconvenient for use in household surveys. These tend either to ask employees if they consider themselves part-time, or base the distinction between full- and part-time working on an hours cut-off considered most suitable for the country concerned. For international purposes, it has been recently concluded that there are advantages in applying the hours cut-off method to all countries, using a common cut-off [Van Bastelaer *et al.* (1997)].
>
> The OECD has decided to define part-time working in terms of usual working hours under 30 per week. This definition is used for the statistics on the incidence of part-time working presented in the Statistical Annex, in Annex 1.A and, as far as possible, in the statistics presented in the two sub-sections below (exceptions are noted in Annex 1.B). However, this does not apply to the information on preferences for part-time working. The available statistics on preferences always leave it to the individuals concerned to make their own assessment of their work status and their attitudes to it. In addition, statistics derived from employer-based surveys, including some of the earnings data presented below, depend partly on the employers' own classification of part-time working.
>
> Different forms of definition, and different choices for the cut-off, can produce considerable differences in the estimated share of part-time working in total employment. However, the ranking of countries is not very sensitive to the choice of definition – countries with relatively high levels of part-time working according to one definition tend to have relatively high levels of part-time working according to another [Van Bastelaer *et al.* (1997)].

least for some categories of part-time workers, and in some countries, benefits are lower than for full-time workers, even on a *pro rata* basis.

- In occupations which employ the highest proportion of part-time workers, the gap between part-time and full-time earnings is relatively small – no more than around 10 per cent for women and 20 per cent for men. However, these are generally occupations where average pay is low for all workers.
- The gap between the hourly pay of the lowest paid part-time workers and the lowest paid full-time workers is smaller than the gap between average workers – owing, perhaps, to the effect of minimum wage legislation.
- There is a limited amount of evidence that hourly earnings of part-timers working under 20 hours a week are lower than those of other part-time workers. The numbers of such part-time workers have been rising at the same rate as the numbers of part-time workers as a whole.
- Part-time workers tend to have lower job tenure than full-timers – in most countries, well over one-half of them have job tenures of under 5 years, while the opposite is true for full-timers. They are also more likely to hold temporary jobs.
- Part-time workers tend to receive less job-related training than full-timers. In European Union countries for which data are available, the average incidence of training for part-timers, *relative* to full-timers, is around 70 per cent for men and 60 per cent for women. Most of these differences remain after controlling for the lower educational attainment and lower job tenure of part-time workers, and the fact that they tend to be found in smaller establishments, different sectors and have a different age structure from full-time workers. There is no evidence that the gap between the training incidence of part- and full-timers decreases with educational qualification.
- In all countries, under one-half of part-time workers indicate a preference for full-time working, or say they are working part-time only because they cannot find full-time work. The higher the proportion of part-time working in total employment in a given country, the lower is the proportion of part-timers wishing to change to full-time.

C. Hourly earnings

Comparisons between the earnings of full- and part-time workers need to be based on earnings per hour, rather than earnings per week or per month. This, unfortunately, makes it somewhat harder to obtain accurate data, for reasons that are explained in Box 2. The sources used here are the employer-based 1995 EUROSTAT Structure of Earnings Survey (SES) and household labour force survey data from Australia, Canada and the United States.[4] They are discussed in detail in Annex 1.B. The data available from the SES permit disaggregations by broad sector and occupation.

---

4. In some cases, Australia, Canada and the United States are excluded from the following tables due to a lack of comparable data.

> *Box 2.* **Part-time/full-time earnings comparisons: measurement issues**
>
> A number of caveats apply to comparisons of hourly earnings data for part- and full-time workers, including the following:
>
> - Data on hourly earnings are likely to be of best quality when they refer to hourly-paid workers and when the data are obtained directly from employer records. In other cases, it is generally necessary to combine data on earnings with data on hours, which tend to be of lower quality. Employers may tend to think in terms of hours paid, rather than hours actually worked, while employees may give only a rough estimate of their actual hours of work.
> - When data are obtained from employers, the distinction between part-time and full-time working may depend on the employers' own classification, which may vary from country to country and industry to industry. In this connection, it may be noted that the specification of the EUROSTAT Structure of Earnings Survey stipulates that "Part-time employees are considered to be those who, in accordance with a contract with the employer, do not perform a full days work or do not complete a full week's work (…). Part-time work rarely exceeds 35 hours, while the normal duration of full-time work is at least about 30 hours". However, even where followed, this allows room for different interpretations by employers.
> - When data are obtained from employers, the coverage may be restricted. For example, the SES excludes enterprises with fewer than 10 employees, as well as certain sectors.
> - When only aggregated data are available, as is generally the case in this section, it is only possible to compare part-time and full-time hourly earnings for rather heterogeneous groups of workers.

For most of the countries for which data are available, the median hourly earnings for part-time workers are indeed lower than those for full-time workers. Hourly earnings of part-time workers represent between around 55 and 90 per cent of those of full-timers, depending on the country (Table 1.5). The shortfall is almost always larger for men than for women. In a few southern European countries, the median earnings of women part-timers appear to be higher than those for full-timers. It is possible that this is partly a statistical artefact, in that some employees with short hours, but without a definite part-time contract, might not have been counted as working part-time.[5] In general, the earning gap between full-time and part-time workers is smaller when the specific characteristics of the workers and jobs are taken into account.[6]

A disaggregation by broad sector indicates that part-timers have lower hourly earnings than full-timers in most sectors and in most countries (Annex 1.A, Table 1.A.2). Overall, the relative hourly earnings of part-timers are lowest in "real estate, renting and business activities", with men earning less than two-thirds and women less than three-quarters of their full-time counterparts. This sector typically employs 15 per cent or more of total part-time employment. However, in the wholesale and retail trade sector, which in most countries employs the largest share of part-timers, the gap is much smaller: women tend to earn more than 90 per cent of the hourly earnings of their full-time counterparts, while men average just over 80 per cent. There are a few cases where part-timers have average hourly earnings matching those of comparable full-timers (*e.g.* men working in construction or women in financial intermediation in some countries), but these tend to be sectors with relatively small shares of the part-time work force.

A disaggregation by broad occupational groups shows particular concentrations of part-timers in service and sales, clerical and low-skilled "elementary" occupations (Annex 1.A, Table 1.A.3). Generally, in the occupations where female part-timers are concentrated, the gap between the median hourly earnings of female part-time and full-time workers is less than ten per cent. The differences for men are generally larger than those for women. It is striking that, for many countries, the gaps between part-time and full-time median hourly earnings within the various occupation groups are all smaller than the gap for all employees taken together. This is explained by the

---

5. The basis for this statement, which remains to be investigated further, is that in response to household surveys asking employees to classify themselves as part-time or full-time workers, many employees in southern European countries working under 30 hours a week (and even under 20 hours a week) fail to report themselves as part-time workers. A similar situation may exist with respect to the enterprise-based data presented in this section (see Box 2).
6. For a detailed analysis using French data, see Friez (1999). Kaukewitsch and Rouault (1998) find that almost all of the difference between the hourly earnings of part- and full-time workers in France, and 95 per cent of the difference in Germany can be explained by the different characteristics of part- and full-time workers and of their jobs.

Table 1.5. **Median hourly earnings of part-time workers, by gender, 1995**
Percentage of median hourly earnings of full-time workers

	Men	Women	All
Australia[a]	..	..	89.4
Belgium	74.7	86.8	78.4
Canada[a]	46.9	69.8	55.9
Denmark	74.2	76.4	74.2
Finland	76.5	90.2	82.6
France[b]	73.2	81.7	73.0
Germany	78.4	87.5	82.5
Greece[c]	79.6	108.8	86.6
Italy	83.1	103.0	87.4
Luxembourg	78.6	77.5	69.5
Netherlands	69.8	93.1	73.2
Portugal	80.8	113.0	90.0
Spain	66.4	84.0	67.8
Sweden	88.7	92.3	87.2
United Kingdom	54.2	69.6	58.0
United States[d]	44.0	62.5	54.3
Unweighted average	**71.3**	**86.4**	**75.6**

.. Data not available.
a) 1997.
b) 1994.
c) Industry only.
d) 1996.
Sources: Australia: ABS, *Weekly Earnings of Employees*, August 1997; Canada: Statistics Canada, Labour Force Survey, 1997; EUROSTAT, Structure of Earnings Survey, 1995; United States: OECD Secretariat calculations using the 1996 US Bureau of Labor Statistics Current Population Survey annual earnings file (outgoing rotation groups).

Table 1.6. **Median part-time hourly earnings, by hours usually worked and gender, 1997**
Percentage of median full-time hourly earnings in each category[a]

	Australia	Canada	United Kingdom[b]	United States[c]
All				
1-20 hours	88.6	54.2	57.7	53.1
21-30 hours	90.6	67.7	69.2	59.0
Men				
1-20 hours	..	43.8	49.6	44.0
21-30 hours	..	56.3	64.1	48.0
Women				
1-20 hours	..	62.1	66.1	60.0
21-30 hours	..	81.5	78.1	70.0

.. Data not available.
a) Categories vary somewhat, as follows: Australia: 1-19 hours, 20-34 hours; Canada: 1-20 hours, 21-29 hours.
b) 1998.
c) 1996.
Sources: Australia: ABS, *Weekly Earnings of Employees*, August 1997; Canada: Statistics Canada, Labour Force Survey, 1997; United Kingdom: ONS, Labour Force Survey, Spring 1998; United States: OECD Secretariat calculations using the 1996 US Bureau of Labor Statistics Current Population Survey annual earnings file (outgoing rotation groups).

concentration of part-time workers in relatively low paid occupational groups.[7]

Labour force survey data from Canada and the United States also permit a disaggregation of full- and part-timers' hourly earnings by educational attainment. In both countries, part-timers in all educational categories earn less than their full-time counterparts. However, the gap is smallest for part-timers with at least some college or university education. At each level of educational attainment, the gap for men is greater than the corresponding gap for women.

Another highly relevant way of disaggregating part-time workers is according to their hours of work. A number of studies, including Dekker *et al.* (1999), Galtier (1998), Hakim (1997) and OECD (1994) have noted that part-time working of very short hours has been tending to grow in a number of OECD countries and have expressed concern that average hourly earnings in such short-hours jobs may be lower than for part-time working as a whole. Data presented in Table 1.6 and Annex Table 1.A.4 show that part-time working of under 20 hours has generally increased in absolute numbers, over the period 1987 to 1997. However, it has not generally increased any faster than part-time working as a whole. It represented just under 45 per cent of total part-time working in both 1987 and 1997.[8] Data presented in Table 1.6 indicate that, at least for the four countries shown, part-timers working 20 hours or less have lower earnings than those working over 20 hours, sometimes substantially so.

A comparison of averages leaves aside the important issue of how the hourly earnings of the lowest paid part-time workers relate to the hourly earnings of the lowest paid full-time workers. This is investigated here by looking at the "bottom decile" of the distributions, that is the maximum earnings of those workers whose earnings are in the bottom tenth of all workers. For part-time workers, the bottom decile of their earnings distribution is lower than that for full-time workers, sometimes markedly so (Table 1.7). However, the table also shows that the gap is generally smaller for the bottom decile than it is for the medians. One factor behind this may be the effects of minimum wage laws and minima in collective agreements, both likely to have a more noticeable effect on the lower hourly earnings of part-time workers. In addition, some countries – particularly in Europe – have laws or legal precedents against discrimination against part-time workers, which may help to mitigate downward pressure on their hourly earnings.[9]

One factor likely to be relevant to differences in earnings is work experience. This is related both to tenure in the job and to the type of contract – temporary or permanent. As shown in Table 1.8, part-time workers are more likely to have short tenures and less likely to have long tenures than is the case for full-time workers. In most countries, the bulk of part-time workers have tenures of under five years, while full-time workers tend to have tenures of over five years. In addition, a comparison of the overlap between part-time and temporary working reveals a greater tendency for part-timers to work in temporary jobs (Table 1.9). A greater share of men in part-time work have temporary contracts than is the case for women: in four countries, over one-half of male part-timers are employed in temporary jobs.

D. Benefits

Comparisons of hourly earnings probably provide a conservative assessment of the overall differences in hourly compensation and labour costs between full-time and part-time work. In the European Union, the legal protection for part-time workers proscribes discrimination by employers against part-time workers in pay, certain benefits, working conditions and redundancy policy [European Council Directive 97/81/EC (15 December 1997)].[10] In addition, in many European countries, collective agreements are used to support the principle that part-time workers are entitled to the same rights and benefits as full-time workers (generally on a *pro-rata* basis) [Cranfield (1997)]. However, in some countries, this does not apply to part-time workers who work below a certain threshold number of hours. For example, public health, old-age

---

7. EUROSTAT (1997), in a comparison of gross hourly earnings in France, Spain, Sweden and the United Kingdom, also found that in all four countries part-timers on average were less well paid than full-timers, and that this was connected with the fact that most part-timers are in low-paid occupations. Grimshaw and Rubery (1997) find similar results in an analysis of highly disaggregated occupational hours and earnings data for Australia, Canada, Germany, France, Norway, the United Kingdom and the United States.
8. The same tendency for part-time working of short hours to represent a roughly constant proportion of total part-time working can also be observed for the 1980s [OECD (1991)].
9. In Europe, the relatively high representation of women among part-time workers is sometimes reflected in a certain amount of legal protection for part-time workers; treatment that has an adverse impact on persons of a particular gender may be deemed to constitute indirect discrimination and, therefore, be considered unlawful. As a consequence, court cases have established that it is unlawful for an employer to discriminate indirectly in pay, unless there are objective reasons not related to gender [Neathey and Hurstfield (1995, p. 170); Thompsons (1997)].
10. This is sometimes bolstered by specific protection in national law. For example, in the Netherlands, the 1996 Law on the Equal Treatment of Part-Time and Full-Time Employment requires equal treatment in terms of hourly earnings and social protection for part-time and full-time workers fulfilling equal functions.

Table 1.7. **First decile and median part-time hourly earnings, 1995**
Percentage of median full-time hourly earnings

	First decile		Median
	Full-time	Part-time	Part-time
Belgium	73	57	78
Canada[a]	51	39	56
Denmark	70	39	74
Finland	74	61	83
France[b]	68	62	73
Germany	70	56	83
Greece[c]	66	75	87
Italy	71	68	87
Luxembourg	63	53	70
Netherlands	66	36	73
Portugal	62	57	90
Spain	58	43	68
Sweden	79	70	87
United Kingdom	57	43	58
United States[d]	52	39	54
Unweighted average	**65**	**53**	**75**

a) 1997.
b) 1994.
c) 1993, industry only.
d) 1996.

Sources: *Canada:* Statistics Canada, Labour Force Survey, 1997; EUROSTAT, Structure of Earnings Survey, 1995; *United States:* OECD Secretariat calculations using the 1996 US Bureau of Labor Statistics Current Population Survey annual earnings file (outgoing rotation groups).

pension, and unemployment benefits in Germany, Ireland, Japan and Sweden have hours or earnings minima for eligibility [Doudeijns (1998); OECD (1998a)].

Outside the European Union part-time workers may be less well protected. They may, in particular, receive fewer employer-provided benefits (*e.g.* paid holidays), although this differential is limited in some cases by law or collective bargaining agreements [Houseman (1997a); Gornick and Jacobs (1996); Thompsons (1997)]. In particular, in the United States, where part-time work is less common than in the average OECD country, part-timers appear to be offered comparatively few benefits. A recent study by the WE Upjohn Institute for Employment Research found that about three-quarters of establishments said that the hourly pay for part-time workers was about the same as for regular employees in similar positions [Houseman (1997a)]. However, nearly 63 per cent said that the cost of hourly pay *plus benefits* was lower. Houseman (1997b) also notes that only about 60 per cent of the establishments claimed to provide over one-half of their part-time workers with at least one of five benefits (paid vacations, sick leave, pensions, profit sharing, or health insurance), while virtually all reported providing at least one of these to their regular full-time workers. A separate study by Lettau (1995) also found that part-timers had lower compensation (*i.e.* wages and benefits) than full-timers, even when their jobs were in the same establishment and occupation. Finally, a report by the US Department of Labor found a clear positive correlation between the number of hours worked and private-sector employer sponsorship of health plans [USDOL (1995)].[11]

For Canada, Lipsett and Reesor (1997) found that part-timers were less likely than full-timers to be entitled to company pensions, health plans, dental plans, paid sick leave, and paid vacation leave. Drawing on the 1995 Survey of Work Arrangements, they present data showing that part-timer entitlement rates for each of these benefits were less than two-fifths of those for full-timers.

E. Training

While information on earnings allows some assessment of the current remuneration of part-time jobs as compared with full-time jobs, data on the incidence of

---

11. In some cases, however, the lack of benefits does not leave part-timers unprotected. The Employment Policy Foundation [EPF (1997)] found that more than one-third of all American part-timers received health insurance from the employer of a relative (*e.g.* a spouse or parent) or other person.

Table 1.8. **Distribution of job tenures for part-time and full-time wage earners and salaried employees aged 15 years and older, by gender, 1997**

Percentages

	All							Men							Women						
	Part-time			Full-time				Part-time			Full-time				Part-time			Full-time		
	Less than 1 year	1 year to under 5 years	5 years or more	Less than 1 year	1 year to under 5 years	5 years or more	Less than 1 year	1 year to under 5 years	5 years or more	Less than 1 year	1 year to under 5 years	5 years or more	Less than 1 year	1 year to under 5 years	5 years or more	Less than 1 year	1 year to under 5 years	5 years or more
Austria	5	7	88	3	13	84	16	18	66	3	11	86	4	6	90	5	16	80
Belgium	13	24	63	11	24	65	15	25	60	10	24	66	13	24	64	12	25	63
Canada[a]	42	36	22	24	34	42	48	34	18	22	31	47	40	36	24	28	40	32
Czech Republic	33	43	24	16	36	48	31	45	24	15	36	49	33	42	25	16	36	48
Denmark	35	37	28	20	30	50	41	42	17	21	29	50	32	34	34	21	29	50
Finland	39	26	35	18	19	62	45	26	28	19	22	59	35	26	40	18	17	66
France	24	27	49	13	23	65	22	25	54	13	23	64	25	29	46	12	22	66
Germany	18	31	51	13	27	59	32	37	31	13	26	62	16	31	54	15	30	55
Greece	15	28	57	11	27	62	13	23	64	10	25	65	17	30	53	12	30	58
Hungary	21	38	41	15	32	53	21	39	41	16	34	50	22	38	41	14	30	56
Iceland	34	33	34	23	25	52	46	35	19	24	24	53	30	32	37	22	27	52
Ireland	29	31	39	18	30	52	29	29	41	17	28	55	47	27	27	19	33	48
Italy	13	25	62	8	24	68	12	25	64	8	23	69	14	25	62	9	25	66
Luxembourg	12	31	57	9	28	63	10	28	61	8	25	67	12	32	56	11	34	55
Netherlands	11	32	57	11	28	61	18	39	43	10	25	65	10	30	60	52	31	17
Norway	26	22	52	22	21	57	39	30	32	22	21	57	24	20	56	21	22	57
Poland	..	..	..	..	..	..	..	..	..	..	..	..	..	..	..	..	..	..
Portugal	19	24	57	16	23	62	26	24	50	16	23	61	17	24	59	15	23	62
Spain	59	19	22	32	15	53	70	17	13	31	14	54	56	20	24	33	16	51
Sweden	20	25	55	11	22	67	34	31	35	11	25	64	17	23	61	10	19	71
Switzerland	21	36	44	15	30	55	26	39	35	14	27	59	19	35	46	18	37	45
United Kingdom	30	34	36	19	29	53	43	37	20	19	28	54	27	33	40	18	31	51
Unweighted average	**25**	**29**	**46**	**16**	**26**	**59**	**30**	**31**	**39**	**15**	**25**	**60**	**24**	**28**	**47**	**18**	**27**	**55**

.. Data not available.
a) Includes self-employed and unpaid family workers.
Sources: EUROSTAT, European Labour Force Survey, 1997; Statistics Canada, *Labour Force Historical Review*, 1997.

Table 1.9. **Proportion of temporary jobs[a] within full-time and part-time employment, by gender, 1997**

Percentage of total employment in each category shown[b]

	Full-time		Part-time	
	Men	Women	Men	Women
Austria	7	10	11	5
Belgium	4	8	25	10
Denmark	10	13	16	8
Finland	13	16	45	35
France	10	11	48	22
Germany	11	15	24	7
Ireland	4	6	61	33
Italy	6	7	56	27
Netherlands	5	10	28	17
Norway	8	12	30	17
Sweden	7	9	43	21
United Kingdom	5	6	25	11
Unweighted average	**7**	**10**	**34**	**18**

a) Temporary jobs are defined as those for which termination is said to be determined by objective conditions such as reaching a certain date, completion of an assignment or return of another employee who was temporarily replaced.
b) Includes wage earners and salaried employees aged 15 to 64 years with either temporary or permanent contracts; excludes non-responses.
Source: EUROSTAT, European Labour Force Survey, 1997.

training allows some assessment of the future employability and earnings prospects that the two sorts of job provide. This sub-section looks at the incidence of employer-provided training – excluding initial training – for part-time and full-time prime-age workers (aged 25 to 54 years), comparing the influence of the hours distinction on the probability of training with other factors. The two data sources used are the International Adult Literacy Survey (IALS) and the European Labour Force Survey (ELFS). (See Chapter 3 for an extensive analysis of training issues and statistics.)

In order to make valid comparisons of the incidence of training with respect to the employment of part- and full-time workers, it is necessary to restrict the age range concerned and the types of training that are considered. One common reason young people give for working part-time is to free-up time to use in further education and training outside the workplace [OECD (1998a)]. For this reason, the comparisons here are restricted to the age-range 25 to 54 years. In order to be relevant for the quality of the job itself, training should be paid for or provided by the employer, rather than by the employee. A jobs-oriented assessment also requires that initial training (*i.e.* training prior to any employment) and apprenticeship training be excluded, as they may not be directly associated with the job.

The IALS survey defines training to include both adult education and training, in a broad definition that includes courses, private lessons, workshops, on-the job training and other forms of structured learning, taken during the 12 months preceding the survey. Additional questions were used to narrow this definition, in order to assess career and job-related training versus employer-provided training. The ELFS guidelines also allow for a number of different definitions of training. In order to focus on employer provided training, a relatively restricted definition was selected. This considers training to be "specific vocational training in a working environment" paid for or provided by the person's employer, during the four weeks preceding the survey, and relevant for the current or possible future job of the respondent [EUROSTAT (1996)]. Courses for personal interests, hobbies or general application (*e.g.* driving lessons) and "dual system" and apprenticeship-type training are excluded. The differences in the definitions mean that the data from the two surveys cannot be compared. In addition, the variation between the ELFS questionnaires used in the different countries precludes international comparisons of levels of training using the ELFS. For this reason, this survey is used here only for comparisons of the *relative* incidence of training received (see Annex 1.B for details of these surveys).

Given their overall characteristics, part-time workers might be expected to have a lower incidence of training than their full-time counterparts. For example, the ELFS data indicate that, on average, they tend to have lower educational attainment and a greater likelihood of working in smaller firms. Both are factors generally associated with lower incidences of training. In most EU countries, small firms tend to have a lower incidence of training than large firms (Annex 1.A, Tables 1.A.5 and 1.A.6).

Data from the IALS survey show this expectation to be generally confirmed. The top panel (A) of Table 1.10 presents IALS data, relating only to career or job-related training. The data are disaggregated by gender, age and educational attainment–sample size restrictions do not permit greater detail to be shown. The bottom panel (B) presents data restricted to training funded at least partly by the employer. The numbers in the bottom panel tend to be smaller, reflecting the fact that employer-provided training is generally career- or job-related (but the opposite is not always true). It can be seen that part-time workers tend to experience a lower incidence of training than full-timers in nearly all of the countries and regions shown.[12] On average, the gap in the incidence of training between part- and full-time workers is greater with respect to employer-provided training than with respect to career and job-related training. Disaggregation reveals, for both full- and part-timers, that the incidence of career and job-related training tends to be higher for the youngest groups of workers and for those with tertiary educational attainment. The age pattern is less pronounced in the case of employer-provided training. A detailed examination coupled with the raw IALS results shows little tendency for the gap between the incidence of employer-provided training for part- and full-time workers to narrow as the level of education attainment rises.

The ELFS data indicate a similar pattern (Table 1.11). These data, which refer to the relative incidence of employer-provided vocational training, also indicate that part-timers tend to have lower training incidences than full-timers.[13] In nine countries, women part-timers experienced training incidences that are more than 25 per cent lower than those for women full-timers; this is also the case for men in three countries. There are some exceptions where part-timers appeared to have incidences that equal or exceed those of full-timers – *e.g.* male part-timers in Germany, Hungary and Ireland. The reasons for these results are unclear.[14]

The ELFS data also allow an estimation of the differences between the *relative* training incidences of part- and full-time workers, after controlling for a number of relevant variables, comprising age, education, job tenure, establishment size and broad industrial sector. This was done by fitting a logit model separately for men and women in eleven countries. The results are provided in Table 1.12. They refer to the probability of training for relatively common categories of part-time workers, relative to the probability of training for workers having exactly the same characteristics, except for being full-time workers. The underlying logit coefficients, most of which are statistically significant, are shown in Annex Tables 1.A.5 and 1.A.6.

Comparing the results in Tables 1.11 and 1.12 shows that controlling for the additional variables does cause some attenuation of the estimated difference for women between the training incidences of part- and full-time workers. The results for men are mixed. However, the estimated impact of the part-time/full-time distinction on the likelihood of training remains substantial. Sometimes, it is one of the most important factors in the model. Nevertheless, generally, at least one other variable has a stronger impact than part-time working status (as measured by the relative sizes of the coefficients). In particular, sector of employment or educational attainment are often more important. Once again, as discussed above, for men in some countries, the estimated incidence of training is higher for part-time working than for full-time working.

---

12. The result for Canada is the sole exception. However, this figure was of low statistical significance. In a contrasting finding, De Broucker (1997) found that part-time workers received less employer-supported training than full-time workers in Canada. His finding was based on a national source, the 1994 Adult Education and Training Survey.
    A number of studies confirm the lower incidence of training for part-timers in other countries. An Australian study found that the incidence of employer support for formal training of part-time workers was only about one-half of that of full-time workers [Fraser (1996)]. Cranfield (1997) found that, in Denmark, Finland, France, Switzerland and the United Kingdom, there was a negative correlation between spending on training and use of part-time employment, which the study suggested might be linked to the use of part-time labour as a means of reducing labour costs. In the United States, a BLS survey found that part-time workers receive less formal training than full-time workers, as well as much less informal training [BLS (1996)]. Frazis *et al.* (1998) also found in the United States a strong, negative relationship between the share of part time workers in a firm and the incidence of formal employer-provided training during the previous 12 months.
13. Due to differences in definitions used in the various national surveys, the training levels and probabilities are not strictly comparable between countries. Therefore, an index presentation is used in Tables 1.11 and 1.12. Data for some EU countries have been excluded on the grounds that the questionnaires departed too far from the standard, or because the results seemed implausible.
14. Disaggregations by age and by job tenure of the incidence of employer-provided vocational training among part-timers in these countries did not point to particularly high incidences of training for part-timers in the 25-to-34 year age group or among those with low job tenure (except for Ireland). Thus, there does not appear to be a particular confounding of initial, dual system or apprenticeship training with the type of employer-provided vocational training considered here. Nevertheless, it cannot be ruled out that the high incidences of employer-provided vocational training shown in the data are exaggerated to some extent by a confounding of employer-provided vocational training with other types of education or training.

Table 1.10. Incidence of training for part-time and full-time workers, by gender, age group and education attainment, 1994

Percentage of wage earners and salaried employees aged 25 to 54 years

	Total		Gender				Age (years)						Educational attainment					
			Men		Women		25-34		35-44		45-54		Less than upper secondary		Upper secondary		Tertiary	
	Part-time	Full-time	Part-time	Full-time	Part-time	Full-time	Part-time	Full-time	Part-time	Full-time	Part-time	Full-time	Part-time	Full-time	Part-time	Full-time	Part-time	Full-time

Panel A. Career or job-related training

Belgium (Flanders)	13	22	–	22	14	20	–	24	14*	18	–	23	–	8*	–	23	19*	37
Canada	42*	37	–	39	43*	34	–	42	52*	40	–	26	–	–	28*	30	56*	50
Germany	17*	21	–	19	17*	25	–	23	–	23	–	15*	11*	16	–	26*	–	25
Ireland	18*	26	–	22	16*	34	–	28	21*	24	–	25*	–	18*	–	27	–	37
Netherlands	24	38	33*	39	23	36	29	40	26	40	14*	33	16*	27	28	40	31	49
New Zealand	37	52	46*	48	36	59	37	53	38	53	36*	50	29	41	31*	55	55	66
Poland	–	20	–	20	–	19	–	20	–	20	–	18	–	10	–	28	–	31
Sweden	::	30	::	32	::	25	::	32	::	28*	::	28*	::	::	::	30	::	40
Switzerland (French)	28	30	–	32	28	25	27*	32	33*	28*	::	28*	::	::	30*	30	42*	40
Switzerland (German)	30*	35	–	35	31*	36	–	39	31*	35	40*	29	–	–	38*	37	–	42
United Kingdom	45	62	–	58	46	69	43*	68	61	61	29*	53	39	50	–	66	76	78
United States	41	50	–	49	41	51	46	48	38	50	36*	51	–	20*	37*	38	56	67
Unweighted average[a]	30	37	40	44	29	39	36	48	35	39	31	43	24	34	32	38	48	55

Panel B. Employer-provided training[b]

Belgium (Flanders)	12	20	–	21	13*	16*	–	21	16*	17	–	21	–	6*	–	20*	17*	35
Canada	::	30	–	32	–	27	–	33	–	33	–	21	–	–	–	25	–	41
Germany	8*	9	–	8	9*	9*	–	7	–	11*	–	7*	9*	7*	–	–	–	11*
Ireland	–	19	–	17	–	22	–	21	–	18*	–	16*	–	14*	–	18	–	26
Netherlands	20	38	–	39	19	36	18*	40	23	39	15*	35	12*	29	23*	39	26	48
New Zealand	24	41	–	38	25	46	18*	41	28	42	23*	40	18*	33	19*	38	36*	54
Poland	–	17	–	18	–	15	–	17	–	18	–	16*	–	9	–	24	–	26
Sweden	44	58	–	54	46	63	32*	56	52	59	45	58	37	44	40	57	54	66
Switzerland (French)	18	26	–	28	19	21	–	26	22*	23*	–	29	–	–	25*	26	–	33
Switzerland (German)	20*	31	–	30	20*	31	–	33	20*	28	30*	28	–	–	29*	31	–	38
United Kingdom	38	59	–	56	38	66	32	65	51	60	27*	52	33	49	–	64	59	74
United States	27*	42	–	43	29*	42	30*	38	21*	43	31*	45	–	16*	23*	31	39*	58
Unweighted average[a]	23	36	–	35	24	50	26	33	29	39	28	43	22	32	27	37	38	56

.. Data not available.
– Not significant: sample size less than 30, or very high levels of error associated with the estimate (coefficient of variation in excess of 33.3 per cent).
* High levels of error associated with the estimate (coefficient of variation in the range 16.6 to 33.3 per cent).
a) Includes only countries where data are available for both part-time and full-time.
b) Includes all training at least partly financed by an employer.

Source: International Adult Literacy Survey, 1994-95.

Table 1.11. **Relative incidence of employer-provided training[a] for part-time workers, by gender, 1997**

Wage earners and salaried employees, aged 25 to 54 years
Percentage of the incidence for full-time workers

	Men Full-time	Men Part-time	Women Full-time	Women Part-time
Austria	..[b]	..[b]	100	65
Belgium	100	79	100	33
Denmark	100	31	100	67
Finland	100	30	100	45
Germany	100	100	100	50
Hungary	100	128	100	76
Ireland	100	100	100	79
Netherlands	100	51	100	43
Norway	..[b]	..[b]	100	53
Sweden	..[b]	..[b]	100	60
United Kingdom	..[b]	..[b]	100	72
Unweighted average	..	..	**100**	**59**

.. Data not available.
a) Based on the incidence of training in previous 4 weeks; excludes "dual-system" or apprenticeship-type training.
b) Sample size too small to allow an estimate to be made.
Source: EUROSTAT, European Labour Force Survey, 1997.

Table 1.12. **Relative likelihood of employer-provided training: hypothetical individuals,[a] 1997**

Wage earners and salaried employees, aged 25 to 54
Index: probability for full-timers = 100

	Men (Age: 25 to 29 years, Education: upper secondary, Job tenure: 1 to 5 years, Establishment size: 11 to 19 employees, Sector: wholesale and retail trade, repairs) Full-time	Part-time	Women (Age: 40 to 44 years, Education: upper secondary, Job tenure: 1 to 5 years, Establishment size: 11 to 19 employees, Sector: wholesale and retail trade, repairs) Full-time	Part-time
Austria	..[b]	..[b]	100	90
Belgium	100	63	100	48
Denmark	100	27	100	69
Finland	100	33	100	49
Germany	100	37	..[b]	..[b]
Hungary	100	124	100	64
Ireland	..[b]	..[b]	100	81
Netherlands	100	62	100	65
Norway	..[b]	..[b]	100	39
Sweden	100	19	100	71
United Kingdom	100	62	100	75
Unweighted average	..	..	**100**	**65**

.. Data not available.
a) Secretariat calculations using logistic regression. See Tables 1.A.5. and 1.A.6.
b) The stepwise regression model used did not retain the working hours status variable.
Source: EUROSTAT, European Labour Force Survey, 1997.

F. Preferences for part-time and full-time working

One of the distinguishing features of part-time employment, as opposed to other forms of non-standard employment, such as shift-working, is the strongly favourable attitude of many employees towards it. This applies both to those who already work part-time and, in many cases, also to those who work full-time. One way of looking at such issues is through the use of attitude data. Such information must always be treated with particular care, as substantial differences in response to questions can result from minor changes in their wording. In addition, information on attitudes must be understood to apply only in the context of the specific institutional arrangements applying in the different countries at the time of the survey. For example, in the case of women with children, many analysts have stressed that attitudes to part-time working may well depend upon the child-care arrangements respondents feel are available to them. As noted in the introduction, the definition of part-time working used here is not the OECD definition of under 30 hours per week, but was left to the appreciation of the survey respondents.

Information on the relative preferences for part-time and full-time working is provided by the 1994 *ad hoc* Labour Market Survey of employees commissioned by the European Commission (1995). While this is a comparatively small survey, conducted for the European Commission by market research organisations, rather than National Statistical Offices, and is subject to relatively large sampling errors, its particular advantage in the present context is that the same questions were asked in all countries.[15, 16] Table 1.13 and Chart 1.1, derived primarily from this survey, show the following:

- In all the countries included, with the exception of Spain, men working part-time show a much higher preference for full-time working than do women (Table 1.13). The proportion of men working part-time who say they would prefer to work full time varies from a one-quarter in the Netherlands to 100 per cent in Portugal.

- The proportion of women part-timers saying they would prefer to work full-time is well under a half

Chart 1.1. Proportion of women employees working part-time, and of women part-time employees preferring full-time work, 1994

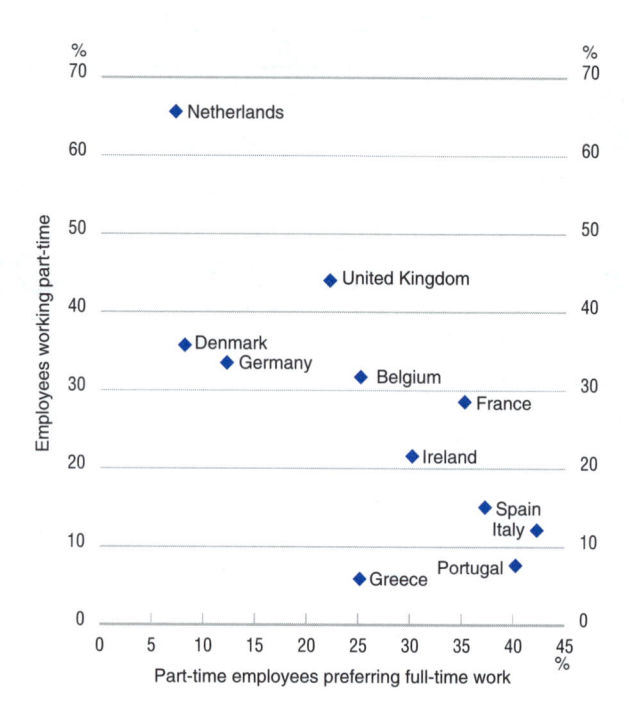

Sources: European Commission (1995); EUROSTAT (1995a).

in all countries, and under 10 per cent in some (Table 1.13).

- The higher the proportion of women working part-time in a given country, the smaller tends to be the proportion of them who say they would prefer to work full-time. For example, in Italy, where 12 per cent of women reported they work part-time, 42 per cent said they would prefer to work full-time. On the other hand, in the Netherlands, where 65 per cent of women worked part-time, only 7 per cent said they would prefer to work full-time (see Chart 1.1, the correlation coefficient is –0.8).

---

15. The precise question posed in the survey was as follows:
    a) If you are a full-time employee, would you rather have part-time employment with a correspondingly lower salary? (Yes/No).
    b) If you are a part-time employee, would you rather have full-time employment? (Yes/No).
16. Figures from the European Labour Force Survey (ELFS) show some changes in preferences for full-time work among women part-time workers over the period 1994 to 1997 for the countries for which suitable data are available. To be precise, in the ELFS as administered in Denmark, France, the Netherlands and the United Kingdom, part-time workers were asked to single out one of the following reasons for working part-time: "in education/training"; "owing to illness or handicap"; "not able to find full-time work"; "full-time working not wanted" (for France, the first two reasons were omitted). In response, in 1994, the proportions of women opting for the last reason were 58%, 63%, 81% and 80%, respectively. In 1997 they were 61%, 61%, 82% and 79%.

Table 1.13. **Preferences for full-time and part-time employment, 1994**

Proportion of employees in category shown[a]

	All		Men		Women	
	Part-timers preferring full-time work	Full-timers preferring part-time work	Part-timers preferring full-time work	Full-timers preferring part-time work	Part-timers preferring full-time work	Full-timers preferring part-time work
Belgium	27	17	31	9	25	36
Denmark	14	13	69	7	8	21
Germany	15	7	52	5	12	10
Greece	25	8	33	8	25	9
France	41	17	69	11	35	28
Ireland	38	10	78	8	30	12
Italy	43	26	83	22	42	32
Netherlands	8	16	25	13	7	23
Portugal	62	5	100	7	40	2
Spain	36	10	36	8	37	14
United Kingdom	29	5	72	3	22	9
Unweighted average	**31**	**12**	**59**	**9**	**26**	**18**

a) For example, the first figure in the first row, for Belgium, indicates that 27 per cent of Belgian employees working part-time said they would prefer to work full-time.
Source: European Commission (1995, Tables 26a-c).

Table 1.14. **Share of involuntary part-time employment[a] in total part-time employment,[b] by gender, 1997**

Percentages

	All	Men	Women
Australia	11.2	17.0	8.5
Canada	31.3	34.9	29.8
Czech Republic	3.1	1.8	3.7
Denmark	13.6	13.1	13.9
Finland	37.6	32.8	40.2
France	41.3	52.9	38.8
Germany	13.3	17.8	12.6
Greece	41.0	50.2	36.0
Japan[c]	15.8	18.9	4.0
Netherlands	5.5	8.2	4.6
Norway	15.7	17.2	15.2
Portugal	21.6	16.1	24.1
Sweden	32.0	34.7	31.3
Switzerland	6.3	8.4	5.8
United Kingdom	12.2	23.8	9.5
United States	7.8	7.4	8.0
Unweighted average	**19.3**	**22.2**	**17.9**

a) Defined as part-time workers who say they are working part-time because they could not find full-time work.
b) For European countries, excludes self-employed and family workers.
c) 1996.
Sources: OECD database on full-time/part-time employment; OECD database on involuntary part-time employment; United States: OECD Secretariat calculations using the March 1997 US Bureau of Labor Statistics Current Population Survey CD-ROM; EUROSTAT (1998).

A wider range of national information is available from statistics which attempt to measure the incidence of "involuntary part-time working". This information is produced by questions asking part-time workers why they are working part-time, taking involuntary part-time workers to be those who reply that they have been unable to find full-time work. Owing to the fact that the questions used differ between countries, international comparisons should be made only with caution.[17] However, in general, it appears that the proportion of involuntary part-time workers is a minority of total part-time working for both sexes. Sometimes, as in the Netherlands, it is only a small minority (Table 1.14). The data show the same general pattern as those in Table 1.13, with the figures for men uniformly higher than those for women. Again, the higher the proportion of women working part-time in a given country, the lower tends to be the proportion of involuntary part-timers among women working part-time. Data on involuntary part-time working generally follow movements in unemployment closely [OECD (1995)]. However, despite the improvement in the economic cycle since 1993, the share of involuntary part-time working has increased quite strongly in France [Forgéot and Lenglart (1997)], as well as in Germany, Greece and the Netherlands.

G. Transitions out of part-time working

Information on transitions into part-time employment has been available for a number of countries for many years. It has been used, for example by O'Reilly (1997) to illustrate the importance of part-time working as an entry mechanism into the labour market, particularly for some types of unemployed workers. However, the retrospective surveys on which this information is based (notably the European Labour Force Survey) often provide no way for assessing the rate of exit from part-time working into other forms of employment. This subsection, therefore, reviews a number of recent longitudinal analyses providing that information for seven countries.[18]

Some general conclusions emerge from these studies:

- The rate of transition out of part-time working into full-time employment is much higher for men than for women [Anxo *et al.* (1999); Dekker *et al.* (1999); Galtier (1998); Bothfeld and O'Reilly (1999); Smith *et al.* (1999)]. At the same time, the experience of women is by no means uniform. Blank (1994) and Hakim (1996) suggest that this is because of a heterogeneity among women: some are relatively constant in their labour market decisions, others change labour market states frequently.

- Transitions out of part-time employment to full-time employment are more frequent for younger, more highly-educated and more highly-skilled workers. In the United States, Blank (1994) finds that less-educated women are more likely to terminate spells of part-time work by leaving the labour market. For both the Netherlands and the United Kingdom, Smith *et al.* (1999) find that professionals and highly-skilled people are more likely to move from part- to full-time.

- For France and the Netherlands, and no doubt for some other countries, part-time workers working very short hours are less likely to move into full-time working than other part-timers [Galtier (1998) for France and Dekker *et al.* (1999) for the Netherlands].

The studies also tend to emphasise the difference in the role of part-time working in the labour markets of different countries, often confirming the impression given by the cross-sectional information provided earlier in this section:

- For Spain, Smith *et al.* (1999) find evidence of considerable instability of part-time working. Longer part-time job tenure seems to decrease the probability of entering a full-time job.

- In the United States, the part-time workforce is dominated by younger and older workers. Part-time working is mainly used as a source of short-term jobs during education and the transition to retirement. Movements from part-time working into full-time working are rare [Blank (1994)].

- For the Netherlands and Germany there is little flow out of part-time working. For women in the Netherlands, Dekker *et al.* (1999) find part-time

---

17. Another possible component of involuntary part-time working consists of people working part-time "for economic reasons", which refers to people whose hours have been reduced because of slack economic conditions. This is not included here.
18. The studies reviewed, the countries they cover, and brief details of the data sources employed, are as follows: Anxo *et al.* (1999): Netherlands, Dutch Socio-Economic Panel, waves 1986 and 1991; and Sweden, Household Market and Non-market Activities survey, matched panel from the 1986 and 1991 surveys; Blank (1994): United States, Panel Survey of Income Dynamics, from 1976 to 1990; Dekker *et al.* (1999): Netherlands, Dutch Socio-Economic Panel, waves 1985 to 1994; Galtier (1998): France, matched samples from national labour force survey (*Enquête-Emploi*), for 1994, 1995 and 1996; Bothfeld and O'Reilly (1999): Germany, German Socio-Economic Panel, and United Kingdom, British Household Panel Survey, both for January 1990 to December 1995; Smith *et al.* (1999): Spain and United Kingdom, matched samples from national Labour Force Surveys, both for Spring 1995 and Spring 1996. Final versions of Anxo *et al.* (1999), Bothfeld and O'Reilly (1999) and Smith *et al.* (1999) are to be published in O'Reilly *et al.* (forthcoming).

employment of longer hours almost as stable as full-time employment. For Germany, Bothfeld and O'Reilly (1999) also find little movement out of part-time working, with almost no movement into full-time working.

- For France and the United Kingdom, there is evidence of a small amount of movement out of involuntary part-time working into full-time employment and voluntary part-time working. For France, Galtier (1998) finds that, out of those women part-timers in 1994 who said they would prefer longer hours, two years later just under a quarter had moved into full-time work and slightly under another quarter were still working part-time but were now satisfied with their hours. For the United Kingdom, Smith *et al.* (1999) find that, over the period 1995-1996, 16 per cent of those part-time women workers who said they would prefer full-time working moved into full-time working.

- For Sweden, the use of part-time working as an interlude in a full-time career, involving transitions first from full-time working to part-time and then back again to full-time, is a common way for women to combine market work with family responsibilities [Anxo *et al.* (1999)].

Conclusions

Part-time working represents a growing share of employment in many countries, and has been an important source of job growth over the past decade. The evidence presented in this chapter confirms that part-time jobs tend to receive lower hourly earnings than full-time ones and experience a lower incidence of employer-provided training than full-time workers. While most men working part-time say they would prefer to work full-time, this is not the case for women.

The importance of part-time working for employment as a whole, and for women's employment in particular, varies considerably from country to country. This chapter shows that a relatively high incidence of part-time working in employment as a whole is associated with a relatively low proportion of part-time workers saying that they would prefer to work full-time, a relatively low proportion of part-time workers in temporary jobs and a relatively large variation in hours of work (when part-time working is relatively common there is a relatively high share of part-time workers carrying out work of both very short hours, and longer hours, close to those of full-time working). On the other hand, it appears that a higher incidence of part-time working is not associated with a higher level of part-time hourly earnings relative to full-time earnings. For training, there is no clear relationship.

The relatively low levels of employer-provided training received by part-time workers, even when they are well-educated, raise questions for policy. If current demographic trends continue, a higher proportion of adults may live in households where no other adult is present. In addition, the mounting pressures on social security and pensions systems emphasise the importance of securing a higher proportion of lifetime income from employment earnings. Recent reports on ageing, including OECD (1998*b*), have highlighted the importance of lifetime learning in this regard. On the basis of the evidence in this chapter, these trends may well pose particular difficulties for part-time workers. Not only are they likely to receive lower levels of employer-provided training, but their lower earnings levels, even on an hourly basis, are likely to make it more difficult for them to finance training themselves. In most countries, transitions from part- to full-time working appears to be rare. The life-time earnings and pension entitlements of part-time workers thus risk being left further behind those of comparable full-timers.

Annex 1.A

Supplementary Tables

Table 1.A.1. **Contributions of part-time and full-time employment to overall employment change 1987-97, by gender**
Percentage of total employment[a] in initial year

	Total employment	Part-time			Full-time		
	All	All	Men	Women	All	Men	Women
Australia[b]	1.75	0.88	0.33	0.55	0.87	0.38	0.50
Belgium	0.44	0.41	0.02	0.39	0.03	−0.30	0.33
Canada[c]	1.25	0.42	0.14	0.28	0.83	0.30	0.53
Denmark	0.43	−0.21	0.14	−0.34	0.63	0.17	0.46
France	0.26	0.29	0.04	0.26	−0.03	−0.21	0.18
Germany[c,d]	0.56	0.68	0.13	0.55	−0.12	−0.02	−0.10
Greece	0.68	0.23	0.09	0.14	0.45	0.11	0.34
Ireland	2.32	0.95	0.24	0.71	1.37	0.51	0.86
Japan[b,c]	1.07	0.76	0.34	0.43	0.31	0.24	0.07
Italy	−0.06	0.31	0.08	0.23	−0.37	−0.40	0.03
Luxembourg[c]	0.76	0.36	0.04	0.32	0.40	0.21	0.19
Netherlands	1.99	0.84	0.00	0.84	1.15	0.69	0.47
New Zealand[b,c]	0.98	0.77	0.28	0.49	0.21	−0.05	0.25
Portugal	0.92	0.44	0.14	0.31	0.47	0.01	0.47
Spain	1.22	0.37	0.08	0.29	0.85	0.20	0.65
United Kingdom	0.66	0.35	0.17	0.18	0.31	−0.04	0.35
United States[e]	1.42	0.12	0.04	0.09	1.30	0.60	0.70
OECD[f]	**0.98**	**0.47**	**0.13**	**0.34**	**0.51**	**0.14**	**0.37**
European Union[f]	**0.85**	**0.42**	**0.10**	**0.32**	**0.43**	**0.08**	**0.35**

a) Total employment is defined as the sum of part-time and full-time employment. Part-time employment is defined as work with usual weekly hours less than 30, except for Japan where it is less than 35 per week.
b) Actual hours instead of usual hours.
c) 1986-96 instead of 1987-97.
d) Data for Germany are for western Germany up to 1991. From 1992 onwards data are for Germany.
e) Wage earners and salaried employees only.
f) Unweighted average of above countries.
Sources: EUROSTAT, European Labour Force Survey; and national Labour Force Surveys.

Table 1.A.2. **Median hourly earnings of part-time workers, by gender and sector, 1995**

Percentage of median hourly earnings of full-time workers

	Mining and quarrying		Manufacturing		Electricity, gas and water supply		Construction		Wholesale and retail trade, repairs		Hotels and restaurants		Transport, storage and communication		Financial intermediation		Real estate, renting and business activities		Total	
	Median	Share of total part-time employment	Median	Share of total part-time employment	Median	Share of total part-time employment	Median	Share of total part-time employment	Median	Share of total part-time employment	Median	Share of total part-time employment	Median	Share of total part-time employment	Median	Share of total part-time employment	Median	Share of total part-time employment	Median	Share of total part-time employment
Men																				
Canada[a]	..	..	47.1	..	..	..	66.7	..	..	..	..	..	63.0	..	..	..	..	..	46.9	..
Belgium	68.4	0.1	94.1	16.5	90.4	0.4	90.8	2.5	77.1	21.9	81.5	19.1	82.9	17.3	100.2	2.4	63.9	19.8	74.7	100.0
Denmark	76.5	0.2	83.8	29.6	66.8	0.1	93.6	18.7	59.3	22.2	75.2	5.9	79.9	7.5	56.6	2.2	54.4	13.7	74.2	100.0
Finland	..	..	84.6	12.0	91.4	0.7	115.2	0.6	80.2	24.5	92.6	14.8	76.8	28.9	54.9	1.6	61.8	16.9	76.5	100.0
France[b]	141.2	0.1	99.3	14.9	67.8	0.4	87.3	2.0	74.6	18.0	98.2	11.7	81.3	6.8	79.9	2.0	59.8	44.2	73.2	100.0
Germany	..	..	90.2	40.6	49.7	3.6	82.7	17.5	85.0	35.5	..	..	..	..	73.3	2.7	..	..	78.4	100.0
Italy	86.4	0.8	101.7	23.2	94.7	1.8	103.6	5.0	134.8	12.3	91.8	5.3	85.9	10.7	75.9	2.6	70.5	38.3	83.1	100.0
Netherlands	..	..	79.8	12.9	..	..	80.8	4.2	68.1	17.3	81.2	7.6	87.0	11.8	88.0	1.9	57.4	43.3	69.8	100.0
Portugal	..	..	81.8	28.8	84.1	0.2	96.3	10.0	70.1	23.2	71.9	10.1	109.1	3.7	32.1	0.2	91.7	23.8	80.8	100.0
Spain	91.7	0.3	72.7	20.2	97.6	0.3	85.1	6.9	81.3	22.2	80.4	20.6	68.9	11.2	87.0	4.2	57.3	14.1	66.4	100.0
Sweden	96.5	0.1	89.6	35.1	121.2	0.9	103.8	6.6	97.5	13.0	89.5	5.5	93.3	18.0	84.7	1.6	75.0	19.1	88.7	100.0
United Kingdom	87.4	0.1	86.7	7.6	91.9	0.2	106.3	1.5	63.6	35.5	65.4	26.0	76.3	7.6	65.2	1.8	44.8	19.7	54.2	100.0
Unweighted average[c]	92.6	0.2	87.7	21.9	85.6	0.8	95.1	6.9	81.0	22.3	82.8	12.7	84.1	12.4	72.5	2.1	63.7	25.3	74.6	100.0
Women																				
Canada[a]	..	..	71.5	..	..	..	88.0	..	..	..	..	..	75.9	..	..	..	..	..	69.8	..
Belgium	83.1	..	100.5	10.6	99.3	0.6	93.7	1.3	91.3	42.7	91.4	7.3	89.6	5.3	102.0	10.3	76.6	21.8	86.8	100.0
Denmark	83.7	..	87.3	21.7	92.1	0.2	87.7	2.1	79.5	28.6	86.4	10.2	90.7	2.6	89.7	10.3	69.1	24.3	76.4	100.0
Finland	122.6	0.1	99.7	5.1	85.9	0.5	103.6	0.4	96.7	44.6	100.8	13.3	81.9	18.8	100.0	9.4	75.7	7.7	90.2	100.0
France[b]	226.1	0.1	96.7	13.9	117.7	0.5	74.1	1.5	89.3	31.0	99.9	11.4	84.2	2.1	82.2	2.9	73.4	36.6	81.7	100.0
Germany	71.5	0.2	82.3	23.9	89.3	1.4	83.5	8.5	99.3	60.7	..	..	..	..	97.9	5.3	..	..	87.5	100.0
Italy	182.7	0.3	109.8	29.6	95.3	0.5	92.7	1.3	108.3	22.9	98.3	7.0	86.0	11.4	98.4	4.4	90.1	22.4	103.0	100.0
Netherlands	..	0.0	98.7	11.5	..	..	96.0	1.2	96.1	28.5	98.2	6.3	113.8	7.3	100.9	6.6	82.1	38.0	93.1	100.0
Portugal	41.2	0.1	98.6	29.1	78.9	0.1	89.9	2.6	96.0	44.2	97.1	10.0	70.3	3.6	59.9	2.0	84.4	8.4	113.0	100.0
Spain	78.2	0.1	82.9	16.9	43.9	0.4	80.1	2.9	101.0	41.2	93.3	14.9	64.5	4.7	72.6	2.2	73.8	16.7	84.0	100.0
Sweden	87.2	0.1	95.6	22.6	105.2	0.6	105.9	2.4	93.9	37.6	88.6	5.0	96.9	7.4	93.3	5.8	84.3	18.4	92.3	100.0
United Kingdom	57.2	0.1	83.6	8.9	86.2	0.3	82.9	1.3	80.7	44.4	81.9	19.1	80.6	3.0	82.3	5.0	63.6	17.8	69.6	100.0
Unweighted average[c]	103.4	0.1	94.2	17.6	89.4	0.5	90.0	2.3	93.8	38.8	93.6	10.4	85.8	6.6	89.0	5.8	77.3	21.2	88.9	100.0

.. Data not available.
a) 1997. Due to differences in industrial classification, not all sectors are shown. Total for Canada covers all sectors, including those not shown here.
b) 1994.
c) Excludes Canada.
Sources: EUROSTAT, Structure of Earnings Survey, 1995; Statistics Canada, Labour Force Survey, 1997.

Table 1.A.3. Median hourly earnings of part-time workers, by gender and broad occupational group, 1995

Percentage of median hourly earnings of full-time workers

	Legislators, senior officials Median	Legislators, senior officials Share of total part-time employment	Professionals Median	Professionals Share of total part-time employment	Technicians and associate professionals Median	Technicians and associate professionals Share of total part-time employment	Clerks Median	Clerks Share of total part-time employment	Service workers and sales workers Median	Service workers and sales workers Share of total part-time employment	Craft and related trade workers Median	Craft and related trade workers Share of total part-time employment	Plant and machine operators and assemblers Median	Plant and machine operators and assemblers Share of total part-time employment	Elementary occupations Median	Elementary occupations Share of total part-time employment	Total Median	Total Share of total part-time employment
Men																		
Belgium	106.2	2.8	91.7	2.9	88.2	6.6	81.6	12.6	74.7	29.2	93.1	10.0	84.6	13.1	85.0	23.0	74.7	100.0
Denmark	116.9	0.4	77.4	0.8	65.4	2.1	69.8	2.4	71.4	14.6	95.2	23.2	92.6	18.4	80.7	37.5	74.2	100.0
Finland	100.9	0.8	104.4	3.6	69.8	6.6	84.3	11.1	89.7	34.7	90.4	2.7	97.7	2.9	85.3	37.6	76.5	100.0
France[a]	151.3	3.0	86.7	4.2	66.6	11.0	77.5	5.7	91.9	16.1	90.6	18.8	97.0	18.9	93.1	22.4	73.2	100.0
Germany	94.0	3.4	107.8	5.1	71.0	8.4	69.5	12.9	81.0	17.8	88.5	21.7	80.9	6.4	80.7	24.4	78.4	100.0
Italy	144.1	0.5	88.2	0.5	79.3	7.0	93.3	21.5	83.3	31.3	102.9	13.4	104.7	8.1	83.5	17.6	83.1	100.0
Netherlands	67.6	5.5	71.1	9.1	67.5	13.2	68.0	13.7	68.4	13.1	74.8	16.8	76.4	13.2	74.4	15.3	69.8	100.0
Portugal	118.2	6.1	87.1	7.1	54.7	7.5	49.0	8.3	79.1	15.0	86.4	16.8	106.9	8.5	104.6	30.6	80.8	100.0
Spain	108.3	4.7	92.6	10.4	72.7	6.6	66.3	14.8	83.6	15.9	70.2	8.3	66.5	13.7	80.3	25.7	66.4	100.0
Sweden	..	..	101.0	5.1	106.4	10.1	88.4	8.7	97.1	7.5	96.6	18.4	91.4	22.6	95.4	26.3	88.7	100.0
United Kingdom	109.7	4.6	105.9	2.4	81.2	2.4	76.6	16.7	75.6	39.4	90.3	5.3	83.1	8.7	68.2	20.5	54.2	100.0
Unweighted average	111.7	3.2	92.2	4.7	74.8	7.4	74.9	11.7	81.4	21.3	89.0	14.1	89.3	12.2	84.7	25.5	74.6	100.0
Women																		
Belgium	100.2	0.7	102.3	1.9	104.8	5.9	101.6	26.2	106.1	36.2	105.0	3.5	105.5	2.2	99.3	23.3	86.8	100.0
Denmark	91.7	0.3	95.8	1.2	96.5	7.8	97.4	11.8	92.0	27.8	91.6	2.8	95.5	10.4	90.7	37.5	76.4	100.0
Finland	89.3	0.1	94.5	2.8	93.3	3.6	98.1	15.2	100.4	49.4	93.9	0.7	96.0	0.9	94.8	27.3	90.2	100.0
France[a]	65.8	0.9	94.2	1.3	64.2	14.8	83.1	20.9	97.7	25.4	94.6	9.9	99.8	7.6	98.1	19.2	81.7	100.0
Germany	62.3	0.4	86.5	3.6	83.6	6.6	85.8	27.1	113.4	47.8	93.6	4.6	91.0	1.5	99.9	8.3	87.5	100.0
Italy	..	..	68.8	0.1	79.7	3.2	101.3	36.9	100.6	23.6	111.3	9.4	111.1	7.0	92.8	19.7	103.0	100.0
Netherlands	84.5	2.7	83.4	4.1	95.2	11.9	99.9	33.3	98.2	25.1	105.4	1.7	98.7	4.0	98.8	17.2	93.1	100.0
Portugal	118.8	1.6	104.0	2.3	63.7	3.2	80.4	11.8	114.6	37.2	90.2	11.1	122.7	5.1	119.0	27.6	113.0	100.0
Spain	66.7	0.5	80.6	2.1	73.8	2.5	80.7	28.4	101.0	25.2	88.2	4.3	82.1	4.6	96.4	32.4	84.0	100.0
Sweden	..	..	94.2	3.7	96.2	11.1	97.8	28.9	98.8	24.9	94.5	3.6	96.9	7.2	96.9	20.1	92.3	100.0
United Kingdom	74.9	2.0	88.8	1.2	65.9	2.3	81.3	29.0	91.2	42.8	94.2	1.9	90.9	2.9	81.5	18.0	69.6	100.0
Unweighted average	83.8	1.0	90.3	2.2	83.4	6.6	91.6	24.5	101.3	33.2	96.6	4.9	99.1	4.9	97.1	22.8	88.9	100.0

.. Data not available.
a) 1994.
Source: EUROSTAT, Structure of Earnings Survey, 1995.

Table 1.A.4. **Incidence and composition of part-time employment of short hours[a] and total part-time[b] employment, by gender, 1997**

Percentages

	Men			Women		
	Part-time employment as a percentage of total male employment		Share of short hours part-time employment in total male part-time employment 1997 (1987 figures in brackets)	Part-time employment as a percentage of total female employment		Share of short hours part-time employment in total female part-time employment 1997 (1987 figures in brackets)
	Total part-time employment	Short hours part-time employment		Total part-time employment	Short hours part-time employment	
Australia[c]	14.7	10.0	68.5 (61.6)	41.2	29.6	71.8 (73.2)
Austria	2.6	1.1	43.9 ..	21.3	5.6	26.0 ..
Belgium	4.8	1.4	28.6 (21.5)	32.3	13.5	41.7 (34.5)
Canada	10.5	5.9	56.0 (63.2)	29.4	15.2	51.8 (56.2)
Czech Republic	1.9	0.7	34.8 ..	5.5	1.5	27.2 ..
Denmark	11.1	8.9	79.8 (72.6)	24.2	12.2	50.6 (39.5)
Finland	6.0	3.3	55.1 ..	10.6	5.0	47.2 ..
France	5.9	2.0	33.7 (37.4)	25.2	8.9	35.5 (38.9)
Germany[d]	3.7	2.2	59.7 (51.6)	29.9	14.2	47.5 (32.0)
Greece	4.8	1.3	26.5 (21.1)	14.1	3.8	27.2 (26.5)
Hungary	1.8	0.4	21.1 ..	5.0	0.8	16.8 ..
Iceland	9.0	5.4	60.0 ..	36.7	12.7	34.6 ..
Ireland	7.0	2.4	34.7 (30.9)	27.2	11.4	41.8 (40.6)
Italy	5.1	2.9	57.6 (53.4)	22.2	8.3	37.2 (36.3)
Japan[c, d]	11.5	1.8	15.8 (18.9)	36.1	7.2	20.1 (21.1)
Korea[c, e]	3.3	1.3	38.8 ..	7.8	3.0	38.7 ..
Luxembourg[d]	2.1	0.4	17.1 (12.9)	24.7	7.5	30.4 (38.3)
Mexico	8.6	3.7	42.5 ..	29.9	15.2	50.8 ..
Netherlands	11.1	7.8	70.7 (61.4)	54.8	31.4	57.4 (65.9)
New Zealand[c, d]	10.1	7.0	69.7 (67.3)	36.9	23.1	62.6 (60.9)
Norway	7.9	5.7	72.3 ..	36.8	21.0	57.1 ..
Portugal	5.1	2.1	41.8 (35.1)	16.5	7.3	44.0 (40.1)
Poland[c]	5.6	2.2	38.3 ..	9.1	3.5	38.0 ..
Spain	3.1	1.1	35.4 (38.6)	16.8	7.1	42.5 (47.4)
Sweden	8.1	3.9	48.2 ..	24.9	7.6	30.5 ..
Switzerland	7.9	4.9	62.3 ..	47.8	33.2	69.5 ..
Turkey[c, d]	2.9	0.9	30.3 ..	12.7	3.6	28.3 ..
United Kingdom	8.2	5.1	63.0 (55.6)	40.9	23.9	58.3 (60.2)
United States[f]	8.3	3.5	42.3 (45.4)	19.5	8.0	40.8 (44.8)
Unweighted average	**6.6**	**3.4**	**46.5**	**25.5**	**11.9**	**42.3**

.. Data not available.
a) Usual hours of work less than 20 hours per week, except Australia, less than 21 hours, and Japan, less than 15 hours.
b) Usual hours of work less than 30 hours per week, except Japan, less than 35 hours.
c) Actual hours.
d) 1996, 1986 in brackets.
e) Civilian employment.
f) Wage earners and salaried employees.
Sources: EUROSTAT, European Labour Force Survey; and national Labour Force Surveys.

Table 1.A.5. Coefficients from logistic regression model[a] for likelihood of employer-provided training, for men

Wage earners and salaried employees, aged 25 to 54 years

	Constant	Age (years)						Working hours status (usual weekly hours)		Educational attainment			Job tenure (years)		
		25-29	30-34	35-39	40-44	45-49	50-54	Full-time	Part-time	Less than upper secondary	Upper secondary	Tertiary	Less one	1-5	5 or more
Austria	-3.86	–	–	–	–	–	–	–	–	–	–	–	–	–	–
Belgium	-5.83	–	0.22		-0.44		-0.87		-0.46		0.86	1.98	–	0.22	0.05
Denmark	-3.18	–	0.31	0.28			-0.64		-1.37		0.63	0.94	–	-0.91	-1.42
Finland	-2.96	–	0.10	0.18	0.31	0.08	0.07		-1.15		0.39	1.41	–	-0.50	-0.78
Germany	-5.38	–		-1.24	-1.31				-1.00		0.56				
Hungary	-6.84	–	-0.26	0.18	-0.54	0.12	-1.06		0.22		1.33	2.06	–		
Ireland	-3.45	–	-0.09	-0.26	-0.26	-0.57	-1.29		0.39		0.05	0.47	–	-0.74	-1.08
Italy	-4.53	–	-0.12			0.09	-0.28				1.18	1.04	–	-0.04	-0.27
Netherlands	-4.03	–	-0.37	-0.44	-0.60	-0.83	-0.99		-0.49		0.98	0.81	–	-0.50	-0.13
Norway	-2.58	–	0.21	0.19	0.10	0.12	0.36		-1.75		0.37		–		
Sweden	-2.36	–	0.10						-0.55		0.43		–		
United Kingdom	-1.81	–									0.09	0.33	–	-0.01	0.16
Unweighted average	**-3.90**		**0.01**	**-0.16**	**-0.39**	**-0.16**	**-0.59**		**-0.69**		**0.63**	**1.06**		**-0.33**	**-0.50**

	Establishment size (employees)				Industrial sector (NACE[b])										
	1-10	11-19	20-49	50+	A	C	D	E	F	G	H	I	J	K	L	M
Austria	–	–		0.40				1.35		–			1.41		0.54	
Belgium	–	–	0.31	0.32		0.99	-0.53	1.15	-0.69	–	0.57	0.42	0.63	-0.34	0.81	
Denmark	–	–						1.04	-0.89	–		0.59	1.12		0.83	0.72
Finland	–	-0.33	-0.16	0.12	0.21			0.45	-0.59	–		-0.30	1.71	-0.15	1.03	-0.30
Germany	–		-0.68	0.31	1.21	0.50	1.84	1.49	-0.87	–	-1.32	-1.27			0.52	0.77
Hungary	–	-0.15	0.17	0.25	1.49			2.63	0.90	–	0.38	2.38	2.53	2.88	2.27	2.51
Ireland	–	0.75	0.63	1.09	-0.71	0.36	0.13	0.88	-0.25	–	-0.83	-0.34	0.87	0.21	0.68	0.49
Italy	–	0.17	0.72	0.59	-0.15	1.55	0.09	0.72	-1.52	–	0.20	0.41	0.71	0.08	0.07	0.43
Netherlands	–	0.13	0.47	1.03	0.15			0.67	0.08	–	-0.60	-0.15	0.78	0.11	0.04	0.09
Norway	–		0.76	0.53				1.00		–			0.96		0.62	
Sweden	–			0.34						–					0.37	-0.48
United Kingdom	–	0.11		-0.11	-0.16	0.54	-0.01	0.46	-0.10	–	-0.16	0.08	0.14	-0.39	0.18	-0.15
Unweighted average		**0.11**	**0.28**	**0.44**	**0.29**	**0.79**	**0.30**	**1.08**	**-0.44**		**-0.25**	**0.20**	**1.09**	**0.31**	**0.66**	**0.45**

– Category is included in the constant.
a) Parameters are significant at $p < 0.05$. If the cell is empty, the parameter is not significant.
b) NACE categories are:
A: Agriculture, hunting, forestry and fishing
C: Mining and quarrying
D: Manufacturing
E: Electricity, gas and water supply
F: Construction
G: Wholesale and retail trade, repairs
H: Hotels and restaurants
I: Transport, storage and communication
J: Financial intermediation
K: Real estate, renting and business activities
L: Public administration
M: Other services.

Source: EUROSTAT, European Labour Force Survey, 1997.

Table 1.A.6. **Coefficients from logistic regression model[a] for likelihood of employer-provided training, for women**

Wage earners and salaried employees, aged 25 to 54 years

	Constant	Age (years)						Working hours status (usual weekly hours)		Educational attainment			Job tenure (years)		
		25-29	30-34	35-39	40-44	45-49	50-54	Full-time	Part-time	Less than upper secondary	Upper secondary	Tertiary	Less one	1-5	5 or more
Austria	-3.64	–	0.15			-0.35	-1.11	–	-0.11	–	0.13	0.35	–	-0.58	-1.09
Belgium	-5.53	–						–	-0.73	–	0.47	1.47	–		
Denmark	-4.35	–	0.26	0.48	0.85	0.51	0.64	–	-0.41	–	0.79	1.38	–	-0.26	0.09
Finland	-2.82	–			0.25			–	-0.78	–	0.51	1.30	–		0.20
Germany	-6.43	–	-0.36					–		–		0.93	–	-1.30	
Hungary	-5.99	–	-0.29		-0.82		-0.24	–	-0.45	–	1.53	1.81	–	0.17	-1.95
Ireland	-3.24	–			-0.56		-0.46	–	-0.21	–	0.35		–	-0.86	-1.16
Italy	-5.17	–					-0.36	–	0.24	–	0.93	1.20	–	-0.27	
Netherlands	-4.44	–	-0.07	-0.27	-0.26	-0.29	-0.39	–	-0.44	–	0.76	0.52	–	0.51	0.25
Norway	-3.22	–						–	-1.00	–	0.71	1.63	–		-0.15
Sweden	-2.79	–		0.73	0.24	0.64	0.55	–	-0.38	–	0.45	0.72	–	0.24	0.33
United Kingdom	-1.87	–						–	-0.33	–		0.12	–		
Unweighted average	-4.12		-0.06	0.32	-0.05	0.13	-0.19		-0.42		0.66	1.04		-0.29	-0.44

	Establishment size (employees)				Industrial sector (NACE[b])										
	1-10	11-19	20-49	50 +	A	C	D	E	F	G	H	I	J	K	L	M
Austria	–	–	0.37	0.93			-0.64	0.97	-1.00	–	-1.16	0.39	1.10		0.64	0.22
Belgium	–	–		0.37					1.60	–		1.14	1.09		0.57	-0.28
Denmark	–	0.64	0.45	0.54			0.56		0.97	–			1.03	1.13	0.70	0.88
Finland	–	–		0.25						–			1.31	0.63	0.56	1.44
Germany	–	–								–		0.81	1.47		1.33	
Hungary	–	–	-0.42	0.21	0.72					–	1.03		1.94		1.20	1.34
Ireland	–	0.70		0.71						–	-0.55	0.64	0.69	0.84	0.60	0.62
Italy	–	–	0.34	0.34	1.47		-0.15			–	1.17	1.04	1.48		1.01	1.26
Netherlands	–	0.16	-0.30	0.35	-1.25	1.25	0.22	0.57		–	-1.69	-0.29	1.28	0.42	0.65	0.21
Norway	–	–								–			0.71	-0.63		
Sweden	–	–	0.48	0.46						–	-0.71	0.59	0.74	0.28		
United Kingdom	–	–	0.13					1.23		–			0.26			
Unweighted average		0.50	0.15	0.46	0.32	1.25	0.00	0.92	0.52		-0.32	0.62	1.09	0.45	0.81	0.71

– Category is included in the constant.
a) Parameters are significant at $p < 0.05$. If the cell is empty, the parameter is not significant.
b) NACE categories are:
A: Agriculture, hunting, forestry and fishing
C: Mining and quarrying
D: Manufacturing
E: Electricity, gas and water supply
F: Construction
G: Wholesale and retail trade, repairs
H: Hotels and restaurants
I: Transport, storage and communication
J: Financial intermediation
K: Real estate, renting and business activities
L: Public administration
M: Other services

Source: EUROSTAT, European Labour Force Survey, 1997.

Annex 1.B

Data Sources

Earnings

Part-time earnings data used in this chapter are based largely on EUROSTAT's 1995 Structure of Earnings Survey (SES), which covers 15 countries in Europe. The SES is an establishment survey capturing information on local units operating in industry (including construction) or services and having 10 or more employees. Agriculture, public administration and "other services" (*i.e.* certain community, social and personal services) are the primary excluded sectors. For Greece, only industry is covered.

The SES earnings data refer to remuneration in cash paid directly and regularly by the employer at the time of each wage payment, before tax deductions and social security contributions payable by wage-earners and retained by the employer.

The following elements are included:

- All payments relating to this period including any overtime pay, shift premium, bonus, and commissions.
- Payments for overtime, allowances for team-work, night work, week-end work, and commissions.
- Bonuses and allowances paid regularly in each pay period.
- Payments for periods of absence and work stoppage paid for entirely by the employer.
- Family allowances and other gratuities fixed by collective agreements or voluntarily agreed.

The following are not included:

- Payments paid in this period but relating to other periods, such as arrears or advances of pay for holiday or sickness absence outside this period.
- Periodic bonuses and gratuities not paid regularly at each pay date.
- Payments for periods of absence paid by the employer at a reduced rate.
- Statutory family allowances.
- The value of benefits in kind.
- Allowances for work clothes or tools.
- Reimbursements or payments for travelling, subsistence, etc. expenses incurred in carrying out the employer's business.

The use of the SES for assessment of the situation of part-time workers is subject to several important reservations. First, part-timers are disproportionately represented in enterprises with fewer than 10 employees, so the exclusion of these small firms from the SES biases the results. If smaller firms pay relatively low wages, for example, then the exclusion may lead to an upward bias in the part-time earnings estimates presented in this chapter. On average, European Labour Force Survey (ELFS) data for 1997 show about 45 per cent of part-timers working in these small firms, but there is wide variation between countries. Similarly, the exclusion of part-timers working in "other services" sector may bias the earnings results. From the ELFS it is known that the "other services" sector includes a relatively high share of part-time workers. In 1996 across the 15 countries for which ELFS data were available, part-timers made up 29 per cent of employment in "other services" but only 16 per cent of total employment in all sectors [EUROSTAT (1997)]. About one in five part-timers worked in the "other services" sector.

Second, there are some variations in the classification of workers according to their working hours. Generally, the SES depends on employer assessments of part-time working status. Some employers may classify workers according to their type of contract rather than by an hours threshold. In some cases, due to the national survey structure, a portion of very short hour part-timers are not covered (*e.g.* in Denmark). In others, hours data are imputed (*e.g.* in Finland) or non-standard definitions are used (*e.g.* there is a 35 weekly hours threshold in Greece).

With respect to the SES data for the United Kingdom, there is a particular problem linked to the use of the New Earnings Survey (NES) as the basis of the sample. The LFS is also used, but only to match in additional variables. The NES gives a comprehensive coverage of full-time adult employees. However, its coverage of part-time employees is more limited because many of those whose earnings fall below the income tax threshold are not covered by the survey. This mainly excludes certain women with part-time jobs as well as a small proportion of young people. These problems arise because the sample frame is one of individuals rather than firms and does not apply to the other countries covered by the SES.

Additional earnings data are drawn from labour force surveys (LFS) from Australia, Canada and the United States. The LFS data are based on household surveys and therefore – being based on the individuals' assessments of hours worked – are not strictly comparable with the establishment data of the SES. The LFS data cover employees without regard to establishment size; this also limits their comparability with the SES data. The LFS data refer to 1997 for Australia and Canada, and 1996 for the United States.

For Australia earnings are based on the last total pay from wage and salary jobs prior to the interview (*i.e.* before taxation and other deductions had been made). For Canada, the earnings are based on the usual wages or salary of employees at the respondent's main job, before taxes and other deductions, but including tips, commissions and bonuses. For the United States, the earnings include wages, salary, commissions, tips, piece-rate payments, and cash bonuses earned, before deductions are made for taxes, bonds, pensions, union dues.

In some cases, sources cited in the text draw on national definitions of part-time working that are not based on a specific hours thresholds, but rather on other criteria such as relative hours thresholds (*e.g.* usual working hours less than full-time). For example, Houseman and Osawa (1995) note that part-time work in Japan is generally defined by the Ministry of Labour as work with fewer hours per day or days per week than regular workers, but may be based on an employer-classification of workers and not necessarily linked to reduced hours.

Training

The training experience of part-time workers uses the International Adult Literacy Survey (IALS) and the European Labour Force Survey (ELFS). The IALS was a joint initiative of the OECD and Statistics Canada. The data presented here refer to 1994 and cover 11 OECD countries and regions. The IALS combined a household survey approach with educational testing to obtain information on individuals' literacy. The questionnaires asked whether respondents worked mostly full- or part-time during the preceding 12 months, defining part-time as less than 30 hours per week. The IALS survey groups adult education and training together in a broad definition that includes courses, private lessons, workshops, on-the job training and other forms of structured learning. The respondents were asked about their training and education experiences over the preceding 12 months and were able to describe up to three instances. For the present analysis, training was approached by applying two alternative conditions to the data set. First, training was restricted to include only training or education taken primarily for career or job-related purposes. Under this condition, observations were excluded if the main reason was personal interest or "other" purposes. Second, training was restricted to include only training or education financially supported by an employer.

The ELFS data are drawn from household surveys and the data set used here covers 12 countries and refers to 1997. The data set is comprised of grouped data, which masks a portion of the variation. Due to differences in the questionnaires, the ELFS training data are not strictly comparable between countries; for more details, see the data discussion in Chapter 3. The ELFS guidelines define training as education or vocational training received during the four weeks preceding the survey and which is relevant for the current or possible future job of the respondent [EUROSTAT (1996)]. Courses for personal interests, hobbies or general application (*e.g.* driving lessons) are excluded. Respondents were generally asked to cite only what they considered to be the most important instance of training or education. For purposes of the present analysis using the ELFS data, only employer-provided training was considered. Employer-provided training is relatively narrowly defined as "specific vocational training in a working environment". This refers to training either received at the place of work or made available or paid for by the person's employer, but specifically excludes "dual system" or apprenticeship-type training. It also excludes employer supported education and some other training that might be considered as employer-provided. For the analysis using the ELFS data, part-time status was defined as normal working hours of 1 to 29 hours per week.

BIBLIOGRAPHY

ANXO, D., STANCANELLI, E. and STORRIE, D. (1999),
"Transitions between Different Working Time Arrangements: A comparison of Sweden and the Netherlands", paper prepared for the Conference on Transitional Labour Markets, 30 January, Wissenschaftszentrum Berlin für Sozialforschung, mimeo.

BLANK, R.M. (1994),
"The Dynamics of Part-time Work", National Bureau of Economic Research, Working Paper No. 4911.

BLS (1996),
1995 Survey of Employer Provided Training-Employee Results, News Release, US Bureau of Labor Statistics, Washington DC, Internet posting (http://stats.bls.gov/news.release /sept.nws.html), December.

BOTHFELD, S. and O'REILLY, J. (1999),
"Moving up or Moving out? Comparing transitions through part-time employment in Britain and Germany", paper prepared for the Conference on Transitional Labour Markets, 30 January, Wissenschaftszentrum Berlin für Sozialforschung, mimeo.

CRANFIELD (1997),
Working Time and Contract Flexibility in the EU: Main report, Cranfield University School of Management, Bedford, England.

DE BROUCKER, P. (1997),
"Job-Related Education and Training – Who Has Access?", *Education Quarterly Review*, Spring, pp. 10-31.

DEKKER, R., MUFFELS, R. and STANCANELLI, E. (forthcoming),
"A Longitudinal Analysis of Part-Time Work by Women and Men in the Netherlands", in Gustaffson, S. and Meulders, D. (eds.), *Gender and the Labour Market*, Macmillan, London.

DOUDEIJNS, M. (1998),
"Are Benefits a Disincentive to Work Part-Time?", in O'Reilly, J. and Fagan, C. (eds.), *Part-Time Prospects*, Routledge, London and New York, pp. 116-136.

EPF (1997),
"Part-time Work Seen As Positive Feature of Workplace", Press Release and Executive Summary, Employment Policy Foundation, Internet posting (http://epf.org/pr970520a.htm), 20 May.

EUROPEAN COMMISSION (1994),
Employment in Europe, Brussels.

EUROPEAN COMMISSION (1995),
European Economy, Reports and Studies No. 3, Brussels.

EUROSTAT (1996),
The European Labour Force Survey: Methods and Definitions, Statistical Office of the European Communities, Luxembourg.

EUROSTAT (1997),
"Part-Time Work in the European Union", *Statistics in Focus*, No. 13, Statistical Office of the European Communities, Luxembourg.

FORGÉOT, G. and LENGLART, F. (1997),
"Développement du temps partiel et comportements d'activité", *Note de conjoncture*, INSEE, June.

FRASER, D. (1996),
The Training Guarantee: Its Impact and Legacy 1990-1994, EMB Report 5/96, Department of Employment, Education, Training and Youth Affairs, Canberra, pp. 38-39.

FRAZIS, H., GITTLEMAN, M., and JOYCE, M. (1998),
"Determinants of Training: An Analysis Using Both Employer and Employee Characteristics", US Bureau of Labor Statistics, mimeo, February.

FRIEZ, A. (1999),
"Les salaires depuis 1950", *Données sociales 1999*, INSEE, Paris, pp. 160-161.

GALTIER, B. (1998),
"Les trajectoires d'emploi des salariés à temps partiel dans le secteur privé", Document de travail 98-04, Conseil supérieur de l'emploi, des revenus et des coûts, Paris.

GORNICK, J. and JACOBS, J. (1996),
"A Cross-National Analysis of the Wages of Part-time Workers: Evidence from the United States, the United Kingdom, Canada and Australia", *Work, Employment and Society*, March, pp. 1-27.

GRIMSHAW, D. and RUBERY, J. (1997),
"The Concentration of Women's Employment and Relative Occupational Pay: A Statistical Framework for Comparative Analysis", Labour Market and Social Policy Occasional Papers, No. 26, OECD, Paris.

HAKIM, C. (1996),
Key Issues in Women's Work: Female Heterogeneity and the Polarisation of Women's Employment, Athlone Press, Atlantic Highlands, New Jersey, United States.

HAKIM, C. (1997),
"A Sociological Perspective on Part-Time Work", in Blossfeld, H.P. and Hakim, C. (eds.), *Between Equalization and Marginalization*, Oxford University Press, pp. 22-70.

HOUSEMAN, S. (1997*a*),
Temporary, Part-Time, and Contract Employment in the United States: A Report on the WE Upjohn Institute's Employer Survey on Flexible Staffing Policies, WE Upjohn Institute for Employment Research, Internet posting (http://www.upjohninst.org /ptimesum.html), June.

HOUSEMAN, S. (1997*b*),
"New Institute Survey on Flexible Staffing Arrangements", *Employment Research*, WE Upjohn Institute for Employment Research, Internet posting (http://www.upjohninst.org/publications/empres.html), Spring.

HOUSEMAN, S. and OSAWA, M. (1995),
"Part Time and Temporary Employment in Japan", *Monthly Labor Review*, October, pp. 10-18.

HUSSMANS, R., MERHAN, F. and VERMA, V. (1990),
Labour Force, Employment, Unemployment and Underemployment: An ILO manual on concepts and methods, Geneva.

KAUKEWITSCH, P. and ROUAULT, D. (1998),
"Les structures des salaires en France et en Allemagne en 1995 : une analyse statistique comparative des hiérarchies salariales", *Économie et Statistique*, No. 315, pp. 3-27.

LETTAU, M. K. (1995),
"Compensation in Part-time Jobs Versus Full-time Jobs: What if the Job is the Same?", Office of Economic Research, Bureau of Labor Statistics, January, Washington, DC, mimeo.

LIPSETT, B. and REESOR, M. (1997),
"Flexible Work Arrangements: Evidence from the 1991 and 1995 Survey of Work Arrangements", Research Paper R-97-10E, Human Resources Development Canada, June.

NEATHEY, F. and HURSTFIELD, J. (1995),
Flexibility in Practice: Women's Employment and Pay in Retail and Finance, Industrial Relations Service, Manchester.

OECD (1990),
Employment Outlook, Paris, July.

OECD (1991),
Employment Outlook, Paris, July.

OECD (1994),
Women and Structural Change: New Perspectives, Paris.

OECD (1995),
Employment Outlook, Paris, July.

OECD (1998*a*),
Employment Outlook, Paris, June.

OECD (1998*b*),
Maintaining Prosperity in an Ageing Society, Paris.

O'REILLY, J. (1997),
"Regulating Working Time Transitions: An Overview", Chapter 1 of Provisional Report of TRANSLAM project, 14th October, mimeo.

O'REILLY, J., ANXO, D., CEBRIAN, I. and LALLEMENT, M. (forthcoming),
Working Time Changes: Social Integration through Working Time Transitions, Edward Elgar Publishing, Cheltenham, United Kingdom.

SMITH, M., FAGAN, C. and RUBERY, J. (1998),
"Where and Why is Part-time Work Growing in Europe?", in O'Reilly, J. and Fagan, C. (eds.), *Part-time Prospects*, Routledge, London and New York, pp. 35-56.

SMITH, M., CEBRIÁN LÓPEZ, I., DAVIA RODRÍGUEZ, M.A., MAOL OCAÑA, M.A. and HERNANZ MARTÍN, V. (1999),
"Transitions through Part-time Work in Spain and the United Kingdom: A Route into Secure Employment?", paper prepared for the Conference on Transitional Labour Markets, 30 January, Wissenschaftszentrum Berlin für Sozialforschung, mimeo.

THOMPSONS (1997),
Part-time Workers – A Guide to the Law, The Thompsons Library, Internet posting (http://www.thompsons.law.co.uk/ltext/l0230001.htm).

USDOL (1995),
Report on the American Workforce, US Department of Labor, Washington, DC.

VAN BASTELAER, A., LEMAÎTRE, G. and MARIANNA, P. (1997),
"The Definition of Part-time Work for the Purpose of International Comparisons", Labour Market and Social Policy Occasional Papers, No. 22, OECD, Paris.

Chapter 2

EMPLOYMENT PROTECTION AND LABOUR MARKET PERFORMANCE

Summary

The potential incompatibility of employment protection legislation (EPL) with labour market flexibility has occasioned much debate and a growing body of research. The central question has been whether excessively strict EPL has been an important contributor to the persistently high unemployment experienced in many OECD countries since the early 1980s. But empirical research to date has not provided a clear-cut answer to this question. Part of the reason for this is that most of the cross-country research has used data on EPL at one point in time and this data base is now increasingly outdated.

New data are presented here that describe the EPL legislation and practices currently prevailing in 27 OECD countries. The resulting portrait shows that such legislation and practices differ substantially across countries, with EPL being most strict in southern Europe, France, and Germany, and least restrictive in English-speaking countries. When these data for the late 1990s are compared with analogous data for the late 1980s, it is shown that there generally have not been large shifts in overall EPL strictness. However, a number of countries have liberalised significantly the regulation of temporary employment in the past ten years, while a smaller number have liberalised EPL for regular employment or tightened specific components of EPL.

These new data provide the basis for a reassessment of the links between EPL and labour market performance. Consistent with prior studies, there appears to be little or no association between EPL strictness and overall unemployment. However, EPL may be more strongly associated with the level of employment and the demographic composition of employment and unemployment. Simple bivariate associations suggest that stricter EPL raises employment for prime-age men but lowers employment for youths and women, with the overall effect being a net reduction. Similarly, youths and perhaps women appear to bear a larger share of the burden of unemployment. However, these associations tend to be weaker or entirely absent when multivariate techniques are used to control for other factors that influence employment and unemployment levels. The evidence is more robust for EPL tending to increase self-employment and lower turnover rates in the labour market. The latter result implies that fewer individuals become unemployed in those countries where employment protection is stricter but once unemployed, they have a higher risk of remaining unemployed for a long period of time.

Chapter 2

EMPLOYMENT PROTECTION AND LABOUR MARKET PERFORMANCE

Introduction

Employment protection regulation raises especially difficult questions in a period of rapid and pervasive economic change. Some features of the current economic environment, including rapid shifts in technology, innovative forms of business organisation, flexible workplace practices (see Chapter 4) and intense competitive pressures, have resulted in a heightened perception of job insecurity in many OECD countries. Even as fears of job loss reinforce the demand for public and private measures to enhance job security, it is sometimes asserted that it may be difficult to reconcile such protection with the flexibility required for firms and national economies to prosper today.

The potential incompatibility of employment protection legislation (EPL) with labour market flexibility has motivated a large body of research.[1] The central question has been whether excessively strict EPL has been an important contributor to the persistently high unemployment experienced in many OECD countries since the early 1980s. The OECD has previously reviewed this issue several times [OECD (1993, 1994a, 1997a)]. Robust estimates of the impact of EPL on employment and unemployment have proven elusive, but the international comparisons presented in these and related studies have documented statistical associations between stricter EPL and several measures of labour market performance, including greater prevalence of long-duration unemployment and temporary jobs. The OECD *Jobs Study* included a recommendation that governments assess whether employment protection regulation should be relaxed [OECD (1994a)]. A certain number of OECD countries have initiated reforms along these lines [OECD (1998a)], but an overall assessment of the resulting shifts in EPL strictness and their impact on labour market performance has been lacking to date.

This chapter reassesses employment protection regulation in OECD countries and its links to labour market performance. It extends prior research in two ways. First, it presents new data describing EPL in the late 1990s. Until now, much analysis of this topic has relied on the comparative data first developed by Grubb and Wells (1993) and then extended for the OECD *Jobs Study* [OECD (1994a)]. These data are now increasingly out of date, since they describe EPL in the late 1980s. The new data update this information to reflect conditions in the late 1990s and are used to assess the extent to which policy reforms during the past decade have changed employment protection practices. The EPL data for the late 1990s also cover more OECD countries than the earlier data and incorporate regulations relating to collective dismissals which were not previously covered.

Secondly, the chapter uses this new, richer data base to reassess the relationship between employment protection and labour market performance. The main question examined is whether a greater degree of EPL strictness affects employment and unemployment outcomes averaged over a number of years. However, two aspects of the potential impact of EPL on labour market performance that previously have not received much attention are also addressed. First, the chapter attempts to identify those aspects of employment protection (*e.g.* procedural requirements, notification periods or severance pay) that are most important in accounting for any identifiable associations between overall measures of EPL strictness and labour market performance. Second, the newly assembled data are used to examine possible links between changes in EPL and changes in labour market performance.

Main findings

The main findings of the chapter are:

- There is significant international variation in employment protection, both with respect to the overall level of EPL strictness and with respect to the

---

1. This chapter follows the literature in using EPL as a compact acronym for employment protection regulation generally. It must be emphasised, however, that this is intended to refer to all types of employment protection measures, whether grounded primarily in legislation, court rulings, collectively bargained conditions of employment or customary practice.

- relative emphasis placed on the different components of regulation.
- The southern European countries stand out for having relatively strict employment protection, along with France and Germany. At the other extreme, regulation is least restrictive in the United States, the United Kingdom, New Zealand and Canada.
- Between the late 1980s and the late 1990s, there was considerable continuity in EPL practices in most countries. The major exception to this picture of continuity is that a number of countries liberalised significantly the regulation of employers' use of fixed-term contracts and the operation of temporary work agencies.
- Although the most common patterns were either stable EPL strictness or some easing, several countries tightened specific aspects of their regulations. For example, Spain tightened restrictions on the use of fixed-term contracts, but simultaneously loosened EPL for regular contracts and temporary agency work. Only in France does overall EPL strictness appear to have increased somewhat since the late 1980s, mainly due to additional restrictions in the areas of fixed-term contracts and temporary agency work.
- Practically all countries enforce additional requirements on employers in the case of collective dismissals. In most countries, these provisions represent a modest increment to the protection already afforded workers in the case of individual dismissals. However, the added requirements are quite important in Belgium, the Czech Republic, Italy, Mexico, Poland and Switzerland.
- Simple, cross-country comparisons suggest that EPL has little or no effect on overall unemployment, but may affect its demographic composition. In countries where EPL is stricter, unemployment tends to be lower for prime-age men but higher for other groups, especially younger workers. However, this latter finding must be regarded as tentative, since it is not supported by the evidence from the multivariate regressions, except in the case of stricter EPL having a negative impact on the unemployment of prime-age men.
- The employment-to-population ratio for the working-age population tends to be lower in countries with stricter EPL, but this pattern reverses for prime-age men, suggesting that any negative effects of EPL on overall employment are concentrated among prime-age women, youths and older workers. Regression analysis confirms that EPL may have a positive effect on the employment rate for prime-age men, but provides only weak evidence for a negative effect on other groups.
- Stricter EPL is strongly associated with higher rates of self-employment, even when other factors are controlled for. However, the new data do not support earlier findings that the combination of strict EPL for regular employment together with unrestrictive EPL for temporary employment encourages an expansion in temporary employment. This finding is contrary to expectations and may indicate that too little time has passed since a number of countries have liberalised the regulation of temporary employment for these changes to be reflected in a higher share of temporary contracts in total employment.
- Stricter EPL is associated with lower turnover in the labour market, with both jobs and unemployment spells tending to last longer. Fewer workers experience unemployment in any given year in countries with stricter EPL, but those becoming unemployed have a greater probability of remaining unemployed for a year or more.

I. Employment protection regulation in OECD countries

A. Definitions and historical context

Employment protection refers both to regulations concerning hiring (*e.g.* rules favouring disadvantaged groups, conditions for using temporary or fixed-term contracts, training requirements) and firing (*e.g.* redundancy procedures, mandated prenotification periods and severance payments, special requirements for collective dismissals and short-time work schemes). Various institutional arrangements can provide employment protection: the private market, labour legislation, collective bargaining agreements and, not the least, court interpretations of legislative and contractual provisions. Some forms of *de facto* regulations are likely to be adopted even in the absence of legislation, simply because both workers and firms derive advantages from long-term employment relations.[2] Accordingly, the collection and use of available data in this chapter go beyond a narrow concept of employment protection *legislation* and follows a broader definition of *regulation* which aims to

---

2. In fact, on certain aspects of EPL, employers in countries with few formal legislative requirements may *de facto* face as many constraints as those in countries with strict legislation.

incorporate prevailing protective standards whatever their origin.

For example, any comparative analysis of the structure of employment protection regulation has to consider that legislation and collective bargaining are linked in various ways. Legislation may set only minimum standards which are extended by collective agreements. National administrations, in turn, may make collective agreements, including those with more stringent employment protection provisions than originally set through legislation, generally binding by extending them throughout a particular sector or the total economy, thus giving their provisions a quasi-legal character.[3] Similar links exist between legislation and judicial practices (*e.g.* compensation for unfair dismissal set by the courts can deviate widely from minima set out in legislation).[4] While they refer mainly to legislative provisions, the short descriptions of country practices in Annex 2.A show to what extent collective agreements and judicial practices have been taken into account in constructing the data base. However, it is important to keep in mind that non-legislated employment protection tends to be more difficult to measure and may therefore be underweighted in the information presented.[5]

Although foundations were sometimes laid before the Second World War (*e.g.* legislated notice periods in Germany, bargained seniority rules in the United States, strong government supervision of employment relationships in Portugal and Spain), much of the currently prevailing employment protection regulation was introduced between the 1950s and 1970s. The recession following the 1973 oil shock gave an additional impetus to governments and labour relations systems to adopt various protective measures, including in the area of collective dismissals (see, for example, the 1975 EC Directive on collective redundancies, which subsequently shaped EC Member states' legislation). Since then, the broad evolution has been towards de-regulation [see OECD (1986) and Büchtemann (1993*a*) for an historical overview].

However, countries have chosen quite different deregulatory paths, with some focusing on the relaxation of procedural requirements and others allowing more variety in employment contracts. An important development over the past two decades was the spread of fixed-term and temporary or "casual" employment contracts, which are extensively used in such countries as Spain, Australia and Finland. In addition, in recent years most countries have either legalised or eased remaining restrictions (for example on sectoral scope or contract duration) for temporary work agencies (TWAs). By contrast, a few countries have continued to tighten specific components of EPL. Table 2.1 gives some illustrations of major initiatives undertaken by selected countries to either tighten or ease their employment protection regulations since the mid-1980s.

Sources of information and methodology

The analysis of EPL in this chapter follows, to some extent, the method chosen by Grubb and Wells (1993) who used a large number of indicators to attribute scores and ranks to a subset of (European) OECD countries, based on the situation in the late 1980s. That analysis was later expanded in the OECD *Jobs Study* [OECD (1994*a*)]. The chapter uses many of the same indicators to measure the strictness of employment protection in the late 1990s, thereby allowing comparisons over time. The indicators refer to the protection of regular workers against dismissal and the regulation of temporary work. In addition, a number of new indicators for the regulation of *collective* dismissals were developed, thus allowing an even broader basis for positioning countries along an overall "strictness" criterion.

Due to the multi-dimensional nature of employment regulation and the sometimes ambiguous information available, the construction of current EPL indicators and attribution of country scores faces many of the same difficulties encountered by prior research. Tables 2.2 to 2.5 and Chart 2.1 present summary information for 27 countries and 22 indicators that aims to be as representative of current standards as possible, taking into account available multi-country surveys of regulatory provisions, as well as information made available by OECD member governments. The analysis therefore relies upon almost 1 200 data points, although for certain countries, information gaps could not be filled satisfactorily. Variables are expressed either in units of time (*e.g.* delays before notice becomes effective, or months of severance pay as differentiated by

---

3. As OECD (1994*a*) has shown, such extension practices are particularly pervasive in Austria, Belgium, France and Portugal, while they are practically non-existent in Japan, Norway, Sweden, the United Kingdom and the United States.
4. For example, in Belgium certain formulae have been developed by the judicial system to determine compensation awards for white-collar employees which take into account previous salary, age and length of service.
5. For example, the indicators presented in this chapter can take little account of the subtleties of actual enforcement of EPL. Although a country may have legislated strong protective standards, these may be unevenly enforced because workers are not informed about them or because they may feel intimidated or lack the necessary resources to take judicial action in cases of perceived violation. The increasing role of jurisprudence in EPL matters may also lead to regional disparities in enforcement. In addition, at least in some countries, court rulings may be affected by underlying labour market conditions, for example when taking into account the difficulty of finding new jobs in high unemployment areas or cyclical downswings [see Bertola *et al.* (forthcoming)].

Table 2.1. **Employment protection legislation: illustrative changes since the mid-1980s**

		Tightening of EPL	Relaxation of EPL
Permanent workers			
Finland	1991		Procedural delays before notice can become effective were shortened from about 2 months to 1-2 weeks.
	1996		Period of notice was shortened from 2 to 1 month for workers with tenure below one year.
France	1986		Prior administrative authorisation for dismissals for economic reasons was abolished.
	1989	Legislation required that collective redundancies be accompanied by "social plans".	
	1993	Statutory requirements about the contents of "social plans".	
Germany	1993	Statutory notice periods for blue-collar and white-collar workers were equalised. This increased average notice periods for workers with over 10 years tenure.	
	1996		The employment threshold at which protection against unfair dismissal applies, was raised from 5 to 10 full-time employees per establishment.
	1999	Employment threshold for unfair dismissal protection was lowered again to 5 employees per establishment.	
Korea	1998		Legal permission granted for dismissal "for managerial reasons", *i.e.* redundancy and economic restructuring.
Portugal	1989/1991		Firing restrictions eased through a wider range of admissible lay-off motivations and the abolition of prior authorisation of collective dismissals.
Spain	1994		Prior administrative authorisation for dismissals for economic reasons was abolished. Objective grounds for collective redundancies extended and procedural requirements made less time-consuming.
	1997		Maximum compensation pay for unfair dismissal was reduced from 45 to 33 days per year of service.
Sweden	1993		The "last-in-first-out" rule was relaxed: employers may retain two workers of their own choice in redundancy situations.
	1995/1997	Employers were again bound by "last-in-first-out" rule, but possibilities to modify the order of dismissals through collective bargaining were strengthened.	
United Kingdom	1985		The period of service to claim unfair dismissal increased to two years.
United States	1988	Employees in firms with more than 100 workers affected by plant closures or mass lay-offs must be given 60 days' notice.	

Table 2.1. **Employment protection legislation: illustrative changes since the mid-1980s** *(cont.)*

	Tightening of EPL	Relaxation of EPL
Temporary workers		
Belgium	Early 1990s	Fixed-term contracts possible without specifying an objective reason.
		Number of permissible renewals as well as overall duration of fixed-term and temporary agency contracts were progressively widened.
France	1985/1986	Substantial relaxation of restrictions for fixed-term contracts.
	1990 — Tightening of reasons under which temporary agency work and fixed-term contracts are allowed, and reduced time limits for overall duration.	
Germany	1985	Fixed-term contracts possible without specifying an objective reason.
	1990s	Number of permissible renewals as well as overall duration of fixed-term and temporary agency contracts were progressively widened.
Italy	1987	Fixed-term contracts could be used more widely through collective agreements specifying target groups and employment shares.
	1997	Temporary work agencies were admitted on an experimental basis.
Korea	1998	Temporary work agencies were widely liberalised.
Spain	1984	Substantial relaxation of restrictions for fixed-term contracts.
	1994 — Tightening of reasons under which fixed-term contracts are allowed.	Temporary work agencies permitted.
Sweden	1993	Temporary work agencies permitted.
	1997	Fixed-term contracts possible without specifying an objective reason, where no more than five employees are covered by such contracts simultaneously.

Source: See Annex 2.A.

employee tenure), or as scores on ordinal scales devised specifically for each indicator (0 to 2, 3, 4 or simply yes/no). The reader is referred to Annex Tables 2.A.1 to 2.A.9 for a fuller overview of the data and methods employed.[6] In the process of updating and expanding the OECD *Jobs Study* tabulations, a certain number of revisions were made to the original values attributed for the late 1980s.[7] In addition, a different technique was used in calculating summary measures of EPL strictness.[8]

First, as shown in Table 2.2 Panel A, values and scores were attributed for 12 indicators referring to the strictness of dismissal regulation for *regular* or *permanent workers* where either quantitative information was available or valid qualitative assessments of regulatory constraints could be made. Strictness of regulation is broken down by procedural requirements, notice and severance pay and unfair dismissal provisions. Next, Table 2.3, Panel A shows the values and scores attributed to countries for six indicators referring to the regulation of *fixed-term contracts and temporary agency work*. The indicators refer to the restrictions on the use of such "non-standard" work arrangements, both as regards the definition of cases and sectors where they are allowed, and their use over time, as measured by the possibility for renewals and overall duration. Table 2.4 presents four measures for the strictness of *collective dismissal* regulation, to the extent that the requirements for employers (such as notification of employee representatives, additional delays, social compensation plans, etc.) go beyond those conditions laid down for individual redundancy dismissal. This latter table, therefore, is meant to highlight only incremental requirements triggered by the "collective" nature of dismissal (as defined by countries in various ways).

Finally, all three tables provide the inputs for the construction of an overall EPL indicator in the right-hand columns of Table 2.5. Two versions of an overall indicator are presented: one combining the indicators for regular employment and temporary contracts; and a second one adding the measures in Table 2.4 for collective dismissal regulation. While the former allows a comparison of the late 1990s with the late 1980s, the latter refers only to the current situation. The scatter plots in both tables of Chart 2.1 further illustrates the changes in countries' EPL strictness over time.

B. Current standards in employment protection regulation

Protection of regular workers against dismissal

Table 2.2 provides a closer look at the extent of protection against individual dismissal for a regular employee. Protection provisions vary widely between countries and often vary within them, as well, by length of service, firm size, employee status (blue-collar/white-collar) and the existence or not of an employee representative body.

Three broad areas were identified as being indicative of the strictness of dismissal protection: procedural inconveniences which the employer faces when trying to dismiss employees; notice and severance pay provisions; and prevailing standards of and penalties for unfair dismissal. First, employers' ability to dismiss may be restricted by certain *procedural requirements* that must be followed from the decision to dismiss up to the actual termination of the contract. Countries are scored according to the delay involved before notice can start (for example, because there has to be a sequence of previous warnings, or because an interview has to be scheduled with the employee), according to whether a written statement of the reasons for dismissal must be supplied to the worker in question, whether a third party (such as a works council or the competent labour authority) must be notified or consulted and whether dismissal cannot proceed without the approval of a third party.

The country ranking (figures in brackets in Panel B) shows that the Netherlands is the most restrictive country on

---

6. The values and scores for the 22 EPL indicators used in this chapter are based on a variety of national sources as well as multi-country surveys by Watson Wyatt Data Services [Watson Wyatt (1997, 1998)], Incomes Data Services [see IDS (1995, 1996, 1997)], and the European Commission (1997a). OECD governments provided additional information, based on a request for information from the OECD Secretariat.
7. In some cases, where information had previously not been available, values were attributed retroactively; in others, previously attributed values were based on inaccurate or incomplete information and were revised; in yet other cases, certain regulatory features were more stringently defined, and the resulting assumptions also applied retroactively. For example, a delay of six days was assumed when a warning procedure prior to notice was required by legislation or jurisprudence. Similarly, the indicator used in the OECD *Jobs Study* specifying whether in the case of temporary agency work the "final user" can terminate the employment relationship at any moment, was abandoned due to the legal complexities involved, in particular where there is a triangular relationship between the worker, the temporary agency and the user company.
8. The OECD *Jobs Study* ranked countries on each individual indicator and constructed a summary ranking by taking an arithmetic average across rank positions and then ranking the averages themselves (so-called "rank of averaged ranks" technique). This approach has not been considered appropriate for making comparisons over time. Therefore, a different technique is used in this chapter to calculate summary measures. First, countries were assigned scores from 0 to 6 on each of the 22 indicators, with higher values representing more strict regulation. Next, summary scores by main area (3 areas for individual dismissal, 2 for temporary work, and 1 for collective dismissal) were established by taking the average of individual scores per indicator. Finally, in Table 2.5 summary scores by main area were combined into comprehensive summary scores from which rankings of countries' overall EPL strictness have been derived. For a more detailed explanation of the construction of summary scores, including the weights attributed to different indicators, see Annex 2.B.

Table 2.2. Indicators of the strictness of employment protection for regular employment

Panel A: Values of the indicators[a]

	Regular procedural inconveniences[b]				Notice and severance pay for no-fault individual dismissals by tenure categories[c]												Difficulty of dismissal						
	Procedures[d]		Delay to start of notice[e]		Notice period after						Severance pay after						Definition of unfair dismissal[f]		Trial period before eligibility arises		Unfair dismissal compensation at 20 years of tenure[g]		Extent of reinstatement[h]	
					9 months		4 years		20 years		9 months		4 years		20 years									
	Scale 0 to 3		Days		Months						Months						Scale 0 to 3		Months				Scale 0 to 3	
	Late 1980s	Late 1990s	Late 1980s	Late 1990s	Late 1980s	Late 1990s	Late 1980s	Late 1990s	Late 1980s	Late 1990s	Late 1980s	Late 1990s	Late 1980s	Late 1990s	Late 1980s	Late 1990s	Late 1980s	Late 1990s	Late 1980s	Late 1990s	Late 1980s	Late 1990s	Late 1980s	Late 1990s
Central and Western Europe																								
Austria	2.0	2.0	9.0	9.0	1.0	1.0	1.2	1.2	2.5	2.5	0.0	0.0	2.0	2.0	9.0	9.0	1.0	1.0	1.0	1.0	15.0	15.0	1.0	1.0
Belgium	0.5	0.5	1.5	1.5	2.0	2.0	2.8	2.8	9.0	9.0	0.0	0.0	0.0	0.0	0.0	0.0	0.0	0.0	3.3	3.3	12.5	15.0	0.0	0.0
France	1.5	1.8	12.0	12.0	1.0	1.0	2.0	2.0	2.0	2.0	0.0	0.0	0.4	0.4	2.7	2.7	1.5	1.5	1.6	1.6	15.0	15.0	0.0	0.0
Germany	2.5	2.5	17.0	17.0	1.0	1.0	1.0	1.0	4.5	7.0	0.0	0.0	0.0	0.0	0.0	0.0	2.0	2.0	6.0	6.0	24.0	24.0	1.5	1.5
Ireland	1.5	1.5	4.5	4.5	0.2	0.3	0.5	0.5	2.0	2.0	0.0	0.0	0.2	0.2	2.2	2.2	0.0	0.0	12.0	12.0	24.0	24.0	1.0	1.0
Netherlands	3.0	3.0	38.0	31.0	0.6	1.0	1.0	1.0	5.3	3.0	0.0	0.0	0.0	0.0	0.0	0.0	1.5	1.5	2.0	2.0	6.0	18.0	1.0	1.0
Switzerland	0.5	0.5	1.0	1.0	1.0	1.0	2.0	2.0	3.0	3.0	0.0	0.0	0.0	0.0	2.0	2.0	0.0	0.0	2.0	2.0	6.0	6.0	0.0	0.0
United Kingdom	1.0	1.0	2.0	2.0	0.2	0.2	0.9	0.9	2.8	2.8	0.0	0.0	0.5	0.5	2.4	2.4	0.0	0.0	24.0	24.0	8.0	8.0	0.0	0.0
Southern Europe																								
Greece	2.0	2.0	1.0	1.0	0.6	0.5	1.7	1.5	9.0	8.0	0.3	0.3	0.9	1.0	4.6	5.8	0.5	0.5	2.0	3.0	15.0	15.8	2.0	2.0
Italy	1.5	1.5	1.0	1.0	0.3	0.3	1.1	1.1	2.2	2.2	0.7	0.7	3.5	3.5	18.0	18.0	0.0	0.0	0.8	0.8	32.5	32.5	2.0	2.0
Portugal	2.5	2.0	21.0	21.0	2.0	2.0	2.0	2.0	2.0	2.0	3.0	3.0	4.0	4.0	20.0	20.0	3.0	2.0	1.0	2.5	20.0	20.0	3.0	2.5
Spain	2.3	2.0	40.0	1.0	1.0	1.0	3.0	1.0	3.0	3.0	0.5	0.5	2.6	2.6	12.0	12.0	2.0	2.0	1.7	2.5	35.0	22.0	0.0	0.0
Turkey	2.0	2.0	1.0	1.0	..	1.0	..	2.0	..	2.8	0.0	0.0	..	4.0	..	20.0	..	0.0	..	2.0	..	26.0	..	0.0
Nordic countries																								
Denmark	0.5	0.5	1.0	1.0	1.6	1.8	2.8	3.0	5.0	4.3	0.0	0.0	0.0	0.0	1.5	1.5	0.0	0.0	1.5	1.5	9.0	12.0	1.0	1.0
Finland	1.8	1.8	56.0	11.0	2.0	2.0	2.0	2.0	6.0	6.0	0.0	0.0	0.0	0.0	0.0	0.0	0.0	1.5	4.0	4.0	12.0	12.0	0.0	0.0
Norway	1.5	1.5	2.0	2.0	1.0	1.0	1.0	1.0	5.0	5.0	0.0	0.0	0.0	0.0	0.0	0.0	2.5	2.5	1.0	1.0	15.0	15.0	2.0	2.0
Sweden	2.0	2.0	15.0	15.0	1.0	1.0	4.0	3.0	6.0	6.0	0.0	0.0	0.0	0.0	0.0	0.0	2.0	2.0	6.0	6.0	32.0	32.0	1.0	1.0
Transition economies																								
Czech Republic	..	2.0	..	7.0	..	2.0	..	2.5	..	2.5	..	1.0	..	1.0	..	1.0	..	2.0	..	3.0	..	8.0	..	2.0
Hungary	..	1.0	..	13.0	..	1.0	..	1.2	..	3.0	..	0.0	..	1.0	..	5.0	..	0.0	..	3.0	..	10.0	..	2.0
Poland	..	2.0	..	13.0	..	1.0	..	3.0	..	3.0	..	0.0	..	0.0	..	0.0	..	0.0	..	1.8	..	3.0	..	2.0
North America																								
Canada	0.0	0.0	1.0	1.0	0.5	0.5	0.5	0.5	0.5	0.5	0.0	0.0	0.2	0.2	1.3	1.3	0.0	0.0	3.0	3.0	..	..	1.0	1.0
Mexico	..	1.0	..	1.0	..	0.0	..	0.0	..	0.0	..	3.0	..	3.0	..	3.0	..	3.0	..	..	..	16.0	..	1.0
United States	0.0	0.0	1.0	1.0	0.0	0.0	0.0	0.0	0.0	0.0	0.0	0.0	0.0	0.0	0.0	0.0	0.0	0.0	..	..	..	..	0.5	0.5
Asia and Oceania																								
Australia	0.5	0.5	1.0	1.0	0.2	0.2	0.7	0.7	1.2	1.2	0.0	0.0	1.0	1.0	1.0	1.0	0.0	0.0	..	..	..	..	1.5	1.5
Japan	1.5	1.5	3.0	3.0	1.0	1.0	1.0	1.0	1.0	1.0	0.0	0.0	1.5	1.5	4.0	4.0	2.0	2.0	..	..	26.0	26.0	2.0	2.0
Korea	2.5	1.8	..	32.0	..	1.0	..	1.0	..	1.0	..	0.0	2.0	2.0	6.0	6.0	..	2.0	..	..	..	..	2.0	2.0
New Zealand	0.8	0.8	7.0	7.0	..	0.5	..	0.5	..	0.5	..	0.0	..	1.5	..	5.0	..	0.0	..	2.0	..	..	..	1.0

Table 2.2. Indicators of the strictness of employment protection for regular employment (cont.)

Panel A: Values of the indicators[a]

.. Data not available.

a) In addition to the notes below, see the further explanation of the indicators in Tables 2.A.1 to 2.A.9.
b) Procedures may be legislated, set through collective bargaining or generally considered necessary because without them the employer's case will be weakened before the courts, if a claim for unfair dismissal is made.
c) Information based mainly on legal regulation, but also, where relevant, on averages found in collective agreements or employment contracts. Where relevant, calculations assume that the worker was 35 years old at the start of employment. Averages are taken where different situations apply (e.g. blue-collar and white-collar workers; or dismissals for personal reasons and for redundancy).
d) Procedures are scored according to the scale 1 when a written statement of the reasons for dismissal must be supplied to the employee; 2 when a third party (such as a works council or the competent labour authority) must be notified; and 3 when the employer cannot proceed to dismissal without authorisation from a third party.
e) Estimated time includes an assumption of 6 days in case of required warning procedure prior to dismissal (although such time periods can be very diverse and may range from a few days to several months). One day is counted when dismissal can be notified orally or the notice can be directly handed to the employee, 2 when a letter needs to be sent by mail, and 3 when a registered letter needs to be sent.
f) Scored 0 when worker capability or redundancy of the job are adequate and sufficient grounds for dismissal; 1 when social considerations, age or job tenure must when possible influence the choice of which worker(s) to dismiss; 2 when a transfer and/or retraining to adapt the worker to different work must be attempted prior to dismissal; and 3 when worker capability cannot be a ground for dismissal.
g) Where relevant, calculations assume that the worker was 35 years old at the start of employment and that a court case takes 6 months on average. Averages are taken where different situations apply (e.g. blue-collar and white-collar workers).
h) The extent of reinstatement is based upon whether, after a finding of unfair dismissal, the employee has the option of reinstatement into his/her previous job even when this is against the wishes of the employer. The indicator is 1 where this option is rarely made available to the employee, 2 where it is fairly often made available, and 3 where it is always made available.

Sources: See Annex 2.A.

Table 2.2. Indicators of the strictness of employment protection for regular employment

Panel B: Summary scores by main area[a, b]

	Regular procedural inconveniences		Notice and severance pay for no-fault individual dismissals		Difficulty of dismissal		Overall strictness of protection against dismissals	
	Late 1980s	Late 1990s	Late 1980s	Late 1990s	Late 1980s	Late 1990s	Late 1980s	Late 1990s
Central and Western Europe								
Austria	2.5 (15)	2.5 (18)	2.0 (14)	2.0 (19)	3.3 (12)	3.3 (16)	2.6 (12)	2.6 (17)
Belgium	0.5 (3)	0.5 (3)	2.3 (16)	2.3 (22)	1.8 (6)	1.8 (5)	1.5 (6)	1.5 (6)
France	2.5 (15)	2.8 (20)	1.5 (10)	1.5 (13)	2.8 (10)	2.8 (14)	2.3 (9)	2.3 (14)
Germany	3.5 (18)	3.5 (24)	1.0 (4)	1.3 (8)	3.5 (14)	3.5 (20)	2.7 (13)	2.8 (21)
Ireland	2.0 (11)	2.0 (12)	0.8 (2)	0.8 (2)	2.0 (7)	2.0 (6)	1.6 (8)	1.6 (8)
Netherlands	5.5 (22)	5.0 (27)	1.0 (4)	1.0 (4)	2.8 (10)	3.3 (16)	3.1 (18)	3.1 (25)
Switzerland	0.5 (3)	0.5 (3)	1.5 (9)	1.5 (12)	1.5 (3)	1.5 (3)	1.2 (5)	1.2 (5)
United Kingdom	1.0 (7)	1.0 (7)	1.1 (7)	1.1 (6)	0.3 (1)	0.3 (1)	0.8 (2)	0.8 (2)
Southern Europe								
Greece	2.0 (11)	2.0 (12)	2.4 (17)	2.2 (21)	3.3 (12)	3.0 (15)	2.5 (11)	2.4 (16)
Italy	1.5 (9)	1.5 (10)	2.9 (18)	2.9 (25)	4.0 (17)	4.0 (23)	2.8 (16)	2.8 (23)
Portugal	4.0 (19)	3.5 (24)	5.0 (20)	5.0 (27)	5.5 (20)	4.5 (26)	4.8 (20)	4.3 (27)
Spain	4.8 (20)	2.0 (12)	3.1 (19)	2.6 (23)	3.8 (15)	3.3 (16)	3.9 (19)	2.6 (18)
Turkey	2.0 (11)	2.0 (12)	..	3.4 (26)	..	2.5 (12)	..	2.6 (19)
Nordic countries								
Denmark	0.5 (3)	0.5 (3)	2.0 (15)	1.9 (18)	2.3 (9)	2.3 (8)	1.6 (7)	1.6 (7)
Finland	4.8 (20)	2.8 (20)	1.9 (13)	1.4 (11)	1.5 (3)	2.3 (8)	2.7 (14)	2.1 (11)
Norway	1.5 (9)	1.5 (10)	1.1 (8)	1.1 (7)	4.5 (19)	4.5 (26)	2.4 (10)	2.4 (15)
Sweden	3.0 (17)	3.0 (22)	1.7 (11)	1.6 (14)	3.8 (15)	3.8 (22)	2.8 (17)	2.8 (22)
Transition economies								
Czech Republic	..	2.5 (18)	..	2.7 (24)	..	3.3 (16)	..	2.8 (24)
Hungary	..	2.0 (12)	..	1.8 (15)	..	2.5 (12)	..	2.1 (10)
Poland	..	3.0 (22)	..	1.4 (10)	..	2.3 (8)	..	2.2 (12)
North America								
Canada	0.0 (1)	0.0 (1)	0.8 (2)	0.8 (2)	2.0 (7)	2.0 (6)	0.9 (3)	0.9 (3)
Mexico	..	1.0 (7)	..	2.1 (20)	..	3.7 (21)	..	2.3 (13)
United States	0.0 (1)	0.0 (1)	0.0 (1)	0.0 (1)	0.5 (2)	0.5 (2)	0.2 (1)	0.2 (1)
Asia and Oceania								
Australia	0.5 (3)	0.5 (3)	1.0 (4)	1.0 (4)	1.5 (3)	1.5 (3)	1.0 (4)	1.0 (4)
Japan	2.0 (11)	2.0 (12)	1.8 (12)	1.8 (16)	4.3 (18)	4.3 (25)	2.7 (15)	2.7 (20)
Korea	..	3.8 (26)	..	1.8 (16)	..	4.0 (23)	..	3.2 (26)
New Zealand	1.3 (8)	1.3 (9)	..	1.4 (9)	..	2.3 (11)	..	1.7 (9)

.. Data not available.
a) The summary scores can range from 0 to 6, with higher values representing stricter regulation. Their calculation is explained in Annex 2.B.
b) Figures in brackets show country rankings. All rankings increase with the strictness of employment protection.
Source: See Table 2.2, Panel A.

the indicator of regular procedural inconveniences, followed by Korea, Germany and Portugal, while Canada and the United States are the least restrictive. In the Netherlands, a long-established dismissal procedure requires authorisation by the public employment service; not only does this procedure tend to be lengthy, but a certain number of requests are turned down annually.[9] The Korean score is affected by the long consultation period with employee representatives in case of dismissal for economic reasons, a feature introduced into Korean law in early 1998 when economic redundancy was first recognised as a valid reason for dismissal.

The Netherlands also had the most restrictive rank in the late 1980s, followed by Finland and Spain. The latter two countries have considerably eased restrictions since then, particularly in terms of the delays required for consultation before notice can start. Chart 2.1, Panel A, provides a further illustration of the easing of regulations by these two countries concerning procedural inconveniences.

Consider next *notice* and *severance pay* requirements in Table 2.2. Many entries in Panel A are composite values of different situations, *e.g.* for blue-collar and white-collar workers, or for dismissals for personal reasons and for economic redundancy (see Annex 2.A, Tables 2.A.2 and 2.A.3 for details). Where there are differences between these categories, termination costs tend to be higher for white-collar workers and for redundancies. All countries, apart from the United States, apply regular notice periods, but only two-thirds provide for severance pay for long-service employees. With few exceptions, there is also a tendency for countries with high severance pay requirements to offer little in terms of notice periods, and vice versa.

Turning to country rankings, the southern European countries tend to have the highest requirements (Portugal, followed by Turkey and Italy), while the United States, Canada and Ireland are among the least restrictive.[10] The Netherlands also ranks low on this indicator, which is in stark contrast to its comparative strictness concerning procedural inconveniences. Chart 2.1 illustrates that country values and relative ranks have not changed much in comparison with the situation in the late 1980s. Germany stands out somewhat as having further increased its regulation in the area since, in the process of harmonising notice periods for blue-collar and white-collar workers, it increased the length of notice for long-tenure workers. By contrast, mandated notice periods seem to have decreased in Spain and Finland, while the Netherlands increased its minimum and decreased its maximum periods.

Further requirements may be faced by employers in cases of "unjustified" or "unfair" dismissal. Practically all OECD countries have legislated remedies for *unfair dismissal*.[11] The third summary area in Table 2.2, entitled "difficulty of dismissal", shows the constraints which arise. The length of the trial period is important because, within this period, unfair dismissal claims can usually not be made.[12] Next, many countries consider a dismissal as unfair if the employer cannot demonstrate appropriate previous efforts to avoid it (*e.g.* through in-house transfers or re-training) or when social considerations, age or job tenure (*e.g.* the *last-in, first-out* rule) have not been followed. Courts may also order reinstatement after a finding of unfair dismissal, or award high compensation payments in excess of regular severance pay. Maximum compensation payments are particularly high in Italy and Sweden, although in the United States damages awarded by some courts in wrongful termination cases have exceeded corresponding payments in other OECD countries.[13]

Norway, Portugal and Japan stand out as offering the highest employment protection on the summary indicator "difficulty of dismissal", with the United States and the United Kingdom at the opposite end of the spectrum. Norwegian courts have restricted dismissal for personal reasons mainly to cases of material breach of the employment contract (disloyalty, persistent absenteeism, etc.), while dismissals for economic reasons are automatically unfair where the employee could have been retained in another capacity.

Compared with the late 1980s, Portugal has become less restrictive since, at the turn of the decade, it started allowing dismissal for lack of performance and economic redundancy (previously the only grounds for dismissal were disciplinary). Spain also registered a decrease, mainly due to

---

9. This figure stood at 7 per cent in 1997-1998. An increasing number of Dutch employers currently turn to the cantonal labour court, to avoid such uncertainties and get speedier permission for dismissal. While there seems to be less risk involved of the courts turning down proposed dismissals, they nevertheless tend to increase employers' termination costs by often determining generous severance pay.
10. Despite the complete absence of legal requirements, it is worth noting that in the United States, according to a 1992 survey, a minority (between 15 and 35 per cent) of employees, depending on company size, are covered by company severance pay plans [OECD (1996a)].
11. The United States is a partial exception, but even there, legally enforceable collective agreements, civil rights principles and special legislation for the public sector have somewhat eroded the traditional "employment at will" doctrine [Büchtemann (1993a); Mendelsohn (1990)].
12. For example, to ease restrictions on employers, the government in the United Kingdom raised the qualifying period for unfair dismissal claims from 26 to 52 weeks in 1979, and to 104 weeks in 1985.
13. Most countries have legislation in place which makes dismissal for certain reasons or of certain categories of employees automatically unjust. This refers mainly to discrimination based on race, gender, religion, etc., and to special protection for pregnant women, disabled workers and trade union representatives.

a cap on damage awards. As Chart 2.1 illustrates, for most other countries the summary indicator for "difficulty of dismissal" has remained essentially unchanged since the late 1980s. The overall EPL indicator of strictness for regular employment also has remained comparatively stable over the 1990s (see Chart 2.1, Panel A, lower right-hand corner). The major exception is Spain which appears as the only country to have eased restrictions on all three summary indicators (procedures, notice and severance pay, unfair dismissal regulation), while Portugal and Finland relaxed EPL restrictions in two of the three areas.

Regulation of temporary forms of employment

Countries can change the overall strictness of their employment protection regulation by keeping existing provisions intact for regular or permanent workers, but facilitating other options to enhance work-force flexibility. Publicly subsidised short-time work is one such administrative option which has been identified by Houseman and Abraham (1995) as accounting for much of the difference between some European countries and the United States in terms of employment adjustment. Another way to ease employers' termination costs is to facilitate the use of fixed-term contracts with a specific termination date and recourse to workers hired from temporary work agencies (TWAs). In general, no notice and severance pay are foreseen in these cases and it will usually be difficult for the employee to file an unfair dismissal claim.

Table 2.3, Panel A throws some light on existing restrictions on the use of temporary employment, broken down by regulations governing fixed-term contracts and those governing the operations of TWAs. In both areas, one indicator refers to the types of work that are allowed under such contractual arrangements, while two other indicators provide measures of their maximum allowable duration.

All countries recognise the validity of fixed-term contracts in the case of so-called "objective" reasons or time-limited situations, referring to specific projects, seasonal work or the replacement of employees who are absent temporarily. Indeed, in the past many countries, particularly in Europe, restricted temporary contracts exclusively to such objective reasons. However, currently the majority of the countries in the table have either lifted or relaxed significantly this requirement. Most Anglo-Saxon countries have always allowed the use of temporary contracts without any significant restrictions. Currently, some countries continue to list specific situations which may, however, go beyond "objective", time-limited tasks (*e.g.* business start-ups or workers in search of their first job).

Concerning duration, contracts can be renewed at will in Canada, Ireland, the United Kingdom and the United States. In a number of other countries, this is only the case if separate valid objective reasons can be given for each new contract. In these cases, after successive renewals (often starting with the first renewal), courts can be called upon to examine the validity of the reason given and may declare the fixed term unjustified, judging that its main purpose is to circumvent termination laws. To facilitate hiring under fixed-term contracts without such judicial interference, countries like Belgium, Germany and Sweden have specified in law the maximum number of successive contracts which are permitted without the presence of an objective reason, and their maximum cumulated duration.

As is the case for fixed-term contracts, there has been a general trend throughout the 1980s and 1990s to liberalise the use of TWAs [Delsen (1991)]. In the late 1980s, for example, 9 of the 27 countries shown in Table 2.3 had banned their operation (with some *de facto* tolerance), while today only Greece and Turkey continue to do so. A number of countries have expanded the types of work or the range of economic sectors where TWAs can operate or increased the maximum permitted length of employment. Germany, which as a general rule had previously required TWAs to give their employees an indefinite contract independently of any demand by potential user companies, has recently lifted this requirement, at least for the initial contract.

60 – *OECD Employment Outlook*

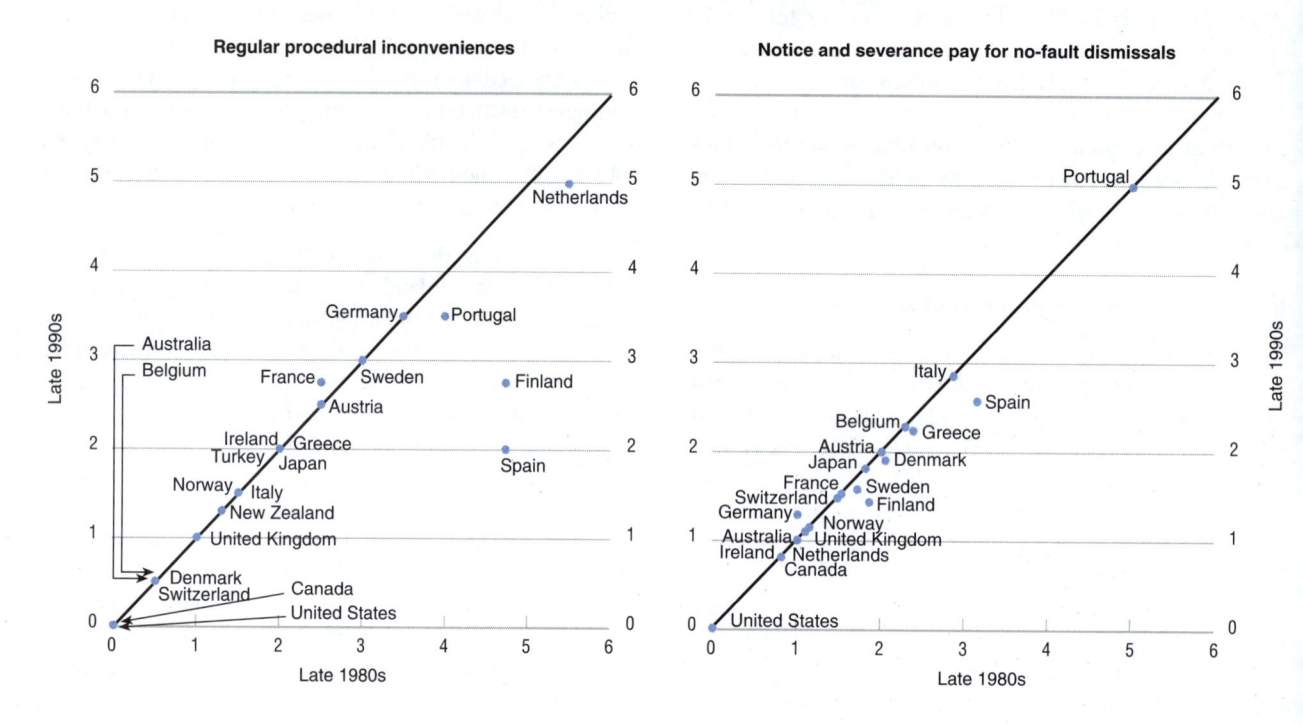

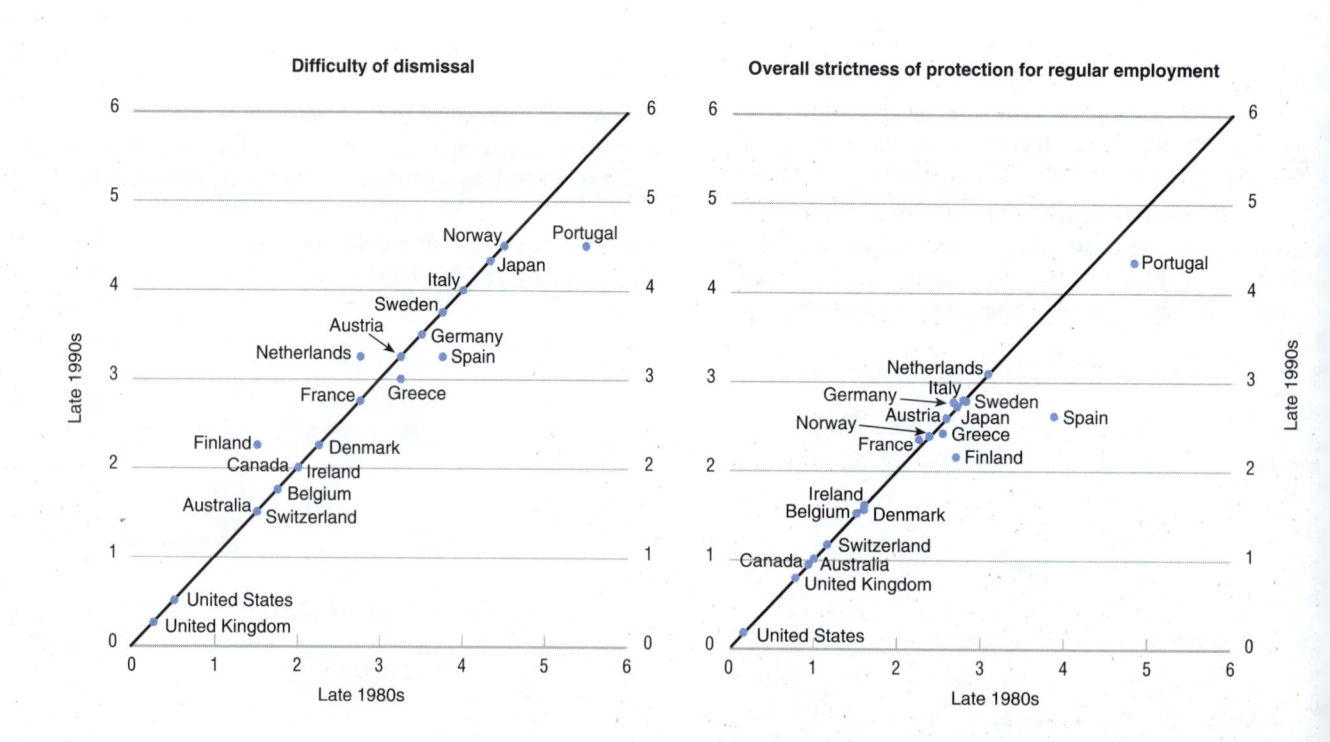

Chart 2.1. Evolution of the EPL summary indicators, from the late 1980s to the late 1990s

Panel A: Employment protection for regular employment

Chart 2.1. Evolution of the EPL summary indicators, from the late 1980s to the late 1990s (cont.)
Panel B: Temporary employment and overall EPL

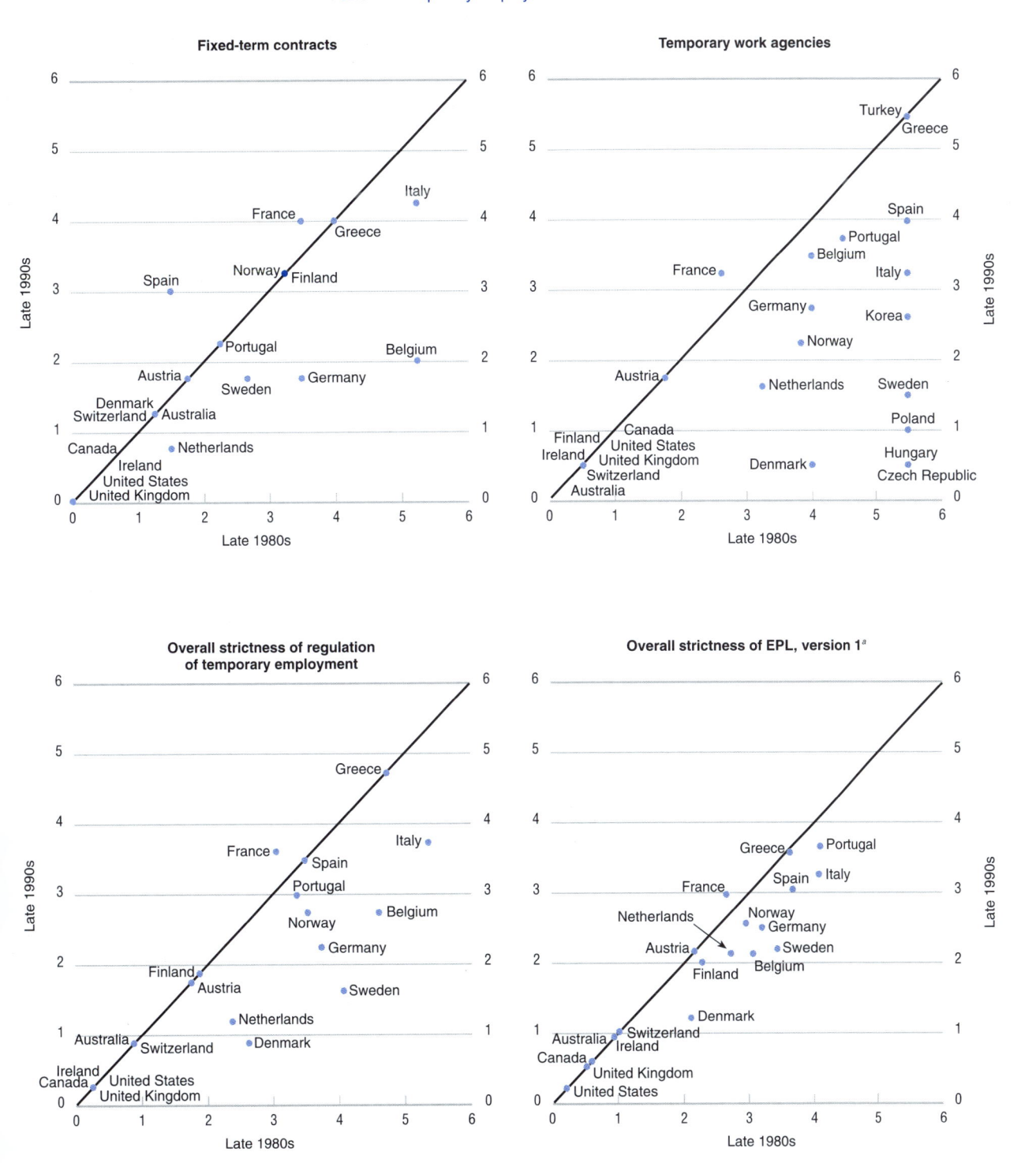

a) Average of indicators for regular contracts and temporary contracts.
Sources: See Table 2.2, Panel B, Table 2.3, Panel B and Table 2.5.

Table 2.3. Regulation of temporary employment
Panel A: Values of the indicators

	Fixed-term contracts						Temporary work agencies (TWAs)					
	Valid cases other than the usual objective reasons [a]		Maximum number of successive contracts [b]		Maximum cumulated duration		Types of work for which TWA employment is legal		Restrictions on number of renewals		Maximum cumulated duration of temporary work contracts	
	Scale 0 to 3 [c]		Number		Months		Scale 0 to 4 [d]		Yes/No		Months	
	Late 1980s	Late 1990s	Late 1980s	Late 1990s	Late 1980s	Late 1990s	Late 1980s	Late 1990s	Late 1980s	Late 1990s	Late 1980s	Late 1990s
Central and Western Europe												
Austria	2.5	2.5	1.5	1.5	No limit	No limit	3.0	3.0	Yes	Yes	No limit	No limit
Belgium	0.0	2.0	1.0	4.0	24.0	30.0	2.0	2.0	Yes	Yes	2.0	15.0
France	1.0	1.0	3.0	2.0	24.0	18.0	2.5	2.0	Yes	Yes	24.0	18.0
Germany	2.0	2.5	1.0	4.0	18.0	24.0	2.0	3.0	Yes	Yes	6.0	12.0
Ireland	3.0	3.0	No limit	No limit	No limit	No limit	4.0	4.0	No	No	No limit	No limit
Netherlands	3.0	3.0	1.0	3.0	No limit	No limit	3.0	3.5	Yes	Yes	6.0	42.0
Switzerland	3.0	3.0	1.5	1.5	No limit	No limit	4.0	4.0	No	No	No limit	No limit
United Kingdom	3.0	3.0	No limit	No limit	No limit	No limit	4.0	4.0	No	No	No limit	No limit
Southern Europe												
Greece	0.0	0.0	2.5	2.5	No limit	No limit	0.0	0.0	–	–	–	–
Italy	0.5	1.0	1.5	2.0	9.0	15.0	0.0	1.0	–	Yes	–	No limit
Portugal	2.0	2.0	3.0	3.0	30.0	30.0	1.0	2.0	Yes	Yes	9.0	9.0
Spain	2.0	1.0	3.0	3.0	36.0	36.0	0.0	2.0	–	Yes	–	6.0
Turkey	0.0	0.0	6.0	1.5	..	No limit	0.0	0.0	–	–	–	–
Nordic countries												
Denmark	3.0	3.0	1.5	1.5	No limit	No limit	2.0	4.0	Yes	No	3.0	No limit
Finland	1.0	1.0	1.5	1.5	No limit	No limit	4.0	4.0	..	No	..	No limit
Norway	1.0	1.0	1.5	1.5	No limit	No limit	1.5	3.0	Yes	Yes	–	24.0
Sweden	2.0	2.5	2.0	No limit	..	12.0	0.0	4.0	–	No	–	12.0
Transition economies												
Czech Republic	..	2.5	..	No limit	..	No limit	0.0	4.0	–	No	–	No limit
Hungary	..	2.5	..	No limit	..	60.0	0.0	4.0	–	No	–	No limit
Poland	..	3.0	..	2.0	..	No limit	0.0	4.0	–	Yes	–	No limit
North America												
Canada	3.0	3.0	No limit	No limit	No limit	No limit	4.0	4.0	No	No	No limit	No limit
Mexico	..	0.5	..	..	..	No limit	..	..	..	..	..	..
United States	3.0	3.0	No limit	No limit	No limit	No limit	4.0	4.0	No	No	No limit	No limit
Asia and Oceania												
Australia	3.0	3.0	1.5	1.5	No limit	No limit	4.0	4.0	No	No	No limit	No limit
Japan	..	2.5	2.5	2.5	..	No limit	2.0	2.0	..	Yes	..	36.0
Korea	..	2.5	..	2.5	..	No limit	0.0	2.5	..	Yes	..	24.0
New Zealand	..	3.0	..	5.0	..	No limit	4.0	4.0	–	No	–	No limit

.. Data not available.
– Not applicable.
a) All countries recognise the validity of fixed-term contracts in "objective" situations, a term which typically refers to specific projects, seasonal work, replacement of temporarily absent permanent workers (on sickness or maternity leave), and exceptional workload.
b) The law in most countries does not specify any limits to the number of fixed-term contracts if separate valid objective reasons for each new contract can be given. However, after successive renewals (often at the first such renewal) courts may examine the validity of the reason given and may declare the fixed term unjustified.
c) Scored 0 if fixed-term contracts are permitted only for "objective" or "material" reasons (i.e. to perform a task which itself is of fixed duration); 1 if specific exemptions apply to situations of employer need (e.g. launching a new activity) or employee need (e.g. workers in search of their first job); 2 when exemptions exist on both the employer and the employee side; 3 when there are no restrictions on the use of fixed-term contracts.
d) Scored 0 if TWA employment is illegal. 1 to 3 depending upon the degree of restrictions, and 4 where no restrictions apply.
Source: See Annex 2.A.

Table 2.3. Regulation of temporary employment
Panel B: Summary scores by main area[a, b]

	Fixed-term contracts Late 1980s	Fixed-term contracts Late 1990s	Temporary work agencies (TWAs) Late 1980s	Temporary work agencies (TWAs) Late 1990s	Overall strictness of regulation Late 1980s	Overall strictness of regulation Late 1990s
Central and Western Europe						
Austria	1.8 (10)	1.8 (15)	1.8 (8)	1.8 (15)	1.8 (7)	1.8 (14)
Belgium	5.3 (18)	2.0 (18)	4.0 (12)	3.5 (22)	4.6 (17)	2.8 (19)
France	3.5 (15)	4.0 (24)	2.6 (9)	3.3 (20)	3.1 (11)	3.6 (23)
Germany	3.5 (15)	1.8 (15)	4.0 (12)	2.8 (18)	3.8 (15)	2.3 (18)
Ireland	0.0 (1)	0.0 (1)	0.5 (1)	0.5 (1)	0.3 (1)	0.3 (1)
Netherlands	1.5 (8)	0.8 (7)	3.3 (10)	1.6 (14)	2.4 (9)	1.2 (12)
Switzerland	1.3 (5)	1.3 (10)	0.5 (1)	0.5 (1)	0.9 (5)	0.9 (8)
United Kingdom	0.0 (1)	0.0 (1)	0.5 (1)	0.5 (1)	0.3 (1)	0.3 (1)
Southern Europe						
Greece	4.0 (17)	4.0 (24)	5.5 (16)	5.5 (25)	4.8 (18)	4.8 (25)
Italy	5.3 (18)	4.3 (26)	5.5 (16)	3.3 (20)	5.4 (19)	3.8 (24)
Portugal	2.3 (11)	2.3 (19)	4.5 (15)	3.8 (23)	3.4 (12)	3.0 (21)
Spain	1.5 (8)	3.0 (21)	5.5 (16)	4.0 (24)	3.5 (13)	3.5 (22)
Turkey	..	4.3 (26)	5.5 (16)	5.5 (25)	..	4.9 (26)
Nordic countries						
Denmark	1.3 (5)	1.3 (10)	4.0 (12)	0.5 (1)	2.6 (10)	0.9 (8)
Finland	3.3 (13)	3.3 (22)	0.5 (1)	0.5 (1)	1.9 (8)	1.9 (15)
Norway	3.3 (13)	3.3 (22)	3.8 (11)	2.3 (16)	3.5 (14)	2.8 (19)
Sweden	2.7 (12)	1.8 (15)	5.5 (16)	1.5 (13)	4.1 (16)	1.6 (13)
Transition economies						
Czech Republic	..	0.5 (6)	5.5 (16)	0.5 (1)	..	0.5 (6)
Hungary	..	0.8 (7)	5.5 (16)	0.5 (1)	..	0.6 (7)
Poland	..	1.0 (9)	5.5 (16)	1.0 (12)	..	1.0 (11)
North America						
Canada	0.0 (1)	0.0 (1)	0.5 (1)	0.5 (1)	0.3 (1)	0.3 (1)
Mexico	..	2.5 (20)	..	..	..	..
United States	0.0 (1)	0.0 (1)	0.5 (1)	0.5 (1)	0.3 (1)	0.3 (1)
Asia and Oceania						
Australia	1.3 (5)	1.3 (10)	0.5 (1)	0.5 (1)	0.9 (5)	0.9 (8)
Japan	..	1.5 (13)	..	2.8 (18)	..	2.1 (17)
Korea	..	1.5 (13)	5.5 (16)	2.6 (17)	..	2.1 (16)
New Zealand	..	0.3 (5)	..	0.5 (1)	..	0.4 (5)

.. Data not available.
Source and notes: See Table 2.2, Panel B.

Table 2.3, Panel B and Chart 2.1 further illustrate the liberalising trend in both areas of temporary work regulation. Turkey, Greece and Italy currently rank highest on overall strictness, while Canada, Ireland, the United Kingdom and the United States again are the least restrictive. Compared with the late 1980s, Sweden, Belgium, Denmark and Italy come out as having moved furthest away from the previous situation. France alternated between liberalisation and restriction during the sequence of governments in the 1980s, and is currently more legally restrictive, requiring proof of an objective reason and allowing only one prolongation of a temporary contract. This, however, does not seem to have prevented French companies from making strong use of temporary workers, as shown by the available statistics on the share of both fixed-term and temporary-agency employees in the labour market [DARES (1998*a*, *b*)].[14] Spain liberalised temporary work agencies, but tightened somewhat its criteria for the use of fixed-term contracts in the mid-1990s which had become very widespread after liberalisation in 1984 – they accounted for up to one-third of total employment and 90 per cent of new hires in the mid-1990s.

A comparison of the overall strictness of employment protection regulation for temporary work with that for regular employment in Panels A and B of Chart 2.1 suggests that most countries have concentrated their effort in the 1990s on easing the restrictions for temporary work, while there has been comparatively less movement on the protection of regular employment. Taking both summary indicators together, Sweden, Belgium, Denmark and Italy have moved most in the direction of easing employment protection, a result heavily influenced by the temporary work indicator (Chart 2.1, Panel B, lower right-hand corner).

Specific requirements for collective dismissals

Tables 2.4 and 2.5 provide evidence as to whether country scores and ranks change when the regulation of *collective dismissal* is added as a third summary measure. Four separate indicators were used to measure the strictness of protection against collective dismissal. The left-hand column of Table 2.4 scores countries by the size of the redundancy which is required to trigger the application of the collective dismissal regulation. The next three columns refer to any additional delays and procedures required which go beyond those applicable for individual dismissal.

It is interesting to note that, on this measure, the ranking of countries seems quite different from that based on the other indicators, with New Zealand, Japan, Korea and France being scored as having the least, and Sweden, the Czech Republic, Italy and Belgium as having the most additional requirements. Canada, the United Kingdom and the United States occupy a middle position, since they have legislated considerable waiting periods and notification requirements in the event of collective dismissals, in contrast to their stance on protection of individual dismissal.

Indicators of overall EPL strictness

The summary indicators for the three main components of EPL are consolidated in Table 2.5 along with two versions of an overall indicator of strictness. Version 1 allows changes over time to be studied and is most comparable to prior work by the OECD, while Version 2 provides the most comprehensive measure of EPL in the late 1990s, since it incorporates the indicators for collective dismissal. There are some changes in overall scores and country ranks depending on whether a measure for collective dismissal is included or not, even though incremental provisions for collective dismissal are weighted less heavily than measures for the protection of regular and temporary employment when entered into Version 2 of the overall indicator. Although country ranks differ by up to three positions, on both definitions the same countries tend to appear at the opposite ends of the spectrum, with the United States and the United Kingdom as the least regulated countries while the strictest employment protection is offered by the countries of southern Europe.

The method used in Tables 2.2 to 2.5 is only one among several possibilities for assessing the strictness of employment protection. Table 2.6 shows various rankings that have been used by earlier studies to compare the strictness of EPL across countries. The rankings from the International Organisation of employers (IOE) and the EC *ad hoc* surveys are based on employers' assessments of the restrictions they face in dismissing workers, while the rankings of Lazear, Bertola and the OECD *Jobs Study* are closer to the method adopted here, being based on a compilation of legislative requirement or common practices. With the exception of the EC *ad hoc* surveys – which give quite a different assessment of relative strictness – rank

---

14. In search of an equilibrium between the flexibility needs of enterprises, employee protection and economic efficiency, the reform of 1985 abolished a previous list of references to "objective reasons" as preconditions for time-limited contracts, while the reform of 1990 reintroduced this list in modified form and reduced the maximum number of successive contracts and the maximum allowable duration. The 1990 reform also sought to close the gap in contractual status between fixed-term and temporary agency employees. While it may be argued that these legal changes contributed to some decline in the recourse to such forms of temporary employment after 1990, their use has increased again strongly since the mid-1990s. The effects of the 1990 change in legislation seem therefore to have been of little significance in practice [see Michon and Ramaux (1993); OECD (1996*b*), Chapter 1].

Table 2.4. Regulation of collective dismissal, late 1990s
Requirements over and above those applying to individual dismissals

	Definition of collective dismissal [a]	Additional notification requirements [b]	Additional delays involved (in days) [c]	Other special costs to employers [d]	Overall strictness relative to individual dismissals [e]
Central and Western Europe					
Austria	4	1	21	1	3.3 (16)
Belgium	3	2	44	1	4.1 (24)
France	3	0	22	1	2.1 (4)
Germany	3	1	28	1	3.1 (13)
Ireland	3	1	18	0	2.1 (4)
Netherlands	2	1	30	1	2.8 (9)
Switzerland	3	2	29	1	3.9 (22)
United Kingdom	2	1.5	57	0	2.9 (11)
Southern Europe					
Greece	4	1	19	1	3.3 (16)
Italy	4	1.5	44	1	4.1 (24)
Portugal	4	0.5	65	1	3.6 (20)
Spain	3	1	29	1	3.1 (13)
Turkey	3	1	29	0	2.4 (6)
Nordic countries					
Denmark	3	2	29	0	3.1 (13)
Finland	3	1	32	0	2.4 (6)
Norway	3	1.5	28	0	2.8 (9)
Sweden	4	2	113	0	4.5 (27)
Transition economies					
Czech Republic	4	2	83	0	4.3 (26)
Hungary	3	2	47	0	3.4 (18)
Poland	3	1	32	2	3.9 (22)
North America					
Canada	1	2	111	0	3.4 (18)
Mexico	4	2	0	1	3.8 (21)
United States	1	2	59	0	2.9 (11)
Asia and Oceania					
Australia	3	2	0	0	2.6 (8)
Japan	2	1	0	0	1.5 (2)
Korea	3	1	0	0	1.9 (3)
New Zealand	0	0.5	0	0	0.4 (1)

a) The score is 0 if there are no special regulations on collective dismissal; 1 if regulations apply from 50 dismissals upward; 2 if they apply from 20 onward; 3 if they start at 10 dismissals; and 4 if regulations start to apply at below 10 dismissals.
b) There can be notification requirements to employee representatives/works councils, and to government authorities such as public employment offices. Countries are scored according to whether there are additional notification requirements on top of those requirements applying to individual redundancy dismissal. The score is 0 if there are no additional requirements; 1 if one more actor, and 2 if two more actors need to be notified.
c) This column lists delays required on top of delays before the start of notice for economic redundancy listed under Table 2.2. Averages are taken if separate delays apply to different types of situations.
d) This column refers to whether there are additional severance pay requirements in case of collective dismissal and whether social compensation plans (detailing measures for redeployment, retraining, outplacement or severance pay) are obligatory or common practice. The score is 2 if both requirements apply.
e) The summary scores can range from 0 to 6, with higher values representing stricter regulation (see Annex 2.B). Figures in brackets show country rankings. All rankings increase with the strictness of employment protection.
Source: See Annex 2.A.

Table 2.5. **Summary indicators of the strictness of employment protection legislation**

	Regular employment[a]		Temporary employment[b]		Collective dismissals[c]	Overall EPL strictness[d]					
						Version 1[e]				Version 2[f]	
	Late 1980s	Late 1990s	Late 1980s	Late 1990s	Late 1990s	Late 1980s		Late 1990s		Late 1990s	
Central and Western Europe											
Austria	2.6	2.6	1.8	1.8	3.3	2.2	(8)	2.2	(15)	2.3	(15)
Belgium	1.5	1.5	4.6	2.8	4.1	3.1	(13)	2.1	(13)	2.5	(16)
France	2.3	2.3	3.1	3.6	2.1	2.7	(10)	3.0	(21)	2.8	(21)
Germany	2.7	2.8	3.8	2.3	3.1	3.2	(14)	2.5	(18)	2.6	(20)
Ireland	1.6	1.6	0.3	0.3	2.1	0.9	(4)	0.9	(4)	1.1	(5)
Netherlands	3.1	3.1	2.4	1.2	2.8	2.7	(11)	2.1	(14)	2.2	(13)
Switzerland	1.2	1.2	0.9	0.9	3.9	1.0	(6)	1.0	(6)	1.5	(7)
United Kingdom	0.8	0.8	0.3	0.3	2.9	0.5	(2)	0.5	(2)	0.9	(2)
Southern Europe											
Greece	2.5	2.4	4.8	4.8	3.3	3.6	(16)	3.6	(24)	3.5	(24)
Italy	2.8	2.8	5.4	3.8	4.1	4.1	(18)	3.3	(23)	3.4	(23)
Portugal	4.8	4.3	3.4	3.0	3.6	4.1	(19)	3.7	(25)	3.7	(26)
Spain	3.9	2.6	3.5	3.5	3.1	3.7	(17)	3.1	(22)	3.1	(22)
Turkey	..	2.6	..	4.9	2.4	..		3.8	(26)	3.5	(25)
Nordic countries											
Denmark	1.6	1.6	2.6	0.9	3.1	2.1	(7)	1.2	(8)	1.5	(8)
Finland	2.7	2.1	1.9	1.9	2.4	2.3	(9)	2.0	(12)	2.1	(11)
Norway	2.4	2.4	3.5	2.8	2.8	3.0	(12)	2.6	(19)	2.6	(19)
Sweden	2.8	2.8	4.1	1.6	4.5	3.5	(15)	2.2	(16)	2.6	(18)
Transition economies											
Czech Republic	..	2.8	..	0.5	4.3	..		1.7	(11)	2.1	(12)
Hungary	..	2.1	..	0.6	3.4	..		1.4	(9)	1.7	(9)
Poland	..	2.2	..	1.0	3.9	..		1.6	(10)	2.0	(10)
North America											
Canada	0.9	0.9	0.3	0.3	3.4	0.6	(3)	0.6	(3)	1.1	(4)
Mexico	..	2.3	..	..	3.8	..		..		..	
United States	0.2	0.2	0.3	0.3	2.9	0.2	(1)	0.2	(1)	0.7	(1)
Asia and Oceania											
Australia	1.0	1.0	0.9	0.9	2.6	0.9	(5)	0.9	(5)	1.2	(6)
Japan	2.7	2.7	..	2.1	1.5	..		2.4	(17)	2.3	(14)
Korea	..	3.2	..	2.1	1.9	..		2.6	(20)	2.5	(17)
New Zealand	..	1.7	..	0.4	0.4	..		1.0	(7)	0.9	(3)

.. Data not available.
a) From Table 2.2, Panel B.
b) From Table 2.3, Panel B.
c) From Table 2.4.
d) Figures in brackets show country rankings. All rankings increase with the strictness of employment protection.
e) Average of indicators for regular contracts and temporary contracts.
f) Weighted average of indicators for regular contracts, temporary contracts and collective dismissals. See Annex 2.B for explanation of the weighting scheme.
Source: See Annex 2.A.

Table 2.6. **Comparing EPL indicators in selected studies with new OECD data**

All indicators converted into rankings (increasing with the strictness of EPL)

	International Organisation of Employers (IOE)[a]	EC ad hoc surveys[b]		Lazear (1990)[c]	Bertola (1990)[d]	OECD Jobs Study[e]	OECD (1999)[f]		
	1985	1989	1994	1956-84	1988	Late 1980s	Late 1980s (version 1)	Late 1990s (version 1)	Late 1990s (version 2)
Central and Western Europe									
Austria	4	..	..	12	..	7	8	15	15
Belgium	9	5	10	10	9	10	13	13	16
France	9	6	5	15	8	8	10	21	21
Germany	9	7	7	11	6	14	14	18	20
Ireland	4	2	7	1	..	3	4	4	5
Netherlands	9	9	3	9	3	5	11	14	13
Switzerland	..	..	..	8	..	1	6	6	7
United Kingdom	1	1	1	7	4	2	2	2	2
Southern Europe									
Greece	..	4	5	16	..	12	16	24	24
Italy	13	10	4	19	10	16	18	23	23
Portugal	7	3	2	13	..	15	19	25	26
Spain	13	8	9	17	..	13	17	22	22
Turkey	..	..	..	..	..	..	..	26	25
Nordic countries									
Denmark	2	..	..	14	2	4	7	8	8
Finland	2	..	..	..	..	10	9	12	11
Norway	4	..	..	18	..	9	12	19	19
Sweden	7	..	..	6	7	6	15	16	18
Transition economies									
Czech Republic	..	..	..	..	..	..	..	11	12
Hungary	..	..	..	..	..	..	..	9	9
Poland	..	..	..	..	..	..	..	10	10
North America									
Canada	..	..	..	..	..	..	3	3	4
Mexico	..	..	..	..	..	..	..	..	..
United States	..	..	..	1	1	..	1	1	1
Asia and Oceania									
Australia	..	..	..	1	..	..	5	5	6
Japan	..	..	..	1	5.0	..	..	17	14
Korea	..	..	..	..	..	..	..	20	17
New Zealand	..	..	..	1	..	..	..	7	3
Spearman rank correlation with OECD late-1990s (version 2) measure	0.74	0.27	–0.03	0.78	0.88	0.86	0.95	0.98	1.00

.. Data not available.

a) Ranks based on the average of the IOE scorings of obstacles to dismissal and to the use of regular and fixed-term contract workers.
b) Ranks based on the share of employer respondents claiming that hiring/firing restrictions are very important or important.
c) Ranks based on combination of legal notice period and severance pay, as averaged for the period from 1956 to 1984.
d) Author's compilation from the rankings in Emerson (1988).
e) Ranks based on the average of overall rankings for regular and temporary work in OECD (1994a), Tables 6.5 and 6.6.
f) Ranks in versions 1 and 2 were taken from Table 2.5.

Sources: Bertola (1990); European Commission (1991, 1995); IOE (1985); Lazear (1990); OECD (1994a).

correlations between previous summary indicators and that developed here range from 0.74 to 0.88, indicating considerable consistency. Furthermore, some of the differences with earlier rankings simply reflect changes in employment protection since the 1980s.

II. Exploring the Link between EPL and Labour Market Performance

A. Theoretical predictions and prior empirical evidence

The links between employment regulation and the performance of the labour market have occasioned both extensive public debate and much economic research. This section surveys the latter, so as to provide a context for the empirical analysis reported in Sections II.B and II.C.

Potential benefits and costs

There are a number of potential benefits and costs from EPL. Starting with the benefits:

- *For the worker.* The key intent of EPL is to reduce economic uncertainty by enhancing job and income security. Advance notice, for example, is a means to give workers ample warning of future layoffs and thus facilitate job search; seniority clauses are a means to protect older workers against dismissal; redundancy payments compensate workers for job loss. Employment protection may also enhance worker satisfaction and longer-term attachment to the job. Finally, if EPL implies longer-lasting employment relationships, this may provide positive incentives (to both the employer and the employee) to augment the worker's skills, especially those specific to the firm. Greater investment in training may, in turn, enhance productivity on the current job as well as re-employment prospects in case of a layoff.

- *For the firm.* Stable employment relationships can be a positive asset for firms insofar as they provide one of the preconditions for more trust, loyalty to the firm and co-operation on the part of the workforce [Akerloff (1984)]. For example, workers who feel secure may be less likely to resist the introduction of new technologies in the workplace and the re-organisation of working practices. Since a firm's decision to invest in training depends partly on the degree of its workers' attachment, EPL may enhance skill formation and, hence, internal flexibility [Piore (1986)].

- *For the collectivity.* If stable employment relations, trust and co-operation are important preconditions for enterprise adaptation, technological progress and skill upgrading, as many empirical studies suggest, EPL may enhance aggregate productivity, living standards and growth [Ichniowski *et al.* (1997); Nickell and Layard (1998); Levine and Tyson (1990)]. Employment protection is also a way to internalise the social costs of dismissals [Lindbeck and Snower (1988)]. EPL may discourage employers from dismissing workers when it would be socially preferable to redeploy them within the firm, thereby bringing the profitability criterion into closer correspondence with social efficiency. Also, legislated worker protection may correct asymmetries of power between employees and firms, especially in situations of monopsony [Gregg and Manning (1997)].

On the side of potential costs:

- *For the worker.* Even if EPL has the desired effects of improving the access of some workers to stable jobs that provide ample training opportunities, it may simultaneously disadvantage workers who fail to gain access to these sorts of jobs. In other words, EPL may enhance the dualism between protected workers (so-called "insiders") and jobseekers and temporary workers (so-called "outsiders"). But even workers in jobs that are covered by EPL rules face significant trade-offs. While EPL may reduce the probability that "insiders" will become unemployed due to redundancies, it may increase the chance of long-duration unemployment for the smaller number of workers continuing to be laid off by their employers. To the extent that EPL reduces overall hiring in the economy, it may also tend to lock protected workers into relatively poor job matches by making it more difficult for them to obtain a new position. Finally, employers may try to off-set some of their costs of complying with EPL by negotiating lower wages.

- *For the firm.* Employment protection may raise labour costs since it is, in effect, a tax on work-force adjustments, obliging firms to pay severance payments and comply with other regulatory requirements. To some extent, firms can reduce these explicit costs by "smoothing" employment. However, doing so may result in significant implicit costs, such as the costs of keeping non-productive workers in the firm or of remaining overstaffed for significant periods of time following reductions in demand.

- *For the collectivity.* Employment protection may produce two major types of costs for the collectivity.

First, if EPL tends to trap a portion of the population in long-duration unemployment or a pattern of cycling between unemployment and temporary jobs, it could worsen the problems of labour market inequality and social exclusion. Second, EPL may result in a more sclerotic labour market, unable to achieve quickly the volume of workforce adjustment that is required in response to rapid changes in technologies and product market competition. Any such diminished ability to reallocate labour in a flexible manner would tend to lower aggregate productivity levels and growth prospects. It is also possible that rigidities caused by EPL could raise the overall level of unemployment, although the likely tendency for unemployment durations to increase will tend to be offset by a reduction in the number of workers experiencing redundancies (see below).

Overview of prior results

Economic theorists have constructed formal models assessing how EPL is likely to affect labour market performance [for a recent survey, see Bertola (1999)]. These models conceptualise EPL as a firing cost (*i.e.* a "tax" facing firms who want to layoff workers) and the analysis typically proceeds in three basic stages. First, it assesses how the hiring and firing policies of firms adjust to the incentive to "smooth" employment, for a given wage structure. Second, it reviews how EPL may affect wage bargaining, where the effect could be either to restrain wages (*e.g.* as employers attempt to shift some of the costs of EPL back to workers in the form of lower wages) or to increase them (*e.g.* if stricter EPL serves to raise the bargaining powers of "insiders"). The final stage seeks to place these changes in workers' and firms' behaviour into a general equilibrium model of the determination of labour market outcomes, such as employment and unemployment.[15]

Although much of the theoretical analysis of EPL is quite sophisticated, it is not yet possible to incorporate all of the potentially important effects of EPL into existing economic models. For example, many of the potential benefits from encouraging more stable employment patterns (*e.g.* more co-operative labour relations and greater on-the-job training) are rarely considered. More generally, this literature has tended to focus on the potential costs of reducing external flexibility in the employment of labour, while largely ignoring potential enhancements to internal flexibility or economic security that may offset some of the negative effects of EPL.

The following provides a summary of the main findings from selected recent empirical studies of the impact of EPL on the performance of the labour market (see Annex 2.C for a more extensive survey):

- Some studies find that employment and labour force levels are lower when EPL is strict. Nickell (1997) and Nickell and Layard (1998) argue that these results might be biased, since there is a "spurious" correlation between low female participation and strict EPL, both of which are typical in southern European countries. Consistent with this interpretation, the effect disappears when the comparison is confined to adult male employment rates. Another possibility is that the result is driven by youth employment, since youth transitions into employment may become more difficult when EPL is stricter.

- Concerning overall unemployment levels, the theoretical analysis is inconclusive. The higher firing costs resulting from EPL reduce hirings during upswings (because employers become more hesitant about taking on additional workers, as they are aware of the costs of dismissals), but also reduce firings during downswings, so that the net impact on the unemployment stock is indeterminate. In practice, most of the studies surveyed in Annex 2.C find no effect.

- The empirical evidence is stronger, however, for EPL causing changes in the dynamics of unemployment. The unemployment pool becomes more stagnant, due to the lower inflows and outflows, and longer durations [Bentolila and Bertola (1990); Büchtemann (1993*a*); Nickell (1997); Nickell and Layard (1998)]. Stricter EPL appears to be associated with lower rates of job displacement from firms that continue in operation, but also leads to longer durations of unemployment following displacement [Albæk *et al.* (1998)].

- Flows through employment may not be affected as strongly by EPL as unemployment flows. There is little correlation between the magnitude of job and worker flows and the "flexibility" of the labour market across countries [Garibaldi *et al.* (1997) and Alogoskoufis *et al.* (1995), but see Schettkat (1997) for some opposing evidence]. In effect, the rates of job creation and job destruction (*i.e.* the gross job turnover rate) do not seem to differ between North America and some European countries [Bertola and Rogerson (1997); Contini *et al.* (1995); OECD (1996*b*), Chapter 5; but see Blanchard and Portugal (1998) for some opposing evidence]. Mean job tenures are also roughly similar in countries with very

---

15. The analysis may incorporate additional behavioural responses to EPL, such as advance notice encouraging workers to begin job search in anticipation of a redundancy or voluntary quits declining in response to greater conservatism in companies' hiring decisions [Garibaldi (1998)].

different labour market institutions [Burgess *et al.* (1997)], but stricter EPL increases the share of quits where the worker moves directly to another job [Boeri (1999)].

- EPL may also alter the composition of employment and unemployment. The cost of a "bad match" might be higher for firms when EPL is stricter, causing them to avoid hiring "risky" workers (unless wages are sufficiently lower to compensate for that risk). Esping-Andersen (forthcoming) and Scarpetta (1996) conclude that youths are the most adversely affected group, especially in a context of wage compression. Grubb and Wells (1993) find that stricter EPL increases the proportion of self-employment and temporary employment in total employment across countries, but reduces the proportion of part-timers.

- The higher dismissal costs caused by EPL may shift firms' preferences from varying employment in favour of adjusting hours worked, when responding to fluctuations in demand. Bertola (1990) finds that employment becomes more stable and hours less stable, when EPL is stricter. Abraham and Houseman (1993) show that Japan, like most European countries, tends to adjust both in the short- and long-run through hours, while the United States uses employment adjustments. It appears, however, that total labour input adjustment (*i.e.* combining hours and workers) in manufacturing is similar between some European countries and the United States, suggesting that EPL may not greatly hamper firms' ability to adjust total labour input.

- At the macroeconomic level, unemployment appears to become more persistent and the speed of adjustment declines in the presence of stricter EPL [Jackman *et al.* (1996)]. A possible explanation is that, when unemployment rises due to an adverse shock, stricter EPL decreases the restraining effect of higher unemployment on wages and, hence, raises the level of unemployment required for price stability. Reinforcing mechanisms, such as duration dependence and marginalisation [Blanchard (1998)] can create a pattern of hysteresis, so that an initial increase in unemployment tends to persist [see, for example, Bertola (1990); Blanchard and Summers (1987); Blanchard (1998); Flanagan (1988)].[16]

- One empirical question that remains open is why some economies manage to combine strong regulations with low unemployment. One possible explanation has to do with institutional interactions. Bertola and Rogerson (1997) find that the degree of flexibility in wage-setting appears to affect the strength of the link between EPL and employment, with rigid wage setting in the presence of strict EPL being a potentially unfortunate mix. Similarly, Elmeskov *et al.* (forthcoming) find that the effect of EPL depends on the structure of collective bargaining.

Limitations of prior empirical studies

Empirical studies of the labour market impact of EPL face a number of major difficulties, some of which apply to the analysis in this chapter:

- *EPL measures.* Many studies are based on inadequate measures of EPL. For example, EPL data are often only available for one out-of-date year (*e.g.* the OECD Jobs Study indicators for the late 1980s), only one dimension (*e.g.* Lazear's time series on maximum severance pay), or are based on subjective measures (*e.g.* employer surveys). With the EPL indicators presented in Section I, this chapter makes a major advance on this front.

- *Isolation of labour market impact.* It is extremely difficult to isolate the effects of EPL on labour market outcomes from other determinants. In particular, cross-sectional analysis of country data suffers from few degrees of freedom and an inability to control adequately for country effects. This chapter makes a modest advance here by adding more countries and some time-variation in EPL.

- *Dynamics of EPL reform.* Empirical evidence about the dynamics of EPL reforms is limited. Changes in employment protection are likely to affect employers' expectations and hiring policies in complex ways. One example of this complexity is described in Box 1. A similar reform (*i.e.* de-regulation of fixed-term contracts) implemented in Spain and Germany at about the same time nonetheless yielded very different outcomes which took a number of years to unfold. This chapter presents simple associations between changes in EPL and changes in labour market outcomes that are intended to begin to unravel these issues.

- *Components of EPL.* Not much attention has been paid to the relative importance of different components of employment protection for labour market performance. As noted above, EPL involves many different aspects of regulation which are unlikely to affect

---

16. By protecting insiders and reducing firms' willingness to hire outsiders, EPL may lead to segmentation between these two groups, with self-reinforcing effects on the future reemployment prospects of the outsiders, resulting in longer average durations of unemployment for the latter.

> **Box 1. De-regulation strategies: the German and Spanish experiences with fixed-term contracts**
>
> During the mid-1980s, Germany and Spain significantly eased restrictions on the use of fixed-term contracts [see Table 2.1]. Despite the similarity of these reforms, the impact was sharply different in the two countries and has taken many years to unfold [Büchtemann (1991, 1993*b*); Milner *et al.* (1995)]. First, in Germany, fixed-term contracts grew only modestly and still account for a relatively small proportion of the labour force (about 8 per cent if apprentices are not included, and 12 per cent if they are included). By contrast, the share of fixed-term contracts increased rapidly in Spain, from 10 per cent to one-third of dependent employment. Second, fixed-term employment is concentrated among first-time job seekers or in certain job categories (*e.g.* unskilled jobs which require no on-the-job training) in Germany, whereas it is spread across a much broader range of Spanish workers and firms. Furthermore, a much higher proportion of German workers hired under the type of fixed-term contract introduced in the 1980s gain permanent status [BMAS (1994)] than is the case for their Spanish counterparts, of whom only approximately 10 per cent do so [Güell-Rotllan and Petrongolo (1998)].
>
> Why did similar reforms to EPL lead to such different outcomes? One possible explanation is related to the tradition of social partnership which has strong roots in Germany, but not in Spain. The strong sense of social partnership, which contributes to the success of the German dual-system of vocational training, may also encourage firms to regard stable and long-term relationships with employees as a positive asset [Büchtemann (1993*b*)]. Hence, German employers use fixed-term contracts primarily to screen workers for permanent positions. In Spain, on the other hand, firms use fixed-term contracts mainly to obtain "numerical flexibility", in adjusting to changes in labour requirements.
>
> Another possible explanation is that the wide availability to German employers of (fixed-term) apprenticeship contracts, which pay well below entry-level wages for unskilled adult workers, is viewed by them as a preferable alternative to regular fixed-term contracts. Despite the existence of apprenticeship contracts in Spain, most youths are hired on fixed-term contracts with no training obligation [see Rogowsky and Schömann (1996) for a comparative review].
>
> A third possible explanation is that the potential future firing costs due to EPL that were associated with hiring a worker on a permanent contract, as opposed to a fixed-term contract, remained larger in Spain than in Germany. The indicators presented in Section I suggest this was the case in the late 1980s, but may no longer be so today.

labour market outcomes in the same way. Identifying the best mixes of EPL components is important for informing policy choices. The analysis in Sections II.B and II.C explores multiple measures of EPL.

- *Institutional interactions.* Relatively little attention has been paid to the ways in which other labour market institutions condition the effects that EPL has on labour market outcomes. This chapter also explores a small number of interactions between EPL and other institutional variables (*e.g.* centralisation/co-ordination of collective bargaining and the generosity of unemployment benefits).
- *Off-setting flexibilities.* The use of alternative practices that may offset some of the effects of EPL has not had much attention in the literature, even though such off-setting flexibility may be of great relevance. For example, early retirement may be regarded as an offsetting flexibility in situations where dismissals of older workers are costly; self-employment may be one way of avoiding restrictions on employment contracts or high fixed wage costs; short-time work and work-sharing may be ways to adjust in recessions; informal or black-economy activity may be a response to overly regulated labour markets.
- *Social welfare.* Even when robust associations have been established between employment protection and labour market outcomes, a comprehensive evaluation of the implications for social welfare is rarely undertaken. For example, stricter EPL appears to be associated with longer lasting jobs. This shift to higher tenures might reflect important gains in economic security and on-the-job training, or it might reflect an increased number of workers spending long periods in jobs they do not like or are ill suited for. The equity and efficiency effects of an EPL-induced shift toward fewer, but longer lasting unemployment spells are similarly difficult to evaluate. A fuller assessment of the benefits and costs of employment protection regulation will be required if empirical research is to inform policy choices more effectively, but such an assessment would be very complex and is not attempted in this chapter.

B. Effects on employment and unemployment

Bivariate associations

Chart 2.2 plots the most comprehensive indicator of EPL in the late 1990s (along the horizontal axis) against measures of employment and unemployment averaged over 1990-1997 (along the vertical axis). Panel A suggests that there is no association between EPL strictness and overall unemployment. However, the other charts in

72 – OECD Employment Outlook

Chart 2.2. Overall EPL strictness,[a] employment and unemployment

Panel A: Unemployment rates, averages over 1990-97
Percentages

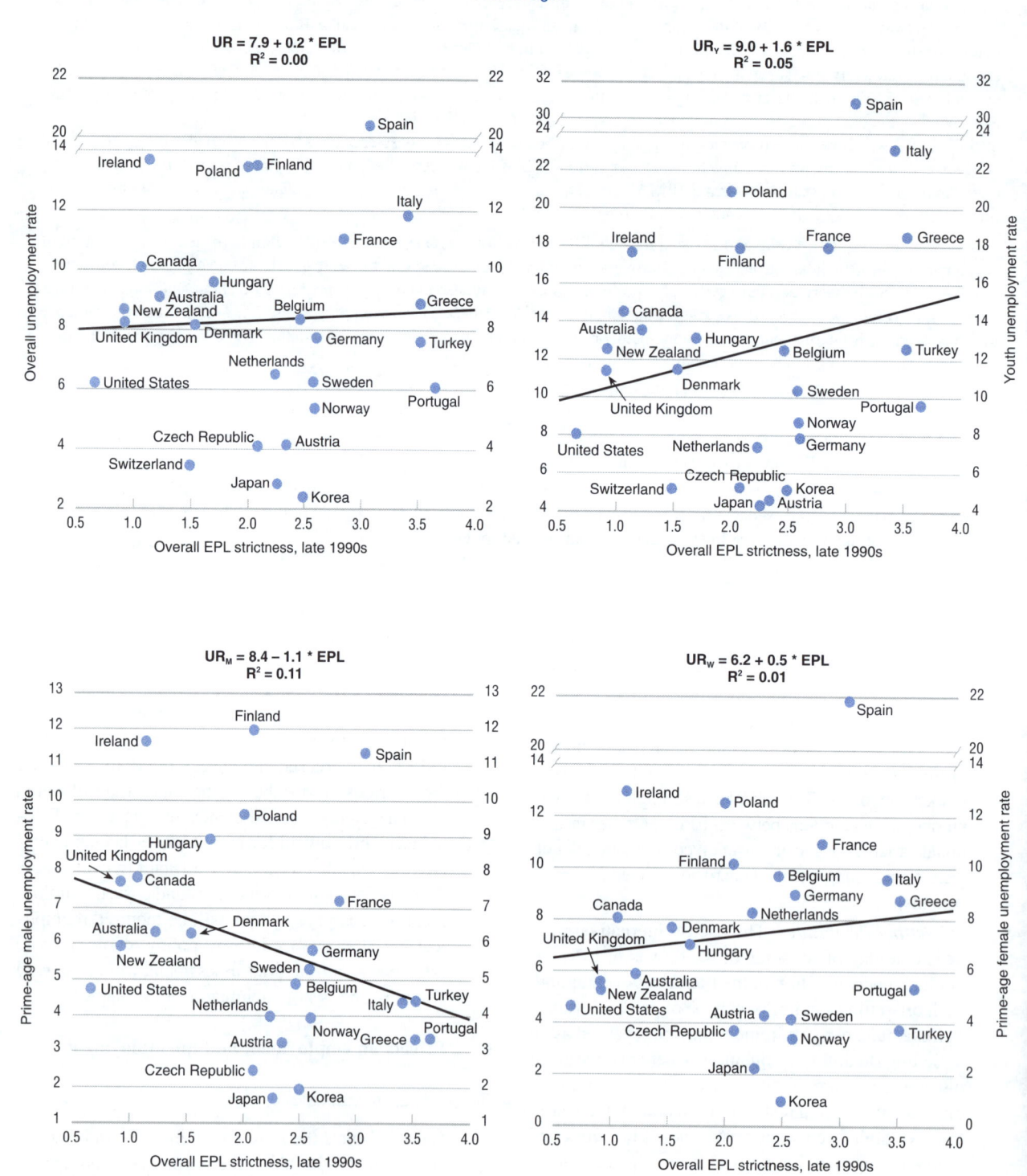

$UR = 7.9 + 0.2 * EPL$
$R^2 = 0.00$

$UR_Y = 9.0 + 1.6 * EPL$
$R^2 = 0.05$

$UR_M = 8.4 - 1.1 * EPL$
$R^2 = 0.11$

$UR_W = 6.2 + 0.5 * EPL$
$R^2 = 0.01$

a) Overall EPL strictness, version 2.

Employment Protection and Labour Market Performance – 73

Chart 2.2. Overall EPL strictness,[a] employment and unemployment *(cont.)*
Panel B: Employment/population ratios, averages over 1990-97
Percentages

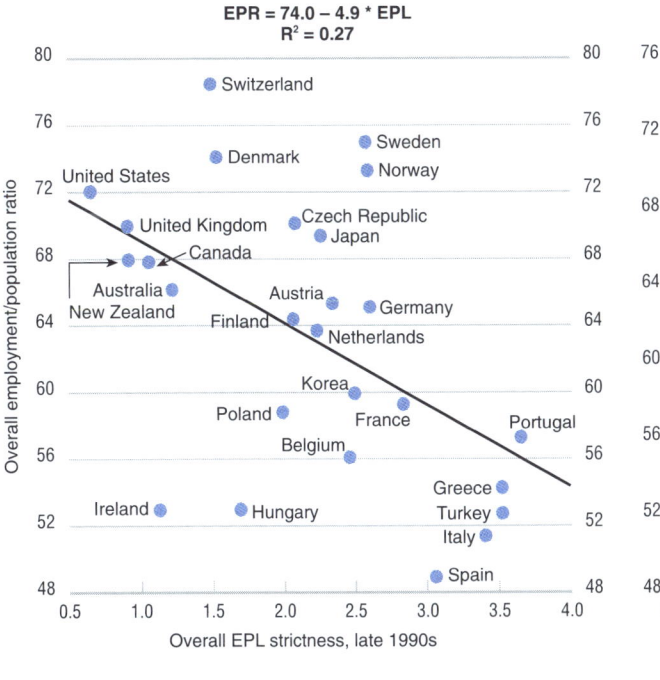

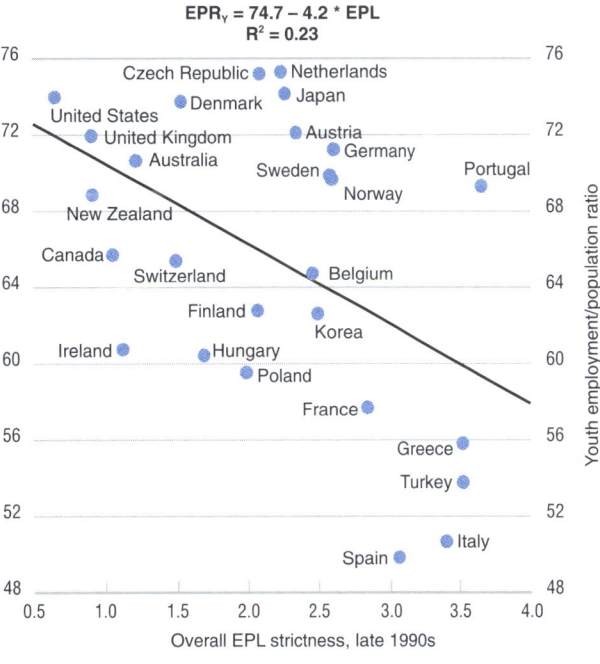

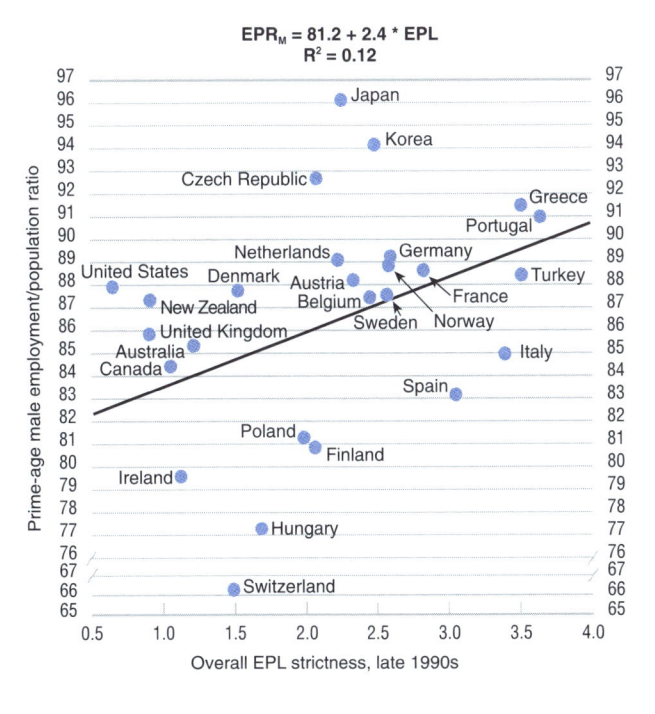

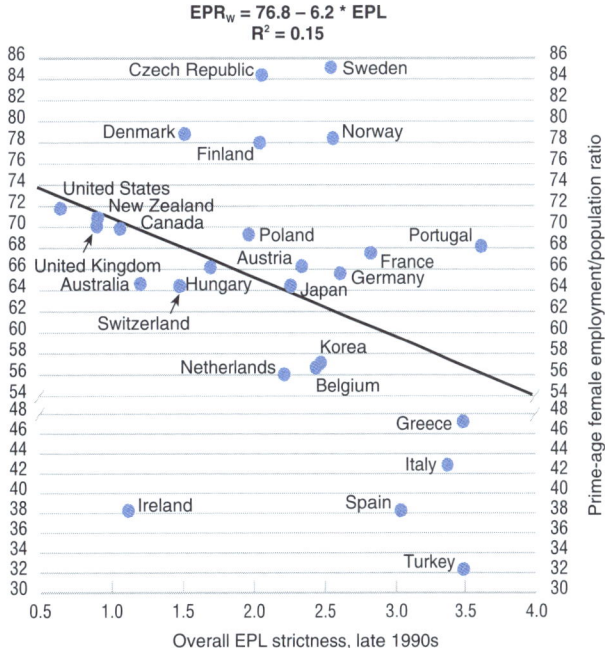

Top left: EPR = 74.0 − 4.9 * EPL, $R^2 = 0.27$ (Overall employment/population ratio vs Overall EPL strictness, late 1990s)

Top right: EPR_Y = 74.7 − 4.2 * EPL, $R^2 = 0.23$ (Youth employment/population ratio vs Overall EPL strictness, late 1990s)

Bottom left: EPR_M = 81.2 + 2.4 * EPL, $R^2 = 0.12$ (Prime-age male employment/population ratio vs Overall EPL strictness, late 1990s)

Bottom right: EPR_W = 76.8 − 6.2 * EPL, $R^2 = 0.15$ (Prime-age female employment/population ratio vs Overall EPL strictness, late 1990s)

a) Overall EPL strictness, version 2.

OECD

74 – OECD Employment Outlook

Chart 2.2. Overall EPL strictness,[a] employment and unemployment (cont.)
Panel C: Employment shares by type of employment, averages over 1990-97
Percentages

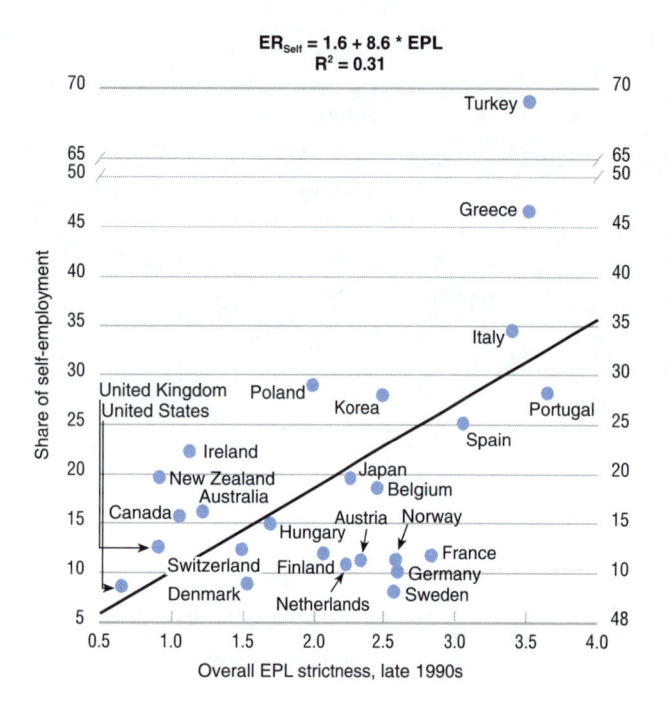

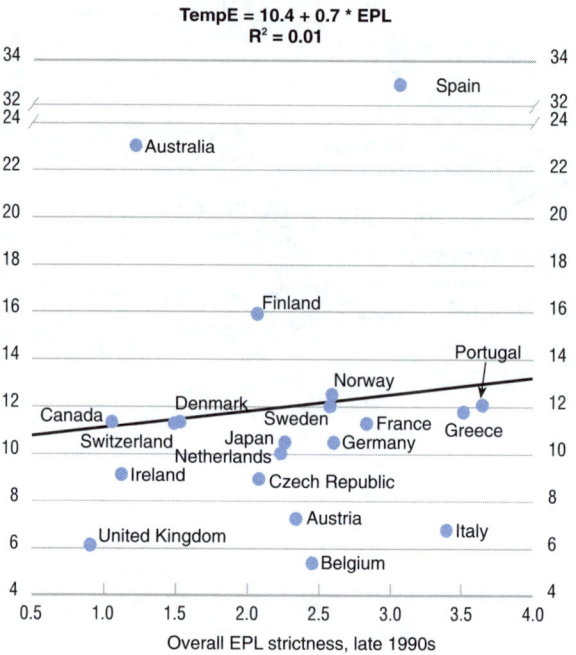

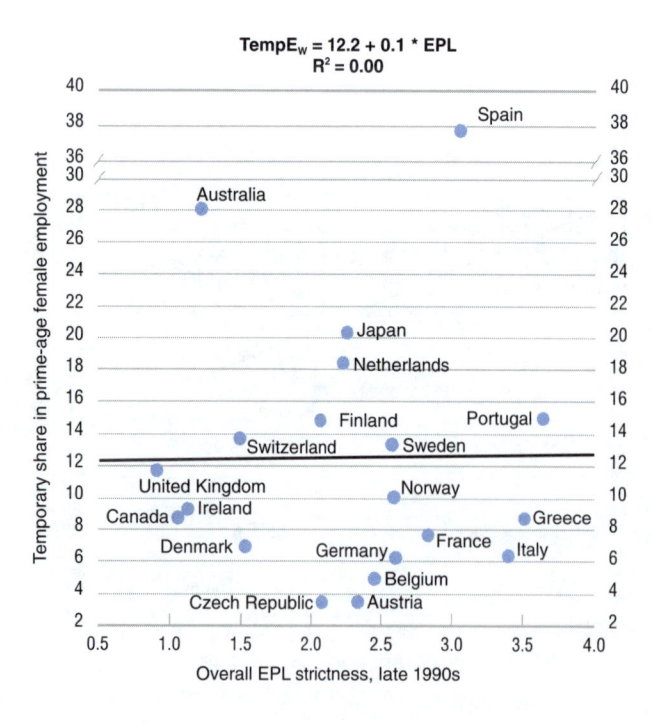

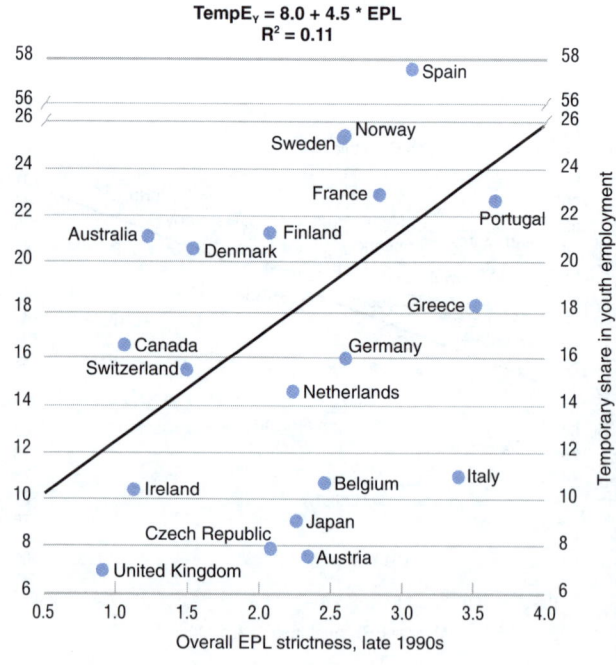

$ER_{Self} = 1.6 + 8.6 * EPL$
$R^2 = 0.31$

$TempE = 10.4 + 0.7 * EPL$
$R^2 = 0.01$

$TempE_W = 12.2 + 0.1 * EPL$
$R^2 = 0.00$

$TempE_Y = 8.0 + 4.5 * EPL$
$R^2 = 0.11$

a) Overall EPL strictness, version 2.
Sources: See Table 2.5 and Annex 2.D.

Panel A show some correlations between EPL strictness and the demographic composition of unemployment: stricter EPL being associated with lower unemployment for prime-age men, but with higher unemployment for youths and, perhaps, prime-age women. However, the low fits of the regression lines suggest that EPL is not the dominant determinant of international differences in either the level or the demographic composition of unemployment.

EPL strictness, however, is more strongly associated with employment rates, although, here too, the scatter of data points is quite dispersed. Panel B of Chart 2.2 shows a clear negative relationship between EPL strictness and the overall employment/population ratio. This negative association also holds for youths and prime-age women, but it reverses for prime-age men, consistent with the hypothesis that EPL protects the jobs of prime-age men (who are mainly insiders) at the cost of reducing employment for prime-age women and youths (who are mainly outsiders). Panel C shows that stricter EPL is associated with a higher share of self-employment. Regulation of regular contracts is expected to increase the share of temporary jobs and regulation of temporary employment is expected to reduce it, so the impact of the comprehensive indicator is theoretically ambiguous. Only among young workers is stricter EPL associated with an appreciable increase in the share holding temporary jobs. Thus, stricter EPL may encourage greater use of temporary contracts, but only for labour market entrants whose "productivities" are unknown due to their lack of work experience. Alternatively, recent liberalisations of EPL for temporary employment may not yet be fully reflected in hiring practices, but are beginning to be visible for younger workers.

Table 2.7 presents the simple correlation coefficients between a variety of EPL strictness indicators, in both the late 1980s and the late 1990s, and various employment and unemployment rates. Many of these correlation coefficients are small and not significantly different from zero, especially the correlations between measures of EPL strictness and the unemployment rates. However, these correlations suggest that EPL strictness may have an effect on employment rates and the share of self-employment. EPL strictness on temporary employment is more strongly associated with employment and self-employment rates than is EPL for regular employment or collective dismissals.[17] Over the past ten years, the correlations have increased between EPL strictness for temporary work and the overall, prime-age female and youth employment rates, as well as the share of self-employment.

The correlations between the EPL strictness measures and the share of temporary employment are never significant at even the 10 per cent level. However, the correlation between EPL strictness for regular work in the late 1980s and the shares of temporary employment are consistently positive and moderately large, a pattern that attenuates strongly in the late 1990s. Why this should be is unclear. One possibility, assuming there is a causal relationship, is that insufficient time has elapsed for recent reforms of EPL to be fully reflected in employers' use of temporary contracts.

Overall, the bivariate analysis suggests that EPL affects employment rates more than unemployment rates. This pattern suggests that stricter EPL may be associated with approximately equal shifts in labour force participation and employment: the employment and participation of prime-age men tending to be higher in countries with stricter EPL, but tending to be lower for prime-age women and youths. Stricter EPL is also associated with a higher share of self-employment, but there is little or no evidence of a link to the share of temporary employment, except in the case of young workers.

Multivariate analysis

Multivariate analysis may provide a superior assessment of the effects of employment protection on labour market performance since it controls for other determinants of cross-country differences in employment and unemployment. Accordingly, Tables 2.8 to 2.11 report the estimated coefficients from multivariate regression models that attempt to isolate the causal impact of various measures of EPL strictness. Although it is desirable to control for other determinants of labour market outcomes, these regression models rely on strong assumptions that may not be justified. As a result, both the bivariate and the multivariate results are of value for assessing the impact of EPL.

Panel-data methods are used to take advantage of the availability of the EPL indicators at two points in time [Hsiao (1986)]. The regression coefficients are estimated using the random-effects, generalised least squares (GLS) procedure that incorporates time-invariant "country effects".[18] Since the EPL strictness indicators are only available for two points in

---

17. The one possible exception is that stricter EPL for regular employment contributes significantly to the positive association between overall EPL strictness and the employment rate for prime-age men.
18. Allowing for cross-country differences in labour market performance that reflect the influence of omitted variables is highly desirable, but the random-effects method for doing so produces biased estimates if these country effects are correlated with the model regressors. Therefore, a Hausman test for misspecification of the random-effects model is shown for each regression [Hausman (1978)]. As an additional check, all of the panel models reported in this chapter were reestimated without country effects. When data for the two periods are pooled, the OLS coefficients for the EPL variables are similar to the random-effects GLS estimates that are discussed below.

Table 2.7. **Correlation coefficients between EPL indicators and static measures of employment and unemployment**[a, b]

Indicators of the strictness of EPL

	Regular employment		Temporary employment		Collective dismissals	Overall EPL, version 1[c]		Overall EPL, version 2[d]
	Late 1980s	Late 1990s	Late 1980s	Late 1990s	Late 1990s	Late 1980s	Late 1990s	Late 1990s
Employment[e]								
Employment/population ratios								
Overall	−0.35	−0.27	−0.40*	−0.52***	0.02	−0.43*	−0.48**	−0.46**
Prime-age males	0.32	0.42**	0.43*	0.31	−0.18	0.42*	0.40**	0.35*
Prime-age females	−0.19	−0.14	−0.19	−0.52***	0.09	−0.21	−0.42**	−0.39*
Youths	−0.26	−0.15	−0.42*	−0.61***	−0.08	−0.41*	−0.48**	−0.48**
Share of self-employment	0.36	0.32	0.46**	0.66***	−0.05	0.46**	0.59***	0.56***
Share of temporary employment								
Overall	0.27	0.02	−0.03	0.18	0.05	0.10	0.13	0.10
Prime-age females	0.27	0.03	−0.14	0.07	−0.15	0.02	0.06	0.01
Youths	0.45	0.15	0.24	0.38	0.09	0.38	0.35	0.33
Unemployment[e, f]								
Unemployment rates								
Overall	0.16	−0.13	0.09	0.14	−0.02	0.15	0.04	0.05
Prime-age males	−0.14	−0.37	−0.31	−0.20	−0.05	−0.26	−0.31	−0.30
Prime-age females	0.23	−0.07	0.16	0.16	0.10	0.23	0.08	0.11
Youths	0.21	−0.05	0.30	0.34	0.03	0.31	0.21	0.22
ISCED 0-2, prime age	−0.13	−0.34	−0.23	−0.24	−0.07	−0.21	−0.32	−0.32
ISCED 3, prime age	0.15	−0.16	−0.01	0.03	−0.09	0.06	−0.05	−0.06
ISCED 5, prime age	0.17	−0.01	0.11	0.29	−0.05	0.15	0.18	0.17
ISCED 6-7, prime age	0.12	−0.18	0.08	0.21	−0.12	0.11	0.07	0.05

*, ** and *** denote correlation coefficient significant at 10%, 5% and 1% levels respectively.
a) Variables of labour market performance are averages over 1990-1997, except the unemployment rates by levels of education, which are averages over 1991, 1992, 1994, 1995 and 1996.
b) The sample size is between 16 and 21 countries.
c) Average of summary indicators for regular employment and temporary employment (see Table 2.5 for details and explanations).
d) Weighted average of summary indicators for regular employment, temporary employment and collective dismissals (see Table 2.5 for details and explanations).
e) Age groups: 16-64 for the overall, 30-54 for prime age and 20-29 for the youth.
f) Educational attainments are divided in four groups: ISCED 0-2 for primary and lower secondary levels of education, ISCED 3 for upper secondary level of education, ISCED 5 for non-university tertiary level of education and ISCED 6-7 for university tertiary level of education.
Sources: For labour market performance variables see Annex 2.D. EPL variables are from Table 2.5.

time, a two-period model is estimated: the first period combines late-1980s EPL values with 1985-1990 averages for the performance and control variables, and the second period combines late-1990s EPL values with 1992-1997 averages for the other variables.[19] This averaging has the twin advantages of smoothing out some of the effects of the cycle and reducing measurement error.[20]

The selection of the control variables closely follows specifications previously used in the literature. The "basic specification" includes four variables characterising the wage bargaining structure (*i.e.* the degrees of centralisation and co-ordination of collective bargaining, trade union density, and collective bargaining coverage), two variables characterising income-support schemes for the unemployed (*i.e.* the average gross replacement rate and the maximum duration of benefits), the tax wedge, spending on active labour market policies (ALMPs) and the output gap to control for the effects of the cycle. Due to limited availability of the performance and control variables, the final regression sample is restricted to 19 of the 27 OECD countries for which EPL data are presented in Section I.[21]

[19]. It would probably be desirable to introduce a time lag between the dates at which EPL strictness and labour market performance are measured, since it may take several years for changes in EPL to be fully reflected in employment and unemployment. It has, for example, been argued that the initial impacts of EPL reforms on employment and unemployment may differ from their long-run effects [Bertola and Ichino (1995)]. It is not yet possible to explore lagged effects when analysing the EPL data for the late 1990s, but the possibility that recent changes in EPL are not yet fully visible in labour market performance needs to be taken into account when interpreting the results.
[20]. Alternative averaging periods were tried, but the results did not change significantly.
[21]. Two of the countries included in the regression sample, Japan and New Zealand, contribute only a single observation, since no EPL data are available for the late 1980s. More details on data availability, as well as the definitions and sources of the performance and control variables, can be found in Annex 2.D.

Unemployment effects

Table 2.8 presents regression coefficients for models relating international differences in overall unemployment rates to EPL strictness and various combinations of control variables. The first column reports a "basic specification" that closely parallels those used in previous studies, including a typical list of control variables and a single, overall, indicator of EPL strictness. A second version of the basic specification is presented in column (2), which differs only in that separate indicators are used for the three main components of EPL (*i.e.* strictness for regular employment, temporary employment and collective dismissals). In both cases, the results are qualitatively similar. The estimated coefficient for overall EPL strictness is very small and insignificant, which accords with the majority of the prior studies reviewed in Annex 2.C and the plots in Chart 2.2. Similarly, none of the coefficients for the three components of EPL indicates a significant impact on unemployment. The latter result is quite novel, since few studies have analysed the impact of separate components of EPL, and suggests that the finding of no link between overall EPL strictness and unemployment is not due to off-setting effects of the separate components of EPL.[22]

The remaining five columns of Table 2.8 further demonstrate the robustness of this result. Columns (3) and (4) report estimates for two specifications in which the components of EPL are further disaggregated. In the first specification, EPL for regular employment is divided into two components: regulations that imply a transfer from the employer to the employee (*i.e.* notice period and severance pay) and regulations that imply a net "tax" on the employment relationship (*i.e.* procedural inconveniences and difficulty of dismissal).[23] In the second specification, EPL for temporary work is divided into regulations for fixed-term contracts and for TWAs. In neither case, are any of the EPL coefficients of statistical significance.

The final three columns of Table 2.8 report results for additional generalisations of the basic specifications, which incorporate two new control variables[24] and interactions between EPL strictness and two measures of labour market institutions that may influence the strength of the link between EPL and unemployment: the centralisation and co-ordination of wage bargaining and the generosity of the unemployment benefits scheme [Bertola (1999)]. The interaction of EPL strictness with the centralisation/co-ordination index yields a marginally significant, negative coefficient, consistent with the argument that strict EPL is less likely to increase unemployment if wage bargaining is effectively co-ordinated at the national level.[25] The coefficient of the interaction with the replacement rate for unemployment benefits is zero. Although there is some confirmation that interaction effects may be important, there is no indication that adding the additional control variables or interactions reveals important effects of EPL strictness on overall unemployment that were obscured by the simpler specifications. The basic finding appears robust: overall unemployment is not significantly related to EPL strictness.

Turning now to the demographic composition of unemployment, Table 2.9 presents regressions relating international differences in the unemployment rates of prime-age males, prime-age females, youths and the low-skilled to EPL. In this and all the following tables, each independent variable (*i.e.* measure of labour market performance) is investigated using the two versions of the basic specification. "Model 1" includes a single, overall indicator of EPL strictness (Version 1 from Table 2.5) and is most easily compared with previous studies. "Model 2" includes separate indicators of EPL strictness for regular employment, temporary employment and collective dismissals. It allows for the possibility that these different components of EPL have distinct effects on labour market outcomes. Both models also contain the same nine control variables used in columns (1) to (4) of Table 2.8, although their coefficients are not reported.

The regression coefficients only weakly support the inference from Chart 2.2 that stricter EPL may affect the demographic composition of unemployment. The strongest evidence is for a reduction in unemployment for prime-age men. However, the bivariate association between stricter EPL and higher unemployment is only weakly confirmed for youths and totally disappears for prime-age women. This result is somewhat different from those obtained by several prior studies, which have also found

---

22. The fit of the basic specifications are quite good: R-squared values exceed 0.6, the model coefficients are highly jointly significant and the Hausman statistic indicates acceptance of the random-effects specification. A number of the control variables have statistically significant coefficients that accord well with previous studies.
23. The former may tend to have less impact on employment and unemployment than the latter, because mandated, employer-to-employee transfers can – at least in principle – be fully off-set by adjusting hiring terms, while payments to third parties or procedural costs represent an inescapable reduction in the joint income of the employer and employee.
24. The two additional control variables are the percentage of home owners – a control variable proposed in Oswald (1996) and used in Nickell and Layard (1998) – and earnings dispersion.
25. Elmeskov *et al.* (forthcoming) found that EPL raises unemployment more in combination with an intermediate level of centralisation and co-ordination of bargaining, than with either high or low levels. An alternative specification of the model in column (6) of Table 2.8 was estimated that allowed for such a pattern but the estimated interaction effect was monotonically decreasing, rather than "hump-shaped".

Table 2.8. Two-period panel regressions to explain (log) overall unemployment rate[a, b]

Random-effects GLS estimates

	Basic specifications		Further disaggregation of EPL components		Augmented basic specification	Interactions	
	(1)	(2)	(3)	(4)	(5)	(6)	(7)
Strictness of EPL							
Overall EPL, version 1	–0.01 (0.1)				–0.05 (0.5)	–0.06 (0.6)	–0.06 (0.5)
Regular employment		0.02 (0.2)		0.02 (0.1)			
Procedural inconveniences and difficulty of dismissal			–0.05 (0.4)				
Notice period and severance pay			0.08 (0.7)				
Temporary employment		–0.03 (0.4)	–0.04 (0.5)				
Fixed-term contracts				–0.02 (0.2)			
TWAs				–0.01 (0.2)			
Collective dismissals		–0.04 (0.3)	–0.11 (0.6)	–0.04 (0.2)			
Interactions[c]							
EPL with the average of co-ordination and centralisation						–0.29 (1.8)*	
EPL with the replacement rate							0.00 (0.4)
Wage bargaining system							
Co-ordination (1-2.5)	–0.43 (2.7)***	–0.44 (2.5)**	–0.39 (2.0)**	–0.44 (2.5)**	–0.23 (1.4)	–0.01 (0.1)	–0.25 (1.4)
Centralisation (1-2.5)	–0.25 (0.9)	–0.19 (0.6)	–0.21 (0.7)	–0.21 (0.7)	–0.20 (0.8)	0.10 (0.3)	–0.11 (0.4)
Trade union density (%)	–0.01 (1.2)	–0.01 (1.1)	–0.01 (1.1)	–0.01 (1.0)	–0.01 (1.7)*	–0.01 (1.4)	–0.01 (0.2)
Bargaining coverage (%)	0.01 (1.5)	0.01 (1.1)	0.01 (1.2)	0.01 (1.1)	0.01 (1.4)	0.01 (1.0)	0.01 (1.1)
Unemployment benefit scheme							
Replacement rate (%)	0.02 (2.1)**	0.01 (1.8)*	0.01 (1.7)*	0.01 (1.8)*	0.01 (1.3)	0.01 (1.6)	0.01 (1.0)
Duration (months)	0.00 (0.7)	0.00 (0.5)	0.00 (0.7)	0.00 (0.5)	0.00 (1.0)	0.00 (0.9)	0.00 (0.8)
Tax wedge (%)	0.02 (1.6)	0.03 (1.5)	0.03 (1.6)	0.03 (1.5)	0.02 (1.4)	0.02 (1.7)*	0.02 (1.4)
ALMP spendings (as % of GDP)	–0.38 (1.4)	–0.37 (1.2)	–0.33 (1.0)	–0.39 (1.3)	0.04 (0.1)	–0.05 (0.1)	0.04 (0.1)
Output gap	–0.11 (3.3)***	–0.11 (3.3)***	–0.11 (3.0)***	–0.11 (3.1)***	–0.09 (2.8)***	–0.09 (3.1)***	–0.10 (3.0)***
Home ownership rate (%)					0.02 (2.1)**	0.02 (1.8)*	0.02 (1.9)*
Earnings dispersion (D9/D1)					0.06 (0.4)	0.13 (0.8)	0.08 (0.5)
Number of observations[d]	34	34	34	34	34	34	34
R-squared	0.63	0.62	0.64	0.63	0.71	0.75	0.72
Wald test[e]	35.4 ***	31.6 ***	31.2 ***	30.7 ***	46.8 ***	50.6 ***	42.2 ***
Breusch and Pagan test[f]	0.67	0.69	0.21	0.14	0.03	0.03	0.03
Hausman test[g]	7.1	6.7	8.3	6.6	5.7	7.6	40.0 ***

*, ** and *** denote statistically significant at 10%, 5% and 1% levels respectively.
a) Generalised least squares estimates for the random-effects panel model. Absolute values of t-statistics reported in parenthesis. Regressions also contain a constant term.
b) Unemployment rates are averages over 1985-90 and 1992-97. EPL is measured in the late 1980s and the late 1990s, except for collective dismissals, where late 1990s values are used for both periods. Most control variables are measured over the same two periods. In the cases where data for a control variable are only available for one of the periods, the same value was assigned to the other period.
c) Interactions are calculated as the product of the overall EPL indicator (version 1) and the institutional variables (expressed as a mean deviation). For example, the interaction of EPL with replacement rate in country i is measured as: (EPL indicator for i) × (replacement rate for i – average replacement rate).
d) Nineteen countries are included in the estimation sample: Australia, Austria, Belgium, Canada, Denmark, Finland, France, Germany, Italy, Japan, the Netherlands, New Zealand, Norway, Portugal, Spain, Sweden, Switzerland, the United Kingdom and the United States. Since EPL data for the late 1980s are not available for Japan and New Zealand, these countries only contribute a single observation (i.e. for the late 1990s).
e) Wald test for joint significance of regressors (Chi-square statistic).
f) Breusch and Pagan Lagrangian multiplier test for presence of country effects (Chi-square statistic).
g) Hausman test for misspecification of the random-effects model (Chi-square statistic).
Sources: The summary indicators for EPL strictness are from Table 2.2, Panel B, Table 2.3, Panel B and Table 2.5. The sources and definitions for the control variables and the labour market performance variables are described in Annex 2.D.

Table 2.9. **Two-period panel regressions to explain log unemployment rates**[a, b]

Random-effects GLS estimates

	Overall unemployment rate (1)	Prime-age male unemployment rate [c] (2)	Prime-age female unemployment rate [c] (3)	Youth unemployment rate [c] (4)	Low-skilled unemployment rate [c] (5)
Strictness of EPL (model 1)					
Overall EPL, version 1	−0.01 (0.1)	−0.21 (1.9)*	−0.06 (0.5)	0.06 (0.6)	−0.13 (0.9)
Strictness of EPL (model 2)					
Regular employment	0.02 (0.2)	−0.06 (0.4)	0.02 (0.2)	0.01 (0.1)	−0.09 (0.5)
Temporary employment	−0.03 (0.4)	−0.13 (1.6)	−0.04 (0.5)	0.02 (0.3)	−0.06 (0.6)
Collective dismissals	−0.04 (0.3)	−0.05 (0.3)	0.15 (1.0)	−0.10 (0.5)	−0.04 (0.2)
Number of observations	34	33	33	34	34
Model 1					
R-squared	0.63	0.55	0.67	0.61	0.55
Wald test [d]	35.4 ***	39.3 ***	44.9 ***	34.3 ***	50.5 ***
Breusch and Pagan test [e]	0.7	4.5 **	0.5	0.8	0.8
Hausman test [f]	7.1	4.7	10.0	16.0 **	15.4 *
Model 2					
R-squared	0.62	0.56	0.69	0.61	0.55
Wald test [d]	31.6 ***	37.3 ***	42.7 ***	31.8 ***	47.0 ***
Breusch and Pagan test [e]	0.7	3.5 *	0.2	0.6	0.6
Hausman test [f]	6.7	6.1	8.0	13.5	16.9 *

*, ** and *** denote statistically significant at 10%, 5% and 1% levels respectively.
a) For explanations of the estimation method and data definitions see notes a) and b) of Table 2.8.
b) The results presented in this table are obtained from two different model specifications, refered to as "model 1" and "model 2", which correspond to the specifications in the first and second columns of Table 2.8 and incorporate the same nine control variables and a constant term (coefficients not reported here).
c) Prime age refers to the age group 30-54, youth refers to the age group 20-29 and low-skilled refers to workers with no more than primary and lower secondary levels of education (ISCED 0-2).
d) Wald test for joint significance of regressors (Chi-square statistic).
e) Breusch and Pagan Lagrangian multiplier test for presence of country effects (Chi-square statistic).
f) Hausman test for misspecification of the random-effects model (Chi-square statistic).
Source: See Table 2.8.

evidence that greater EPL strictness has little effect on overall unemployment, but have found stronger evidence that it increases relative unemployment for select groups, especially youths (see *Annex 2.C* for a summary of prior studies).

Employment effects

Table 2.10 presents regression results for the effect of EPL on employment rates. The coefficients on overall EPL strictness indicate a positive effect on the employment rate for prime-age men and negative effects for women and the total workforce. However, none of these coefficients are statistically significant at even the 10 per cent level and it would, thus, appear that EPL may have little impact on employment rates once other factors are controlled for. The coefficients for the three components of EPL also fail to confirm a statistically significant relationship. These results differ substantially from those of several prior studies, using an overall EPL strictness indicator for the late 1980s, which found a significant negative impact on overall employment, but no effect for prime-age males [Nickell (1997); Nickell and Layard (1998)].[26]

Table 2.10 does confirm that stricter EPL is a significant factor encouraging the expansion of self-employment (Table 2.10, column 5). This result is consistent with previous findings [Grubb and Wells (1993)], and suggests that self-employment functions as an alternative form of employment that avoids the costs of strict regulation. The regulations on regular employment appear to matter most for stimulating increased self-employment.

The final two columns in Table 2.10 examine the effect of EPL on the share of temporary work in total employment, first for the total workforce and then for

---
26. The Hausman misspecification test indicates that the random-effects specification used here may be inappropriate.

Table 2.10. **Two-period panel regressions to explain employment**[a, b, c]
Random-effects GLS estimates

	Overall employment/ population ratio (1)	Prime-age male employment/ population ratio[d] (2)	Prime-age female employment/ population ratio[d] (3)	Youth employment/ population ratio[d] (4)	Share of self-employment (5)	Temporary share in total employment (6)	Temporary share in youth employment[d] (7)
Strictness of EPL (model 1)							
Overall EPL, version 1	−1.59 (1.1)	1.37 (1.5)	−3.66 (1.4)	−0.54 (0.3)	2.75 (2.3)**	−0.01 (0.0)	1.81 (0.5)
Strictness of EPL (model 2)							
Regular employment	−1.30 (0.7)	0.91 (0.8)	−3.86 (1.1)	0.04 (0.0)	4.62 (3.9)***	−5.26 (2.5)**	−6.93 (1.7)*
Temporary employment	−0.64 (0.7)	0.44 (0.8)	−1.77 (1.1)	−0.31 (0.3)	−0.02 (0.0)	0.90 (0.9)	2.88 (1.2)
Collective dismissals	−0.44 (0.2)	−3.37 (1.7)*	−4.69 (0.7)	0.80 (0.3)	0.78 (0.3)	−5.76 (1.5)	−6.17 (1.0)
Number of observations	34	34	34	33	36	28	27
Model 1							
R-squared	0.69	0.50	0.54	0.60	0.54	0.21	0.27
Wald test[e]	29.8 ***	58.2 ***	11.6	45.0 ***	12.9	6.2	5.6
Breusch and Pagan test[f]	2.5	2.4	7.6 ***	1.2	1.3	4.1 **	4.0 **
Hausman test[g]	8.7	17.6 **	35.6 ***	27.5 ***	95.6 ***	5.2	3.2
Model 2							
R-squared	0.68	0.46	0.51	0.60	0.48	0.08	0.09
Wald test[e]	25.1 **	66.4 ***	8.6	41.9 ***	22.9 **	23.1 **	11
Breusch and Pagan test[f]	2.1	2.7	5.7 **	0.9	1.6	4.5 **	4.5 **
Hausman test[g]	26.7 ***	48.8 ***	37.7 ***	26.0 ***	3.4	10.5	7.9

*, ** and *** mean statistically significant at 10%, 5% and 1% levels respectively.
a) See note a) of Table 2.8 for an explanation of the estimation method.
b) Employment/population ratios are averages over 1985-90 and 1992-97.
c) See note b) from Table 2.9 for an explanation of the two regression models.
d) Prime age refers to the age group 30-54 and youth to the age group 20-29.
e) Wald test for joint significance of regressors (Chi-square statistic).
f) Breusch and Pagan Lagrangian multiplier test for presence of country effects (Chi-square statistic).
g) Hausman test for misspecification of the random-effects model (Chi-square statistic).
Source: See Table 2.8.

youths. These regressions accord with the bivariate analysis in detecting no significant effect of overall EPL strictness on the overall share of temporary employment and, at best, a weak effect for youths. When three separate indicators of EPL strictness are included in the model for total temporary employment, many of the estimated coefficients are large but the signs are uniformly inconsistent with the theoretical predictions that regulation of regular employment increases the incidence of temporary employment while regulation of temporary employment reduces it. Thus, the analysis does not confirm earlier research that found an important role for EPL in encouraging the growth of temporary employment, but neither is it particularly successful at identifying alternative explanations for international differences in its prevalence (as indicated by the low goodness-of-fit statistics).[27]

Effect of changes in EPL on changes in labour market outcomes

Have the changes in EPL during the past decade had a detectable effect on employment and unemployment? The regression models in Tables 2.8 to 2.10 were reestimated in first-difference form, which relates changes in labour market outcomes to changes in EPL strictness and the control variables.[28] A representative selection of the results are reported in Table 2.11.[29]

---

27. Several additional attempts were made to improve the model specification, but the qualitative results did not change. For example, the estimation sample was restricted to European Union countries, since that reduces cross-country differences in the nature and measurement of temporary employment [OECD (1996b, Table 2.5)]. Also, Model 2 was reestimated omitting the EPL indicator for collective dismissals, since the coefficients of this variable behave quite erratically.
28. Since first differencing the data removes any country effects, these models are estimated using ordinary least squares (OLS).
29. Three variables, for which only second-period (i.e. mid to late 1990s) data are available had to be omitted from these regressions (i.e. EPL for collective dismissals, unemployment benefit duration and the tax wedge).

Table 2.11. **Regressions to explain changes in the performance variables, from the late 1980s to the late 1990s**[a, b]

Cross-section OLS estimates

	Changes in unemployment rates				
	Overall (1)	Prime-age males[c] (2)	Prime-age females[c] (3)	Youth[c] (4)	Low-skilled[c] (5)
Changes in the strictness of EPL (model 1)					
Overall EPL, version 1	0.50 (0.3)	0.62 (0.6)	0.67 (0.3)	0.85 (0.4)	1.68 (1.1)
Changes in the strictness of EPL (model 2)					
Regular employment	−2.51 (1.1)	−1.36 (0.9)	−7.53 (3.3)**	−0.96 (0.3)	0.26 (0.1)
Temporary work	0.34 (0.4)	0.37 (0.7)	0.59 (0.8)	0.48 (0.4)	0.81 (1.0)
Number of countries	17	17	17	16	16
Model 1					
Adjusted R-squared	0.45	0.62	−0.10	0.55	0.70
F test[d]	2.6 *	4.3 **	0.8	3.3 *	5.4 **
Model 2					
Adjusted R-squared	0.48	0.64	0.57	0.49	0.66
F test[d]	2.7	4.2 **	3.4 *	2.6	4.2 **

	Changes in employment/population ratios				Changes in the shares of different types of employment	
	Overall (1)	Prime-age males[c] (2)	Prime-age females[c] (3)	Youth[c] (4)	Self-employment (5)	Temporary (6)
Changes in the strictness of EPL (model 1)						
Overall EPL, version 1	−1.81 (0.9)	0.03 (0.0)	−0.60 (0.2)	−1.58 (0.6)	−2.25 (1.6)	5.34 (1.3)
Changes in the strictness of EPL (model 2)						
Regular employment	−2.58 (0.9)	0.56 (0.3)	−2.95 (0.7)	−0.85 (0.2)	2.16 (1.2)	−10.19 (3.1)*
Temporary work	−0.85 (0.8)	0.00 (0.0)	−0.21 (0.1)	−0.79 (0.6)	−1.22 (1.9)*	1.32 (1.5)
Number of countries	17	17	17	17	19	12
Model 1						
Adjusted R-squared	0.69	0.60	0.43	0.66	0.09	0.29
F test[d]	5.5 **	4.0 **	2.5	4.9 **	1.2	1.6
Model 2						
Adjusted R-squared	0.66	0.55	0.38	0.61	0.27	0.89
F test[d]	4.5 **	3.2 *	2.1	3.8 **	1.8	10.5 *

* and ** denote statistically significant at 10% and 5% levels, respectively.
a) Changes in the performance, EPL and control variables are measured between the first and second periods of the panel models reported in Tables 2.8 to 2.10.
b) The regressions include the same control variables as the panel models in Tables 2.9 to 2.10, except that two variables, for which no data were available for the late 1980s, are omitted (i.e. unemployment benefit duration and tax wedge).
c) Prime age refers to the age group 30-54, youth to the age group 20-29 and low-skilled to workers with no more than primary and lower secondary levels of education (ISCED 0-2).
d) F-statistic test for joint significance of regressors.
Source: See Table 2.8.

Overall, these results indicate that it is difficult to confirm that recent EPL reforms have been associated with changes in employment and unemployment. Virtually all of the coefficients on the variables for changes in EPL strictness are statistically insignificant; while the three exceptions all have the "wrong" sign. However, a weakness of these first-differenced models is that changes in employment and unemployment are being related to approximately *contemporaneous* changes in EPL, whereas it probably would be better to allow for a lagged effect between recent reforms and labour market outcomes. Given the data available, this was not possible. A second weakness is that EPL, particularly provisions for regular employment, was largely unchanged in many of the countries between the late 1980s and the late 1990s. Nonetheless, the first-differenced regressions suggest that EPL probably has not been a dominant explanation of international differences in changes in the levels and composition of employment and unemployment in recent years.

C. Effects on labour market dynamics

Bivariate associations

Chart 2.3 examines the bivariate association between the most comprehensive indicator of EPL strictness in the late 1990s (along the horizontal axis) and 12 measures of labour market dynamics (along the vertical axis). These scatter plots generally are consistent with the theoretical prediction that stricter EPL leads to a labour market with lower turnover, but some of the associations are stronger than others and there are notable examples of countries diverging from the overall tendency.

The simple associations between overall EPL strictness and measures of job and labour turnover[30] are presented in Chart 2.3, Panel A. These scatter plots do not suggest that international differences in employment protection are an important determinant of differences in overall job turnover, consistent with earlier analysis by the OECD (1997a). Even when attention is restricted to job turnover at continuing firms, the component of overall turnover that is most likely to be discouraged by EPL, the association is very weak.[31] By contrast, stricter EPL is more strongly associated with lower rates of labour turnover. Spain and Poland emerge as outliers, however, when the share of the workforce with less than one year of job tenure is used as an alternative measure of annual labour turnover. Spain has much higher labour turnover than other countries with equally strict EPL, reflecting the high share of temporary employment in the Spanish labour market. Poland's very low labour turnover, despite intermediate levels of EPL, may reflect aspects of its recent transition to a market economy, including that employment protection was much stricter quite recently and that turnover was very low during the communist era.

Mean job tenure is higher in countries with stricter employment protection (Chart 2.3, Panel B). Once again, Poland is an outlier. Similarly, five-year retention rates (*i.e.* the probability that worker-job matches observed at one point in time will still be intact five years later) tend to rise with the strictness of employment protection. This is consistent with EPL creating greater job security for workers already employed, encouraging employers to screen new employees more carefully and discouraging incumbent employees from quitting in order to search for another job. The relationship between employment protection and more durable jobs is especially strong for jobs having already lasted at least five years. Omitting very low tenure jobs, which are potentially fixed-term or TWA positions, brings Australia, Germany, Japan and Spain into closer conformity with the general pattern, but Finland remains an outlier, combining very low retention rates with intermediate EPL.[32] Stability among workers having already accumulated five years of tenure is unusually high in France, even after accounting for the relative strictness of EPL.

Stricter employment protection is associated with lower flows into and out of unemployment and longer durations of unemployment (Chart 2.3, Panel C).[33] The monthly unemployment inflow rate is highest in Canada and the United States, which score very low on EPL strictness, and generally declines as EPL strictness rises. A similar, but weaker statistically, relationship holds for the monthly rate at which unemployed persons exit

---

30. Job turnover is the sum of job creation and job destruction measured at the level of individual firms (or establishments). Labour turnover is job turnover plus movements of workers between on-going jobs. See Annex 2.D for definitions and sources of all the dynamic variables.
31. Although stricter EPL creates incentives for firms to smooth employment for any given system of wage setting, countries with stricter EPL may not have lower job turnover than other countries because they are characterised by less wage flexibility in response to labour demand "shocks" [Bertola and Rogerson (1997)].
32. The severe recession of the early 1990s probably accounts for the low retention rate for Finnish workers.
33. The unemployment inflow rate is defined as persons unemployed for less than one month as a percentage of the source population (the working-age population less the unemployed) and the outflow rate as the percentage of the unemployed moving to employment or out of the labour force in an average monthly. Note that both inflows and outflows include transitions between unemployment and inactivity that may be less relevant for assessing the impact of EPL than flows between unemployment and employment.

Employment Protection and Labour Market Performance – 83

Chart 2.3. **Overall EPL strictness[a] and labour market dynamics**
Panel A: Job and labour turnover
(as a percentage of employment)

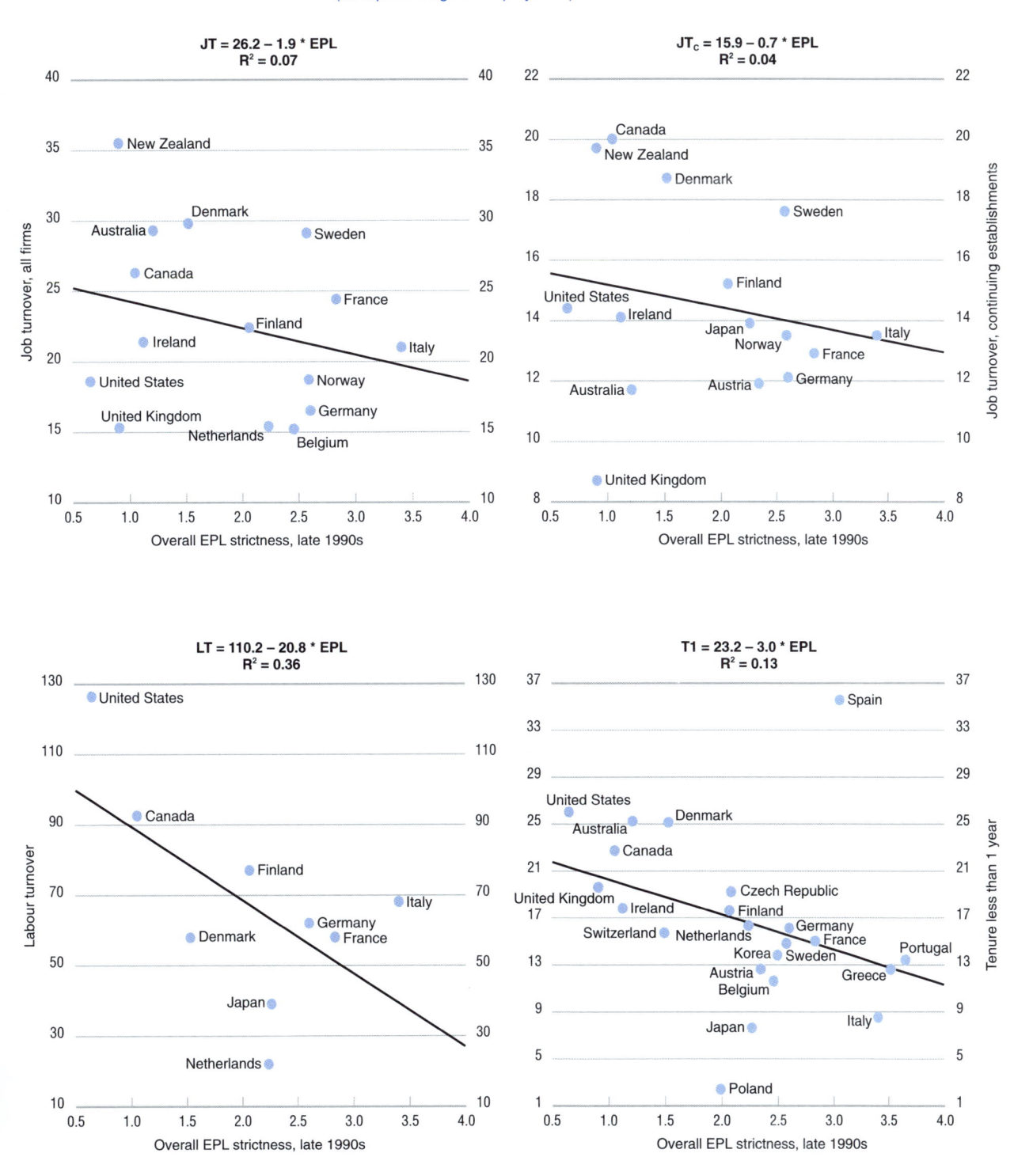

$JT = 26.2 - 1.9 * EPL$
$R^2 = 0.07$

$JT_c = 15.9 - 0.7 * EPL$
$R^2 = 0.04$

$LT = 110.2 - 20.8 * EPL$
$R^2 = 0.36$

$T1 = 23.2 - 3.0 * EPL$
$R^2 = 0.13$

a) Overall EPL strictness, version 2.

OECD

Chart 2.3. Overall EPL strictness[a] and labour market dynamics (cont.)
Panel B: Job tenure and retention rates

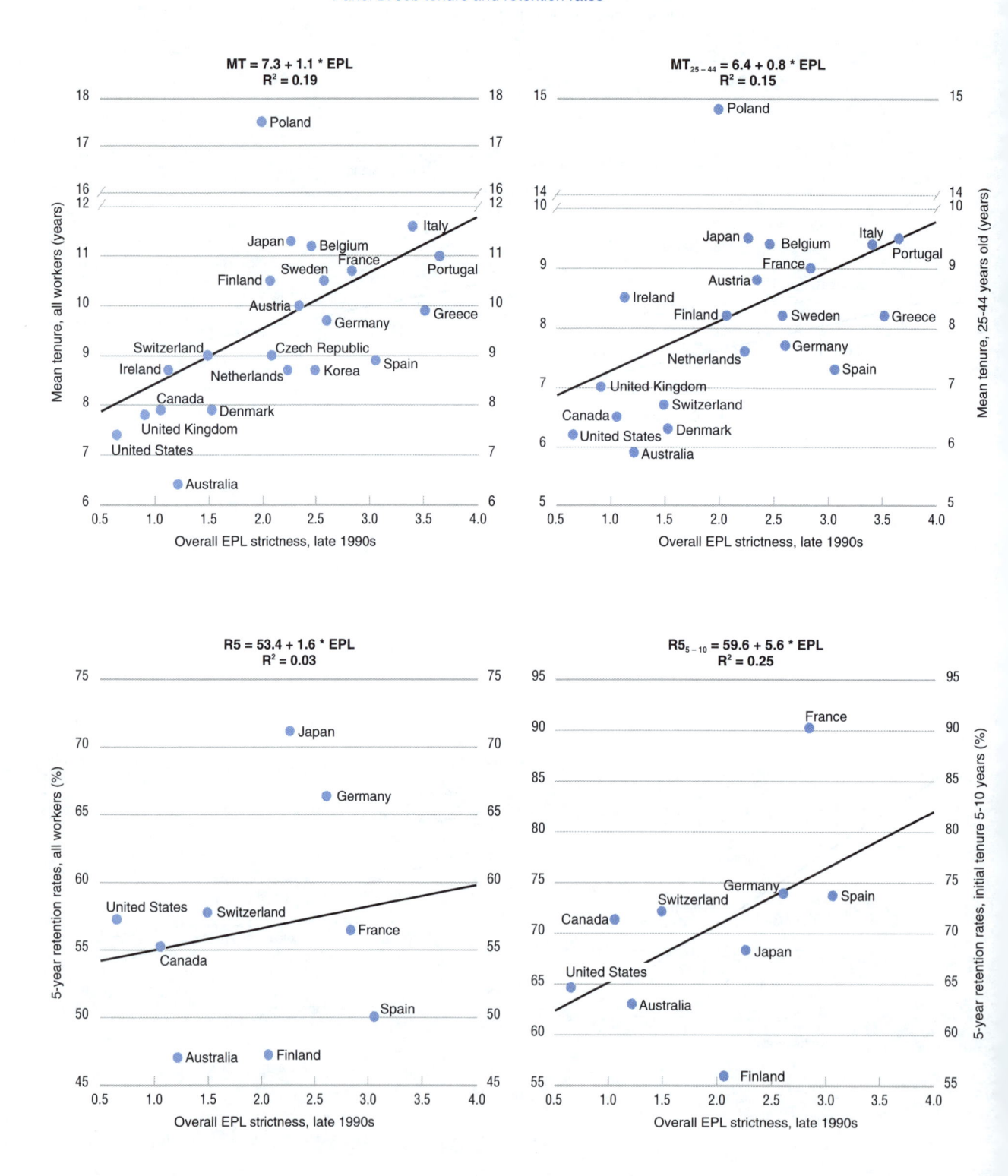

a) Overall EPL strictness, version 2.

Chart 2.3. **Overall EPL strictness[a] and labour market dynamics** *(cont.)*
Panel C: Unemployment flows and durations

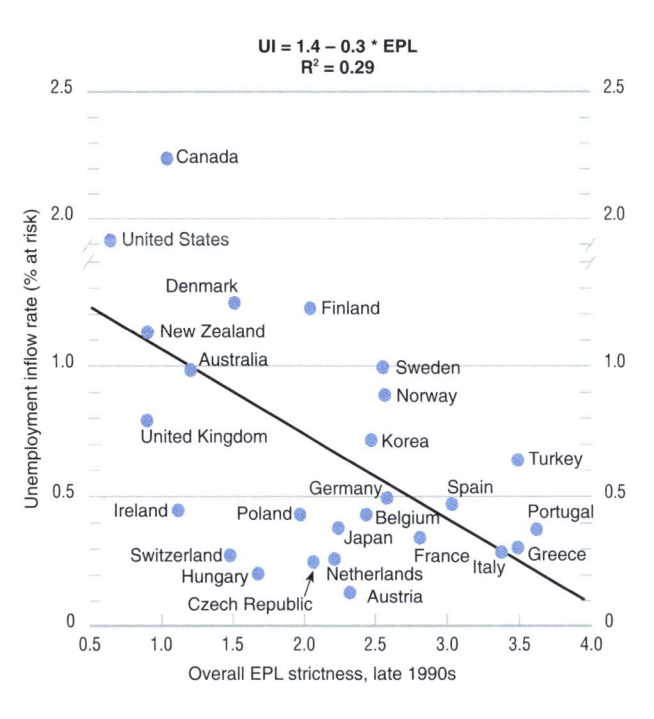

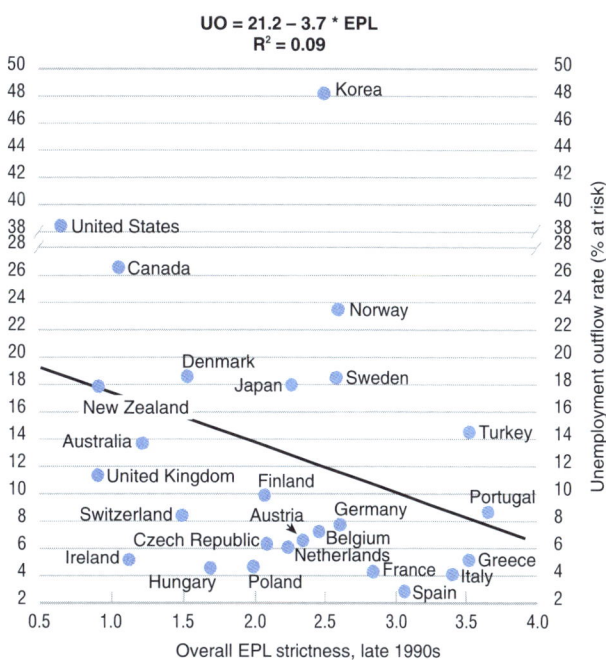

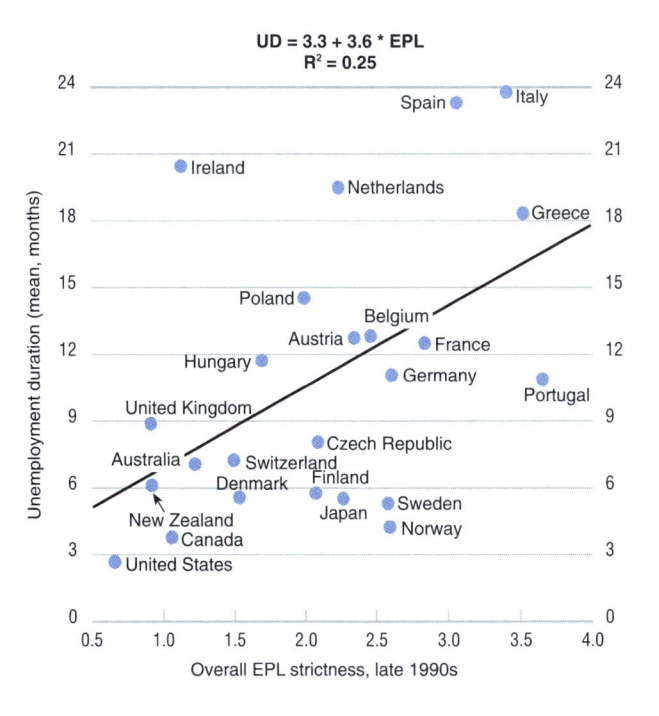

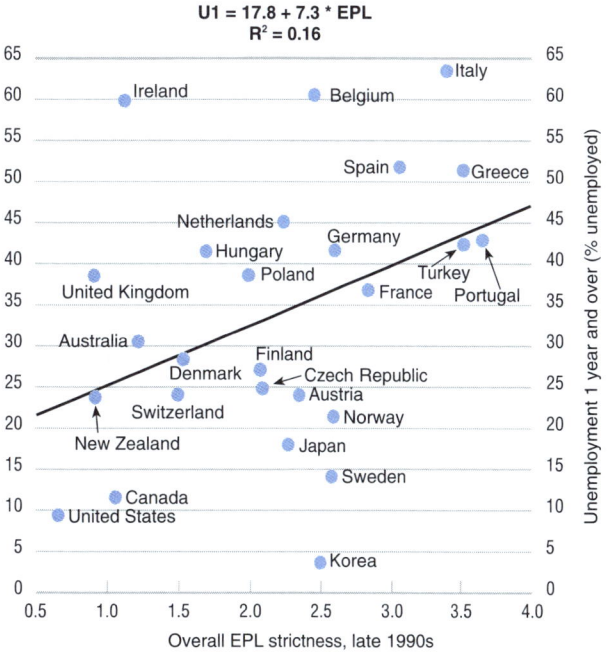

$UI = 1.4 - 0.3 * EPL$
$R^2 = 0.29$

$UO = 21.2 - 3.7 * EPL$
$R^2 = 0.09$

$UD = 3.3 + 3.6 * EPL$
$R^2 = 0.25$

$U1 = 17.8 + 7.3 * EPL$
$R^2 = 0.16$

a) Overall EPL strictness, version 2.
Sources: See Table 2.5 and Annex 2.D.

unemployment.[34] Korea is an exception, however, combing an extremely high unemployment outflow rate with moderately strict employment protection.[35] Both mean unemployment durations and the share of the unemployed who have been jobless for at least a year tend to be higher in countries with stricter EPL, consistent with several earlier studies [Blanchard and Portugal (1998); Gregg and Manning (1997); Jackman *et al.* (1996); Nickell and Layard (1998); OECD (1993)].

Table 2.12 reports pair-wise correlations between nine measures of labour market dynamics and twelve measures of EPL. Most of these correlations are not significantly different from zero, at even the 10 per cent level. However, the correlations with EPL strictness are quite strong and frequently significant for several of the variables: the labour turnover and unemployment inflow rates and the two measures of unemployment duration (mean duration and the share of unemployed who have been searching for more than one year). The strongest and most consistent finding is that of a negative association between EPL strictness and the inflow rate to unemployment. A second finding concerns the relative importance of different components of employment protection. The overall strictness of employment protection is significantly related to lower labour turnover and higher mean tenures, but most of this association operates through EPL practices affecting regular employment. For example, lower labour turnover rates appear to be most strongly associated with the procedural inconvenience and difficulty-of-dismissal aspects of the regulation of regular employment. By contrast, lower inflows to unemployment and longer mean durations appear to be about equally associated with restrictive regulations affecting temporary and regular employment.

Multivariate analysis

The extent to which EPL reduces labour market flows can be better gauged if other factors influencing these variables are controlled for using the regression framework introduced above to examine static measures of employment and unemployment. Table 2.13 reports GLS regression coefficients for two-period panel models, in which select measures of labour market dynamics have been regressed on summary indicators of EPL strictness and nine additional control variables. Many of the dynamic variables used in the bivariate analysis cannot be examined using panel regression models because data are not available for the late 1980s. Thus, this analysis is limited to one measure of job stability and five of unemployment dynamics.

Regression results for the five-year retention rate do not confirm the link between stricter EPL and greater job stability suggested by the bivariate analysis, but this may be due to data only being available for nine countries. By contrast, the regression analysis is more supportive of stricter EPL slowing flows into *and* out of unemployment, although many of the coefficients are not estimated with a high level of precision. The evidence is strongest for stricter EPL slowing the inflow rate into unemployment and lengthening the mean duration of unemployment. EPL for both regular and temporary employment appears to have the effect of reducing the number of workers becoming unemployed, but also of lengthening the expected time spent unemployed. The off-setting nature of the reduction in the number of workers becoming unemployed and the increase in unemployment duration suggests that the impact of EPL on overall unemployment will tend to be muted, consistent with the analysis using a static measure of unemployment. Thus, one conclusion of the statistical analysis is that EPL appears to have a greater impact on the *dynamics* and *composition* of unemployment than on its *level*.

Conclusions

The chapter has focused on making international comparisons of the strictness of employment protection and then analysing whether these differences affect some aspects of labour market performance. The main contribution here has been to provide new data about current employment protection regulation and how it differs from a decade ago. These new data also extend the international comparative analysis of EPL to a wider range of OECD countries and incorporate measures of special regulations applicable to collective dismissals.

The expanded OECD dataset on employment protection regulation confirms that EPL practice differs significantly across countries. In most respects, it appears that there has been quite high persistence in national systems of employment protection regulation over the past ten years, despite some reforms. In both the late 1980s and the late 1990s, EPL was strictest in southern Europe and least restrictive in the United States and the United Kingdom. However, there are also some examples of large changes

---

34. Boeri (1999) also finds that stricter EPL reduces the outflow rate from unemployment, particularly the rate at which the unemployed move into jobs.
35. The very high unemployment outflow rate for Korea (and the correspondingly low probability of long duration unemployment) may reflect the combination of very rapid growth rates and the absence of a system of unemployment benefits during 1990-1997, both conditions that have recently changed.

Table 2.12. **Correlation coefficients between EPL indicators and measures of employment and unemployment dynamics**[a]

Strictness of EPL (in the late 90s) on	Job turnover rate	Labour turnover rate	Tenure less than 1 year	Mean tenure	Retention rate (5 years)	Retention rate (5 years)[b]	Unemployment inflow rate	Unemployment outflow rate	Mean unemployment duration	Unemployment more than 1 year
Regular employment										
Procedural inconvenience	-0.10	-0.87***	-0.39*	0.40*	0.34	0.32	-0.57***	-0.21	0.36*	0.16
Notice and severance pay	-0.24	-0.73**	-0.37*	0.36	0.24	0.27	-0.47**	-0.17	0.41**	0.15
Notice[c]	0.07	-0.49	-0.21	0.29	0.02	0.28	-0.47**	-0.32	0.28	0.32
Severance pay[d]	-0.16	-0.58*	-0.31	0.41*	0.11	0.21	-0.28	-0.28	0.07	0.31
Difficulty of dismissal	0.24	-0.11	-0.06	0.09	-0.07	0.19	-0.34*	-0.17	0.26	0.15
	-0.04	-0.80***	-0.36*	0.33*	0.52	0.31	-0.43**	-0.04	0.17	-0.06
Temporary employment										
Fixed-term contracts	-0.25	-0.39	-0.24	0.32	0.07	0.56	-0.39*	-0.22	0.48**	0.41**
Temporary work agencies	-0.08	-0.25	-0.21	0.32	-0.23	0.36	-0.33*	-0.27	0.32	0.30
	-0.41	-0.47	-0.24	0.27	0.35	0.63*	-0.40**	-0.17	0.51***	0.43**
Collective dismissals	-0.37	0.31	-0.12	0.27	-0.25	0.00	-0.20	-0.32	0.11	0.13
Overall EPL, version 1	-0.21	-0.64*	-0.35	0.40*	0.19	0.48	-0.52***	-0.25	0.49**	0.37*
Overall EPL, version 2	-0.26	-0.60*	-0.36	0.43**	0.17	0.50	-0.54***	-0.30	0.50**	0.39**
Number of observations	15	9	22	22	9	9	27	27	25	27

*, ** and *** denote correlation coefficient significant at 10%, 5% and 1% levels, respectively.
a) Labour market performance variables are averages over 1990-97.
b) Five-year retention rate for workers beginning with between 5 and 10 years of tenure.
c) Average strictness score for notice period after 9 months, 4 years and 20 years, as reported in Table 2.2, Panel B.
d) Average strictness score for severance pay after 9 months, 4 years and 20 years, as reported in Table 2.2, Panel B.
Sources: EPL strictness indicators from Tables 2.2 to 2.5. See Annex 2.D for the sources and definitions of the measures of employment and unemployment dynamics.

Table 2.13. **Two-period panel regressions to explain employment and unemployment dynamics**[a, b, c]

Random-effects GLS estimates

	Retention rate (5 years) (1)	Unemployment inflow rate (months) (2)	Unemployment outflow rate (months) (3)	Mean unemployment duration (months) (4)	Share unemployed more than 1 year[d] (5)	Long-term unemployment rate (log) (6)
Strictness of EPL (model 1)						
Overall EPL, version 1	−1.03 (0.3)	−0.45 (4.8)***	−5.37 (2.2)**	0.13 (3.6)***	4.30 (1.3)	0.10 (0.2)
Strictness of EPL (model 2)						
Regular employment	n.a.	−0.20 (1.6)	−4.00 (1.3)	0.10 (2.6)***	3.66 (0.8)	0.25 (0.9)
Temporary employment	n.a.	−0.24 (4.0)***	−2.17 (1.3)	0.05 (1.6)	1.85 (0.8)	−0.03 (0.2)
Collective dismissals	n.a.	−0.05 (0.3)	−1.17 (0.3)	0.06 (1.3)	2.77 (0.4)	0.09 (0.2)
Number of observations	17	34	34	34	34	36
Model 1						
R-squared	0.89	0.65	0.51	0.56	0.43	0.56
Wald test[e]	43.1 ***	50.4 ***	21.2 **	29.3 ***	13.7	28.5 ***
Breusch and Pagan test[f]	2.4	6.3 **	7.0 ***	1.7	8.8 ***	6.7 ***
Hausman test[g]	182.7 ***	7.1	2.0	3.7	4.5	5.6
Model 2						
R-squared	n.a.	0.65	0.51	0.60	0.45	0.54
Wald test[e]	n.a.	48.1 ***	19.4 *	26.5 ***	12.9	27.1 ***
Breusch and Pagan test[f]	n.a.	5.4 **	6.8 ***	2.8 *	5.9 **	6.6 **
Hausman test[g]	n.a.	5.2	2.6	31.9 ***	6.5	7.2

*, ** and *** mean statistically significant at 10%, 5% and 1% levels respectively.
n.a.: Not available due to insufficient observations to estimate the model.
a) See note a) of Table 2.8 for an explanation of the estimation method.
b) Measures of employment and unemployment dynamics are averages over 1985-90 and 1992-97.
c) See note b) of Table 2.9 for an explanation of the two regression models estimated.
d) As a percentage of all unemployed.
e) Wald test for joint significance of regressors (Chi-square statistic).
f) Breusch and Pagan Lagrangian multiplier test for presence of country effects (Chi-square statistic).
g) Hausman test for misspecification of the random-effects model (Chi-square statistic).
Source: See Table 2.12.

over the past decade, especially in relaxing the regulation of temporary employment.

As regards the effects of employment protection on labour market performance, this chapter's results are qualitatively consistent with the results of earlier studies in many cases. This analysis strengthens the conclusion that EPL strictness has little or no effect on overall unemployment. Simple, cross-country comparisons suggest that EPL may affect the demographic composition of unemployment, with lower unemployment for prime-age men being offset by higher unemployment for other groups, particularly younger workers. However, this latter finding must be regarded as tentative, since the evidence from the multivariate regressions does not support it except in the case of stricter EPL having a negative impact on the unemployment of prime-age males.

The evidence is also somewhat inconsistent for employment. Simple, cross-country comparisons suggest that EPL raises employment for prime-age men, but lowers employment for youths and prime-age women, with the overall effect being a net reduction. However, these correlations become very weak and statistically insignificant when mutivariate regressions are used to isolate the causal impact of EPL from that of other determinants of employment. By contrast, the evidence is quite robust for stricter EPL leading to an expansion of self-employment. Contrary to the predictions of economic theory and several prior studies, the new data do not indicate a clear link between EPL and the share of workers in temporary jobs. However, it is possible that insufficient time has passed for employers' use of temporary employment contracts to adapt fully to recent liberalisation in their use in a number of countries.

Both the bivariate and the multivariate analyses support the hypothesis that stricter EPL lowers some forms of labour market turnover. Stricter EPL appears to expand the number of stable jobs, as intended by its supporters. However, unemployment spells also tend to last longer. With stricter EPL, fewer individuals become unemployed, but those who become unemployed are at a greater risk of remaining unemployed for a year or more. EPL provisions for both temporary and regular employment appear to have an important dampening impact on turnover.

The implications of these findings for policymaking cannot be reduced to a simple formula. Overall, the analysis confirms that EPL should be monitored closely as part of the continuing process of evaluating and fine-tuning an overall strategy for lowering long-duration unemployment and improving labour market performance generally. As labour market conditions evolve, it should be verified that excessively restrictive or poorly designed provisions for employment protection are not creating barriers to employment for youths or other labour force groups that may face difficulties in gaining access to stable jobs. However, any initiatives to reform employment protection practices have to confront difficult trade-offs, such as whether to lessen job protection for high-tenure workers in order to improve employment opportunities for recent school leavers.

Annex 2.A

Detailed Description of Employment Protection Regulation and Practice

The following nine tables present the more detailed descriptions of employment protection regulation that form the basis for the indicators of EPL presented in Tables 2.2 to 2.5 and discussed in Section I. These descriptions are based on a variety of national sources as well as multi-country surveys by Watson Wyatt Data Services [Watson Wyatt (1997, 1998)], Incomes Data Services [IDS (1995, 1996, 1997)] and the European Commission (1997a). OECD governments provided additional information, based on a request for information from the OECD Secretariat.

Table 2.A.1. **Administrative procedures for individual notice and dismissal**[a]

Situation of a regular employee, after any trial period for the job, who is dismissed on personal grounds or individual redundancy, but without fault

	Notification procedures[b] Requirement	Score (0-3)	Estimated time before notice can start[c] Requirement	In days
Australia[d]	No prescribed procedures. In case of legal proceedings, tribunal will consider whether there were warnings, provision of an opportunity to the employee to answer allegations and, particularly in the case of redundancy, whether trade union/employee representatives were notified.	0.5	Written or oral notification.	1
Austria	Notification first to works council (if one exists), then to employee.	2	Maximum 5 days for works council to react. Notice can then be served, usually by registered mail.	9[e]
Belgium	Notification of employee usually by registered letter. Oral notification possible if employer chooses severance pay in lieu of notice.	0.5	Registered letter or oral notification.	1.5
Canada	No prescribed procedure.	0	Written or oral notification.	1
Czech Republic				
Personal reasons	Notification of employee and trade union body, after previous warning.	2	Letter sent by mail or handed out directly.	7
Redundancy	Notification of employee, trade union and public employment office.	2	Advance consultation, with offer of another job or re-training if feasible; then letter sent by mail or handed directly to employee.	7
Denmark	Legal requirement of written notice only for white collar workers. Employees can request negotiation with the union once notice is received.	0.5	For white collar workers, letter sent by mail or handed out directly.	1
Finland				
Personal reasons	Statement of reasons and information on appeals procedures given to the employee. Advance discussion with employee and trade union if requested by employee.	1.5	Advance discussion, then notice orally or in writing.	7
Lack of work	In companies with 30 or more employees, notification to trade union representatives and consultation on reasons and ways to avoid lay-off.	2	Invitation to consultation; 5-day delay; consultation for 7 days; then notice in writing.	15
France				
Personal reasons	Statement of reasons to employee; in many cases, additional notification of works council is requested by collective agreement.	1.5	Letter; interview; notice served in a second letter including statement of reasons.	9
Economic reasons	Labour Inspectorate and usually the personnel delegates or works council.	2	Letter, interview including re-training offer; a second letter after delay of at least 7 days.	15
Germany	Notification to employee, usually in writing (required in many collective agreements), after oral or written warnings to employee in case of dismissal for lack of performance. Previous notification of planned dismissal, including reasons for termination, to works council (if one exists). In case of notice given despite works council objection and subsequent law suit, dismissal has to wait for decision by Labour Court.	2.5	After notification, maximum 7 days for works council to object to dismissal. Notice can then be served, specifying the 1st or 15th of the month.	17[f]
Greece	Written notice to employee, plus additional notification to OAED local office (public employment service). Previous warning in case of dismissal for poor performance may be advisable.	2	Letter sent by mail or handed directly to employee.	1
Hungary	Statement of reasons upon request, after written warnings and provision of an opportunity to the employee to answer allegations.	1	Advance discussion, then letter sent by mail or handed directly to employee.	13

Table 2.A.1. **Administrative procedures for individual notice and dismissal**[a] *(cont.)*

Situation of a regular employee, after any trial period for the job, who is dismissed on personal grounds or individual redundancy, but without fault

	Notification procedures[b]		Estimated time before notice can start[c]	
	Requirement	Score (0-3)	Requirement	In days
Ireland				
Individual termination	No prescribed procedure, but advisable to serve notice in writing after warnings specifying what aspect of behaviour is sub-standard. Employee can request statement of reasons.	1	Written or oral notification.	7
Redundancy	Copy of official redundancy form to be sent to Department of Employment.	2	Idem.	2
Italy	Written notice to employee who can require communication of detailed reasons and can request conciliation by the provincial employment office or through conciliation committees set up under collective agreements.	1.5	Letter sent by mail or handed directly to employee.	1
Japan				
Personal reasons	To stand up in court, it is considered advisable that notice is given in writing and reasons are stated. Some collective agreements provide for prior consultation with trade union.	1	Written or oral notification.	1
Managerial reasons	The courts must be satisfied that trade union/ employee representatives have been adequately notified and consulted.	2	Sincere consultation on need for dismissal and standards of selection, then letter of dismissal.	5
Korea				
Personal reasons	Statement of urgency and reasons to employee.	1	Letter sent by mail or handed directly to employee.	1
Managerial reasons	Notification of union or other worker representatives 60 days before dismissal.	2.5	Sincere consultation procedure on need for dismissal and standards of selection within the 60-day period; then letter of dismissal.	63
Mexico	Statement of reasons to the employee.	1	Letter sent by mail or handed directly to employee.	1
Netherlands	Prior authorisation from regional employment office needed, except in cases of bankruptcy and mutual agreement.[g]	3	Authorisation procedure normally takes 4-6 weeks, although there is a trend towards shorter duration ("shortened procedure"); then written notice by registered mail.	31
New Zealand				
Personal reasons	Statement of reasons to the employee, after written warnings and provision of an opportunity to the employee to answer allegations and improve performance.	1	Notification orally or in writing, as provided for in contract.	7
Redundancy	Notification of trade union/employee representatives only if required by contract.	0.5	Consultation on selection and ways of avoiding dismissal may be required by contract.	7
Norway	Written notice to employee, with statement of reasons upon request.	1.5	Letter sent by mail. (Notice period runs from the first day of the month following that in which notice was given.)	2
Poland	Notification to representative trade union of intention to terminate, including reasons for dismissal. In case the employee takes the case to the labour court, the court may require evidence of a warning procedure and of a fair account of trade union opinions.	2	5 days for consultation with local trade union on justification for dismissal. (In case of objection, case will be submitted to upper union levels which shall give their opinion within another 5 days.) Notice can then be served, usually by mail.	13
Portugal	Written notice to employee and employee representatives justifying the reasons for dismissal and the lack of suitable alternatives. In case of individual termination for unsuitability, a replacement must be hired. In case of economic redundancy, employee representatives can call in the Labour Inspectorate to verify justification of dismissal.	2	After initial notification, minimum two weeks for employee or works council to present their views, and a further delay of 5 days before final notice is issued, usually in a letter sent by mail or handed directly to employee.	21

Table 2.A.1. **Administrative procedures for individual notice and dismissal**[a] *(cont.)*

Situation of a regular employee, after any trial period for the job, who is dismissed on personal grounds or individual redundancy, but without fault

	Notification procedures[b]		Estimated time before notice can start[c]	
	Requirement	Score (0-3)	Requirement	In days
Spain	Written notice with statement of reasons, plus notification to workers' representatives.	2	Letter sent by mail or handed directly to employee.	1
Sweden				
Personal grounds	Written notification to employee and trade union, after at least one previous warning (as proof of "long-standing" problems) that action is intended; reasons to be given if requested by employee.	2	Minimum 14 days to be allowed for consultation before notice can be served.	23
Redundancy	Notification to employee, trade union and county labour board which may request consultation on selection and dismissal procedures.	2	Duty to negotiate on pending dismissals before notice can be served. Lack of suitable alternatives must be demonstrated in all cases.	7
Switzerland	Notification to the employee who has the right to request a statement of reasons.	0.5	Letter sent by mail or handed directly to employee.	1
Turkey	Written notice to employee and notification, within 15 days, to Ministry of Labour.	2	Letter sent by mail or handed directly to employee.	1
United Kingdom				
Individual termination	Employees with 2 years' continuous service have the right to demand the reasons in writing.	0.5	Written or oral notification.	1
Redundancy	Consultation with recognised trade union recommended, but not legally required when few workers are affected.	1.5	"Reasonable notice" that redundancy is being considered.	3
United States	No prescribed procedures. Only a few States prescribe a "service letter" a certain period after dismissal, noting the reasons for termination.	0	Written or oral notification.	1

a) The procedures are either directly legislated or generally considered necessary because without them the employer's case will be weakened before the courts, if a claim for unfair dismissal is made.
b) Procedures are scored according to the scale 1 when a written statement of the reasons for dismissal must be supplied to the employee; 2 when a third party (such as a works council or the competent labour authority) must be notified; and 3 when the employer cannot proceed to dismissal without authorisation from a third party.
c) Estimated time includes an assumption of 6 days in case of required warning procedure prior to dismissal (although such time periods can be very diverse and range from a couple of days to several months). One day is counted when dismissal can be notified orally or the notice can be directly handed to the employee, 2 when a letter needs to be sent by mail, and 3 when a registered letter needs to be sent.
d) Australia: when they do not refer to all employees, procedures and requirements in Tables 2.A.1 to 2.A.9 refer to the federal workplace relations system which regulates employment conditions for approximately half the workforce.
e) Austria: 3 days if no works council is present.
f) Germany: 8 days if no works council is present.
g) Netherlands: notification of trade union/employee representatives may also be required by contract. Instead of turning to the public employment service (which may refuse authorisation), both employers and employees can also file a request with the Cantonal Court that the employment contract be dissolved "for important reasons". This is done in an increasing number of dismissal cases.

Table 2.A.2. Required notice and severance pay for individual dismissal

Case of a regular employee with tenure beyond any trial period, dismissed on personal grounds or economic redundancy, but without fault [a]

	Type of worker	Notice/tenure [b]	Severance pay/tenure [b]
Australia [c]	All workers	1 week < 1 year, 2 weeks < 3 years, 3 weeks < 5 years, 4 weeks > 5 years. These notice periods are increased by one week if employee is over 45 years old and has over 2 years continuous service.	None.
	Workers dismissed for redundancy	Idem.	0 < 1 year, 4 weeks < 2 years, 6 weeks < 3 years, 7 weeks < 4 years, 8 weeks > 4 years (typical cases).
Austria	Blue collar	Usually 2 weeks (but ranging from 1 day in construction industry to 5 months in some collective agreements).	2 months > 3 years, 3 months > 5 years, 4 months > 10 years, 6 months > 15 years, 9 months > 20 years, 12 months > 25 years.
	White collar	6 weeks < 2 years, 2 months < 5 years, 3 months < 15 years, 4 months < 25 years, 5 months > 25 years.	Idem.
Belgium	Blue collar	0 in trial period; 7 days < 6 months, 28 days < 20 years, 56 days > 20 years (can be modified by royal decree or collective agreements).	None.
	White collar	7 days < 6 months (trial period), 3 months < 5 years. *Plus* 3 more months of notice for each additional 5 years of service. [d]	None.
Canada	All workers (federal jurisdiction)	2 weeks.	0 < 12 months, after which 2 days for each year of tenure, but with a minimum of 5 days.
	All workers (Ontario)	1 week < 1 year, 2 weeks < 3 years, 3 weeks < 4 years, 4 weeks < 5 years, up to 8 weeks > 8 years.	1 week per year of service, up to 26 weeks maximum, if tenure > 5 years, and if in a firm with a payroll of $2.5 million or more.
	Other jurisdictions	Notice requirements similar to Ontario in most other provinces.	No legislated severance pay.
Czech Republic	All workers	2 months.	None.
	Workers dismissed for redundancy	3 months.	2 months.
Denmark	Blue collar [e]	0 < 9 months, 21 days < 2 years, 28 days < 3 years, 56 days < 6 years, 70 days > 6 years.	None.
	White collar	14 days < 3 months, 1 month < 5 months, 3 months < 33 months, 4 months < 68 months, 5 months < 114 months, 6 months > 114 months.	1 month after 12 year, 2 months after 15 years, 3 months after 18 years.
Finland	All workers	0 < 4 months, 1 month < 1 year, 2 months < 5 years, 3 months < 9 years, 4 months < 12 years, 5 months < 15 years, 6 months > 15 years.	None. [f]
France	Blue collar	7 days < 6 months, 1 month < 2 years, 2 months > 2 years.	1/10th of a month's pay per year of service plus an additional 1/15th after 10 years.
	White collar	15 days < 6 months, 1 month < 2 years, 2 months > 2 years.	Idem.
Germany	All workers	2 weeks in trial period, 4 weeks < 2 years, 1 month < 5 years, 2 months < 8 years, 3 months < 10 years, 4 months < 12 years, 5 months < 15 years, 6 months < 20 years, 7 months > 20 years. (Notice periods > 4 weeks only apply to workers above 25 years of age.)	No legal entitlement, but can be included in collective agreements and social compensation plans.

Table 2.A.2. **Required notice and severance pay for individual dismissal** (cont.)
Case of a regular employee with tenure beyond any trial period, dismissed on personal grounds or economic redundancy, but without fault [a]

	Type of worker	Notice/tenure [b]	Severance pay/tenure [b]
Greece	Blue collar	None.	5 days < 1 year, 7 days < 2 years, 15 days < 5 years, 30 days < 10 years, 60 days < 15 years, 90 days < 20 years, 105 days > 20 years.
	White collar	0 < 2 months, 30 days < 1 year, 60 days < 4 years, 3 months < 6 years, 4 months < 8 years, 5 months < 10 years, plus one month per year of service, up to a maximum of 24 months. Notice can be waived if full severance pay is given.	Half the notice period if written notice is given; otherwise, severance pay according to the schedule for notice.
Hungary	All workers	30 days < 3 years, 35 days < 5 years, going up to 90 days > 20 years.	0 < 3 years, 1 month < 5 years, 2 months < 10 years, going up to 5 months > 20 years and 6 months > 25 years.
Ireland	All workers	0 < 13 weeks, 1 weeks < 2 years, 2 weeks < 5 years, 4 weeks < 10 years, 6 weeks < 15 years, 8 weeks > 15 years. 2 weeks minimum in redundancy cases.	In redundancy cases with at least two years tenure: 1 week pay, *plus* half a week of pay per year worked under the age of 41, *plus* one week of pay per year worked over the age of 41, with a maximum of Ir£ 15 600 (as of 1995). Employers are partially reimbursed by redundancy fund.
Italy	Blue collar	2 days < 2 weeks and 6 to 12 days thereafter.	2/27 of annual salary per year of service (often higher in collective agreements).
	White collar	8 days < 8 weeks and 15 days to 4 months thereafter (minimum legal requirements, often higher in collective agreements).	Idem.
Japan	All workers	30 days.	According to enterprise surveys, average severance pay (retirement allowance) equals almost 1 month per year of service, although it is not legally required. It is somewhat higher in the case of lay-offs, and lower in case of voluntary quits. Figures shown in Tables 2.2 and 2.A.3 refer to the differential in severance pay between these two cases.
Korea	All workers	0 < 6 months, 30 days > 6 months. Notice can be exchanged for severance pay (retirement allowance).	Retirement allowance of > 30 days per year of service legally required; often more in practice. Although no detailed data are available, difference between allowance for lay-off and voluntary quit was assumed to be somewhat higher than in Japan.
Mexico	All workers	No minimum notice period.	3 months.
Netherlands	All workers	1 month in the first five years of service, extended by one more month for every additional 5 years of service, up to a maximum of 4 months. In practice the maximum is closer to 3 weeks since time spent on PES dismissal procedure is usually compensated to the employer.	None by law, and if the dismissal is handled by the employment office. However, if the employer files for permission by a labour court, the court may determine severance pay, roughly according to the formula: 1 month per year of service for workers < 40 years of age; 1.5 months for workers between age 40 and 50; 2 months for workers 50 years and over. [g]
New Zealand	All workers	No specific period required by law, but case law requires reasonable notice. Usually 1-2 weeks for blue collar and over 2 weeks for white collar.	None by law; however according to survey data, about three quarters of employees are covered by contracts which provide them with severance pay in case of redundancy (typically 6 weeks for 1st year, and 2 weeks for additional years of tenure).

Table 2.A.2. Required notice and severance pay for individual dismissal (cont.)

Case of a regular employee with tenure beyond any trial period, dismissed on personal grounds or economic redundancy, but without fault [a]

	Type of worker	Notice/tenure [b]	Severance pay/tenure [b]
Norway	All workers	14 days < 6 months, 1 month < 5 years, 2 months < 10 years, 3 months > 10 years; with above 10 years seniority, notice period increases with age, up to 6 months at age 60 and above.	None by law; however collective agreements in the private sector may require lump-sum additional payments to long-serving staff who have reached age 50-55, or where the dismissal arises from company reorganisation.
Poland	All workers	2 weeks before 6 months, 1 month after 6 months, 3 months after 3 years. 2 weeks for school leavers in first job.	Usually none, but 1 month in case of termination due to disability or retirement.
Portugal	All workers	0 < 2 months; 60 days > 2 months (legal minimum).	1 month per year of service (legal minimum 3 months).
Spain	Workers dismissed for "objective" reasons	30 days.	2/3 of a month's pay per year of service up to a maximum of 12 months.
	Workers under fixed-term contracts	0 < 1 year, 15 days > 1 year.	None, except for workers under contract with temporary agencies who get 12 days per year of service.
Sweden	All workers	1 month < 2 years, 2 months < 4 years, 3 months < 6 years, 4 months < 8 years, 5 months < 10 years, 6 months > 10 years.	No legal entitlement, but occasionally included in collective agreements.
Switzerland	All workers	0 < 1 month, 1 month < 1 year, 2 months < 10 years, 3 months > 10 years, always to the end of a calendar month.	No legal entitlement to severance pay, except for workers over age 50 and with more than 20 years seniority, where severance pay cannot be less than 2 months wages.
Turkey	All workers	0 < 1 month, 2 weeks < 6 months, 4 weeks < 18 months, 6 weeks < 3 years, 8 weeks > 3 years.	After one year's employment, one month for each year of service, often extended by collective agreement to 45 days.
United Kingdom	All workers	0 < 1 month, 1 week < 2 years, plus one additional week of notice per year of service up to a maximum of 12 weeks.	Legally required only for redundancy cases with 2 years tenure: half a week per year of service (ages 18-21); 1 week per year (ages 22 to 40); 1.5 weeks per year (ages 41 to 64), limited to 30 weeks and £220 per week (as of April 1998). According to a government study, 40% of firms exceed legal minima.
United States	All workers	No legal regulations (but can be included in collective agreements or company policy manuals). [h]	

a) Information based mainly on legal regulation, but also, where relevant, on averages found in collective agreements or individual employment contracts.
b) "28 days < 20 years" means 28 days of notice or severance pay is required when length of service is below 20 years.
c) Australia: notice periods may be increased through collective agreements, particularly in cases of redundancy.
d) Belgium: this refers to the legal minimum. If annual salary is above 928 000 BF (in 1998), currently the case in over half of Belgian white-collar employees, parties or courts tend to use one of a number of standard formulas (such as the Claeys formula) for severance pay in lieu of notice.
e) Denmark: based on collective agreements.
f) Finland: dismissed employees of 45 and over, and with tenure 5 years and above, are entitled to 1-2 months severance pay out of a collective redundancy payment fund, often used for training purposes [European Commission (1997b), p. 52].
g) Netherlands: judges may apply a correction factor taking into account particulars of the case.
h) United States: for example, the US Labor Department's Employee Benefits Survey shows that in 1992 over a third of employees of medium and large establishments were covered by formal severance pay plans, while 15% of the employees were covered at small establishments [OECD (1996a)].

Table 2.A.3. **Notice periods and severance pay for individual dismissals at three lengths of service**[a]

	Type of worker	Notice 9 months	Notice 4 years	Notice 20 years	Severance pay 9 months	Severance pay 4 years	Severance pay 20 years
Australia (federal jurisdiction)	All workers	1 week	3 weeks	5 weeks	0	0	0
	Redundancy cases	1 week	3 weeks	5 weeks	0	8 weeks	8 weeks
Austria	Blue collar	2 weeks	2 weeks	2 weeks	0	2 months	9 months
	White collar	6 weeks	2 months	4 months	0	2 months	9 months
Belgium[b]	Blue collar	28 days	28 days	56 days	0	0	0
	White collar	3 months	3 months	12 months	0	0	0
	Claeys formula for white collar workers	3 months	6 months	21 months	0	0	0
Canada (federal jurisdiction)	All workers	2 weeks	2 weeks	2 weeks	0	8 days	40 days
Czech Republic	All workers	2 months	2 months	2 months	0	0	0
	Redundancy cases	2 months	3 months	3 months	2 months	2 months	2 months
Denmark	Blue collar	3 weeks	8 weeks	10 weeks	0	0	0 3 months
	White collar	3 months	4 months	6 months	0	0	3 months
Finland	All workers	1 month	2 months	6 months	0	0	0
France	All workers	1 month	2 months	2 months	0	0.4 month	2.7 months
Germany	All workers	4 weeks	1 month	7 months	0	0	0
Greece	Blue collar	0	0	0	7 days	15 days	3.5 months
	White collar	30 months	3 months	16 months	15 days	1.5 months	8 months
Hungary	All workers	30 days	35 days	90 days	0	1 month	5 months
Ireland	All workers	1 week	2 weeks	8 weeks	0	0	0
	Redundancy cases	2 weeks	2 weeks	8 weeks	0	2 weeks	18 weeks
Italy	Blue collar	6 days	9 days	12 days	0.7 month	3.5 months	18 months
	White collar	15 days	2 months	4 months	0.7 month	3.5 months	18 months
Japan	All workers	30 days	30 days	30 days	0	1.5 months	4 months
Korea	All workers	1 month	1 month	1 month	0	2 months	6 months
Mexico	All workers	0	0	0	3 months	3 months	3 months
Netherlands[c]	All workers	1 month	1 month	4 months	0	0	0
New Zealand	Blue collar	1-2 weeks	1-2 weeks	1-2 weeks	0	0	0
	White collar	< 2 weeks	< 2 weeks	< 2 weeks	0	0	0
	Redundancy cases				0	3 months	10 months
Norway	All workers	1 month	1 month	5 months	0	0	0
Poland	All workers	1 month	3 months	3 months	0	0	0
Portugal	All workers	60 days	60 days	60 days	3 months	4 months	20 months
Spain	Workers dismissed for "objective" reasons	30 days	30 days	30 days	0.5 month	2²/₃ months	12 months
Sweden	All workers	1 month	3 months	6 months	0	0	0
Switzerland	All workers	1 month	2 months	3 months	0	0	2 months
Turkey	All workers	4 weeks	8 weeks	8 weeks	0	4 months	20 months
United Kingdom	All workers	1 week	4 weeks	12 weeks	0	0	0
	Redundancy cases	1 week	4 weeks	12 weeks	0	4 weeks	20 weeks
United States	All workers	0	0	0	0	0	0

a) Where relevant, calculations assume that the worker was 35 years old at the start of employment. Averages are taken where different situations apply (e.g. blue collar and white collar workers; dismissals for personal reasons and for redundancy, etc.). For further explanation, see detailed notes to Table 2.A.2.
b) Belgium: two notice periods calculated for white collar workers, depending on whether they earn below or above the BF 928 000 threshold (see Table 2.A.2).
c) Netherlands: data for severance pay refer to dismissal cases handled by the public employment service.

Table 2.A.4. **Conditions under which individual dismissals are fair or unfair**[a]

	Fair	Unfair	Score (0-3)[b]
Australia	Dismissal can be fair if justified on the basis of capacity or conduct, subject to whether it is harsh, unjust or unreasonable, as well as for economic redundancy ("retrenchment").	Dismissals on grounds of, *inter alia*, race, sex, colour, sexual preference, age, disability, marital status, family responsibilities, pregnancy, religion, political views and union membership, as well as those where no adequate notice has been given.	0
Austria	Dismissals for "serious reason", including non-performance or lack of competence, and for operational reasons or other business needs.	"Socially unjustified" dismissals (which would affect the dismissed employee more unfavourably than other comparable employees of the company, or which would impair the interests of the employee to a greater degree than the interest of the firm in dissolving the employment relationship); and dismissals on inadmissible motive (*e.g.* discrimination, trade union activity or imminent military service).	1
Belgium	Dismissals for non-performance or business needs.	Dismissals for "reasons which have no connection whatsoever with the capability or conduct of the worker or which are not based on the operational needs of the undertaking, establishment or department". Dismissals of workers on maternity or educational leave, and of trade union and works council delegates.	0
Canada	All dismissals for "just cause".	Dismissals without notice and/or pay in lieu of notice, for pregnancy and trade union activities, for exercising a right under labour statutes, such as those dealing with minimum employment standards and occupational safety and health, and dismissals based on breach of human rights legislation.	0
Czech Republic	Dismissals for failure to meet performance requirements and for reasons of technological and organisational change.	Dismissals where employee can be retained in another capacity, if necessary after retraining. Unfair are also any dismissals based on discrimination (age, sex, colour, religion, union membership, etc.).	2
Denmark	Lack of competence and economic redundancy are legitimate reasons.	Dismissals founded on "arbitrary circumstances" (blue-collar workers) or "not reasonably based on the employee's or the company's circumstances". Dismissals based on race, religion, national origin, etc., and as a result of a corporate take-over are also unfair.	0
Finland	Dismissals are justified for "specific serious reasons", including personal characteristics and urgent business needs.	Dismissals for an employee's illness, participation in a strike, union activities and political or religious views; and dismissals where employees could be reasonably, in view of their skills and abilities, transferred or retrained.	1.5
France[c]	Dismissals for personal characteristics such as non-performance or lack of competence, or for economic reasons such as work reorganisation or other business needs. In redundancy cases, obligation for employer to consider alternative solutions (*reclassement*), offer redundant employees a "re-training contract" and give them priority when rehiring.	Dismissals without real and serious cause, and for reasons relating to the private life of the employee.	1.5
Germany	Dismissals based on factors inherent in the personal characteristics or behaviour of the employee (such as insufficient skill or capability), or business needs and compelling operational reasons.	Dismissals where the employee can be retained in another capacity within the same establishment or enterprise, and redundancy dismissals where due account has not been taken of "social considerations" (*e.g.* seniority, age, family situation).	2
Greece	Dismissals for non-performance or business needs (production requirements, work organisation). In larger companies, dismissals are fair only as a "last resort", after exhaustion of oral and written warnings, pay reductions and suspensions, and after consultation with employee representatives.	Dismissals of trade union representatives, works council members, of recent mothers, and for reasons of pregnancy and discrimination.	0.5

Table 2.A.4. **Conditions under which individual dismissals are fair or unfair**[a] *(cont.)*

	Fair	Unfair	Score (0-3)[b]
Hungary	Dismissals are justified for non-performance or business needs.	Dismissals without notice and of workers on sick leave, maternity leave and child care leave.	0
Ireland	Dismissals for lack of ability, competence or qualifications, or for redundancy.	Dismissals reflecting discrimination on grounds of race, religion, age, gender, etc., including when these factors bias selection during redundancies.	0
Italy	Termination of contract only possible for "just cause" or "just motive", including significant non-performance of the employee, and compelling business reasons.	Dismissals reflecting discrimination on grounds of race, religion, gender, trade union activity, etc.	0
Japan	Dismissals for "reasonable cause". Redundancy dismissals require urgent business reasons for reducing number of staff; reasonableness of selection criteria, and reasonableness of procedures.	Dismissals for reason of nationality, gender, belief or social status, of workers on sick leave, and maternity leave, and when conditions in left-hand column have not been satisfied.	2
Korea	Dismissals for "just cause" or urgent managerial needs, including individual redundancy and dismissals due to mergers and acquisitions when employees or union have been consulted on urgency, selection criteria and transfer/retraining alternatives.	Dismissals for reason of nationality, gender, belief or social status, of workers on sick leave, and maternity leave, and when not having demonstrated special efforts to avoid dismissal in consultation with labour union.	2
Mexico	Dismissals are fair only when the employer can demonstrate the worker's lack of integrity or actions prejudicial to the company's interests (such as negligence, imprudence, or disobedience). Redundancy or poor performance are normally not legal grounds for dismissal.	..	3
Netherlands	Dismissals on grounds of employee conduct or unsuitability, and for economic redundancy. In the latter case, data on the financial state of the company and proof that alternatives to redundancy have been considered must be given, and the selection of dismissed employees be justified ("last in-first out" principle, or age/sex balance of the workforce, for example).	Unfair are "obviously unreasonable" terminations, and dismissals of pregnant women, the disabled, new mothers and works council members.	1.5
New Zealand	Termination of contract is possible if there is good reason and the employer carries out the dismissal fairly. Good reasons include misconduct, poor performance and individual redundancy.	Dismissals will be judged unfair if carried out in an unreasonable manner. In redundancy cases, failure to consult or consider redeployment may cast doubt on fairness of the dismissal.	0
Norway	Dismissals for personal and economic reasons (rationalisation measures, etc.) are possible. However, the courts have restricted personal reasons mainly to cases of material breach of the employment contract (disloyalty, persistent absenteeism, etc.).	Dismissals for economic reasons are unfair if the employee could have been retained in another capacity. Dismissals for reasons of age (under the age of 70), for trade union activities, military service, pregnancy and of recent mothers and employees on sick leave are also unfair.	2.5
Poland	Dismissals based on factors inherent in the employee (e.g. lack of competence) or on economic grounds of redundancy of the job.	..	0
Portugal	Previously the only grounds for dismissal were disciplinary. Laws in 1989 and 1991 added dismissals for economic grounds and for lack of professional or technical capability. Dismissals for individual redundancy must be based on urgent needs and must not involve posts also manned by people on fixed-term contracts. Dismissals for lack of competence are only possible after introduction of new technology or change to job functions.	Dismissals where employees could have been reasonably, in view of their skills and abilities, transferred or retrained.	2
Spain[d]	Dismissals for "objective" reasons, which include economic redundancy and an employee's inability to adapt to changed working practices, after having been given up to 3 months training.	Dismissals based on discrimination or violating an employee's constitutional or civil rights (such as based on trade union or works council membership).	2

OECD

Table 2.A.4. **Conditions under which individual dismissals are fair or unfair**[a] *(cont.)*

	Fair	Unfair	Score (0-3)[b]
Sweden	Dismissals on "objective grounds", *i.e.* economic redundancy and personal circumstances, including lack of competence. In cases of redundancy, selection of workers to be dismissed has to be justified (mainly based on "*last-in, first-out*" principle).	Objective grounds are deemed not to exist if an employee could reasonably have been transferred to other work, or if dismissal is based on events which happened over two months ago.	2
Switzerland	..	Dismissals based, *inter alia*, on personal grounds such as sex, religion, union membership, marital status or family responsibilities, or on the exercise of an employee's constitutional rights or legal obligations, such as military service.	0
Turkey	..	Dismissals of shop stewards, and on grounds of trade union membership, strike activity, pregnancy and after occupational accidents.	0
United Kingdom	Dismissals justified by lack of capability or qualifications; persistent or gross misconduct; economic redundancy; or some other "substantial reason". Two years tenure necessary for being able to file for unfair dismissal.	Dismissals based on discrimination by race and sex, or related to trade union activity or health and safety.	0
United States	With the exception of the public sector, it is generally fair to terminate an open-ended employment relationship without justification or explanation ("employment-at-will" principle) unless the parties have placed specific restrictions on terminations.	Dismissals based on breach of Equal Employment Opportunity principles (*i.e.* national origin, race, sex, etc.) and dismissals of employees with physical or mental impairment if work could be performed through appropriate workplace adjustment.[e]	0

.. Data not available.
a) This table does not report the treatment of dismissal for serious fault which is considered fair grounds for dismissal in all countries.
b) Scored 0 when worker capability or redundancy of the job are adequate and sufficient grounds for dismissal; 1 when social considerations, age or job tenure must when possible influence the choice of which worker(s) to dismiss; 2 when a transfer and/or retraining to adapt the worker to different work must be attempted prior to dismissal; and 3 when worker capability cannot be a ground for dismissal.
c) In France, the employer often has to provide or contribute towards the cost of training after a dismissal (*convention de conversion*), but the retraining condition does not enter into judging the fairness of the dismissal. By contrast, in countries like Germany and Spain rehabilitation must already have been attempted before the dismissal, or the dismissal is considered unfair.
d) Spain: after legislative reforms in 1994 and 1997, the share of individual dismissals found to be unjustified by the courts has fallen considerably.
e) United States: in addition, there are increasing numbers of cases where employees pursue wrongful termination claims by alleging that dismissal was based on an "implied contract" for continued employment.

Table 2.A.5. Compensation and related remedies following unjustified dismissal

Australia	Courts may order reinstatement with back pay. Compensation up to six months wages, plus entitlements (that would have been) accrued until the end of notice period. (For non-award employees, the cap is either 6 months wages or $34 000, whichever is the lower amount.)
Austria	A reinstatement order is possible, although rarely taken up by the employee concerned. Compensation through regular severance pay, plus a sum equal to earnings between the dismissal and the legal settlement of the case. Sums earned by the employee in the interim are set off against the award.
Belgium	Compensation at least equal to notice period, plus compensation for damages corresponding to six months. No right to reinstatement.
Canada	Reinstatement now recognised by the courts as an appropriate remedy for dismissals without just cause (but still relatively rare). Wrongfully discharged workers may be entitled to damages corresponding to past and future financial losses, and accompanying psychic injuries.
Czech Republic	Unfair dismissal gives rise to a right to reinstatement. If reinstatement is not accepted by both parties, compensation is through severance pay and award of lost earnings during the court case. Sums earned by the employee in the interim are set off against the award.
Denmark	Compensation is limited to 1 year of pay (for long service cases). Reinstatement orders are possible but rare.
Finland	Courts may suggest reinstatement, but this cannot be enforced. Compensation between 3 and 20 months.
France	Reinstatement cannot be enforced. Compensation of 6 months minimum (in some cases up to 24 months or more) for employees with at least two years tenure and working in enterprises with more than 11 employees. For employees with less than 2 years service and/or working in a firm with fewer than 11 people, the judge can order compensation according to the loss suffered, but without any minimum.
Germany	A reinstatement order is possible, although rarely taken up by the employee concerned. Compensation of up to 12 months, depending on length of service (15 months if aged over 50, 18 months if aged over 55). In some cases, additional liability for wages from the expiry date of the notice to the conclusion of the court hearing.
Greece	Frequent reinstatement orders, accompanied by indemnity for the period of time between notice of termination and court ruling. No reinstatement, if severance pay has been requested.
Hungary	Reinstatement orders fairly frequent. In lieu of reinstatement, severance pay is normally doubled and extended to those below 3 years tenure.
Ireland	A reinstatement order, with back pay from the date of dismissal, is possible. Maximum compensation equals 104 weeks of pay.
Italy	Two Acts of 1966 and 1970, both revised in 1990, regulate unfair dismissals, differentiated by establishment size. Under the 1970 Act (Workers Statute), workers in companies employing > 60 employees, or > 15 employees in an establishment or in the same commune can choose reinstatement (plus at least 5 months compensation pay) or financial compensation of 15 months. For establishments not included in the above cases, the 1966 Act gives the employer the choice between re-engagement and compensation of 2.5-6 months (depending on seniority and firm size), but up to 10 months for > 10 years seniority, and 14 months for > 20 years seniority if the firm employs > 15 employees. Normal severance pay is payable in addition to compensation.
Japan	Frequent orders of reinstatement with back pay. Alternatively, compensation through regular severance pay, plus a sum equal to earnings between the dismissal and the legal settlement of the case. Sums earned by the employee in the interim can only partially be set off against the award.
Korea	Courts may order reinstatement with back pay. Compensation in lieu of reinstatement varies widely.
Mexico	Reinstatement orders are rare, although possible by law. In the case of dismissal without "just cause", compensation of 3 months plus 20 days per year of service.
Netherlands	Notwithstanding court rulings, employers in practice can choose to replace reinstatement by payment of compensation. The amount of compensation is governed by application of severance pay formula as in Table 2.A.2, although a "correction factor" may be applied to this formula. Recent research has documented that average compensation is about NLG52 000. Scored as 18 months.
New Zealand	No legal provisions. Compensation set on a case-by-case basis.
Norway	Reinstatement orders fairly frequent. Compensation up to 6 months pay (although it can go up to 3 years in rare cases), plus back pay for the duration of the court case.
Poland	Reinstatement frequently ordered. Compensation of up to 2 months depending on amount of salary earned in another job by the time of court decision.
Portugal	Employee can choose between reinstatement with full back pay counting from the date of the dismissal to the actual court sentence; or compensation of one month of pay per year of service (with a minimum indemnity of 3 months).
Spain	Employer can choose between reinstatement with back pay and, since 1997, compensation of 33 days per year of service, with a maximum of 24 months pay. Workers hired under pre-1997 legislation can still receive up to 45 days severance pay per year of service, with a total of 42 months. In certain cases involving discrimination or union/works council activities, the dismissal is "annulled" and employers have to accept reinstatement.

— Table 2.A.5. **Compensation and related remedies following unjustified dismissal** *(cont.)* —

Sweden	Courts may order reinstatement or damages, plus a sum equal to earnings between the dismissal and the legal settlement of the case. If employer refuses to comply with reinstatement, damages are payable on the scale (employees over 60 in parenthesis): 16 (24) months < 5 years; 24 (36) months < 10 years; 32 (48) months > 10 years.
Switzerland	Courts are not empowered to order reinstatement. Compensation usually limited to wages for the notice period that should have been observed, or for the time period from the time of the unjustified dismissal to the actual court sentence, with an overall limit of 6 months.
Turkey	Courts are not empowered to order reinstatement, with the exception of dismissals on grounds of trade union activities. Standard remedy is a right to compensation, amounting to triple the notice period, plus regular severance pay.
United Kingdom	Employers are not obliged to reinstate. Compensation may consist of various elements: basic award (up to £6 600); compensatory award (up to £12 000); and special awards. Unlimited, if there is also discrimination on grounds of sex, race or disability.
United States	Reinstatement often ordered where worker has been discharged in violation of laws such as the National Labor Relations Act or the Equal Rights Act. A wrongfully discharged worker employed under a fixed-term contract is entitled to damages corresponding to what he/she would have earned over the life of the contract (less any salary from newly entered employment). Workers under open-ended contracts may be entitled to damages corresponding to past and future financial losses, and accompanying psychic injuries.

Table 2.A.6. Compensation pay and related provisions following unjustified dismissal
Trial periods, compensation payable and extent of reinstatement

	Type of worker	Trial period before eligibility arises	Typical compensation at 20 years tenure[a]	Extent of reinstatement[b]
Australia	All workers	Not legally regulated	Wide range, on case-by-case basis	1.5
Austria	All workers	1 month	15 months	1
Belgium	Blue collar	7-14 days	8 months	0
	White collar	1-6 months[c]	18/27 months[d]	0
Canada	All workers	Typically 3 months	Disparate rulings	1
Czech Republic	All workers	3 months	8 months	2
Denmark	Blue collar	0 months	9 months	1
	White collar	3 months	9 months	1
Finland	All workers	4 months	12 months	0
France[e]	Blue collar	1 week-2 months	15 months	0
	White collar	1-3 months	15 months	0
Germany	All workers	6 months	18 months	1.5
Greece	Blue collar	3 months	9.5 months	2
	White collar	3 months	22 months	2
Hungary	All workers	3 months	10 months	2
Ireland	All workers	12 months[f]	24 months	1
Italy	Blue collar	1-2 weeks[g]	32.5 months	2
	White collar	3-8 weeks	32.5 months	2
Japan	All workers	Not legally regulated, but varies mainly between 2 and 6 months	26 months	2
Korea	All workers	Not legally regulated, varies from case to case	Wide range, on case-to-case basis	2
Mexico	All workers	Not legally regulated	16 months	1
Netherlands	All workers	1 month for contract of up to 2 years duration; 2 months for contract with > 2 years duration	18 months[h]	1
New Zealand	All workers	All employees covered by EPL from start of employment[i]	Wide range, on case-by-case basis	1
Norway	All workers	1 month	15 months	2
Poland	All workers	Minimum 2 weeks, ranging up to 3 months	3 months	2
Portugal	All workers	60 days[j]	20 months	2.5
Spain	All workers	2 or 3 months (depending on company size)[k]	22 months	0
Sweden	All workers	Probationary period limited to a maximum of 6 months; does not exclude claim for damages	32 months, if employer refuses to comply with reinstatement order	1
Switzerland	All workers	1 month, sometimes extended by collective agreements to 3 months	6 months	0
Turkey	All workers	1 month, sometimes extended by collective agreements to 3 months	26 months	0
United Kingdom	All workers	2 years[f]	8 months[l]	0
United States	All workers	Wide range	Disparate rulings	0.5

a) Where relevant, calculations assume that the worker was 35 years old at the start of employment and that a court case takes 6 months on average.
b) The extent of reinstatement is based upon whether, after a finding of unfair dismissal, the employee has the option of reinstatement into his/her previous job even when this is against the wishes of the employer. The indicator is 1 where this option is rarely made available to the employee, 2 where it is fairly often made available, and 3 where it is always made available.
c) For Belgian white collar workers, the trial period can be up to 12 months if pay exceeds BF 1 130 000 per year.
d) Two possibilities given, depending on salary (< or > BF 928 000 annually in 1998).
e) France: trial period taken from collective agreement of chemical industry [IDS (1995), p. 105]; 15 months are sum of 12 months compensation and 2.7 months severance pay.
f) In Ireland and the United Kingdom, shorter trial periods are commonly agreed between employer and employee, but claims under statutory unfair dismissal legislation are not normally possible until after the periods shown.
g) For Italy, the trial periods cited are those common in collective agreements which are enforceable.
h) Netherlands: see Table 2.A.5 for detail.
i) New Zealand: case law tends to reduce rigour of provisions where employee is on probation.
j) Portugal: while 60 days is the standard trial period, the period can vary from 15 days in case of fixed-term contracts below 6 months duration, to 90 days in firms with > 20 employees, and 240 days for senior managers.
k) Spain: trial period can go up to 6 months for qualified technical staff and 9 months for managers.
l) After 20 years of service, an average worker is entitled to about £12 000 which equal roughly 8 months average gross salary.

Table 2.A.7. **Regulation of fixed-term contracts**

	Valid cases other than "objective" or "material" situation[a]		Maximum number of successive contracts[b]	Maximum cumulated duration of successive contracts
	Current practice	Score[c] 0-3	Number	Time
Australia	No restrictions in legislation.	3	1.5 No legal limit specified; but risk that, upon continuous renewal, the courts will find that the primary purpose of the contract is to avoid termination laws.	No limit specified.
Austria	No restrictions for first contract.	2.5	1.5 Successive fixed-term contracts without objective reason imply the risk of a court declaring the contract null and void.	No limit specified.
Belgium	Still in principle restricted to objective situations (replacement, temporary increase in workload, etc.), fixed-term contracts are now permitted without specifying an objective reason, a) for up to two years, or b) up to three years with the authorisation of the social and labour inspectorate.	2	4 If each > 3 months under option a), or 6 months under option b).	30 months (generally 2 years, but 3 years after authorisation of labour inspectorate).
Canada	No restrictions.	3	No limit.	No limit.
Czech Republic	Generally permitted, with restrictions for certain categories of employees, such as the disabled, those under 18 and recent graduates of apprenticeship and higher education.	2.5	No legal limit.	No limit specified.
Denmark	Fixed-term contracts allowed for specified periods of time and/or for specific tasks. Widely used, particularly in professional services and construction.	3	1.5 No legal limit, but successive contracts imply the risk of a court declaring the fixed-term contract null and void.	No limit specified.
Finland	Permitted for temporary replacements, traineeship, and special business needs (unstable nature of service activity, etc.).	1	1.5 In case of successive contracts, justification of limitation of contract subject to court examination.	No limit.
France[d]	Restricted to "objective" situations (replacement, seasonal work, temporary increases in company activity). Certain categories of fixed-term contracts are allowed for training purposes and in case of hiring subsidies and public work programmes.	1	2 A new contract on the same post can only start after a waiting period amounting to one third of initial contract.	18 months (respectively 9 and 24 months in restricted cases).
Germany	Fixed-term contracts are now widely possible without specifying any objective reason [up to mid-80s, restricted to "material reasons" (specific projects, replacement, seasonal work, etc.)].	2.5	4 (no legal limit in case of objective reason).	24 months (no legal limit in case of objective reason).
Greece	Objective situations only (mainly seasonal work and special projects), with the exception of the public service.	0	2.5 No legal limit specified, but outside the public service, more than 2 renewals will imply the risk of a court declaring the fixed-term contract null and void.	No limit specified.

Table 2.A.7. **Regulation of fixed-term contracts** (cont.)

	Valid cases other than "objective" or "material" situation[a]		Maximum number of successive contracts[b]	Maximum cumulated duration of successive contracts
	Current practice	Score[c] 0-3	Number	Time
Hungary	No restrictions, except for public service (objective reasons only).	2.5	No limit specified.	5 years.
Ireland	Employers do not have to justify recourse to fixed-term contracts.	3	No limit (but some possibility for unfair dismissal claims after having been employed for successive contracts).	No limit.
Italy	Traditionally limited to "objective" situations and subject to approval by the Employment Office. Since 1987, fixed-term contracts can be used more widely through sectoral collective agreements which specify target groups (youth and unemployed) and employment shares (often 8-10 per cent)	1	Scored 2 (two prolongations possible, but renewal is allowed only in restricted circumstances).	Scored 15 months (generally 12 months; 24 months for the special case of "training-work" contract).
Japan	Fixed-term contracts under 1 year duration widely possible without specifying any objective reason.	2.5	2.5 No legal limit specified; after repeated renewal the employee becomes entitled to expect renewal of his/her contract and the employer must have just cause to refuse renewal.	No limit.
Korea	Fixed-term contracts under 1 year duration widely possible without specifying any objective reason. Contracts over 1 year still limited to objective situations.	2.5	2.5 No limit specified, but several successive renewals imply the risk that a court will declare a fixed-term contract invalid.	No limit specified.
Mexico	Restricted to objective situations (replacement, temporary increase in workload, etc.), with the exception of a few occupations. Extent of use determined in consultation with union delegates.	0.5	No limit specified, negotiable by both parties.	No limit specified, negotiable by both parties.
Netherlands	No restrictions.	3	3 Beyond 2 renewals, worker is entitled to indefinite status. Notice required after 3 successive contracts.	No limit for first fixed-term contract, but 3 years in case of renewals.
New Zealand	No restrictions in legislation.	3	Scored 5 No legal limit specified; recent case law has reduced the risk that upon continuous renewal courts will find fixed-term contract a "sham".	No limit.
Norway[e]	Permitted for specific tasks/projects, the hiring of trainees, athletes and chief executives, temporary replacements of absent employees, and job creation measures.	1	1.5 In case of successive contracts, justification of limitation of contract subject to court examination.	No limit.
Poland	No restrictions.	3	2	No limit specified.
Portugal	Permitted, *inter alia*, for *a)* business start-ups; *b)* launching a new activity of uncertain duration; and *c)* recruiting workers in search of their first job and long-term unemployed.	2	3	3 years, except for new activities and business start-ups (2 years); scored 30 months.

OECD

Table 2.A.7. **Regulation of fixed-term contracts** (cont.)

	Valid cases other than "objective" or "material" situation[a]		Maximum number of successive contracts[b]	Maximum cumulated duration of successive contracts
	Current practice	Score[c] 0-3	Number	Time
Spain	Permitted *inter alia*, for specific tasks/projects; temporary replacements; training contracts; "eventualities of production"; and the hiring of handicapped, older workers and long-term unemployed.	1	3 No limit specified, except that implied by legislated minimum (12 months) and maximum cumulated duration.	3 years. Law prohibits hiring successive workers under fixed-term contracts to occupy the same post.
Sweden	Permitted, *inter alia*, for: a) temporary replacement of absent employees; b) temporary increases in workload; c) trainee work; d) since 1997 also allowed without specifying the reason, but only where no more than 5 employees are covered by such contracts simultaneously.	2.5	No limit specified.	Under a), 3 years in 5-year period; under b), 6 months in 2-year period; under d), 12 months in 3-year period, or 18 months for 1st employee; scored 12 months.
Switzerland	General.	3	1.5 No limit specified, but successive contracts imply the risk of a court declaring the fixed-term contract null and void.	No limit specified.
Turkey	Restricted to "objective situations", particularly seasonal and agricultural work.	0	1.5 No limit specified, but successive contracts imply the risk of a court declaring the fixed-term contract null and void.	No limit specified.
United Kingdom	No restrictions.	3	No limit.	No limit.
United States	No restrictions.	3	No limit.	No limit.

a) All countries recognise the validity of fixed-term contracts in "objective" situations, a term which typically refers to specific projects, seasonal work, replacement of temporarily absent permanent workers (on sickness or maternity leave), and exceptional workload.
b) The law in most countries does not specify any limits to the number of fixed-term contracts if separate valid objective reasons for each new contract can be given. However, after successive renewals (often at the first such renewal) courts may examine the validity of the reason given and may declare the fixed term unjustified.
c) Scored 0 if fixed-term contracts are permitted only for "objective" or "material" reasons (*i.e.* to perform a task which itself is of fixed duration); 1 if specific exemptions apply to situations of employer need (*e.g.* launching a new activity) or employee need (*e.g.* workers in search of their first job); 2 when exemptions exist on both the employer and the employee side; 3 when there are no restrictions on the use of fixed-term contracts.
d) France: fixed-term contracts are not allowed in a period of six months following dismissals for economic reasons.
e) Norway: employers have to give notice to fixed-term employees, instead of simply letting their contracts run out. Fixed-term workers dismissed before expiry date because of lack of work are entitled to preferential rehiring later, under certain conditions.

Table 2.A.8. **Regulation of temporary work agency (TWA) employment**

	Types of work for which TWA employment is legal	Score[a] (0-4)	Are there any restrictions on the number of renewals?	Maximum cumulated duration of temporary work contracts[b]
Australia	General.	4	No.	No limit.
Austria	General, if contract is indefinite, but limited to "objective" situations, if it is of fixed duration.	3	Yes (unless there is a separate reason for every contract).	No limit.
Belgium	Limited to "objective" situations; prohibited in certain sectors of the construction and transport industries; consultation with union delegates required.	2	Yes.	6 to 24 months, depending on reason. Scored 15 months.
Canada	General.	4	No.	No limit.
Czech Republic	General.	4	No.	No limit.
Denmark	General.	4	No.	No limit.
Finland	General.	4	No.	No limit.
France	Limited to "objective" situations, as for other fixed-term contracts.	2	Yes (1 prolongation possible).[c]	18 months.
Germany	General, with exception of construction industry.	3	Yes.	12 months.
Greece	TWAs not permitted.	0	Not applicable.	Not applicable.
Hungary	General.	4	No.	No limit.
Ireland	General.	4	No.	No limit.
Italy	Admitted since 1997 on an experimental basis for particular sectors, for replacement of absent workers and for types of work not normally used in the enterprise. Collective agreements lay down upper limits for the use of temporary workers. Excluded for all unskilled workers and firms which have resorted to collective dismissals in the last 12 months.	1	Yes (regulated through sectoral agreements; generally only one renewal possible).	No limit.
Japan	"Dispatching agencies" restricted by law to 23 types of occupations.	2	Yes (two prolongations possible).	36 months (12 months for initial contract).
Korea	Allowed in 26 occupations and in response to certain specified labour shortages.	2.5	Yes.	2 years.
Mexico	..	..	..	..
Netherlands	General, with exception of seamen (previous restrictions on construction and transport now removed).	3.5	Yes.	3.5 years, after which an indefinite contract with the TWA will be required.
New Zealand	General.	4	No.	No limit.
Norway	General prohibition remains in force, but wide exceptions for most service sector occupations.	3	Yes.	24 months.
Poland	General.	4	Yes.	No limit specified.
Portugal	Restricted to "objective situations", including seasonal activity and substitution of absent workers.	2	Yes; only certain categories of contract may be renewed, always with the permission of the Labour Inspectorate. Succession of temporary workers in the same post is expressly forbidden.	6 or 12 months, depending on reason. Scored 9 months.

Table 2.A.8. **Regulation of temporary work agency (TWA) employment** *(cont.)*

	Types of work for which TWA employment is legal	Score[a] (0-4)	Are there any restrictions on the number of renewals?	Maximum cumulated duration of temporary work contracts[b]
Spain	TWAs legal since 1994, limited to "objective situations".	2	Yes.	Not regulated for substitution and contracts related to a specific task; 3 or 6 months for temporary increase in workload. Scored 6 months.
Sweden	General.	4	No.	Same rules as for fixed-term contracts. Scored 12 months.
Switzerland	General.	4	No (but no renewals possible with the same client employer)	No limit.
Turkey	Prohibited (with the exception of agricultural work).	0	Not applicable.	Not applicable.
United Kingdom	General.	4	No.	No limit.
United States	General.	4	No.	No limit.

.. Data not available.
a) Scored 0 if TWA employment is illegal, 1 to 3 depending upon the degree of restrictions, and 4 where no restrictions apply.
b) In most OECD countries, work contracts are between the temporary employee and the temporary work agency, while the latter concludes a different type of contract with the final user.
c) France: a new contract on the same post can only start after a waiting period amounting to one third of initial contract.

Table 2.A.9. **Procedures and standards for collective dismissal**

	Definition of collective dismissal	Notification of employee representatives	Notification of public authorities	Delays involved	Type of negotiation required[a]	Selection criteria	Severance pay
Australia	Employers planning to dismiss 15 or more employees on economic, technical or structural grounds.	Obligation to inform and consult with employees and trade union, where relevant.	Notification of competent labour authorities.	No specific regulations.	Consultation on alternatives to redundancy and selection standards.	Law requires fair basis of employee selection.	No special regulations for collective dismissal.
Austria	Within 30 days, 5+ workers in firms with 20-99 employees; 5%+ in firms with 100-599; 30+ workers in firms with > 600; 5+ workers > 50 years old.	General duty to inform the works council about changes affecting the business.	Notification of local employment office.	30 days waiting period before first notice can become effective.	Consultation on alternatives to redundancy and ways to mitigate the effects; social plan to be established in firms with > 20 employees.	No criteria laid down by law.	No legal requirements, but often part of social compensation plans.
Belgium	Within 60 days, > 10 workers in firms with 20-99 employees; > 10% in firms with 100-300; > 30 workers in firms with 300+ employees.	Obligation to inform and consult with works council or trade union delegation.	Notification of sub-regional employment office.	30 days delay, can be lengthened to 60 days by employment office.	Consultation on alternatives to redundancy and ways to mitigate the effects.	No criteria laid down by law, but a national collective agreement allows co-determination of works council.	Severance pay during four months equivalent to half the difference between unemployment benefit and net remuneration (up to a ceiling).
Canada	50 or more employees within a period of 4 weeks in federal jurisdiction, Manitoba, Newfoundland and Ontario; between 10 or more and 25 or more in most other jurisdictions.	Obligation to inform and consult with recognised or certified trade union in less than half of the jurisdictions.	Notification of competent labour authorities or ministries in all jurisdictions.	Extended notice period to individuals (16 weeks in federal jurisdiction).	In 4 jurisdictions, labour authorities may require employer to establish or participate in a joint committee to discuss alternatives to redundancy and measures for finding new employment. This is obligatory in the federal jurisdiction.	As laid down in any collective agreements.	No special regulations for collective dismissal in federal jurisdiction.
Czech Republic	Employers planning to dismiss several employees for reasons of structural change or reorganisation.	Duty to inform competent trade union body.	Notification of district labour office.	Information to trade union and PES office 3 months before implementation.	Consultation on alternatives to redundancy and measures for finding new jobs.	Obligation to take account of social considerations (e.g. mothers, adolescents, disabled).	No special regulations for collective dismissal.
Denmark	Within 30 days, > 9 workers in firms with 21-99 employees; > 9% in firms with 100-299; > 29 workers in firms with 300+ employees.	Inform and consult with works council or trade union delegation.	Notification of public employment service.	30 days delay after notice to PES; delays are longer in firms with > 100 workers that seek to dismiss over half of staff.	National agreement obliges companies to organise transfer and/or retraining whenever possible.	No criteria laid down by law.	No special regulations for collective dismissal.

Employment Protection and Labour Market Performance – 109

OECD

Table 2.A.9. Procedures and standards for collective dismissal *(cont.)*

	Definition of collective dismissal	Notification of employee representatives	Notification of public authorities	Delays involved	Type of negotiation required[a]	Selection criteria	Severance pay
Finland	> 9 workers in firms with > 20 employees, in case of dismissal for financial or production-related reasons.	Consultation with trade union or personnel representatives.	Notification of local employment office.	Consultation for at least 42 days, plus 5 days advance notice of the need for consultation.	Consultation on alternatives to redundancy and ways to mitigate the effects.	As laid down in collective agreements, selection procedure usually takes account of seniority, family circumstances and the retention of skilled personnel.	No legal requirements.
France	10 or more redundancies within 30 days (special obligations, similar to those for individual redundancy, also for dismissal of 2 to 9 employees).	Full information to be given to personnel delegates or works council and consultation meetings to be held.	Notification of departmental labour market authorities (DDTEFP).	30-60 days in companies with 50 or more employees; 21-35 days in companies with fewer than 50 employees (depending on number of proposed dismissals).	Consultation in several phases on alternatives to redundancy, such as redeployment or retraining; consultation on social compensation plan which is obligatory in companies with 50 or more employees. No veto power by employee representatives, but possibility of rejection of social plan by labour market authorities.	Labour law requires to take account of family responsibilities, seniority, age, disability and professional qualification (by job category).	No special regulations for collective dismissal.
Germany	Within 30 days, > 5 workers in firms with 21-59 employees; 10% or > 25 workers in firms with 60-499; > 30 workers in firms with > 500 employees.	Consultation with works council.	Notification of local employment office.	1 month delay after notice to PES, can be extended to two months.	Consultation on alternatives to redundancy and ways to mitigate the effects; social plan to be set up in conjunction with works council, regulating selection standards, transfers, lump-sum payments, early retirement, etc.	Social as well as economic considerations can enter the selection criteria, e.g. labour market prospects of concerned employees and economic viability of the company.	No legal requirements, but often part of social compensation plans.
Greece	Within a month, > 5 workers in firms with 20-50 employees; > 2% or > 30 workers in firms with > 50 employees.	Notification of reasons and obligation to reach agreement with employee representatives.	Notification to Prefect and Labour Inspection, with request for approval.	If social partners agree and ministry approves, notice can be given after 10 days. Ministry can extend time for negotiation by another 20 days.	Negotiation with employee representatives on dismissal procedures. If no agreement is reached, Labour Ministry can impose its own terms.	Law lays down union participation, but no specific selection criteria for dismissal.	No special regulations for collective dismissal.

Table 2.A.9. **Procedures and standards for collective dismissal** (cont.)

	Definition of collective dismissal	Notification of employee representatives	Notification of public authorities	Delays involved	Type of negotiation required[a]	Selection criteria	Severance pay
Hungary	10+ workers in firms with 20-299 employees; > 10% in firms with 100-299; 30+ workers in firms with 300+ employees.	Committee to be set up, including works council or trade union representatives to consult on procedures and benefits.	Notification of local employment office.	30 days delay after notification of employment office, if at least 10 persons are involved, 90 days if 25% of workforce or 50+ employees are involved.	Consultation on principles of staff reduction, and ways to mitigate its effects.	Law lays down union participation, but no specific selection criteria for dismissal.	No special regulations for collective dismissal.
Ireland	Within 30 days, 5-9 workers in firms with 20-49 employees; 10+ workers in firms with 50-99; 10% in firms with 100-299; 30+ in firms with 300+ employees.	Duty to inform and consult with competent trade union.	Notification of ministry competent for labour and employment.	Information to trade union and ministry 30 days before implementation.	Consultation on alternatives to redundancy and ways to mitigate the effects.	Law lays down union participation, but no specific selection criteria for dismissal.	No special regulations for collective dismissal, but legally required severance pay usually topped up in cases of mass redundancies.
Italy	In firms with 15 and more employees and over a period of 120 days, 5+ workers in a single production unit; 5+ workers in several units within one province.	Duty to inform employee representatives and competent trade union and set up a joint examination committee.	Notification of labour authorities (at local, regional or national level, depending on size of redundancy).	Up to 45 days negotiation in joint examination committee before implementation. Conciliation if no agreement reached.	Consultation on alternatives to redundancy, scope for redeployment and ways to mitigate the effects; severance agreement usually reached after negotiation with union and (in major cases) labour authorities, determining selection criteria and use of financial support.	Law specifies social and economic criteria (length of service, number of dependants, technical and production requirements), but does not specify priorities.	Regular severance pay after exhaustion of *Cassa Integrazione Guadagni* or mobility payments.
Japan	No special statute on collective dismissal, but notification requirement in cases of 30+ dismissals.	Courts usually require information and consultation with trade union or employee representatives.	Notification of public employment service.	No special regulations.	Courts will require sincere consultation on need for redundancy, dismissal standards and employee selection.	No specific selection criteria for dismissal.	No special regulations for collective dismissal.
Korea	> 10 workers in firms with < 100 employees; > 10% of workers in firms with 100-999; > 100 workers in firms with > 1 000 employees.	Information and consultation with trade union/employee representatives.	Notification to Ministry of Labour.	No special regulations (60 days waiting period as for individual redundancy).	Sincere consultation on need for redundancy, dismissal standards and employee selection.	Law lays down union participation, but no specific selection criteria for dismissal other than "rational and fair standards".	No special regulation for collective dismissal.

Table 2.A.9. **Procedures and standards for collective dismissal** (cont.)

	Definition of collective dismissal	Notification of employee representatives	Notification of public authorities	Delays involved	Type of negotiation required[a]	Selection criteria	Severance pay
Mexico	Unspecified number to be dismissed for economic reasons; provisions restricted to companies with 20+ employees.	Duty to inform and consult with trade union/employee representatives.	Notification to Conciliation and Arbitration Board (*Junta*) if no agreement with union can be found.	No special regulations for collective dismissal.	Negotiation with employee representatives on conditions and procedures of dismissal. If no agreement is reached, agreement by *Junta* on terms of dismissal required.	Usually seniority-based.	No special regulation for collective dismissal.
New Zealand	No special statute on collective dismissal.	Duty to inform and consult with trade union/employee representatives only if required by contract.	Not required.	No special regulations for collective dismissal.	No legal requirements apart from procedural fairness.	Law requires fair basis of employee selection, but essentially employer's decision.	No special regulations for collective dismissal.
Netherlands	Over 3 months, 20+ workers dismissed by one employer in one employment service region.	Duty to inform and consult with works council and trade union delegation.	Notification of regional employment office.	30 days waiting period to allow for social plan negotiations (unless the social partners have agreed in writing to refrain from the waiting period).	Consultation on alternatives to redundancy and ways to mitigate the effects; social plan will normally be agreed outlining transfers, re-training, early retirement measures and financial compensation.	Employment service can determine mix of selection criteria ("last in-first out" principle, or "mirror-image" of existing workforce).	No legal entitlement, but social plans often contain severance pay or top-ups to unemployment benefits.
Norway	10+ employees within a month.	Duty to inform and consult with trade union/employee representatives.	Notification of district employment office.	30 days waiting period after notification of employment service.	Consultation on alternatives to redundancy and selection standards.	Accepted custom is by seniority, but recent case law gives more weight to business needs.	No legal requirements.
Poland	10%+ of workers in firms with < 1 000 employees 100+ workers in firms with 1 000 employees and above.	Duty to inform competent trade union.	Notification of local employment office.	Information to trade union and PES 45 days before implementation.	Agreement to be reached with trade union on alternatives to redundancy and ways to mitigate the effects.	Law lays down union participation, but no specific selection criteria for dismissal.	1 month < 10 years of service; 2 months < 20 years; 3 months > 20 years.
Portugal	Within 90 days, 2+ workers in firms with < 51 employees; 5+ workers in firms with 51+ employees.	Duty to inform and consult with works council or trade union delegation.	Notification of Labour Inspectorate.	75 days if agreement on dismissal procedures can be reached; otherwise 90 days.	Consultation on alternatives to redundancy, selection standards and ways to mitigate the effects; written agreement to be reached, if necessary via conciliation by Labour Inspectorate.	No criteria laid down in law, except for priority to trade union representatives and members of works councils.	No special regulations for collective dismissal.

Table 2.A.9. Procedures and standards for collective dismissal *(cont.)*

	Definition of collective dismissal	Notification of employee representatives	Notification of public authorities	Delays involved	Type of negotiation required[a]	Selection criteria	Severance pay
Spain	Within 90 days, 10+ workers in firms with < 100 employees; 10%+ in firms with 100-299, 30+ workers in firms with 300+ employees.	Duty to inform and consult with works council or trade union delegation.	Notification of local labour market authorities.	Employer must consult 30 days in advance (15 days in firms with < 50 employees). Further 15 days delay for approval of labour market authorities, if required.	Consultation on alternatives to redundancy, selection standards and ways to mitigate the effects. Written agreement to be reached, otherwise approval by labour market authorities is required.	No criteria laid down in law, except for priority to trade union representatives and members of works councils.	No special regulations for collective dismissal.
Sweden	Collective dismissal governed by regulation on redundancy dismissal.	Duty to inform and consult with competent trade union.	Notification of county labour board.	Waiting periods after notification of employment service are from 2 months (when 5-24 workers involved) to 6 months (when 100+ workers involved).	Consultation on alternatives to redundancy, selection standards and ways to mitigate the effects; notice may not take effect before negotiation with trade union.	Usually based on seniority within a job category, but deviations by collective agreement are possible.	No special regulations for collective dismissal.
Switzerland	10+ workers in firms with 20-99 employees; 10%+ in firms with 100-299, 30+ in firms with 300+ employees.	Obligation to inform and consult with works council or trade union delegation.	Duty to notify cantonal employment service.	30 days waiting period.	Consultation on alternatives to redundancy and ways to mitigate the effects; obligation to negotiate a social plan frequently contained in collective agreements.	No selection criteria laid down in law.	No legal requirements, but often part of social plans.
Turkey	10+ employees.	Not legally regulated (some collective agreements may require notification).	Duty to notify public employment service of names and skills of employees to be dismissed.	1 month waiting period.	No legal requirements (some collective agreements may stipulate some type of joint decision-making).	Usually employer prerogative.	No special regulations for collective dismissal.
United Kingdom	Within 90 days, 20+ employees.	Duty to inform and consult with recognised trade union or other elected employee representatives.	Notification of Department of Trade and Industry.	30 days if 20-99 workers are involved, 90 days when 100+ workers are involved.	Consultation on selection standards and dismissal procedures.	No criteria laid down in law, except for prohibition of discrimination. Often mix of seniority and performance-based criteria.	No special regulations for collective dismissal.

Table 2.A.9. **Procedures and standards for collective dismissal** (cont.)

	Definition of collective dismissal	Notification of employee representatives	Notification of public authorities	Delays involved	Type of negotiation required[a]	Selection criteria	Severance pay
United States	In firms with 100 or more employees and over a period of 30 days, 50+ workers in case of plant closure; 500+ workers in case of layoff; 50-499 workers, if they make up at least one third of the workforce.	Duty to inform affected workers or labour unions (where they exist).	Duty to notify state and local authorities.	Special 60-day notice period.[b]	No legal requirements.	As laid down in collective agreements or company manuals; usually seniority-based.	No special regulations for collective dismissal.

a) Including obligations, if any, to conclude compensation agreements ("social plans"), detailing *inter alia* measures for re-deployment, re-training, outplacement and severance pay, between the enterprise concerned, its employee representatives and/or the competent labour authorities.
b) Exceptions to the notice period include layoffs due to risk of bankruptcy, unforeseen circumstances, or ending of a temporary business activity. Several studies have shown that in a substantial number of cases employers fail to adequately apply notice requirements.

Annex 2.B

Calculation of Summary Indicators of EPL Strictness

Summary indicators of EPL strictness greatly facilitate the analysis of employment protection and its effects on labour market performance. Comparisons of employment protection across countries, or at different times in the same country, would be extremely cumbersome if done solely in terms of the 22 first-level indictors presented in Tables 2.2 to 2.4 (or the even more numerous descriptive entries reported in Annex 2.A). Although item-by-item comparisons can be instructive, summary measures appear to be essential in order to study the effects of employment protection on labour market outcomes.

However, the construction of such summary measures raises difficult choices of quantification and weighting that are familiar from the theory of index numbers. In earlier work, the OECD used a "rank of averaged ranks" approach to constructing summary indicators [OECD (1994a)], which was originally developed by Grubb and Wells (1993). Since the basic EPL indicators being combined are difficult to quantify in comparable units (*e.g.* difficulty of procedural requirements and severance pay), this largely ordinal approach is potentially attractive. However, the rank of averaged ranks method can prove misleading if national rankings differ too strongly across these basic indicators. In such a case, performing a cardinal operation on an ordinal measure – such as averaging several rankings – can lead to perverse results.

An ordinal approach is not sufficient for the purposes of this chapter because valid comparisons could not be made between levels of EPL strictness in the late 1990s and in the late 1980s. One limitation of a summary indicator based on ranking is that a given country's strictness score could either rise or fall over time, even though its employment protection practices were completely unchanged, for the simple reason that other countries changed their policies. Even more fundamentally, it would be invalid to compare a rank-based score for the late 1980s, which was based on an analysis of 16 European countries, with a rank-based score for the late 1990s based on a sample of 27 countries. Quite independently of any changes in EPL, the maximum rank score has nearly doubled.

A four-step procedure was developed for constructing *cardinal* summary indicators that allow meaningful comparisons to be made, both across countries and between different years (Chart 2.B.1).[1] Since the theoretical analysis of employment protection emphasises the analogy of EPL to an employer-borne tax on employment adjustment, the overall intent is to reflect, as accurately as possible, the cost implications of various regulatory provisions for employers (*i.e.* stricter is interpreted as more costly). However, the correspondence between the strictness scores and employers' costs is no more than qualitative.

The first step is to convert each of the 22 first-level indicators of EPL into cardinal scores that are normalised to range from 0 to 6, with higher scores representing stricter regulation. This scoring algorithm is somewhat arbitrary, but was implemented so as to compromise between allowing the score to rise proportionally with the underlying measure (*e.g.* with weeks of severance pay) and respecting natural break points in the data (*i.e.* clusters in country practices). Table 2.B.1 specifies the mapping that was used for each of the 22 first-level indicators.

Having converted all of the first-level measures into numerical scores that are in comparable units, it is mathematically straightforward to form various averages, as depicted in Levels 2 to 4 of Chart 2.B.1. However, it would be inappropriate to take unweighted averages of all of the components and uneven weights were used in two situations (see Table 2.B.2 for details):

- In cases where a single underlying aspect of employment protection regulation was reflected in multiple measures, their weights were reduced to be collectively equivalent to the weight applied to another aspect represented by a single measure. For example, the notice period and severance pay are not triple weighted, just because each is measured three times (*i.e.* at 9 months, 4 years and 20 years of tenure).

- In two cases, uneven weights were used because it was judged that some aspects of employment protection deserved greater economic weight than others. First, and following the *Jobs Study* [OECD (1994a)], it was assumed that a week of notice was only equivalent to 0.75 of a week of severance pay.[2] Second, when forming an overall strictness measure from the three subcomponents for strictness of regulation for regular contracts, temporary contracts and collective dismissals, the summary measure for collective dismissals was allocated just 40 per cent of the weight assigned to regular and temporary contracts. The rationale for this is that the collective dismissals indicator only reflects *additional* employment protection that was trigged by the collective nature of a dismissal. In most countries, these additional requirements are quite modest.

---

1. In practice, the cardinal summary indicator used in this chapter produces a very similar ranking of countries by overall EPL strictness to that produced by applying the rank of averaged ranks method to the underlying data (Spearman rank correlation of 0.95 for the late 1990s).
2. In each case, the employer must pay a week's wages, but in the case of notice the workers typically provide productive services that are of some value.

Chart 2.B.1. Four-step procedure to construct summary indicators of EPL strictness[a, b]

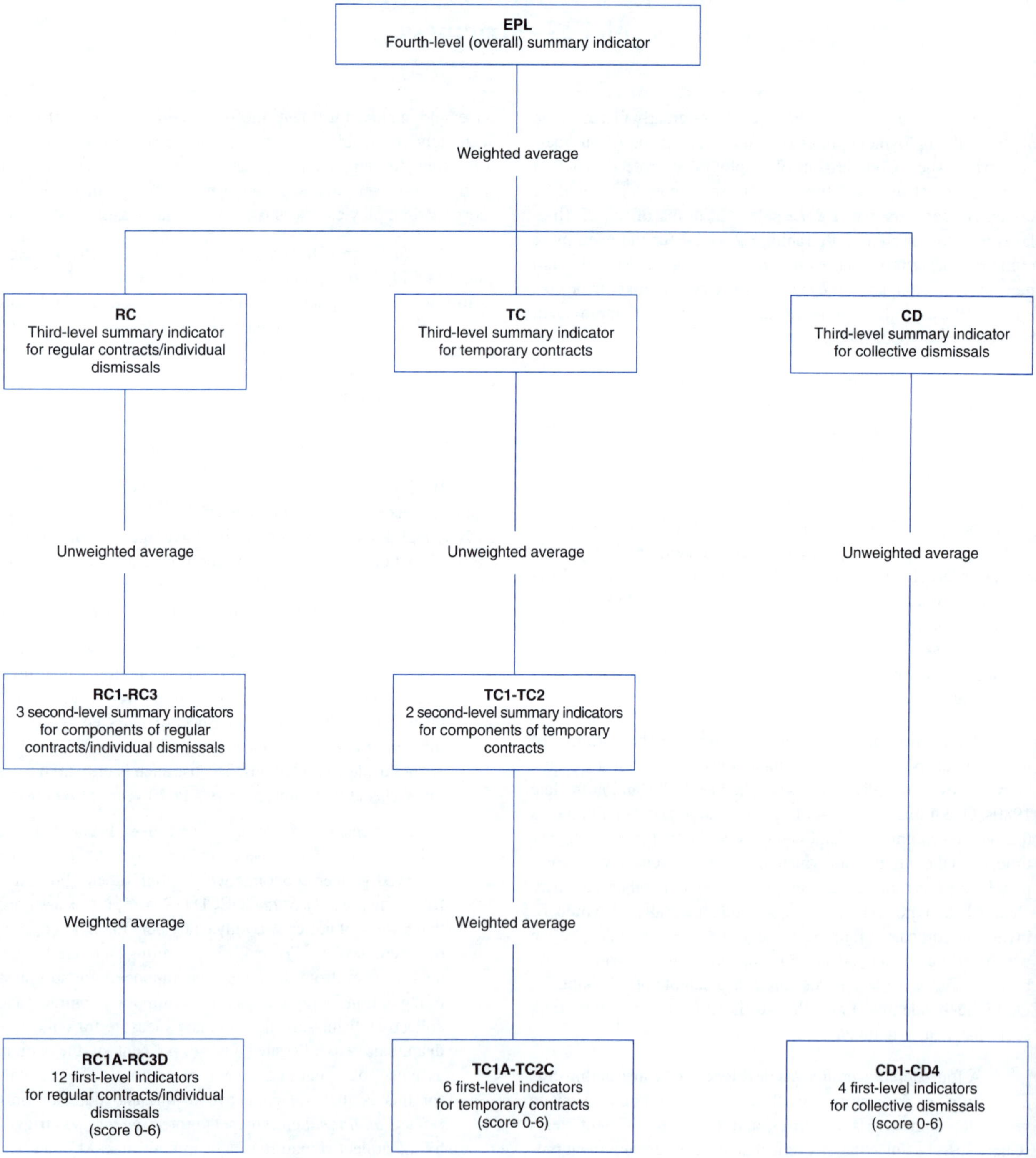

```
                        ┌─────────────────────────────────────┐
                        │              EPL                    │
                        │ Fourth-level (overall) summary      │
                        │           indicator                 │
                        └─────────────────────────────────────┘
                                        │
                               Weighted average
                                        │
         ┌──────────────────────────────┼──────────────────────────────┐
         │                              │                              │
┌────────────────────┐      ┌────────────────────┐      ┌────────────────────┐
│        RC          │      │        TC          │      │        CD          │
│ Third-level        │      │ Third-level        │      │ Third-level        │
│ summary indicator  │      │ summary indicator  │      │ summary indicator  │
│ for regular        │      │ for temporary      │      │ for collective     │
│ contracts/         │      │ contracts          │      │ dismissals         │
│ individual         │      │                    │      │                    │
│ dismissals         │      │                    │      │                    │
└────────────────────┘      └────────────────────┘      └────────────────────┘
         │                              │                              │
 Unweighted average          Unweighted average           Unweighted average
         │                              │                              │
┌────────────────────┐      ┌────────────────────┐                     │
│     RC1-RC3        │      │     TC1-TC2        │                     │
│ 3 second-level     │      │ 2 second-level     │                     │
│ summary indicators │      │ summary indicators │                     │
│ for components of  │      │ for components of  │                     │
│ regular contracts/ │      │ temporary          │                     │
│ individual         │      │ contracts          │                     │
│ dismissals         │      │                    │                     │
└────────────────────┘      └────────────────────┘                     │
         │                              │                              │
  Weighted average              Weighted average                       │
         │                              │                              │
┌────────────────────┐      ┌────────────────────┐      ┌────────────────────┐
│    RC1A-RC3D       │      │    TC1A-TC2C       │      │     CD1-CD4        │
│ 12 first-level     │      │ 6 first-level      │      │ 4 first-level      │
│ indicators for     │      │ indicators for     │      │ indicators for     │
│ regular contracts/ │      │ temporary          │      │ collective         │
│ individual         │      │ contracts          │      │ dismissals         │
│ dismissals         │      │ (score 0-6)        │      │ (score 0-6)        │
│ (score 0-6)        │      │                    │      │                    │
└────────────────────┘      └────────────────────┘      └────────────────────┘
```

a) The sequence of calculations flows from the bottom to the top of the chart (*i.e.* from first to fourth-level indicators).
b) See Tables 2.B.1 and 2.B.2 for variable definitions and aggregation weights.
Source: OECD.

Table 2.B.1. **Assignment of numerical strictness scores to first-level EPL indicators**[a]

Code	Original unit	Assigned scores						
		0	1	2	3	4	5	6
Individual dismissals of workers with regular contracts								
RC1A	Scale 0-3				Scale (0-3)*2			
RC1B	Days	0-2	< 10	< 18	< 26	< 35	< 45	≥ 45
RC2A1	Months	0	≤ 0.4	≤ 0.8	≤ 1.2	< 1.6	< 2	≥ 2
RC2A2	Months	0	≤ 0.75	≤ 1.25	< 2	< 2.5	< 3.5	≥ 3.5
RC2A3	Months	< 1	≤ 2.75	≤ 5	≤ 7	≤ 9	> 11	< 11
RC2B1	Months	0	≤ 0.5	≤ 1.0	≤ 1.75	≤ 2.5	< 3	≥ 3
RC2B2	Months	0	≤ 0.5	≤ 1	≤ 2	≤ 3	< 4	≥ 4
RC2B3	Months	0	≤ 3	≤ 6	≤ 10	≤ 12	≤ 18	> 18
RC3A	Scale 0-3				Scale (0-3)*2			
RC3B	Months	≥ 24	> 12	> 9	> 5	> 2.5	> 1.5	< 1.5
RC3C	Months	≤ 3	≤ 8	≤ 12	≤ 18	≤ 24	≤ 30	> 30
RC3D	Scale 0-3				Scale (0-3)*2			
Temporary employment								
TC1A	Scale 0-3				6-Scale (0-3)*2			
TC1B	Number	No limit	≥ 5	≥ 4	≥ 3	≥ 2	≥ 1.5	< 1.5
TC1C	Months	No limit	≥ 36	≥ 30	≥ 24	≥ 18	≥ 12	< 12
TC2A	Scale 0-4				6-Scale (0-4)*6/4			
TC2B	Yes/no	–	–	No	–	Yes or TC2A = 0	–	–
TC2C	Months	No limit	≥ 36	≥ 24	≥ 18	≥ 12	> 6	≤ 6 or TC2A = 0
Collective dismissals								
CD1	Scale 0-4				Scale (0-4)*(6/4)			
CD2	Scale 0-2				Scale (0-2)*3			
CD3	Days	0	< 25	< 30	< 50	< 70	< 90	> 90
CD4	Scale 0-2				Scale (0-2)*3			

a) The first 12 rows of this table (variables RC1A to RC3D) correspond to the measures of EPL for individual dismissals of workers with regular contracts as reported in Table 2.2, Panel A; the next 6 rows (variables TC1A to TC2C) correspond to the measures of the regulation of temporary contracts as reported in Table 2.3, Panel A; and the last 4 rows (variables CD1 to CD4) correspond to the measures of EPL for collective dismissals reported in Table 2.4.

The assignment of scores and weights adds a subjective dimension to the EPL strictness scores that is additional to the judgements already embodied in the 22 descriptive indicators. Experimentation with alternative scoring schemes for the first-level indicators suggests that the conclusions reached by the analysis are unlikely to be affected by the arbitrariness embodied in this step. By contrast, the weighting scheme can have a greater impact, since the components of EPL are not always highly, positively correlated. To take the most extreme example, notice and severance are actually negatively correlated (correlation coefficient of -0.16 in the late 1990s), so that the relative weights assigned to these components, can affect cross-country comparisons of EPL strictness. Rather than reporting results for a number of different weighting schemes for constructing alternative summary strictness measures, this chapter provides considerable analysis of the separate components of EPL.

Table 2.B.2. **EPL summary indicators and weighting scheme**[a]

Level 4	Level 3	Level 2	Level 1			
EPL Overall summary indicator[b]	RC Regular contracts[c] (5/12)	RC1 Procedural inconveniences (1/3)	Procedures		(1/2)	RC1A
			Delay to start a notice		(1/2)	RC1B
		RC2 Notice and severance pay for no-fault individual dismissals (1/3)	Notice period after	9 months	(1/7)	RC2A1
				4 years	(1/7)	RC2A2
				20 years	(1/7)	RC2A3
			Severance pay after	9 months	(4/21)	RC2B1
				4 years	(4/21)	RC2B2
				20 years	(4/21)	RC2B3
		RC3 Difficulty of dismissal[d] (1/3)	Definition of unfair dismissal		(1/4)	RC3A
			Trial period		(1/4)	RC3B
			Compensation		(1/4)	RC3C
			Reinstatement		(1/4)	RC3D
	TC Temporary contracts[c] (5/12)	TC1 Fixed-term contracts[e] (1/2)	Valid cases other than the usual "objective"		(1/2)	TC1A
			Maximum number of successive contracts		(1/4)	TC1B
			Maximum cumulated duration		(1/4)	TC1C
		TC2 Temporary work agency (TWA) employment[e] (1/2)	Types of work for which is legal		(1/2)	TC2A
			Restrictions on number of renewals		(1/4)	TC2B
			Maximum cumulated duration		(1/4)	TC2C
	CD Collective dismissals[c] (2/12)		Definition of collective dismissal		(1/4)	CD1
			Additional notification requirements		(1/4)	CD2
			Additional delays involved		(1/4)	CD3
			Other special costs to employers		(1/4)	CD4

a) Level 1 corresponds to the disaggregated data that have been assembled on EPL, while levels 2-4 represent successively more aggregated indicators of EPL strictness. The values in parenthesis indicate the aggregation weights to use in creating the next higher level summary indicator as a weighted average of the indicators at that level. Prior to forming these weighted averages, the level 1 indicators must be converted into equivalently scaled, cardinal variables (as specified in Table 2.B.1).
b) Variables CD1-CD4 are only available for the late 1990s. Thus, an alternative overall index is calculated as an unweighted average of RC and TC only. The table also omits several other indices that are used in the analysis. For example, equally weighted indices were calculated from RC2A1-RC2A3 (notice) and RC2B1-RC2B3 (severance).
c) The weighting 5/12, 5/12, 2/12 assigns CD 40 per cent the weight of assigned to RC and TC. This is intended to reflect the fact that the collective dismissals measures typically represent modest increments to the EPL requirements for individual dismissals.
d) Since all of the underlying data are available for Australia, Canada, Japan, Korea, Mexico, New Zealand and the United States, except RC3B or RC3C, the index RC3 (difficulty of dismissal) is calculated in these cases by averaging over all of the variables RC3A-RC3D with valid data. This allows levels 3 and 4 summary indicators to be calculated for these countries.
e) Since all of the underlying data are available for Finland, Norway and Sweden in the late 1980s, except for one or two items related to the maximum duration of temporary employment, the indices TC1 and TC2 are calculated in these cases by averaging over all of the variables TC1A-TC2C with valid data. This allows changes in the levels 3 and 4 summary indicators to be calculated for these three countries.

Annex 2.C

Summary of the Empirical Literature

Table 2.C.1. **Effects of EPL on labour market performance, findings from selected studies**

Study	Period and countries	Performance measure	Measure of EPL	Control variables and/or interactions	Method	Findings
EMPLOYMENT, UNEMPLOYMENT, AND HOURS						
Bertola (1990)	1962-86, 1974-86; 10 countries.	Employment rate; unemployment rate; hours worked.	Ranking based on evidence from Emerson (1988).	Unemployment rate; CPI; time-period dummies; GDP growth.	Time series estimation.	No effect on unemployment levels. Positive effect on unemployment persistence.
Blanchard (1998)	1960-64 to 1995-96; 21 countries.	Unemployment rate.	OECD ranking.[a]	The same as used in Nickell (1997), excluding the union density variable.	Unbalanced panel, with explicit treatment of shocks, and interaction of shocks and institutions.	No effect on unemployment, even after controlling for possible shocks.
Elmeskov et al. (forthcoming)	1983-95; 19 countries.	Structural unemployment (NAWRU).	OECD ranking.[a] Changes of EPL over time.	Income-schemes for unemployed;[b] ALMP;[c] collective bargaining;[c] tax wedge; minimum wages.	Panel data methods for a reduced-form unemployment equation. Theoretical bargaining model, taken from Layard et al. (1991).	Positive effect on structural unemployment. The results are more robust than Scarpetta's (1996) – note that EPL changes are taken into account.
Jackman et al. (1996)	1983-88, 1989-94; 20 countries.	Short-term unemployment; long-term unemployment (average over 1985-93, standardised and in logs).	OECD ranking.[a]	Income-schemes for unemployed;[b] ALMP;[c] collective bargaining;[c] change of inflation; time dummy.	Pooled regression for the two sub-periods, using random-effects methods. Equations also include lagged dependent variables.	No effect on unemployment, because the effect on hirings is almost offset by the effect on firings. No significant effect on unemployment persistence.
Esping-Andersen (forthcoming)	1993; 18 countries.	Unemployment rates.	OECD ranking.[a]	Collective bargaining;[c] minimum wage.[d]	Experimentations with the specification of EPL (linear and quadratic). Interactions of EPL with collective bargaining are allowed.	No impact on aggregate unemployment.
Lazear (1990)	1956-84; 22 countries.	Employment/population rate; labour force/participation rate; unemployment rate; hours worked per week.	Historical time series of severance pay and months of advance notice before dismissal (blue-collar worker with 10 years of service).	Severance pay, notice variable (both after 10 years of service) and quadratic time trend.	Models in reduced form.	High severance pay reduces employment, reduces labour force participation, and raises unemployment. Changes in severance pay rules partly explain unemployment changes in France, Italy and Portugal.

Table 2.C.1. **Effects of EPL on labour market performance, findings from selected studies** *(cont.)*

Study	Period and countries	Performance measure	Measure of EPL	Control variables and/or interactions	Method	Findings
Nickell (1997)	1983-88, 1989-94; 20 countries.	Log unemployment rate; overall labour supply;[e] employment/working-age-population ratio.	OECD ranking.[a]	Income-schemes for unemployed.[b] ALMP.[c] collective bargaining; total tax rate; change in inflation. Period dummy.	GLS random effects using two periods.	Insignificant effect on unemployment. Negative effect on employment, which becomes nil on prime-age men (due to high correlation between strict EPL and low female participation in southern Europe).
Nickell and Layard (1998)	1983-88, 1989-94; 20 countries.	Unemployment rate; employment/population; hours/population (six-year averages).	OECD ranking.[a]	Income-schemes for unemployed.[b] ALMP.[c] collective bargaining; total tax rate. Owner occupation rate. Time period dummy. Change in inflation.	GLS random effects using two time periods. The rate of change in inflation is included to capture the difference between actual and structural unemployment rate.	No effect on total unemployment. Negative effect on employment/population ratio (due to high correlation between strict EPL and low female participation in southern Europe)
Scarpetta (1996)	1983-93; 17 countries.	Structural unemployment (NAWRU); no-employment rate.	OECD ranking.[a]	Cyclical factors. Income-schemes for unemployed.[b] ALMP.[c] collective bargaining;[c] tax wedge; exposure to trade (proxy for product market competition). Real interest rates.	Static reduced-form model. Takes into consideration the difference between actual and equilibrium unemployment.	Positive impact on unemployment, which disappears after including institutional interactions. Positive impact also on non-employment rates.

LONG-TERM AND SHORT-TERM UNEMPLOYMENT, FLOWS AND UNEMPLOYMENT DURATION

Study	Period and countries	Performance measure	Measure of EPL	Control variables and/or interactions	Method	Findings
Blanchard and Portugal (1998)	1985-94; 21 countries.	Unemployment inflow; unemployment duration (average 1985-94).	OECD ranking.[a]	None.	Regression of the log flow and the log duration on the EPL rank.	EPL lowers flows through unemployment and raises unemployment duration.
Bertola and Rogerson (1997)	Mid to late 1980s; 6 countries.	Job creation, job destruction, unemployment flows and job turnover.	Grubb and Wells (1993) ranking.	None.	Standard theoretical model of job turnover to analyse the effects of firing costs on steady-state job turnover across firms.	Similar job turnover across countries. But EPL reduces the flows into and out of unemployment. Thus, job reallocation takes more often the form of job-to-job mobility.
Boeri (1999)	1983-94; 13 EU countries.	Probability of job-to-job and employment to unemployment flows; probability of unemployment outflow to employment.	Proportion of temporary employees.	GDP growth rate (lagged); country dummy; linear (and quadratic) time trend.	Panel data (grouped) logit equations for the group of workers in short-term jobs. Separated regressions for (adult and young) men and women.	EPL raises job-to-job mobility, but reduces flows from employment to unemployment. Since with strict EPL quits are more often not re-filled, it also reduces the chances of unemployed.

Table 2.C.1. **Effects of EPL on labour market performance, findings from selected studies** (cont.)

Study	Period and countries	Performance measure	Measure of EPL	Control variables and/or interactions	Method	Findings
Gregg and Manning (1997)	10 countries.	Percentage of long-term unemployed (> 1 year).	Average job tenure 1991, Bertola index.	None.	Regressions on average job tenure and on the Bertola index.	Positive effect on long-term unemployment.
Jackman et al. (1996)	1983-88; 1989-94; 20 countries.	Short-term unemployment; long-term unemployment (average over 1985-93, standardised and in logs).	OECD ranking.[a]	Income-schemes for unemployed;[b] ALMP; collective bargaining;[c] change of inflation; time dummy.	Pooled regression for the two sub-periods, using random-effects methods. Equations also include lagged dependent variables.	EPL increases long-term unemployment (because it decreases hirings), but also decreases short-term unemployment (because it decreases firings).
Nickell (1997)	1983-88; 1989-94; 20 countries.	Long-term and short-term unemployment (six-year averages in logs).	OECD ranking.[a]	Income-schemes for unemployed;[b] ALMP; collective bargaining;[c] total tax rate. Change in inflation. Period dummy.	GLS random effects using two periods.	The effects of EPL on short-term and long-term unemployment are not significant.
Nickell and Layard (1998)	1983-88; 1989-94; 20 countries.	Long-term and short-term unemployment (six-year averages in logs).	OECD ranking.[a]	Income-schemes for unemployed;[b] ALMP; collective bargaining;[c] total tax rate. Owner occupation rate. Time period dummy. Rate of change in inflation.	GLS random effects using two time periods. The rate of change in inflation is included to capture the difference between actual and structural unemployment rate.	Reduction of labour market flows, raising long-term unemployment and reducing short-term unemployment.
Schettkat (1997)	1982-83; 1987-88; 9 EU countries.	Overall labour mobility; flows out of employment; job-to-job mobility.	Own grouping based on strictness of dismissals protection (individual and collective).	Country dummies (proxy for labour market regulations); industry dummies (product market conditions); employment change and unemployment rate (macroeconomic conditions).	Pooled regressions, in reduced form.	Negative effect on labour mobility.
OECD (1993)	1979-91; 19 countries.	Long-term unemployment.	Severance pay and notice periods combined as one factor (blue- and white-collar workers).	Unemployment benefit duration; ALMP expenditures/ unemployment benefits.	Pooled time-series/cross-section estimation.	Positive effect on long-term unemployment rates. in southern Europe and Ireland, job security account for more than half of the long-term unemployed observed, particularly among blue-collar workers.
EMPLOYMENT AND UNEMPLOYMENT COMPOSITION						
Blanchard and Portugal (1998)	1985-94; 21 countries.	Unemployment inflow; unemployment duration (average 1985-94).	OECD ranking.[a]	None.	Regression of the log flow and the log duration on the EPL rank.	Strong effects on the nature of unemployment are found – the effect on the unemployment rate is ambiguous.

Table 2.C.1. **Effects of EPL on labour market performance, findings from selected studies** *(cont.)*

Study	Period and countries	Performance measure	Measure of EPL	Control variables and/or interactions	Method	Findings
Esping-Andersen (forthcoming)	1993; 18 countries.	Log unemployment rate; youth to male-adult unemployment ratio; unskilled to all unemployed ratio; unemployment outflow.	OECD ranking.[a]	Collective bargaining,[b] minimum wage.[d]	Experimentations with the specification of EPL: linear monotonic measure, quadratic specification, interactions with collective bargaining.	A quadratic effect is found. Youth and female unemployment is high when EPL is either strict or flexible (u-curve), and low-skilled unemployment is low when EPL is strict or flexible (hump-shaped curve).
Grubb and Wells (1993)	1989; 11 EU countries.	Incidence of temporary work; shifts in the structure of employment towards non-regulated forms of work.	Own rank based on regulations of: individual dismissals; temporary employment; working time.	None.	Cross-country correlations between regulation indicators and patterns of work. Partial cross-correlations between different indicators of regulation and corresponding work patterns' indicators are discussed.	EPL increases non-regulated forms of employment, and the proportion of employees in part-time and temporary work who are involuntary.
Nickell (1997)	1983-88, 1989-94; 20 countries.	Long-term and short-term unemployment (six-year averages, in logs).	OECD ranking.[a]	Income-scheme for unemployed;[b] ALMP; collective bargaining coverage;[c] total tax rate. change in inflation. Period dummy.	Estimation made using GLS random effects using two periods.	No effect on prime-age male unemployment.
Scarpetta (1996)	1983-93; 17 countries.	Youth unemployment.	OECD ranking.[a]	Cyclical factors. Income-schemes for unemployed;[b] ALMP; collective bargaining;[c] tax wadge; exposure to trade (proxy for product market competition). Real interest rates.	Static reduced-form model. Takes into consideration the difference between actual and equilibrium unemployment.	Significant impact on the structure of employment and unemployment (e.g. youth), which disappears after institutional interactions.
LABOUR INPUT ADJUSTMENT AND REALLOCATION OF LABOUR						
Abraham and Houseman (1994)	1973-90; 4 countries.	Employment adjustments; hours adjustments.	Separate regressions for each country. Dummy for changes in labour market regulation.	Output; time trend.	Koyck model of the dynamic demand for labour to estimate labour adjustments.	Employment adjustment (in manufacturing) is slower in Europe than in the United States, but hours adjustment is similar. EPL is not an obstacle to adjust for firms, since they develop strategies to get the needed flexibility (e.g. short-time work).

Table 2.C.1. **Effects of EPL on labour market performance, findings from selected studies** *(cont.)*

Study	Period and countries	Performance measure	Measure of EPL	Control variables and/or interactions	Method	Findings
Bertola (1990)	1962-86, 1974-86; 10 countries.	Employment rate; unemployment rate; hours worked.	Ranking based on evidence from Emerson (1988).	Unemployment rate; CPI; time-period dummies; GDP growth.	Time series estimation.	Employment is more stable, hours are less stable and unemployment is more persistent.
Boeri (1999)	1983-94; 13 EU countries.	Probability of unemployment outflow to employment, probability of voluntary quits.	Proportion of temporary employees.	GDP growth rate (lagged); country dummy; linear (and quadratic) time trend.	Panel data (grouped) logit equations for the group of workers in short-term jobs. Separated regressions for (adult and young) men and women.	"Partial reforms" which liberalise fixed-term contracts reduce the employment chances of the unemployed and discourage voluntary quits, which is often an efficient way to achieve optimal labour reallocation.
Jackman *et al.* (1996)	1983-88, 1989-94; 20 countries.	Short-term unemployment; long-term unemployment (average over 1985-93, standardised and in logs).	OECD ranking.[a]	Income-schemes for unemployed;[b] ALMP; collective bargaining;[c] change of inflation; time dummy.	Pooled regression for the two sub-periods, using random-effects methods. Equations also include lagged dependent variables.	Reduction in the speed of adjustment, but minor impact on the equilibrium unemployment.

INTERACTIONS WITH OTHER INSTITUTIONAL FACTORS

Study	Period and countries	Performance measure	Measure of EPL	Control variables and/or interactions	Method	Findings
Bertola and Rogerson (1997)	Mid to late 1980s; 6 countries.	Job creation, job destruction, unemployment flows and job turnover.	Grubb and Wells (1993) ranking.	None.	Standard theoretical model of job turnover to analyse the effects of firing costs on steady-state job turnover across firms.	Firings (but not hirings) increase if strict EPL coincides with wage compression.
Elmeskov *et al.* (forthcoming)	1983-95; 19 countries.	Structural unemployment (NAWRU).	OECD ranking.[a]	Income-schemes for unemployed;[b] ALMP; collective bargaining;[c] tax wedge; minimum wages.	Panel data methods for a reduced-form unemployment equation. The theoretical bargaining model follows Layard *et al.* (1991).	The positive effect of unemployment benefit and tax wedge on unemployment is larger if EPL is strict or loose. The negative impact of EPL on unemployment is stronger in countries with intermediate degree of centralisation/co-ordination of collective bargaining.

Table 2.C.1. **Effects of EPL on labour market performance, findings from selected studies** *(cont.)*

Study	Period and countries	Performance measure	Measure of EPL	Control variables and/or interactions	Method	Findings
Scarpetta (1996)	1983-93; 17 countries.	Structural unemployment (overall and youth).	OECD ranking.[a]	Cyclical factors. Income-schemes for unemployed;[b] ALMP; collective bargaining;[c] tax wedge; exposure to trade (proxy for product market competition). Real interest rates.	Static reduced form model (for the impact of institutions on structural unemployment). Takes into consideration the difference between actual and equilibrium unemployment.	A worst case scenario (as far as unemployment is concerned) would combine strong EPL with generous unemployment benefits and uncoordinated bargaining.

a) OECD *Jobs Study* (1994b), Part II, Table 6.7, Panel B, Column 2.
b) Replacement rate and unemployment benefit duration.
c) Union density, union coverage and bargaining centralisation/co-ordination.
d) Minimum wage as a percentage of the average wage.
e) Overall labour supply is measured with a combination of annual hours worked and employment/population ratios.

Annex 2.D

Definitions and Data Sources of the Performance and Control Variables Used for the Analysis in Sections II.B and II.C

Definitions

Three types of variables have been used to analyse the links between EPL and labour market performance in Sections II.B and II.C. The first are the summary indicators of EPL strictness, presented in Table 2.5. The second are the performance variables, both static and dynamic. Section II.B uses the static measures and Section II.C the dynamic ones. The third are institutional and policy measures that are used as control variables in the regressions presented in Sections II.B and II.C.

Performance variables

Data for the performance variables have been gathered for the 27 OECD countries for which EPL data were collected, from 1985 to 1997[1], although the analysis mostly concentrates on the years 1990 to 1997. The static variables used in Chart 2.2 and Tables 2.7 to 2.11 are divided into three groups: unemployment rates by age, gender and educational attainment, employment/population ratios by age and gender, and shares of different types of employment. The basic definitions of these variables are given in the notes of the tables, but additional details are provided here. Concerning the age groups, generally these are 15-64 years for "all ages", 20-29 years for youth and 30-54 years for the prime-age group. However, there are a few exceptions:

- Employment/population ratios for prime-age groups refer to ages 35-54 years (rather than 30-54) for Australia, Canada, Ireland, Mexico and New Zealand, and to ages 30-59 years for Italy.
- Employment/population ratios for youth refer to ages 20-24 years (rather than 20-29) for Australia, Canada, Ireland, Mexico and New Zealand, and 15-24 years for Switzerland.
- Unemployment rates for youth refer to ages 20-24 years (rather than 20-29) for Australia, Canada, Ireland, Mexico and New Zealand and 15-24 years for Switzerland.

The share of temporary employment is defined as the proportion of workers in temporary jobs over total employment. If no age group is specified, the share refers to workers of all ages. Note that the share of youth temporary employment is the number of 20-29 year olds in temporary jobs over the total employment for the same age group.[2] Similarly, the share of self-employment is defined as the proportion of self-employees over total employment for all age groups.

The dynamic variables used in Chart 2.3 and Tables 2.12 and 2.13 include job turnover, labour turnover, tenure and separation rates. The distinction between job turnover and labour turnover is important [OECD (1996b), Chapter 5]. Job turnover is the sum of changes (over one year) in employment levels across all establishments. Labour turnover measures the changes in individuals' jobs, regardless of whether the jobs themselves are newly created, ongoing or disappeared. Thus, this definition includes moves into and out of ongoing jobs, in addition to those due to job turnover. Normally, both job and labour turnover are measured in annual averages, although there are some exceptions [see notes to Tables 5.1 and 5.2 in OECD (1996b), Chapter 5]. These annual averages cover many different time periods, some referring to the early and mid 1980s (*e.g.* Australia, Belgium and Ireland), the late 1980s (*e.g.* Finland, France, Germany, Japan, the Netherlands, New Zealand, Norway, Sweden, the United Kingdom and the United States), most of the 1980s (*e.g.* Denmark and Italy) and some referring to the early 1990s (*e.g.* Austria).

Tenure is measured as the proportion of employment by employer tenure. For example, tenure for less than one year refers to the proportion of employees who have been employed at their firm for one year or less. Mean tenure denotes the average length of ongoing and, hence, incomplete spells. Retention rates are measures of the stability of the employer-employee match. For example, the five-year retention rate is the percentage of employees in a certain year which are still with the same employer five years latter. These are measured both over 1985-90 and over 1990-95. Also, these are broken down by length of initial tenure. [See OECD (1997a), Chapter 5 for more details on these definitions.]

The unemployment inflow rate is defined as persons unemployed for less than a month as a percentage of the source population (the working-age population less the unemployed). Similarly, the unemployment outflow rate is defined as the average percentage of the unemployed moving to employment or out of the labour force in a month. Since the group leaving unemployment cannot be identified in typical labour force survey data, the size of this group is estimated indirectly, as the number of persons who must have exited in order to reconcile the data on unem-

---

1. The available performance data begin in more recent years for Austria (1994), the Czech Republic (1993), Hungary (1995), Mexico (1991), Poland (1992), Switzerland (1991) and Turkey (1988).
2. The temporary employment data for Germany include apprentices.

ployment inflows and the change in the total number unemployed. The mean duration of unemployment is also estimated indirectly, as the reciprocal of the share of all unemployed with a duration under one month.[3]

Control variables

Data for control variables have been gathered for the 27 OECD countries for which EPL data was collected. These include measures of institutional and policy variables thought likely to be important determinants of the performance variables. Values have been collected (when possible) for two points in time; the late 1980s and the latest date available for use in the regressions presented in Sections II.B and II.C, Tables 2.8, 2.9, 2.10, 2.11 and 2.13.

Unions and the wage bargaining process, in 1990 and 1994. These data are only available for: Australia, Austria, Belgium, Canada, Denmark, Finland, France, Germany, Italy, Japan, the Netherlands, New Zealand, Norway, Portugal, Spain, Sweden, Switzerland, the United Kingdom and the United States.

- *Centralisation of collective bargaining.* This variable scores from 0 to 2.5, according to the prevailing bargaining level [see OECD (1997*a*), Chapter 3 for more details].
- *Co-ordination of collective bargaining.* This variable also scores from 0 to 2.5, according to the degree of co-ordination in bargaining [see OECD (1997*a*), Chapter 3, for more details].
- *Trade union density.* This variable measures the percentage of workers belonging to a trade union [see OECD (1997*a*), Chapter 3, for more details].
- *Bargaining coverage.* This variable is calculated on the basis of the number of employees covered by a collective agreement divided by the corresponding total number of wage and salary earners [see OECD (1997*a*), Chapter 3, for more details].

Unemployment benefit schemes, in the late 1990s:

- *Replacement rate for unemployment benefit schemes.* Overall average of gross replacement rates for three types of families (single person, with dependent spouse, and with spouse in work) and two earning levels. The replacement rates are averages of benefit levels over a five-year period of benefit receipt and refer to programme characteristics in 1995. These data are available for all countries, except the Czech Republic, Hungary, Korea, Mexico, Poland and Turkey.
- *Unemployment benefit duration.* Duration has been calculated by taking – for a given type of worker – the maximum duration of the unemployment insurance benefits (in months), plus – when applicable – the maximum duration of the unemployment assistance benefits (in months) when the insurance is exhausted. The type of worker is a 40 year-old single worker with a long employment history, previously earning an average income [*i.e.* earnings equal to the Average Production Worker (APW)]. For the econometric analysis, when this variable takes on an indefinite value (due to indefinite duration of the benefit), this has been substituted by a value of 100. These data are available for all countries, except Mexico and Turkey.

Other institutional and policy variables, in the 1990s:

- *ALMP spending in 1990 and 1996-97.* This variable measures ALPM spending as a percentage of GDP. Data are available for all countries except the Czech Republic, Hungary, Korea, and Poland in 1990, and Mexico and Turkey in both time periods.
- *Tax wedge in 1995.* This is measured as the sum of employees' and employers' social security contributions and personal income tax less transfer payments as a percentage of gross labour costs (gross wage earnings plus employers' social security contributions). The chosen family type is a two-earner married couple with two children, whose combined earnings are one-third above the APW's earnings. Data are available for all countries, except Korea.
- *Home ownership.* This is measured as the percentage of home-owners in 1990. Data are available for all countries except the Czech Republic, Greece, Hungary, Korea, Mexico, Poland and Turkey.
- *Output gap.* This is measured as the fraction of real GDP to potential GDP, minus 1. It is averaged over 1985-1990 and over 1992-1997 to cover the same periods as the dependent variables. Data are available for all countries except the Czech Republic, Hungary, Korea, Mexico, Poland and Turkey.
- *Earnings dispersion.* This variable is measured as the deciles ratios D9/D1. Generally, these are gross earnings ratios, except for France. These are either annual (*i.e.* Canada, Finland, France, the Netherlands, Spain, Sweden and Switzerland), monthly (*i.e.* Austria, Czech Republic, Germany, Hungary, Italy, Japan, Korea and Poland), weekly (*i.e.* Australia, Belgium, Ireland, New Zealand, Portugal, the United Kingdom and the United States) or even hourly (*i.e.* Norway). Normally the data refer to full-time full-year earnings, except for Austria, Denmark and Norway, which include all employees. Two years have been used: 1990 and the latest available, which varies significantly among countries: 1993 (for Belgium, Norway and Portugal), 1994 (for Austria, Canada and Ireland), 1995 (for Germany, the Netherlands and Spain), 1996 (for the Czech Republic, Finland, France, Italy, Japan, Korea, Poland, Sweden, Switzerland and the United States), 1997 (for Australia, Hungary and New Zealand) and 1998 (for the United Kingdom).

Data sources

Performance variables

Static employment and unemployment variables have been obtained from several OECD databases.

---

3. In steady state, the mean duration of unemployment is equal to the reciprocal of the share of newly unemployed among all unemployed.

- All *employment/population ratios* by age groups, gender and educational attainment are obtained from the OECD SID database (Directorate of Education, Employment, Labour and Social Affairs, DEELSA). The employment/population ratios by educational attainment are published annually in the OECD's *Education at a Glance*.
- *Shares of self-employment* are obtained from the OECD Analytical Database (Economics Department).
- *Shares of temporary employment* (totals and for youth) are obtained from the OECD SID database (DEELSA).
- *Unemployment rates by gender, age, educational attainment and duration* are obtained from the OECD SID database (DEELSA). The unemployment rates by educational attainment are published annually in the OECD's *Education at a Glance*.
- *Dynamic variables* been obtained from previous OECD publications or on-going data bases. Data on job turnover and labour turnover are obtained from OECD (1996*b*), Chapter 5, Table 5.1 and Table 5.2 respectively. The tenure variables are obtained from Tables 5.5 and 5.6 of OECD (1997*a*), Chapter 5, and retention rates are obtained from Tables 5.8 and 5.9 of the same publication. Data on unemployment flows and durations are from the OECD SID database (DEELSA).

Control variables

The sources of the control variables are as follows:

- *Unions and wage bargaining variables*. All these data are obtained from the OECD DEELSA database. Data have also been published in OECD (1997*a*), Chapter 3, Table 3.3.
- *Unemployment benefit schemes*. Data on replacement rates are obtained from the OECD DEELSA database on unemployment benefit entitlements and replacement rates. Unemployment benefit duration has been obtained from OECD (1998*c*). Information on unemployment insurance is obtained from Table 2.2 (last column), and on unemployment assistance from Table 2.3 (last column).
- *Minimum wage*. Data obtained from OECD DEELSA Minimum Wage Database.
- *ALMP*. Obtained from OECD (1995), Table T and OECD (1998*b*), Table J, row marked "Total active measures".
- *Tax wedge*. Data obtained from the OECD Analytical Database (Economics Department), as published in OECD (1997*b*), Table 5.
- *House ownership*. Data obtained from Oswald (1996).
- *Output gap*. Obtained from OECD Analytical Databank Database (Economics Department).
- *Earnings dispersion*. Obtained from the OECD DEELSA Earnings Database.

BIBLIOGRAPHY

ABRAHAM, K. and HOUSEMAN, S. (1993),
"Job Security and Work Force Adjustment: How Different are US and Japanese Practices?", in Büchtemann, C.F. (ed.), *Employment Security and Labor Market Behavior: Interdisciplinary Approaches and International Evidence*, ILR Press, Ithaca, New York, pp. 180-199.

ABRAHAM, K. and HOUSEMAN, S. (1994),
"Does Employment Protection Inhibit Labor Market Flexibility? Lessons from Germany, France and Belgium", in Blank, R. (ed.), *Social Protection versus Economic Flexibility. Is there a Trade-off?*, NBER Comparative Labor Market Series, Chicago University Press, Chicago, pp. 59-94.

AKERLOFF, G. (1984),
An Economist's Book of Tales, Cambridge University Press, Cambridge, UK.

ALBÆK, K., VAN AUDENRODE, M. and BROWNING, M. (1998),
"Employment Protection and the Consequences for Displaced Workers: A Comparison of Belgium and Denmark", mimeo.

ALOGOSKOUFIS, G., BEAN, C., BERTOLA, G., COHEN, D., DOLADO, J.J. and SAINT-PAUL, G. (1995),
"Unemployment: Choices for Europe", *Monitoring European Integration*, No. 5, Centre for Economic Policy Research, London.

BENTOLILA, S. and BERTOLA, G. (1990),
"Firing Costs and Labour Demand: How Bad is Eurosclerosis?", *Review of Economic Studies*, July, pp. 381-402.

BERTOLA, G. (1990),
"Job Security, Employment and Wages", *European Economic Review*, June, pp. 851-886.

BERTOLA, G. (1999),
"Microeconomic Perspectives on Aggregated Labour Markets", mimeo. Forthcoming in Ashenfelter, O. and Card, D. (eds.), *Handbook of Labor Economics*, Vol. 3, North Holland, Amsterdam.

BERTOLA, G. and ICHINO, A. (1995),
"Crossing the River: A Comparative Perspective on Italian Employment Dynamics", *Economic Policy*, October, pp. 359-420.

BERTOLA, G. and ROGERSON, R. (1997),
"Institutions and Labor Reallocation", *European Economic Review*, June, pp. 1147-1171.

BERTOLA, G., BOERI, T., CAZES, S. (forthcoming),
"Employment Protection and Adjustment: Evolving Institutions and Variable Enforcement in OECD Countries", *ILO Working Paper*, Geneva.

BLANCHARD, O. (1998),
"Thinking about Unemployment", mimeo.

BLANCHARD, O. and PORTUGAL, P. (1998),
"What Hides Behind an Unemployment Rate: Comparing Portuguese and US Unemployment", National Bureau of Economic Research, Working Paper No. 6636.

BLANCHARD, O. and SUMMERS, L. (1987),
"Hysteresis in Unemployment", *European Economic Review*, February-March, pp. 288-295.

BMAS (BUNDESMINISTERIUM FÜR ARBEIT UND SOZIALORDNUNG) (1994),
Beschäftigung und Arbeitsmarkt, Research Report No. 242, Bonn.

BOERI, T. (1999),
"Enforcement of Employment Security Regulations, On-the-job Search and Unemployment Duration", *European Economic Review*, January, pp. 65-89.

BÜCHTEMANN, C.F. (1991),
"Does (De-) Regulation Matter? Employment Protection in West Germany", in Matzner, E. and Streeck, W. (eds.), *Beyond Keynesianism: The Socio-Economics of Production and Full Employment*, Edward Elger, Cambridge, UK, pp. 111-136.

BÜCHTEMANN, C.F. (1993a),
"Employment Security and Labor Markets", in Büchtemann, C.F. (ed.), *Employment Security and Labor Market Behavior: Interdisciplinary Approaches and International Evidence*, ILR Press, Ithaca, New York, pp. 3-68.

BÜCHTEMANN, C.F. (1993b),
"Employment Security and Deregulation: The West German Experience", in Büchtemann, C.F. (ed.), *Employment Security and Labor Market Behavior: Interdisciplinary Approaches and International Evidence*, ILR Press, Ithaca, New York, pp. 272-296.

BURGESS, S., PACELLI, L., and REES, H. (1997),
"Job Tenure and Labour Market Regulation: A Comparison of Britain and Italy Using Microdata", Centre for Economic Performance, Discussion Paper No. 1712, October.

CONTINI, B., PACELLI, L., FILIPPI, M., LIONI, G. and REVELLI, R. (1995),
"A Study on Job Creation and Job Destruction in Europe", *Study for the Commission of the European Communities*, DG-V, Brussels.

DARES (1998a),
"L'évolution du travail temporaire de 1996 à 1997", Direction de l'animation de la recherche, des études et des statistiques, *Premières Synthèses,* No. 22.1.

DARES (1998b),
"Les emplois en contrat à durée déterminée en 1996", Direction de l'animation de la recherche, des études et des statistiques, *Premières Synthèses,* No. 48.2.

DELSEN, L. (1991),
"Atypical Employment Relations and Government Policy in Europe", *Labour,* Winter, pp. 123-149.

ELMESKOV, J., MARTIN, J.P. AND SCARPETTA, S. (forthcoming),
"Key Lessons for Labour Market Reforms: Evidence from OECD Countries' Experience", *Swedish Economic Policy Review.*

EMERSON, M. (1988),
"Regulation or De-regulation of the Labour Market: Policy Regimes for the Recruitment and Dismissal of Employees in Industrialised Countries", *European Economic Review*, April, pp. 775-817.

ESPING-ANDERSEN, G. (forthcoming),
"Who is Harmed by Employment Regulation?", in Esping-Andersen, G. and Regini, M. (eds.), *Why De-Regulate Labour Markets?*, Oxford University Press, Oxford.

EUROPEAN COMMISSION (1991),
European Economy, March, Brussels.

EUROPEAN COMMISSION (1995),
European Economy, No. 3, Brussels.

EUROPEAN COMMISSION (1997a),
Employment and Social Affairs, *Termination of Employment Relationships. Legal Situation in the Member States of the European Union*, Brussels.

EUROPEAN COMMISSION (1997b),
Labour Market Studies. Finland, Brussels.

FLANAGAN, R. J. (1988),
"Unemployment as a Hiring Problem", OECD *Economic Studies*, Autumn, pp. 123-154.

GARIBALDI, P. (1998),
"Search Unemployment with Advance Notice", Working Paper of the International Monetary Fund, August.

GARIBALDI, P., KONINGS, J. and PISSARIDES, C. (1997),
"Gross Job Reallocation and Labour Market Policy", in Snower, D., and de la Dehesa, G. (eds.) *Unemployment Policy: Government Options for the Labour Market*, Cambridge University Press, Cambridge, UK, pp. 467-489.

GREGG, P. and MANNING, A. (1997),
"Labour Market Regulation and Unemployment", in Snower, D. and de la Dehesa, G. (eds.), *Unemployment Policy: Government Options for the Labour Market*, Cambridge University Press, Cambridge, UK, pp. 395-424.

GRUBB, D. and WELLS, W. (1993),
"Employment Regulation and Patterns of Work in EC Countries", OECD *Economic Studies*, No. 21, Winter, pp. 7-58.

GÜELL-ROTLLAN, M. and PETRONGOLO, B. (1998),
"The Transition of Workers from Temporary to Permanent Employment: the Spanish Case", Universidad Carlos III de Madrid, Working Paper No. 98-81, November.

HAUSMAN, J.A. (1978),
"Specification Tests in Econometrics", *Econometrica*, November, pp. 1251-1271.

HOUSEMAN, S. and ABRAHAM, K. (1995),
"Labor Adjustment under Different Institutional Structures", in Buttler, F. *et al.* (eds.), *Institutional Frameworks and Labour Market Performance*, Routledge, London, pp. 285-315.

HSIAO, C. (1986),
Analysis of Panel Data, Cambridge University Press, Cambridge, UK.

ICHNIOWSKI, C., SHAW, K. and PRENNUSHI, G. (1997),
"The Effects of Human Resource Management Practices on Productivity", National Bureau of Economic Research, Working Paper No. 5333.

IDS (Incomes Data Services) (1995),
Contracts and Terms and Conditions of Employment, European Management Guides, London.

IDS (1996),
Industrial Relations and Collective Bargaining, European Management Guides, London.

IDS (1997),
Recruitment, Training and Development, European Management Guides, London.

IOE (International Organisation of Employers) (1985),
Adapting the Labour Market, Geneva.

JACKMAN, R., LAYARD, R. AND NICKELL, S. (1996),
"Combating Unemployment: Is Flexibility Enough", Centre for Economic Performance Discussion Paper No. 293.

LAYARD, R., NICKELL, S. and JACKMAN. R. (1991),
Unemployment: Macroeconomic Performance and the Labour Market, Oxford University Press, Oxford.

LAZEAR, E.P. (1990),
"Job Security Provisions and Employment", *The Quarterly Journal of Economics*, August, pp. 699-726.

LEVINE, D.I. and TYSON, L.D.A. (1990),
"Participation, Productivity and the Firm's Environment", in Blinder, A. (ed.), *Paying for Productivity*, Brookings Institution, Washington DC., pp. 183-243.

LINDBECK, A., and SNOWER, D.J. (1988),
The Insider-Outsider Theory of Employment and Unemployment, MIT Press, Cambridge, Mass.

MENDELSOHN, S.R. (1990),
"Wrongful Termination Litigation in the United States and its Effect on the Employment Relationship", Labour Market and Social Policy Occasional Papers, No. 3, OECD, Paris.

MICHON, F. and RAMAUX, C. (1993),
"Temporary Employment in France: a Decade Statement", *Labour*, Autumn, pp. 93-116.

MILNER, S., METCALF, D. and NOMBELA, G. (1995),
"Employment Protection Legislation and Labour Market Outcomes in Spain", Centre for Economic Performance, Discussion Paper No. 244, pp. 1-62.

NICKELL, S. (1997),
"Unemployment and Labor Market Rigidities: Europe versus North America", *Journal of Economic Perspectives*, Summer, pp. 55-74.

NICKELL, S. and LAYARD, R. (1998),
"Labour Market Institutions and Economic Performance", Centre for Economic Performance, Discussion Paper No. 407, September. Forthcoming in Ashenfelter, O. and Card, D. (eds.), *Handbook of Labor Economics*, Vol. 3, North Holland, Amsterdam.

OECD (1986),
Flexibility in the Labour Market: The Current Debate. A Technical Report, Paris.

OECD (1993),
Employment Outlook, Paris, July.

OECD (1994a),
The OECD *Jobs Study, Evidence and Explanations, Part II*, Paris.

OECD (1994b),
The OECD *Jobs Study: Facts, Analysis, and Strategies*, Paris.

OECD (1995),
Employment Outlook, Paris, July.

OECD (1996a),
Economic Survey: United States, Paris.

OECD (1996b),
Employment Outlook, Paris, July.

OECD (1997a),
Employment Outlook, Paris, July.

OECD (1997b),
Tax/Benefit Position of Employees, 1995-96, Paris.

OECD (1998a),
"The OECD Jobs Strategy: Progress Report on Implementation of Country-specific Recommendations", Economics Department Working Paper No. 196, Paris.

OECD (1998b),
Employment Outlook, Paris, June.

OECD (1998c),
Benefit Systems and Work Incentives, Paris.

OSWALD, A. (1996),
"A Conjecture on the Explanation for High Unemployment in the Industrialized Nations: Part I", Warwick Economics Research Paper No. 475, December.

PIORE, M. (1986),
Labor Market Flexibility, University of California Press, Berkeley, CA.

ROGOWSKI, R. and SCHÖMANN, K. (1996),
"Legal Regulation and Flexibility of Employment Contracts", in Schmid, G., O'Reilly, J., and Schömann, K. (eds.), *International Handbook of Labour Market Policy and Evaluation*, Edward Elgar, Cheltenham, UK and Brookfield, US, pp. 623-651.

SCARPETTA, S. (1996),
"Assessing the Role of Labour Market Policies and Institutional Settings on Unemployment: A Cross-Country Study", OECD *Economic Studies*, No. 26, pp. 43-98.

SCHETTKAT, R. (1997),
"Employment Protection and Labour Mobility in Europe: An Empirical Analysis using the EU's Labour Force Survey", *International Review of Applied Economics*, January, pp. 105-118.

WATSON WYATT (1997),
Employment Terms & Conditions, Europe, 1997, Brussels.

WATSON WYATT (1998),
Employment Terms & Conditions, Asia/Pacific, 1998-1999, Brussels.

Chapter 3

TRAINING OF ADULT WORKERS IN OECD COUNTRIES: MEASUREMENT AND ANALYSIS

Summary

Recent economic experience underlies the importance of a highly skilled workforce. While a good initial education provides an essential foundation, learning continues through the working years and national skill development systems should be assessed in terms of how effectively they support the goal of life-long learning, recently endorsed by OECD Member governments. Policies encouraging wide participation of the adult workforce in continuing training may be able to play an important role in assuring strong economic growth and broadly-based prosperity. International comparisons of continuing training, including an analysis of the causes and consequences of cross-country differences, would be very useful for assessing the potential scope for and choices among such policies, but little systematic information has been available concerning these issues. This chapter assembles some of the available evidence and discusses its implications for policy-making and data collection.

The empirical analysis proceeds along two tracks. First, four "harmonised" surveys of training are used to assemble a set of "stylised" facts concerning international differences in the level and distribution of training for 24 OECD countries. The robustness of these comparisons across different surveys and training measures is assessed, as are their implications for understanding international differences in human capital investment and economic outcomes. Several of these issues are then examined in greater depth using independent – but broadly comparable – national surveys, which provide more detailed information on training. Multivariate statistical techniques are used to analyse both individual probabilities of training and the relationship between training and individual earnings.

Training patterns differ significantly across OECD countries. Although it is not possible to make precise comparisons, the evidence is robust that the level of formal continuing training is relatively low in southern European countries such as Greece, Italy, Portugal and Spain, and relatively high in the United Kingdom, France and most Nordic countries. Workers tend to receive more training in countries with higher educational attainment and achievement, as well as in countries devoting a larger share of GDP to research and development and achieving a strong trade performance in "high tech" industries. This suggests that educational reform and greater training are mutually reinforcing, due to the associated tendency for firms to specialise in economic activities requiring higher skills across a broad spectrum of the workforce. While improving initial education should increase training levels for future cohorts of workers, policies to improve the training received by the current workforce are also desirable. Since a key distinguishing feature of high-training economies is that participation in training is more evenly distributed, policies enhancing the incentives and resources for investing in the continuing training of workers typically receiving little training may be of particular importance. However, the analysis of the determinants and consequences of training is not yet sufficiently developed to provide policy makers with reliable estimates of the economic returns that would accrue to specific policy approaches. Further progress in the harmonisation of training statistics could make a useful contribution to filling that gap.

OECD

Chapter 3

TRAINING OF ADULT WORKERS IN OECD COUNTRIES: MEASUREMENT AND ANALYSIS

Introduction

The critical importance of a highly skilled workforce in an increasingly "globalised" and "computerised" economy has become a commonplace. At the individual level, a good education is increasingly decisive for employment prospects and earnings levels [Blau and Kahn (1996); OECD (1997d, e)]. Human capital formation also appears to be an important precondition for the economic success of firms and national economies, although these links are more difficult to verify [Griliches (1996); OECD (1998d)]. This evidence suggests that policies encouraging wide participation in education and training are an important component of an overall strategy to achieve broadly-based prosperity.

The skills and competences of the workforce are the product of a large variety of learning activities that take place in diverse institutional contexts. While good initial education provides an essential foundation, learning continues through the working years. This suggests that national skill development systems should be assessed in terms of how effectively they support the goal of life-long learning. Consistent with this perspective, researchers assessing the potential economic contribution of human capital investments have increasingly emphasised the importance of *continuing vocational training*, including informal on-the-job learning [Lynch (1994); Booth and Snower (1996)].

Very little is known concerning international differences in continuing training or their causes and consequences [OECD (1991, 1993)]. Such information would be useful for assessing policy choices related to training, such as whether to encourage an overall increase in training levels or to attempt to redirect training investments toward groups in the workforce currently receiving little training. Prior research suggests that differences across national labour markets, such as those documented for labour turnover rates and the degree of wage compression, could have important effects on the incentives of businesses and workers to invest in training [Acemoglu and Pischke (1999); Lynch (1994)]. If these or other factors result in significant differences in training patterns, there could be important consequences for workforce skills and labour market performance. This chapter conducts an exploratory analysis of these issues.

Section I surveys prior research on continuing training, while Sections II and III present new empirical results on comparative training patterns. Section II uses four "harmonised" surveys of training to assemble a set of "stylised" facts concerning differences in the level and distribution of training across 24 OECD countries. The robustness of these comparisons across different surveys and training measures is assessed, as are their implications for understanding international differences in human capital investment and economic outcomes. Section III examines several of these issues in greater depth using independent – but broadly comparable – national surveys, which provide more detailed information on training. Multivariate statistical techniques are used to analyse individual probabilities of training and the relationship between training and individual earnings. A concluding section considers implications for policy.

Several limitations of the analysis require emphasis. This chapter analyses only one type of job training, namely, continuing and more or less formal training received by *incumbent* workers. Most of the analysis is limited to workers between the ages of 25 and 54 years, since this restriction avoids complications related to international differences in initial education [OECD (1994, 1998f)] and retirement patterns [OECD (1998e)]. Because most continuing training of employees is sponsored – at least in part – by employers, employer-provided training is emphasised. However, worker-financed training and public training programmes receive some attention, as does training received by adults not currently employed. Finally, training is measured in terms of the resources invested, not in terms of the learning achieved.

Main findings

The main findings of the chapter are:

- The level of training differs significantly across OECD countries. Although it is not possible to make

- precise comparisons, the evidence is quite robust that formal, continuing training is relatively low in southern European countries such as Greece, Italy, Portugal and Spain, and relatively high in the United Kingdom, France and most Nordic countries. There also appears to be some trade-off between the extensive and intensive margins of training, with the average duration of training being higher in countries with lower participation rates.
- Overall, men and women appear to participate in job-related training at fairly equal rates, although men may receive more financial support from their employers. When expected hours of training are calculated over the 40-year period between the ages of 25 and 64, women have significantly lower training expectancies than men, due to less continuous employment. Lower training rates for part-time and temporary workers may also lower relative training access for women.
- The extent to which training falls off with age varies strongly across countries, suggesting that progress in reaching the goal of life-long learning has been uneven. Workers aged 50-54 years receive almost as much training as those aged 25-29 in the United States and the Nordic countries (except Finland), while the older group receives much less training than the younger in France, Greece, Portugal and Spain.
- Training tends to reinforce skill differences resulting from unequal participation in schooling in all countries, although the strength of this relationship varies significantly between countries. Training appears to be most evenly distributed across educational levels in Ireland, Japan, New Zealand, the Netherlands and several Nordic countries, and least equally in Belgium, Hungary and southern Europe. The positive association between more schooling and training remains strong even after controlling for other characteristics affecting the probability of training.
- Workers tend to receive more training in countries with higher overall average levels of educational attainment and achievement, as well as in countries devoting a larger share of GDP to research and development and achieving a strong trade performance in "high tech" industries. A higher overall training rate is also associated with more equal age and educational distributions of training. These patterns suggest that education and greater training are mutually reinforcing due, at least in part, to an associated tendency for firms to specialise in economic activities requiring a highly skilled workforce.
- Workers reporting recent training are paid more than other workers, but the strength of this relationship varies across countries. The pay "premium" associated with training differs between educational and gender groups within all of the countries, with the most common pattern being higher training premiums for the least educated workers.
- The strong link between national levels of educational attainment and achievement, on the one hand, and the level of workforce training, on the other, suggests that an indirect strategy of strengthening schooling is a potent – if slow – means of encouraging continuing training. Since a key distinguishing feature of high-training economies is that participation in training is more evenly distributed, policies enhancing the incentives and resources for investing in the continuing training of workers typically receiving little training are of particular importance. However, the theoretical and empirical analysis of the determinants and consequences of continuing training are not yet sufficiently developed to provide policy makers with reliable estimates of the economic returns that would accrue to specific policy approaches. Further harmonisation of training statistics could make a useful contribution to filling that gap.

I. Review of litterature

The standard model of training as human capital investment and its main critiques are briefly reviewed in this Section. The focus here is on the most recent literature developments as this topic was already dealt with in the 1991 *Employment Outlook* to which the reader is referred for a more complete treatment.

According to the standard theoretical model of training as a human capital investment [Becker (1964)], firms train workers to increase productivity and output while workers undertake training to realise future earnings gains associated with these increases in productivity. This model predicts that the costs of training are borne partly by the worker and partly by the firm. Even when training is provided by the employer, workers may indirectly pay for their training by accepting lower wages for the duration of the training period. Because trained workers may quit the firm and the benefits of training be reaped by other firms, the model predicts that firms will mainly finance *firm-specific* training, that cannot be exported to other firms, as opposed to *general* training. This model also predicts that the provision of firm-specific training will be associated with longer tenure at the firm since workers will lose part or all of their expected future earnings gains if they move to other firms. Similarly, firms will not have an incentive to train those workers who are more likely to quit.

The main policy issue highlighted by this model is that investments in *general* training may be inadequate. Employers may be unwilling to finance enough such training because trained workers may quit the firm later on. An economic externality arises because some of the returns to the general training provided by the initial employer accrues to other firms, who subsequently hire the trained worker. However, the higher wages that a trained worker can command with other employers creates a corresponding incentive for employees to pay for their own training. Thus, a serious market failure is only likely to arise if capital market imperfections prevent workers from borrowing the money required to finance their own training.

The empirical literature has focused on testing the predictions of the conventional model:

- The positive impact of training on future earnings.
- The positive impact of training on productivity.
- Lower earnings during the training period.
- The possibility to distinguish between general and firm-specific skills and the prediction that most training provided by firms is firm-specific.
- The positive relationship between training and job tenure.
- The negative relationship between training and turnover.
- The market allocates training optimally.

Some of the most recent studies on these issues are reviewed in Table 3.A.1 in Annex 3.A to this chapter. The main conclusions from this review are summarised here.

Earnings growth after training and the event of training may not be independent variables. Unobserved individual characteristics may determine both the probability that someone is trained and the fact that they earn higher-than-average wages after the training.

Generally, most empirical work has found a positive impact of training on earnings growth. In particular, some recent studies have concluded that the earnings gains from training are significantly larger for groups of workers less-likely to be trained: less-skilled workers in the United States [Bartel (1995)] mid-educated workers in the United Kingdom [Blundell *et al.* (1996)] and women in the United Kingdom [Booth (1991)] and in Germany [Pischke (1996)].

However, theories other than human capital may explain the fact that wages increase over an individual work's life [Veum (1995)]. For example, firms may increase wages over time to reduce supervision costs [Lazear (1981)], to reduce turnover costs [Salop and Salop (1976)], to encourage employees' work efforts and their morale [Akerlof (1984)] or simply as a consequence of good employer-employee matches [Jovanovic (1979)]. Overall, individual and firm unobservables have been found to be very important in explaining wage differences across firms and individuals [Abowd *et al.* (1994, 1998)].

The literature generally confirms a positive impact of training on productivity [Bartel (1995); Black and Lynch (1996); Boon (1998)]. However, most studies suffer from the fact that it is hard to disentangle the pure effect of training from other alternative explanations of any rise in productivity.

There is very scant evidence that earnings of trainees are lower than those of comparable workers, with the exception of apprentices.

Several recent studies have investigated whether firms provide general or firm-specific training. Generally, since it hard to measure the content of training, inferences are made using information on tenure, quits, turnover rates and on earnings growth of job movers. Inferences based on such evidence favour the view that most firm training is of a general nature and exportable to other firms [Blundell *et al.* (1996); Goux and Maurin (1997); Loewenstein and Spletzer (1998); Regner (1995, 1997); Vilhuber (1997, 1998)]. A possible explanation is that training that is firm-specific may often be complementary to general training so that some elements of both have to be provided by the firm. It is also unlikely that any training will be useful only to one specific firm or vice versa to all firms in the economy.

The empirical evidence on the relationship between tenure and training is blurred, as is the relationship between turnover and training. These new facts, especially the finding that much enterprise-based training appears to be general, yet trainees do not undergo periods of lower earnings, is an argument against the validity of Becker's model [Acemoglu and Pischke (1998, 1999)]. In sum, recent empirical work calls into question the standard explanation of the determinants of employer-financed training, as well as the associated analysis of training policy.

An important stream of literature has investigated whether market forces alone are likely to be efficient in allocating training optimally across workers as is implied by the standard model, in the absence of capital market imperfections [Lynch (1994); Booth and Snower (1996)]. If not, there is a market failure and some government intervention to subsidise on-the-job training may be needed.

Lynch (1994, p. 22) surveys studies of training in different OECD countries and concludes that "different" systems are more or less successful in overcoming market failure and that it is difficult for individual firms to move unilaterally from one training system to another. For example, Japanese firms appear to have a strong tradition of training their workers. According to Hashimoto (1994), the secret of successful firm training in Japan lies in the close link with the education system and in the fact that training is not only of a technical nature, but also involves teaching workers to co-operate with each other. In particular, it is a prize for senior workers to be able to pass on their knowledge to more junior workers.

Most studies find that employers tend to train their better educated workers more [OECD (1991); Lynch (1994); O'Connell (1998); Blundell *et al.* (1996); Shömann (1998)]. The empirical literature also indicates that larger firms, firms that pay above-average wages and more capital-intensive firms are more likely to train their workers. There is some evidence that workers on part-time jobs are less likely to be trained, as argued in Chapter 1, and the same applies to workers on temporary contracts [Arulampalam and Booth (1998*a*)].

Absent good rate of return data, it is difficult to judge whether the uneven distribution of training indicates a market failure in the allocation of training. Clearly, however, there are equity concerns. For example, training by firms appears to reinforce patterns of poorer labour market performance of the less-educated. The empirical evidence indicates that firm training and formal schooling complement each other. Not only do firms invest more in training their better educated workers, but they also may spend more resources in the screening and hiring of workers that they expect to train later on [De Grip and Hoevenberg (1996); Burdett and Cunningham (1998)].

In sum, the predictions of a positive impact of training on workers' earnings and productivity are generally confirmed by the empirical literature while other important predictions of the standard model do not find much empirical support.

Alternative theories have recently been formulated that may better explain the evidence [see, for example, articles in Booth and Snower (1996)]. Most recently, Acemoglu and Pischke (1998, 1999) have put forward a different model of firm-provided training. They argue that non-competitive labour markets often compress the structure of wages and this provides an incentive for firms to invest in general training. The authors argue that employers and employees will share the costs of training depending on how compressed the distribution of wages is. The more compressed the wage distribution, the higher is the incentive for employers to train workers in order to reap the benefit of productivity gains that are not passed on to these workers in the form of higher wages. A more compressed wage distribution may also lower workers' incentives to invest in training, but the net effect on training will be positive if employers play the dominant role in determining the level of training.

The authors illustrate possible sources of wage compression. The current employer has information about workers' abilities that other employers do not have access to; this is shown, under given circumstances, to lead to wage compression and incentives to train. Quits impose costs on the current employer who has to replace the worker in question and on workers who have to invest resources in finding a new job; these costs may create some job-match rent that is shared between the current employer and the worker through bargaining. Employers may have an incentive to pay workers more than their marginal productivity when they first hire them – to increase their work effort or to reduce their quit probability, as in efficiency-wage models – and to train them later on to increase their productivity up to the level of the wage or above. Minimum wages may result in more training of workers whose productivity is initially below the wage level. Trade unions may compress the structure of wages by making employers pay higher wages to less-skilled workers.[1]

This theory has not yet gone through much empirical testing [Acemoglu and Pischke (1998, 1999)]. However, it can better account for the key finding that firms pay for a substantial share of general training. The theory also suggest that international differences in labour market institutions and practices, such as wage setting and labour turnover patterns, may have an important influence on the extent to which the private market provides an optimal level and distribution of training.

II. Training across countries: lessons from "harmonised" surveys

A. Sources and definitions

Several recent initiatives have collected "harmonised" data on the continuing training of the adult workforce. The OECD has co-ordinated two of these efforts,

---

1. The literature does indeed generally find that, in the presence of trade unions, more training is provided [Green *et al.* (1999); Kennedy *et al.* (1994)].

while two others have been co-ordinated by EUROSTAT. In all four cases, national statistical offices collected the underlying survey data, which was then reported in a common format. Although the intent is to assemble internationally comparable data on training, the four initiatives differ in the extent to which the survey questionnaire and data collection process were harmonised among the participating countries. They also differ in terms of the precise definitions of training activity, the population sampled and the countries and years for which data were collected.

Table 3.1 describes some of the basic characteristics of these four sources of training statistics: the International Adult Literacy Survey (IALS); the European Labour Force Survey (ELFS); the OECD/INES (Indicators of Education Systems); and EUROSTAT's Continuing Vocational Training Survey (CVTS).[2] Two characteristics are especially salient for making international comparisons. The first is differences in the degree of cross-country harmonisation that has been achieved. The second is differences in the way in which training is defined and measured in the surveys.

The IALS comes the closest to the ideal of fully harmonised data collection. A common questionnaire and survey interview protocol were used in all countries, although there was some discretion concerning the use of certain supplementary questions. The two EUROSTAT surveys are intermediate in terms of harmonisation. Statistical authorities in EU member States make considerable efforts to comply with common guidelines for questionnaire content and data collection, yet considerable variation remains in both domains – particularly in the ELFS. Finally, the OECD/INES data appear to be the least harmonised overall. Under this programme, participating countries report data estimates from pre-existing national surveys that match, as closely as possible, a common set of definitions.

All four surveys provide measures of the level of continuing vocational training among the adult workforce. However, there are important differences in how the training questions are phrased.[3] Most mechanically, the ELFS asks about training over the prior 4 weeks, whereas the other three surveys use a 12-month reference period. A second difference is that the CVTS poses the training questions to employers and not workers. There are likely to be systematic differences in how these two groups report training activities. A third difference is that respondents in the ELFS and the CVTS are asked to distinguish between initial and continuing vocational training, so that the former can be explicitly omitted from the training estimates. This information is not available in the other two surveys and some initial vocational training undoubtedly contaminates these data, although the adoption of a minimum age threshold of 25 years reduces this problem.

More subtle differences occur in the precise phrases used to characterise training activities. For example, the surveys included in the OECD/INES typically ask about participation in training "courses" or "programmes," while the IALS question also refers to "on-the-job training." The latter formulation may result in greater reporting of less structured forms of training – such as coaching provided by more experienced colleagues – and, hence, result in higher estimates of training. The ELFS is probably intermediate between those in the IALS and OECD/INES in the amount of informal training reported, since the survey question asks about any "schooling and training received in the last four weeks". Employers in the CVTS, with its focus on structured training programmes, probably report little or no informal training. These effects could be quite large since prior research indicates that participation in informal training activities is at least as widespread as participation in formal training [Frazis *et al.* (1998); OECD (1991)]. There is some evidence, however, that formal and informal training are positively correlated [Loewenstein and Spletzer (1994)]. Such an association suggests that *relative* levels of training for different groups or countries might not be as greatly affected by cross-survey differences in the extent to which informal training is recorded, as are *absolute* levels. The cross-survey indices of training developed below combine exclusively relative measures from the underlying surveys.

These four sources also differ with respect to how much employer involvement is required for a training episode to be reported. Data from the IALS confirm that international comparisons of training participation can be affected by these noncomparabilities, although the effect may be relatively minor. For the 25-54 age group, most education and training activities reported by employed respondents are characterised by them as being career or job-related, and most of this job-related training received direct employer support (Chart 3.1). The comparison between all job-related training and employer-supported, job-related training is most critical for assessing the comparability of the four harmonised surveys, since the CVTS only records employer-supported training while the

---

2. For detailed documentation of these four surveys see, respectively, OECD and Statistics Canada (1995), EUROSTAT (1996), OECD (1997*a*) and EUROSTAT (1997).
3. See Phelps and Stowe (1998) and OECD (1997*b*, 1998*a*) for fuller discussions of this issue.

Table 3.1. Overview of surveys providing harmonised training statistics

Title and year	Countries covered	Nature of survey, including degree of harmonisation and sample size	Definitions of training participation and volume used in this chapter	Reference period	Comments
The International Adult Literacy Survey (IALS), 1994-1995	Australia, Belgium (Flanders), Canada, Germany, Ireland, Netherlands, New Zealand, Poland, Sweden, Switzerland, United Kingdom, United States.[a]	Household survey using a common questionnaire. Relatively small sample sizes (e.g. 3 045 individuals for the United States).	*Participation*: Took one or more education and training courses for "career or job-related purposes". *Volume*: Total hours for the three most recent courses.[b]	12 months	Initial training question is very broad and may capture quite informal learning activities not captured by the other three harmonised surveys. The IALS also provides unique data on workers' literacy skills.
European Labour Force Survey data from EUROSTAT (ELFS), 1997	Austria, Belgium, Denmark, Finland, France, Germany, Greece, Hungary, Iceland, Ireland, Italy, Luxembourg, Netherlands, Norway, Portugal, Spain, Sweden, United Kingdom.	Household survey (national labour force surveys that have been adapted to some extent to the EUROSTAT standard, but differ somewhat in the questions posed). Data are mapped into a common file structure and the sample sizes are large.	*Participation*: Received education and training for a reason other than secondary education or initial vocational training. *Volume*: Total hours.	4 weeks[c]	Annual data on training participation are available for the period 1988-1997 for twelve of the countries.
The OECD/INES[d] (Indicators of Education Systems) data on continuing training, 1991-96	Australia, Canada, Finland, France, Germany, Norway, Sweden, Switzerland, United States.	Household surveys, typically national labour force surveys or special surveys of adult education and training.[e] Data mapped into a common file structure. Large sample sizes.	*Participation*: Took one or more training courses that the interviewed person identified as job or career-related. *Volume*: Total hours.	12 months	OECD/INES training statistics are not available for the age group emphasised in this chapter (25 to 54 years). Training patterns are analysed, instead, for workers aged 25 to 64 years. Only very limited data are available for France and Norway.
The EUROSTAT's Continuing Vocational Training Survey (CVTS), 1994	Belgium, Denmark, France, Germany, Greece, Ireland, Italy, Luxembourg, Netherlands, Portugal, Spain, United Kingdom.	Employer survey of enterprises with 10 or more employees in the European Union. Survey is based on common specifications with large sample sizes (50 000 enterprises in total).	*Participation*: Percentage of workforce receiving employer-sponsored vocational training, including internal and external courses and structured on-the-job learning, but excluding inititial vocational training. *Volume*: Hours and costs for courses.	12 months	The CVTS excludes enterprises with fewer than 10 employers or in NACE Rev 1 sectors A and B (agriculture, forestry, fishing), L, M and N (public administration, health and education), P (household domestic staff) and Q (extra-territorial).

a) IALS data have been collected for 12 additional countries, but are not yet available for analysis.
b) The IALS for Sweden provides no usable data for the hours of training nor for the question whether the main purpose of training was career and job-related. Training rates for Sweden are calculated, instead, in terms of participation in training that received at least some employer financial support.
c) The reference period for France in the ELFS is current (*i.e.* date of survey interview) training activities.
d) The OECD/INES data used here only include those countries reporting training activity over a 12-month period. This database also includes a number of countries reporting training over a 4-week period, but they are essentially the same labour force survey data reported under ELFS and, hence, are not included here.
e) The OECD/INES for France consists of administrative data (DARES – ministère de l'Emploi et de la Solidarité).

Chart 3.1. **Alternative definitions of the participation rate in training**[a]
Percentage of dependent employees aged 25 to 54 years

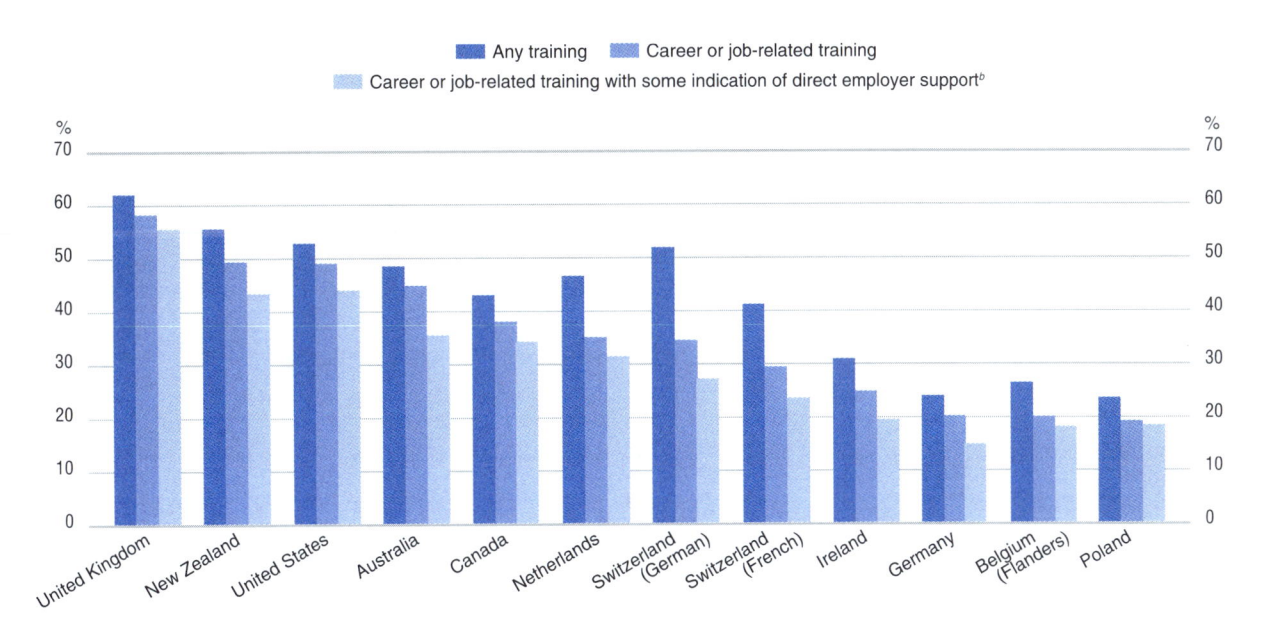

■ Any training   ■ Career or job-related training
■ Career or job-related training with some indication of direct employer support[b]

a) Countries are ranked in descending order of the percentage of training for career or job-related purposes.
b) Worker reports that main purpose of the training was career or job-related and that the employer either directly provided the training or provided one or more of the following: financial support, the training site (including on-the-job) or the suggestion to take the training (including provisions in collectively bargained agreements).
Source: International Adult Literacy Survey, 1994-1995.

household surveys should also record job-related training not supported by the employer. The IALS data suggest that the resulting difference in the range of training activities that are reported is fairly small in most countries. Although the magnitude of cross-country differences in training participation rates varies, depending on whether comparisons are made for all job-related training or only the subset supported by employers, the only significant change in country rankings is that Germany moves from approximate parity with Belgium and Poland to being somewhat lower – apparently because German employers provide financial support for an unusually low share of *continuing* formal vocational training, in marked contrast to their investment in *initial* training [OECD (1995)].

The population sampled also differs between some of the four surveys. Dependent and salaried employees between the ages of 25 and 54 years, which are the target population of most of the following analysis, can be exactly identified only in the IALS and the ELFS. The OECD/INES training statistics are for the age range 25 and 64 years, while the CVTS data cover employees of all ages in the surveyed enterprises. The CVTS sample also excludes workers in enterprises with fewer than ten employees and all workers in certain sectors (see Table 3.1). The exclusion of workers in the smallest enterprises biases upward the training participation rates calculated using CVTS data, since training rates rise with enterprise size over the observed range [EUROSTAT (1997)].

B. **The level of training**

Does a larger share of the workforce receive training in some countries than in others? Since the boundary between training and the learning that accompanies work experience is so difficult to draw in practice, it should not be expected that very precise statements can be made about how much higher training is in one country than another. Nonetheless, it should be possible to rank countries in terms of training intensities based on the evidence from the harmonised surveys. This section constructs such rankings.

Participation rates

Training participation rates are shown in Table 3.2. Looking first at the unweighted column means (calculated over all countries for which data are available), the average participation rates in the IALS and the OECD/INES (both 37 per cent) are much higher than that for the ELFS

Table 3.2. **Participation rate in career or job-related training**
Employees aged 25 to 54 years in the 1990s

	IALS		ELFS		OECD/INES		CVTS		Cross-survey index of participation rate (average = 0) [b]	
	Participation rate (%) (1)	Rank (2)	Participation rate (%) (3)	Rank (4)	Participation rate (%) (5)	Rank (6)	Participation rate (%) (7)	Rank (8)	Mean (9)	Rank (10)
European Union										
Austria	..	..	7.9	8	..	..	..	..	−0.1	13
Belgium [c]	19.8	11	3.4	13	..	..	25	6	−0.7	17
Denmark	..	..	18.4	1	..	..	33	4	1.1	4
Finland	..	..	18.0	3	45.0	1	..	..	1.5	1
France [d]	..	..	*1.9*	n.a.	40.2	3	37	3	0.9	5
Germany	20.0	10	4.2	10	33.3	8	24	8	−0.7	16
Greece	..	..	0.7	17	..	..	13	11	−1.3	24
Ireland	24.6	9	6.6	9	..	..	43	1	0.1	11
Italy	..	..	3.8	12	..	..	15	10	−0.9	21
Luxembourg	..	..	2.5	16	..	..	25	6	−0.6	15
Netherlands	34.8	7	14.9	4	..	..	26	5	0.3	9
Portugal	..	..	3.2	14	..	..	13	11	−1.1	22
Spain	..	..	3.1	15	..	..	20	9	−0.7	19
Sweden	55.5	2	18.3	2	41.6	2	..	..	1.2	2
United Kingdom	58.0	1	14.2	5	..	..	39	2	1.2	3
North America										
Canada	37.7	6	..	..	28.4	9	..	..	−0.8	20
United States	48.8	4	..	..	33.5	7	..	..	0.1	12
Pacific area										
Australia	44.6	5	..	..	38.1	4	..	..	0.4	8
New Zealand	49.1	3	..	..	..	..	..	..	0.8	6
Other OECD countries										
Hungary	..	..	4.2	11	..	..	..	..	−0.7	18
Iceland	..	..	14.0	6	..	..	..	..	0.8	7
Norway	..	..	11.7	7	37.0	5	..	..	0.2	10
Poland	19.0	12	..	..	..	..	..	..	−1.3	23
Switzerland [e]	33.0	8	..	..	35.0	6	..	..	−0.3	14
Switzerland (French)	*29.2*	n.a.	..	..	..	..	..	..	−0.6	n.a.
Switzerland (German)	*34.2*	n.a.	..	..	..	..	..	..	−0.2	n.a.
Unweighted mean	37.1	n.a.	8.8	n.a.	36.9	n.a.	26.1	n.a.	0.0	n.a.
Standard deviation	14.2	n.a.	6.3	n.a.	5.0	n.a.	10.1	n.a.	0.9	n.a.

.. Data not available.
n.a.: Not applicable.
a) Figures in *italics* are not used in the calculations of the cross-country statistics in Columns 3 and 4 or the cross-survey index in Column 9.
b) The national estimates of training participation rates in Columns 1, 3, 5 and 7 were standardised to have a zero mean and unit variance. Column 9 reports the unweighted means of these standardised values which are calculated using all surveys for which estimates are available for that country.
c) The IALS data for Belgium only cover Flanders.
d) The ELFS data for France measure only current training activity and are not fully comparable to those reported for the other countries. Accordingly, the French value is not used in the calculations of the cross-country statistics in Columns 3 and 4 or the cross-survey index in Column 9.
e) IALS values for Switzerland are a weighted average of the values for the French and German-speaking populations.
Source: See Table 3.1.

(9 per cent). This is in line with expectations since the four-week reference period used by the latter will miss many of the episodes of training occurring during the previous twelve months. The average participation rate from the CVTS (26 per cent) is somewhat lower than the rates for the IALS and OECD/INES, consistent with employers not reporting some vocational training activities reported by workers, such as training undertaken on their own initiative outside of work or less formal activities at the work site. These data confirm that differences in survey design are likely to lead to significantly different estimates of the absolute level of training.

Each of the surveys indicates considerable cross-country differences. This variation suggests that training patterns differ significantly between countries, especially since it is quite pronounced for the two most harmonised surveys, the IALS and the CVTS (standard deviations of 14 and 10 percentage points, respectively).

Simple inspection of Table 3.2 reveals that there is considerable consistency across the surveys concerning international differences in participation rates. Denmark, Finland, Sweden and the United Kingdom consistently show above-average training participation, while Greece, Italy, Portugal and Spain have below-average rates of participation. However, Ireland illustrates a more mixed pattern, with below-average participation in the IALS and ELFS, but the highest rate in the CVTS. Despite a few such anomalies, it appears that most of these countries can be characterised, with some confidence, as being low, near average or high in the OECD hierarchy of training rates. In this spirit, column 9 of Table 3.2 combines the information from the four surveys to calculate a summary index of relative participation.[4] The resulting cross-survey index suggests that training participation tends to be high in the Nordic countries and the United Kingdom and low in southern Europe. The cross-survey index also suggests that international differences in participation are quite large, since it ranges from 1.5 standard deviations above the mean to 1.3 standard deviations below.[5]

The volume of training

A simple "head count," such as a participation rate, provides an incomplete measure of the level of training. Training is a form of economic investment. This suggests that a continuous measure of the resources invested in training would be more informative than a simple, yes/no measure of whether any investment was made. While from a theoretical standpoint a measure of training volume is desirable, in practice it is difficult to gather accurate information of this type. Neither workers nor their employers routinely track the magnitudes of training investments and their attempts to estimate them in a survey interview are likely to be quite inaccurate [OECD (1997*b*)]. These considerations suggest that it is best to utilise both participation and volume measures to gauge the level of training, rather that relying solely on one or the other, since they have different strengths and weaknesses.

The primary measure of training *volume* examined here is hours of training averaged over all workers, whether they received any training or not. The four sources of harmonised training statistics yield quite different estimates of the average hours of training (Table 3.3). The major difference is the much lower level reported in the CVTS, which probably can be explained by the fact that the CVTS only reports hours spent in employer-provided "courses," which is narrower than the range of training activities covered by the other three surveys. Similarly, the use of a shorter reference period accounts for lower average hours in the ELFS than in the other two household surveys.[6] It is unclear, however, why training volume in the IALS is so much higher than in OECD/INES (42 versus 28 hours per worker). This difference may reflect a greater tendency of the IALS to capture relatively unstructured training.

All four surveys confirm that training volume differs between countries, but this variation ranges from quite modest in the CVTS to quite high in the IALS (standard deviations of 4 and 18 hours, respectively). As has been previously noted [OECD (1998*a*)], some of the cross-country differences in training hours measured in the ELFS appear to reflect either incompatible definitions or large measurement errors. In particular, the figure of 150 hours for the Netherlands is implausibly high.[7] Consistent with measurement error being greater for training volume than for participation rates, international comparisons of volume are less consistent across the four surveys. Greece provides the most extreme example of cross-survey inconsistency, being rated very low in the ELFS (15th out of 16 countries) but having the second

---

4. In order to average a country's ranking across all of the sources for which data are available, it is first necessary to convert the four sets of participation rates into comparable units. (Recall that differences in questionnaire design, such as different reference periods, mean that *absolute* levels are not comparable across the four sources.) For this purpose, each participation rate was "standardised" into a mean deviation in standard deviation units. For example, the training participation rate for Belgium from the IALS (19.8 per cent) is approximately 1.2 standard deviations below the cross-country mean value (37.1 per cent) and its standardised value is calculated as (19.8-37.1)/14.2 or –1.23. The cross-survey index is simply the unweighted mean of these standardised participation rates, where the average for each country is calculated across only the surveys in which it participated. The index has a mean value of zero by construction and is more reliable for the countries participating in a greater number of the surveys.
5. The ELFS provides some limited information concerning whether these training rates have changed over time. Between 1988 and 1997, training participation rose in seven of the twelve European countries for which data are available, while it fell in two and was approximately unchanged in the remaining three. While there is some overall support for a rising trend in training participation rates across EU countries, there is no evident trend toward a convergence of national rates.
6. The use of a 4-week – rather than 12-month – reference period in the ELFS underestimates training volume less strongly than participation for two reasons. First, the *full* length of any training courses that were on-going during the reference period is recorded. Second, a short reference period disproportionately "captures" long training episodes (a statistical phenomenon known as "length bias").
7. Two factors heightening the implausibility of these data are that *no* Dutch trainees are recorded as training for fewer than 20 hours per week and most of this training is attributable to a residual, "other purposes" category, rather than to "continuous vocational training" or "changing career". As a result, the ELFS data for the Netherlands are not used in any of the analysis of international differences in training volume.

Table 3.3. Volume of career or job-related training
Average hours of training per employee aged 25 to 54 years in the 1990s

	IALS Volume (1)	IALS Rank (2)	ELFS Volume (3)	ELFS Rank (4)	OECD/INES Volume (5)	OECD/INES Rank (6)	CVTS Volume (7)	CVTS Rank (8)	Cross-survey index of volume (average = 0)[b] Mean (9)	Cross-survey index of volume (average = 0)[b] Rank (10)
European Union										
Austria	..	..	19.8	6	..	..	..	..	0.3	9
Belgium[c]	17.3	10	8.4	12	..	..	10.2	8	−0.9	20
Denmark	..	..	34.9	1	..	..	12.9	5	0.9	4
Finland	..	..	31.8	2	18.8	6	..	..	0.3	8
France[d]	..	..	*6.4*	n.a.	..	..	20.1	1	1.8	1
Germany	40.5	8	31.6	3	34.9	2	8.2	11	0.2	10
Greece	..	..	4.1	15	..	..	18.0	2	0.0	11
Ireland	45.6	6	14.8	9	..	..	10.9	7	−0.1	14
Italy	..	..	8.0	13	..	..	6.1	12	−1.2	23
Luxembourg	..	..	3.4	16	..	..	10.0	10	−1.0	21
Netherlands[e]	51.0	4	*151.6*	n.a.	..	..	17.2	3	0.8	5
Portugal	..	..	30.5	4	..	..	11.0	6	0.5	7
Spain	..	..	16.2	7	..	..	10.0	9	−0.3	16
Sweden	..	..	11.6	11	20.2	5	..	..	−0.6	18
United Kingdom	52.1	3	21.6	5	..	..	15.8	4	0.6	6
North America										
Canada	41.1	7	..	..	21.9	3	..	..	−0.3	15
United States	46.6	5	..	..	21.9	4	..	..	−0.1	12
Pacific area										
Australia	61.3	2	..	..	48.9	1	..	..	1.4	3
New Zealand	69.0	1	..	..	..	..	..	..	1.5	2
Other OECD countries										
Hungary	..	..	13.5	10	..	..	..	..	−0.4	17
Iceland	..	..	15.8	8	..	..	..	..	−0.1	13
Norway	..	..	7.8	14	..	..	..	..	−0.9	19
Poland	20.7	9	..	..	..	..	..	..	−1.1	22
Switzerland[f]	11.3	11	..	..	..	..	..	..	−1.7	24
Switzerland (French)	*8.2*	n.a.	..	..	..	..	..	..	−1.8	n.a.
Switzerland (German)	*12.4*	n.a.	..	..	..	..	..	..	−1.6	n.a.
Unweighted mean	41.5	n.a.	17.1	n.a.	27.8	n.a.	12.5	n.a.	0.0	n.a.
Standard deviation	18.2	n.a.	10.3	n.a.	11.9	n.a.	4.3	n.a.	0.9	n.a.

.. Data not available.
n.a.: Not applicable.
a) Figures in *italics* are not used in the calculations of the cross-country statistics in Columns 3 and 4 or the cross-survey index in Column 9.
b) The national estimates of training volume in Columns 1, 3, 5 and 7 were standardised to have a zero mean and unit variance. Column 9 reports the unweighted means of these standardised values which are calculated using all surveys for which estimates are available for that country.
c) The IALS data for Belgium only cover Flanders.
d) The ELFS data for France measure only current training activity and are not fully comparable to those reported for the other countries. Accordingly, the French value is not used in the calculations of the cross-country statistics in Columns 3 and 4 or the cross-survey index in Column 9.
e) The ELFS data for the Netherlands are not used in the calculations of the cross-country statistics in Columns 3 and 4 or the cross-survey index in Column 9, because they appear to be non-comparable (see text).
f) IALS values for Switzerland are a weighted average of the values for the French and German-speaking populations.
Source: See Table 3.1.

highest volume in the CVTS. Nonetheless, stable patterns also emerge: Australia and the Netherlands being consistently above average; Germany and Portugal consistently near the average value; and Belgium and Italy consistently below average. That relatively few countries have volume data for multiple surveys also makes it somewhat difficult to come to an overall assessment of the cross-survey robustness of international differences. Although its validity appears more open to doubt, column 9 of Table 3.3 presents a cross-survey index of training volume, analogous to that previously constructed for participation. Australia, France, the Netherlands and New Zealand have the highest values while Belgium, Italy, Poland and Switzerland have the lowest.

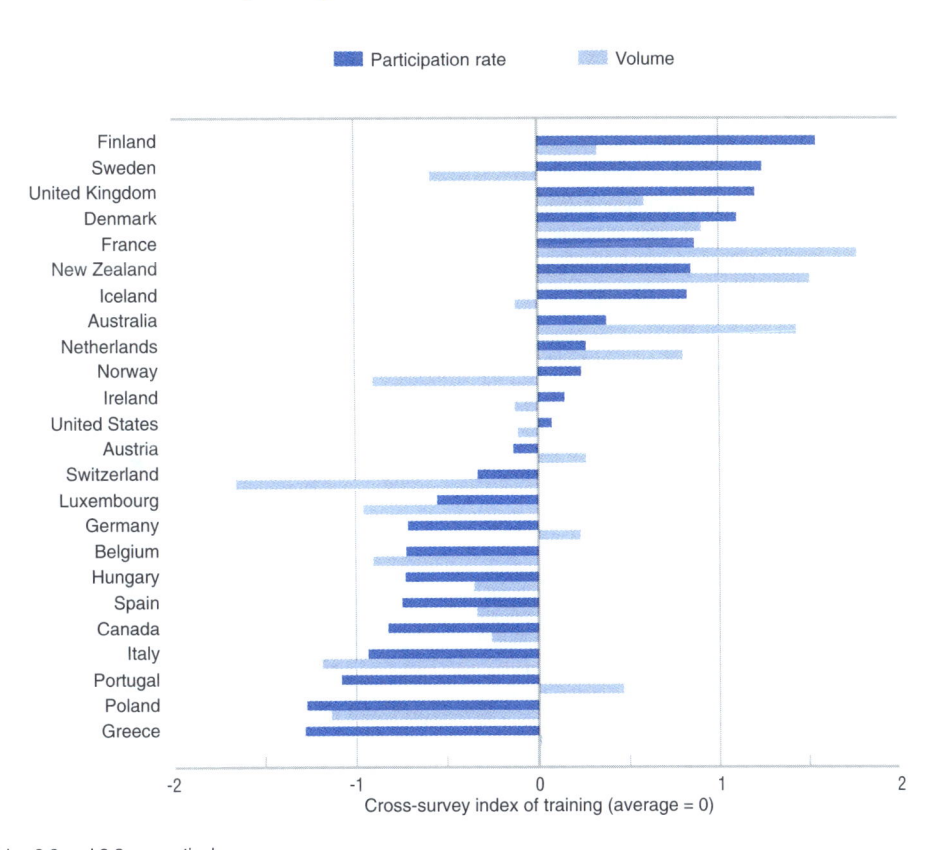

Chart 3.2. Cross-survey indices of the relative level of training: participation rates versus volume[a]

Cross-survey index of training (average = 0)

a) Column 9 of Tables 3.2 and 3.3 respectively.
Source: See Table 3.1.

Another question related to the consistency of international comparisons of training levels is whether the training participation and volume measures produce similar country rankings. Chart 3.2 juxtaposes the cross-survey indices of participation and volume. These two measures provide somewhat different assessments of which countries invest most in continuing training. The second highest rated country, in terms of participation, is below average on training volume (Sweden), while the lowest participation country has average training volume (Greece). However, there is some positive association between the two measures for the larger number of countries in the middle ranges of the two distributions, resulting in an overall correlation of 0.50.

The absence of a closer association between a country's relative positions in training participation and volume could reflect a trade-off between the extensive and intensive margins of training investments. A country that provides a little training for many workers is emphasising the extensive margin and will tend to score higher on the participation index than on the volume index. These data suggest that this pattern may characterise the Nordic countries, Switzerland and the United Kingdom. By contrast, there is evidence that countries such as Australia, France, Germany, Greece, the Netherlands, New Zealand and Portugal emphasise the intensive margin, providing relatively intensive training to the average, or even below-average, share of workers who receive any training. It is striking that several of the countries that appear to emphasise the intensive margin also have (or recently had) a training levy: Australia, France and New Zealand.[8] This pattern may reflect the tendency of a training levy to encourage a mix of training that favours easily documented forms of spending, such as employer-sponsored courses, which are heavily weighted by the volume measures in these surveys.

---

8. The Australian data are for 1995, the year that the training levy was abolished.

The magnitude of this trade-off can be roughly estimated. If trainees received the same hours of training on average, independent of the participation rate, then the correlation between participation and volume should be 1.0 in the absence of measurement error. This correlation is 0.50 for the cross-survey indices, but the 0.66 value for the IALS data alone is a better indication of the extent to which training intensity tends to fall as participation rises, since it is less affected by measurement problems. The IALS correlation implies that a 10 per cent increase in the training participation rate is associated with approximately a 3 per cent fall in hours per trainee.

The CVTS provides an alternative measure of training volume, namely, employers' costs for training courses as a share of total labour costs (Chart 3.3). By this measure, Portuguese and Italian employers rank last, spending less than one per cent of total labour costs on training, while United Kingdom employers invest most, at 2.7 per cent. Overall, this measure of volume accords quite closely with the earlier analysis of participation rates, but less closely with the hours measures of training volume. In particular, the southern European countries with relatively low participation rates (*i.e.* Greece, Italy, Portugal and Spain) also have the lowest cost shares among the EU Member states, while the two countries with the highest participation rates (the United Kingdom and France) also rate highest in employer spending.

Correlation analysis

Table 3.4 presents a more formal analysis of the robustness of cross-country differences in the level of training. Cross-country rank correlations were calculated between the various measures of training participation and volume. These correlations provide a quantification of the degree of consonance across three types of comparisons: between different measures of the level of training using the same survey (*e.g.* the 0.79 correlation between the IALS measures of training participation and hours); between different surveys using the same measure of training (*e.g.* the 0.83 correlation between the IALS and ELFS measures of participation); and using different measures and different surveys (*e.g.* the 0.30 correlation between the IALS participation and the ELFS hours measures). Note that the cross-survey correlations are often calculated for relatively small numbers of countries, since they can only be calculated over countries for which both estimates are available.

The participation and hours measures are positively correlated in the IALS, ELFS and CVTS. However, these correlations are substantially smaller that 1.0, suggesting either a cross-country trade-off between the number of

Chart 3.3. **Employers' training costs as a share of total labour costs, 1994**[a]

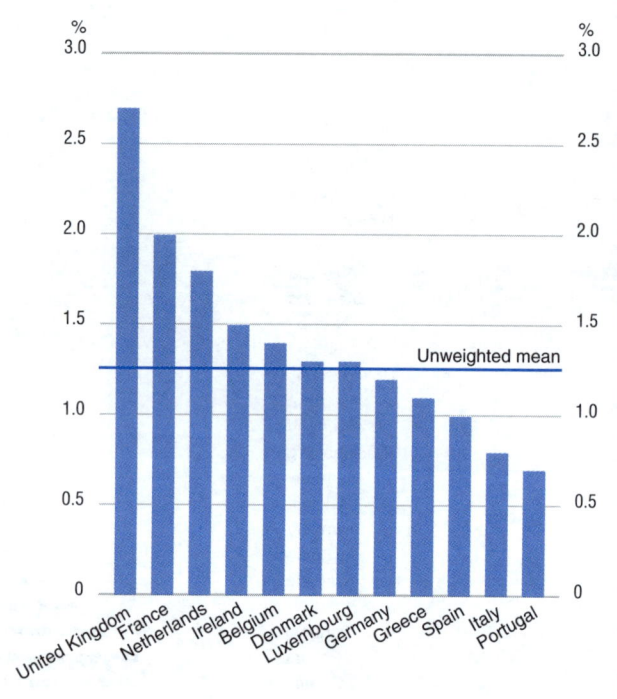

a) Employers' spending on formal training courses. Countries are ranked in descending order.
Source: EUROSTAT, CVTS, 1994.

workers being trained and the duration of training received or substantial measurement error in the hours measure. This correlation is actually negative in the OECD/INES, a pattern which suggests serious measurement error, since it is difficult to believe that increases in the share of workers being trained are associated with greater than proportional decreases in the average duration of training. For the CVTS, the correlations between training costs and both the participation and hours measures are strongly positive, at 0.89 and 0.51, indicating a high degree of agreement.

The cross-survey correlations for participation range from 0.60 to 0.83, indicating a quite high consistency in ranking countries by this dimension of training. This suggests that it is possible to make qualitatively valid comparisons of training participation rates and the cross-survey index of participation introduced earlier is used for this purpose latter in this section.

C. The distribution of training

Earnings levels and employment security are increasingly tied to a worker's skills [OECD (1997*c*)]. If

Table 3.4. **Spearman rank correlations of national measures of the level of career or job-related training across different data sources**
Employees aged 25-54 years in the 1990s

Measures compared[a]		Comparing the IALS with:				Comparing the ELFS with:			Comparing the OECD/INES with:		Comparing the CVTS with:
First survey	Second survey	IALS	ELFS	OECD/INES	CVTS	ELFS	OECD/INES	CVTS	OECD/INES	CVTS	CVTS
T%	T%	1.00**	0.83**	0.60	0.60	1.00**	0.80	0.72**	1.00**	..	1.00**
Hrs	Hrs	1.00**	0.40	0.20	0.80	1.00**	–0.50	0.18	1.00**	..	1.00**
T%	Hrs	0.79**	0.30	–0.70	0.80	0.51**	–0.50	0.21	–0.60	..	0.31
Hrs	T%	0.79**	0.90**	0.30	0.60	0.51**	0.40	0.20	–0.60	..	0.31
T%	C%	..	..	..	0.90**	..	..	0.58*	..	..	0.89**
Hrs	C%	..	..	..	0.90**	..	..	0.01	..	..	0.51*

.. Data not available.
* Significant at the 10% level.
** Significant at the 5% level.
a) T% denotes the percentage of workers participating in training, Hrs the average hours of training per employee and C% training costs as a percentage of total labour costs.
Source: See Table 3.1.

certain groups receive little training, this could significantly restrict their labour market opportunities and result in greater economic inequality. An uneven distribution of training may also lower economic efficiency. There is some evidence (see Chapter 4) that recent trends in technology and work organisation have increased the importance of broad and continuing participation of a firm's workforce in training. Despite these equity and efficiency concerns, little is known about whether there are significant international differences in the distribution of training. This section uses the four sources of harmonised training data to assess international differences in training participation rates across workers grouped by gender, age and education.[9] Qualitatively similar results were obtained when this analysis was repeated for hours of training, but those results are not reported in detail, due to the lower quality of the underlying data.

Gender distribution of training

Equalising the labour market opportunities of women with men is an important policy goal and the upward trend in the labour market premium on skill [Blau and Kahn (1996)] suggests that equal access to education and training is of some importance in meeting this goal. Overall efficiency is also likely to suffer if a large segment of the labour force, such as women, have inadequate access to training.

Table 3.5 presents ratios of the training participation rate for women to that for men, for the four harmonised surveys. Averaging these gender ratios over all of the countries covered by a given survey always results in a mean ratio relatively close to 1.0 (the values range from 0.91 for the CVTS to 1.12 for the ELFS), suggesting that women and men participate in training to a roughly comparable extent. The moderately lower CVTS estimate suggests, however, that women participate somewhat less than men when attention is restricted to employer-provided training courses. Consistent with this interpretation, the IALS data indicate that women less often receive financial support from their employers for job-related training than do men [Loewenstein and Spletzer (1994); O'Connell (1998)]. It was argued earlier that the IALS training measures may tend to pick up more of the relatively unstructured forms of training than measures from the other two household surveys. The average relative training rate for women is lower in the IALS than in the ELFS, consistent with men having greater access to informal training.

There is significant cross-country variation in the gender ratios for each of the surveys. For example, the relative participation of women ranges from 0.75 (the Netherlands) to 1.32 (Ireland) in the IALS. By casual inspection, there appears to be moderate cross-survey consistency in the share of training received by women in a specific country and how it compares to the international average. For example, the gender ratio in Ireland is always greater than 1.0 and frequently among the higher values. Similarly, the Netherlands values are consistently below 1.0 for participation. However, there are also examples of rather striking inconsistencies. The IALS participation

---
9. CVTS data are used only for analysing gender differences in participation rates, because it lacks data on training rates by age and education.

Table 3.5. **Differences in career or job-related training by gender**
Ratios of the participation rates for women to those for men

	IALS Ratio (1)	IALS Rank (2)	ELFS Ratio (3)	ELFS Rank (4)	OECD/INES Ratio (5)	OECD/INES Rank (6)	CVTS Ratio (7)	CVTS Rank (8)	Unweighted mean ratio[a] (9)	Rank (10)
European Union										
Austria	..	..	0.97	14	..	..	..	..	0.97	17
Belgium[b]	0.83	11	0.93	16	..	..	1.12	1	0.96	18
Denmark	..	..	1.29	3	..	..	1.06	3	1.18	2
Finland	..	..	1.28	4	0.99	4	..	..	1.14	5
France	..	..	1.13	8	..	..	0.85	9	0.99	15
Germany	1.15	2	0.96	15	0.87	6	0.63	12	0.90	21
Greece	..	..	1.21	5	..	..	1.00	5	1.10	6
Ireland	1.32	1	1.12	9	..	..	1.05	4	1.16	3
Italy	..	..	1.46	2	..	..	0.69	11	1.07	9
Luxembourg	..	..	0.85	18	..	..	1.08	2	0.97	16
Netherlands	0.75	12	0.93	17	..	..	0.89	7	0.85	24
Portugal	..	..	1.03	11	..	..	0.73	10	0.88	22
Spain	..	..	1.58	1	..	..	0.86	8	1.22	1
Sweden	1.09	3	1.04	10	1.13	2	..	..	1.08	7
United Kingdom	1.00	6	1.16	6	..	..	0.93	6	1.03	12
North America										
Canada	0.94	7	..	..	1.11	3	..	..	1.02	13
United States	1.00	5	..	..	1.16	1	..	..	1.08	8
Pacific area										
Australia	0.91	10	..	..	0.98	5	..	..	0.95	19
New Zealand	1.05	4	..	..	..	..	..	..	1.05	10
Other OECD countries										
Hungary	..	..	1.15	7	..	..	..	..	1.15	4
Iceland	..	..	1.03	12	..	..	..	..	1.03	11
Norway	..	..	1.00	13	..	..	..	..	1.00	14
Poland	0.92	9	..	..	..	..	..	..	0.92	20
Switzerland[c]	0.93	8	..	..	0.81	7	..	..	0.87	23
Switzerland (French)	0.79	n.a.	..	..	..	..	..	..	0.79	n.a.
Switzerland (German)	0.98	n.a.	..	..	..	..	..	..	0.98	n.a.
Unweighted mean	**0.99**	**n.a.**	**1.12**	**n.a.**	**1.01**	**n.a.**	**0.91**	**n.a.**	**1.02**	**n.a.**
Standard deviation	**0.15**	**n.a.**	**0.19**	**n.a.**	**0.13**	**n.a.**	**0.16**	**n.a.**	**0.10**	**n.a.**

.. Data not available.
n.a.: Not applicable.
a) Mean calculated using all surveys for which estimates are available for that country.
b) The IALS data for Belgium only cover Flanders.
c) IALS values for Switzerland are a weighted average of the values for the French and German-speaking populations.
Source: See Table 3.1.

data for Germany indicate women participating at 1.15 times the rate of men (substantially above the average level for the 12 countries with these data), but at only 0.96, 0.87 and 0.63 times the rate of men in the other three surveys.

When the robustness of the international comparisons of these gender ratios is assessed using correlations between the various measures (Table 3.8, Panel A), the picture remains rather mixed. There is considerable consistency between the participation measures from the IALS, ELFS and OECD/INES. However, the estimates of gender differences in training based on the CVTS participation rates (or hours data from any of the surveys) provide a rather disparate picture of cross-country differences.

Age distribution of training

The logic of human capital theory, as well as simple observation of life courses, suggest that skill investments are likely to be concentrated in the early portions of an individual's life and career. While basic schooling and initial vocational training are everywhere concentrated in the pre- or early-career years, there may be considerable variation in the extent to which workers continue to receive training in the middle and later portions of their working lives. Too rapid a "tailing off" of training with age could lead to skill obsolescence and create severe employment difficulties for some older workers, while also reducing the adaptive capacity of the economy as the workforce ages in coming decades [OECD (1998*c*)].

Table 3.6 compares training participation for relatively young workers (*i.e.* ages 25-29 years) to that for older workers (*i.e.* ages 50-54 years). The greater the value of the age ratio, the more strongly continuing training is concentrated in the early stages of the prime working years. Since values in excess of 1.0 predominate, these four sources of harmonised training data confirm a tendency for training to be "front-loaded".

The cross-country averages of these age ratios vary considerably across the different surveys, from 1.10 for the OECD/INES to 2.76 for the ELFS. The lower values for the OECD/INES could be a simple artefact of having calculated the age ratio using broader age bands. Omitting this survey reduces the cross-survey difference in mean ratios, but large differences remain. This variation suggest that changes in survey design that affect the types of training captured are not age-neutral and can have a large effect on estimates of the age concentration of training.

There is considerable cross-country variation in the age concentration of training. For example, the age ratio calculated from IALS data on participation ranges from 0.93 for Sweden to 1.96 in Canada.[10] This variation suggests that countries differ significantly in the extent to which their training practices realise the goal of "life-long learning".

There appears to be considerable consistency across the three data sources and two measures in terms of which countries provide older workers with the greatest relative access to training. Most of the Nordic countries (with Finland as a notable exception) and the United States have consistently among the lowest age ratios, indicating no or only a weak tendency to concentrate training on younger workers. By contrast, the ratio tends to be well above average in France, Luxembourg and most southern European countries, indicating a steep fall off in training with age. Correlations between these measures of age differences in training (Table 3.8, Panel B) indicate a quite high degree of cross-survey consistency, especially for the participation measures of training. Overall, it appears that a number of reasonably robust comparisons can be made concerning international differences in the age distribution of training.

Education, literacy and the distribution of training

Extensive initial schooling might be complementary with subsequent participation in continuing training, if the knowledge base and learning skills acquired in school facilitate the later acquisition of more specific vocational skills through training. Alternatively, schooling and initial vocational preparation could be substitutes. Since the overall efficiency of the skill development system requires that continuing training mesh well with other forms of human capital investment, it would be valuable to know whether complementary or substitution links predominate and if there are important international differences in these relationships. International differences in the association of prior human capital investments and training could also have important implications for equity, since a strong complementarity between education and schooling would tend to reinforce the labour market disadvantages of the least educated workers.

In order to gauge the strength of the association between education and training, Table 3.7 presents the ratio of the training participation rate for workers with a university degree to that for workers who did not complete upper secondary schooling. These ratios are always

---

10. It is striking that the concentration of training on younger workers appears to be much stronger in Canada than in the United States (1.96 versus 0.97 for participation in the IALS).

Table 3.6. Differences in career or job-related training by age
Ratios of the participation rates for younger to those for older workers

	IALS Ratio (1)	IALS Rank (2)	ELFS Ratio (3)	ELFS Rank (4)	OECD/INES Ratio (5)	OECD/INES Rank (6)	Unweighted mean ratio[b] (7)	Rank (8)
European Union								
Austria	..	..	1.60	11	..	..	1.60	11
Belgium[c]	1.25	7	2.19	10	..	..	1.72	10
Denmark	..	..	0.98	16	..	..	0.98	21
Finland	..	..	1.50	13	0.96	5	1.23	17
France	..	..	5.38	2	..	..	5.38	2
Germany	1.79	2	3.32	7	1.25	2	2.12	8
Greece	..	..	4.55	4	..	..	4.55	4
Ireland	1.20	8	2.51	9	..	..	1.86	9
Italy	..	..	1.14	14	..	..	1.14	18
Luxembourg	..	..	4.54	5	..	..	4.54	5
Netherlands	1.44	5	2.93	8	..	..	2.19	7
Portugal	..	..	6.13	1	..	..	6.13	1
Spain	..	..	4.87	3	..	..	4.87	3
Sweden	0.93	12	0.88	18	0.90	7	0.90	23
United Kingdom	1.56	3	1.55	12	..	..	1.56	12
North America								
Canada	1.96	1	..	..	1.14	3	1.55	13
United States	0.97	11	..	..	0.94	6	0.96	22
Pacific area								
Australia	1.16	9	..	..	1.40	1	1.28	16
New Zealand	1.08	10	..	..	..	..	1.08	19
Other OECD countries								
Hungary	..	..	3.67	6	..	..	3.67	6
Iceland	..	..	1.01	15	..	..	1.01	20
Norway	..	..	0.89	17	..	..	0.89	24
Poland	1.42	6	..	..	..	..	1.42	14
Switzerland[d]	1.47	4	..	..	1.13	4	1.30	15
Switzerland (French)	1.70	n.a.	..	..	..	..	1.70	n.a.
Switzerland (German)	1.43	n.a.	..	..	..	..	1.43	n.a.
Unweighted mean	**1.35**	**n.a.**	**2.76**	**n.a.**	**1.10**	**n.a.**	**2.25**	**n.a.**
Standard deviation	**0.32**	**n.a.**	**1.73**	**n.a.**	**0.18**	**n.a.**	**1.63**	**n.a.**

.. Data not available.
n.a.: Not applicable.
a) Younger is defined as ages 25-29 in IALS and ELFS, and as 25-34 in OECD/INES; older is defined as ages 50-54 in IALS and ELFS, and as 45-64 in OECD/INES.
b) Mean calculated using all surveys for which estimates are available for that country.
c) The IALS data for Belgium only cover Flanders.
d) IALS values for Switzerland are a weighted average of the values for the French and German-speaking populations.
Source: See Table 3.1.

Table 3.7. Differences in career or job-related training by education

Ratios of the participation rates for workers with a university degree to those for workers not having finished upper secondary schooling

	IALS Ratio (1)	IALS Rank (2)	ELFS Ratio (3)	ELFS Rank (4)	OECD/INES Ratio (5)	OECD/INES Rank (6)	Unweighted mean ratio[a] (7)	Rank (8)
European Union								
Austria	..	..	2.89	15	..	..	2.89	18
Belgium[b]	5.70	2	14.93	3	..	..	10.32	5
Denmark	..	..	3.34	11	..	..	3.34	14
Finland	..	..	3.30	12	2.11	7	2.70	19
France	..	..	5.08	9	..	..	5.08	8
Germany	1.96	8	5.19	8	6.91	1	4.69	9
Greece	..	..	22.83	2	..	..	22.83	2
Ireland	2.62	5	3.25	13	..	..	2.93	17
Italy	..	..	8.29	6	..	..	8.29	6
Luxembourg	..	..	4.58	10	..	..	4.58	10
Netherlands	1.88	9	1.93	18	..	..	1.90	23
Portugal	..	..	37.29	1	..	..	37.29	1
Spain	..	..	13.80	4	..	..	13.80	3
Sweden	1.58	12	2.11	17	2.25	5	1.98	22
United Kingdom	1.70	11	5.55	7	..	..	3.63	13
North America								
Canada	2.34	6	..	..	4.21	3	3.28	15
United States	4.09	3	..	..	4.30	2	4.19	11
Pacific area								
Australia	2.01	7	..	..	2.21	6	2.11	21
New Zealand	1.80	10	..	..	..	..	1.80	24
Other OECD countries								
Hungary	..	..	12.05	5	..	..	12.05	4
Iceland	..	..	2.26	16	..	..	2.26	20
Norway	..	..	3.02	14	..	..	3.02	16
Poland	3.72	4	..	..	..	..	3.72	12
Switzerland[c]	8.70	1	..	..	3.77	4	6.23	7
Switzerland (French)	4.80	n.a.	..	..	..	..	4.80	n.a.
Switzerland (German)	12.25	n.a.	..	..	..	..	12.25	n.a.
Unweighted mean	3.18	n.a.	8.43	n.a.	3.68	n.a.	6.87	n.a.
Standard deviation	2.14	n.a.	9.17	n.a.	1.72	n.a.	8.12	n.a.

.. Data not available.
n.a.: Not applicable.
a) Mean calculated using all surveys for which estimates are available for that country.
b) The IALS data for Belgium only cover Flanders.
c) IALS values for Switzerland are a weighted average of the values for the French and German-speaking populations.
Source: See Table 3.1.

Table 3.8. **Spearman rank correlations of national measures of the distribution of career or job-related training across different data sources and definitions**

Employees aged 25-54 years in the 1990s

Measures compared [a]		Comparing the IALS with:				Comparing the ELFS with:			Comparing the OECD/INES with:
First survey	Second survey	IALS	ELFS	OECD/INES	CVTS	ELFS	OECD/INES	CVTS	OECD/INES
Panel A. Correlations of ratios of the values for women to those for men									
T%	T%	1.00*	0.60	0.26	0.00	1.00*	0.50	−0.26	1.00*
Hrs	Hrs	1.00*	−0.10	−0.40	..	1.00*	−0.50	..	1.00*
T%	Hrs	0.23	0.09	−0.30	..	0.78*	0.50	..	0.54
Hrs	T%	0.23	−0.10	−0.90*	..	0.78*	−0.50	..	0.54
Panel B. Correlations of ratios of the values for younger to those for older workers [b]									
T%	T%	1.00*	0.60	0.60	..	1.00*	1.00*	..	1.00*
Hrs	Hrs	1.00*	0.10	−0.20	..	1.00*	−0.50	..	1.00*
T%	Hrs	0.44	0.54	0.50	..	0.61*	0.50	..	0.83*
Hrs	T%	0.44	0.90*	−0.10	..	0.61*	0.50	..	0.83*
Panel C. Correlations of ratios of the values for workers with a university degree to those for workers not having finished secondary schooling									
T%	T%	1.00*	0.49	0.14	..	1.00*	0.50	..	1.00*
Hrs	Hrs	1.00*	0.60	−0.50	..	1.00*	−1.00	..	1.00*
T%	Hrs	0.71*	0.03	0.60	..	0.85*	−1.00	..	0.80
Hrs	T%	0.71*	0.70	−0.50	..	0.85*	−0.50	..	0.80

.. Data not available.
* Significant at the 5% level.
a) T% denotes the percentage of workers participating in training and Hrs the average hours of training per employee.
b) Younger is defined as ages 25-29 in IALS and ELFS, and as 25-34 in OECD/INES; older is defined as ages 50-54 in IALS and ELFS, and as 45-64 in OECD/INES.
Source: See Table 3.1.

in excess of 1.0. Averaged across countries for a given survey, the mean values range from 3.2 (IALS) to 8.4 (ELFS), confirming that training reinforces the skill differences resulting from unequal initial schooling. These education ratios are consistently larger for the hours measure (not shown), suggesting that the concentration of training on the most educated workers, like that on younger workers, operates on both the extensive and the intensive margins.

The extent of concentration varies considerably across countries for any given survey. For example, the education ratio varies from 1.6 for Sweden to 8.7 for Switzerland, using IALS participation data. However, there is considerable consistency in the relative position of different countries. Training appears to be most evenly distributed across educational attainment levels in Australia, Austria, Ireland, New Zealand, the Netherlands and the Nordic countries. Training is most reinforcing of school-based differences in human capital in southern European countries, Belgium and Hungary. Correlation analysis confirms strong, cross-survey consistency in these comparisons, except that the results for the OECD/INES are more dissimilar (Table 3.8, Panel C).

Chart 3.4 uses IALS data on literacy scores to provide another perspective on the relationship between prior human capital investments and additional training. In all 11 countries, workers with high levels of literacy receive more training than workers with low literacy scores. This association illustrates an important complementarity between literacy and the ability to benefit from training programmes. Such a link could also account for some of the complementarity between greater initial schooling, which tends to enhance literacy, and subsequent training.[11] The strength of the association between training and literacy varies markedly across the 11 countries, in a pattern that roughly parallels international differences in the

---
11. There is a strong and positive correlation between literacy scores and educational attainment, but considerable variation in literacy scores is found at any given level of education [OECD and Statistics Canada (1995)]. Regression analysis of the determinants of training using IALS data indicates that literacy exercises an important, independent, effect on increasing the probability of training, controlling for the level of education.

Chart 3.4. Differences in career or job-related training by literacy level
Ratio of values for workers with prose literacy level 4-5 to those with literacy level 1[a]

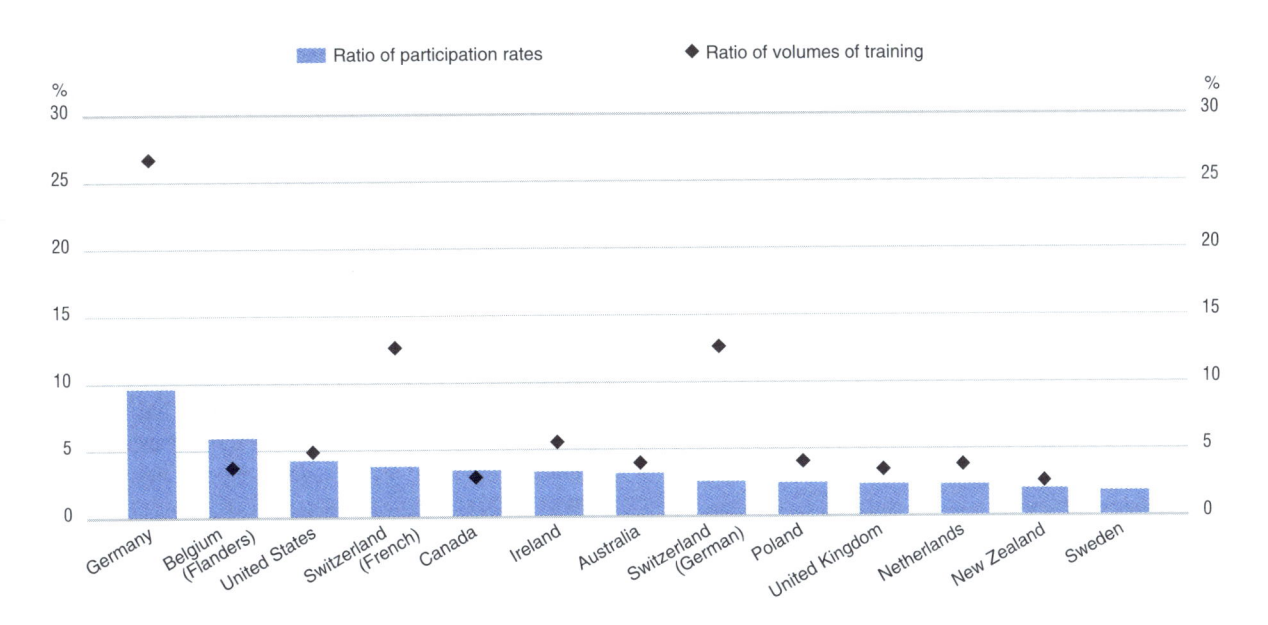

a) Level 1 indicates a low level of literacy proficiency while levels 4-5 represent the highest proficiencies. See OECD and Statistics Canada (1995) for detailed definitions and analysis of the distribution of literacy scores.
Source: International Adult Literacy Survey, 1994-1995.

strength of the association between schooling and training. However, Germany is an important exception. The literacy-training association is especially strong for Germany, which only has an average level of association between education and training.

Is there a link between the level and distribution of training?

Chart 3.5 examines whether there is any systematic association between national differences in the level of training and differences in how strongly training is concentrated on younger and more educated workers. The result is clear-cut: training tends to be more evenly distributed in the countries with the highest participation rates, so that the cross-survey index of training participation is negatively correlated with the indices of the relative concentration of training on younger and better-educated workers (–0.41 and –0.55, respectively). With the exception of younger workers in France, all twelve countries with above-average participation have below-average concentrations of training on younger and the most educated workers. Similarly, training tends to be most concentrated in the countries with the lowest participation, although some exceptions occur at this end of the spectrum. Canada and Poland have both below-average participation in training and below-average concentration.

The association between higher training rates and more equal participation in training suggests that differences in national training systems that affect the overall level of training operate most strongly through their effects on the extent to which older and less-educated workers receive training. While it is not clear how to explain this relationship, it suggests that institutions or conditions affecting the incentives or resources available to train older and low-educated workers may be of particular importance. Relatively high and relatively equal training appears to characterise the Nordic countries, as well as Australia, New Zealand and the United Kingdom. At the other extreme, southern, central and eastern European countries tend to have low and concentrated training.[12]

---

12. While no Japanese data are available in the four harmonised surveys, data from the 1997 Survey of Vocational Training in Private Enterprises (Minkan Kunren Jittai Chosa) suggest that Japan should be classified among the countries with high and relatively equal training: 53 per cent of employees in private establishments with 30 or more regular employees had participated in formal, off-the-job training during the previous year, with the participation rate just 20 per cent higher for university graduates than for workers not finishing secondary schooling and workers aged 46-54 years actually training at a little higher rate than those aged 25-35.

Life-cycle perspective

New insights can be gained by adapting a life-cycle view of training that follows workers from age 25 until 64, taken to be the conventional retirement age. Since many individuals are not continuously employed throughout this forty-year period, realism requires that periods of unemployment and inactivity be incorporated into the analysis, even though training while employed is the focus of this chapter. The IALS data indicate that training occurs while individuals are not employed (Chart 3.6). In most countries, training participation is significantly higher for employees than for the unemployed, but the two rates are similar in the Netherlands and Switzerland and the unemployed actually report more training in Germany. The training rate for persons outside of the labour force is universally far lower than that for the employed.

Table 3.9 presents estimates of training expectancies, defined as the total hours of training received by a "typical" individual between the ages of 25 and 64 years. Using the IALS data, age, gender and education-specific rates were calculated for the three labour force states, as were mean annual training hours conditional on labour force status. These rates are then used to cumulate expected training time for individuals over this forty-year time span on the assumption that current conditions continue to prevail.[13]

Averaging over the 11 countries with the necessary data, these training expectancies imply that a typical individual devotes 1 288 hours, or the equivalent of over thirty weeks of full-time employment, to training after the period of initial vocational training has concluded. While this reflects a considerable investment of time, it is much smaller than that made to initial schooling.[14] Such a comparison probably greatly understates the relative importance of continuing training and on-the-job experience to the development of workforce skills and productivity, because a large share of informal training and experiential learning are not captured by this calculation.

When the life-cycle perspective is adopted, the volume of training received by women is significantly lower relative to that received by men than is indicated by single-year calculations: using the IALS data for employed individuals between the ages of 25 and 54 years, average annual training hours were 92 per cent as high for women as for men, but this falls to just 79 per cent for the forty-year training expectancies. This is due to the typical women being employed fewer years, than men, and when not employed being more likely to be out of the labour force. For the same reason, the concentration of training on the most educated individuals becomes more pronounced when the full working life is considered, a pattern that is very pronounced for women. It does not appear, however, that national comparisons of the level or distribution of training are much affected by the shift to a life-cycle perspective.

D. Bivariate analysis of the associates of training

The following two subsections report cross-country correlations of the level and distribution of training with other variables. This exploratory analysis has the limited objective of clarifying the interpretation and economic salience of the international comparisons that can be made with the existing data on training. Correlations are reported with variables that economic theory suggests may be important determinants or effects of training. Nonetheless, these simple associations should not be interpreted as providing rigorous evidence of the causes and consequences of international differences in training, because they do not control for other causal factors. Instead, they are intended to provide an initial survey of factors that are associated with these differences, which can help to guide more sophisticated multivariate analysis of these empirical relationships.

Training and overall human capital formation

While the most educated workers receive a disproportionate share of training in all of the countries analysed, it need not follow that training and education are similarly reinforcing at the national level. Training rates might have to be higher in a country where initial schooling is less well developed, if the nation's business firms are to compete successfully.[15] Chart 3.7 shows that there is a tendency for higher national training rates to be associated with higher educational attainment. In other words, the complementary relationship between initial schooling and training appears to be stronger than the relationship of substitution. A con-

---

13. This method is analogous to that used to calculate life expectancy based on the age-specific mortality rates observed in the population in a given year. Note that the results should not be understood as providing forecasts of individual training histories, rather they provide an alternative optic for viewing contemporaneous training patterns.
14. These training expectancies are also moderately lower than 40 times the mean annual hours of training for all workers, which were examined in Table 3.3, due to training rates being lower for the years spent unemployed and out of the labour force. A second reason for this shortfall is that the cross-sectional averages for hours of training were calculated for the age span, 25 to 54 years, while these life-time calculations also include ages 55 through 64 years, during which training hours tend to be quite low.
15. A survey of multinational employers' assessments of international differences in the amount of training required suggests that such a relationship holds for the United Kingdom. Employers report needing to train workers more extensively to compensate for the poorer skills of new recruits [DfEE and Cabinet Office (1996)].

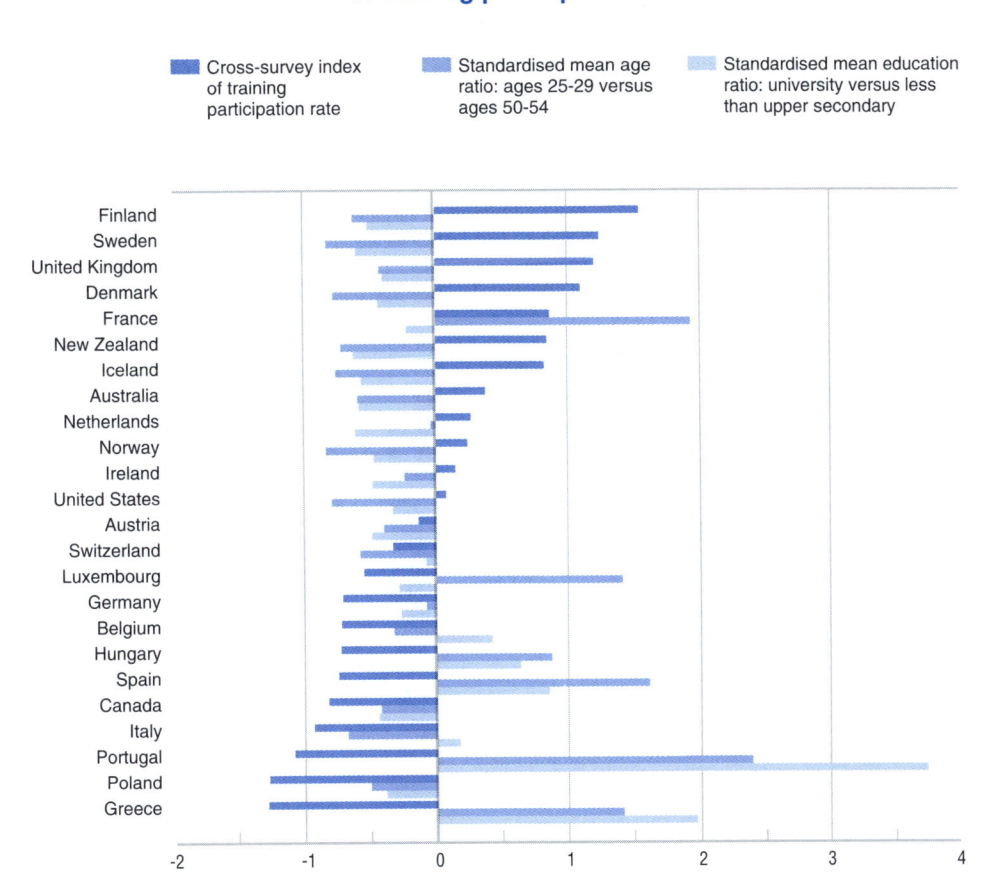

Chart 3.5. National differences in the level and concentration of training participation[a]

- Cross-survey index of training participation rate
- Standardised mean age ratio: ages 25-29 versus ages 50-54
- Standardised mean education ratio: university versus less than upper secondary

Finland, Sweden, United Kingdom, Denmark, France, New Zealand, Iceland, Australia, Netherlands, Norway, Ireland, United States, Austria, Switzerland, Luxembourg, Germany, Belgium, Hungary, Spain, Canada, Italy, Portugal, Poland, Greece

a) Countries are ranked in descending order of the cross-survey index of training participation rate.
Source: See Table 3.1.

siderable number of countries with average or below-average training participation, nonetheless, have above-average shares of the working-age population having finished upper secondary schooling. Notable examples include Canada, Germany, Poland and the United States.

The associations between continuing training and other measures of human capital are examined in greater detail in Table 3.10. Panel A reports correlations between three measures of the level of training and six measures of educational attainment and spending on schools. The correlations for training participation confirm that the positive cross-country association of greater training with greater initial schooling is robust to different measures of educational attainment. The relationship is even stronger for measures of current schooling patterns (*i.e.* educational expectancies of five-year olds today) and school spending than for the educational attainment of the working-age population. It also appears that a high rate of upper secondary

school completion is more closely associated with higher training than a high rate of university study.

Table 3.10, Panel A also reports correlations between educational attainment and three measures of the *distribution* of training. Training is less concentrated on younger and more educated workers in countries with higher educational attainment. While the presence of a better educated workforce appears to encourage employers to invest more in training, this increase affects less educated workers more strongly than more educated workers. This suggests that an increase in the supply of skilled workers due to conventional schooling may induce employers to adopt more skill-intensive production processes that imply a more-than-proportionate increase in skill demand, which is met – in part – through greater and more broadly distributed training [Acemoglu (1998)].

Panel B of Table 3.10 reports correlations between the training measures and six measures of educational

OECD

Chart 3.6. Participation rate in career or job-related training by labour force status[a]

Percentages of persons aged 25 to 54 years

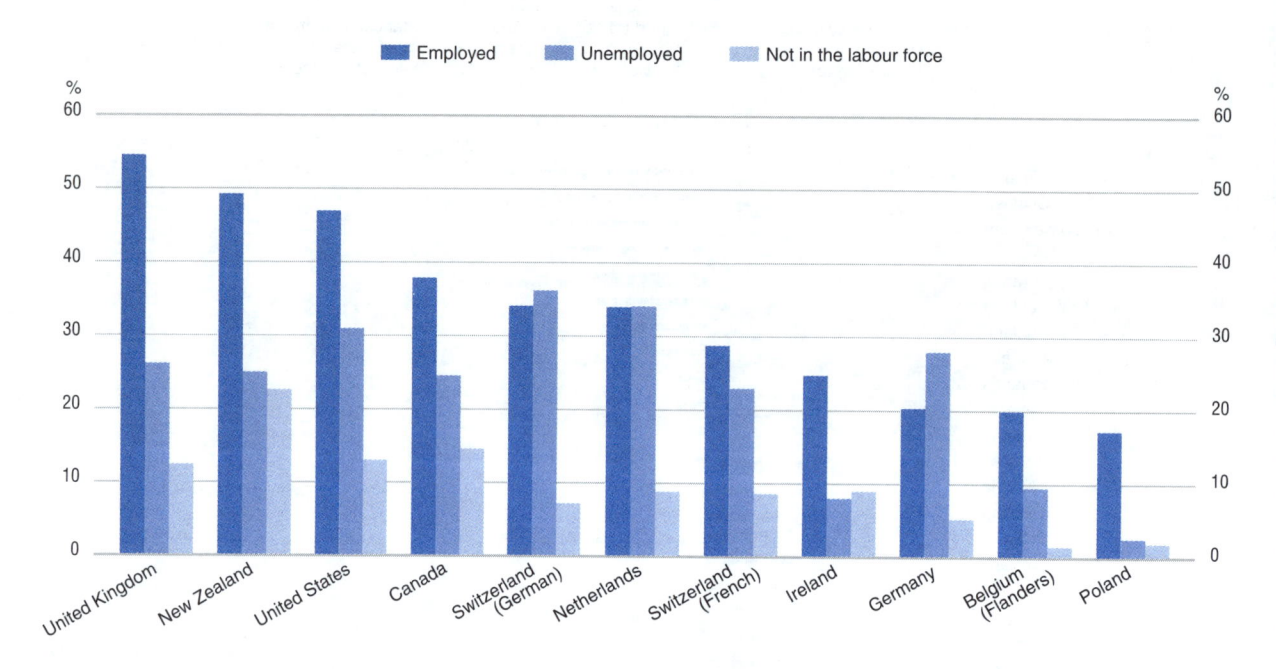

Legend: Employed / Unemployed / Not in the labour force

Countries (ranked by employed training rate): United Kingdom, New Zealand, United States, Canada, Switzerland (German), Netherlands, Switzerland (French), Ireland, Germany, Belgium (Flanders), Poland.

a) Countries are ranked in descending order of the percentage of training for employed persons.
Source: International Adult Literacy Survey, 1994-1995.

achievement and literacy proficiencies. There is a strong positive association between the level of training and both the mathematics achievement scores of current eight graders and the literacy scores of adults. There is also evidence that training levels are lower where the dispersion of literacy scores is higher, suggesting that training may be inhibited where the members of the workforce differ greatly in their "trainability" (e.g. their ability to use instructional materials). No such effect is evident for the dispersion of mathematics scores.[16] Training tends to be less strongly concentrated on younger and better educated workers in countries with higher education achievement. Greater dispersion in literacy scores increases the concentration of training on more educated workers, also suggestive of an inhibiting effect of low literacy proficiencies on trainability.

Schooling and formal training are only two of the ways in which economies invest in greater workforce skills and future productive capacity. Panel C of Table 3.10 presents correlations of the training measures with six measures of related investments. Training levels among the employed are positively correlated with national spending rates on active labour market policies (ALMPs). To some extent, this correlation reflects an overlapping of the two categories of training. However, the major part of ALMP expenditures are for nonemployed individuals, suggesting that countries providing more training to the unemployed also tend to have higher on-the-job training, which is less concentrated on younger and better educated workers.

Countries investing a higher share of GDP in research and development (R&D) or having a higher share of researchers in the workforce also tend to have higher training rates, less concentration of training on younger and better educated workers, and relatively less training for women. However, the pattern is very different for the association between training and investment in fixed capital, with more investment being correlated with lower and more concentrated training. This result provides an interesting extension of the well-established finding that physical capital and skilled workers are complements in production [Griliches (1969); Bergström and Panas (1992)]. While greater investments in physical capital appear to shift recruitment choices toward hiring more educated workers, these correlations suggest that there is a reduction in overall training which becomes more concentrated on university-educated workers.

---
16. This may be because mathematical ability is less strongly related to general trainability or it could simply reflect the positive correlation between the dispersion of test scores and the mean score [OECD (1998b)].

Table 3.9. **Training expectancy given current conditions**[a]

Cumulative hours of career or job-related training between the ages of 25 and 64 years

	Cumulative training hours	Ratio of training hours for:		
		Years employed relative to all years	Women relative to men	University educated relative to less than upper secondary
Australia	1 605	..	0.73	3.16
Belgium (Flanders)	478	0.88	0.68	10.75
Canada	2 109	0.48	1.03	3.83
Germany	1 833	0.44	1.23	1.13
Ireland	1 261	0.64	1.19	1.14
Netherlands	1 512	0.66	0.58	1.18
New Zealand	2 627	0.62	0.81	2.73
Poland	391	0.95	0.80	2.58
Switzerland (French)	217	0.92	0.39	2.47
Switzerland (German)	353	0.96	0.50	3.36
United Kingdom	1 666	0.73	0.75	1.72
United States	1 403	0.80	0.80	2.26
Unweighted mean	**1 288**	**0.73**	**0.79**	**3.03**
Standard deviation	**739**	**0.17**	**0.24**	**2.48**

.. Data not available.
a) Expected training hours are the *cumulation*, over five-year age intervals between the ages of 25 and 64, of age and gender-specific estimates of mean training hours. Mean training hours for a specific age and gender were calculated as weighted averages of the mean hours of training for each of three labour force states (employed, unemployed and out of the labour force), where population shares were used as weights.
Source: International Adult Literacy Survey, 1994-1995.

Overall, these patterns suggest that schooling and training are complements because a better educated workforce encourages firms to specialise in products and services that place a high premium on workforce skills and R&D, but are not especially physical capital-intensive. It also appears likely that policies to improve general educational and literacy levels can create a virtuous circle, in which greater skill supply induces greater skill demands and, hence, greater incentives for workers to obtain more schooling, as well as for employers and workers to invest in continuing training. However, a better understanding of these incentives and how they are shaped by policy and labour market conditions is needed. The determinants of the incentives for broadly targeted investments in training – for example, training for less educated and older workers – appear to be of particular importance.

Training and the broader economy

Can these international differences in the level and distribution of training be explained in terms of the labour market institutions and conditions that economic theory identifies as potential determinants of training rates? This section uses bivariate associations to provide a first indication of which factors might plausibly play an important role in causing these differences. Similarly, summary indicators of national training investments are correlated with measures of economic outcomes that training might affect.

Among the labour market institutions that are examined in Table 3.11, Panel A, higher training participation is most strongly associated with greater adoption of flexible working practices.[17] In large part, this correlation reflects the relatively high use of flexible work practices in the Nordic countries which also tend to have the highest training rates, but it is consistent with the belief that increased training facilitates the successful implementation of these practices. Higher trade union density is also associated with higher training participation, consistent with earlier research [Green *et al.* (1999)]. However, collective bargaining coverage does not appear to be strongly associated with training levels. Finally, formal training rates are higher in countries with a higher share of the workforce changing jobs in the previous year, and lower in countries with stricter EPL and higher mean job tenure, two indicators of relatively low labour turnover [see Chapter 2]. Comparisons of training participation *within* individual countries (*e.g.* across workers, firms or industries) have often found that lower turnover is associated with higher training [OECD (1991, 1993)], a pattern that

---

17. The index of flexible working practices used here is the mean of adoption rates for fours sets of such practices, as measured in the EPOC survey for ten European countries: job rotation, team-based work organisation, involvement of lower-level employees and flattening of management structures [see Chapter 4 for details].

158 – OECD Employment Outlook

Chart 3.7. National differences in training participation and educational attainment[a]

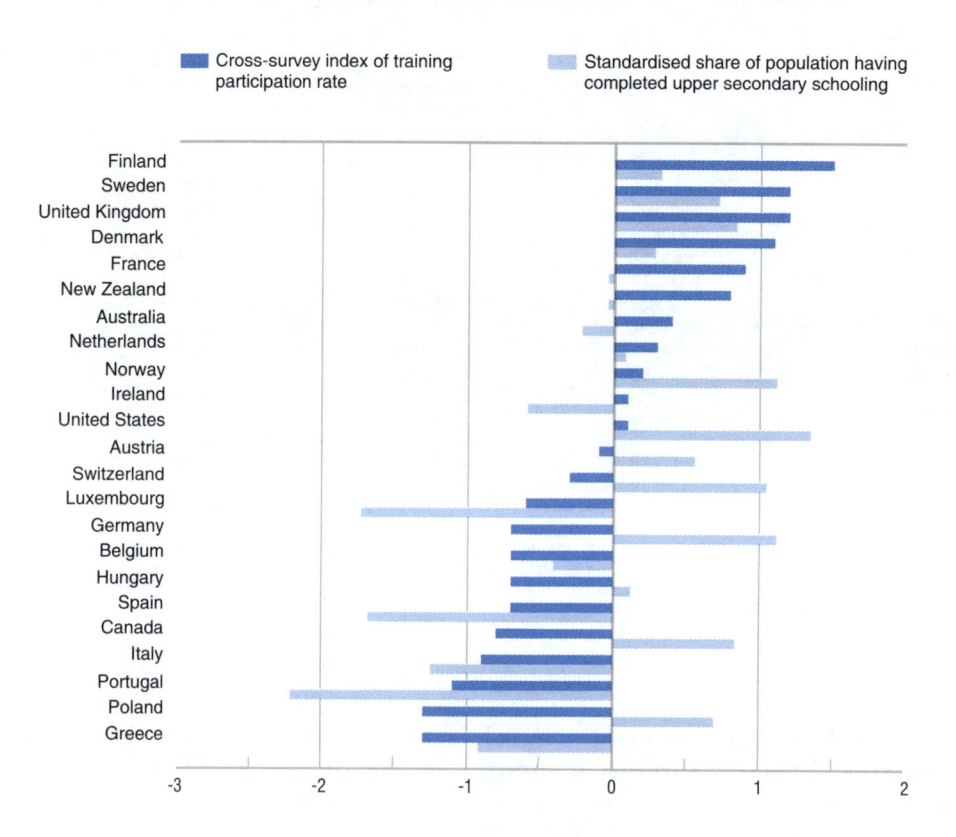

- Cross-survey index of training participation rate
- Standardised share of population having completed upper secondary schooling

Countries (ranked): Finland, Sweden, United Kingdom, Denmark, France, New Zealand, Australia, Netherlands, Norway, Ireland, United States, Austria, Switzerland, Luxembourg, Germany, Belgium, Hungary, Spain, Canada, Italy, Portugal, Poland, Greece

a) Countries are ranked in descending order of the cross-survey index of training participation rate.
Sources: See Table 3.1 and OECD (1998b).

is consistent with greater job stability increasing the returns to employers of investing in their workers' skills. That the opposite should be true for international comparisons suggest that high priority be assigned to further study of the links between turnover and training.[18]

Correlations between training and seven measures of earnings dispersion suggest that greater wage inequality generally is associated with lower training participation (Table 3.11, Panel B). However, this effect tends to be modest and statistically insignificant, suggesting that larger wage differentials have largely off-setting effects on the incentives to invest in training: larger wage dispersion increasing the incentives of workers to invest in training, so as to qualify for better paying jobs, but also reducing the incentives of employers to train their workers [Acemoglou and Pischke (1998, 1999)]. The participation index of training suggests that greater wage dispersion, higher incidence of low pay and especially a steeper age-earnings profile are a net discouragement to training,[19] but that the two opposing effects appear to cancel each other out for increases in the educational premium.

Table 3.11, Panel C reports correlations between the summary indicators of training levels and six measures of economic performance. Employment rates are higher, and unemployment rates lower, in countries with higher training. Similarly, the levels of mean earnings and GDP per capita are positively correlated with training, as is trade performance in "high tech" industries. However, the growth in labour productivity and GDP per capita over the

---

18. Several recent studies using data for single countries have also called the link between lower turnover and higher training into question [Goux and Maurin (1997); Vilhuber (1997, 1998)].
19. The negative correlation between training and a larger age premium in earnings is another instance of these cross-country associations differing from cross-worker associations within a country. The latter tend to show that workers receiving training have steeper age-earnings profiles.

Table 3.10. **Correlations of national measures of training with other measures of human capital and related investments**

Panel A. Training measures correlated with educational attainment and school spending

Training measures[a]	Percentage of population aged 25-64 years completing upper secondary education	Percentage of population aged 25-64 years completing a university degree	Educational expectancy of five-year-olds under current conditions, expected years of full- and part-time schooling	Educational expectancy of five-year-olds under current conditions, expected years of full-time schooling	School spending as a percentage of GDP, public spending	School spending as a percentage of GDP, public and private spending
Level						
Participation rate	0.37*	0.20	0.48**	0.29	0.49**	0.54**
Mean hours	−0.02	0.14	0.31	0.02	0.01	0.19
Cost share	0.66**	0.35	0.18	−0.33	0.07	0.29
Distribution						
Gender ratio, participation	−0.14	0.08	−0.10	−0.04	0.13	0.17
Age ratio, participation	−0.70**	−0.28	−0.29	−0.04	−0.30	−0.33
Education ratio, participation	−0.64**	−0.31	−0.25	−0.25	−0.23	−0.43*

Panel B. Training measures correlated with educational achievements

Training measures[a]	Mathematics achievement of eight graders, mean score	Mathematics achievement of eight graders, 25th percentile score	Mathematics achievement of eight graders, range from 75th to 25th percentile scores	Prose literacy of population aged 25-54 years, mean score	Prose literacy of population aged 25-54 years, percentage scoring at level 3 or higher	Prose literacy of population aged 25-54 years, range from 75th and 25th percentile scores
Level						
Participation rate	0.13	0.10	0.14	0.56*	0.59**	−0.13
Mean hours	−0.09	−0.13	0.05	0.36	0.36	0.04
Cost share	0.53	0.46	0.47	−0.09	−0.00	0.36
Distribution						
Gender ratio, participation	−0.23	−0.28	0.03	0.22	0.21	0.50*
Age ratio, participation	−0.34	−0.23	−0.58**	−0.09	−0.13	−0.37
Education ratio, participation	−0.59**	−0.51**	−0.59**	−0.24	−0.21	0.06

Panel C. Training measures correlated with related investments

Training measures[a]	ALMP spending as a percentage of GDP	R&D spending as a percentage of GDP, total	R&D spending as a percentage of GDP, excluding higher education	Researchers per 10 000 labour force	Gross fixed capital formation as a percentage of GDP	Gross fixed capital formation, machinery and equipment, as a percentage of GDP
Level						
Participation rate	0.50**	0.61**	0.61**	0.64**	−0.46**	−0.22**
Mean hours	0.16	0.01	0.02	0.05	0.10	0.04
Cost share	0.02	0.67**	0.68**	0.58*	−0.60**	−0.24**
Distribution						
Gender ratio, participation	0.08	−0.13	−0.10	−0.00	−0.41**	−0.60**
Age ratio, participation	−0.22	−0.44**	−0.41**	−0.54**	0.45**	0.27**
Education ratio, participation	−0.18	−0.54**	−0.53**	−0.60**	0.48**	0.28**

ALMP = Active labour market policies.
* Significant at the 10% level.
** Significant at the 5% level.
a) Cross-country indices of training from Tables 3.2, 3.3, 3.5, 3.6 and 3.7, except that the cost share estimates are based solely on the CVTS.
Sources: For data on training, see Table 3.1. Other data from OECD, 1998b; OECD (1998), National Accounts; OECD Main Science and Technology Indicators Database.

past decade was actually lower in countries with higher training.[20]

Associations between the distribution of training and the measures of labour market institutions and economic outcomes in Table 3.11 are overall difficult to interpret, but several cases merit comment. The age and education concentration of training is significantly lower where flexible work practices are more widespread. Conversely, training is more strongly concentrated on younger and better educated workers in countries with lower job turnover (and stricter EPL) and greater collective bargaining coverage and centralisation/co-ordination. Women receive more training relative to men where flexible work practices are more widespread, earnings dispersion is greater and unemployment rates higher, but lower relative training where the employment to population ratio is higher. A higher wage premium for education is associated with a greater concentration of training on more educated workers, but a higher wage premium for older workers is associated with a greater concentration of training on younger workers.

Overall, these international comparisons suggest that many of the implications of theoretical models of training, like many of the findings of empirical studies for one or a few countries, do not easily generalise to a broad cross-section of OECD economies. Clearly, there is much room for further study of the determinants of the incidence of training and its relationship to earnings and other economic outcomes. The next section uses detailed micro-data for select countries to examine several of these issues in greater depth than is possible with the limited training data that are available in the surveys analysed here.

III. Analyses of training probabilities and earnings of trainees

This section seeks to answer the following questions:

- Which factors are most important in explaining the probability that a worker gets trained? Does training accrue mainly to the higher educated? Is there a gender bias in training? Do small firms train less than larger ones?

- What is the statistical association between wages and training? Does the relationship between wages and training differ by gender and education level? Do workers get trained more in the presence of compressed wage distributions?

A. Main features of the datasets

The micro-data used for the analysis are drawn from surveys for Australia, Canada, France, Germany, Great Britain, Italy and the Netherlands (see Annex 3.B for details). These surveys have the advantage that the samples drawn are large enough to enable one to make reasonable inferences about the population of origin and the questionnaires allow one to investigate the determinants of training. Another advantage is that information on individual (hourly) wages is available so that it is possible to investigate the correlation between wages and training. Some datasets also ask questions on the permanent or temporary nature of the work contract. Firm size and sector of industrial activity are also recorded in all surveys.

Other aspects of the datasets include:

- They relate to representative national samples of employed individuals.

- Questions about training all relate to formal, off-the-job, training. This is normally meant to cover courses or seminars taken either at the firm or outside it.

- Training is defined as only that paid for or provided by the employer for Canada, France, Italy and the Netherlands; but it includes "job-related training" courses that employees may have paid for themselves for Australia, Germany and Great Britain. However, given that the samples are composed of individuals in paid employment, the overlap between job-related training and employer-provided training is likely to be quite large (see Section II).

- The reference period over which training is recorded is the year preceding the date of the interview,[21] with the exception of the Netherlands, where the question relates to training courses being undertaken at the time the survey was carried out.

---

20. While these associations are consistent with training having important effects on economic performance, it must be emphasised that these correlations could be "spurious". For example, the true *causal* link might be between higher educational attainment and higher labour productivity, rather than from higher training to higher productivity. The interpretation of the negative correlation between training and growth rates in the recent past merits particular caution, since training investments may only be reflected in growth with a lag.
21. For France and Germany, the question asks whether any training courses were taken in the past, respectively, five years, for France, and three years, for Germany. However, in these surveys the date of the last training course/s is recorded. This additional information was used to construct a variable that records training having taken place in the past year. In Great Britain, the reference period is actually slightly more than a year since the relevant question asks about any training undertaken since 1 September 1995 and the survey is carried out some time (shortly) after 1 September 1996.

Table 3.11. **Correlations of national measures of training with measures of labour market institutions and economic outcomes**

Panel A. Training measures correlated with labour market institutions

Training measures[a]	Index of the introduction of flexible work practices	Collective bargaining coverage rate	Trade union density	Strictness of EPL	Percentage of workforce with less than 1 year of tenure	Mean job tenure in years	Tax wedge
Level							
Participation rate	0.83**	0.02	0.44*	−0.42*	0.31	−0.39*	−0.07
Mean hours	−0.02	0.03	−0.21	−0.15	0.37	−0.43*	−0.12
Cost share	0.76**	−0.38	−0.17	−0.69**	0.08	−0.51*	−0.24
Distribution							
Gender ratio, participation	0.36	−0.10	0.36	−0.05	0.49**	−0.22	0.20
Age ratio, participation	−0.52	0.25	−0.48**	0.62**	0.00	0.11	−0.01
Education ratio, participation	−0.65**	0.06	−0.20	0.62**	−0.09	0.16	0.07

Panel B. Training measures correlated with earnings dispersion

Training measures[a]	Ratio of 90th to 10th percentiles	Ratio of 90th to 50th percentiles	Ratio of 50th to 10th percentiles	Low-pay as a percentage of full-time employment	Ratio women to men	Ratio 45-54 years old to 25-29 years old	Ratio university degree to less than upper secondary
	Full-time weekly earnings					Mean annual earnings	
Level							
Participation rate	−0.19	−0.14	−0.11	−0.38	0.02	−0.45*	0.05
Mean hours	0.02	0.03	−0.00	0.03	−0.09	−0.21	0.10
Cost share	0.01	−0.06	0.09	0.85*	−0.15	−0.62*	0.21
Distribution							
Gender ratio, participation	0.30	0.27	0.31	−0.05	−0.11	0.35	0.12
Age ratio, participation	0.20	0.24	0.05	−0.04	−0.06	0.41*	0.28
Education ratio, participation	0.10	0.18	−0.08	0.11	0.21	0.31	0.28

Panel C. Training measures correlated with economic outcomes

Training measures[a]	Mean employment to population ratio for the working age population, 1988-97	Mean unemployment rate for the total labour force, 1988-97	Mean earnings in PPP	GDP per capita in PPPs, 1997	Growth in labour productivity, annual rate for 1988-97	Growth in GDP per capita, annual rate for 1988-97	Trade coverage ratio (exports/imports) for "high tech" industries
Level							
Participation rate	0.56**	−0.18	0.28	0.33	−0.12	−0.19	0.37
Mean hours	0.06	−0.02	0.30	−0.07	−0.25	−0.15	−0.18
Cost share	0.49	−0.15	0.08	0.23	−0.17	−0.01	0.64**
Distribution							
Gender ratio, participation	−0.25	0.54**	−0.17	−0.16	0.17	0.09	−0.05
Age ratio, participation	−0.58**	0.29	−0.29	−0.31	0.07	0.24	−0.09
Education ratio, participation	−0.44**	0.04	−0.38	−0.44**	0.06	0.08	−0.34

EPL = Employment protection legislation.
PPP = Purchasing power parities.
* Significant at the 10% level.
** Significant at the 5% level.
a) Cross-country indices of training from Tables 3.2, 3.3, 3.5, 3.6 and 3.7, except that the cost share estimates are based solely on the CVTS.
Sources: For data on training, see Table 3.1. Other data from the OECD Earnings Database; OECD (1998), *National Accounts*; OECD *Labour Force Statistics 1987-1997*, Part III; and Chapters 2 and 4 of this volume.

B. Results of estimation of models of the probability of being trained

The probability of being trained is specified as a dichotomous variable, taking the value of one if workers are trained and zero otherwise. A probit model is estimated by maximum likelihood techniques. The impact of individual and firm characteristics on the training probability is modelled by means of the following explanatory variables: age; education level; gender; type of contract, either permanent or temporary; tenure with the current employer; hours of work; firm size; public or private sector; and industrial sector (more details are given in Table 3.B.2 in Annex 3.B). A quadratic in tenure with the current employer is specified to allow for non-linearities in the relationship between job-related training and tenure. According to the standard theory, employers are more likely to train workers that will stay longer at the firm. However, the training probability is bound to be higher for a given worker in the first years of employment tenure. Issues of the potential endogeneity of tenure, and also of hours of work and type of contract, are not taken up in this analysis.

Results of estimation of models of the probability of being trained are shown in Table 3.12. The main findings are:

- Less-educated workers are significantly less likely to be trained in all countries considered except the Netherlands. This is important as most policies fail to affect the distribution of training across different categories of workers. Moreover, the labour market situation of less-skilled workers has deteriorated in many OECD countries [OECD (1997d)].
- Large establishments are significantly more likely to train workers.
- Workers on temporary contracts and in part-time jobs are significantly less likely to be trained. This is an especially important finding given the trend towards the increasing number of these types of contracts in most OECD countries [Chapter 1].
- Public sector employees are significantly more likely to be trained.
- Workers in finance, insurance and business or community, social and personal services are more likely to be trained compared with other industries.
- Training probabilities decrease significantly with age in Germany and the Netherlands; but less so in other countries.
- The training probability decreases significantly with tenure at an increasing rate in Australia, while it increases with tenure in Italy and Great Britain.

Notwithstanding large cross-countries differences in the amount of training provided, there are common patterns in the allocation of training that emerge from this analysis. In particular, the finding that less-educated workers get less on-the-job training confirms the conclusions of Section II and raises some policy concerns. Also important for policy is the conclusion that small firms provide less (formal) training of workers.

C. Results on the relation between training and wages

The relationship between wages and training has been the focus of a number of empirical and theoretical studies that have stressed the importance of the wage effect as a measure of training gains. Recent work, as reviewed in Section I and in Table 3.A.1, has brought up the following issues:

- The earnings gains from training are higher for some categories of workers that are, on the other hand, less likely to be trained: the mid-educated workers in the United Kingdom [Blundell *et al.* (1996)] workers that receive "remedial" training in the United States [Bartel (1995)]; and women in (west) Germany [Pischke (1996)].
- Employers have more incentives to train if the wage distribution is more compressed because the gains from training are not passed entirely on to wages [Acemoglou and Pischke (1998, 1999)].

The first group of studies have carefully dealt with the potential endogeneity of training variables entered in earnings regressions, (see Section I). The hypothesis about the impact of wage compression may require one to use information on institutions such as collective bargaining or minimum wages legislation to control for possible sources of wage compression. This is outside the scope of the analysis carried out here that draws on individual-level data. Rather, here the analysis investigates the statistical association of wages and training. Gross hourly wages, observed at the time of the surveys (*i.e.* at the end of the period over which training is recorded) are used for this purpose. For the Netherlands, these are contemporaneous wages as training is recorded at the time of the survey.

In Table 3.13, the mean wages of workers trained are compared with the mean wages of workers not trained. The earnings "gains" for workers trained are computed as the proportional difference between the two.

Workers trained have higher mean wages than those not trained. However, the proportional earnings differences vary considerably in size from country to country. The proportional earnings "gains" for all workers are the largest in Italy. As shown in the preceding section, Italy is one of the countries that rank lowest in terms of the quantity of job-related training provided. In addition, university graduates reap the least "benefits" from training in most countries considered. Finally, women get the highest wage gains from training compared with men in Australia, France and Great Britain. In France, it is workers with less than lower secondary schooling that benefit most from training.

However, these earnings differences may be explained by factors other than training. More light on this issue may be shed by econometric analysis of wages and training. Results of the estimation of wage regressions using ordinary least squares are shown in Table 3.14. The natural logarithm of gross hourly wages is regressed on the following explanatory variables: age; gender; job tenure; hours of work; nature of the contract; firm size; public sector employee; and industrial sector. Interaction variables of training and gender, and training and education levels have been included in the model to capture the impact of training on wages.

The estimation results indicate that there is a significantly positive relationship between training and wages, except for the Netherlands, France and Italy. The result for the Netherlands may be due to the absence of a time lag between the times at which training and wages are observed. Previous studies for the Netherlands find a significantly positive impact of training on future wages [Groot (1994)]. The results for France and Italy are, instead, in line with previous findings in the literature, using the same datasets [Goux and Maurin (1997); Brunello and Miniaci (1999)].

For France, Italy, the Netherlands and Great Britain, there is a significant positive relationship between wages and training of less-educated workers. This finding provides some support for the argument that the lower educated, *when trained*, realise larger wage gains. On the other hand, it may also be a spurious result, driven by the correlation of unobservables that determine both the wage rate and the probability of being trained.

The interaction between women and training is insignificant in all countries except for Germany, where it is significantly positive. This confirms previous findings for Germany that women who get training realise more significant earnings gains than men [Pischke (1996)].

The possible endogeneity of training is controlled for by applying Heckman's two-stage procedure. This consists of including among the explanatory variables a term summarising information obtained from separate estimation of a probit of training. The additional term is significantly negative, which indicates the presence of some selection bias.[22]

On the basis of these findings, it may be concluded that, as argued in recent literature, the earnings gains from training are higher for some categories of workers who are, on the other hand, less likely to be trained. The evidence gathered also cannot reject the hypothesis that employers have more incentives to train workers in countries where the wage distribution is more compressed. However, given the limitations of the analysis carried out here, more work is needed to draw robust conclusions on these issues.

IV. What policies are in place for improving access to training for employees?

From the empirical analysis carried out in Sections II and III some policy concerns arise. The findings that less-educated workers; workers on part-time or temporary contracts and employees of small firms tend to receive relatively little training raise not only equity but also efficiency concerns. Lower training participation may worsen the labour market position of already disadvantaged categories of workers. This may lead to considerable costs in terms of loss of potential output, skill deterioration and future unemployment. Furthermore, it has emerged that training of workers takes place in some countries at a much lower rate than in others. This may signal some market failure in the allocation of training that may lead to lower productivity, worse economic performance and lower economic growth. This is especially important as recent theories stress the importance of human capital accumulation for economic growth. In particular, it has been argued that lower training rates may contribute to creating "low-skill-bad-job" traps such that firms have little incentives to upgrade their workers' skills and to invest in more productive activities [Booth and Snower (1996)].

Generally, it is very hard to establish whether the observed rates of training are "optimal" from the perspective of the individual, the firm and society. This is the more so as the costs and benefits of training to these different actors are very difficult to evaluate. Even if it were possible to conclude that observed training rates are "sub-optimal", this may not imply that government intervention

---

22. A general problem with any procedure to control for endogeneity of training is that of finding suitable instruments that affect training but not earnings. Here, the marital status presence, young children and their interaction with gender were used for this purpose. Functional form differences may also act as to identify training.

Table 3.12. **Results of estimation of probits of the probability of being trained**[a]

	Australia	Canada[b]	France	Germany	Italy	Netherlands	Great Britain
Intercept	0.49**	−0.27	−1.50**	−0.68**	−1.47**	−1.27**	0.35**
Woman	0.05*	−0.26	0.01	0.11	−0.11*	−0.12	0.15**
Age group 35-44	−0.03	−0.06	−0.14**	−0.12*	−0.04	−0.21**	0.00
Age group 45-54	−0.02	−0.18	−0.19**	−0.45**	−0.10	−0.39**	0.04
Tenure	−0.03**	0.11**	0.03**	−0.00	0.02	−0.01	−0.00**
Tenure squared	0.00**	−0.00**	−0.00**	0.00*	−0.00	−0.00	0.00
Less than upper secondary	−0.26**	−1.54**	−0.45**	−1.02**	−0.63**	0.01	−0.54**
Upper secondary	−0.18**	−0.43**	−0.12**	−0.37**	−0.08	0.13	−0.33**
Large firm size	0.08**	0.46**	0.48**	0.23**	..	0.24**	0.26**
Part-time work	−0.08**	−0.97**	−0.31**	−0.34**	0.12	−0.22*	−0.39**
Temporary job	−0.33**	−0.42	−0.34**	−0.25	..	..	−0.24**
Public sector	0.11**	..	0.02	0.38**	..	0.07	0.34**
Married	..	−0.21	0.15**	0.24**	0.14**	0.08	0.15**
Child less than 6	−0.05	..	−0.05	..	−0.04	0.10	0.03
Woman × child less than 6	−0.05	..	−0.20**	..	−0.01	−0.08	−0.27*
Married woman	..	0.16	..	−0.24**	..	..	..
Agriculture	..	..	−0.17	−5.49*	−0.51*	0.08	−0.09
Electricity, gas and water	0.38**	..	−0.25*	0.38**	..	−0.07	0.44**
Construction	−0.20**	..	−0.22**	−0.24	−0.52**	−0.18*	0.05
Wholesale and retail trade, restaurants	0.08*	..	−0.06	0.02	0.02	−0.26	0.14*
Transport and communication	0.07	..	0.01	0.15**	−0.03	−0.20	0.09
Finance, insurance and business services	0.28**	..	0.06	0.52**	0.57**	0.18	0.37**
Community, social and personal services	0.13**	..	0.03	0.28**	0.20**	0.15	0.23**
Number of observations	12 821	1 556	8 286	3 442	5 229	2 544	3 117

.. Data not available.
* Significant at the 10% level.
** Significant at the 5% level.
a) Figures have been rounded to the second decimal point.
b) Due to the pilot nature of the data, the specification for Canada is different.
Source: See Annex 3.B.

Table 3.13. **Proportional mean wage differences for workers trained**[a]

Percentages

	Australia	Canada	France	Germany	Italy	Netherlands	Great Britain
All	9.6	26.4	11.1	18.5	25.0	3.1	19.3
Men	9.6	32.0	17.2	17.6	29.1	0.0	15.1
Women	11.2	12.2	20.7	16.5	20.0	−2.3	25.0
Less than upper secondary	6.9	..	30.2	16.0	15.7	17.6	20.2
Upper secondary	8.6	..	16.1	9.5	23.8	0.7	4.3
Non-university tertiary	4.2	..	2.3	−7.6	..	−0.3	19.8
University	1.8	..	−1.3	17.9	6.8	−15.9	3.0

.. Data not available.
a) Mean earnings of workers trained minus mean earnings of workers not trained, divided by mean earnings of workers not trained.
Source: See Annex 3.B.

Table 3.14. **Results of estimation of OLS wage regressions with selection**[a, b]

Dependent variable: log of gross hourly wage

	Australia	Canada[c]	France	Germany	Italy	Netherlands	Great Britain
Intercept	2.42**	1.89	11.57**	3.85**	2.48**	4.31**	1.64**
Woman	–0.13**	–0.20**	–0.21**	–0.23**	–0.14**	–0.09**	–0.26**
Age group 35-44	0.04**	..	0.11**	0.12**	0.07**	0.17**	0.05**
Age group 45-54	0.07**	..	0.15**	0.25**	0.09**	0.31**	0.02
Tenure	–0.00	0.02**	0.01**	0.00**	0.01**	0.02**	0.00**
Tenure squared	0.00*	0.00*	–0.00**	–0.00**	–0.00**	–0.00**	–0.00**
Less than upper secondary	–0.48**	–0.27**	–0.60**	0.10	–0.37**	–0.37**	–0.13**
Upper secondary	–0.33**	–0.11**	–0.40**	–0.07**	–0.24**	–0.28**	–0.04
Large firm size	0.06**	0.20**	0.16**	0.01	..	–0.03	0.06*
Part-time work	0.19**	–0.27**	–0.16**	0.12**	0.26**	0.12**	–0.09*
Temporary job	–0.36**	0.01	–0.09**	0.06	..	..	–0.02
Public sector	0.09**	..	–0.04**	–0.16**	..	–0.09**	0.08
Agriculture	..	..	–0.28**	2.58**	–0.13**	–0.17**	–0.29**
Electricity, gas and water	0.14**	..	–0.07**	–0.08	..	0.15**	0.07
Construction	–0.16**	..	–0.04*	0.10**	–0.04**	0.06	–0.04
Wholesale and retail trade, restaurants	–0.08**	..	0.04**	–0.11**	–0.02	0.06	–0.26**
Transport and communication	0.04**	..	0.04*	–0.18**	0.06**	0.10**	–0.02
Finance, insurance and business services	0.21**	..	0.09**	–0.16**	0.07**	–0.01	0.17**
Community, social and personal services	0.01	..	–0.06**	–0.11**	0.06**	–0.05*	–0.10**
Had training	0.05**	0.14**	0.00	0.08**	0.38**	–0.04	0.74**
Training × woman	–0.00	–0.02	0.03	0.09**	–0.00	–0.02	0.04
Training × less than upper secondary	0.02	0.02	0.16**	–0.01	0.26**	0.17**	0.09**
Training × upper secondary	–0.01	–0.04	0.07**	–0.04	0.22**	0.04	0.03
Selection	0.94**	..	0.07	–0.55**	–0.23**	–0.58**	–0.44**
Adjusted R-squared	0.23	0.27	0.37	0.34	0.38	0.32	0.30
Number of observations	12 609	1 556	8 179	3 093	5 212	2 457	3 117

.. Data not available.
* Significant at the 10% level.
** Significant at the 5% level.
a) A correction for possible endogeneity of training is made using Heckman's two steps method; the selection used is the probit in Table 3.12.
b) Figures have been rounded to the second decimal point.
c) Due to the pilot nature of the data, the specification for Canada is different; regressors include a polynomial in age, a marital status dummy and the log of worked hours.
Source: See Annex 3.B.

in this area is desirable, because of the possible further distortions introduced by it in the market that may outweigh the benefits. In particular, it may be difficult to intervene effectively in an area which is typically the domain of the private sector. Indeed, while all OECD countries provide public education; very few provide public training of workers (an exception here being Denmark).

Despite these uncertainties, there is broad political support for public support of training and most OECD countries have policies that affect, either directly or indirectly, the training of workers. These range from tax-deductibility of training expenses to training levies that legislate compulsory spending on training of workers and to other policies that may indirectly affect training, such as equality of opportunity laws. It is outside the scope of this study to review and evaluate such policies especially given the limited information available on this topic to date. Nonetheless, a brief overview is provided of the policies in place.

One strategy is to focus on creating the right environment for firms to train their workers, rather than legislating compulsory spending on training. Governments may act so as to raise the incentives to train for employers and employees by, for example, improving access to relevant information, improving the recognition of skills acquired through training, and improving flexibility with respect to the capacity to exploit and make use of the acquired skills and competencies [Wurzburg (1998)]. More targeted policies may be needed, however, especially to equalise the distribution of training across workers and firms of different size.

Most countries allow for the immediate and full tax deductibility of training expenses incurred by firms. The tax rules allowing training costs to be "expenses" rather than treated as an investment that is amortised over a period of years, lowers the cost of training relative to investments in physical capital. However, the associated accounting convention may discourage investment in training since firms' financial statements provide little or no indication of the competitive asset that a better trained workforce represents [O'Connor (1998)]. Some countries allow individuals to deduct some share of training expenses from taxable income, but few, if any, allow all expenses to be deducted.

Targeted, fiscal incentives are used to encourage the training of specific categories of workers. The Netherlands have legislated in the 1997 budget larger tax discounts on training expenses of small-and-medium-sized enterprises and on any training directed at older workers, above forty. No evaluation of such programme is available yet.

Some countries, among them France, Belgium and Denmark, grant workers a right to paid training leave [Gasskov (1998)]. This option is interesting especially since it is directed at the individual worker who can choose to take-up the scheme. On the other hand, it may present the disadvantage that the training initiative is taken by the worker rather than by the employer and may not correspond to the firm's needs. Moreover, in France beneficiaries of the programme must have an indefinite work contract, which implies that temporary workers are excluded; in Belgium the scheme is restricted to full-time workers. In Denmark, since the introduction of the programme in the mid-1990s, participation rates have been quite high. However, the programme was designed mainly for the long-term unemployed, that constituted a serious problem for the country since the late eighties, rather than as a means to encourage more training of workers. Generally, it is likely to be the more educated workers that will make use of their right to paid training leave.

Other countries have tax levies that oblige employers to spend a certain percentage of their total wage bill on training. If firms fail to comply, they have to pay the corresponding amount to the government. France was one of the first OECD countries to introduce a tax levy policy, back in 1971. The percentage of the wage bill to be spent on training has been increased several times and it is currently set at 1.5 per cent. The threshold wage bill that regulates participation into the programme is currently set at a level that corresponds roughly to a firm size of above ten employees. Korea implemented a training levy in the mid-1970s that was abolished in 1998, after having earlier restricted the programme to firms with more than a thousand employees. Australia introduced a training levy on employers in 1990 to abolish it few years later in 1994. Quebec introduced a training levy in the mid-1990s.

The levies have generally resulted in an increase in the overall quantity of training and have provided clear incentives for participating firms to formulate a training plan [Fraser (1996)]. However, the empirical evidence suggests that existing levies are not very effective with respect to small and medium-sized enterprises that have often opted to pay the levy rather than provide training [Fraser (1996); Brochier et al. (1997); Gasskov (1998); Ministry of Labor, Republic of Korea (1996)].[23] They also do not affect the distribution of training across different categories of workers as most of the training goes to higher-educated and more skilled workers, just as it does in countries that do not operate a levy scheme.

Denmark and the Netherlands have training funds that are run by collective agreements between employers and unions and that are also supplemented by government funds. In Denmark, the programme is more centralised and training is provided by public training institutions (AMU) to both the employed and the unemployed. These programmes appear to be quite responsive to the different training needs of specific industrial sectors and local labour markets.

In the EU, training of workers has also been promoted by programmes set-up under the activities of the European Social Fund to facilitate the adaptation of workers to industrial change and to changes in production systems. Another such programme is ADAPT, which has focused on the problems, needs and potential of small firms. However, most of the burden of setting up training programmes and funding them has remained with member countries. From the scant evidence available, it seems that such programmes were perhaps more successful in raising training rates in countries where EU funding contribution was more substantial such as Ireland, Portugal and Greece. However, not much evaluation of these programmes has so far been available.

Policies not explicitly targeted at training may also affect training efforts indirectly. For example, in the United States, there is some evidence that Affirmative Action policies have positively affected the training of women and minorities [Holzer and Neumark (1998)]. The authors conclude that firms that make use of Affirmative Action tend to screen more extensively; they hire more women and minority workers and provide more training to their employees. In these establishments, the job performance of women and minority workers is as high as that of other comparable workers.

---

23. The direct and indirect costs of formal training courses may be relatively higher for small and medium sized firms that may find it difficult to replace workers that undertake a course. Small firms may also require different skills from their workers than those provided by available training courses.

Conclusions

Should public policy attempt to expand or redirect the training received by incumbent workers after the period of initial vocational training? While there is no consensus on this question, Member country governments pursue a number of policies directed toward these ends. That the level and distribution of training differs significantly among OECD countries is supportive of the belief that appropriate policies can create an environment that encourages employers and workers to invest in continuing training. That the typical worker devotes more than 1 000 hours to formal training, between the ages of 25 and 64, is also supportive of the importance of continuing training for achieving the goal of life-long learning. Unfortunately, the analysis of the determinants and consequences of training is not yet sufficiently developed to provide policy makers with reliable estimates of the economic returns that accrue to any specific policy approaches. Further harmonisation of training statistics could make an important contribution to filling that gap. Nonetheless, it is possible to draw several tentative conclusions with the limited data currently available.

The strong link between national levels of educational attainment and achievement, on the one hand, and the level of workforce training, on the other, suggests that an indirect strategy of strengthening schooling is a potent – if slow – means of encouraging continuing training. These links also confirm that education and training policies should be assessed as an integrated system affecting learning over the life course [OECD (1996a)]. It is particularly striking that training rates are relatively low in countries where the literacy scores of the adult population are lower and more unequal. A key step in encouraging worker training is to ensure that all individuals enter the world of work with the basic knowledge and learning skills needed to insure their subsequent trainability.

Another finding of potential importance for policy making is that a key distinguishing feature of high-training economies is that participation in training is more evenly distributed across age and educational groups. Policies enhancing the incentives and resources for investing in the continuing training of those workers who typically receive little training may, thus, be of particular importance. Programmes to minimise school failure and early school drop-outs have received increased attention recently, as a part of efforts to protect at-risk youths from a future of economic marginality and social exclusion [OECD (1995)]. Success in bringing all individuals up to a minimum threshold of general education and literacy might also make an important contribution toward a broadening and deepening of enterprise-centred training and higher overall prosperity. However, such an approach will only gradually raise the skill level of the workforce and policies to expand the training received by the current adult workforce may also be desirable.

Internationally comparative research on worker training is not yet sufficiently advanced to assess the desirability of policies designed to affect training patterns more directly. Options here include minimally interventionist measures, which are intended to create a more supportive environment for employers and employees to invest in continuing training. For example, the limited evidence available suggests that policies encouraging the diffusion of flexible working practices [Chapter 4] or providing certification services that facilitate the recognition of skills acquired through training [OECD (1997e)], may indirectly encourage greater training. More interventionist measures, such as mandatory training levies and direct provision of training have also been tried in a number of Member countries. The now extensive evaluation literature on active labour market policies suggests that the effectiveness of any such measures will be dependent on good programme design and administration [OECD (1996b)]. Evaluations of a similar rigour would be highly desirable for the broader range of policies that have been used – or proposed – to enhance the training received by the employed workforce.

Annex 3.A

Overview of Findings from Recent Studies of Job-Related Training

Table 3.A.1. **An overview of main findings from recent studies of job-related training**

Authors	Country and data sources	Main findings
Arulampalam and Booth (1998b)	United Kingdom, British National Child Development Study of men only.	Training incidence has a significant large positive impact on wage growth, after controlling for its endogeneity. The number of training courses undertaken has no significant impact on wage growth. There is a strong positive correlation between the number of training courses and educational qualifications.
Bartel (1995)	Personnel records from a large American company.	A large and significant impact of formal training on employee's wage growth is found after controlling for selection bias. The effect is larger for "remedial" training, targeted at individuals that have low relative status in the job. Significant positive effects of training on job performance.
Black and Lynch (1996)	US establishment data.	The duration of off-the-job training has a positive impact on productivity.
Blundell et al. (1996)	United Kingdom, British National Child Development Study.	Formal off-the-job training especially increases the wages of individuals with intermediate schooling, who are, on the other hand, less likely to obtain training. More-educated people are more likely to be trained; and men are more likely to be trained than women. The duration of training courses has a significant positive impact on wages. Training provided by a previous employer has a positive impact on wages, as well as training with the current employer.
Boon (1998)	Netherlands, linked firm-level data, Central Bureau of Statistics, 1991 and 1993.	Investment in training has a positive effect on firm's value added.
Booth (1991)	United Kingdom, British Social Attitudes Survey, 1987.	There are significant positive effects of formal job-related training on wages. Men receive more training, but the positive wage effects are larger for women. Training is treated as exogenous.
Goux and Maurin (1997)	France, matched firm-worker data; Enquête sur la Formation et la Qualification Professionnelle, 1993, and Bénéfices Industriels et Commerciaux.	Training efforts are concentrated in occupations in the middle of the work hierarchy, *i.e.* technicians, foremen. Firms with higher mean wages train their workers more. While a positive impact of formal firm-training on wages is found, it disappears when firm and individual selection effects are controlled for. A three simultaneous equations model is estimated that contains a wage equation, a probability of training equation and an equation for the probability that the worker quits the firm. The impact of training on the probability of quitting the firm is small and insignificant.
Loewenstein and Spletzer (1997)	United States, National Longitudinal Survey of Youth, 1988 to 1991.	Formal training, beyond the first year of tenure, has a significant positive impact on wages, after controlling for the endogeneity of training and measurement error. Individuals who received previous training in the current job are more likely to be trained again in the current year.
Loewenstein and Spletzer (1998)	United States, National Longitudinal Survey of Youth, 1988 to 1991.	Employers seem to pay for most general training, like courses and seminars provided outside of the firm premises. Completed spells of training with previous employers have a larger positive effect on wages than completed spells of training with the current employer. This indicates that training is general and employers share the costs of it.
Pischke (1996)	Germany, Socio-economic Panel, 1989, that asked special questions on continuous training.	Returns to training are significantly positive for women, but insignificant for men. Training is mostly provided by employers. Individuals do not undertake much training at their expense. Training appears to be more general than firm-specific. Training is distributed very unequally: the more-skilled receive a disproportionate share of the training.
Regner (1995 and 1997)	Sweden, the Swedish Level of Living Survey, 1981, 1991.	Training is split into general or specific according to respondents' subjective answers. Most training is considered general. The returns to training are large and significant. There is no empirical evidence of a relationship between training and tenure at the firm.
Veum (1995)	United States, National Longitudinal Survey of Youth, 1986 to 1990.	Company training and seminars outside work have a positive impact on wages. Other forms of training do not impact on wages. The duration of the training does not affect wages.
Vilhuber (1997, 1998)	United States, National Longitudinal Survey of Youth, 1979 to 1993. Germany, Socio-economic Panel, 1989, 1993.	Workers mobility patterns indicate that employer-provided training is sector-specific or general rather than firm-specific.

Annex 3.B

Data Sources, Definitions and Methods for the Analysis in Section III

The data used in Section III are drawn from household surveys for France, Germany, Great Britain, Italy, the Netherlands, and from the employees' files from matched employer-employee surveys for Australia and Canada. The Canadian data are drawn from a pilot survey. The datasets used and the training questions asked are described in Table 3.B.1.

The sample selected for analysis consists of employees, excluding the self-employed and apprentices, aged between 25 and 54 years. Only workplaces with more than 20 employees were surveyed for Australia.

The analysis has been carried out partly by the OECD Secretariat and partly by the following individuals: Wiji Arulampalam Narendranathan, Department of Economics, Warwick University, United Kingdom; Jean-David Fermanian and Marc-Antoine Estrade at *Division Emploi*, INSEE, Paris, France; Bill Harley, Department of Management, University of Melbourne, Australia; Raffaele Miniaci, Department of Economics, University of Padova, Italy; Garnett Picot, Marie Drolet and Robert Kopersievich at Statistics Canada, Canada.

The descriptive tabulations and econometric analysis were carried out both with and without population weights. For Italy, weights were only available on a household rather than on an individual basis, and the unweighted statistics are presented. Unweighted statistics are also presented for Great Britain, France, Italy and the Netherlands. However, weighted statistics are presented for Germany, and for countries for which the sample dataset is drawn from the population of workplaces, rather than from the population of individuals, *i.e.* for Australia and Canada.

The variables used in the econometrics analysis are defined in Table 3.B.2.

Table 3.B.1. Data sources for the analysis in Section III

Country	Dataset, year	Question on training
Australia	Australian Workplace Industrial Relations Survey, 1995.	Has your employer provided you with any of the following training over the last 12 months? Include any training which is provided or paid by your employer and training to help you do your job.
Canada	Workplace and Employee Survey, 1995.	In the past twelve months have you participated in any formal training programmes related to your job?
France	Enquête sur la Formation et la Qualification Professionnelle, 1993.	Have you followed any training course organised and paid for, at least partially, by your employer, after completing your schooling? Which is the starting and ending date of the most recent course followed?
Germany	Socio-economic Panel, 1993; special section on employer-provided training.	Have you taken courses for occupational advancement in the last three years? Please, give the year when the most recent training course started and ended.
Great Britain	British Household Panel, 1996.	Since 1 September 1995, have you taken part in any education or training schemes or courses, as part of your present employment?
Italy	Bank of Italy survey, 1991; special supplement on employer-provided training.	Have you been on a training course organised and paid for by your employer in 1991?
Netherlands	Socio-economic Panel, 1994.	Are you currently following any training or education course that is paid for by your employer?

Table 3.B.2. **Definitions of variables for the econometric analysis in Section III**

Variable name	Definition	Countries' specificities
Training dummy	Equal to 1 if trained, 0 otherwise.	
Wage	Gross hourly wage.	Netherlands: only individuals who worked 12 months in the previous years are selected here, since usual hours of work in the reference week are asked in the current year survey and wages and months of work in the following tax year survey. France: the hourly wage is derived from INSEE computations of equivalent yearly earnings, since hours of work are not available.
Age		Dummies take the value of 1 when individuals belonging to that age group are entered. The excluded group is age 25-35.
Woman	Dummy that takes value 1 for women; 0 otherwise.	
Married	Dummy that takes value 1 if individual is married; 0, otherwise.	Australia: marital status is not available.
Child less than 6	Dummy equal to 1 if children younger than 6 are present and 0 otherwise.	
Tenure	Tenure with current employer.	
Part-time work	Dummy equal to 1 if hours less or equal to 30; 0, otherwise.	
ISCED 2	Dummy equal to 1, if education level is less than upper secondary education. Base is higher education (ISCED = 5, 6, 7).	
ISCED 3	Dummy equal to 1, if education level is upper secondary education. Base is higher education (ISCED = 5, 6, 7).	
Large firm	Dummy equal to 1 if firm size is larger than 100 employees.	Germany: the threshold firm size is 200 employees.
Temporary work	Dummy equal to 1 if contract is temporary; 0, otherwise.	Definitions vary across countries.
Public sector	Dummy equal to 1 if employed in the public sector.	Germany and the Netherlands: civil servants rather than broad public sector workers are covered here.
Industry dummies	One-digit SIC industrial sector dummies. The reference group includes mining and manufacturing.	Germany: an additional dummy for other sectors is included; results not shown in Tables 3.12 and 3.14.

BIBLIOGRAPHY

ABOWD, J.M., FINER, H. and KRAMARZ, F. (1998),
"Determinants of Compensation: An Analysis of Matched Longitudinal American Employer and Employee Data", National Bureau of Economic Research and INSEE-CREST, mimeo.

ABOWD, J.M., KRAMARZ, F. and MARGOLIS, D.N. (1994),
"High Wage Workers and High Wage Firms", National Bureau of Economic Research, Working Paper No. 4917.

ACEMOGLOU, D. (1998),
"Changes in Unemployment and Wage Inequality: An Alternative Theory and Some Evidence", National Bureau of Economic Research, Working Paper No. 6658.

ACEMOGLOU, D. and PISCHKE, J.S. (1998),
"The Structure of Wages and Investment in General Training", National Bureau of Economic Research, Working Paper No. 6357.

ACEMOGLOU, D. and PISCHKE, J.S. (1999),
"Beyond Becker: Training in Imperfect Labor Markets", *The Economic Journal*, February, pp. 112-142.

AKERLOF, G. A. (1984),
"Gift Exchange and Efficiency Wages: Four Views", *American Economic Review*, May, pp. 79-83.

ARULAMPALAM, W. and BOOTH A.L. (1998*a*),
"Training and Labour Market Flexibility: Is there a Trade-Off?", mimeo, forthcoming in the *British Journal of Industrial Relations*.

ARULAMPALAM, W. and BOOTH A.L. (1998*b*),
"Learning and Earning: Do Multiple Training Events Pay? A Decade of Evidence from a Cohort of Young British Men", Warwick University and Essex University, mimeo.

BARTEL, A.P. (1995),
"Training, Wage Growth, and Job Performance: Evidence from a Company Database", *Journal of Labor Economics*, No. 3, pp. 401-425.

BECKER, G.S. (1964),
Human Capital: A Theoretical Analysis with Special Reference to Education, Columbia University Press, New York.

BERGSTRÖM, V. and PANAS, E.E. (1992),
"How Robust is the Capital-Skill Complementarity Hypothesis?", *Review of Economics and Statistics*, No. 2, pp. 540-552.

BLACK, S. and LYNCH, L.M. (1996),
"Human Capital Investments and Productivity", *American Economic Review*, May, pp. 263-267.

BLAU, F. and KAHN, L. (1996),
"International Differences in Male Wage Inequality: Institutions versus Market Forces", *Journal of Political Economy*, August, pp. 791-837.

BLUNDELL, R., DEARDEN, L. and MEGHIR, C. (1996),
The Determinants and Effects of Work-Related Training in Britain, The Institute for Fiscal Studies (IFS), London.

BOON, M. (1998),
"Employee Training in the Dutch Manufacturing: Determinants and Productivity Effects", Statistics Netherlands, mimeo.

BOOTH, A.L. (1991),
"Job-Related Formal Training: Who Receives it and What is it Worth?", *Oxford Bulletin of Economics and Statistics*, August, pp. 281-294.

BOOTH, A.L. and SNOWER, D.J. (1996),
Acquiring Skills. Market Failures, Their Symptoms and Policy Responses, Cambridge University Press, United Kingdom.

BROCHIER, D., CADETTE, J.P., HANCHANE, S., LECOUTRE, M., MIROCHNITCHENKO, K., VERDIER, E. and VERNOUX, I. (1997),
"Les aides publiques à la formation continue dans les enterprises: quelles modalités d'évaluation?", Centre d'Études et de Recherches sur les Qualifications (CEREQ), Document No. 124, Serie Évaluation, Marseille, France.

BRUNELLO, G. and MINIACI, R. (1999),
"Training Probabilities and Earnings Gains in Italy", Department of Economics, Padova University, Italy, mimeo, March.

BURDETT, K. and CUNNINGHAM, E.J. (1998),
"Toward a Theory of Vacancies", *Journal of Labor Economics,* No. 3, pp. 445-478.

DE GRIP, A. and HOEVENBERG, J. (1996),
"Upgrading in the European Union", Research Centre for Education and the Labour Market (ROA), Maastricht, Research Memorandum No. 1996/3E.

DfEE and Cabinet Office (1996),
The Skills Audit: A Report from an Interdepartmental Group, London.

EUROSTAT (1996),
The European Union Labour Force Survey: Methods and Definitions 1996, Luxembourg.

EUROSTAT (1997),
Continuing Vocational Training Survey in Enterprises: Results, Luxembourg.

FRASER, D. (1996),
"The Training Guarantee: Its Impact and Legacy 1990-94", Australian Department of Employment, Education, Training and Youth Affairs, Evaluation and Monitoring Branch (EMB) Report 5/96.

FRAZIS, H., GITTLEMAN, M., HORRIGAN, M.W. and JOYCE, M. (1998),
"Results from the 1995 Survey of Employer-Provided Training", *Monthly Labor Review,* June, pp. 3-13.

GASSKOV, V. (1998),
"Levies, Leave and Collective Agreements Incentives for Enterprises and Individuals to Invest in Training", European Centre for the Development of Vocational Training (CEDEFOP), *Vocational Training,* No. 13, pp. 27-36.

GOUX, D. and MAURIN, E. (1997),
"Returns to Continuous Training: Evidence from French Worker-Firm Matched Data", CREST, Paris.

GREEN, F., MACHIN, S. and WILKINSON, D. (forthcoming),
"Trade Unions and Training Practises in British Workplaces", *Industrial and Labor Relations Review.*

GRILICHES, Z. (1969),
"Capital-Skill Complementarity", *Review of Economics and Statistics,* November, pp. 465-468.

GRILICHES, Z. (1996),
"Education, Human Capital and Growth: A Personal Perspective", National Bureau of Economic Research, Working Paper No. 5426.

GROOT, W. (1994),
"*Bedrijsopleidingen: goed voor producktiviteit en loon*", *Economisch Statistische Berichten,* the Netherlands, December, pp. 1108-1111.

HASHIMOTO, M. (1994),
"Employment-Based Training in Japanese Firms in Japan and in the United States: Experiences of Automobile Manufacturers", in Lynch, L.M. (ed.), *Training and the Private Sector: International Comparisons,* pp. 109-149.

HOLZER, H.J. and NEUMARK, D. (1998),
"What Does Affirmative Action Do?", National Bureau of Economic Research, Working Paper No. 6605.

JOVANOVIC, B. (1979),
"Job Matching and the Theory of Turnover", *Journal of Political Economy,* October, pp. 972-990.

KENNEDY, S., DRAGO, R., SLOAN, J. and WOODEN, M. (1994),
"The Effect of Trade Union on the Provision of Training: Australian Evidence", *British Journal of Industrial Relations,* No. 4, pp. 565-580.

LAZEAR, E.P. (1981),
"Agency, Earnings Profiles, Productivity and Hours Restriction", *American Economic Review,* September, pp. 606-620.

LOEWENSTEIN, M.A. and SPLETZER, J.R. (1994),
"Informal Training: A Review of Existing Data and Some New Evidence", US Bureau of Labor Statistics, mimeo, June.

LOEWENSTEIN, M.A. and SPLETZER, J.R. (1997),
"Belated Training: The Relationship between Training, Tenure and Wages", US Bureau of Labor Statistics, mimeo, September.

LOEWENSTEIN, M.A. and SPLETZER, J.R. (1998),
"Dividing the Costs and Returns to General Training", *Journal of Labor Economics*, January, pp. 142-171.

LYNCH, L.M. (ed.) (1994),
Training and the Private Sector: International Comparisons, The University of Chicago Press, Chicago.

MINISTRY OF LABOR, REPUBLIC OF KOREA (1996),
"Labor Policy in Korea", mimeo.

O' CONNELL, P.J. (1998),
"Adults in Training: An International Comparison of Continuing Education and Training from the Adult Literacy Survey", OECD, Paris, mimeo.

O'CONNOR, M.A. (1998),
"Rethinking Corporate Financial Disclosure of Human Resource Values for the Knowledge-based Economy", *University of Pennsylvania Journal of Labor and Employment Law*, Fall, pp. 527-544.

OECD (1991),
Employment Outlook, Paris, July.

OECD (1993),
Employment Outlook, Paris, July.

OECD (1994),
Apprenticeships: Which Way Forward? Paris.

OECD (1995),
Our Children at Risk, Paris.

OECD (1996*a*),
Lifelong Learning for All, Paris.

OECD (1996*b*),
The OECD Jobs Strategy: Enhancing the Effectiveness of Active Labour Market Policies, Paris.

OECD (1997*a*),
Education at a Glance – OECD Indicators, Paris.

OECD (1997*b*),
Manual for Better Training Statistics, Paris.

OECD (1997*c*),
Employment Outlook, Paris, July.

OECD (1997*d*),
"Policies for Low-paid Workers and Unskilled Job Seekers", General Distribution, Paris.

OECD (1997*e*),
"Lifelong Learning to Maintain Employability", General Distribution, Paris.

OECD (1998*a*),
Harmonisation of Training Statistics, Paris, February.

OECD (1998*b*),
Education at a Glance – OECD Indicators, Paris.

OECD (1998*c*),
Employment Outlook, Paris, June.

OECD (1998*d*),
Human Capital Investment: An International Comparison, Paris.

OECD (1998*e*),
"The Retirement Decision in OECD countries", Working Papers on the Economics of Ageing, AWP 1-4, Paris.

OECD (1998*f*),
Pathways and Participation in Vocational and Technical Education and Training, Paris.

OECD and STATISTICS CANADA (1995),
Literacy, Economy and Society – Results of the First International Adult Literacy Survey, Paris and Ottawa.

PHELPS, R.P. and STOWE, P. (1998),
Review of OECD countries Survey Items on Continuing Education and Training and Analysis of their Comparability, US Department of Education.

PISCHKE, J.S. (1996),
"Continuous Training in Germany", National Bureau of Economic Research, Working Paper No. 5829.

REGNER, H. (1995),
"The Impact of On-the-Job Training on Tenure-Wage Profile and Job Mobility. Does the Distinction between General and Firm Specific Human Capital Really Matter?", Swedish Institute for Social Research, Stockholm, Working Paper No. 2.

REGNER, H. (1997),
"Training at the Job and Training for a New Job", Swedish Institute for Social Research, Stockholm, Doctoral Dissertation.

SALOP, J. and SALOP, S. (1976),
"Self-Selection and Turnover in the Labour Market", *Quarterly Journal of Economics*, No. 4, pp. 619-627.

SHÖMANN, K. (1998),
"The Interface Between Organizational Learning and Life-Long Learning", Social Science Research Center (WZB), Berlin, mimeo, September.

VEUM, J.R. (1995),
"Sources of Training and their Impact on Wages", *Industrial and Labour Relations Review*, No. 4, pp. 812-826.

VILHUBER, L. (1997),
"Sector-Specific On-the-Job Training: Evidence from US Data", York University, mimeo, December.

VILHUBER, L. (1998),
"Sector-Specific Training and Mobility: Evidence from Continuous Training in Germany", York University, mimeo, June.

WURZBURG, G. (1998),
"Issues in Financing Vocational Education and Training in the EU", European Centre for the Development of Vocational Training (CEDEFOP), *Vocational Training*, No. 13, pp. 22-26.

Chapter 4

NEW ENTERPRISE WORK PRACTICES AND THEIR LABOUR MARKET IMPLICATIONS

Summary

Over recent years, the environment in which companies operate has changed considerably. Firms are faced with a need to achieve greater economic efficiency, and to adapt faster to changing conditions. Many commentators have claimed that these pressures are being reflected in changes in work organisation, towards what are often called "new" or "flexible" or "high-performance" work practices. This involves changes in the design of jobs, towards greater complexity, higher skill levels and greater use of team-working, as well as increased delegation of responsibility to lower level staff and improved communications throughout the company.

The aim of this chapter is, first, to examine the evidence for changes in work organisation towards more flexible types of working, both in terms of job design and the delegation of responsibility. Second, it examines where flexible practices are most common, in terms of both countries and types of firms. Third, it attempts to evaluate to what extent changes in working practices have implications for the labour market. It draws on information developed as part of the recent OECD project on "flexible enterprises", as well as the EPOC study of the European Foundation for the Improvement of Living and Working Conditions.

The evidence assembled indicates that many managers in all countries report a considerable degree of investment in flexible working practices. While there is comparatively little evidence about changes over time, what exists points to the extension of a number of forms of flexible working. Firms in different countries use flexible working practices to a significantly different extent. The patterns are not easily explained by differences in the types of firms in different countries, nor by other characteristics of different OECD countries, such as their industrial relations systems.

Within individual countries, two factors which seem to be linked with greater use of flexible working practices are higher training levels, and industrial relations systems which facilitate negotiations between managers and employees. The analysis in this chapter does not suggest that increased use of flexible working practices necessarily leads to a growing polarisation between "core" and "peripheral" workers.

Chapter 4

NEW ENTERPRISE WORK PRACTICES AND THEIR LABOUR MARKET IMPLICATIONS

Introduction

Over recent years, the environment in which companies operate has changed considerably. Firms are faced with a need to achieve greater economic efficiency, and to adapt more quickly to changing product market conditions. Many commentators have claimed that these pressures are being reflected in changes in work organisation, towards what are often called "new", "innovative", "high-performance" or "flexible" workplaces. This generally involves changes in the design of jobs, towards greater complexity, higher skill levels and greater use of team-working, as well as increased delegation of responsibility to lower level staff and improved communications throughout the company. The aim of this chapter is, first, to examine the evidence for changes in work organisation, both across countries and different types of firms and, second, to evaluate to what extent they are correlated with changes in employment practices likely to have implications for the labour market. The chapter draws, in particular, on information developed as part of the recent OECD project on "flexible enterprises", as well as the EPOC study of the European Foundation for the Improvement of Living and Working Conditions.

Changes in the design of jobs and the way that responsibility is delegated are a crucial part of a company's human resource policies, with implications for recruitment, training, compensation, and employee relations. For example, more job complexity, and a greater emphasis on team-working and information sharing, may give incentives to firms to recruit workers with higher levels of qualifications, and greater communications and social skills. The same factors, combined with technical change, are likely to lead to demands for higher levels of training. To the extent that the new forms of working are dependent upon higher levels of motivation, there will be implications for employee relations policies. Finally, compensation practices may be modified, both to encourage the process of change, and provide the best possible "fit" with the new working practices.

In addition, if changes of this kind are widespread they may have implications for the labour market and for public policy. For example, Betcherman (1997) argues that education and training policies may need to be modified to develop the skills that the new methods of work organisation require. In addition, there have been concerns that moves to new working methods may lead to a polarisation in the work force within companies. Managers may judge that only some of their existing workers have the capacity to take part in more productive, but also more demanding, working methods and may employ the remainder on less advantageous conditions. Thus, changes in work organisation might be connected with labour market outcomes such as rises in part-time and temporary working and, in some countries, the rise in earnings inequality and the increasing labour market difficulties of lower-skilled workers.

The focus of this chapter is on the two broad areas of job design and delegation of responsibility. Supporting human resources practices, such as compensation, training and recruitment, and other areas of employee relations, are not covered directly. Training is the topic of Chapter 3 of this edition of the *Employment Outlook*, while profit-sharing, an element of compensation systems often associated with "high-performance" workplaces, was covered in the 1995 *Employment Outlook*. Other practices which have been excluded are downsizing and outsourcing, on the grounds that their main purposes are to change the type and quantity of work that is carried out by individual organisations and sometimes, in the former case, the pace of working, rather than the way in which work is organised. In acknowledgement of the fact that many of the job design and delegation practices under consideration in this chapter have a long history, they will be referred to as "flexible" rather than "new" work organisation practices.

Summarising broad changes over time in work organisation is difficult. The academic and management science literatures contain many concepts designed to describe, or prescribe developments. A brief review of some of the most important recent concepts is provided in Box 1, which ends with a list of the flexible working practices taken as the basis for the empirical evidence presented here. In addition, mention is made of quality circles (defined in the box), for which data are relatively plentiful.

Box 1. **Flexible work organisation practices**

While changes in work organisation over recent decades are impossible to summarise adequately, there is a good deal of agreement that one current of change has been a move away from mass-production in manufacturing, and bureaucratic control in all sectors, towards more flexible forms of work organisation. Part of the early moves away from conventional mass-production "Taylorist" techniques were spurred by technical advances in computer-controlled machinery which, according to Piore and Sabel (1984), led to the possibility of "flexible specialisation" – producing a wide range of different products from the same set of capital goods at low costs. A second factor was the success of "lean production" methods, which included the elimination of stockpiling of parts and unfinished goods through the "just-in-time" system. The advent of lean production provided striking evidence for the importance of work organisation methods. Japanese car-firms using lean production were found to achieve considerably higher productivity than American firms with more advanced technology using conventional "Fordist" production methods [Berggren (1993); Marsden (1996); Womack *et al.* (1990)].

Employee Involvement (EI), a term which became popular in the 1980s, represents a movement which continues earlier initiatives for worker participation and industrial democracy [Marchington (1995)]. The main principles, drawn particularly from the results of social science, include greater participation by lower level staff, job enrichment to improve motivation and commitment to the organisation, and willingness to share information with employees, who are counted among the firm's stakeholders. It has considerable implications for change in work organisation. One current emphasis is on locating decisions lower down in the hierarchy, in order to take advantage of the detailed knowledge employees have about their own work processes. Management adopts an enabling rather than a controlling role. This tends to favour a flatter organisational structure, with considerable emphasis on lateral work and communication, often through teams [Lawler *et al.* (1998)].

The Socio-Technical movement, which has taken root particularly strongly in some of the Nordic countries, has a long history, linked to EI. As its name suggests, it seeks to harmonise the technical and social aspects of work. Beginning with research at the Tavistock Institute in the 1940s, it was developed in the 1960s in the Norwegian "Democracy at Work Project". Recent applications were seen in two Volvo car plants in Sweden. The main principles include the use of stable, semi-autonomous work groups without status differences, in which tasks are interchangeable and interdependent, and workers' needs for satisfying and challenging work are given a high level of consideration [Kelly (1978)].

Total Quality Management (TQM) has been a particularly influential management philosophy in many countries in the past two decades [Hackman and Wageman (1995)]. While originally based on concepts from quality engineering, it encompasses many of the ideas of both EI and lean production, with distinct emphases on improving quality, satisfying customers and reducing waste. As with EI, but unlike lean production, it has been applied to all sectors of the economy, notably services and the government sector. Two important features of TQM are team-working and decision-making at relatively low levels in the hierarchy. In North America and the United Kingdom, TQM has been regarded as the successor to the quality circle movement, which was modelled on developments in Japan (quality circles are groups of workers from the same work area who meet regularly on a voluntary basis to suggest ways of achieving higher productivity and quality). Compared with EI, there is more emphasis on the directing role of top management and there may be rather less emphasis on job enrichment, in the sense of changes in work design intended to increase the variety of tasks performed and the range of skills that are needed [Hill and Wilkinson (1995)].

Business process re-engineering (BPR) is based on ideas which rapidly achieved popularity after being developed by management consultants at the beginning of the 1990s [Hammer and Champy (1993)]. BPR makes use of many of the ideas of EI and TQM, but stresses the possibility of cost savings by improving or "re-engineering" the processes taking place in organisations. This applies particularly to routine transactions, which may be re-organised in order to exploit the possibilities afforded by micro-electronics. Further cost reductions are advocated by concentrating on the "core competencies" of organisations, and outsourcing goods and services that can be obtained more cheaply elsewhere. As with TQM and EI, BPR involves flatter management structures, partly through the use of modern communications systems – work is to be co-ordinated as far as possible by means of local area networks rather than middle managers. Job enrichment is not necessarily a primary aim, and the explicit emphasis on cost reduction is often associated with downsizing [Conti and Warner (1994)].

As is obvious from the above, contemporary management has a considerable range of philosophies. This wide choice is reflected in the somewhat general concepts of "high-performance workplaces", and "flexible firms" [Kling (1995); OECD (1996*b*)]. These may be conceived as incorporating workplace practices from one or a range of management approaches, in a self-reinforcing way, so as to align the organisation of the workplace with its objectives.

Betcherman (1997) lists the following practices as being some of the main features of work organisation in "high-performance" workplaces. Each is a characteristic of one or several of the "models" mentioned above.

- Job design involving multi-skilling, or multi-tasking.
- Extensive use of team working.
- Reduced hierarchical levels.
- Delegation of responsibility to individuals and teams.

The focus of this chapter is on the spread and development of these broad types of work organisation practices. For convenience, they will be referred to generically as "flexible practices" and divided into two broad categories, job design and delegation of responsibility, corresponding to the first and second pairs of the four tirets above, respectively.

Structure of the chapter

The following sections provide empirical evidence to address the following questions:

- What is the incidence of flexible work organisation practices in different countries and what is the evidence for ongoing change?
- In what types of firms are flexible practices most common?
- What evidence is there that flexible practices tend to be found in combination and which combinations are most frequent?
- What are the implications of flexible practices, in terms of other types of employment practices? For example, is there any evidence that the development of flexible working practices tends to be associated with higher levels of training, or with a larger "peripheral" workforce?

Box 2 reviews the evidence that flexible working practices bring financial benefits to firms, especially when used in combination. This proposition is an important part of the argument that they are not simply "fads" and that more enterprises will find it expedient to use them, and to do so more intensively.

Main findings

National differences in patterns of flexible working

The following points summarise the evidence available about the incidence and change in flexible working practices in different countries. They refer to workplaces with 50 or more employees (unless otherwise stated).

- The incidence of job rotation appears to be high in Germany and Japan relative to France, the United Kingdom and the United States, and may be particularly high in Sweden and some other Nordic countries. Teamworking is again particularly high in Sweden. Measures to delegate responsibility to lower level employees appear to be relatively uncommon in the Southern European countries. In Northern Europe, the highest incidence is found in the Nordic countries and the Netherlands. In North America, the use of quality circles appears to be above the European average.
- In Sweden and Denmark, firms report a particularly high level of recent management initiatives to introduce or extend the use of job rotation. Figures for France, Germany, the Netherlands and Portugal are considerably lower. There is comparatively little variation across European countries regarding recent management initiatives to promote team-working. Firms in Sweden, the Netherlands, France and the United Kingdom report the most recent management initiatives to increase employee involvement, while figures for Germany and Denmark are lower than average.
- In Australia, the proportion of workplaces with various forms of employee involvement practices rose substantially between 1990 and 1995. Quality circles were the exception. For Fortune 1000 companies in the United States, there is also evidence of declines in the use of quality circles from 1993 onwards but, steady increases since 1987 in other forms of employee participation including a very sharp increase in semi-autonomous work groups. In addition, there was an increase in the incidence of schemes for job enrichment and redesign.
- While most firms using flexible working practices appear to have introduced them only in a limited way, it appears from the American Society for Training and Development 1998 "benchmarking" survey that many large firms in North America, Europe, and Japan have adopted flexible working practices to a substantial (and, on average, roughly similar) extent.

Overall, the available data on flexible working practices reveal substantial variations between countries even where there are similarities between their national and workplace IR systems. None of the usual ways of classifying countries according to their IR systems are capable of explaining the pattern that emerges.

In what kinds of workplaces are the practices most common? What are their labour-market implications?

An examination of the incidence of practices across countries suggests that larger workplaces are more likely to have adopted the flexible practices than their smaller counterparts, though the relationship varies by country and by practice. Workplaces in manufacturing tend to have an above-average incidence rate. Establishments with other forms of worker representation, such as through trade unions and works councils, are more apt to have taken initiatives in the area of flexible work organisation practices. Moreover, employers with incentive compensation schemes, particularly profit sharing and pay linked to skill, tend to have higher incidence rates as well, consistent with the view that there are complementarities among such practices.

Box 2. **Flexible work organisation practices – real and important changes or management "fads"?**

Despite the substantial academic and management interest in flexible working practices, there are concerns that they represent, not the culmination of many decades of research and experimentation in search of improved economic performance but, rather, the influence of changing management fashion, driven by the pervasive influence of management literature. Some commentators have argued that it is not management practices and work organisation that have changed, but simply the words used to describe them. A variant of this argument is that, to the extent that there have been changes, they are no more than pendulum swings from management philosophies based on the idea of control to ones based on employee commitment, and back again [Ramsay (1996); Abrahamson (1996)].

These concerns are not entirely groundless. Quality circles were adopted by large numbers of firms in the 1980s without making changes in management structures to accommodate them. As a result, there was widespread disillusionment and many systems of quality circles were abandoned. The high figures reported for the existence of TQM (Total Quality Management) in several countries surely exaggerate the changes in work organisation that are taking place. United States surveys tend find a higher reported incidence of TQM than the team working and quality circles which are generally considered to be an integral part of it [Osterman (1994); Gittleman et al. (1998); Hackman and Wageman (1995)].

On the other hand, there is now a certain amount of evidence to suggest that flexible working practices can improve firms' financial performance. This would be difficult to understand if reports of the adoption of flexible working practices were illusory or if the practices had been introduced in a capricious fashion. In addition, while managerial fashion might tend to swing to and fro over the medium-term, there can be no doubt about the influence of important long-term factors on managerial behaviour, such as those identified by Chandler (1962, 1990) and Porter (1980, 1985), factors which at least some commentators have suggested are leading firms in the direction of flexible working practices.

Flexible practices and firm performance

The question of whether flexible working practices tend to produce higher firm performance is not straightforward to answer. Formidable empirical questions need to be resolved [Ichniowski et al. (1996)]. For example, when studies are based purely on cross-sectional information, it is difficult to control for the reasons why the practices were introduced in the first place. If firms only began to experiment with new forms of working practices when they faced dire trouble, the existence of practices might be associated with poorer performance, at least over the short-term. On the other hand, if flexible practices were introduced mainly into firms with more highly skilled workforces, there is the danger that higher performance may be attributed to the working practices rather than the higher skills. Another difficulty is that many studies, such as the careful analysis of the effects of human resource management practices on the productivity of steel finishing lines by Ichniowski et al. (1997), cover only a small part of the economy.

Despite these caveats, the recent reviews of Becker and Huselid (1998), Delery and Doty (1996), Ichniowski et al. (1996), Kling (1995) and Nordflex (forthcoming), even though based mainly on United States and Nordic analyses, provide substantial evidence that:

- Firms that report the use of "flexible working practices" tend to enjoy better financial performance and higher levels of productivity, than those that do not.
- This beneficial effect is stronger when flexible practices are used in combination both with each other and with support from other human resource practices, such as training and appropriate compensation policies.

It should be stressed that these broad conclusions do not apply to all of the studies reviewed, some of which produced mixed results, [this was also the case for the study of France carried out by Coutrot (1996a)]. In addition, many studies do not investigate the direction of causality, and are open to the objection that, rather than flexible practices being the cause of good firm performance, it is good firm performance which allows firms the luxury of introducing flexible working practices. However, at least three studies do address this issue on the basis of longitudinal information: Lawler et al. (1998); Nordflex (forthcoming) and Patterson et al. (1997). All find evidence of causality running from the introduction of flexible working practices to superior financial performance.

The association of flexible working practices with better economic performance may encourage more firms to use them. In addition, the fact that combinations of practices often yield stronger performance should provide reasons for using them more intensively. However, both these conclusions depend upon appropriate conditions being fulfilled [Ichniowski et al. (1996)]. It is not obvious that firms that have not yet introduced flexible working practices are as well placed as those that have already done so. This applies not only to existing types of enterprises, but also to some new developments, such as the rapid growth in call-centres. Here, Fernie (1999) has found, for the United Kingdom, that work organisation in the more successful centres involves

> **Box 2. Flexible work organisation practices – real and important changes or management "fads"?** *(cont.)*
>
> elements of both team-working and Taylorism. In addition, firms may experiment with the introduction of one or two flexible working practices, only to abandon them as unsatisfactory rather than introducing more [Kochan and Dyer (1995)]. Successful introduction may depend upon the presence of the specific management expertise required, or upon the workforce already possessing a certain level of skills or having the ability to acquire them relatively easily [Betcherman (1997)]. Worker attitudes, and the industrial relations framework in which the firm operates are also likely to be important [Levine (1995); Locke *et al.* (1995)].
>
> **Flexible practices and firm structure and strategy**
>
> Over the last century, the strategy and structure of firms in the industrialised world has changed substantially. Chandler (1962, 1990) describes how large businesses evolved from the typical owner-managed firm of the nineteenth century to more complex organisations, with professional managers, and a functional organisational structure (separate departments for production, sales, finance, and accounting, and so forth). As the twentieth century advanced, these companies found that their administrative complexity was incompatible with innovation and product diversification. One response was the evolution of the divisional structure, in which a number of divisions, linked together at the corporate level, are each made responsible for a particular market or product. While still successful, the divisional form is now being challenged by mixed organisational forms which embody less vertical integration, and looser coupling throughout the system, while retaining tight central financial control.
>
> Miles and Snow (1984) argue that these changes have been reflected in human resource policies. Personnel departments first arose in functional organisations, where they developed a tradition of acquiring, training and maintaining the various types of specialists that functional organisations required. Within divisionalised companies, they found additional roles in devising more elaborate compensation packages, management development programmes, staffing plans and job rotation, as well as training plans, employee relations, and specialised, centralised recruitment centres. The most recent forms of work organisation require more advanced human resources practices, such as job enrichment, team building, and job rotation, in order to develop the necessary range of skills and functional flexibility.
>
> Chandler's account is complemented by Porter (1980, 1985), who identified three typical strategies that firms can use to gain competitive advantage: innovation through the development of new products or services, quality enhancement, and cost reduction. Over time, the competitive strategies of firms in OECD countries have tended to shift in the direction of quality enhancement and innovation. While the linkage between each of these types of strategy and human resource policies is not straightforward, Schuler and Jackson (1987) argue that the innovation strategy requires close interaction within groups of individuals, and a special emphasis on multi-skilling.

Despite assertions by some that flexible practices will vastly improve job quality and by others that they will serve to increase job instability for at least a portion of the workforce, it proves difficult to find evidence of strong links between the presence of the practices and labour market outcomes. The most robust finding is that employers with flexible practices in place are also more likely to provide job training. There is no clear relationship between the existence of the flexible practices and the use of various kinds of "contingent" workers.

I. How common are flexible work organisation practices in OECD countries?

A. Indicators of work organisation

The main indicators of job design used in this chapter are the extent of job rotation and team working. Job rotation, defined as a work design system that allows employees to rotate between different jobs, may produce flexibility in a number of ways. By ensuring that all members of a work group can carry out a range of tasks, it can increase the flexibility of response to different and unpredictable demands. In addition, it may provide skill development for individual workers. Team working achieves flexibility partly by pooling the skills of a number of workers. It usually involves some change in job design as well as a delegation of responsibility to the team. The indicators of delegation of responsibility include information on the levels at which various types of responsibilities are discharged, as well as evidence of flattening of management structures. Data on quality circles will also be presented.

Statistics on the incidence of flexible practices must be treated with considerable caution. Even for the same country, different surveys give widely differing estimates. For example, the nationally representative 1993 Survey of Employer-Provided Training (SEPT) carried out by the US Bureau of Labor Statistics by means of mailed questionnaires provides estimates, reported by Gittleman *et al.*

(1998), which are much lower than those found by a survey with many similar characteristics carried out by Osterman (1994). There are suggestions that, in some domains, interview surveys give higher estimates than postal surveys. One reason may be that interviews tend to focus managers' attention more closely on the questions, making it more likely that they will report practices which are present at low levels of intensity. In addition, faced with a human interlocutor, rather than a piece of paper, managers may feel more inducement to say they have adopted more "advanced" management techniques.

International comparisons based on survey data can, thus, only be made on the basis of identical or near-identical questions, administered as part of similar surveys, carried out in similar ways. The results must always be treated with considerable caution, as it is not possible to translate terms exactly from one country to another, owing to differences in national institutions and traditions. The evidence presented below is based partly on two international surveys: first, the survey of ten EU countries carried out by the EPOC Project (Employee Direct Participation in Organisational Change) of the European Foundation for the Improvement of Living and Working Conditions and, second, the similar, but not identical, surveys of four Nordic countries whose results have been brought together under the Nordflex project (see the Annex for descriptions of these surveys).[1] In addition, a number of countries have recently developed nationally representative workplace-based surveys. While these surveys are by no means identical, they do contain some common questions, allowing some cautious international comparisons. These surveys may be supplemented by two non-representative commercial surveys, designed to enable firms to "benchmark" their use of training and workplaces practices against those of other firms. Finally, reference is made to academic studies of particularly industries in pairs of countries. These are able to go into greater depth than surveys, and circumvent some of the problems that arise when terms that are current in one country have no exact equivalent in another.

As the incidence of practices is found to vary somewhat by size of workplace (see below), and the information is very sparse for small workplaces, the statistics presented in this section refer to those with 50 or more employees. It must be stressed that the data generally refer to the existence of practices in workplaces, rather than the intensity of their use.

B. Comparisons of indicators of work organisation

Job rotation

While there is no international survey of the incidence of job rotation, Marsden (forthcoming) deduces a ranking of countries on the basis of a number of bilateral studies, including Maurice *et al.* (1986) for France and Germany; Sorge and Warner (1986) for Germany and the United Kingdom; Lam (1994 and 1997) and Whittaker (1993) for Japan and the United Kingdom; and Cole (1979), Koike and Inoki (1993) and Lincoln and Kalleberg (1990) for Japan and the United States.

The general conclusion is that the incidence of job rotation is higher in Japan and Germany than it is in the United States, the United Kingdom or France. In France and the United States, where work organisation is focused strongly on the job or the "work post", job rotation is seen as incompatible with the primary responsibility for one particular job. No information is available to compare the incidence of job rotation in Germany and Japan. However, Marsden (forthcoming) argues that it has a somewhat different function in the two countries. In both Japan and Germany, job rotation is seen as part of the process of on-the-job training. However, in Japan, the intention is to develop broad, enterprise-specific skills, while in Germany job rotation is seen as part of the process of skill enhancement and progression within an occupation. The occupational dimension is also seen as important in Britain, but job rotation is limited as compared with Germany, in order to respect occupational demarcations. Comparing job rotation practices for engineers in Japan and the United Kingdom, Lam (1994) suggests that in Britain there is a strong emphasis on building up the employee's own specific area of expertise, while in Japan the stress is on systematic sharing and diffusion of expertise.

Figures available from selected national surveys are consistent with these conclusions and suggest that some of the Nordic countries also have high levels of job rotation. For France, the 1992 REPONSE survey suggests that 24 per cent of workplaces use job rotation, the same figure as the 1993 SEPT survey for the United States [Coutrot (1996*b*); Gittleman *et al.* (1998)]. However, the 1996 Flexible Enterprise Survey of German workplaces carried out by the University of Kassel [data provided by Bernard (1998)] provides a considerably higher figure of around 50 per cent of workplaces, of which, roughly one-half reported that job rotation was used for personnel development. For the Nordic countries, the representative national surveys co-ordinated by the Nordflex group have produced estimates of the reported incidence of job rotation varying from 65 per cent for Sweden and 80 per cent for Finland, to 50 per cent for Denmark and 40 per cent for Norway Nordflex (forthcoming)]. A quarter of Swedish and a fifth of Finnish workplaces reported that over 50 per cent of

---

1. The EPOC results must be treated with some caution because a large portion of the sample did not return their questionnaires, with the size of this share varying across countries. Details on the response rates can be found in the Annex to this chapter.

their employees were involved in job-rotation, as opposed to a figure of under 10 per cent in Denmark.

Team working

Even more than job rotation, team working takes different forms in different countries. For example, Marsden (forthcoming) quotes Jürgens *et al.* (1993) as arguing that, in the automobile industry (one of the pioneers of team working) the United States tends to use relatively narrow, job-based teams, Japan uses homogeneous teams based on on-the-job training, the United Kingdom employs teams of similarly-skilled workers, developed around existing skills, while Germany uses mixed teams based on existing skills, but at different skill levels.

There is little comparative information on team working for the economy as a whole. However, Benders *et al.* (1998) present indicative data derived from the EPOC survey on the assumption that team working is likely to occur when managers report a high degree of delegation of responsibility for important issues to groups. More precisely, two conditions were applied – that groups were given rights to make decisions over at least one-half of a set of eight important issues relating to their work and working conditions, and that at least 70 per cent of the largest occupational group in the workforce was involved.[2] For the eight countries which could be covered, team working was found to be most prevalent in Sweden. The United Kingdom, France and the Netherlands were also above average, while Ireland, Germany, Denmark and Italy were below it.

The Nordflex co-ordinated surveys indicate that, within the four Nordic countries covered, Sweden has by far the highest proportion of employees working in teams. Ninety-one per cent of Swedish workplaces reported the use of team-working as opposed to 75, 74 and 69 per cent in Denmark, Finland and Norway, respectively. Fifty-eight per cent of Swedish workplaces reported that 60 per cent or more of the workforce were working in teams, while in Finland and Denmark the corresponding figures (but relating to 50 per cent or more of the workforce) were 30 and 10 per cent, respectively.

One of the more hotly debated issues in European works organisation is the extent to which team working corresponds to the "Scandinavian" model or the "Toyota" model. According to Fröhlich and Pekruhl (1996), the Scandinavian model may be distinguished by voluntary (as opposed to compulsory) membership, group (as opposed to management) selection of the membership and the leader, mixed (as opposed to uniform) qualifications, skill dependent (as opposed to seniority dependent) rewards, relatively complex tasks, pace of work independent of technology, wide autonomy and voluntary internal division of labour. The opposite applies to the Toyota model. While the EPOC questionnaire was not designed to capture all of these characteristics, on the basis of the type of approach described above, Benders *et al.* (1998) concluded that the Scandinavian model was very rare. The majority of workplaces with team working tended to follow a model closer to the Toyota one. This is consistent with findings from the 1998 U.K. Workplace and Employee Relations Survey (WERS98), that 65 per cent of managers reported that most employees in the largest occupational group at their workplace worked in formally designated teams. However, out of this 65 per cent, only 5 per cent said that team members had to work together to the extent of being given responsibility for specific products or services, jointly deciding how work was to be done and appointing their own team leaders [Cully *et al.* (1998)].

Delegation of responsibility

Table 4.1 provides a number of indicators of the degree to which responsibility for a range of different tasks is delegated to individuals and groups within workplaces. The data are taken from the EPOC survey and the 1992 Price Waterhouse Cranfield survey [Brewster and Hegewisch (1994)]. They have been arranged in rough geographic groupings. The EPOC data are based on answers to questions which first ask managers if individuals and groups are given the right to make decisions on how their work is performed, and then, if the response is positive, ask which of a number of possible domains are covered. Delegation is taken to occur only if at least one domain is mentioned.[3]

As noted by EPOC (1997), there seems to be a distinct southern European pattern – the incidence of individual and group delegation is relatively low in Italy, Portugal and Spain. There is, however, no uniform "north-

---

2. The issues were allocation of work, scheduling of work, quality of work, time keeping, attendance and absence control, job rotation, co-ordination of work with other internal groups, and improving work processes. See Benders *et al.* (1998) for further details. The method ignores questions of co-operation and pooling of skills, generally considered to be essential features of team-working. However, the argument is presumably that it would be impossible for groups of workers to be responsible for important issues without them.
3. Without the application of this criterion, the results would be much higher. For individual delegation, the domains in question are: scheduling of work; quality of product or service; improving work processes; dealing with "internal" customers; dealing with external clients; time keeping; attendance; and working conditions. For group delegation, they are: allocation of work; scheduling of work; quality of work; time keeping; attendance and absence control; job rotation; co-ordination of work with other internal groups; and improving work processes.

Table 4.1. **Indicators of delegation of responsibility**
Percentage of workplaces reporting presence of practice

	Individual delegation, 1996	Group delegation, 1996	Quality circles, 1992
Sweden	69	56	9
Denmark	57	30	10
Netherlands	59	48	15
Germany	64	31	19
France	54	40	20
United Kingdom	53	37	18
Ireland	62	42	11
Italy[a]	44	28	..
Spain	40	10	17
Portugal	26	26	11
Unweighted average	55	36	14

.. Data not available.
a) Data for Italy from the EPOC survey refers to the three months prior to the survey in 1996 and for the other countries to the three years prior to the survey.
Sources: Data on individual and group delegation are from the EPOC survey. Data on quality circles are from the Price Waterhouse Cranfield survey.

ern" European pattern, nor indeed a uniform Nordic pattern. While Sweden is in first place, Denmark is relatively low for group delegation.[4] Another interesting feature is the difference between the Netherlands and Germany, despite the fact that both countries have rather similar workplace industrial relations systems, and (according to the results of another question on the EPOC questionnaire) attach a similar level of priority to quality-of-working life issues. According to the Price Waterhouse Cranfield survey, which confirms indications from the Nordflex study, the influence of the "quality circle movement" in Sweden and Denmark has been limited, no doubt because quality circles are not a part of the Socio-technical approach which has been influential in the Nordic countries.

For Canada, data from the Pilot Workplace and Employment Survey (WES) supplied by Statistics Canada suggest a considerably higher incidence of quality circles than for European countries – 34 per cent of workplaces with 50 employees and over reported their presence (over the 12 months to April 1996), compared with only 14 per cent on average for the 10 EU countries in Table 4.1.[5] United States data also suggest higher levels than the European average, though not necessarily higher than the European leaders – 16 per cent according to the 1993 SEPT survey [Gittleman et al. (1998)] and 27 per cent on the basis of the 1995 SEPT survey [Frazis et al. (1998)]. Data from the 1995 Australian Workplace Industrial Relations Survey (AWIRS95), on the other hand, suggest figures very close to the European average shown above [Morehead et al. (1997)].

The Nordflex (forthcoming) project provides detailed data on delegation for the four Nordic countries covered. A substantial proportion of workplaces in Sweden, Denmark and Finland report the delegation of daily planning to individuals (57 per cent, 62 per cent and 40 per cent, respectively) as opposed to only 20 per cent in Norway. A roughly similar, though slightly lower, pattern of results was obtained for quality control. Sweden has the highest reported level of delegation of purchasing, at around 14 per cent.

Evidence from non-representative samples

A further source of information comes from surveys designed to allow firms to "benchmark" the incidence of their training, work organisation and other practices against the average for similar firms. Surveys of this kind, both with an international dimension, were carried out in 1998 by the American Society for Training and Development (ASTD) and the Centre for Effective Organizations (CEO).

The ASTD survey, described in Bassi and Van Buren (1999), provides information not only for US-based firms, but also for firms in Canada, Japan and Europe.[6] The results shown in Table 4.2 apply only to those size categories for which relatively large numbers of firms were available. They are generally much higher than the nation-

---

4. It should be noted, however, that, although the overall level of delegation in Denmark is much lower than in Sweden, for those workplaces with delegation Denmark compares well in terms of the number of issues delegated to groups.
5. See Statistics Canada (1998) for a description of this survey and a review of its results.
6. The survey also covered a relatively small number of firms in Asia and the Pacific.

ally representative survey data reported above. Examination of the full range of figures available shows this is not simply because of the size of the firms shown in the table – high incidence of these work practices were also reported for smaller firms. Rather, it probably relates to the use of the survey for benchmarking. Firms responding are clearly interested in the topic and may well be concerned to ensure they score well against the average. However, the figures are internally consistent. They show the expected drop from the numbers of firms reporting that the practice is present at all, to the numbers indicating that at least 50 per cent of the workforce is affected.

Canada and the United States have very similar figures. The main differences relate to task forces, problem solving teams or quality circles and TQM, for which there is a suggestion of greater depth of use in Canada. For Japan, where comparisons have been confined to the 1 000 employees and over group, the reported incidence of practices is broadly similar to those for Canada and the United States. However, results for "job rotation or cross training" are comparatively low. This is in contradiction to the two-country study of Japan and the United States by Lincoln and Kalleberg (1990). However, as noted by Cole (1979), survey evidence of job rotation in Japan requires careful interpretation – job rotation is so much a part of Japanese employee management systems that some managers may not regard it as representing anything other than standard working practice.

The results available for Europe apply only to a tiny sample of firms, spread roughly evenly across the larger European countries, with relatively high numbers in Ireland, Germany, Austria and Hungary. They cannot be regarded as in any sense representative of the population of large European firms. However, it is interesting to note the similarity in the pattern of results for Europe and those for the other countries. This suggests that there is a group of large firms in Europe which use flexible working practices to a roughly similar extent to large firms in North America.

The Center for Effective Organizations (CEO) study, reported by Lawler *et al.* (1998), provides information about Fortune 1 000 corporations in the United States (Table 4.3). Overall, bearing in mind the differences in question wording, and the larger average size of the Fortune 1 000 firms, the results for the United States appear broadly consistent with those provided by the ASTD for the 1 000+ category. In addition, the table shows similar results from Spain, where the bulk of the questionnaire was administered to larger industrial corporations. Overall, the United States firms report higher levels of use of the various practices than their Spanish counterparts (with the exception of quality circles). However, the differences are much less for firms reporting that 40 per cent or more of their workforce are covered by the practice. This latter result suggests that, while a smaller proportion of larger, industrial Spanish firms have introduced flexible working practices, many that have done so have moved to a similar intensity of use as large firms in the United States.

Table 4.2. **Percentage of workplaces reporting the use of selected work organisation practices, by firm size, 1998**

	Canada		Japan	United States		Europe	
Firm size (number of employees)	100-999	1 000+	1 000+	100-999	1 000+	100-999	1 000+
At least some workers involved in the practice							
Job rotation or cross-training[a]	92	88	70	85	89	95	97
Self-directed work teams[b]	48	54	..	43	56	67	72
Task forces, problem solving teams or quality circles	87	85	83	88	92	95	100
Employee involvement with management in business decisions	74	87	83	72	76	81	66
Total quality management	68	73	76	69	74	76	83
At least 50 per cent of workforce involved in the practice							
Job rotation or cross-training[a]	27	13	28	20	18	38	17
Self-directed work teams[b]	15	8	..	11	4	33	14
Task forces, problem solving teams or quality circles	31	13	37	16	20	29	10
Employee involvement with management in business decisions	19	10	13	20	17	33	7
Total quality management	39	25	24	27	31	38	21
Number of firms in sample	62	52	54	149	133	21	22

.. Data not available (the question was not asked in Japan).
a) Cross-training is defined as training workers for jobs other than those they are currently doing.
b) Self-directed work teams are small groups of workers whose members have the authority to handle a wide range of issues relating to the team as they see fit, in order to fulfil its objectives.
Source: Calculations by the Secretariat on the basis of data supplied by the American Society for Training and Development.

Table 4.3. **Incidence of selected workplace practices in the United States and Spain**
Percentages

		United States[a]		Spain[b]	
		At least some employees involved in the practice	At least 40% of employees involved in the practice	At least some employees involved in the practice	At least 40% of employees involved in the practice
Job enrichment or redesign	1987	61	11	..	..
	1990	75	9	..	..
	1993	83	18	..	..
	1996	87	25	..	..
	1997	..	..	70	27
Self-managing work teams	1987	27	1	..	..
	1990	47	1	..	..
	1993	69	5	..	..
	1996	78	9	..	..
	1997	..	..	30	8
Quality circles	1987	60	10	..	..
	1990	68	13	..	..
	1993	66	15	..	..
	1996	60	12	..	..
	1997	..	..	62	28
Employment participation groups other than quality circles	1987	69	15	..	..
	1990	87	22	..	..
	1993	92	35	..	..
	1996	94	38	..	..
	1997	..	..	74	27

.. Data not available.
a) Fortune 1 000 firms.
b) Large industrial companies.
Sources: United States: Lawler et al. (1998); Spain: data supplied by Professor Juan Antonio Marin Garcia, Universidad Politécnica de Valencia.

Table 4.4. **Percentage of workplaces in 1996 reporting selected management initiatives over the past three years**[a]

	Job rotation	Installation of team-based work organisation	Greater involvement of lower level employees	Flattening of management structures
Sweden	38	29	60	46
Denmark	28	40	10	42
Netherlands	9	9	46	47
Germany	7	20	19	30
France	6	30	44	21
United Kingdom	13	33	48	45
Ireland	10	27	32	23
Italy	13	28	24	10
Spain	14	34	33	..
Portugal	9	22	9	3
Unweighted average	15	27	33	29

.. Data not available (question asked was different).
a) Data for Italy refer to the three months prior to the survey.
Source: Secretariat calculations based on data from the EPOC survey, referring to workplaces with 50 or more employees.

Table 4.5. **Methods of employee involvement, Australia**[a]

Percentage of firms reporting existence of practices

	1990	1995
Quality circles	16	16
Joint consultative committees	20	44
Task forces or *ad hoc* joint committees	33	47
Employee representatives on board of managing directors	9	16

a) Data refer to workplaces with 50 or more employees.
Source: Morehead et al. (1997).

C. Comparisons of change

Information on the extent of recent initiatives to extend the use of flexible working practices is available from the EPOC survey, which asked managers to report initiatives undertaken over the previous three years (Table 4.4) in four areas, each of which corresponds fairly closely to the four categories of flexible working practices set out in the introduction to this chapter. It should be stressed that this information relates both to initiatives to introduce flexible working practices as well as to extend the use of already-existing practices.[7]

According to the EPOC data shown in Table 4.4, the highest figures for management initiatives in the area of job rotation are to be found in Sweden and Denmark. While Germany was assessed above as likely to display comparatively high rates of job rotation compared with France and the United Kingdom, this does not appear to be the case for initiatives to introduce or extend the practice. Here, both Germany and France, together with the Netherlands and Portugal, have figures well below those of the United Kingdom, which are close to the average for the 10 countries. Most countries show lower figures for the introduction or extension of job rotation than for team working, where there is also comparatively little variation overall.

Despite its already very high figures for individual and group delegation, Sweden reports the highest level of initiatives for the involvement of lower level employees, followed by France, the Netherlands and the United Kingdom. The countries with the lowest figures are Denmark and Portugal, with Germany also well below average. Recent initiatives to flatten management structures are reported comparatively frequently in Denmark, Sweden and the United Kingdom. Figures for Italy and Portugal are a good deal lower.

For Australia, changes over time in the number of indicators related to the delegation of responsibility to lower level employees are available from comparisons of the Australian Workplace Industrial Relations Surveys of 1990 and 1995 (Table 4.5). Over this period, while there was no change for quality circles, there was a substantial rise in the proportion of Australian workplaces reporting three other forms of employee involvement: joint consultative committees; task forces or *ad hoc* joint committees; and employee representatives on board of managing directors. Increased use of a range of flexible working practices, again with the exception of quality circles, can be seen in Table 4.3, referring to Fortune 1 000 companies in the United States. The strongest increase is apparent for self-managing work teams, where the proportion of workforces reporting their use almost tripled between 1987 and 1996. However, the proportion of firms applying them to 40 per cent or more of their workforces remains small.

D. Summary of national patterns

There has been considerable debate as to the extent to which national systems of workplace industrial relations and corporate governance are conducive to the spread of flexible working practices. Regalia (1995) has argued that two important dimensions of workplace industrial relations are, first, whether there is a normative framework to support co-operative relationships between social partners in workplaces and, second, the source of any such framework. The source may be located within the enterprise itself, or it may flow from a higher level,

---

7. In addition to information on initiatives to extend the use of flexible working practices, it is important to consider to what extent practices are partially, or wholly abandoned. However, such information is sparse and must be treated with caution. Managers may be more reluctant to talk about initiatives which have failed. This might be why many studies which have investigated this issue by direct questioning, such as those reported by Wood and Albanese (1995), Storey (1995) and Bernard (1998), tend to find little evidence of the abandonment of most forms of flexible practices. However, there is evidence, in addition to that from the CEO study cited below, of the abandonment of many quality circle schemes [see for example, Boje and Winsor (1993); Hill (1995)]. It is possible that this issue will be clarified by means of the longitudinal workplace surveys which will soon be available for analysis in a number of countries, including France and the United Kingdom.

being based on legislation, general agreements between the social partners, or some combination of the two. A refinement of this classification is to consider whether or not there are institutional arrangements for works councils. In addition, aspects of corporate governance might be relevant. In some countries, such as Germany, worker representatives may have rights to board membership, as part of a "stakeholder" system of corporate governance. In other countries, such as the United Kingdom and the United States, which combine a "voluntarist" system of industrial relations with a "shareholder" approach to corporate governance, they have no such rights.

A close examination of the indicators used in this section suggests that none of these ways of classifying countries is capable of explaining the distribution of flexible working practices. For example, despite the similarities in the workplace industrial relations systems in Germany and the Netherlands (both of which are subject to statutory regulation, and have works councils with co-determination rights) the indicators show different patterns – Germany displays more evidence of job rotation and the Netherlands, team working. However, both of these countries along with France, report comparatively few management initiatives for either of these elements of job design.

A number of geographical patterns suggest themselves. There are some similarities in patterns within the Nordic countries and the Southern European countries, for example. However, these similarities are not very deep. In general, for the Nordic countries, reports of flexible working in Sweden and Finland are substantially higher than in Denmark and Norway. Again, despite the similarities in the results for the Southern European countries of Italy, Portugal and Spain, there are considerable differences, such as the comparatively high figures for management initiatives to introduce team working in Spain.

In order to take the analysis further, the next section examines the types of establishments in which initiatives for flexible working practices are most common.

II. In what types of workplaces are flexible work organisation practices most common?

A. Theory

Section I established the existence of substantial differences across countries in the incidence of flexible work organisation practices. The characteristics of the workplaces themselves – *e.g.* the size of the employer, the industry, and whether or not a trade union is present – undoubtedly play a role in determining whether or not particular practices are adopted.

The type of characteristics that can be examined as potential correlates of flexible work organisation practices hinges on the research design. As Osterman (1995) has noted, studies of the prevalence of flexible workplace practices generally fall into one of three areas, depending on the main source of information. Case studies examining in great detail the work organisation of one or a handful of firms are at one end of the spectrum and, at the opposite end, are nationally representative surveys asking a relatively small number of questions that are straightforward enough for the answers to be easily converted into quantitative or qualitative variables. In between these two are studies examining a range of firms within a particular industry or industries.

It is evident that there are advantages and disadvantages to each type of research, with the ability to generalise the results to a large portion of the economy coming at the cost of richness of detail. As nationally representative datasets are the main sources used in this section to assess the characteristics of establishments with flexible work practices in place, the focus will be primarily on the kinds of variables that are available in such sources and these factors are discussed below.

Size of the workplace

The size of a workplace is a dimension that has received considerable attention in the economics and management literature. It is likely to play a role in the adoption of flexible practices, though the direction of the effect is not clear, *a priori*. If there are economies of scale involved in implementing and maintaining the new practices, larger firms will be more likely to employ them. Larger employers may also possess advantages in terms of having the resources available to make costly organisational changes or in gathering information about the latest developments in management philosophy. Many of the flexible practices stress the importance of improving communication among employees. Such concerns may be less pressing at smaller workplaces, where informal contact among employees may be more frequent. Relatedly, (very) small employers are almost necessarily less hierarchical than larger ones, lessening the need to take measures to "flatten" the organisational structure.

Industry and ownership

The industry of a workplace may have an important relationship to human resources practices. Certain products and services may be better suited than others to the production styles to which the newer practices are complementary. Similarly, the technology in use and capital intensity are also apt to be linked to human resources management.

Whether or not a workplace is privately-owned and whether or not it operates for profit also may influence the types of work practices in place. As with size, however, it is difficult to predict in advance the direction of these relationships. While the private sector is presumably the driving force in OECD economies, not all private firms are on the cutting edge. Private firms have pressure to improve their performance to maintain profitability, but public entities can face such pressures as well [Marsden (1996)]. For state-owned companies, moreover, additional resources may be available to invest in the workforce. Such firms, government agencies, and, perhaps, non-profit firms as well, may be more apt to take measures that improve the work environment for their employees, rather than only taking measures thought to improve performance directly.

Competition

A number of facets of the competition a workplace faces are also likely to influence the human resources practices in place. Many of the innovative practices are often viewed as less compatible with businesses that compete to provide a simple product at the lowest possible cost and more compatible with competition on the basis of quality or variety, where businesses must differentiate their products and modify them to meet specific customer needs. It is frequently assumed that stiff product market competition raises the rate of innovation, as managers and workers are forced to work harder and smarter in order to stay in business. But, for taking initiatives with respect to work organisation practices as with any innovations, significant resources are required for successful implementation, suggesting that firms with above-average profits will find it easier to finance these types of organisational changes. Companies that have recently lost ground to their competitors may also consider adjustments to work organisation, though this may be more likely when the source of the problem is considered to be internal [Pil and MacDuffie (1996)]. Finally, the extent of foreign competition may have an effect distinct from that of domestic competition, as the process of selling goods or services abroad may increase the company's exposure to innovations abroad, including those in the human resources arena. But, as Osterman (1994) notes, the causality may run in the opposite direction, with an improved performance made possible by the new practices now enabling a firm to compete internationally.

Industrial relations

Human resource practices cannot be considered independently of the state of industrial relations in the workplace. The presence of works councils and trade unions can foster or impede the likelihood of taking initiatives. For some employees, a works council may be viewed as a substitute for increased direct participation [Addison *et al.* (1997)]. In addition, in an atmosphere where workers are highly suspicious of the motives of managers, unions may consider as threatening mechanisms that encourage communication between managers and employees while bypassing the unions. In North America, where unions have been intertwined with an internal labour market system under which the wage scale is closely tied to a specific, narrowly-defined job rather than to a worker's skills and qualifications and where progression up the job ladder is often tied to seniority, a movement toward more flexible ways of assigning workers requires, at a minimum, a major reorientation of union thinking [Bélanger and Dumas (1998)]. In a climate of trust between labour and management, however, trade unions may help rally workers to co-operate with management's efforts to improve the productivity of the workplace. In fact, there are examples, such as in the steel and textile industries in the United States, where unions have taken a proactive approach to the reorganisation of work [Appelbaum and Berg (1997)].

Characteristics of work

Bailey (1993) states three conditions that must hold in order for alternative work practices to be able to improve the performance of the establishment: employees should possess knowledge or skills that the managers do not have; employees are motivated to apply this skill and knowledge through what he terms "discretionary effort"; and the organisation is structured in such a way that this discretionary effort can be used in order to bring about better performance. These considerations argue that, if the work is more complex, more variable and requires higher levels of skill, the innovative practices are more likely to be adopted.[8] Some care must be taken, however, in examining this relationship, as the requirements of jobs may not be something dictated by the technology or product market conditions, but by a conscious human resource strategy, of which the innovative work organisation practices may be a part.[9]

Supporting human resource management practices

The conditions laid out by Bailey (1993) also suggest that firms with human resource practices in place that serve to recruit highly-skilled workers, ensure that such workers continue to develop their skills via training and contribute to the motivation of these workers, will also be more likely to have adopted the innovative work organisation practices. For flexible work organisation practices to have a positive impact on firm performance, a "bundle" of complementary practices may need to be in place, which will include both those practices that directly affect how work is carried out, as well as supporting practices such as the existence of training, selective recruiting procedures, and contingent compensation practices (*e.g.* profit-sharing and skill-based pay) that serve to motivate workers [MacDuffie (1995)]. It is also important to bear in mind that firms who have made substantial investments in their workers and are looking for a strong commitment from them, are likely to take steps to encourage a long-term employment relationship. Here, too, caution must be exercised in inferring that the pre-existence of complementary resource practices facilitated adoption of new work organisation practices, rather than vice versa.

Barriers to adoption

The discussion above suggests that whether and how much flexible work organisation practices improve the performance of a firm depend on various characteristics of the employer as well as the business environment. One explanation for why the use of these practices is not more widespread, therefore, is that any benefits are highly dependent on particular market and product characteristics and thus in a substantial number of cases the gains will be small or non-existent [Bailey (1993)]. There is, however, a belief among some observers, particularly of the American scene, that the rate of adoption is lower than what would be predicted on the basis of where such practices are likely to be profitable. This perceived failure to change organisationally when it would be beneficial to do so has given rise to a literature seeking to explain this behaviour [Levine and Tyson (1990); Appelbaum and Batt (1994); Levine (1995)]. One explanation focuses on the reluctance on the part of managers to cede control and responsibility to lower-level workers. Another, only applicable in countries where equity markets play a dominant role and have a short-term focus, is that the financial markets tend to view more favourably investments in physical capital than harder-to-monitor, less tangible investments in human capital required to implement flexible workplace practices.

These arguments have been taken a step further to suggest that, owing to various market failures, the level of adoption that would result if all firms chose the practices that maximise profits is still below that which is optimal for society as a whole. For instance, it may be the case that a traditionally-managed firm has lower productivity than its more flexible counterpart but may still earn higher profits because its workers are in a weaker bargaining position and thus earn less. As a result, managers have an incentive to resist adoption, even though the combined gains to the firm and the workers would be greater with flexible practices in place. Another argument concerns the possibility of market failure related to employee training, which many have argued causes firms in countries such as the United States and the United Kingdom to train their workers too little [Lynch (1994)]. Assuming that

---

8. The research of Finegold and Wagner (1997), comparing the United States and Germany pump industries, provides an example of how the influence of the skill levels of jobs on the move toward work reorganisation may be mediated by a range of labour market institutions. Skilled American workers were found to be less likely than their German counterparts to resist the movement toward teams, as most of the former did not come through an apprenticeship programme and, partly as a result, identified themselves less with a particular craft and the accompanying specialised set of skills.

9. As the relationship between skill requirements of jobs and work organisation indicates, difficult issues are raised in terms of which variables should be treated as exogenous and which as endogenous. The practice used here is to regard as exogenous those characteristics that are presumably beyond the control – at least over the short-term – of the managers who decide on human resources practices. These variables include the industry and size of employer, the presence of trade unions and work councils, and whether or not a workplace is for-profit or state-owned. Characteristics that measure some of the dimensions of work and human resource practices other than those of work organisation, though they will be used as independent variables, will be considered separately.

Table 4.6. **Flexible work organisation practices by workplace size**
Percentages

A. EPOC: initiatives taken in the three years prior to the 1996 survey[a]

Workplace size (number of employees)	Flattening of management structures	Greater involvement of lower level employees	Installation of team-based work organisation	Job rotation	At least one of the four initiatives	Average *number* of initiatives (not percentage)
All	26.5	30.9	25.4	10.8	56.3	0.94
1-49	24.7	25.4	19.5	12.3	50.9	0.82
50-99	23.6	29.3	24.8	9.3	54.0	0.87
100-499	28.3	34.9	29.0	10.0	60.3	1.03
500-999	39.8	37.7	28.5	13.1	67.4	1.19
1 000+	40.9	39.0	33.4	12.9	66.5	1.26

B. Australia: presence of practices, 1995

Workplace size (number of employees)	Autonomous work groups	Quality circles	Team building	Total quality management
All	43.0	13.2	47.2	36.6
20-49	41.5	10.6	43.3	30.5
50-99	45.4	13.7	45.8	37.2
100-199	41.2	18.4	55.4	44.0
200-499	47.1	16.4	60.9	53.5
500+	48.2	22.4	61.7	69.2

C. Sweden: presence of practices, 1994

Workplace size (number of employees)	Job rotation	Teams[b]
All	65.8	91.3
1-49	58.6	90.8
50-99	62.0	88.4
100-199	64.6	90.4
200-499	75.1	96.3
500+	85.8	100.0

a) For Italy, the three *months* prior to the survey in 1996.
b) The question pertains to whether any employees involved in direct production are organised in work teams. See Annex 4.A for the definition of direct production.
Source: See Annex 4.A.

---

employers with the flexible practices need workers with higher levels of problem-solving and interpersonal skills, such firms may be put at a competitive disadvantage by the need to devote substantial resources to recruitment and skill development to redress the "under-training" that has occurred [Levine and Tyson (1990); Levine (1995)].

B. Empirical evidence

The new evidence presented in this subsection derives from an analysis of the EPOC survey of 10 European nations as well as of data from national surveys of Australia and Sweden (see Annex 4.A). As noted above, it is important to keep in mind the caveat that the EPOC survey measures whether initiatives have been recently taken in the area of flexible work organisation practices, while other surveys note whether or not a practice is currently in use. Of those workplaces with any such practice in place at the time the questionnaire was filled out, the EPOC survey will pick up those who have either recently introduced a practice or have made changes in the way this practice is implemented, but may miss cases where a long-standing practice has not changed recently.

Size and industry

Table 4.6 shows by establishment size the tendency of initiatives in the area of flexible workplace practices to have been recently taken in the ten EU countries and, for Australia and Sweden, the prevalence of these practices. Among the EU countries overall, it is apparent that the odds of having taken at least one initiative as well as the average number of initiatives tends to increase with size, though not dramatically so. For instance, the proportion of establishments with at least one of the four practices being considered here, ranges from 51 per cent for establishments with fewer than 50 employees to 67 per cent for those with 1 000 or more workers. The likelihood of having each of the four individual practices tends to rise with size class, though, in the case of job rotation, the relationship is quite weak. For Australia and Sweden, the likelihood of a practice already being in place tends to rise with size, though the strength of this relationship varies with the practice.

Table 4.7 indicates that there is not much variation across sectors in the EPOC countries in terms of the average number of initiatives taken, with the exception of construction (see Annex 4.A for definitions of sectors). Though flexible practices tend to be more strongly associated in the business press with manufacturing than with other industries, only for job rotation is the sector containing manufacturing the one that has most frequently taken initiatives.[10] For Sweden, manufacturing is the clear leader in the prevalence of job rotation and construction lags furthest behind, while for teams, construction is actually in the forefront, while the incidence rate for manufacturing is about average for the economy as a whole. For Australia, manufacturing has an above average prevalence rate in three out of four cases, while construction is actually the leader in terms of the incidence of quality circles and TQM.

Multivariate analysis

In order to incorporate the effects of more than one set of independent variables at a time, logit analysis is used to assess which factors are correlates of having taken initiatives with respect to work practices in the past three years. A standard dichotomous logit is run for each of the four practices and for any of the practices, while an ordered logit is used in the case where the dependent variable is the number of practices where initiatives have been taken. Logit analysis is used in cases where the dependent variable can take on only a small number of values. In the dichotomous logit used in this section, the value is 0 when no practice is in place and 1 when it is. For the ordered logit, the values range from 0 to 4, representing the number of practices in place. The coefficients for the dichotomous logit indicate, all else equal, how a change in one of the independent variables affects the likelihood of a practice being observed, with a positive coefficient indicating that those workplaces with a higher value of the independent variable tend to be more likely to have a particular practice in place. The situation is analogous for the ordered logit, though, in that case, one can calculate the impact of an independent variable with respect to the probability of having each possible number of practices. The EPOC data for all countries are pooled together for this analysis.

Table 4.8 shows the results for the "structural" characteristics, which here include those relating to country, size, industry, the existence of a collective bargaining agreement, the presence of a works council, ownership, profit status, and the presence of foreign competition (see Annex 4.A for a definition of these variables). Certain aspects of the industrial relations system in place are significantly associated with whether or not initiatives have recently been taken. Establishments with works councils – more precisely, those employers who have representatives of the employees in the largest occupation group recognised for consultation or joint decision-making at the workplace – are more likely to have taken initiatives in all practice areas, except for teams. These relationships lead to a similarly positive relationship with the variables for "any initiative" and the average number of initiatives. The presence of a collective bargaining agreement also has a significant relationship with these two summary variables, with unionised workplaces more likely to have flattened their management structure and to have installed teams.[11]

The existence of foreign competition does not always have a significant positive relationship with the taking of initiatives; it is associated with a greater likelihood of having taken measures to flatten management structures and to enhance the involvement of non-supervisory employees, but the relationships with the other two initiatives are insignificant. Overall, though, establishments with foreign competitors were more likely to have taken any one initiative as well as to have taken a greater number of initiatives, a finding that is consistent with that of Osterman (1994).

Whether or not a workplace is private or state-owned does not appear to have a strong effect on the existence of any of the four individual initiatives, though it does have a significant positive relationship with whether or not any initiative occurred.[12] Workplaces in the for-

---

10. Given that retail trade has a reputation for being behind in terms of innovative practices, it may seem surprising that the industry grouping including it has an above-average rate for taking initatives. This grouping does, however, include other industries such as wholesale trade, which past research has shown has a relatively high incidence rate for the presence of these practices [Gittleman *et al.* (1998)].
11. The results are in contrast to those from the United States, with both Osterman (1994) and Gittleman *et al.* (1998) having found no evidence of a significant overall relationship between trade union presence and whether or not an employer had at least one of the practices under consideration, though the latter did find that the presence of a labour union was positively related to some of the individual practices. One explanation for why the American results differ is that American managers may employ certain human resource strategies in order to lessen the attraction of unions [Kochan *et al.* (1986)].
12. This is driven by the fact that the variable for whether a workplace is a private one has a positive, though not statistically significant, relationship with whether or not there is a greater involvement of lower level employees, which is the most prevalent of all the initiatives.

Table 4.7. **Flexible work organisation practices by industry**
Percentages

A. EPOC: initiatives taken in the three years prior to the 1996 survey[a]

Industry[b]	Flattening of management structures	Greater involvement of lower level employees	Installation of team-based work organisation	Job rotation	At least one of the four initiatives	Average number of initiatives (not percentage)
All	26.5	30.9	25.4	10.8	56.3	0.94
Mining and quarrying; manufacturing	27.3	33.0	24.9	13.8	57.5	0.99
Transport, storage and communication; electricity, gas and water	31.3	29.1	21.8	12.4	62.2	0.95
Finance, insurance, real estate and business services	22.5	29.1	26.4	7.6	56.3	0.86
Community, social and personal services	21.3	30.7	25.5	7.8	55.6	0.85
Wholesale and retail trade, restaurants and hotels	31.6	33.9	30.0	11.4	58.6	1.07
Construction	19.8	15.1	15.5	3.6	38.9	0.54

B. Australia: presence of practices, 1995

	Autonomous work groups	Quality circles	Team building	Total quality management
All	43	13	47	37
Mining; manufacturing	47	21	40	39
Transport and storage; communication services; electricity, gas and water supply	40	18	51	44
Finance and insurance; property and business services	49	16	48	45
Health and community services; education; cultural and recreational services; personal and other services; government administration	51	9	49	33
Wholesale and retail trade; accommodation, cafes, restaurants	28	9	49	32
Construction	45	25	41	55

C. Sweden: presence of practices, 1994

	Job rotation	Teams[c]
All	66.0	90.8
Manufacturing	79.9	90.5
Communication	53.1	89.5
Finance	47.7	91.0
Trade	61.5	88.4
Construction	43.5	97.6

a) For Italy, the three *months* prior to the survey in 1996.
b) Differences in terminology are due to differences in national classifications.
c) The question pertains to whether any employees involved in direct production are organised in work teams. See Annex 4.A for the definition of direct production.
Source: See Annex 4.A.

Table 4.8. Correlates of initiatives in flexible work organisation practices[a]

Structural variables

	Flattening of management structures[b]	Greater involvement of lower level employees	Installation of team-based work organisation	Job rotation	At least one practice	Number of practices
Private company	0.028	0.096	–0.169	–0.125	0.258**	0.012
	0.148	0.127	0.127	0.185	0.118	0.105
Workplace active in the profit sector	0.164	–0.092	–0.387***	0.269	0.108	–0.069
	0.151	0.133	0.136	0.194	0.125	0.109
Collective labour agreement binding in the workplace	0.228**	0.167	0.269**	–0.039	0.170*	0.185**
	0.101	0.102	0.107	0.146	0.094	0.082
Foreign competition for workplace products	0.572***	0.281***	0.005	0.181	0.183**	0.299***
	0.089	0.082	0.083	0.116	0.075	0.067
Works council representation	0.179**	0.319***	0.021	0.355***	0.195***	0.240***
	0.086	0.078	0.080	0.112	0.071	0.064
Number of observations[c]	4 244	4 640	4 640	4 640	4 640	4 640

a) Estimates in the last column are based on the ordered logit model and in the other columns, on a standard dichotomous logit model. Structural variables also include controls for country, establishment size and economic sector.
 ***, ** and * indicate significance at the 1%, 5% and 10% levels respectively, asymptotic standard errors are in italics.
 For each model, the likelihood ratio test indicated that the explanatory variables are jointly significant at the 1% level.
b) Spain was excluded from the regression.
c) Because of non-responses to some questions, the number of observations varies and is less than the sample size of 5 786.
Source: Secretariat estimates based on the EPOC survey 1996, see Annex 4.A.

Chart 4.1. Effect of changes in structural variables on the probability of having taken initiatives in flexible work organisation practices[a]

- Benchmark
- Collective labour agreement binding in the workplace
- Works council representation
- Foreign competition for workplace products

Flattening of management structures[b]: 15.8, 19.1, 18.3, 25.0

Greater involvement of lower level employees: 21.5, 24.5, 27.4, 26.7

Installation of team-based work organisation: 20.8, 25.5, 21.1, 20.9

Job rotation: 7.9, 7.6, 10.9, 9.3

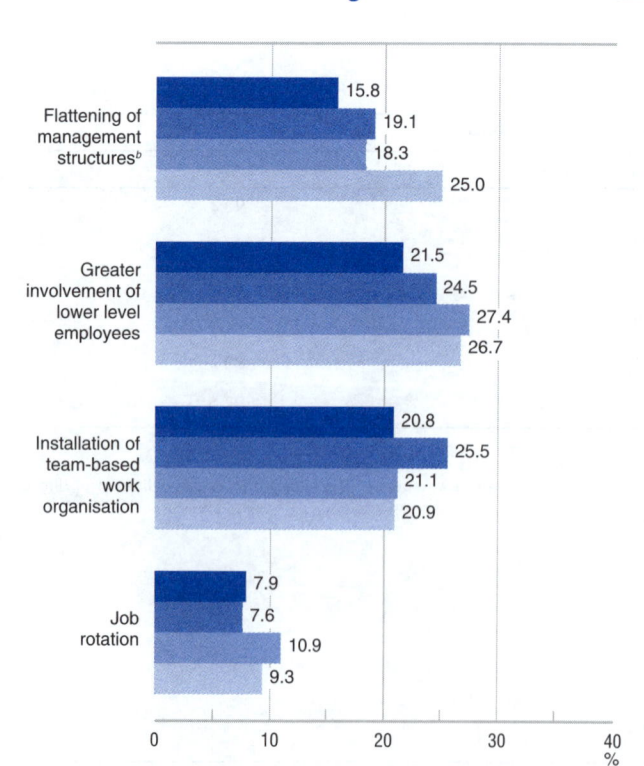

a) Probabilities were calculated using the coefficients and, except for the three structural variables shown in the chart, the means of the variables from the regressions reported in Table 4.8. In the benchmark probability, the three structural variables are set at zero and in the other cases, the appropriate variable is set to one. So, for example, the probability that a workplace introduced flattening of management structures is: 15.8% for workplaces with no collective labour agreement binding, no works council representation and no foreign competition for products (the benchmark); 19.1% for workplaces with a collective labour agreement binding but no works council representation and no foreign competition; 18.3% for workplaces with works council representation but no binding collective agreement and no foreign competition; 25% for workplaces with foreign competition for products but no binding collective agreement and no works council representation.
b) Spain was excluded from the regression.
Source: Secretariat estimates based on the EPOC survey 1996, see Annex 4.A.

profit sector do not appear to be significantly different than their non-profit counterparts in taking initiatives in work practices. This finding is also apparent from a more detailed investigation of the ASTD data presented in Table 4.2.

Chart 4.1 illustrates the quantitative relationship between the probability of having taken an initiative and the three structural variables found to be most important in the regressions of Table 4.8, those relating to trade unions, works councils and foreign competition. For each initiative, the chart shows, as a benchmark, the predicted probability for a hypothetical workplace that has average values for all characteristics other than these three variables, but is not bound by a collective labour agreement, has no works council representation and faces no foreign competition. This probability is then recalculated three times, in each case changing one of these three dichotomous variables to its opposite, but leaving the others unchanged.

As an example, the chart indicates that the probability that this hypothetical employer will have taken an initiative to flatten the management structure is 0.16. The corresponding probability for a workplace with the same characteristics except that a collective labour agreement is in effect is 0.19.

A key issue is whether the influence of these structural characteristics is important in explaining the observed differences in the prevalence of initiatives across countries discussed in Section I. Table 4.9 shows for each of the four initiatives, the probability for workplaces in each country of having taken an initiative, before and after the inclusion of the other structural variables. In other words, the first column of each pair shows the "raw" probability of having taken an initiative, while the second estimates what these probabilities would be if the characteristics of the workplaces for each country were the same as the average for all countries combined. What is striking is that the structural variables, even though in many cases important predictors of the initiatives, explain very little with respect to the cross-country differences. Owing in part to a broad similarity in the distribution of workplace characteristics across nations, the probabilities change very slightly and there are few changes in rank. In general, despite the presence of a number of significant relationships, the explanatory power of the regressions in these sections are very low, indicating the potential importance of factors not measured in the data, *e.g.* a workplace's business strategy or the type of technology in place, in explaining the adoption of flexible practices.[13] It is evident as well, given the large variation across countries, that a range of nation-wide factors also play a major role, such as differences in management culture, industrial relations systems, labour law and public policy.

Does the kind of work being performed affect the likelihood of observing recent initiatives? To test this notion, the specifications summarised in Table 4.8 are augmented by a set of variables describing the characteristics of work. The results are shown in Table 4.10 (see also Chart 4.2 for an indication of the quantitative impact of these variables). When the largest group of non-managerial employees is production employees, the workplace is more likely to have taken initiatives to flatten the hierarchical structure and to enhance lower level involvement, but this is not the case for measures related to teams and job rotation. This finding is slightly at odds with that of Osterman (1994) for the United States, who found that in workplaces where "blue-collar" employees are the "core" employee group, establishments were less likely to have teams in place, but more likely to have job rotation.

One of the conditions noted above for innovative work practices to be effective – that workers should have knowledge and skills that managers do not have – suggests that the practices are more likely to be in place when the work is complex. Some support for this notion is found. Two variables that are suggestive of the complexity of a job – whether work involves a range of different tasks and whether recruits need to be trained – have significant associations with both the number of initiatives and whether or not any initiatives at all have been taken. Both are important predictors of whether workplaces have recently taken initiatives to flatten the management structure and to involve lower level employees to a greater extent. Consistent with this, workplaces where few or no qualifications are required are less likely to have flattened their management structure and to have installed team-based work organisation. In a related finding, Osterman (1994) concluded that the skill levels of jobs were positively related to the presence of the innovative practices.

Finally, it is of interest to examine the relationship between various supporting human resources practices and the initiatives concerning work organisation. EPOC asks a number of questions about the availability for the largest occupational group of incentive compensation schemes that are thought to motivate workers: whether components of pay reflect skill; whether bonuses are related to individual attitude; whether bonuses are related

---

13. As an example, using a linear probability model, where the measure of fit is more easily interpretable than for the logit models, the adjusted R-squared for the probability of having taken an initiative to flatten the management structure rises from 0.065 with country dummies being the only explanatory variables to 0.105, when controls for size, sector, private ownership, for profit, works councils and trade unions are included.

Table 4.9. **Cross-country differences in the probability of having taken an initiative in flexible work organisation practices**[a]

Percentages

Flexible work organisation practice

	Flattening of management structures[b]		Greater involvement of lower level employees		Installation of team-based work organisation		Job rotation	
	Country only[c]	Structural variables[d]	Country only[c]	Structural variables[d]	Country only[c]	Structural variables[d]	Country only[c]	Structural variables[d]
Denmark	44	45	10	11	43	45	24	23
France	20	19	40	39	26	24	6	6
Germany	31	30	18	17	18	17	7	6
Ireland	18	18	31	36	22	25	7	7
Italy	9	7	25	22	29	28	13	12
Netherlands	38	40	46	52	8	8	7	7
Portugal	3	3	10	12	22	23	11	11
Spain	..	..	35	31	40	38	17	15
Sweden	41	41	58	62	24	24	34	33
United Kingdom	48	51	51	54	39	42	16	16
Number of observations[e]	4 244	4 244	4 640	4 640	4 640	4 640	4 640	4 640

.. Data not available.
a) Probabilities have been calculated using the estimated coefficients from the dichotomous logit model and the means of the explanatory variables, other than the country dummies. Italy was included in the regressions but results are not presented since the time frame was only three months instead of three years.
b) Spain was excluded from the regressions.
c) Explanatory variables are country dummies only.
d) Explanatory variables are those in Table 4.8.
e) Because of non-responses to some questions, the number of observations varies and is less than the sample size of 5 786.
Source: Secretariat estimates based on the EPOC survey 1996, see Annex 4.A.

to individual volume of output; whether bonuses are related to team volume of output; whether profit-sharing schemes are available; and whether share-ownership schemes exist. To examine these relationships, variables summarising compensation schemes are added to the specifications and the set describing characteristics of work is removed. Though the cross-sectional data do not allow inferences about causation, a finding that the presence of incentive compensation practices is correlated with the presence of flexible work organisation practices would be consistent with the notion that the two are complementary.

In general, this hypothesis is supported by the EPOC data (see Table 4.11 and Chart 4.3). The compensation practices that have the most consistent relationship to work practice initiatives are profit-sharing and the linkage of pay to skills. The variable for team bonuses is positively related to initiatives for teams and employee involvement. Perhaps reflecting that bonuses for individual output may not be consistent with the more cooperative atmosphere desired under the new practices, however, the coefficient for the existence of such bonuses is not significant in any of the regressions for the individual initiatives. Finally, the results for employee share ownership are mixed, having a significant positive relationship with flattening, but a negative one with job rotation. In general, the results for large-scale surveys from the United States are consistent with these results. Both Osterman (1994) and Gittleman *et al.* (1998) found a positive relationship between pay for skill and profit-sharing with the presence of flexible workplace practices.

In sum, the results of this section suggest that size, industry and the kind of industrial relations system present in the workplace all are related to whether or not an employer will adopt particular work organisation practices. In addition, those workplaces with certain types of incentive compensation schemes in place also tend to have higher incidence rates. Much remains unexplained, however, suggesting the need to supplement the examination of nationally-representative datasets with that of more narrowly focused, but more detailed industry and case studies.

III. Do flexible work organisation practices tend to cluster?

Are there certain combinations of flexible work practices that are frequently observed or do they tend to be implemented in isolation? Two variants of this question

Table 4.10. **Correlates of initiatives in flexible work organisation practices**[a]
Structural variables and characteristics of work

	Flattening of management structures[b]	Greater involvement of lower level employees	Installation of team-based work organisation	Job rotation	At least one practice	Number of practices
Production workers	0.284**	0.305**	−0.010	0.250	0.082	0.210**
	0.139	0.129	0.134	0.185	0.118	0.104
Range of tasks	0.567***	0.293***	0.082	−0.121	0.273***	0.316***
	0.106	0.099	0.102	0.135	0.090	0.080
Technology independent	−0.082	0.079	0.239***	−0.117	−0.124	0.007
	0.096	0.087	0.090	0.124	0.081	0.072
Team activity	0.041	0.172**	0.463***	0.273**	0.290***	0.318***
	0.094	0.086	0.090	0.123	0.081	0.071
Low qualifications	−0.278**	−0.111	−0.340***	−0.067	−0.141	−0.255***
	0.120	0.107	0.114	0.153	0.098	0.087
Recruits need training	0.196**	0.511***	0.154	0.141	0.173**	0.319***
	0.096	0.092	0.094	0.131	0.082	0.073
Number of observations[c]	2 977	3 190	3 190	3 190	3 190	3 190

a) Estimates in the last column are based on the ordered logit model and in the other columns, on the dichotomous logit model. All regressions include the structural variables in Table 4.8.
 ***, ** and * indicate significance at the 1%, 5% and 10% levels respectively, asymptotic standard errors are in italics.
 For each model, the likelihood ratio test indicated that the explanatory variables are jointly significant at the 1% level.
b) Spain was excluded from the regression.
c) Because of non-responses to some questions, the number of observations varies and is less than the sample size of 5 786.
Source: Secretariat estimates based on the EPOC survey 1996, see Annex 4.A.

have been addressed in the literature. The first considers work organisation practices separately from other human resource management practices and is motivated in part by an attempt to make more precise the definition of a "transformed" or "high-performance" workplace [Osterman (1994)]. That is, is the presence of a single alternative practice sufficient to be considered a member of these categories, or are a certain number or combination of practices required?

The second takes a more comprehensive look at human resource management systems, examining not only combinations of work organisation practices, but also how these fit with related policies for compensation, recruitment, training and job security. Analysts have sought to determine whether employers can be grouped based on whether these work systems as a whole are in accord with the stylised models found in the literature. For instance, Appelbaum and Batt (1994) enumerate the sets of workplace policies that correspond to the "American Human Resource, the Swedish Sociotechnical Systems, the Japanese Lean Production, the Italian Flexible Specialization and the German Diversified Quality Production Models".

This search for combinations is also motivated by the view in the management literature that the "organisational logic" of a firm and, thus, its optimal "bundle" of human resource practices will depend on the type of production system in place (*e.g.* mass versus flexible production in manufacturing), and by a theoretical literature in economics on the complementarities that may result when certain practices are used in combination [MacDuffie (1995); Ichniowski *et al.* (1997)]. Similar notions are sometimes expressed in terms of the importance of both "internal fit", where various elements of the HRM system reinforce each other, and "external fit", where the HRM system is appropriate for a firm's overall strategy [Becker and Huselid (1998)]. As a simple example of a case where complementarities do not exist or where there is poor "internal fit", Becker and Huselid (1998) offer the case where job structures are based on teams, but incentive systems and career opportunities are linked solely to individual performance.

An examination of Table 4.12 provides some evidence relating to the first variant of the question, whether certain combinations of work organisation practices are dominant. While the idea that there may be complementarities among such policies is implicit in some of the literature, this notion probably is more meaningful when

Chart 4.2. Effect of changes in characteristics of work on the probability of having taken initiatives in flexible work organisation practices[a]

Legend:
- Benchmark
- Range of tasks
- Recruits need training
- Low qualifications

Flattening of management structures[b]: 16.6, 25.9, 19.4, 13.1

Greater involvement of lower level employees: 20.6, 25.8, 30.2, 18.8

Installation of team-based work organisation: 22.6, 24.1, 25.4, 17.2

Job rotation: 9.5, 8.5, 10.8, 9.0

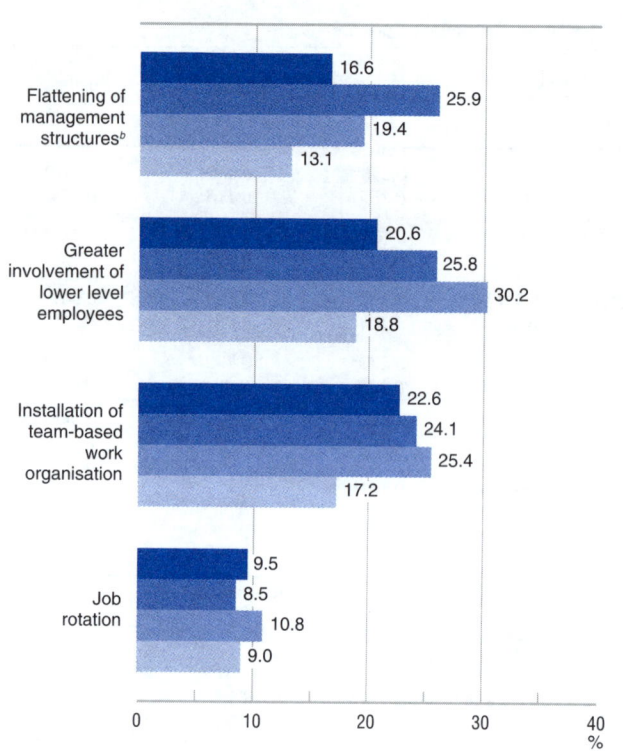

a) Probabilities were calculated using the coefficients and, except for the three work characteristics shown in the chart, the means of the variables from the regressions reported in Table 4.10. In the benchmark probability, the three work characteristics variables are set at zero and in the other cases, the appropriate variable is set to one. So, for example, the probability that a workplace introduced flattening of management structures is: 16.6% for workplaces with no range of tasks, no recruits who need training and where qualifications are not low (the benchmark); 25.9% for workplaces with a range of tasks, but no recruits who need training and where qualifications are not low; 19.4% for workplaces where recruits need training but there is no range of tasks and qualifications are not low; 13.1% for workplaces where qualifications are low but there is no range of tasks and no recruits who need training.
b) Spain was excluded from the regression.
Source: Secretariat estimates based on the EPOC survey 1996, see Annex 4.A.

considering human resource systems as a whole, where complementarities may exist both among the various component HRM practices and between the system as a whole and the firm's business strategy. Though certain work organisation practices may be complements in some settings, they may be substitutes in others. For instance, if employees work together in teams, there may be little need to exchange ideas via quality circles.

The second column of Table 4.12 making use of EPOC data, indicates that, if establishments have taken recent initiatives in the area of work organisation, it is likely that they have done so in only one or at most two areas. That is, of the 56 per cent of workplaces that had taken any initiative at all in the past three years, 46 per cent took only one or two initiatives, while only about 2 per cent took steps in all four areas. Partly as a result, an examination of the prevalence of different combinations of practices reveals no obvious patterns.

The data for Australia, in the third column of Table 4.12, focus on combinations of practices in place, rather than on initiatives recently taken. In part because nearly three-quarters of the sample had at least one practice in place, it is easier to find significant numbers of workplaces with particular combinations of practices. For instance, it is more common to have a two-practice combination of TQM and teams and a three-practice combination of TQM, teams and autonomous work groups than it is to have TQM by itself. And even though quality circles appear in only 13 per cent of the workplaces, they too are more likely to be present in various combinations than by themselves. Even so, as the most prevalent "combinations of practices" are work groups and teams on their own, and neither is present in more than 13 per cent of the establishments, one would be hard-pressed to speak of a particular set of practices as being characteristic of the "transformed" workplace. Osterman (1994) and Gittleman et al. (1998) found a similar lack of dominant combinations in their examination of flexible work practices used by American employers.

IV. What are the labour market correlates of flexible work practices?

A thorough-going reorganisation of work can lead to widespread changes affecting numerous dimensions of work – e.g. compensation, skill requirements, degree of autonomy, the pace of work, and the extent of job

Table 4.11. **Correlates of initiatives in flexible work organisation practices**[a]
Structural and compensation variables

	Flexible work organisation practice					
	Flattening of management structures[b]	Greater involvement of lower level employees	Installation of team-based work organisation	Job rotation	At least one practice	Number of practices
Pay for skill	0.203**	0.134*	0.260***	0.434***	0.207***	0.327***
	0.086	*0.079*	*0.082*	*0.112*	*0.075*	*0.065*
Attitude bonus	0.145	0.186*	0.066	0.423***	0.195**	0.244***
	0.103	*0.100*	*0.103*	*0.134*	*0.094*	*0.081*
Individual volume bonus	0.145	−0.069	0.053	−0.144	0.164*	0.067
	0.097	*0.093*	*0.093*	*0.131*	*0.086*	*0.074*
Team volume bonus	0.003	0.356***	0.424***	0.204	0.457***	0.370***
	0.103	*0.093*	*0.093*	*0.125*	*0.093*	*0.077*
Profit sharing	0.237**	0.656***	0.435***	0.266*	0.367***	0.561***
	0.102	*0.096*	*0.101*	*0.138*	*0.099*	*0.083*
Share ownership	0.377***	0.208	0.090	−0.410**	0.218	0.257**
	0.141	*0.132*	*0.134*	*0.198*	*0.144*	*0.113*
Number of observations[c]	3 826	4 182	4 182	4 182	4 182	4 182

a) Estimates in the last column are based on the ordered logit model and in the other columns, on the dichotomous logit model. All regressions include the structural variables in Table 4.8 and control for whether production workers are the largest occupational group.
 ***, ** and * indicate significance at the 1%, 5% and 10% levels respectively, asymptotic standard errors are in italics.
 For each model, the likelihood ratio test indicated that the explanatory variables are jointly significant at the 1% level.
b) Spain was excluded from the regression.
c) Because of non-responses to some questions, the number of observations varies and is less than the sample size of 5 786.
Source: Secretariat estimates based on the EPOC survey 1996, see Annex 4.A.

security – which may cause changes in job satisfaction, the rate of absenteeism, the extent of friction between managers and workers, the rate of job turnover and the like. On balance, the evidence suggests that firms can improve their performance with the introduction of flexible work organisation practices, though the question of whether workers also benefit has been little studied. The need for more evidence on this issue is all the more pressing in light of the divergent views on the impact that these practices will have on the workforce. In this section, hypotheses about the potential impacts of these practices on workers are discussed and then the empirical evidence is examined.

A. Theory

Compensation

Do workers benefit financially from the presence of innovative human resource practices? If these practices actually raise the productivity of a firm and if this improvement is not matched by its competitors, the productivity gains will be translated into higher profits and higher employee compensation, with the share going to each depending in part on the bargaining power of the workers. Other rationales for paying higher wages in the presence of flexible work organisation practices are closely linked to those stressed in the "efficiency wage" literature, where wage premia are justified in terms of boosting worker effort, reducing turnover, attracting the best workers and improving morale [Groshen (1991)].

Skill requirements of jobs

Another channel through which compensation may be affected by flexible work practices is through the influence of the latter on the skills required of workers. If the introduction of new practices increases the skills demanded, this may lead to higher productivity and higher wages. The new work systems are also predicted by many to lead to jobs with a greater variety of tasks; greater individual autonomy; and jobs with higher levels of empowerment as non-managerial employees make decisions which were previously the prerogative of managers [Handel (1998); Cappelli and Rogovsky (1994)]. In order to raise the level of skills, additional training is thought to be needed, an example of a supporting human resource practice. It is, of course, possible that significant numbers of the new, more highly skilled jobs will go to workers who

Chart 4.3. Effect of changes in compensation variables on the probability of having taken initiatives in flexible work organisation practices[a]

Practice	Benchmark	Pay for skill	Profit sharing	Team volume bonus	Attitude bonus
Flattening of management structures[b]	21.6	25.2	25.9	21.7	24.2
Greater involvement of lower level employees	24.1	26.7	38.0	31.2	27.7
Installation of team-based work organisation	19.8	24.2	27.6	27.4	20.8
Job rotation	6.6	9.9	8.5	8.0	9.8

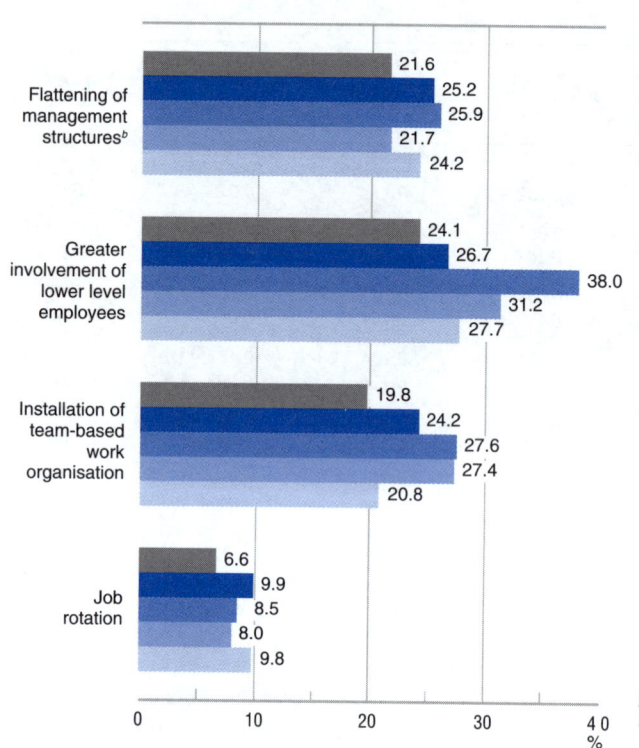

a) Probabilities were calculated using the coefficients and, except for the four compensation variables shown in the chart, the means of the variables from the regressions reported in Table 4.11. In the benchmark probability, the four compensation variables are set at zero and in the other cases, the appropriate variable is set to one. So, for example, the probability that a workplace introduced flattening of management structures is: 21.6% for workplaces with no pay for skill, no profit sharing, no team volume bonus and no attitude bonus (the benchmark); 25.2% for workplaces with pay for skill, but no profit sharing, no team volume bonus and no attitude bonus; 25.9% for workplaces with profit sharing but no pay for skill, no team volume bonus and no attitude bonus; 21.7% for workplaces with a team volume bonus but no pay for skill, no profit sharing and no attitude bonus; 24.2% for workplaces with an attitude bonus but no pay for skill, no profit sharing and no team volume bonus.
b) Spain was excluded from the regression.
Source: Secretariat estimates based on the EPOC survey 1996, see Annex 4.A.

had been employed elsewhere rather than to retrained incumbent workers.

As is the case with predicting the impacts of the introduction of new technologies, however, there is ample reason to be cautious about predicting that the adoption of the flexible practices will raise skill levels across the board and that most or all workers will benefit. Cappelli (1996) suggests that the expectations that skill demands will be increased may be more appropriate for production workers than for their supervisors. Supervisors may serve as teachers and monitors of employees, on the one hand, and also as "lead workers", functioning alongside production workers. If the new practices raise the skill levels of production workers, supervisors will face fewer demands for monitoring, but may find themselves facing increased demands in their function as lead workers, as the skills and abilities of the workers being supervised increase. For other supervisors, the shifting of additional tasks to lower-level workers – either individually or as teams – implies that their jobs may be lost or their status downgraded.[14]

Job satisfaction

Proponents of flexible workplace practices assert that workers will achieve greater satisfaction on the job, and that this will help to reduce absenteeism and turnover. One prominent model speaks of five core task attributes that are linked to job satisfaction: that the job requires a variety of skills; that the job involves completion of an identifiable piece of work; that the job has a significant impact on others; that the job provides the worker with autonomy; and that the worker receives feedback about performance [Appelbaum and Berg (1997)]. Increased flexibility of work organisation has the potential to move the worker towards greater satisfaction along many, if not all, of these dimensions. There are reasons to suspect, however, that the changes in work life resulting from

---

14. Cappelli and Rogovsky (1994) offer a concrete example for scepticism about the extent to which the skill requirements of jobs are raised by changes in work organisation. In the New United Motors (NUMMI) joint venture between Toyota and General Motors, some of the tasks previously performed by industrial engineers were relegated to production teams. But, using the example of statistical process control techniques, these authors argue that it is not necessary for every worker to understand every aspect of the technique: "If one person understands the notion of confidence limits in making statistical inferences, another can read the charts, and a third knows the machine tools well enough to troubleshoot when the problems have been identified, together they have a team that can make the technique work" (pp. 212-213).

Table 4.12. Percentage distribution of number of flexible work organisation practices

Number of practices	Initiatives taken in the 3 years prior to the 1996 survey, EPOC countries[a]	Practices present, Australia, 1995[b]
0	43.6	24.3
1	29.4	32.8
2	16.5	25.5
3	8.5	13.4
4	1.9	4.0

a) Spain is excluded because of a mistranslation in the question about flattening of management structures. Italy is excluded because the time frame is three months rather than three years. Initiatives under consideration are those relating to a flattening of management structures, greater involvement of lower level employees, installing of team-based work organisation and job rotation.
b) Practices under consideration are autonomous work groups, quality circles, team building and total quality management.
Source: See Annex 4.A.

these practices may not be universally positive. For some workers, the increased responsibility may be unwanted. In addition, some of the innovations connected with "lean production", such as "just-in-time" inventory systems, which are designed to eliminate the buffers or intermediate products between work groups, may also lead to increased stress and faster work pace as work groups seek to ensure that their performance does not delay the work of other groups downstream [Cappelli and Rogovsky (1994); Parker and Slaughter (1993)].

Functional and numerical flexibility

In a number of OECD countries, there has been much discussion about the extent to which firms have shifted away from reliance on permanent workers and moved in the direction of part-time, temporary, contingent and contract workers [see Chapter 1; OECD (1996a)]. In the United States, analysis has centred around the question of whether internal labour markets[15] are in decline and being replaced by market-mediated arrangements with workers outside the firm [Abraham (1990)]. In Britain, there has been an active debate about the extent to which a "core-periphery" model of employment is relevant [Atkinson and Meager (1986)].

Though the question of movement toward a more contingent and insecure workforce is hotly debated, it is also of considerable interest to examine the controversial question of what, if any, influence a movement to more flexible workplace practices might have on the stability of employment relationships. It should be noted that hypotheses in these areas tend to have a weaker theoretical foundation than those connecting profit-sharing to employment stability, for instance, where the structure of the compensation package itself may affect hiring and firing considerations [Kruse (1998)]. One hypothesis is that flexible workplace practices will help slow any movement towards a "contingent" workforce, as the increased "functional flexibility" implied by teams, job rotation, flexible job design and other practices, enables workers to shift into different tasks and lessens reliance on "numerical" flexibility, i.e. changes in the numbers of employees (including sub-contracted and temporary workers) and their hours.

However, there may be little reason to expect that the need for increased employment stability will encompass all workers. Instead, this relationship may only be important for a group of selected workers, suggesting that innovative practices may not reduce the need for reliance on "numerical" flexibility or, in fact, could increase it, as firms seek to protect the core group of workers in whom they have made large investments [Marsden (1996)].

B. Empirical evidence

Here, new evidence on the relationship between flexible work practices and selected labour market outcomes is presented, using the EPOC survey as well as data from surveys representative of single nations. Among the latter, the 1995 Australian Workplace Industrial Relations Survey (AWIRS95) and the US Survey of Employer-Provided Training (SEPT95) contain components addressed both to employers and to employees (see Annex 4.A). The results derived from the employer and employee surveys are presented separately in Tables 4.13 and 4.14.

Compensation

As a first cut, mean earnings were calculated by workplace (Australia and the United States) and by

---
15. Groshen and Levine (1998) define internal labour markets as being characterised by: "long-term commitments between employers and employees, defined career paths, limited ports of entry for each career path, wages tied to job (rather than personal) characteristics, and pay structures that exhibit rigidities across occupations and time".

Table 4.13. **Mean values for labour market outcomes by presence of flexible work organisation practices**
Australia, 1995

	Autonomous work groups		Quality circles		Team building		Total quality management		Any practices	
	No	Yes	No	Yes	No	Yes	No	Yes	No	Yes
Workplace survey										
Full-time average workplace weekly earnings (A$)	650*	682	665	655	659	668	665	660	646	669
Voluntary labour turnover (%)	21*	15	20	13	18	20	17	21	19	19
Absenteeism (%)	2.6	2.6	2.6	2.5	2.6	2.6	2.6	2.6	2.5	2.6
Formal training provided (%)	62**	75	66**	79	62**	75	62**	78	55**	72
Employment growth (%)	5.1	3.8	4.7	3.6	3.8	5.4	4.0	5.5	1.1	5.7
Part-time employees (%)	31**	21	29**	21	28	29	30	26	32*	27
Non-core workers (%)	25**	20	24*	18	23	23	24*	21	27**	22
Dismissals (%)	2.4*	1.7	2.1	2.3	2.2	2.0	2.0	2.3	1.8	2.2
Employee survey										
Job is satisfying[a]	1.51	1.49	1.50**	1.54	1.50	1.51	1.50	1.51	1.52	1.50
Lot of effort required[a]	1.86**	1.88	1.87	1.87	1.87	1.87	1.87	1.87	1.86	1.87
Job is stressful[a]	1.14**	1.17	1.15	1.18	1.16	1.14	1.14	1.17	1.11**	1.16
Post-secondary education (%)	48**	54	50*	53	52*	50	50**	52	46**	52
Received job training over last 12 months (%)	64**	67	65*	67	61**	68	63**	67	59**	66
Do different tasks[a]	1.75**	1.78	1.76**	1.78	1.76	1.76	1.76	1.77	1.74*	1.77
Feel insecure about job[a]	0.86*	0.89	0.86**	0.91	0.87	0.87	0.85**	0.89	0.84*	0.88
Job tenure (years)	6.0	6.1	6.0**	6.1	6.0	6.1	5.6**	6.5	5.9	6.1
Part-time (%)	25**	20	24**	20	23	23	26**	19	27**	22

* Differences are significant at the 5 per cent level.
** Differences are significant at the 1 per cent level.
a) Theoretically, scores may range from 0 to 2, with 0 meaning that all respondents disagreed with the statement and 2 meaning that all respondents agreed.
Source and definitions of labour market outcomes: See Annex 4.A.

worker (United States only), by whether or not the workplace has adopted a particular work practice. In Australia, average weekly earnings for full-time employees are not significantly different depending on whether or not a practice is in place, except in the case of autonomous work groups. In the United States, average establishment monthly wages are significantly different for five of the seven practices. Of the former, the wages are higher in all cases, except for that of job rotation. The American results from Table 4.14 also suggest that hourly wages for workers tend to be higher in establishments where flexible practices are in place.[16]

On the other hand, Handel and Gittleman (forthcoming) have examined the relationship between practices and wages of American employers using this SEPT95 database and find, after controlling for other factors that may influence wages, that very few significant differences remain. That is, neither average wages by establishment nor hourly wages for individuals are consistently higher when one of the flexible work organisation practices is in place than when it is not.

Two studies by Cappelli (1996, 1998) also consider the implications of the use of innovative work practices on wages. His analysis make use of a representative sample of the United States' establishments with 20 or more employees, which contains several measures of work organisation (the percentage of non-managerial and non-supervisory employees in self-managed teams, the number of levels between a first-line supervisor and the top official, the presence of a formal TQM program and the employee/supervisor ratio or span of control). After controlling for industry, size and other firm characteristics, employee attributes, and the importance of various traits in hiring, Cappelli (1998) finds that TQM is associated with higher average annual salaries for supervisors, production workers, managers, and technicians, though not for clerical workers. Self-managed teams is the only other work organisation variable to have a significant rela-

---

16. As with any cross-sectional relationship, the finding of a significant correlation is consistent with the practices having raised wages, higher wages having encouraged the adoption of the practices, or both the practices and wages being correlated with a third factor. Perhaps even more important, many other factors influence wages on both the establishment side (*e.g.* the size and industry of the workplace) and the individual side (*e.g.* schooling and job tenure) and these variables have not been taken into account.

Table 4.14. Mean values for labour market outcomes by presence of flexible work organisation practices
United States, 1995

	Practice is present?	Formal training provided in last 12 months (%)	Share of workforce which is part-time (%)	Share of workforce which is contract/ temporary (%)	Average monthly establishment wage, 4th quarter 1993 ($)
Workplace survey					
Employee involvement in firm's technology and equipment decisions	No	87.7**	26.9**	25.2*	2 007**
	Yes	98.6	16.8	32.2	2 393
Job redesign or re-engineering	No	89.6**	25.1**	23.9**	2 102*
	Yes	98.8	16.7	38.0	2 342
Job rotation	No	90.4**	21.4	29.1	2 259*
	Yes	96.5	24.4	26.8	2 020
Co-worker review of employee performance	No	91.2**	22.5	27.6	2 101**
	Yes	98.7	22.2	31.6	2 526
Quality circles	No	90.5**	23.4	27.4	2 163
	Yes	98.1	19.8	30.8	2 217
Total quality management	No	89.4**	22.6	22.8**	2 080*
	Yes	96.5	22.2	35.3	2 302
Self-directed work teams	No	90.6**	23.6**	26.3**	2 127
	Yes	100.0	17.8	36.4	2 377
At least one of the above practices	No	80.3**	25.2	22.5*	1 993*
	Yes	96.4	21.6	30.1	2 237

	Practice is present?	Formal training provided in last 12 months (%)	Share of workforce which is part-time (%)	Tenure with current employer (years)	With post-secondary education (%)	Average hourly wage ($)
Employee survey						
Employee involvement in firm's technology and equipment decisions	No	68.9	18.3**	7.3*	56.9*	12.35**
	Yes	70.5	6.6	8.4	63.8	14.50
Job redesign or re-engineering	No	62.5**	16.4**	6.4**	58.3	12.58**
	Yes	78.3	6.5	9.6	63.5	14.65
Job rotation	No	73.7**	10.0	8.1	65.4**	13.54
	Yes	65.6	13.8	7.7	55.7	13.52
Co-worker review of employee performance	No	66.0**	13.6**	7.3**	57.6**	12.83**
	Yes	83.5	5.4	9.9	71.9	16.10
Quality circles	No	65.8**	13.5*	7.4*	57.0**	12.20**
	Yes	75.6	9.4	8.5	66.1	15.50
Total quality management	No	61.4**	14.1*	6.3**	58.5	13.03*
	Yes	75.9	10.2	9.0	62.2	13.89
Self-directed work teams	No	64.8**	14.1**	7.0**	56.6**	12.45**
	Yes	81.5	6.5	10.0	70.4	16.07
At least one of the above practices	No	58.6**	13.0	5.6**	53.8	12.19*
	Yes	71.5	11.7	8.2	61.7	13.74

* Differences are significant at the 5 per cent level.
** Differences are significant at the 1 per cent level.
Source: See Annex 4.A.

Table 4.15. **Mean percentages for labour market outcomes by presence of flexible work organisation practices**
Sweden, 1994

	Job rotation		Teams [a]	
	No	Yes	No	Yes
Workers with above median level of post-secondary schooling [b]	62.2	44.7	56.9	47.7
Staff turnover [c]	34.1	41.5	47.0	39.3
Time in skill development for direct production workers [d]	6.0	8.0	7.0	7.6

a) The question pertains to whether any employees involved in direct production are organised in work teams.
b) Workplaces were ranked in terms of the proportion of the workforce with education beyond secondary school.
c) Turnover rate is defined as [2(hires+quits)/(employment in 1993 + employment in 1994)].
d) Respondents were asked to provide the "percentage of the work task [that] can be regarded as organised skill improvement".
Source: See Annex 4.A.

tionship with salaries, having a positive relationship for supervisors, production workers and clerical workers. Cappelli concludes that the higher wages are paid not because workers in establishments with TQM or that make greater use of teams actually have greater levels of human capital, but because they are being paid an "efficiency-wage-type premium" to compensate them for the increased effort that these practices require.

Osterman (1998) examines the links between innovative work practices and compensation gains. He is unable to detect a significant relationship between whether an establishment was a "high performance work organisation" in 1992 and whether its workers received a wage increase five years later.[17] Bailey and Bernhardt (1997) conclude from their case studies of retail firms that workplace innovations have done little in this sector to raise wages or improve benefits. Osterman (1994), moreover, did not find any significant differences, on the basis of the presence of flexible work practices, as to whether or not workplaces operated an "efficiency wage" policy, i.e. the payment of higher wages than in other establishments for comparable workers in the same industry and geographic area.

Skill requirements of jobs

Does the presence of flexible practices affect the skill requirements of jobs? Examining Tables 4.13, 4.14, and 4.15, one can see whether workplaces with the practices have more educated workforces than those without them. In Australia, the percentage of the workplace with a post-secondary education is significantly higher for three of the practices, but is significantly lower in the case of team building. In the United States, the differences are statistically significant in five out of seven cases. Job rotation stands out, as it did in the case of wages, as the only practice where education levels are significantly lower when the practice is not in place than otherwise. In Sweden, however, the results of Table 4.15 suggest, for job rotation and teams, that the proportion of the work force with post-secondary schooling is higher at workplaces without the practice than at their counterparts with the practice.[18]

These results contrast the average educational attainments of workers at establishments with and without the practices, but reveal less about how skill levels of workers actually participating in a practice compare with those who do not, a distinction not possible with these data. Freeman, Kleiner and Ostroff's (1997) study of US private-sector firms contains information on both the presence of a practice, as well as on whether a given employee actually participates. They find not only that the likelihood of being at a firm with employee involvement[19] increases with education, but also that the probability of participating in such a program does as well.

Cappelli and Rogovsky (1994) report the result of their study of the connection between the practices and skill requirements themselves (rather than between the former and the educational attainment of the workforce), using a sample of 561 workers employed in ten US public utilities and holding 15 common job titles covering jobs

---

17. An establishment was considered to be a "high establishment work organisation" if it had two or more practices in place (among quality circles, job rotations, teams and TQM) affecting 50 per cent or more of "core" employees.
18. As with compensation, however, caution is warranted in interpreting the relationships, as other factors that may influence skill requirements, such as the kind of technology in use, are not taken into account in these comparisons.
19. The definition of employee involvement (EI) used in this study encompasses a broader range of practices than considered in the chapter. It includes self-managed work teams, worker involvement in the design of EI programs, TQM, committees on productivity, worker involvement in work processes, formal suggestion systems, formal information-sharing with employees and surveys of workers regarding their satisfaction.

ranging from production to managerial work. The design of the study allows a comparison of the demand for skills between establishments that are divided into two groups on the basis of the extent to which they used work practices associated with high-performance work systems. Skills are divided into three areas: foundation skills (basic reading and mathematical skills, communication and thinking skills, responsibility and management), interpersonal skills and various workplace competencies. Generally, the skills demanded in the groups employing the new practices more intensively are greater in all three areas, though the differences are not large.

Cappelli (1996) tests the proposition that innovative practices have changed skill requirements in the United States. Establishments were asked whether skill requirements for production jobs have risen in the past three years, and this measure is correlated with the four measures of work organisation noted above. The analysis also controls for other factors that might also affect skill requirements, such as capital intensity, research and development, the use of computers, the education and experience of the employees, and the presence of a union. The results suggest that the presence of TQM, teamworking and a flatter organisation are associated to some extent with a greater likelihood of rising skill requirements.

As noted above, the new practices may change the variety of tasks in which skills are used. Table 4.13 shows that, in Australia, workers are significantly more likely to agree with a statement that they perform different tasks if they are in a workplace with autonomous work groups or with quality circles than otherwise, though, even for these two cases, the differences are not large.

There does appear to be a strong relation between training and the presence of flexible work practices. For both the United States and Australia (Tables 4.13 and 4.14), almost without exception, workplaces with one of the practices are more likely to have a formal training programme in place and workers at such establishments are more likely to receive training. In Sweden (Table 4.15), the portion of time spent in skill development is higher in workplaces with the practices in place than in those without. These results tend to be consistent with those elsewhere in the literature [Lund and Gjerding (1996); Osterman (1995); Lynch and Black (1998); Frazis *et al.* (1998)].[20]

Job satisfaction

Some of the information about Australian workplaces in Table 4.13 provides direct and indirect evidence about whether workers are more satisfied with their jobs when flexible work organisation practices have been introduced. When questioned directly, only in the case of quality circles were workers significantly more likely to agree that they were satisfied, but the size of the difference is quite small. Only in the case of autonomous work groups did workers in establishments with the flexible practices face somewhat higher requirements for effort and greater levels of stress. Surprisingly, however, and reflecting that these factors did not have a large impact on work satisfaction, this is the only case as well where workers were significantly less likely to leave their jobs. Indicating that employee involvement improves satisfaction, Freeman, Kleiner and Ostroff (1997) found in their survey of American workers that elimination of the EI program would have "bad" or "very bad" effects on them. A review by Appelbaum and Berg (1997), however, finds that, historically, the evidence in this area has been mixed.

Functional and numerical flexibility

Hypotheses about the impact of flexible work organisation suggest effects, often contradictory, on many measures of the employment relationship, including the share of part-time workers, the use of temporary help and the extent of sub-contracting. Table 4.16 shows the results of a regression analysis on the relationship between the measures related to numerical flexibility that can be observed in the EPOC data and having recently taken the four initiatives that have been discussed throughout the chapter. Evidence on these relationships is also available from cross-tabulations derived from the individual national surveys of Australia, Sweden and the United States (Tables 4.13, 4.14 and 4.15).

In the analysis of the EPOC data, the "structural" characteristics discussed in Section III are included as independent variables to take into account other factors that may influence these relationships. The country of the establishment is included in light of cross-national differences that may affect the various dependent variables such as the stage of the business cycle, rates of gross job creation and job destruction, the tendency to adjust for changes in demand via changes in employment levels and changes in hours, and in the use of "flexible" working arrangements.

---

20. Interestingly, Coutrot (1996*b*) finds a negative relationship between training and just-in-time inventory in establishments in France, though a positive association with other forms of organisational innovation.

Table 4.16. **Labour market outcomes and initiatives in flexible work organisation practices**[a]

	Dependent variable							
	Working time reduction	Working time flexibility	Downsizing[b]	Outsourcing[c]	Rise in proportion working part-time	Rise in proportion of temporary contracts	Rise in sub-contracting	Change in employment[d]
Flattening of management structures[e]	0.165	0.260***	0.760***	0.704***	0.318***	0.253**	0.295***	−0.386***
	0.116	0.080	0.084	0.104	0.108	0.103	0.112	0.072
Number of observations[f]	4 431	4 431	4 055	3 790	3 234	3 321	4 431	4 326
Greater involvement of lower level employees	−0.022	0.530***	0.176**	0.230**	0.196**	0.006	0.042	0.305***
	0.111	0.075	0.084	0.103	0.099	0.089	0.106	0.065
Number of observations[f]	4 431	4 431	4 055	3 790	3 234	3 321	4 431	4 326
Installation of team-based work organisation	0.167	0.592***	0.326***	0.509***	0.217**	0.083	−0.074	0.129*
	0.111	0.077	0.086	0.104	0.103	0.092	0.110	0.067
Number of observations[f]	4 431	4 431	4 055	3 790	3 234	3 321	4 431	4 326
Job rotation	0.816***	0.595***	0.060	0.474***	0.382***	0.593***	0.089	−0.192**
	0.135	0.104	0.120	0.139	0.143	0.124	0.145	0.091
Number of observations[f]	4 431	4 431	4 055	3 790	3 234	3 321	4 431	4 326
At least one practice	0.353***	0.398***	0.449***	0.593***	0.348***	0.131	−0.038	0.031
	0.104	0.072	0.082	0.102	0.100	0.087	0.097	0.060
Number of observations[f]	4 431	4 431	4 055	3 790	3 234	3 321	4 431	4 326
One practice	0.406***	0.106	0.299***	0.484***	0.305***	0.075	−0.119	−0.075
	0.117	0.083	0.093	0.115	0.113	0.100	0.113	0.069
Two practices	0.226	0.446***	0.556***	0.570***	0.286**	0.165	−0.043	0.384***
	0.145	0.099	0.111	0.137	0.135	0.115	0.138	0.085
Three practices	0.214	1.602***	0.791***	0.811***	0.653***	0.071	0.178	−0.200*
	0.201	0.136	0.141	0.178	0.172	0.173	0.184	0.117
Four practices	1.004***	0.569**	0.751***	1.818***	0.489	0.914***	0.566**	−0.534**
	0.291	0.233	0.242	0.271	0.321	0.266	0.278	0.208
Number of observations[f]	4 431	4 431	4 055	3 790	3 234	3 321	4 431	4 326

a) Estimates in the last column are based on the ordered logit model and in the other columns, on a standard dichotomous logit model. All regressions include the structural variables in Table 4.8 and control for whether production workers are the largest occupational group. ***, ** and * indicate significance at the 1%, 5% and 10% levels respectively, asymptotic standard errors are in italics. For each model, the likelihood ratio test indicated that the explanatory variables are jointly significant at the 1% level.
b) Spain was excluded from the regressions.
c) Sweden was excluded from the regressions.
d) Change in employment comprises the three groups: an increase, about the same and a reduction.
e) This variable takes the value one if the response was flattening, in any country other than Spain, and zero otherwise.
f) Because of non-responses to some questions, the number of observations varies and is less than the sample size of 5 786.
Source: Secretariat estimates based on the EPOC survey 1996, see Annex 4.A.

An increase in working-time flexibility is consistently associated with the presence of the different work organisation initiatives that have been taken in the past three years. Working-time flexibility evidently complements a less rigid functional use of the workforce. Initiatives in the areas of outsourcing and downsizing are also consistently associated with the work organisation initiatives as well. Further research is needed to see if the forces that have led to a downsizing cause firms to move to a more participatory workplace – either because they have rethought their business philosophy or to improve the morale of the remaining workers.[21]

Is there evidence of any relationship between the flexible work practices and the use of contingent workers? For the EPOC countries, having taken one of the four work organisation initiatives does not tend to have an important impact on the probability of a rise in the proportion of temporary contracts nor a rise in the use of subcontracting (Table 4.16). In Australia, the use of non-core workers tends to be higher where the practices are not

---

21. Some evidence on this score is provided by Osterman (1998). He finds that restructuring, as measured by layoffs, does not significantly affect the likelihood of adopting innovative practices nor of abandoning those already in place. However, those with flexible practices in place in 1992 were more likely to have layoffs in subsequent years.

present, whereas in the United States, the situation is the opposite. The evidence on the use of part-time workers, another aspect of numerical flexibility, is mixed as well. In the EPOC data, those workplaces taking initiatives in the area of work organisation were also more likely to have increased the proportion working part-time. For Australia and the United States, however, the bulk of the evidence suggests that workplaces with the practices have a higher proportion of full-timers.

Do establishments with flexible organisation practices in place have a better record in terms of job creation than their counterparts? Some have speculated that employers may introduce flexible practices at a time of worsening economic conditions and layoffs, partly as an effort to improve morale among the remaining workers. Such a relationship could make it more likely that workplaces taking initiatives have experienced employment declines in the recent past. Somewhat strangely, however, the establishments that recently took initiatives with regard to flattening the management structure and job rotation are more likely to have increased employment in the largest occupation, while for the other two initiatives, the opposite is true. For Australia, the differences in net employment growth rates are never statistically significant.

Finally, the data from individual countries can be used to shed some light on whether employment relationships are, indeed, more stable in workplaces where the flexible practices are in place. In Australia, as shown in Table 4.13, the dismissal rate is significantly lower at workplaces with autonomous work groups (1.7 per cent) than at those without (2.4 per cent), but this is not the case with the other practices. In three out of four cases, however, employees at workplaces with the practices in place feel more insecure about their jobs. In Sweden, the turnover rate, which includes all categories of workers joining and leaving a firm, is higher among establishments making use of job rotation and lower where teams are in use, relative to their counterparts without these practices. Though it is difficult to draw inferences about job stability from tabulations of average tenure, it is of interest to know that in the United States and to a lesser extent in Australia, average tenure tends to be greater at firms where the practices are in place.

Conclusions

This chapter has provided an assessment of the current state of evidence about the incidence of "flexible working practices" across countries. It has also attempted to uncover relationships between flexible working practices in firms and the wider labour market.

In response to most workplace surveys, managers tend to report quite high levels of initiatives in favour of flexible working. For example, in response to the 1996 EPOC survey, covering ten European countries, on average 27 per cent of managers reported initiatives in favour of the introduction or extension of team working in their workplaces in the previous three years, with virtually all countries in the range from 20 to 40 per cent (these figures refer to workplaces with 50 or more employees). Figures relating to already-existing schemes to encourage employment involvement are even higher. Overall, managers appear to be reporting a considerable degree of investment in flexible working practices. However, it must be acknowledged that there is almost no evidence on the rate at which flexible working practices are being abandoned, and little about the intensity of use of such practices.

The limited evidence pertaining to changes over time in the incidence of flexible working practices tends to indicate an increase. This applies to a number of employee involvement practices in Australia over the period 1990 to 1995, and to a wide range of flexible working practices in Fortune 1000 companies in the United States from 1987 to 1998 (in both cases, quality circles were an exception).

It appears that both the reported incidence of flexible working practices and the indications of change differ considerably from country to country. These national differences persist even where there are similarities between their national and workplace industrial relations systems. None of the usual ways of classifying countries, for example, according to their industrial relations systems, seem capable of explaining the patterns that are observed. There are some similarities between neighbouring countries, such as the Nordic countries and the southern European countries. However, they are matched by significant differences.

The differences by type of firm are much less clear-cut than the differences by country. Indeed, the currently available data show only a limited indication of patterns. Larger establishments are generally more likely than smaller ones to have adopted flexible practices, though the strength of this relationship seems to differ by country and by practice. Manufacturing workplaces tend to have above-average prevalence rates, but despite the strong association many of the practices have with this sector, it does not always appear to be the leading sector in this respect. Another finding is that, in general, the existence of various incentive compensation schemes, particularly profit-sharing and pay linked to skills, are positively correlated with the presence of (or initiatives towards) flexible practices. Initiatives to promote flexibility in working-time practices tend to be associated with all of the flexible working practices discussed here.

Recent years have seen a good deal of interest in the interaction between the rate of introduction of flexible working practices and workplace industrial relations systems. For example, it has been argued that initiatives for teamworking might be less frequent in countries with well-established systems of works councils, for two reasons. First, they might not be perceived to be necessary, if co-operative working is indeed assured by the works councils. Second, they might not be as easy to introduce, to the extent that these same bodies have to give their approval.

The evidence available suggests that managers do indeed tend to report fewer initiatives on average for job rotation and team working in two countries, Germany and the Netherlands, where workplace industrial relations systems are particularly well-developed, and where employees have the right to works councils with co-determination powers. This is not the end of the story, however. As noted, overall, establishments with works council representation are more likely to have flattened management structures, enhanced the involvement of lower-level employees, and introduced or extended job rotation. The seeming contradiction is resolved by the fact that, within countries, those firms with works councils have a higher rate of taking initiatives than their counterparts. The chapter also presented evidence of a positive correlation between the presence of trade unions and both the flattening of management structures and the installation of teams. Here, the explanation seems to involve "between-country" effects. That is, countries such as Sweden that have higher rates of unionisation also have higher incidence rates for the initiatives under consideration.

Few strong relationships could be found between flexible working practices in firms and variables likely to be associated with conditions in the wider labour market. Admittedly, this result could well be a function of the weaknesses inherent in this type of data. In addition, in some cases, such as the relationship between numerical and functional flexibility, the absence of a consistent association may not be surprising, given that arguments can be adduced for both a positive and negative correlation. In light of the tendency noted in the literature for the innovative practices to raise productivity and profits, however, it is harder to explain the absence of solid evidence that they are associated with higher wages as well. There are numerous plausible explanations for this, including that many of the workplaces with innovative work organisation practices do not have adequate supporting human resource practices, that the performance of more "flexible" firms hinges substantially on the technology in use and product market conditions, and that workers do not receive a large share of any gains that do accrue to the firm. It is not possible, however, to distinguish among the competing explanations with the data at hand.

The most robust relationship discovered was that workplaces with flexible practices tend to train more than those who do not have them. Regarding education level (where evidence is limited to a number of national surveys), in Australia and the United States, workplaces with flexible work organisation practices tend to have higher proportions of workers who have gone beyond secondary school. However, that does not seem to be the case for Sweden.

The evidence presented in this chapter provides little support for the oft-asserted proposition that greater recourse to flexible working practices will lead to a growing polarisation between "core" and "peripheral" workers. Consistent positive relationships were not found between the presence of flexible working practices and the numbers of workers on various types of "non-standard" work contracts, including part-time and temporary working.

It must be stressed that the available data do not permit any analysis of other aspects of the "polarisation" thesis. It has not, for example, been possible to study the effects of flexible working practices on the distribution of earnings within firms. Here, some commentators have suggested that the pay-for-performance schemes, which seem to be associated with the introduction of flexible working practices, are likely to lead to somewhat greater inequality. Again, there is no information here on the effects on career progression, or employment tenure, for different types of workers, particularly those who may be considered less able to work in the more demanding conditions which appear to be associated with some forms of flexible working.

Overall, despite the progress that has been made in developing survey instruments, it must be admitted that is still very difficult to assess the degree to which there have been changes in work organisation, and harder still to evaluate their impact on the different types of firms and groups of workers. There are a number of ways of making progress: case studies to examine changes in work organisation practices in detail in a small number of firms; nationally representative surveys to provide linked employer-employee data, preferably with a longitudinal capability; and, in between these two extremes, studies of a range of firms within a particular industry. Experience gathered so far appears to highlight the importance of using all these instruments in a concerted way.

Annex 4.A

Sources and Definitions

The EPOC Survey

The Survey of Employee Direct Participation in Organisational Change is part of a major investigation by the European Foundation for the Improvement of Living and Working Conditions, an autonomous body of the European Union. Conducted during 1996, this was a postal survey of workplaces in Denmark, France, Germany, Ireland, Italy, the Netherlands, Portugal, Spain, Sweden and the United Kingdom. A standard questionnaire was used, translations being made from the English original. The respondent was the general manager of the workplace or the person he or she felt was most appropriate.

Throughout the survey, the time frame of reference is the three years up to 1996, so the initiatives taken in the area of work organisation, as well as the labour market outcomes discussed in the chapter, occurred in this period. As will be detailed below, many of the survey questions requested information about the largest occupational group, defined as the occupational category selected by the respondent as having the largest number of non-managerial employees at the workplace.

Survey sample

The sample was designed to be representative of workplaces with 20 or more employees for the smaller and medium-sized countries and 50 or more employees for the larger countries (France, Germany, Italy, Spain and the United Kingdom). Names and addresses of workplaces were selected at random from national business registers. Response rates ranged from 9 per cent for Spain to 38 per cent for Ireland, and averaged 21 per cent. While caution in interpreting the results is warranted given the high levels of non-response, it should be noted that these response rates are typical of those from mail surveys sent to enterprises by research institutes and are comparable to response rates for similar, strictly national surveys. Appropriate weights were assigned to each establishment on the basis of the probability of sampling and an adjustment for non-response. Sample distributions are given in Table 4.A.1.

Variable definitions

Dependent variables

Many of the dependent variables in the logit analysis were derived from the survey's question 9, which asked "Which of the following initiatives have been taken by the management of this workplace in the last three years?" Possible responses included: flattening of management structures; greater involvement of lower level employees; installing of team-based work organisation; and job rotation. In addition, the following other initiatives in the list were used as dependent variables describing outcomes for workers: working-time reduction; working-time flexibility; downsizing; and outsourcing. For all dependent variables derived from this question, the variable was coded as "1" if the initiative was checked and "0" if it was not.

Rise in proportion working part-time: 1 = if largest occupational group has been affected in last three years by increase in proportion of people working part-time; 0 = otherwise.

Rise in proportion of temporary contracts: 1 = if largest occupational group has been affected in last three years by increase in proportion of people working on temporary contracts; 0 = otherwise.

Rise in sub-contracting: 1 = if largest occupational group has been affected in last three years by increase in subcontracting of their activities; 0 = otherwise.

Change in employment: Respondents were asked how the number of employees in the largest occupational group compares with the situation three years earlier: 2 = "there has been an increase"; 1 = "about the same"; 0 = "there has been a reduction".

Structural variables

Private: 1 = workplace is a private company; 0 = state or semi-state-owned company/institution.

For profit: 1 = profit sector; 0 = non-profit sector.

Collective agreement: 1 = workplace is bound by a collective labour agreement; 0 = no collective labour agreement.

Foreign competition: 1 = competition for goods and/or services described as facing "domestic competition with little foreign competition" or "both domestic and foreign competition"; 0 = "no competition" or "only domestic competition".

Works council: 1 = representatives of the employees in the largest occupational group elected to a work council are recognised for the purposes of consultation/negotiation and or joint decision making at the workplace; 0 = otherwise.

Size: Four dummy variables are used to represent establishments divided into five size classes: 49 or fewer employees; 50 to 99 employees; 100 to 499 employees; 500 to 999 employees; and 1 000+ employees.

Table 4.A.1. **EPOC survey 1996: gross, actual and weighted samples by country, ranked by weighted share**

Percentages

	Gross	Actual	Weighted
Germany	15	14	27
United Kingdom	15	14	19
France	15	10	16
Italy	12	9	15
Spain	15	8	9
Netherlands	7	9	5
Portugal	3	5	3
Sweden	7	13	3
Denmark	8	12	2
Ireland	3	7	1
Total	100	100	100
Sample size	33 427	5 786	5 786

Source: EPOC survey.

Table 4.A.2. **Economic sectors used in the analysis**

Sector	EPOC survey: sector in which workplace is most active
Mining and quarrying; manufacturing	Mining Manufacturing industry Process industry
Transport, storage and communication; electricity, gas and water	Transport, warehousing and communications Public utilities
Finance, insurance, real estate and business services	Banking/insurances Professional services
Community, social and personal services	Public administration Education (Public) health and social welfare Culture and recreation/leisure
Wholesale and retail trade, restaurants and hotels	Wholesale Retail trade Catering, hotels
Construction	Construction and installation

Source: EPOC survey.

Industry: Five dummy variables are used to represent the six industry groupings described below.

Country: Nine dummy variables are used to represent the 10 countries.

Characteristics of work

Production workers: 1 = largest number of non-managerial employees are "production; operational"; 0 = otherwise.

For the other characteristics of work, respondents were asked to answer on a scale from 1 to 5, where 1 means total agreement with a statement given and 5 indicates total agreement with the statement's opposite.

Range of tasks: 1 = answered with 1 or 2 to "work involves range of different tasks"; 0 = otherwise;

Technology independent: 1 = answered with 1 or 2 to "pace of work is independent of technology"; 0 = otherwise.

Team activity: 1 = answered with 1 or 2 to "work is essentially a team activity"; 0 = otherwise.

Low qualifications: 1 = answered with 4 or 5 to "a high level of qualification is required"; 0 = otherwise.

Recruits need training: 1 = answered with 1 or 2 to "recruits have to be trained to do the job"; 0 = otherwise.

Compensation variables

All questions refer to largest occupational group.

Pay for skill: 1 = "components reflecting skill/qualifications" are part of wages; 0 = otherwise.

Attitude bonus: 1 = "bonuses related to individual attitude" are part of wages; 0 = otherwise.

Individual volume bonus: 1 = "bonuses for individual volume of output" are part of wages; 0 = otherwise.

Team volume bonus: 1 = "bonuses for team volume of output" are part of wages; 0 = otherwise.

Profit-sharing: 1 = employees of largest occupational group are eligible for profit-sharing schemes; 0 = otherwise.

Share-ownership: 1 = employees of largest occupational group are eligible for share-ownership schemes; 0 = otherwise.

Economic sectors used in the analysis

Sectors used in the EPOC Survey have been grouped as shown in Table 4.A.2 in order to yield industry groupings large enough to obtain sufficiently precise estimates of variables representing these sectors in the regression analysis.

The EPOC sector manufacturing industry accounts for 30 per cent of the weighted sample, while the predominant occupation group is production/operational (40 per cent of the total sample).

Data constraints imposed by the questionnaire

Responses regarding the variables derived from question 9 were affected by the following:

Italy: 3 years to 1996 was translated as 3 months to 1996.

Spain: both "flattening of management structures" and "downsizing" were translated incorrectly.

Sweden: "outsourcing" was omitted from the list of choices.

In addition, the format of the questionnaire made it impossible to distinguish between cases where there was non-response and those where management did not take any of the initiatives. Eight per cent of the questionnaires fell into this category.

Question 18 asked, among other things, whether there had been an increase in sub-contracting. Again, the format of the question does not enable distinction between those who were not affected by any of the changes mentioned and those who did not answer the question. Approximately one-third of respondents left all boxes blank for this question.

Question 21 addresses employee representation by a trade union, works council or advisory committee established by management. In the French questionnaire, the box for works council option was omitted but, nevertheless, about one quarter of respondents indicated that there was employee representation by a works council.

In addition, for many of the questions, the level of unambiguous non-response is not insignificant, leading to a substantial reduction in the sample size available for the regressions. Details on how these data constraints were taken into account are provided below.

Estimation of models

All estimations use weighted data. To take into account the problems with question 9 noted above, Spain was excluded when flattening of management structure and downsizing were dependent variables and Sweden when outsourcing was the dependent variable. Italy was included in all regressions, however, under the assumption that the impact of the difference in time frame will be absorbed into its dummy variable. As noted above, for some questions it is impossible to distinguish between cases where the respondent did not check any boxes because he/she skipped the question and cases where no boxes were checked because none of the choices applied. The results reported in this chapter assume that, in such cases, no choice applied. Extensive testing was done, however, to see if the results are sensitive to this decision. In general, they were not, as coefficients almost always had the same sign under alternative treatment, and effects that were statistically significant tended not to become insignificant and vice versa. There are a handful of cases where previously significant coefficients do become insignificant, partly owing to the reduction in sample size that results from treating the ambiguous cases as non-responses. In addition to the assessment of the impact alternative treatments of individual question non-response have on the estimates, extensive testing was also done to determine if the results are sensitive to changes in regression specification.

The dichotomous logit results presented in Tables 4.8, 4.10, 4.11 and 4.16 are coefficients, b_1 to b_k, from an estimated model of the form

Probability
$(y_i = 1) = F(a + b_1 x_{1i} + b_2 x_{2i} + ... + b_k x_{ki})$ or

$P_i = F(Z_i)$

where F is the logistic function.

For example, in Table 4.8 the first column presents coefficients from an estimation of the probability that a workplace had taken an initiative to flatten its management structures, using the structural characteristics as explanatory variables.

The probabilities in Table 4.9 and Charts 4.1 to 4.3 were calculated using the appropriate estimated model. For example, the coefficients in Table 4.8 were used to calculate the probabilities in Chart 4.1. For the benchmark probability, it is assumed that there is no binding collective labour agreement, no works council representation and no foreign competition, so these variables are set to zero. All other variables are set to the corresponding mean calculated by averaging over the sample used in the regression. P_i is then calculated using the formula above. To show the impact of the variable indicating the presence of a collective labour agreement, the same procedure is used except that its variable is set to 1, while leaving set to zero the variables relating to works councils and foreign competition. Analogous calculations are then made to estimate the impact of the variables for works council representation and foreign competition.

Australia – 1995 Australian Workplace Industrial Relations Survey (AWIRS95)

The 1995 Australian Workplace Industrial Relations Survey (AWIRS95) was conducted between August 1995 and January 1996 for the Department of Employment, Workplace Relations and Small Business (previously the Department of Industrial Relations). The components of AWIRS95 used here are designed to be representative of workplaces with 20 or more employees in all States and Territories of Australia, excluding those in agriculture, forestry and fishing, and defence. In addition to surveying employers, an employee questionnaire was distributed to a random sample of employees at those workplaces in the employer sample where the senior manager agreed that employees could participate. The workplace survey had a response rate of 80 per cent, while that for the employees was 64 per cent. For the existence of workplace practices, answers were taken from two questions about practices currently in place at the workplace. Calculations using AWIRS95 were provided by Bill Harley, Department of Management, University of Melbourne.

Definitions of variables in Table 4.13 derived from employer responses

Full-time average workplace weekly earnings: for each of eight occupational groups, managers were asked to assign a range (usually of A$50) for the earnings of "most" full-time employees. The midpoint of the range was then assigned for each group and multiplied by the number of employees in that group. These amounts were then summed over the groups and divided by the number of full-time employees.

Voluntary labour turnover (%): voluntary resignations divided by number of permanent employees.

Absenteeism (%): the share of all employees who are away from work or on sick leave without leave having been approved in advance.

Formal training provided (%): proportion who answered "yes" to the question whether or not the organisation provided in the last year "any formal program of instruction for employees designed to develop their skills".

Net employment growth (%): growth in employment in the year through the pay period ending on or before 18 August 1995.

Part-time (%): the number of part-time employees as a share of the establishment's total workforce.

Non-core (%): the sum of non-core workers (casual employees, agency workers, home or outworkers and contractors and their employees) as a share of the total workforce at the workplace.

Dismissals (%): the number of dismissals in the 12 months preceding the survey as a share of the total number of employees.

Definitions of variables in Table 4.13 derived from employee responses

Post-secondary education (%): share whose highest level of education is beyond "completed secondary".

Received job training in the last 12 months (%): portion of those who said that employer provided "training to help do [...] job" in last 12 months.

Job tenure: length of time at the workplace.

Part-time: those whose usual hours fell below 35 hours a week were considered to be part-time employees.

The responses to a number of subjective questions were also used. With the exception of the job satisfaction question, employees could respond to these questions by disagreeing, by neither disagreeing nor agreeing, or by agreeing with a particular statement. In calculating the average scores shown in Table 4.13, these three responses were coded as 0, 1 and 2, respectively. In each case, if all respondents agreed with a statement, the average score would be 2. A similar scale, indicated below, was used for the job satisfaction question.

Job is satisfying: respondents were asked "Are you satisfied with the following aspects of your job?" Responses to the aspect "Your job overall" were coded as 0 (dissatisfied), 1 (neither satisfied nor dissatisfied) or 2 (satisfied).

Lot of effort required: "I put a lot of effort into my job".

Job is stressful: "My job is very stressful".

Do different tasks: "I do lots of different tasks in my job".

Feel insecure about job: "I feel insecure about my future here".

See Morehead *et al.* (1997) for additional details.

Denmark – The DISKO project

In Denmark, a survey of flexibility was performed within the DISKO project in 1996. DISKO is an acronym for "The Danish Innovation System in a Comparative Perspective". The purpose of the project was to study the Danish innovation systems and identify salient future challenges. The survey covered private business firms with 20 or more employees within the goods production sector and with 10 or more employees within the service sector. A questionnaire was administered by mail in May 1996, covering the period 1993-1995. Nineteen hundred firms responded to it, representing a response rate of 52 per cent for goods production and 45 per cent for services. Full details are to be found in *Den fleksible virksomhed, Omstillingspres og fornyelse i dansk erhvervsliv*, DISKO-Projektet: Rapport nr. 1, Erhvervsudviklingsrådet, September 1997 and Gjerding (1998).

Finland

The Finnish survey was carried out for the Ministry of Labour in co-operation with the University of Helsinki. Both a mail and telephone questionnaire were used. The mail questionnaire was sent out in November 1996 to private sector workplaces with 10 or more employees. Responses were obtained from 830 workplaces, representing a response rate of 63 per cent. The telephone survey received responses from 1 384 workplaces, a response rate of 83 per cent. The telephone interviews were carried out during November and December 1996 and the complementary mail survey followed during the period January to March 1997. In both cases, the information obtained referred mainly to the end of 1996 and the first months of 1997. Details are to be found in Juha and Pekka (1999*a* and 1999*b*).

Norway

The recent Norwegian study on flexible work organisations was carried out under the responsibility of the Ministry of Labour and Government Administration and the Institute for Social Research. It was carried out by telephone interviewing during February and March 1997, with the questions mainly covering 1996. The scope was private and public workplaces with 10 or more employees. Two thousand one hundred and thirty establishments participated out of the gross sample of 2 800, representing a response rate of 76 per cent. The full details are to be found in *Fleksibilitet i norsk arbeidsliv*, edited by Karen Modesta Olsen and Hege Torp, Institutt for Samfunnsforskning, February 1998.

Sweden – The NUTEK Survey

The NUTEK (Swedish National Board for Industrial and Technical Development) survey used in this chapter is described in full in NUTEK (1996). It was carried out within the framework of the OECD study, "Technological and Organisational Change and Labour Demand: Flexible Enterprises – Human Resource Implications". The survey was based on a questionnaire mailed to a sample of private-sector workplaces with at least 50 employees. The sample covered the following industries: mining and manufacturing; construction; retail, wholesale, hotels and restaurants; transport and communication; and other business activities including financial and real estate. The total number of workplaces registered with Statistics Sweden and meeting these criteria was 6 038. A stratified sample of 2 064 workplaces was taken, and 707 usable questionnaires were returned. There was a slight bias in response towards the manufacturing sector at the expense of the others (especially within the less densely populated regions). The possible bias resulting from this was assessed by means of follow-up telephone surveys and it was concluded that the effects might be to slightly underestimate both labour productivity and the extent of flexible work organisation. NUTEK's Department of Industrial Policy Analyses performed the NUTEK calculations used in this chapter.

While the indicator used in this chapter for whether job rotation exists refers to all employees, that for teams is for workers involved in what is termed "direct production". "Direct production" is defined in manufacturing as the employees who produce, in construction as those who do the construction work, in trade as the personnel who are involved in sales and stockkeeping work, in transportation as those who are working with direct transportation, loading and unloading and customer contacts, and in the financial sector as the personnel working with financial services and customer services.

The NUTEK survey has been co-ordinated with three other surveys in the Nordflex project. These surveys cover Denmark, Finland and Norway, as described above.

United States – Survey of Employer-Provided Training, 1995 (SEPT95)

The 1995 Survey of Employer-Provided Training (SEPT95) was conducted by the US Bureau of Labor Statistics (BLS) for the Employment and Training Administration (ETA) of the US Department of Labor in order to provide representative data on the training practices of employers. The sample was designed to be representative of the universe of private non-agricultural establishments with fifty or more employees. In addition to collecting data from establishments, two randomly-chosen employees in the responding establishments were selected for interviews as well. SEPT95 consists of four survey instruments – a questionnaire and a training log for both the employer and employees.

The employer questionnaire asked about an establishment's work practices, enabling workplaces to be classified on the basis on whether they use job rotation, total quality management, self-directed work teams, etc. Information was also collected on whether formal training was provided in the last 12 months, the number of employees in the establishment, the number of employees considered to be part-time workers, and the number of contract workers or workers employed by temporary help agencies. In addition, in order to calculate an average monthly establishment wage, information was obtained from the BLS Universal Data Base (UDB) on the total payroll of each establishment for the fourth quarter of 1993 and the sum of employment over each month of the quarter. Usable employer questionnaires were obtained from 1 062 of the respondents, implying a response rate of 74 per cent. Weights are used in all calculations.

For the employee questionnaire, the analysis here relies on questions about whether formal training was received in the last 12 months, usual hours worked, tenure with current employer, highest level of education completed and gross earnings. Those whose usual hours fell below 35 hours a week were considered to be part-time employees. 1 074 usable employee questionnaires were collected, representing a response rate of 51 per cent. Weights are used in all calculations. [See Frazis *et al.* (1998) for additional details.]

BIBLIOGRAPHY

ABRAHAM, K.G. (1990),
"Restructuring the Employment Relationship: The Growth of Market-Mediated Work Arrangements", in Abraham, K. and McKersie, R. (eds.), *New Developments in the Labor Market*, The MIT Press, Cambridge, MA, pp. 85-118.

ABRAHAMSON, E. (1996),
"Management Fashion", *Academy of Management Review*, No. 1, pp. 254-285.

ADDISON, J.T., SCHNABLE, C. and WAGNER, J. (1997),
"On the Determinants of Mandatory Works Councils in Germany", *Industrial Relations*, No. 4, pp. 419-445.

APPELBAUM, E. and BATT, R. (1994),
The New American Workplace: Transforming Work Systems in the United States, ILR Press, Ithaca, NY.

APPELBAUM, E. and BERG, P. (1997),
"Work Reorganization and Flexibility in Job Design", in Lewin, D., Mitchell, D.J.B. and Zaidi, M.A. (eds.), *The Human Resource Management Handbook, Part 2*, JAI Press, Stamford, CT, pp. 45-62.

ATKINSON, J. and MEAGER, N. (1986),
"Is Flexibility Just a Flash in the Pan?", *Personnel Management*, Vol. 18, September, pp. 26-29.

BAILEY, T. (1993),
"Discretionary Effort and the Organisation of Work: Employee Participation and Work Reform Since Hawthorne", Teachers College, Columbia University, January, mimeo.

BAILEY, T.R. and BERNHARDT, A.D. (1997),
"In Search of the High Road in a Low-Wage Industry", *Politics & Society*, June, pp. 179-201.

BASSI, L.J. and VAN BUREN, M.E. (1999),
"The 1999 ASTD State of the Industry Report", supplement to *Training and Development Magazine*, January.

BECKER, B.E. and HUSELID, M.A. (1998),
"High Performance Work Systems and Firm Performance: A Synthesis of Research and Managerial Implications", *Research in Personnel and Human Resources Management*, Vol. 16, JAI Press, Stamford, CT, pp. 53-101.

BÉLANGER, J. and DUMAS, M. (1998),
"Teamwork and Internal Labour Markets: A Study of a Canadian Aluminium Smelter", *Economic and Industrial Democracy*, August, pp. 417-442.

BENDERS, J., HUIJGEN, F., PEKRUHL, U. and O'KELLY, K. (1998),
"Useful but Unused – Group Work in Europe", A Report for the European Foundation for the Improvement of Living and Working Conditions, draft of October 1998, Luxembourg, mimeo.

BERGGREN, C. (1993),
"Lean Production – the End of History?", *Work, Employment and Society*, No. 2, pp. 163-188.

BERNARD, H. (1998),
"Erste Ergebnisse zur Erfassung der Flexibilität in deutschen Unternehmen", Universität-Gesamthochschule Kassel, mimeo.

BETCHERMAN, G. (1997),
Changing Workplace Strategies: Achieving Better Outcomes for Enterprises, Workers and Society, Government of Canada and OECD.

BOJE, D.M. and WINSOR, R.D. (1993),
"The Resurrection of Taylorism: Total Quality Management's Hidden Agenda", *Journal of Organizational Change Management*, No. 4, pp. 57-70.

BREWSTER, C. and HEGEWISCH, A. (1994),
Policy and Practice in European Human Resource Management: The Price Waterhouse Cranfield Survey, Routledge, London.

CAPPELLI, P. (1996),
"Technology and Skill Requirements: Implications for Establishment Wage Structures", *New England Economic Review*, May-June, pp. 139-154.

CAPPELLI, P. (1998),
"Technology, Work Organization and the Structure of Wages", unpublished, The Wharton School.

CAPPELLI, P. and ROGOVSKY, N. (1994),
"New Work Systems and Skill Requirements", *International Labour Review*, No. 2, pp. 205-220.

CHANDLER, A.D., Jr. (1962),
Strategy and Structure, The MIT Press, Cambridge, MA.

CHANDLER, A.D., Jr. (1990),
The Dynamics of Scale and Scope: The Dynamics of Industrial Capitalism, Harvard University Press, Cambridge, MA.

COLE, R.E. (1979),
Work Mobility and Participation: A Comparative Study of American and Japanese Industry, University of California Press, Berkeley.

CONTI, R.F. and WARNER, M. (1994),
"Taylorism, Teams and Technology in 'Reengineering' Work Organisation", *New Technology, Work and Employment*, No. 2, pp. 93-102.

COUTROT, T. (1996a),
"Relations sociales et performance économique: Une première analyse empirique du cas français", *Travail et Emploi*, No. 66, pp. 39-58.

COUTROT, T. (1996b),
"Les nouveaux modes d'organisation de la production : quels effets sur l'emploi, la formation, l'organisation du travail ?", *Données Sociales*, INSEE, pp. 209-216.

CULLY, M., O'REILLY, A., MILLWARD, N., FORTH, J., WOODLAND, S., DIX, G. and BRYSON, A. (1998),
The 1998 Workplace Employee Relations Survey: First Findings, Department of Trade and Industry, United Kingdom.

DELERY, J. and DOTY, D. (1996),
"Modes of Theorising in Strategic Human Resource Management: Tests of Universalistic, Contingency and Configurational Performance Predictions", *Academy of Management Journal*, No. 4, pp. 802-835.

EUROPEAN FOUNDATION FOR THE IMPROVEMENT OF LIVING AND WORKING CONDITIONS (1997),
New Forms of Work Organisation: Can Europe Realise its Potential?, Office for Official Publications of the European Communities, Luxembourg.

FERNIE, S. (1999),
"Brave New World?", *CentrePiece*, London School of Economics, Spring, pp. 12-15.

FINEGOLD, D. and WAGNER, K. (1997),
"When Lean Production Meets the 'German Model': Innovation Responses in the German and US Pump Industries", *Industry and Innovation*, December, pp. 207-232.

FRAZIS, H., GITTLEMAN, M. and JOYCE, M. (1998),
"Determinants of Training: An Analysis Using Both Employer And Employee Characteristics", unpublished, February.

FREEMAN, R.B., KLEINER, M.M. and OSTROFF, C. (1997),
"The Anatomy and Effects of Employee Involvement", unpublished, July.

FRÖHLICH, D. and PEKRUHL, U. (1996),
Direct Participation and Organisational Change – Fashionable but Misunderstood? An Analysis of Recent Research in Europe, Japan and the USA, European Foundation for the Improvement of Living and Working Conditions, Office for Official Publications of the European Communities, Luxembourg.

GITTLEMAN, M., HORRIGAN, M. and JOYCE, M. (1998),
"'Flexible' Workplace Practices: Evidence from a Nationally Representative Survey", *Industrial and Labor Relations Review*, October, pp. 99-115.

GJERDING, A.N. (1998),
"Flexibility in Denmark: Pressures for Renewal and Change in the Danish Private Business Sector", Aalborg University, September, mimeo.

GROSHEN, E.L. (1991),
"Five Reasons Why Wages Vary Among Employers", *Industrial Relations*, Autumn, pp. 350-381.

GROSHEN, E.L. and LEVINE, D.I. (1998),
"The Rise and Decline (?) of US Internal Markets", Federal Reserve Bank of New York Research Paper No. 9819, July.

HACKMAN, J.R. and WAGEMAN, R. (1995),
"Total Quality Management: Empirical, Conceptual and Practical Issues", *Administrative Science Quarterly*, June, pp. 309-342.

HAMMER, M. and CHAMPY, J. (1993),
Re-engineering the Corporation, Harper Collins, New York.

HANDEL, M. (1998),
"Post-Fordism and the Growth of Wage Inequality: Cause, Solution or No Effect?", Harvard University, September, mimeo.

HANDEL, M. and GITTLEMAN, M. (forthcoming),
"Is There a Wage Payoff to Innovative Work Practices?", mimeo.

HILL, S. (1995),
"From Quality Circles to Total Quality Management", in Wilkinson, A. and Willmott, H. (eds.), *Making Quality Crucial: New Perspectives on Organizational Change*, Routledge, London, pp. 33-53.

HILL, S. and WILKINSON, A. (1995),
"In Search of TQM", *Employee Relations*, No. 3, pp. 8-25.

ICHNIOWSKI, C., SHAW, K. and PRENNUSHI, G. (1997),
"The Effects of Human Resource Management Practices on Productivity: A Study of Steel Finishing Lines", *American Economic Review*, June, pp. 291-313.

ICHNIOWSKI, C., KOCHAN, T.A., LEVINE, D., OLSON, C. and STRAUSS, G. (1996),
"What Works at Work: Overview and Assessment", *Industrial Relations*, July, pp. 299-333.

JUHA, A. and PEKKA, Y. (1999*a*),
Functional Flexibility and Workplace Success in Finland, Labour Policy Studies, Ministry of Labour, Helsinki, Finland.

JUHA, A. and PEKKA, Y. (1999*b*),
Enterprises as Employers in Finland, Labour Policy Studies, Ministry of Labour, Helsinki, Finland.

JÜRGENS, U., MALSCH, T. and DOHSE, K. (1993),
Breaking from Taylorism: Changing Forms of Work in the Automobile Industry, Cambridge University Press, Cambridge, UK.

KELLY, J. (1978),
"A Reappraisal of Socio-Technical Systems Theory", *Human Relations*, No. 12, pp. 1069-99.

KLING, J. (1995),
"High Performance Work Systems and Firm Performance", *Monthly Labor Review*, May, pp. 29-36.

KOCHAN, T. and DYER, L. (1995),
"HRM: An American View", in Storey, J. (ed.), *Human Resource Management: A Critical Text*, Routledge, London, pp. 332-351.

KOCHAN, T., KATZ, H. and McKERSIE, R. (1986),
The Transformation of American Industrial Relations, Basic Books, New York.

KOIKE, K. and INOKI, T. (1993),
Skill Formation in Japan and Southeast Asia, University of Tokyo Press, Tokyo.

KRUSE, D.L. (1998),
"Profit-sharing and the Demand for Low-Skill Workers", in Freeman, R.B. and Gottschalk, P. (eds.), *Generating Jobs: How to Increase Demand for Less-Skilled Workers*, Russell Sage Foundation, New York, pp. 105-153.

LAM, A.C.L. (1994),
"The Utilisation of Human Resources: A Comparative Study of British and Japanese Engineers in the Electronics Industries", *Human Resource Management Journal*, No. 3, pp. 22-40.

LAM, A.C.L. (1997),
"Embedded Firms, Embedded Knowledge: Problems of Collaboration and Knowledge Transfer in Global Cooperative Ventures", *Organisation Studies*, No. 6, pp. 973-996.

LATNIAK, E. (1995),
"'Technikgestaltung' (Shaping of Technology) and Direct Participation: German Experiences in Managing Technological Change", in Benders, J., de Haan, J. and Bennett, D. (eds.), *The Symbiosis of Work and Technology*, Taylor and Francis, London/Bristol, pp. 59-76.

LAWLER, E.E., with MOHRMAN, S.A. and LEDFORD, G.E. (1998),
Strategies for High Performance Organizations – the CEO Report, Jossey-Bass, San Francisco, CA.

LEVINE, D.I. (1995),
Reinventing the Workplace: How Business and Employees Can Both Win, Brookings Institution, Washington, DC.

LEVINE, D.I. and TYSON, L.D.A. (1990),
"Participation, Productivity, and the Firms's Environment", in Blinder, A.S. (ed.), *Paying for Productivity*, Brookings Institution, Washington DC.

LINCOLN, J.R. and KALLEBERG, A.L. (1990),
Culture, Control and Commitment: A Study of Work Organisation and Work Attitudes in the United States and Japan, Cambridge University Press, Cambridge, UK.

LOCKE, R., KOCHAN, K. and PIORE, M. (1995),
Employment Relations in a Changing World Economy, The MIT Press, Cambridge, MA.

LUND, R. and GJERDING, A.N. (1996),
"The Flexible Company: Innovation, Work Organisation and Human Resource Management", DRUID Working Paper No. 96-17, Department of Business Studies, Aalborg University, mimeo.

LYNCH, L.M. (ed.) (1994),
Training and the Private Sector: International Comparisons, University of Chicago Press, Chicago.

LYNCH, L.M. and BLACK, S.E. (1998),
"Beyond the Incidence of Employer-Provided Training", *Industrial and Labor Relations Review*, No. 1, pp. 64-81.

MACDUFFIE, J.P. (1995),
"Human Resource Bundles and Manufacturing Performance: Organizational Logic and Flexible Production Systems in the World Auto Industry", *Industrial and Labor Relations Review*, January, pp. 197-221.

MARCHINGTON, M. (1995),
"Involvement and Participation", in Storey, J. (ed.), *Human Resource Management: A critical text*, Routledge, London, pp. 280-308.

MARSDEN, D. (1996),
"Employment Policy Implications of New Management Systems", *Labour*, Spring, pp. 17-61.

MARSDEN, D. (forthcoming),
A Theory of Employment Systems: Micro-foundations of societal diversity, Oxford University Press, UK.

MAURICE, M., SELLIER, F. and SILVESTRE, J.J. (1986),
The Social Foundations of Industrial Power: A Comparison of France and Germany, The MIT Press, Cambridge, MA.

MILES, R.E. and SNOW, C.C. (1984),
"Designing Strategic Human Resources Systems", *Organizational Dynamics*, Summer, pp. 36-52.

MOREHEAD, A., STEELE, M., ALEXANDER, M., STEPHEN, K. and DUFFIN, L. (1997),
Changes at Work: The 1995 Australian Workplace Industrial Relations Survey, Longman, South Melbourne, Australia.

NORDFLEX (forthcoming),
Flexibility Matters-Flexible Organisations in the Nordic Countries, NUTEK (Swedish Board for Industrial and Technical Development), Stockholm.

NUTEK (Swedish Board for Industrial and Technical Development) (1996),
Towards Flexible Organisations, Stockholm.

OECD (1995),
Employment Outlook, Paris, July.

OECD (1996a),
Employment Outlook, Paris, July.

OECD (1996b),
Technology, Productivity and Job Creation: Vol. 2 Analytical Report, Paris.

OSTERMAN, P. (1994),
"How Common Is Workplace Transformation and Who Adopts It?", *Industrial and Labor Relations Review*, January, pp. 173-188.

OSTERMAN, P. (1995),
"Skill, Training and Work Organisation in American Establishments", *Industrial Relations*, Vol. 34, No. 2, April, pp. 125-146.

OSTERMAN, P. (1998),
"Work Reorganization in an Era of Restructuring: Trends in Diffusion and Impacts on Employee Welfare", Sloan School, The MIT Press, November, mimeo.

PARKER, M. and SLAUGHTER, J. (1993),
"Should the Labour Movement Buy TQM?", *Journal of Organizational Change Management*, No. 4, pp. 43-56.

PIL, F.K. and MACDUFFIE, J.P. (1996),
"The Adoption of High-Involvement Work Practices", *Industrial Relations*, January, pp. 423-455.

PIORE, M.J. and SABEL, C.F. (1984),
The Second Industrial Divide, Basic Books, New York.

PORTER, M.E. (1980),
Competitive Strategy, The Free Press, New York.

PORTER, M.E. (1985),
Competitive Advantage, The Free Press, New York.

RAMSAY, H. (1996),
"Managing Sceptically: A Critique of Organisational Fashion", in Clegg, S.R. and Palmer, G. (eds.), *The Politics of Management Knowledge*, Russell Sage Foundation, New York, pp. 155-172.

REGALIA, I. (1995),
Humanize Work and Increase Profitability? Direct Participation in Organisational Change Viewed by the Social Partners in Europe, European Foundation for the Improvement of Living and Working Conditions, Office for Official Publications of the European Communities, Luxembourg.

SCHULER, R.S. and JACKSON, S.E. (1987),
"Linking Competitive Strategies with Human Resource Management Practices", *The Academy of Management Executive*, No. 3, pp. 207-219.

SORGE, A. and WARNER, M. (1986),
Comparative Factory Organisation: an Anglo-German Comparison of Management and Manpower in Manufacturing, Gower, Aldershot.

STATISTICS CANADA (1998),
The Evolving Workplace: Findings from the Pilot Workplace and Employee Survey, Catalogue no. 71-583-XPE, Ottawa.

STOREY, J. (1995),
"Human Resource Management: Still Marching On, or Marching Out?", in Storey, J. (ed.), *Human Resource Management: A Critical Text*, Routledge, London, pp. 3-32.

WHITTAKER, H. (1993),
"New Technology and Organization of Work: British and Japanese Factories", in Kogut, B. (ed.), *Country Competitiveness: Technology and the Organizing of Work*, Oxford University Press, New York.

WOMACK, J.P., JONES, D.T. and ROOS, D. (1990),
The Machine that Changed the World, Rawson Associates, New York.

WOOD, S. and ALBANESE, M.T. (1995),
"Can We Speak of High Commitment Management on the Shop Floor?", *Journal of Management Studies*, No. 2, pp. 215-247.

Statistical Annex

Sources and definitions

An important source for the statistics in these tables is Part III of OECD, *Labour Force Statistics*, 1978-1998, forthcoming. Users can refer to notes and sources published in the previous edition of that publication.

Sources and definitions are otherwise specified at the bottom of each table.

The data on employment, unemployment and the labour force are not always the same as the series used for policy analysis and forecasting by the OECD Economics Department, reproduced in Tables 1.2 and 1.3.

Conventional signs

..	Data not available
.	Decimal point
|	Break in series
–	Nil or less than half of the last digit used

Note on statistical treatment of Germany

In this publication, data up to end-1990 are for western Germany only; unless otherwise indicated, they are for the whole of Germany from 1991 onwards.

OECD

Table A. **Standardised unemployment rates in 25 OECD countries**
As a percentage of total labour force

	1990	1991	1992	1993	1994	1995	1996	1997	1998
Australia	7.0	9.6	10.8	10.9	9.8	8.5	8.6	8.6	8.0
Austria	..	..	..	4.0	3.8	3.9	4.4	4.5	4.7
Belgium	6.7	6.6	7.3	8.9	10.0	9.9	9.7	9.2	8.8
Canada	8.2	10.4	11.3	11.2	10.4	9.5	9.7	9.2	8.3
Czech Republic	..	..	..	..	3.8	3.6	3.9	4.7	6.5
Denmark	7.7	8.5	9.2	10.1	8.2	7.3	6.8	5.6	5.1
Finland	3.2	7.1	12.5	16.4	16.8	15.3	14.6	12.7	11.4
France	9.0	9.5	10.4	11.7	12.3	11.7	12.4	12.3	11.7
Germany [a]	4.8		5.6	6.6	7.9	8.4	8.2	8.9	9.9	9.4
Greece	6.4	7.0	7.9	8.6	8.9	9.2	9.6	9.6	..
Hungary	..	..	9.9	12.1	11.0	10.4	10.1	8.9	8.0
Ireland	13.4	14.8	15.4	15.6	14.3	12.3	11.6	9.9	7.8
Italy	9.1	8.8	9.0	10.3	11.4	11.9	12.0	12.1	12.2
Japan	2.1	2.1	2.2	2.5	2.9	3.2	3.4	3.4	4.1
Luxembourg	1.7	1.7	2.1	2.7	3.2	2.9	3.0	2.8	2.8
Netherlands	6.2	5.8	5.6	6.6	7.1	6.9	6.3	5.2	4.0
New Zealand	7.8	10.3	10.3	9.5	8.1	6.3	6.1	6.6	7.5
Norway	5.3	5.6	6.0	6.1	5.5	5.0	4.9	4.1	3.3
Poland	..	..	..	14.0	14.4	13.3	12.3	11.2	10.6
Portugal	4.6	4.0	4.2	5.7	7.0	7.3	7.3	6.8	4.9
Spain	16.2	16.4	18.4	22.7	24.1	22.9	22.2	20.8	18.8
Sweden	1.7	3.1	5.6	9.1	9.4	8.8	9.6	9.9	8.2
Switzerland	..	2.0	3.1	4.0	3.8	3.5	3.9	4.2	..
United Kingdom	7.1	8.8	10.1	10.5	9.6	8.7	8.2	7.0	6.3
United States	5.6	6.8	7.5	6.9		6.1	5.6	5.4	4.9	4.5
European Union [b]	..	8.2	9.2	10.7	11.1	10.7	10.8	10.6	10.0
OECD Europe [b]	..	7.9	8.9	10.8	10.9	10.5	10.5	10.2	9.7
Total OECD [b]	..	6.7	7.5	8.3		8.1	7.7	7.7	7.4	7.0

| Indicates break in series.
a) Up to and including 1990, western Germany; subsequent data concern the whole of Germany.
b) For above countries only.
Note: In so far as possible, the data have been adjusted to ensure comparability over time and to conform to the guidelines of the International Labour Office. All series are benchmarked to labour-force-survey-based estimates. In countries with annual surveys, monthly estimates are obtained by interpolation/extrapolation and by incorporating trends in administrative data, where available. The annual figures are then calculated by averaging the monthly estimates (for both unemployed and the labour force). For countries with monthly or quarterly surveys, the annual estimates are obtained by averaging the monthly or quarterly estimates, respectively. For several countries, the adjustment procedure used is similar to that of the *Bureau of Labor Statistics, US Department of Labor*. For EU countries, the procedures are similar to those used in deriving the Comparable Unemployment Rates (CURs) of the Statistical Office of the European Communities. Minor differences may appear mainly because of various methods of calculating and applying adjustment factors, and because EU estimates are based on the civilian labour force.
Source: OECD, *Quarterly Labour Force Statistics*, No. 1, 1999.

Table B. Employment/population ratios, activity rates and unemployment rates by sex for persons aged 15-64 years[a]

Percentages

Both sexes

	Employment/population ratio							Labour force participation rate							Unemployment rate						
	1990	1994	1995	1996	1997	1998		1990	1994	1995	1996	1997	1998		1990	1994	1995	1996	1997	1998
Australia	67.9	65.7	67.5	67.3	66.3	67.2		73.0	72.4	73.5	73.6	72.4	73.0		7.0	9.3	8.1	8.5	8.5	7.9
Austria	..	..	68.4	67.3	67.2	67.4		..	..	71.5	71.1	70.9	71.3		..	..	4.4	5.3	5.2	5.5
Belgium	54.4	55.7	56.3	56.3	57.0	57.3		58.7	61.7	62.1	62.2	62.6	63.2		7.3	9.7	9.4	9.5	9.0	9.4
Canada	70.5	67.1	67.5	67.5	67.9	69.0		76.8	75.0	74.7	74.8	74.9	75.4		8.2	10.5	9.6	9.8	9.3	8.4
Czech Republic	..	71.5	69.6	69.4	68.7	67.5		..	74.3	72.5	72.1	72.1	72.2		..	3.8	4.1	3.8	4.7	6.4
Denmark	75.4|	72.4	73.9	74.0	75.4	75.3		82.4|	78.8	79.5	79.5	79.8	79.3		8.5|	8.1	7.0	6.9	5.4	5.1
Finland	74.7	60.7	61.9	62.8	63.6	64.8		77.1	72.8	73.1	73.4	72.8	73.2		3.2	16.6	15.4	14.5	12.7	11.5
France	59.9	58.3	59.0	59.2	58.8	59.4		66.0	66.6	66.8	67.4	67.1	67.4		9.2	12.5	11.7	12.2	12.4	11.9
Germany	66.4	64.7	64.7	64.1	63.6	64.1		69.9|	70.9	70.5	70.4	70.6	70.1		4.9|	8.8	8.2	8.9	9.9	8.6
Greece	54.8|	54.1	54.5	54.9	54.8	54.9		59.1|	59.5	60.1	61.0	60.8	62.4		7.2|	9.1	9.3	9.9	9.8	11.9
Hungary[b]	..	48.2|	52.9	52.7	52.7	55.3		..	54.0|	58.9	58.5	57.8	59.8		..	10.7|	10.2	9.9	8.7	7.6
Iceland[c, d]	79.9	78.5	80.5	80.4	80.0	82.2		82.1	83.0	84.7	83.6	83.1	84.5		2.7	5.4	5.0	3.7	3.8	2.7
Ireland	52.3	52.3	53.8	54.8	56.1	59.8		60.2	61.4	61.5	62.3	62.7	65.0		13.2	14.9	12.4	12.0	10.5	7.9
Italy	53.9|	50.9	50.5	50.6	50.5	50.8		59.8|	57.5	57.3	57.7	57.7	57.8		9.9|	11.5	11.9	12.3	12.5	12.2
Japan	68.6	69.3	69.2	69.5	70.0	69.5		70.1	71.4	71.5	72.0	72.6	72.6		2.2	3.0	3.3	3.5	3.5	4.2
Korea	61.2	63.2	63.7	63.8	63.7	59.5		62.8	64.8	65.1	65.1	65.4	64.0		2.5	2.5	2.1	2.1	2.7	7.1
Luxembourg[d]	59.1	60.2	58.5	59.1	59.9	60.2		60.1	62.3	60.3	61.1	61.5	61.9		1.6|	3.5	2.9	3.3	2.5	2.8
Mexico	58.0	58.7	58.2	59.1	61.1	61.4		59.9	61.4	61.8	61.9	63.3	63.2		3.1	4.4	5.8	4.5	3.5	3.0
Netherlands	60.8	63.0	64.2	66.2	68.1	69.8		66.7	68.6	70.1	70.8	72.1	72.9		7.4	6.8	7.1	6.5	5.5	4.3
New Zealand	67.3	67.8	70.0	71.1	70.5	69.5		73.0	73.9	74.7	75.8	75.6	75.2		7.8	8.2	6.3	6.2	6.7	7.6
Norway[c]	73.1	72.2	73.5|	75.3	77.3	78.2		77.1	76.4	77.4|	79.2	80.6	80.8		5.3	5.4	5.0|	4.9	4.1	3.2
Poland	..	58.3	58.1	58.4	58.8	58.9		..	68.4	67.4	66.9	66.4	66.1		..	14.8	13.7	12.7	11.5	10.9
Portugal	65.5|	62.9	62.5	62.3	63.4	66.8		68.8|	67.6	67.4	67.5	68.2	70.2		4.8|	7.0	7.4	7.7	6.9	4.9
Spain[c]	51.1	46.5	47.4	48.2	49.4	51.2		60.9	61.3	61.4	62.0	62.3	63.1		16.1	24.1	22.9	22.1	20.7	18.8
Sweden[c]	83.1	71.5	72.2	71.6	70.7	71.5		84.6	79.2	79.5	79.5	78.7	78.1		1.8|	10.0	9.3	10.2	10.4	8.4
Switzerland[d]	79.6	77.4	78.1	78.3	78.1	79.3		81.1	80.7	80.8	81.3	81.5	82.3		1.8	4.0	3.4	3.8	4.2	3.7
Turkey	54.5	52.0	52.7	52.5	50.2	50.5		59.4	56.7	56.8	56.0	53.7	54.0		8.2	8.3	7.1	6.3	6.6	6.6
United Kingdom[c]	72.4	68.8	69.3	69.8	70.8	71.2		77.8	76.2	75.9	76.1	76.2	75.9		6.8	9.7	8.7	8.2	7.1	6.2
United States[c]	72.2	72.0	72.5	72.9|	73.5	73.8		76.5	76.7	76.9	77.1	77.4	77.4		5.7	6.2	5.6	5.5|	5.0	4.5
European Union[e]	62.0	59.5	60.1	60.2	60.5	61.1		67.5	67.3	67.4	67.6	67.8	67.9		8.1	11.4	10.8	10.9	11.5	9.9
OECD Europe[e]	61.5	58.9	59.5|	59.6	59.5	60.1		66.9	66.3	66.4|	66.4	66.2	66.3		7.9	11.0	10.3|	10.2	10.1	9.3
Total OECD[e]	65.4	63.9	64.3|	64.5|	64.9	65.1		69.5	69.4	69.5|	69.6|	69.8	69.8		5.9	7.8	7.4|	7.3	7.0	6.8

| Indicates break in series.
a) Ratios refer to persons aged 15 to 64 years who are in employment or in the labour force divided by the working age population, or in unemployment divided by the labour force.
b) For years prior to 1995, data cover persons aged 15 and over.
c) Refers to persons ages 16 to 64.
d) The year 1990 refers to 1991.
e) For above countries only.

Sources: OECD, *Labour Force Statistics, 1978-1998, Part III*, forthcoming.
For Austria, Belgium, Denmark, Germany, Greece, Italy, Luxembourg and Portugal, data are from the European Labour Force Survey.

Table B. Employment/population ratios, activity rates and unemployment rates by sex for persons aged 15-64 years[a] (cont.)

Percentages

Men

	Employment/population ratio						Labour force participation rate						Unemployment rate					
	1990	1994	1995	1996	1997	1998	1990	1994	1995	1996	1997	1998	1990	1994	1995	1996	1997	1998
Australia	78.5	74.8	76.1	75.9	74.7	75.2	84.4	82.7	83.2	83.3	81.8	82.1	6.9	9.6	8.6	9.0	8.7	8.4
Austria	..	..	77.6	76.1	75.9	75.9	..	..	80.8	80.4	80.0	80.2	..	..	4	5.4	5.1	5.4
Belgium	68.1	66.5	66.9	66.8	67.1	67.0	71.3	72.0	72.3	72.2	72.2	72.5	4.6	7.7	7.4	7.4	7.1	7.6
Canada	77.9	73.2	73.5	73.4	74.1	74.7	84.9	82.2	81.5	81.5	81.8	81.8	8.3	10.9	9.9	10.0	9.4	8.6
Czech Republic	..	76.8	77.6	78.1	77.4	76.3	..	79.4	80.4	80.7	80.5	80.3	..	3.3	3.5	3.2	3.8	5.0
Denmark	80.1	77.6	80.7	80.5	81.3	80.2	87.1	83.7	85.6	85.3	85.2	83.5	8.0	7.3	5.7	5.6	4.6	3.9
Finland	77.9	62.6	64.8	66.0	66.7	68.2	80.8	76.4	76.7	76.9	76.0	76.6	3.6	18.0	15.5	14.1	12.3	10.9
France	69.7	65.9	66.6	66.7	66.2	66.5	75.0	74.0	73.9	74.5	74.3	74.1	7.0	10.9	9.8	10.5	10.9	10.3
Germany	78.7	74.1	73.9	72.7	71.8	72.5	82.1	80.2	79.6	79.3	79.3	79.2	4.1	7.6	7.1	8.3	9.4	8.5
Greece	73.4	72.2	72.2	72.6	71.9	71.0	76.8	77.0	77.2	77.4	76.9	77.2	4.4	6.2	6.4	6.2	6.4	8.1
Hungary[b]	..	55.1	60.2	60.2	60.3	63.6	..	62.4	67.9	67.4	66.6	69.2	..	11.8	11.4	10.7	9.5	8.1
Iceland[c, d]	85.2	82.4	84.0	84.3	84.2	86.0	87.3	86.8	88.4	87.3	87.1	87.9	2.4	5.1	5.0	3.4	3.3	2.3
Ireland	67.8	64.4	66.3	66.6	67.6	71.4	77.7	75.9	75.8	75.8	75.6	77.8	12.8	15.0	12.5	12.1	10.6	8.2
Italy	72.0	66.5	65.7	65.3	65.0	65.1	77.0	73.1	72.4	72.3	72.2	72.0	6.5	9.0	9.3	9.7	9.8	9.5
Japan	81.3	81.9	81.9	82.1	82.4	81.7	83.0	84.4	84.5	85.0	85.4	85.3	2.1	2.9	3.1	3.5	3.5	4.3
Korea	73.9	76.6	77.2	76.7	76.0	71.7	76.2	78.8	79.0	78.6	78.2	77.9	3.0	2.8	2.3	2.4	2.8	7.9
Luxembourg	76.4	74.9	74.3	74.4	74.3	74.6	77.4	77.3	75.9	76.3	75.7	76.0	1.3	3.0	2.1	2.5	1.9	1.9
Mexico[d]	84.1	82.9	81.5	82.7	84.7	84.8	86.4	86.4	86.4	86.4	87.2	87.1	2.6	4.1	5.7	4.3	2.8	2.6
Netherlands	74.3	73.5	74.7	76.9	78.4	79.9	80.0	79.6	80.8	81.1	82.0	82.8	5.4	5.9	5.9	5.2	4.4	3.5
New Zealand	76.1	76.1	78.6	79.0	78.4	77.1	83.0	83.3	83.8	84.2	84.1	83.5	8.3	8.6	6.3	6.2	6.7	7.7
Norway[c]	78.6	76.8	78.1	80.0	82.0	82.7	83.4	81.6	82.4	84.1	85.4	85.5	5.8	6.0	5.2	4.8	4.0	3.3
Poland	..	64.9	64.7	65.2	66.1	65.8	..	75.0	73.9	73.5	73.2	72.8	..	13.4	12.5	11.3	9.8	9.5
Portugal	78.6	72.5	71.2	71.0	71.9	75.8	81.4	77.2	76.4	76.1	76.7	79.0	3.4	6.1	6.8	6.7	6.2	4.0
Spain[c]	71.0	62.2	63.0	63.6	64.5	67.0	80.4	77.4	76.8	77.1	76.7	77.7	11.8	19.6	18.0	17.4	15.9	13.7
Sweden[c]	85.2	72.3	73.5	73.2	72.4	73.5	86.7	81.4	81.7	81.7	81.0	80.7	1.8	11.4	10.2	10.7	10.8	8.8
Switzerland[d]	90.0	86.6	87.4	86.8	85.9	87.2	91.1	89.8	90.1	89.8	89.9	90.1	1.2	3.6	2.9	3.4	4.4	3.2
Turkey	76.9	73.8	74.6	74.5	74.0	73.6	83.6	80.8	80.5	79.8	78.8	78.8	8.0	8.6	7.3	6.6	6.2	6.6
United Kingdom[c]	82.1	75.4	76.1	76.3	77.4	78.1	88.3	85.2	84.7	84.6	84.4	83.9	7.1	11.5	10.2	9.8	8.2	6.9
United States[c]	80.7	79.0	79.5	79.7	80.1	80.5	85.6	84.3	84.3	84.3	84.2	84.2	5.7	6.2	5.6	5.4	4.9	4.5
European Union[e]	75.2	70.0	70.4	70.2	70.3	71.0	80.4	78.1	77.9	77.9	77.7	77.8	6.4	10.4	9.5	9.8	9.6	8.7
OECD Europe[e]	75.7	70.1	70.7	70.7	70.7	71.3	81.0	78.0	77.9	77.8	77.6	77.7	6.5	10.1	9.2	9.2	8.9	8.2
Total OECD[e]	78.4	75.2	75.5	75.6	75.9	76.0	82.8	81.2	81.2	81.2	81.1	81.2	5.3	7.4	7.0	6.9	6.5	6.3

| Indicates break in series.

a) Ratios refer to persons aged 15 to 64 years who are in employment or in the labour force divided by the working age population, or in unemployment divided by the labour force.
b) For years prior to 1995, data cover persons aged 15 and over.
c) Refers to persons ages 16 to 64.
d) The year 1990 refers to 1991.
e) For above countries only.

Sources: OECD, *Labour Force Statistics, 1978-1998, Part III*, forthcoming.
For Austria, Belgium, Denmark, Germany, Greece, Italy, Luxembourg and Portugal, data are from the European Labour Force Survey.

Table B. **Employment/population ratios, activity rates and unemployment rates by sex for persons aged 15-64 years**[a] (cont.)

Percentages

Women

	Employment/population ratio						Labour force participation rate						Unemployment rate					
	1990	1994	1995	1996	1997	1998	1990	1994	1995	1996	1997	1998	1990	1994	1995	1996	1997	1998
Australia	57.1	56.4	58.9	58.7	57.8	59.2	61.5	61.9	63.7	63.8	63.0	63.9	7.2	8.9	7.6	8.0	8.1	7.3
Austria	..	..	59.2	58.6	58.5	59.0	..	..	62.3	61.8	61.8	62.5	..	..	4.9	5.3	5.3	5.6
Belgium	40.8	44.8	45.4	45.6	46.7	47.5	46.1	51.2	51.7	52.0	52.9	53.8	11.5	12.5	12.3	12.4	11.6	11.7
Canada	63.0	61.1	61.5	61.6	61.7	63.3	68.6	67.8	67.8	68.0	68.0	69.0	8.2	9.9	9.3	9.5	9.2	8.2
Czech Republic	..	66.2	61.6	60.6	60.0	58.8	..	69.3	64.7	63.6	63.7	64.0	..	4.5	4.8	4.6	5.8	8.2
Denmark	70.6	67.1	67.0	67.4	69.4	70.2	77.6	73.8	73.3	73.6	74.2	75.0	9.0	9.0	8.6	8.4	6.5	6.4
Finland	71.5	58.8	58.9	59.5	60.4	61.2	73.5	69.1	69.5	69.9	69.5	69.7	2.7	14.9	15.2	14.9	13.1	12.1
France	50.3	50.7	51.5	51.7	51.5	52.3	57.2	59.2	59.8	60.3	60.1	60.8	12.1	14.4	13.9	14.3	14.2	13.9
Germany	54.0	55.0	55.3	55.4	55.2	55.6	57.6	61.4	61.3	61.3	61.8	60.9	6.2	10.4	9.7	9.7	10.7	8.7
Greece	37.5	37.1	38.0	38.5	39.1	39.6	42.6	43.2	44.3	45.8	46.0	48.2	12.0	14.0	14.1	15.8	15.1	17.8
Hungary[b]	..	41.9	45.9	45.5	45.5	47.3	..	46.3	50.3	49.9	49.3	50.8	..	9.4	8.7	8.8	7.7	6.9
Iceland[c,d]	74.5	74.6	76.8	76.5	75.6	78.3	76.8	79.1	80.9	79.8	79.1	80.9	3.0	5.7	5.0	4.1	4.4	3.3
Ireland	36.6	39.9	41.2	43.0	44.6	48.2	42.6	46.9	47.0	48.8	49.7	52.1	14.0	14.8	12.3	11.9	10.4	7.5
Italy	36.4	35.6	35.6	36.1	36.2	36.7	43.2	42.2	42.5	43.3	43.6	43.9	15.8	15.7	16.3	16.6	16.8	16.4
Japan	55.8	56.5	56.4	56.8	57.6	57.2	57.1	58.3	58.4	58.9	59.7	59.8	2.3	3.1	3.4	3.6	3.6	4.2
Korea	49.0	50.1	50.6	51.1	51.5	47.4	49.9	51.1	51.5	51.9	52.8	50.3	1.9	2.0	1.7	1.6	2.4	5.8
Luxembourg	41.4	44.9	42.2	43.6	45.4	45.6	42.5	47.0	44.1	45.7	47.1	47.6	2.5	4.3	4.4	4.7	3.7	4.2
Mexico[d]	34.2	36.2	36.5	37.4	39.7	40.0	35.7	38.1	38.9	39.3	41.7	41.5	4.3	4.9	6.1	4.9	4.7	3.6
Netherlands	46.9	52.2	53.4	55.2	57.6	59.4	53.1	57.3	59.1	60.2	61.9	62.9	10.6	8.1	8.8	8.3	7.0	5.5
New Zealand	58.5	59.7	61.7	63.4	62.7	62.1	63.2	64.7	65.8	67.5	67.2	67.1	7.3	7.8	6.4	6.1	6.7	7.4
Norway[c]	67.2	67.5	68.8	70.4	72.3	73.5	70.7	70.9	72.1	74.1	75.6	75.9	4.9	4.8	4.7	4.9	4.3	3.2
Poland	..	51.9	51.8	51.8	51.8	52.2	..	62.1	61.0	60.5	59.9	59.7	..	16.4	15.1	14.3	13.5	12.6
Portugal	53.3	54.1	54.3	54.2	55.5	58.1	57.1	58.8	59.1	59.5	60.3	61.9	6.7	8.0	8.1	8.8	7.9	6.0
Spain[c]	31.6	31.0	32.0	33.0	34.3	35.7	41.8	45.4	46.2	47.0	48.0	48.7	24.4	31.6	30.8	29.8	28.4	26.7
Sweden[c]	81.0	70.6	70.8	69.9	68.9	69.4	82.5	77.0	77.2	77.1	76.3	75.5	1.8	8.4	8.1	9.6	9.9	8.0
Switzerland[d]	68.7	67.8	68.3	69.3	69.8	71.0	70.6	71.0	71.1	72.3	72.7	74.2	2.6	4.5	4.0	4.2	4.0	4.3
Turkey	32.9	30.6	31.5	31.0	27.2	28.0	36.0	33.2	33.7	32.8	29.4	30.0	8.7	7.8	6.7	5.5	7.7	6.7
United Kingdom[c]	62.8	62.1	62.5	63.3	64.0	64.2	67.2	67.1	67.1	67.5	68.0	67.8	6.5	7.4	6.9	6.3	5.8	5.3
United States[c]	64.0	65.2	65.8	66.3	67.1	67.4	67.8	69.4	69.7	70.1	70.7	70.7	5.6	6.1	5.7	5.5	5.1	4.7
European Union[e]	49.0	49.1	49.8	50.2	50.7	51.3	54.8	56.5	56.9	57.4	57.8	58.0	10.5	13.0	12.5	12.5	12.4	11.5
OECD Europe[e]	47.5	47.8	48.4	48.7	48.5	49.0	52.8	54.6	54.9	55.1	54.9	55.0	10.1	12.3	11.8	11.7	11.7	10.9
Total OECD[e]	52.6	52.9	53.3	53.7	54.1	54.3	56.5	57.8	58.1	58.3	58.7	58.7	6.8	8.4	8.1	8.0	7.8	7.4

| Indicates break in series.
a) Ratios refer to persons aged 15 to 64 years who are in employment or in the labour force divided by the working age population, or in unemployment divided by the labour force.
b) For years prior to 1995, data cover persons aged 15 and over.
c) Refers to persons ages 16 to 64.
d) The year 1990 refers to 1991.
e) For above countries only.
Sources: OECD, *Labour Force Statistics, 1978-1998, Part III*, forthcoming.
For Austria, Belgium, Denmark, Germany, Greece, Italy, Luxembourg and Portugal, data are from the European Labour Force Survey.

228 – OECD Employment Outlook

Table C. **Unemployment, labour force participation rates and employment/population ratios by age and sex**
Both sexes
Percentages

		1990 15 to 24	1990 25 to 54	1990 55 to 64	1995 15 to 24	1995 25 to 54	1995 55 to 64	1996 15 to 24	1996 25 to 54	1996 55 to 64	1997 15 to 24	1997 25 to 54	1997 55 to 64	1998 15 to 24	1998 25 to 54	1998 55 to 64
Australia	Unemployment rates	13.2	5.1	5.4	14.4	6.4	7.4	14.8	6.8	7.7	15.9	6.6	7.2	14.5	6.3	6.1
	Labour force participation rates	70.4	79.9	44.1	69.6	80.4	44.7	70.1	80.2	45.8	66.8	79.6	45.1	67.6	80.0	46.6
	Employment/population ratios	61.1	75.8	41.8	59.5	75.3	41.4	59.7	74.7	42.3	56.2	74.4	41.9	57.8	75.0	43.7
Austria	Unemployment rates	..	..	..	5.9	4.1	3.9	6.9	5.1	4.6	7.6	4.8	5.2	7.5	5.0	6.4
	Labour force participation rates	..	..	..	61.7	83.3	30.2	59.6	83.5	30.8	58.4	83.9	30.0	58.5	84.7	29.9
	Employment/population ratios	..	..	..	58.1	79.9	29.0	55.5	79.3	29.4	54.0	79.9	28.5	54.2	80.4	28.0
Belgium	Unemployment rates	14.5	6.5	3.5	21.5	8.3	4.0	20.5	8.6	4.5	21.3	7.9	4.7	20.4	8.4	5.3
	Labour force participation rates	35.5	76.7	22.2	33.9	80.4	24.2	32.8	80.8	22.8	32.0	81.0	23.1	32.6	81.2	23.8
	Employment/population ratios	30.4	71.7	21.4	26.6	73.8	23.3	26.1	73.9	21.8	25.2	74.6	22.0	26.0	74.4	22.5
Canada	Unemployment rates	12.7	7.3	6.0	15.6	8.4	8.2	16.1	8.6	7.7	16.7	7.9	7.6	15.2	7.1	6.9
	Labour force participation rates	69.2	84.5	50.0	62.2	83.4	47.4	61.5	83.7	47.9	61.2	83.8	48.4	62.0	84.3	48.8
	Employment/population ratios	60.4	78.4	47.0	52.5	76.4	43.6	51.6	76.5	44.2	51.0	77.2	44.7	52.6	78.3	45.4
Czech Republic	Unemployment rates	..	..	..	7.9	3.3	3.0	7.2	3.2	3.5	8.4	4.0	3.6	12.3	5.4	3.8
	Labour force participation rates	..	..	..	50.6	89.6	35.6	49.4	88.7	38.5	48.3	88.7	39.7	49.0	88.6	38.6
	Employment/population ratios	..	..	..	46.6	86.6	34.5	45.9	85.9	37.1	44.3	85.1	38.3	43.0	83.7	37.1
Denmark	Unemployment rates	11.5	7.9	6.1	9.9	6.2	8.0	10.6	6.0	6.1	8.1	4.8	5.1	7.2	4.6	5.1
	Labour force participation rates	73.5	91.2	57.1	73.2	87.1	53.6	73.8	87.5	50.6	74.2	87.0	54.1	71.5	87.4	53.1
	Employment/population ratios	65.0	84.0	53.6	65.9	81.7	49.3	66.0	82.2	47.5	68.2	82.8	51.4	66.4	83.4	50.4
Finland	Unemployment rates	8.9	2.1	2.7	26.9	13.2	20.3	24.9	12.2	21.0	23.3	10.7	15.0	22.0	9.5	14.0
	Labour force participation rates	60.6	89.7	43.8	45.9	87.5	43.2	46.2	87.5	45.1	48.4	86.8	42.0	49.7	87.1	42.0
	Employment/population ratios	55.2	87.9	42.6	33.5	76.0	34.4	34.7	76.8	35.6	37.1	77.5	35.7	38.8	78.9	36.2
France	Unemployment rates	19.1	8.0	6.7	25.9	10.5	7.2	26.3	11.0	8.4	28.1	11.1	8.5	25.4	10.8	8.7
	Labour force participation rates	36.4	84.1	38.1	29.8	86.0	36.1	29.2	86.4	36.6	28.0	86.0	36.7	28.0	86.2	36.1
	Employment/population ratios	29.5	77.4	35.6	22.0	77.0	33.5	21.5	76.9	33.5	20.1	76.4	33.6	20.9	76.8	33.0
Germany	Unemployment rates	4.6	4.7	7.5	8.5	7.7	11.6	9.6	8.1	13.3	10.7	8.9	15.2	9.4	7.7	12.7
	Labour force participation rates	60.7	80.0	42.4	52.5	83.3	42.8	50.4	83.5	43.7	49.7	84.1	45.1	49.6	83.5	44.5
	Employment/population ratios	57.9	76.3	39.2	48.0	76.9	37.8	45.5	76.7	37.9	44.4	76.6	38.2	45.0	77.0	38.8
Greece	Unemployment rates	23.3	5.1	1.6	27.9	7.3	3.4	31.2	7.7	3.0	31.0	7.7	3.2	32.1	9.6	3.7
	Labour force participation rates	39.4	72.2	41.5	36.7	74.2	41.9	36.9	75.3	41.9	35.5	75.5	42.1	40.7	76.5	40.0
	Employment/population ratios	30.3	68.5	40.8	26.5	68.8	40.5	25.4	69.5	40.7	24.5	69.7	40.7	27.6	69.1	38.5
Hungary	Unemployment rates	..	..	..	18.6	8.9	5.4	18.0	8.7	5.6	15.9	7.5	5.7	13.5	6.6	4.8
	Labour force participation rates	..	..	..	38.4	77.6	18.1	37.1	77.1	18.4	37.3	75.9	18.3	40.8	77.8	17.4
	Employment/population ratios	..	..	..	31.3	70.7	17.1	30.4	70.4	17.4	31.3	70.2	17.3	35.3	72.7	16.6
Iceland [a, b]	Unemployment rates	4.9	2.2	2.1	11.0	3.7	4.1	8.4	2.6	3.8	7.7	3.0	3.1	6.0	2.1	1.6
	Labour force participation rates	59.5	90.1	87.2	61.7	92.5	88.7	59.9	91.7	87.1	60.3	91.0	86.4	65.5	90.8	88.1
	Employment/population ratios	56.6	88.1	85.4	54.9	89.1	85.1	54.8	89.3	83.8	55.7	88.2	83.7	61.6	88.9	86.7

Table C. **Unemployment, labour force participation rates and employment/population ratios by age and sex** (cont.) — Both sexes

Percentages

		1990 15 to 24	1990 25 to 54	1990 55 to 64	1995 15 to 24	1995 25 to 54	1995 55 to 64	1996 15 to 24	1996 25 to 54	1996 55 to 64	1997 15 to 24	1997 25 to 54	1997 55 to 64	1998 15 to 24	1998 25 to 54	1998 55 to 64
Ireland	Unemployment rates	17.6	12.4	8.4	19.1	11.1	7.8	18.2	11.0	6.8	16.1	9.5	6.0	11.5	7.3	5.1
	Labour force participation rates	50.4	68.7	42.2	45.5	72.6	42.5	43.9	74.5	43.2	45.5	74.4	42.6	48.6	76.4	43.8
	Employment/population ratios	41.5	60.2	38.6	36.8	64.5	39.2	35.9	66.3	40.3	38.1	67.3	40.1	43.0	70.9	41.6
Italy	Unemployment rates	28.9	6.6	1.8	32.8	8.9	4.3	34.1	9.3	4.3	33.6	9.6	4.4	32.1	9.6	4.7
	Labour force participation rates	46.8	72.8	32.5	38.8	71.6	28.3	38.5	72.2	28.5	38.0	72.4	28.6	37.5	72.8	28.3
	Employment/population ratios	33.3	68.0	32.0	26.1	65.2	27.0	25.4	65.5	27.3	25.2	65.5	27.3	25.4	65.9	26.9
Japan	Unemployment rates	4.3	1.6	2.7	6.1	2.6	3.7	6.7	2.7	4.1	6.6	2.8	3.9	7.7	3.4	5.0
	Labour force participation rates	44.1	80.9	64.7	47.6	81.4	66.2	48.3	81.8	66.3	48.6	82.2	66.9	48.3	82.1	67.1
	Employment/population ratios	42.2	79.6	62.9	44.7	79.3	63.7	45.0	79.6	63.6	45.3	79.9	64.2	44.6	79.2	63.8
Korea	Unemployment rates	7.0	1.9	0.8	6.3	1.6	0.8	6.1	1.6	0.7	7.7	2.1	1.0	15.9	6.4	4.0
	Labour force participation rates	35.0	74.6	62.4	36.5	75.6	64.1	35.4	76.1	63.6	34.4	76.6	64.3	31.4	75.0	61.3
	Employment/population ratios	32.5	73.2	61.9	34.2	74.4	63.5	33.2	74.9	63.2	31.8	75.0	63.6	26.4	70.3	58.9
Luxembourg	Unemployment rates	3.7	1.4	0.8	7.2	2.5	0.3	9.2	2.7	0.0	7.3	2.1	0.9	6.4	2.5	0.6
	Labour force participation rates	44.7	72.8	28.4	41.2	73.8	24.0	40.7	75.2	22.6	37.4	76.0	24.0	35.3	76.7	25.1
	Employment/population ratios	43.1	71.8	28.2	38.2	71.9	24.0	36.9	73.2	22.6	34.7	74.4	23.7	33.1	74.7	25.0
Mexico[b]	Unemployment rates	5.4	2.2	1.0	9.3	4.4	3.3	7.7	3.3	2.1	6.3	2.5	1.1	5.3	2.2	1.0
	Labour force participation rates	52.2	65.9	54.6	54.1	67.8	52.9	53.1	68.4	53.2	53.5	70.1	56.1	54.0	69.8	54.4
	Employment/population ratios	49.3	64.4	54.1	49.1	64.8	51.2	49.0	66.2	52.1	50.1	68.4	55.4	51.1	68.3	53.9
Netherlands	Unemployment rates	11.1	6.7	3.7	12.8	6.1	3.0	12.1	5.5	3.2	9.5	4.9	2.5	8.2	3.6	2.3
	Labour force participation rates	61.4	76.3	30.8	64.5	79.9	30.3	66.4	80.2	31.6	67.5	81.5	32.5	68.0	82.3	34.1
	Employment/population ratios	54.5	71.2	22.4	56.3	75.0	22.7	58.4	75.7	30.5	61.1	77.5	31.7	62.5	79.3	33.3
New Zealand	Unemployment rates	14.1	6.0	4.6	11.9	5.1	3.3	11.8	4.9	3.7	13.1	5.3	4.0	14.6	6.1	4.6
	Labour force participation rates	67.9	81.2	43.8	67.4	81.7	52.1	67.4	82.4	55.9	66.9	82.1	56.8	65.2	81.8	58.4
	Employment/population ratios	58.3	76.3	41.8	59.4	77.6	50.4	59.4	78.4	53.9	58.1	77.8	54.5	55.7	76.8	55.7
Norway[a]	Unemployment rates	11.8	4.2	2.1	11.9	4.1	2.6	12.4	3.9	2.2	10.9	3.2	2.0	9.5	2.3	1.9
	Labour force participation rates	60.5	85.9	63.1	55.9	85.9	64.8	59.7	87.1	66.0	61.9	88.1	67.7	63.8	87.8	68.2
	Employment/population ratios	53.4	82.3	61.8	49.2	82.4	63.1	52.3	83.7	64.6	55.2	85.3	66.4	57.7	85.7	66.9
Poland	Unemployment rates	..	..	..	31.2	11.7	5.9	28.5	10.8	5.9	24.7	10.0	5.3	23.2	9.5	5.9
	Labour force participation rates	..	..	..	39.7	84.0	35.9	39.0	83.6	35.0	38.3	82.9	35.5	37.3	82.9	34.3
	Employment/population ratios	..	..	..	27.3	74.2	33.8	27.9	74.6	33.0	28.8	74.7	33.6	28.6	75.0	32.3
Portugal	Unemployment rates	10.4	3.7	1.7	16.0	6.1	4.0	17.0	6.2	5.0	14.1	5.7	5.2	9.5	4.1	3.4
	Labour force participation rates	58.4	79.8	47.6	43.1	83.4	47.4	42.3	83.4	48.7	44.2	83.4	49.4	47.4	83.8	52.7
	Employment/population ratios	52.4	76.9	46.8	36.2	78.3	45.5	35.1	78.2	46.3	37.9	78.6	46.8	42.9	80.3	50.9
Spain[a]	Unemployment rates	30.1	13.1	8.1	40.3	19.9	12.2	39.8	19.1	11.6	37.1	18.1	11.3	34.1	16.5	10.6
	Labour force participation rates	54.9	70.3	40.0	47.6	74.0	36.5	46.7	75.3	37.3	46.0	75.3	37.8	46.4	75.6	38.8
	Employment/population ratios	38.3	61.1	36.8	28.4	59.2	32.1	28.1	60.9	33.0	28.9	61.6	33.5	30.6	63.1	34.8

Table C. Unemployment, labour force participation rates and employment/population ratios by age and sex (cont.)

Both sexes

Percentages

		1990 15 to 24	1990 25 to 54	1990 55 to 64	1995 15 to 24	1995 25 to 54	1995 55 to 64	1996 15 to 24	1996 25 to 54	1996 55 to 64	1997 15 to 24	1997 25 to 54	1997 55 to 64	1998 15 to 24	1998 25 to 54	1998 55 to 64
Sweden[a]	Unemployment rates	4.5	1.3	1.5	20.6	7.9	7.8	22.5	8.7	8.2	22.5	9.2	8.0	16.8	7.6	6.6
	Labour force participation rates	69.1	92.8	70.5	52.7	89.6	67.1	51.1	89.4	69.0	50.2	88.6	68.1	50.0	88.0	67.5
	Employment/population ratios	66.0	91.6	69.4	42.3	82.6	61.9	40.3	81.8	63.4	39.6	80.6	62.7	41.6	81.3	63.0
Switzerland[b]	Unemployment rates	3.2	1.6	1.2	5.5	3.0	3.2	4.7	3.7	3.3	6.0	4.1	2.9	5.8	3.3	3.4
	Labour force participation rates	71.6	85.9	72.0	66.2	86.4	72.1	66.4	86.8	73.1	67.0	86.9	72.8	67.2	87.8	73.8
	Employment/population ratios	69.3	84.5	71.1	62.6	83.8	69.8	63.3	83.6	70.7	62.9	83.4	70.7	63.3	84.9	71.3
Turkey	Unemployment rates	16.0	5.4	3.1	14.7	4.9	2.3	12.9	4.4	1.7	14.4	4.4	1.4	13.8	4.7	1.9
	Labour force participation rates	54.7	65.1	44.1	47.9	64.0	43.4	47.1	63.0	42.5	44.5	60.9	40.3	43.6	61.3	41.9
	Employment/population ratios	45.9	61.6	42.7	40.9	60.9	42.4	41.0	60.2	41.8	38.1	58.2	39.7	37.6	58.4	41.1
United Kingdom[a]	Unemployment rates	10.1	5.8	7.2	15.3	7.4	7.5	14.7	7.0	7.1	13.5	5.9	6.3	12.3	5.0	5.3
	Labour force participation rates	78.0	83.9	53.0	69.8	83.4	51.4	70.7	83.3	51.4	70.5	83.3	51.7	69.5	83.3	51.0
	Employment/population ratios	70.1	79.0	49.2	59.1	77.2	47.6	60.3	77.5	47.7	61.0	78.4	48.5	61.0	79.1	48.3
United States[a]	Unemployment rates	11.2	4.6	3.3	12.1	4.5	3.6	12.0	4.3	3.4	11.3	3.9	2.9	10.4	3.5	2.6
	Labour force participation rates	67.3	83.5	55.9	66.3	83.5	57.2	65.5	83.8	57.9	65.4	84.1	58.9	65.9	84.1	59.3
	Employment/population ratios	59.8	79.7	54.0	58.3	79.7	55.1	57.6	80.2	55.9	58.0	80.9	57.2	59.0	81.1	57.7
European Union[c]	Unemployment rates	15.7	6.6	5.6	20.8	9.3	8.4	21.3	9.4	9.0	20.6	9.3	9.4	19.1	8.6	8.1
	Labour force participation rates	55.0	79.1	41.1	47.7	80.7	39.6	47.1	81.1	40.2	46.5	81.2	40.8	46.6	81.3	40.4
	Employment/population ratios	46.4	73.9	38.6	37.8	73.2	36.0	37.1	73.5	36.6	36.9	73.7	36.9	37.7	74.3	37.1
OECD Europe[c]	Unemployment rates	15.4	6.3	5.2	19.7	8.8	7.4	19.5	8.8	7.8	19.1	8.6	8.1	17.8	8.0	7.2
	Labour force participation rates	55.2	77.7	42.1	47.3	79.5	39.7	46.6	79.5	40.1	45.7	79.3	40.5	45.6	79.4	40.2
	Employment/population ratios	46.7	72.8	39.6	38.0	72.5	36.6	37.5	72.6	37.0	37.0	72.5	37.2	37.5	73.0	37.4
Total OECD[c]	Unemployment rates	11.5	4.8	3.8	14.1	6.3	5.2	13.9	6.2	5.3	13.4	5.9	5.2	12.8	5.7	5.0
	Labour force participation rates	55.8	79.1	50.4	52.5	79.9	49.1	51.9	80.1	49.6	51.6	80.3	50.3	51.7	80.1	50.5
	Employment/population ratios	49.4	75.3	48.4	45.1	74.9	46.4	44.7	75.2	47.0	44.6	75.5	47.7	45.1	75.5	47.9

| Indicates break in series.
a) Age group 15 to 24 refers to 16 to 24.
b) The year 1990 refers to 1991.
c) For above countries only.
Sources: OECD, *Labour Force Statistics, 1978-1998, Part III*, forthcoming.
For Austria, Belgium, Denmark, Germany, Greece, Italy, Luxembourg and Portugal, data are from the European Labour Force Survey.

Table C. **Unemployment, labour force participation rates and employment/population ratios by age and sex** (cont.)

Men
Percentages

		1990 15 to 24	1990 25 to 54	1990 55 to 64	1995 15 to 24	1995 25 to 54	1995 55 to 64	1996 15 to 24	1996 25 to 54	1996 55 to 64	1997 15 to 24	1997 25 to 54	1997 55 to 64	1998 15 to 24	1998 25 to 54	1998 55 to 64
Australia	Unemployment rates	13.9	4.9	6.3	14.9	6.9	9.0	15.4	7.2	9.5	17.1	6.6	8.7	15.7	6.7	7.0
	Labour force participation rates	73.0	93.1	63.2	71.6	91.7	60.8	72.6	91.5	60.2	68.7	90.6	59.5	69.9	90.4	60.5
	Employment/population ratios	62.8	88.5	59.2	60.9	85.4	55.3	61.4	84.9	54.4	56.9	84.6	54.3	59.0	84.3	56.3
Austria	Unemployment rates	..	..	..	5.7	3.6	4.4	7.1	5.1	5.1	7.8	4.5	6.0	7.4	4.9	6.6
	Labour force participation rates	..	..	..	64.6	93.2	42.6	62.9	93.0	44.7	61.4	93.3	43.0	61.7	93.8	42.5
	Employment/population ratios	..	..	..	60.9	89.8	40.8	58.4	88.2	42.4	56.6	89.1	40.5	57.1	89.2	39.6
Belgium	Unemployment rates	10.1	4.0	3.1	19.7	6.2	3.8	17.3	6.6	4.7	17.6	6.2	4.8	18.3	6.6	5.3
	Labour force participation rates	37.0	92.2	35.4	36.0	92.3	35.9	35.6	92.4	33.8	34.7	92.1	33.9	35.7	91.7	33.9
	Employment/population ratios	33.3	88.5	34.3	28.9	86.5	34.5	29.4	86.3	32.2	28.5	86.4	32.2	29.2	85.7	32.1
Canada	Unemployment rates	13.9	7.1	6.2	17.0	8.6	8.3	17.5	8.7	7.8	17.6	7.9	7.5	16.6	7.2	6.9
	Labour force participation rates	71.4	93.3	64.9	63.9	91.0	58.9	63.5	91.0	59.3	63.4	91.1	60.6	63.6	91.3	59.6
	Employment/population ratios	61.5	86.6	60.9	53.1	83.2	54.0	52.4	83.1	54.7	52.2	83.9	56.1	53.0	84.7	55.5
Czech Republic	Unemployment rates	..	..	..	7.5	2.6	2.6	6.4	2.5	3.2	7.3	3.1	3.1	10.6	3.9	3.6
	Labour force participation rates	..	..	..	58.0	95.4	52.0	57.7	95.2	55.8	56.1	95.2	56.4	55.7	95.1	55.1
	Employment/population ratios	..	..	..	53.7	92.9	50.6	54.1	92.8	54.0	52.0	92.3	54.7	49.8	91.4	53.2
Denmark	Unemployment rates	11.4	7.5	5.2	7.8	5.0	6.9	9.0	4.7	6.0	6.6	4.1	4.4	6.7	3.3	4.2
	Labour force participation rates	76.5	94.5	69.2	77.0	91.8	67.9	76.6	92.8	62.1	77.7	92.5	63.8	71.5	91.9	61.1
	Employment/population ratios	67.8	87.4	65.6	71.0	87.3	63.2	69.7	88.5	58.4	72.5	88.7	61.0	66.7	88.9	58.6
Finland	Unemployment rates	9.4	2.5	2.7	25.6	13.3	21.6	24.3	11.8	20.3	22.0	10.4	15.0	20.0	9.0	14.0
	Labour force participation rates	64.2	92.9	47.1	52.0	90.6	44.6	52.2	90.3	47.2	52.9	89.6	44.5	54.1	90.2	44.5
	Employment/population ratios	58.1	90.6	45.8	38.7	78.6	34.9	39.5	79.7	37.6	41.3	80.3	37.8	43.2	82.1	38.3
France	Unemployment rates	15.3	5.9	6.0	21.0	8.8	7.7	22.1	9.3	8.6	24.6	9.7	8.6	21.9	9.3	8.3
	Labour force participation rates	39.6	95.4	45.8	32.8	94.9	41.5	32.4	95.2	42.3	31.4	94.8	42.0	30.9	94.5	41.3
	Employment/population ratios	33.6	89.8	43.0	25.9	86.6	38.4	25.3	86.3	38.6	23.7	85.6	38.4	24.2	85.8	37.9
Germany	Unemployment rates	4.4	3.6	6.7	8.7	6.3	10.4	10.5	7.3	12.3	12.0	8.2	13.9	10.4	7.5	12.0
	Labour force participation rates	62.5	93.9	58.3	54.6	93.1	54.5	53.6	92.9	54.5	53.2	93.3	55.3	52.9	93.2	55.6
	Employment/population ratios	59.7	90.5	54.4	49.8	87.3	48.8	48.0	86.1	47.8	46.8	85.7	47.6	47.5	86.1	48.9
Greece	Unemployment rates	15.1	3.2	1.8	19.4	5.1	3.6	21.5	4.8	2.9	22.2	4.9	3.3	23.1	6.5	3.7
	Labour force participation rates	44.1	94.3	59.5	41.3	94.5	61.1	40.1	94.9	61.0	38.7	94.6	61.0	44.3	94.2	57.0
	Employment/population ratios	37.4	91.3	58.4	33.3	89.7	58.9	31.5	90.3	59.2	30.1	89.9	59.0	34.0	88.0	55.0
Hungary	Unemployment rates	..	..	..	20.7	9.9	5.4	19.0	9.4	5.7	16.9	8.2	6.3	14.8	6.9	4.7
	Labour force participation rates	..	..	..	44.6	86.5	28.6	43.7	85.9	28.0	43.6	85.0	27.8	46.5	87.7	26.9
	Employment/population ratios	..	..	..	35.3	77.9	27.1	35.4	77.8	26.4	36.2	78.0	26.1	39.6	81.6	25.6
Iceland[a, b]	Unemployment rates	5.8	1.8	1.0	13.1	3.1	4.2	9.2	2.1	3.3	8.3	2.3	2.8	6.4	1.3	1.8
	Labour force participation rates	60.1	97.0	93.5	63.8	96.8	92.7	60.1	96.3	93.2	59.2	96.7	91.7	63.8	96.1	93.3
	Employment/population ratios	56.6	95.2	92.6	55.4	93.9	88.8	54.6	94.3	90.1	54.3	94.5	89.1	59.7	94.8	91.6

Table C. **Unemployment, labour force participation rates and employment/population ratios by age and sex** (cont.)

Men

Percentages

		1990 15 to 24	1990 25 to 54	1990 55 to 64	1995 15 to 24	1995 25 to 54	1995 55 to 64	1996 15 to 24	1996 25 to 54	1996 55 to 64	1997 15 to 24	1997 25 to 54	1997 55 to 64	1998 15 to 24	1998 25 to 54	1998 55 to 64
Ireland	Unemployment rates	18.9	11.8	8.5	20.5	11.2	7.5	19.2	11.2	6.9	16.9	9.7	6.4	11.9	7.7	5.3
	Labour force participation rates	53.4	91.9	65.1	49.0	90.6	63.0	47.1	91.5	63.0	48.9	90.5	61.7	52.4	92.2	63.0
	Employment/population ratios	43.3	81.1	59.6	38.9	80.5	59.1	38.0	81.3	58.7	40.6	81.7	57.8	46.2	85.1	59.6
Italy	Unemployment rates	23.4	3.9	1.7	29.0	6.7	4.1	30.0	7.1	4.3	28.7	7.5	4.6	28.1	7.2	4.8
	Labour force participation rates	50.7	94.0	51.7	43.8	89.5	44.1	43.0	89.7	44.0	42.2	89.8	43.5	42.7	89.8	42.6
	Employment/population ratios	38.8	90.2	50.9	31.1	83.5	42.3	30.1	83.4	42.1	30.1	83.0	41.5	30.7	83.3	40.5
Japan	Unemployment rates	4.5	1.4	3.4	6.1	2.2	4.7	6.8	2.5	5.1	6.9	2.5	5.0	8.2	3.1	6.3
	Labour force participation rates	43.4	97.5	83.3	48.0	97.5	84.8	48.9	97.7	84.9	49.4	97.6	85.1	48.8	97.3	85.2
	Employment/population ratios	41.4	96.2	80.4	45.1	95.3	80.8	45.6	95.3	80.6	46.0	95.1	80.9	44.8	94.3	79.8
Korea	Unemployment rates	9.5	2.5	1.2	8.0	1.9	1.1	8.3	2.0	0.9	9.4	2.4	1.5	20.8	7.2	5.4
	Labour force participation rates	28.4	94.6	77.2	30.1	94.6	79.7	29.5	94.4	79.2	28.2	94.0	79.7	26.4	93.6	75.4
	Employment/population ratios	25.7	92.2	76.3	27.7	92.8	78.8	27.1	92.5	78.5	25.6	91.8	78.5	20.9	86.8	71.3
Luxembourg	Unemployment rates	2.7	1.1	1.1	6.7	1.7	0.0	10.1	1.8	0.0	5.6	1.5	0.8	5.8	1.7	0.0
	Labour force participation rates	45.7	95.1	43.2	42.4	93.9	35.1	42.8	93.8	35.6	39.4	93.4	35.8	37.2	94.4	35.1
	Employment/population ratios	44.5	94.0	42.7	39.6	92.2	35.1	38.5	92.1	35.6	37.2	92.0	35.5	35.1	92.8	35.1
Mexico[b]	Unemployment rates	5.2	1.5	1.0	8.6	4.6	3.5	7.1	3.2	2.6	5.4	2.0	0.9	4.7	1.9	1.1
	Labour force participation rates	71.2	96.8	85.9	72.5	96.2	80.7	71.8	96.5	80.2	71.7	96.9	83.7	71.8	96.7	83.3
	Employment/population ratios	67.5	95.4	85.1	66.3	91.8	77.9	66.7	93.4	78.2	67.8	95.0	82.9	68.4	94.8	82.4
Netherlands	Unemployment rates	10.0	4.5	3.2	12.0	5.0	2.6	11.1	4.3	2.9	9.1	3.7	2.2	7.8	2.8	2.0
	Labour force participation rates	61.8	93.4	45.7	65.5	92.8	42.3	66.9	92.7	43.1	69.0	93.1	44.2	68.9	93.7	46.9
	Employment/population ratios	55.6	89.2	33.5	57.7	88.2	31.5	59.5	88.7	41.8	62.7	89.7	43.3	63.5	91.1	46.0
New Zealand	Unemployment rates	14.9	6.6	4.9	12.0	5.1	3.6	12.4	4.8	4.3	13.2	5.3	4.7	15.6	6.0	4.9
	Labour force participation rates	71.4	93.4	56.8	71.3	92.0	65.3	70.8	91.9	69.0	69.6	92.0	69.3	67.9	91.4	70.6
	Employment/population ratios	60.7	87.2	54.0	62.8	87.4	62.9	62.0	87.5	66.0	60.4	87.2	66.0	57.3	85.9	67.1
Norway[a]	Unemployment rates	12.4	4.7	3.0	11.9	4.3	3.2	12.1	3.8	2.5	10.1	3.2	2.2	9.5	2.3	2.0
	Labour force participation rates	63.9	92.3	72.8	58.0	91.2	72.3	62.0	92.1	73.2	65.4	92.6	75.1	66.4	92.4	75.8
	Employment/population ratios	56.0	88.0	70.7	51.1	87.3	70.0	54.5	88.6	71.4	58.8	89.7	73.5	60.1	90.2	74.2
Poland	Unemployment rates	..	..	..	29.0	10.4	6.7	26.3	9.3	6.3	22.0	8.2	5.6	21.5	8.0	6.2
	Labour force participation rates	..	..	..	43.9	90.1	45.5	43.4	89.7	44.5	42.3	89.4	45.3	41.0	89.3	44.5
	Employment/population ratios	..	..	..	31.1	80.8	42.5	32.0	81.4	41.7	33.0	82.1	42.7	32.2	82.2	41.7
Portugal	Unemployment rates	7.9	2.4	1.9	15.1	5.3	4.9	14.6	5.2	5.9	11.0	5.0	6.4	8.3	3.1	3.8
	Labour force participation rates	63.8	94.0	65.9	47.2	93.6	61.9	46.2	93.4	62.2	48.5	92.7	62.2	51.1	93.1	67.3
	Employment/population ratios	58.7	91.7	64.6	40.1	88.6	58.9	39.4	88.5	58.5	43.1	88.0	58.2	46.9	90.2	64.7
Spain[a]	Unemployment rates	23.2	9.3	8.4	33.6	15.3	12.6	33.0	14.9	11.4	30.3	13.5	10.8	27.1	11.5	9.6
	Labour force participation rates	61.7	94.3	62.4	52.5	92.7	54.9	51.8	92.8	56.3	50.4	92.6	56.6	51.7	92.7	57.7
	Employment/population ratios	47.4	85.5	57.2	34.9	78.5	48.0	34.7	79.0	49.9	35.2	80.1	50.5	37.7	82.0	52.1

Table C. **Unemployment, labour force participation rates and employment/population ratios by age and sex** (cont.)

Men

Percentages

		1990 15 to 24	1990 25 to 54	1990 55 to 64	1995 15 to 24	1995 25 to 54	1995 55 to 64	1996 15 to 24	1996 25 to 54	1996 55 to 64	1997 15 to 24	1997 25 to 54	1997 55 to 64	1998 15 to 24	1998 25 to 54	1998 55 to 64
Sweden[a]	Unemployment rates	4.6	1.3	1.3	21.8	8.7	8.9	23.0	9.2	9.4	23.0	9.4	9.4	17.5	7.8	7.8
	Labour force participation rates	69.3	94.7	75.3	52.7	92.0	70.7	52.0	91.6	72.9	51.4	91.0	71.3	51.4	90.5	71.4
	Employment/population ratios	66.1	93.5	74.4	41.8	84.0	64.4	40.7	83.4	66.0	40.3	82.6	64.7	42.4	83.4	65.8
Switzerland[b]	Unemployment rates	3.0	0.8	1.4	5.4	2.3	4.0	5.2	3.2	3.1	8.0	4.0	3.1	4.7	2.8	4.1
	Labour force participation rates	72.9	97.8	86.4	68.0	97.7	82.3	68.3	97.3	81.7	69.0	97.0	81.9	70.6	97.0	81.7
	Employment/population ratios	70.7	97.0	85.2	64.3	95.4	79.0	64.7	94.2	79.1	63.5	93.2	79.3	67.3	94.3	78.4
Turkey	Unemployment rates	16.6	5.2	4.0	16.3	4.9	3.1	14.6	4.6	2.3	14.0	4.3	1.8	14.5	4.8	2.4
	Labour force participation rates	71.8	94.2	61.3	61.9	93.4	60.9	60.9	92.6	57.4	59.4	92.1	56.5	57.8	92.2	58.2
	Employment/population ratios	59.9	89.3	58.8	51.8	88.8	59.1	52.0	88.3	56.1	51.1	88.1	55.4	49.5	87.8	56.8
United Kingdom[a]	Unemployment rates	11.1	5.6	8.4	17.9	8.5	10.1	17.8	8.0	9.5	15.6	6.7	7.8	13.8	5.5	6.8
	Labour force participation rates	83.5	94.8	68.1	74.4	92.7	62.4	75.3	91.9	62.9	74.6	91.6	63.6	73.4	91.4	62.6
	Employment/population ratios	74.2	89.5	62.4	61.1	84.8	56.1	61.9	84.6	57.0	63.0	85.4	58.6	63.3	86.4	58.3
United States[a]	Unemployment rates	11.6	4.6	3.8	12.5	4.4	3.6	12.6	4.2	3.3	11.8	3.7	3.1	11.1	3.3	2.8
	Labour force participation rates	71.8	93.4	67.8	70.2	91.6	66.0	68.8	91.8	67.0	68.2	91.8	67.6	68.4	91.8	68.1
	Employment/population ratios	63.5	89.1	65.2	61.5	87.6	63.6	60.1	87.9	64.7	60.1	88.4	65.5	60.8	88.8	66.2
European Union[c]	Unemployment rates	13.5	5.0	5.6	19.4	8.0	8.5	20.0	8.2	9.0	19.1	8.1	9.2	17.6	7.3	8.0
	Labour force participation rates	58.8	94.3	56.7	51.4	92.6	51.9	50.9	92.6	52.3	52.6	92.5	52.5	50.4	92.4	52.2
	Employment/population ratios	50.8	89.6	53.2	41.4	85.3	47.2	40.7	85.0	47.6	42.5	85.0	47.7	41.6	85.6	48.0
OECD Europe[c]	Unemployment rates	13.9	4.9	5.3	18.8	7.6	7.6	18.7	7.7	7.9	17.9	7.5	7.9	16.7	6.9	7.1
	Labour force participation rates	61.1	94.3	57.8	52.7	92.5	52.4	52.2	92.3	52.4	53.0	92.2	52.6	51.3	92.2	52.5
	Employment/population ratios	52.6	89.7	54.4	42.8	85.5	48.1	42.4	85.3	48.2	43.5	85.3	48.4	42.7	85.8	48.7
Total OECD[c]	Unemployment rates	11.1	4.1	4.2	13.9	5.7	5.7	13.8	5.6	5.7	13.3	5.3	5.5	12.5	5.2	5.5
	Labour force participation rates	61.3	94.6	66.5	57.9	93.2	62.7	57.4	93.1	63.0	57.4	93.1	63.6	57.0	93.0	63.7
	Employment/population ratios	54.5	90.8	63.5	49.9	87.9	59.0	49.5	87.9	59.4	49.8	88.2	60.1	49.9	88.2	60.2

| Indicates break in series.
a) Age group 15 to 24 refers to 16 to 24.
b) The year 1990 refers to 1991.
c) For above countries only.
Sources: OECD, Labour Force Statistics, 1978-1998, Part III, forthcoming.
For Austria, Belgium, Denmark, Germany, Greece, Italy, Luxembourg and Portugal, data are from the European Labour Force Survey.

Table C. Unemployment, labour force participation rates and employment/population ratios by age and sex *(cont.)*

Women
Percentages

		1990 15 to 24	1990 25 to 54	1990 55 to 64	1995 15 to 24	1995 25 to 54	1995 55 to 64	1996 15 to 24	1996 25 to 54	1996 55 to 64	1997 15 to 24	1997 25 to 54	1997 55 to 64	1998 15 to 24	1998 25 to 54	1998 55 to 64
Australia	Unemployment rates	12.4	5.5	3.0	14.0	5.7	4.0	14.1	6.4	4.2	14.5	6.5	4.2	13.2	5.7	4.4
	Labour force participation rates	67.7	66.6	24.9	67.5	69.2	28.6	67.4	68.9	31.2	64.7	68.7	30.6	65.1	69.6	32.4
	Employment/population ratios	59.3	63.0	24.2	58.1	65.2	27.4	57.9	64.5	29.9	55.4	64.2	29.3	56.5	65.6	31.0
Austria	Unemployment rates	..	..	..	6.2	4.8	2.9	6.5	5.1	3.5	7.3	5.0	3.3	7.6	5.2	5.7
	Labour force participation rates	..	..	..	58.9	73.3	18.8	56.4	73.9	17.9	55.4	74.4	17.9	55.5	75.5	18.1
	Employment/population ratios	..	..	..	55.2	69.8	18.3	52.7	70.1	17.3	51.4	70.7	17.3	51.3	71.6	17.1
Belgium	Unemployment rates	19.2	10.3	4.9	23.7	11.1	4.4	24.4	11.3	4.0	25.7	10.2	4.3	23.0	10.7	5.4
	Labour force participation rates	34.1	60.8	9.9	31.7	68.2	13.3	29.9	69.0	12.5	29.3	69.7	13.0	29.4	70.5	14.2
	Employment/population ratios	27.5	54.5	9.4	24.2	60.6	12.7	22.6	61.2	12.0	21.8	62.6	12.4	22.6	62.9	13.4
Canada	Unemployment rates	11.3	7.5	5.6	14.0	8.3	8.0	14.6	8.5	7.6	15.7	7.9	7.8	13.7	7.1	6.9
	Labour force participation rates	67.0	75.7	35.5	60.4	75.9	36.3	59.5	76.4	36.9	59.0	76.6	36.5	60.4	77.3	38.2
	Employment/population ratios	59.4	70.0	33.5	51.9	69.6	33.4	50.8	69.9	34.1	49.7	70.5	33.6	52.1	71.8	35.6
Czech Republic	Unemployment rates	..	..	..	8.5	4.2	3.8	8.3	4.0	4.1	10.0	5.1	4.5	14.6	7.2	4.4
	Labour force participation rates	..	..	..	42.9	83.7	21.3	40.8	82.1	23.2	40.2	82.0	25.0	42.0	81.9	23.9
	Employment/population ratios	..	..	..	39.2	80.3	20.5	37.4	78.9	22.3	36.2	77.9	23.8	35.9	76.0	22.9
Denmark	Unemployment rates	11.6	8.4	7.5	12.3	7.6	9.8	12.4	7.6	6.3	9.9	5.7	6.0	7.7	6.1	6.4
	Labour force participation rates	70.4	87.7	45.8	69.4	82.1	40.1	70.8	82.1	39.5	70.4	81.7	43.9	71.5	82.8	44.2
	Employment/population ratios	62.2	80.3	42.4	60.9	75.9	36.1	62.0	75.8	37.0	63.4	77.0	41.2	66.0	77.7	41.3
Finland	Unemployment rates	8.3	1.6	2.8	28.7	13.1	18.9	25.8	12.7	21.7	25.0	11.1	15.0	24.5	10.1	13.9
	Labour force participation rates	56.9	86.5	40.8	39.5	84.4	41.9	40.0	84.7	43.1	43.6	84.0	39.6	45.1	84.0	39.7
	Employment/population ratios	52.2	85.1	39.7	28.2	73.4	34.0	29.7	73.9	33.7	32.7	74.6	33.7	34.1	75.6	34.2
France	Unemployment rates	23.9	10.7	7.6	32.2	12.6	6.6	31.9	13.0	8.2	32.8	12.9	8.5	30.0	12.7	9.3
	Labour force participation rates	33.1	72.9	31.1	26.7	77.3	30.9	25.9	77.8	31.3	24.5	77.3	31.6	25.0	77.9	31.2
	Employment/population ratios	25.2	65.1	28.8	18.1	67.5	28.9	17.7	67.6	28.8	16.5	67.3	28.9	17.5	68.0	28.3
Germany	Unemployment rates	4.7	6.3	8.9	8.2	9.4	13.7	8.6	9.1	14.9	9.2	9.9	17.3	8.2	8.0	14.0
	Labour force participation rates	58.8	65.6	27.5	50.3	73.2	31.3	47.1	73.7	33.1	46.1	74.5	35.0	46.3	73.5	33.4
	Employment/population ratios	56.0	61.5	25.0	46.2	66.3	27.0	43.0	67.0	28.2	41.9	67.2	28.9	42.5	67.6	28.7
Greece	Unemployment rates	32.6	8.6	1.2	37.7	10.9	2.9	41.3	12.3	3.0	40.6	11.9	3.1	42.4	14.4	3.9
	Labour force participation rates	35.3	51.5	24.3	32.5	55.0	24.5	34.1	56.9	24.5	32.6	57.5	25.1	37.3	59.4	24.4
	Employment/population ratios	23.8	47.1	24.0	20.3	49.0	23.8	20.0	49.9	23.8	19.4	50.7	24.4	21.5	50.8	23.4
Hungary	Unemployment rates	..	..	..	15.6	7.7	5.3	16.4	7.8	5.3	14.5	6.7	4.4	11.6	6.1	5.1
	Labour force participation rates	..	..	..	31.9	68.9	9.7	30.2	68.5	10.8	30.6	67.2	10.8	34.9	68.2	10.0
	Employment/population ratios	..	..	..	27.0	63.6	9.2	25.2	63.2	10.2	26.2	62.7	10.3	30.9	64.0	9.5
Iceland[a,b]	Unemployment rates	3.9	2.6	3.4	8.6	4.3	4.0	7.6	3.2	4.4	7.1	3.9	3.5	5.6	2.9	1.4
	Labour force participation rates	58.8	83.0	81.1	59.6	88.0	84.8	59.6	86.9	81.3	61.5	85.1	81.2	67.3	85.4	83.0
	Employment/population ratios	56.5	80.8	78.3	54.5	84.2	81.5	55.1	84.1	77.7	57.2	81.8	78.4	63.5	82.9	81.9

234 – OECD Employment Outlook

Table C. Unemployment, labour force participation rates and employment/population ratios by age and sex (cont.)

Women

Percentages

		1990 15 to 24	1990 25 to 54	1990 55 to 64	1995 15 to 24	1995 25 to 54	1995 55 to 64	1996 15 to 24	1996 25 to 54	1996 55 to 64	1997 15 to 24	1997 25 to 54	1997 55 to 64	1998 15 to 24	1998 25 to 54	1998 55 to 64
Ireland	Unemployment rates	16.1	13.5	8.3	17.4	10.9	8.5	17.0	10.7	6.7	15.2	9.3	4.9	11.1	6.7	4.6
	Labour force participation rates	47.3	45.5	19.9	42.0	54.6	21.2	40.6	57.5	23.4	41.9	58.4	23.3	44.6	60.8	24.6
	Employment/population ratios	39.6	39.3	18.2	34.7	48.6	19.4	33.7	51.4	21.8	35.6	53.0	22.2	39.7	56.8	23.5
Italy	Unemployment rates	35.4	11.3	2.0	37.6	12.6	4.9	39.2	12.9	4.3	39.9	13.1	3.8	37.2	13.4	4.5
	Labour force participation rates	43.0	52.1	15.0	33.8	53.7	13.8	33.9	54.8	14.4	33.8	55.1	15.0	32.2	56.1	15.1
	Employment/population ratios	27.8	46.2	14.7	21.1	47.0	13.1	20.6	47.7	13.8	20.3	47.9	14.4	20.2	48.6	14.4
Japan	Unemployment rates	4.1	2.1	1.4	6.1	3.1	2.1	6.7	3.2	2.3	6.3	3.2	2.2	7.3	3.8	2.9
	Labour force participation rates	44.8	64.2	47.2	47.2	65.2	48.5	47.6	65.8	48.8	47.7	66.7	49.5	47.8	66.6	49.9
	Employment/population ratios	43.0	62.9	46.5	44.4	63.2	47.5	44.4	63.7	47.6	44.7	64.6	48.4	44.3	64.0	48.5
Korea	Unemployment rates	5.5	0.9	0.3	5.3	0.9	0.4	4.8	1.0	0.4	6.6	1.7	0.4	12.8	4.9	1.9
	Labour force participation rates	40.7	54.2	49.6	41.9	55.6	50.4	40.5	56.9	49.6	39.8	58.4	50.2	35.8	55.9	47.9
	Employment/population ratios	38.5	53.7	49.4	39.7	55.1	50.2	38.5	56.4	49.4	37.1	57.5	50.0	31.2	53.1	46.9
Luxembourg	Unemployment rates	4.7	2.2	0.0	7.8	3.9	1.0	8.3	4.2	0.0	9.2	2.9	1.2	7.1	3.9	1.9
	Labour force participation rates	44.0	49.7	13.8	40.0	52.7	13.3	38.5	55.9	10.2	35.3	58.0	12.6	33.4	58.4	15.6
	Employment/population ratios	42.0	48.6	13.8	36.8	50.6	13.2	35.3	53.6	10.2	32.1	56.3	12.5	31.0	56.2	15.3
Mexico[b]	Unemployment rates	5.8	3.8	1.0	10.8	4.1	2.6	8.8	3.5	1.0	7.8	3.5	1.8	6.4	2.7	0.5
	Labour force participation rates	34.5	38.2	24.4	36.0	42.3	26.9	35.2	43.4	27.8	36.5	46.3	30.2	37.1	45.8	28.3
	Employment/population ratios	32.5	36.8	24.2	32.1	40.6	26.2	32.1	41.9	27.5	33.6	44.7	29.6	34.7	44.6	28.1
Netherlands	Unemployment rates	12.3	10.3	5.0	13.7	7.7	3.7	13.1	7.3	4.0	10.0	6.5	3.2	8.7	4.8	3.1
	Labour force participation rates	60.9	58.5	16.7	63.5	66.4	18.6	65.8	67.2	20.2	66.0	69.4	20.9	67.1	70.5	21.5
	Employment/population ratios	53.4	52.4	12.0	54.8	61.3	14.0	57.1	62.3	19.4	59.4	65.0	20.2	61.3	67.1	20.8
New Zealand	Unemployment rates	13.2	5.4	4.0	11.8	5.0	2.7	11.2	5.0	2.7	13.0	5.3	3.0	13.5	6.2	4.1
	Labour force participation rates	64.3	69.3	30.7	63.4	71.8	39.0	64.1	73.3	43.0	64.1	72.6	44.4	62.4	72.5	46.3
	Employment/population ratios	55.8	65.6	29.5	56.0	68.1	37.9	56.9	69.6	41.8	55.8	68.7	43.1	54.0	68.1	44.4
Norway[a]	Unemployment rates	11.0	3.9	1.9	11.8	3.7	1.9	12.7	3.9	1.8	11.1	3.5	1.7	9.4	2.3	1.7
	Labour force participation rates	56.9	79.2	53.9	53.7	80.4	57.4	57.3	81.7	59.2	58.1	83.3	60.6	61.1	83.0	60.8
	Employment/population ratios	50.7	76.1	52.8	47.3	77.4	56.4	50.0	78.5	58.1	51.6	80.4	59.6	55.3	81.1	59.8
Poland	Unemployment rates	..	..	..	33.8	13.2	4.9	31.2	12.5	5.2	28.0	12.0	4.9	25.2	11.2	5.5
	Labour force participation rates	..	..	..	35.6	78.0	27.6	34.6	77.5	26.9	34.3	76.5	27.1	33.7	76.5	25.7
	Employment/population ratios	..	..	..	23.5	67.7	26.3	23.8	67.8	25.5	24.7	67.3	25.7	25.2	67.9	24.3
Portugal	Unemployment rates	13.3	5.4	1.4	17.1	7.0	2.6	20.0	7.4	3.6	18.0	6.5	3.4	10.9	5.4	2.8
	Labour force participation rates	53.0	67.0	31.5	38.9	74.1	34.5	38.3	74.3	36.8	39.8	74.8	38.3	43.6	74.9	40.0
	Employment/population ratios	46.0	63.4	31.1	32.3	68.9	33.6	30.6	68.8	35.4	32.6	69.9	37.0	38.8	70.9	38.9
Spain[a]	Unemployment rates	39.7	20.6	7.2	49.1	27.5	11.4	48.8	26.3	12.1	46.1	25.4	12.7	43.4	24.1	12.1
	Labour force participation rates	47.5	46.9	19.5	42.4	55.5	19.9	41.4	56.8	20.2	41.2	58.1	20.6	40.9	58.9	21.4
	Employment/population ratios	28.7	37.2	18.1	21.6	40.2	17.6	21.2	41.9	17.8	22.2	43.4	18.0	23.2	44.8	18.8

Table C. Unemployment, labour force participation rates and employment/population ratios by age and sex (cont.)

Women
Percentages

		1990 15 to 24	1990 25 to 54	1990 55 to 64	1995 15 to 24	1995 25 to 54	1995 55 to 64	1996 15 to 24	1996 25 to 54	1996 55 to 64	1997 15 to 24	1997 25 to 54	1997 55 to 64	1998 15 to 24	1998 25 to 54	1998 55 to 64
Sweden[a]	Unemployment rates	4.5	1.2	1.6	19.4	7.0	6.6	22.0	8.3	6.9	21.9	8.9	6.5	16.1	7.3	5.2
	Labour force participation rates	68.9	90.8	65.8	52.6	87.1	63.7	50.2	87.1	65.2	48.9	86.2	64.9	48.5	85.4	63.6
	Employment/population ratios	65.9	89.7	64.7	42.9	81.1	59.5	39.9	80.1	60.7	38.9	78.6	60.7	40.7	79.1	60.3
Switzerland[b]	Unemployment rates	3.4	2.6	0.7	5.5	4.0	1.8	4.1	4.3	3.6	3.8	4.2	2.6	7.0	4.0	2.3
	Labour force participation rates	70.3	73.7	53.4	64.4	75.0	58.7	64.5	76.1	61.8	64.8	76.7	60.8	63.7	78.6	63.7
	Employment/population ratios	67.9	71.8	53.0	60.8	72.0	57.6	61.9	72.8	59.6	62.3	73.5	59.2	59.3	75.5	62.3
Turkey	Unemployment rates	15.0	5.9	1.0	12.1	4.7	0.4	10.4	3.7	0.3	15.0	4.8	0.5	12.7	4.5	0.7
	Labour force participation rates	39.4	36.0	26.6	35.3	34.4	26.1	34.7	32.8	27.9	31.2	29.5	24.3	30.6	30.5	25.5
	Employment/population ratios	33.5	33.9	26.4	31.0	32.8	26.0	31.1	31.6	27.8	26.5	28.1	24.2	26.7	29.1	25.4
United Kingdom[a]	Unemployment rates	9.0	5.9	5.0	12.2	6.0	3.7	11.1	5.6	3.4	11.0	4.9	3.9	10.5	4.5	3.1
	Labour force participation rates	72.4	72.9	38.7	64.9	74.0	40.8	65.8	74.5	40.2	66.1	75.0	40.3	65.4	75.1	39.8
	Employment/population ratios	65.9	68.6	36.7	57.0	69.5	39.3	58.6	70.3	38.8	58.8	71.3	38.7	58.5	71.7	38.5
United States[a]	Unemployment rates	10.7	4.6	2.8	11.6	4.5	3.6	11.3	4.4	3.4	10.7	4.1	2.7	9.8	3.8	2.4
	Labour force participation rates	62.9	74.0	45.2	62.3	75.6	49.2	62.2	76.1	49.6	62.6	76.7	50.9	63.3	76.5	51.2
	Employment/population ratios	56.1	70.6	44.0	55.1	72.2	47.5	55.2	72.8	47.9	55.9	73.5	49.5	57.2	73.6	50.0
European Union[c]	Unemployment rates	18.1	8.9	5.7	22.5	11.0	8.2	22.8	11.0	8.9	22.5	10.8	9.7	20.8	10.3	8.3
	Labour force participation rates	51.1	64.0	26.7	43.9	68.7	28.0	43.1	69.4	28.7	42.6	69.9	29.6	42.7	70.1	29.0
	Employment/population ratios	41.8	58.3	25.1	34.1	61.1	25.6	33.3	61.8	26.2	33.1	62.3	26.7	33.8	62.9	26.6
OECD Europe[c]	Unemployment rates	17.3	8.5	5.1	20.8	10.4	7.0	20.7	10.3	7.6	20.9	10.2	8.3	19.2	9.7	7.2
	Labour force participation rates	49.4	61.1	27.3	41.8	66.4	27.8	41.0	66.6	28.6	40.0	66.4	29.0	40.0	66.5	28.6
	Employment/population ratios	40.8	55.9	25.8	33.1	59.4	25.7	32.6	59.7	26.4	31.6	59.6	26.6	32.3	60.1	26.5
Total OECD[c]	Unemployment rates	12.1	5.8	3.3	14.4	7.1	4.6	14.1	6.9	4.7	14.0	6.8	4.8	13.1	6.5	4.3
	Labour force participation rates	50.4	63.7	35.5	47.1	66.8	36.4	46.5	67.2	37.1	46.2	67.6	37.9	46.4	67.5	38.0
	Employment/population ratios	44.3	60.0	34.3	40.3	62.1	34.7	39.9	62.5	35.3	39.8	63.0	36.1	40.3	63.0	36.3

| Indicates break in series.
a) Age group 15 to 24 refers to 16 to 24.
b) The year 1990 refers to 1991.
c) For above countries only.

Sources: OECD, *Labour Force Statistics, 1978-1998, Part III*, forthcoming.
For Austria, Belgium, Denmark, Germany, Greece, Italy, Luxembourg and Portugal, data are from the European Labour Force Survey.

Table D. Unemployment, labour force participation rates and employment/population ratios by educational attainment for persons aged 25-64, 1996

Percentages

		Both sexes			Men			Women		
		Less than upper secondary education	Upper secondary education	Tertiary level education	Less than upper secondary education	Upper secondary education	Tertiary level education	Less than upper secondary education	Upper secondary education	Tertiary level education
Australia	Unemployment rates	8.9	6.3	3.9	10.1	6.1	4.2	7.8	6.8	3.5
	Labour force participation rates	65.1	80.9	86.0	81.1	89.8	92.3	54.8	65.9	79.0
	Employment/population ratios	59.3	75.8	82.6	72.9	84.3	88.4	50.5	61.5	76.2
Austria	Unemployment rates	6.0	3.3	2.3	6.4	3.1	2.2	5.8	3.6	2.4
	Labour force participation rates	57.6	78.3	88.9	72.6	86.3	92.1	48.5	68.3	84.7
	Employment/population ratios	54.1	75.7	86.9	68.0	83.6	90.0	45.8	65.9	82.7
Belgium	Unemployment rates	13.4	7.4	3.6	10.3	4.6	3.0	18.8	11.5	4.2
	Labour force participation rates	54.6	78.1	86.8	70.3	88.5	91.7	39.4	66.8	82.0
	Employment/population ratios	47.3	72.4	83.7	63.0	84.4	88.9	31.9	59.1	78.5
Canada	Unemployment rates	13.4	8.9	6.7	13.3	8.9	6.6	13.5	8.8	6.8
	Labour force participation rates	60.8	79.4	85.8	74.2	88.5	90.7	46.6	71.6	80.7
	Employment/population ratios	52.6	72.4	80.1	64.3	80.6	84.7	40.3	65.3	75.2
Czech Republic	Unemployment rates	8.9	2.4	0.8	11.5	1.7	0.8	7.5	3.3	0.9
	Labour force participation rates	60.3	84.3	93.5	73.1	88.8	95.7	55.0	79.3	90.1
	Employment/population ratios	54.9	82.3	92.7	64.7	87.4	94.9	50.9	76.6	89.3
Denmark	Unemployment rates	11.8	7.0	3.9	10.2	6.0	4.0	13.4	8.2	3.7
	Labour force participation rates	69.7	86.6	92.3	77.2	89.1	93.8	63.6	83.4	90.8
	Employment/population ratios	61.5	80.6	88.7	69.3	83.8	90.0	55.1	76.5	87.4
Finland	Unemployment rates	21.5	15.2	7.1	20.3	15.2	7.1	23.0	15.3	7.1
	Labour force participation rates	69.2	84.2	89.4	72.8	87.3	91.0	65.4	81.4	87.5
	Employment/population ratios	54.3	71.4	83.0	58.0	74.0	84.5	50.3	68.9	81.3
France	Unemployment rates	14.8	9.7	6.7	13.0	8.1	5.9	16.9	12.0	7.4
	Labour force participation rates	65.9	83.3	88.0	77.2	89.6	92.9	56.5	76.0	83.3
	Employment/population ratios	56.2	75.2	82.1	67.2	82.3	87.4	47.0	66.9	77.1
Germany	Unemployment rates	14.2	8.9	5.2	15.8	7.9	4.8	12.7	10.0	6.1
	Labour force participation rates	55.9	76.9	88.0	76.0	84.5	91.1	45.0	69.0	82.7
	Employment/population ratios	48.0	70.1	83.4	63.9	77.8	86.8	39.3	62.1	77.7
Greece	Unemployment rates	6.5	9.2	8.0	4.2	5.4	4.8	10.7	15.6	11.7
	Labour force participation rates	60.7	68.9	85.9	84.5	88.6	90.8	40.3	50.1	80.1
	Employment/population ratios	56.7	62.6	79.0	81.0	83.8	86.1	36.0	42.3	70.7
Hungary	Unemployment rates	12.9	7.7	2.0	15.0	8.2	1.6	10.8	7.0	2.4
	Labour force participation rates	41.3	77.2	83.1	49.8	85.5	87.3	35.5	67.8	79.2
	Employment/population ratios	36.0	71.3	81.5	42.3	78.5	85.9	31.6	63.0	77.3
Ireland	Unemployment rates	16.9	7.4	4.2	16.1	6.4	3.8	19.0	8.4	4.8
	Labour force participation rates	60.2	73.3	86.3	82.7	92.0	94.0	34.5	59.2	78.2
	Employment/population ratios	50.0	67.9	82.7	69.4	86.1	90.4	28.0	54.2	74.5
Italy	Unemployment rates	9.4	8.2	7.3	7.3	6.0	5.2	13.8	11.2	10.1
	Labour force participation rates	54.0	70.5	87.1	76.1	80.0	92.0	33.5	60.6	81.3
	Employment/population ratios	48.9	64.7	80.8	70.5	75.2	87.2	28.8	53.8	73.1

Statistical Annex – 237

OECD

Table D. Unemployment, labour force participation rates and employment/population ratios by educational attainment for persons aged 25-64, 1996 (cont.)

Percentages

		Both sexes - Less than upper secondary education	Both sexes - Upper secondary education	Both sexes - Tertiary level education	Men - Less than upper secondary education	Men - Upper secondary education	Men - Tertiary level education	Women - Less than upper secondary education	Women - Upper secondary education	Women - Tertiary level education
Korea	Unemployment rates	0.9	1.7	2.0	1.3	2.0	2.2	0.5	1.1	1.5
	Labour force participation rates	71.8	72.9	82.0	89.1	92.5	95.4	60.9	48.9	56.2
	Employment/population ratios	71.1	71.6	80.3	88.0	90.6	93.3	60.6	48.4	55.4
Luxembourg	Unemployment rates	3.8	2.1	0.6	2.5	2.1	0.4	6.3	2.1	1.3
	Labour force participation rates	58.8	77.4	89.1	80.3	87.7	93.3	39.4	65.6	81.2
	Employment/population ratios	56.6	75.8	88.5	78.4	85.9	93.0	36.9	64.2	80.2
Netherlands	Unemployment rates	7.0	4.5	3.5	5.8	3.1	3.2	8.7	6.5	3.9
	Labour force participation rates	56.5	78.1	86.2	75.8	87.3	90.4	41.5	67.5	80.6
	Employment/population ratios	52.6	74.6	83.2	71.4	84.6	87.5	37.9	63.1	77.4
New Zealand[a]	Unemployment rates	6.8	3.5	2.9	7.6	3.2	3.2	5.9	4.0	2.6
	Labour force participation rates	68.2	85.6	85.6	81.6	92.6	91.9	58.1	74.7	80.3
	Employment/population ratios	63.6	82.6	83.1	75.4	89.6	89.0	54.7	71.8	78.2
Norway	Unemployment rates	4.9	3.8	2.6	5.0	3.8	2.4	4.8	3.9	2.5
	Labour force participation rates	68.3	85.4	90.7	78.6	90.4	93.4	58.7	80.0	87.9
	Employment/population ratios	64.9	82.1	88.3	74.7	87.0	91.1	55.9	76.9	85.7
Poland[b]	Unemployment rates	13.9	11.4	3.8	14.2	9.6	3.5	13.6	13.7	4.1
	Labour force participation rates	58.1	78.5	87.0	69.4	84.6	90.2	49.1	71.9	84.7
	Employment/population ratios	50.0	69.6	83.7	59.5	76.4	87.1	42.5	62.0	81.2
Portugal	Unemployment rates	6.4	5.7	3.2	5.7	5.1	3.0	7.4	6.5	3.3
	Labour force participation rates	71.7	84.4	90.6	84.3	88.4	93.1	60.4	80.2	88.8
	Employment/population ratios	67.1	79.6	87.7	79.5	83.9	90.3	55.9	74.9	85.8
Spain	Unemployment rates	20.1	17.4	14.3	16.2	12.0	10.3	27.6	25.4	19.3
	Labour force participation rates	58.9	79.8	87.4	82.0	91.0	91.7	37.8	67.8	82.5
	Employment/population ratios	47.1	65.9	74.9	68.7	80.1	82.3	27.4	50.6	66.6
Sweden	Unemployment rates	10.8	9.6	4.8	10.5	10.3	5.4	11.2	8.8	4.3
	Labour force participation rates	77.1	87.6	91.3	82.2	90.1	92.0	71.3	85.0	90.6
	Employment/population ratios	68.7	79.2	86.9	73.5	80.8	87.1	63.3	77.5	86.8
Switzerland	Unemployment rates	6.5	3.1	2.7	6.4	2.6	2.8	6.5	3.6	2.4
	Labour force participation rates	72.5	82.6	92.4	91.6	93.8	96.4	63.9	72.5	81.2
	Employment/population ratios	67.8	80.0	89.9	85.8	91.3	93.6	59.7	69.9	79.2
Turkey[a]	Unemployment rates	4.3	5.5	3.5	4.3	4.3	3.0	4.3	10.8	4.6
	Labour force participation rates	59.2	70.4	83.5	87.0	89.6	88.9	25.3	35.6	72.7
	Employment/population ratios	56.6	66.5	80.6	83.2	85.7	86.3	24.2	31.7	69.4
United Kingdom	Unemployment rates	10.9	7.1	3.5	15.1	8.1	4.1	7.3	5.8	2.9
	Labour force participation rates	62.0	82.1	88.3	72.7	88.7	92.6	55.1	74.4	83.4
	Employment/population ratios	55.2	76.2	85.2	61.7	81.5	88.8	51.1	70.1	81.0
United States	Unemployment rates	10.9	5.1	2.4	11.0	5.7	2.6	10.7	4.5	2.1
	Labour force participation rates	60.2	79.7	87.4	74.3	87.8	92.9	45.7	72.3	81.8
	Employment/population ratios	53.7	75.7	85.3	66.1	82.8	90.5	40.9	69.1	80.1

Table D. **Unemployment, labour force participation rates and employment/population ratios by educational attainment for persons aged 25-64, 1996** (cont.)

Percentages

		Both sexes			Men			Women		
		Less than upper secondary education	Upper secondary education	Tertiary level education	Less than upper secondary education	Upper secondary education	Tertiary level education	Less than upper secondary education	Upper secondary education	Tertiary level education
European Union	Unemployment rates	12.7	8.5	6.0	11.3	7.5	5.2	14.7	9.8	7.1
	Labour force participation rates	59.7	78.8	88.0	77.8	86.5	91.8	44.9	70.4	83.2
	Employment/population ratios	52.1	72.1	82.7	69.0	80.0	87.1	38.3	63.5	77.3
OECD Europe[c]	Unemployment rates	12.6	8.0	5.7	11.3	7.1	5.0	14.3	9.1	6.8
	Labour force participation rates	59.5	79.1	88.1	77.2	86.8	92.0	45.0	70.9	83.3
	Employment/population ratios	52.0	72.8	83.1	68.5	80.6	87.4	38.6	64.4	77.7
Total OECD[c]	Unemployment rates	11.1	6.5	4.0	10.5	6.3	3.9	11.9	6.8	4.3
	Labour force participation rates	60.8	79.1	87.3	77.5	87.6	92.5	46.9	70.3	81.4
	Employment/population ratios	54.0	73.9	83.7	69.3	82.1	88.9	41.4	65.5	77.9

a) Data are for the year 1997.
b) Data are for the year 1995.
c) For above countries and year 1996 only.
Source: OECD, Education at a Glance – OECD Indicators, 1998.

Table E. Incidence and composition of part-time employment[a], 1990-1998
Percentages

	\multicolumn{5}{c}{Part-time employment as a proportion of employment}										
	\multicolumn{5}{c}{Men}	\multicolumn{5}{c}{Women}				
	1990	1995	1996	1997	1998	1990	1995	1996	1997	1998
Australia[b, c]	11.3	13.5	14.0	14.6	14.4	38.5	40.2	40.0	41.0	40.7
Austria	..	3.1	2.6	2.6	2.7	..	21.6	21.7	21.3	22.8
Belgium	4.6	4.7	4.8	4.8	4.9	29.8	31.5	32.1	32.3	32.2
Canada	9.1	10.6	10.7 |	10.5	10.5	26.8	28.2	28.9 |	29.4	28.6
Czech Republic	..	1.8	2.0	1.9	1.7	..	5.7	5.3	5.5	5.4
Denmark	10.2	9.7	10.2	11.1	9.9	29.6	25.6	24.2	24.2	25.4
Finland	4.8	6.0	5.8	6.5	6.8	10.6	11.7	11.3	12.4	13.0
France	4.4	5.6	5.7	5.9	5.8	21.7	24.3	24.1	25.2	25.0
Germany	2.3	3.4	3.7	4.1	4.6	29.8	29.1	29.9	31.4	32.4
Greece	4.0	4.7	4.7	4.8	5.3	11.5	13.2	13.8	14.1	15.9
Hungary	..	1.9	1.8	1.8	1.9	..	4.6	4.6	5.0	5.0
Iceland[d]	7.5	9.1	8.4	10.1	9.8	39.7	37.8	35.3	36.8	38.6
Ireland	4.2	6.5	6.2	7.0	..	20.5	26.6	26.4	27.2	..
Italy	3.9	4.8	4.7	5.1	5.5	18.2	21.1	20.9	22.2	22.7
Japan[b, f]	9.5	10.0	11.6	12.9	12.9	33.2	34.7	36.6	38.3	39.0
Korea[b]	3.1	2.9	2.7	3.3	5.2	6.5	6.7	6.9	7.8	9.3
Luxembourg	1.6	1.9	2.1	2.0	2.6	19.1	28.4	24.7	26.2	29.6
Mexico	..	9.6	8.3	8.7	8.2	..	31.3	28.5	30.2	28.3
Netherlands	13.4	11.4	11.3	11.1	12.4	52.5	54.7	55.5	54.8	54.8
New Zealand	7.9	9.5	9.9	10.5	10.6	34.6	35.5	36.8	37.0	37.6
Norway	6.7	7.5 |	8.0	7.9	8.1	39.1	37.4 |	37.3	36.9	35.9
Poland[b]	..	..	..	8.2	8.0	..	..	..	16.6	16.6
Portugal	3.1	3.8	4.5	5.1	5.2	11.8	14.5	15.1	16.5	15.8
Spain	1.4	2.5	2.9	3.1	2.9	11.5	15.9	16.2	16.8	16.6
Sweden	5.3	6.8	6.7	6.5	5.6	24.5	24.1	23.5	22.6	22.0
Switzerland[d]	6.8	6.5	7.3	7.1	7.2	42.6	44.9	44.9	45.7	45.8
Turkey	4.9	3.9	2.9	3.6	3.4	18.8	13.2	12.0	13.5	13.3
United Kingdom	5.3	7.3	7.7	8.2	8.2	39.5	40.7	41.4	40.9	41.2
United States[e]	8.3 |	8.4	8.4 |	8.3	8.2	20.0 |	20.3	20.2 |	19.5	19.1
European Union[g]	4.2	5.1	5.3	5.7	5.9	27.0	28.4	28.7	29.4	28.1
OECD Europe[g]	4.4	4.9 |	4.9	5.5	5.6	26.8	26.5 |	26.6	26.6	26.1
Total OECD[g]	6.0 |	6.7 |	6.6 |	6.9	7.0	23.6 |	24.2 |	24.1 |	24.2	24.0

	\multicolumn{5}{c}{Part-time employment as a proportion of total employment}	\multicolumn{5}{c}{Women's share in part-time employment}				
	1990	1995	1996	1997	1998	1990	1995	1996	1997	1998
Australia[b, c]	22.6	25.0	25.2	26.0	25.9	70.8	69.2	68.5	68.0	68.6
Austria	..	11.1	10.9	10.8	11.5	..	84.2	86.4	86.3	86.9
Belgium	14.2	15.6	16.1	16.2	16.3	79.9	82.3	82.4	82.6	82.4
Canada	17.0	18.6	18.9 |	19.0	18.7	70.1	68.8	69.1 |	69.7	69.5
Czech Republic	..	3.5	3.4	3.4	3.3	..	70.5	67.3	69.1	70.0
Denmark	19.2	16.8	16.5	17.1	17.0	71.5	68.1	66.0	64.3	68.5
Finland	7.6	8.7	8.4	9.3	9.7	66.8	64.2	64.0	63.2	63.1
France	12.2	14.2	14.3	14.9	14.8	79.8	79.1	78.7	78.8	79.3
Germany	13.4	14.2	14.9	15.8	16.6	89.7	86.3	85.8	85.1	84.1
Greece	6.7	7.7	8.0	8.2	9.2	61.1	61.4	62.5	63.0	63.6
Hungary	..	3.2	3.1	3.3	3.4	..	67.7	69.4	71.3	69.2
Iceland[d]	..	22.5	20.9	22.4	23.2	81.6	78.5	78.3	75.8	77.4
Ireland	9.8	14.4	14.1	15.2	..	71.8	72.4	73.2	72.7	..
Italy	8.8	10.5	10.5	11.3	11.8	70.8	70.8	71.5	71.0	70.4
Japan[b, f]	19.1	20.1	21.8	23.2	23.6	70.5	70.2	68.2	67.0	67.5
Korea[b]	4.5	4.4	4.4	5.1	6.8	58.7	61.2	63.5	62.4	54.8
Luxembourg	7.6	11.4	10.4	11.1	12.8	86.5	89.2	87.3	89.0	87.3
Mexico	..	16.6	14.9	15.9	15.0	..	60.8	62.4	63.8	63.5
Netherlands	28.2	29.0	29.3	29.1	30.0	70.4	76.5	77.2	77.6	75.8
New Zealand	19.6	21.0	22.0	22.4	22.8	77.1	74.6	75.0	74.1	74.3
Norway	21.3	21.2 |	21.4	21.2	21.0	82.7	80.7 |	79.7	80.0	79.1
Poland[b]	..	..	..	11.9	11.8	..	..	..	61.1	62.2
Portugal	6.8	8.6	9.2	10.2	9.9	74.0	75.3	72.9	72.6	70.9
Spain	4.6	7.1	7.5	7.9	7.7	79.5	77.1	75.1	74.8	75.9
Sweden	14.5	15.1	14.8	14.2	13.5	81.1	76.8	76.5	76.3	97.3
Switzerland[d]	22.1	22.9	23.7	24.0	24.2	82.4	83.8	82.4	83.4	83.4
Turkey	9.2	6.7	5.6	6.3	6.2	62.5	59.2	63.7	58.6	60.3
United Kingdom	20.1	22.3	22.9	22.9	23.0	85.1	81.8	81.4	80.4	80.4
United States[e]	13.8 |	14.1	14.0 |	13.6	13.4	68.2 |	68.7	68.8 |	68.4	68.0
European Union[g]	13.3	14.9	15.2	15.7	16.0	80.9	79.8	79.6	79.1	81.8
OECD Europe[g]	13.2	13.7 |	13.8	14.1	14.4	79.6	78.7 |	78.8	77.1	79.8
Total OECD[g]	13.4 |	14.1 |	14.0 |	14.3	14.3	74.1 |	72.6 |	72.9 |	72.1	73.6

\| Indicates break in series.
a) Part-time employment refers to persons who usually work less than 30 hours per week in their main job. Data include only persons declaring usual hours.
b) Data are based on actual hours worked.
c) Part-time employment based on hours worked at all jobs.
d) 1990 refers to 1991.
e) Estimates are for wage and salary workers only.
f) Less than 35 hours per week.
g) For above countries only.

Notes, Sources and Definitions:
For Austria, Belgium, Denmark, France, Germany, Greece, Ireland, Italy, Luxembourg, the Netherlands, Portugal, Spain and the United Kingdom, data are from the European Labour Force Survey. For other countries data are taken from National Labour Force Surveys.
See OECD Labour Market and Social Policy Occasional Paper No 22, "The definition of Part-time work for the Purpose of International Comparisons", which is available on Internet (http://www.oecd.org/els/papers/papers.htm).

Table F. Average annual hours actually worked per person in employment[a]

	1979	1983	1990	1994	1995	1996	1997	1998
Total employment								
Australia	1 904	1 852	1 869	1 879	1 876	1 867	1 866	1 861
Canada	1 836	1 783	1 790	1 783	1 780	1 787	1 777	..
Czech Republic	..	..	..	..	2 065	2 072	2 064	2 070
Finland[b]	..	1 809	1 764	1 780	1 775	1 790	1 779	1 761
Finland[c]	1 868	1 821	1 707	1 701	1 707	1 720	1 712	1 693
France	1 813	1 711	1 668	1 635	1 638	1 644	1 634	..
Germany	..	..	1 625	1 604	1 581	1 576	1 570	1 580
Western Germany	1 764	1 724	1 611	1 581	1 561	1 557	1 553	1 562
Iceland	..	..	..	1 813	1 832	1 860	1 839	1 817
Japan	2 126	2 095	2 031	1 898	1 889	..	..	..
Mexico	..	..	..	..	1 834	1 955	1 927	1 878
New Zealand	..	..	1 820	1 851	1 843	1 839	1 823	1 825
Norway	1 514	1 485	1 432	1 431	1 414	1 407	1 399	1 401
Spain	2 022	1 912	1 824	1 815	1 814	1 810	1 812	1 821
Sweden	1 451	1 453	1 480	1 537	1 544	1 554	1 552	1 551
Switzerland	..	..	..	1 632	1 636	1 585	1 579	..
United Kingdom	1 815	1 713	1 767	1 737	1 740	1 738	1 736	1 737
United States	1 905	1 882	1 943 |	1 945	1 952	1 951	1 966	1 957
Dependent employment								
Canada	1 803	1 763	1 774	1 773	1 773	1 781	1 777	..
Czech Republic	..	..	..	..	1 984	1 990	1 983	1 989
Finland[b]	..	..	1 668	1 674	1 673	1 692	1 687	1 672
France	1 667	1 558	1 539	1 520	1 523	1 526	1 519	..
Germany	..	..	1 583	1 552	1 529	1 523	1 517	1 526
Western Germany	1 699	1 686	1 557	1 527	1 506	1 502	1 498	1 508
Iceland	..	..	..	1 774	1 776	1 799	1 790	1 762
Italy	1 748	1 724	1 694	1 682	..	..	..	..
Japan[d]	2 114	2 098	2 052	1 904	1 909	1 919	1 900	1 879
Japan[e]	..	..	2 064	1 910	1 910	1 919	1 891	1 871
Korea	..	2 734	2 514	2 471	2 484	2 467	2 436	2 390
Mexico	..	..	..	..	1 933	2 006	1 978	1 942
Netherlands	1 591	1 530	1 433	1 388	1 384	1 374	1 365	..
Spain	1 936	1 837	1 762	1 746	1 749	1 747	1 748	1 754
United Kingdom	1 750	1 652	1 704	1 693	1 698	1 699	1 701	1 702
United States	1 884	1 866	1 936 |	1 947	1 953	1 949	1 966	1 957

\| Indicates break in series.
a) The concept used is the total number of hours worked over the year divided by the average numbers of people in employment. The data are intended for comparisons of trends over time; they are unsuitable for comparisons of the level of average annual hours of work for a given year, because of differences in their sources. Part-time workers are covered as well as full-time.
b) Data estimated from the Labour Force Survey.
c) Data estimated from National Accounts.
d) Data refer to establishments with 30 or more regular employees.
e) Data refer to establishments with 5 or more regular employees.

Sources and definitions:
  Australia: Data supplied by the Australian Bureau of Statistics from the Labour Force Survey. Annual hours are adjusted to take account of public holidays occuring during the reporting period. The method of estimation is consistent with the National Accounts.
  Canada: New series supplied by Statistics Canada, based mainly on the monthly Labour Force Survey supplemented by the Survey of Employment Payrolls and Hours, the annual Survey of Manufacturers and the Census of Mining.
  Czech Republic: Data supplied by the Czech Statistical Office and based on the quarterly Labour Force Sample Survey. Main meal breaks (one half hour a day) are included.
  Finland: Data supplied by Statistics Finland. National Accounts series based on an establishment survey for manufacturing, and the Labour Force Survey for other sectors and for the self-employed. Alternative series based solely on the Labour Force Survey.
  France: Data supplied by Institut national de la statistique et des Études économiques, produced within the framework of the National Accounts.
  Germany: Data supplied by the Institut für Arbeitsmarkt- und Berufsforschung, calculated within a comprehensive accounting structure, based on establishment survey estimates of weekly hours worked by full-time workers whose hours are not affected by absence, and extended to annual estimates of actual hours by adjusting for a wide range of factors, including public holidays, sickness absence, overtime working, short-time working, bad weather, strikes, part-time working and parental leave.
  Iceland: Data are provided by Statistics Iceland and are based on the Icelandic Labor Force Survey. Annual actual hours worked per person in employment are computed by multiplying daily actual hours worked by annual actual working days net of public holidays and annual vacations. The latter are for a typical work contract by sector of activity.
  Italy: Data are for dependent employment supplied by Eurostat and based mainly on the European Labour Force Survey, for 1983 to 1994. From 1960 to 1982, trend in data is taken from the total employment series provided by ISTAT and based on a special establishment survey discontinued in 1985.
  Japan: Data for total employment are Secretariat estimates based on data from the Monthly Labour Survey of Establishments, extended to agricultural and government sectors and to the self-employed by means of the Labour Force Survey. Data for dependent employment supplied by Statistics Bureau, Management and Coordination Agency, from the Monthly Labour Survey, referring to all industries excluding agriculture, forest, fisheries and government services.
  Korea: Data supplied by the Ministry of Labour from the Report on monthly labour survey.
  Mexico: Data supplied by STPS-INEGI from the bi-annual National Survey of Employment, based on the assumption of 44 working weeks per year.
  Netherlands: From 1977 onwards, figures are "Annual Contractual Hours", supplied by Statistics Netherlands, compiled within the framework of the Labour Accounts. Overtime hours are excluded. For 1970 to 1976, the trend has been derived from data supplied by the Economisch Instituut voor het Midden en Kleinbedrijf, referring to persons employed in the private sector, excluding agriculture and fishing.
  New Zealand: Data supplied by Statistics New Zealand and derived from the quarterly Labour Force Survey, whose continuous sample design avoids the need for adjustments for public holidays and other days lost. Total employment figures revised slightly.
  Norway: Data supplied by Statistics Norway, based on National Accounts and estimated from a number of different data sources, the most important being establishment surveys, the Labour Force Surveys and the public sector accounts. For 1978 to 1995, data revised due to major revision of National Accounts; for earlier years, trend in data taken from old series.
  Spain: Series supplied by Instituto Nacional de Estadistica and derived from the quarterly Labour Force Survey. Series break at 1986/87 due to changes in the Survey.
  Sweden: Series supplied by Statistics Sweden derived from National Accounts data, based on both the Labour Force Survey and establishment surveys.
  Switzerland: Data supplied by Office fédéral de la statistique. The basis of the calculation is the Swiss Labour Force Survey which provides information on weekly hours of work during one quarter of the year. The estimates of annual hours are based also on supplementary, annual information on vacations, public holidays and overtime working and have been extended to correspond to National Accounts concepts.
  United Kingdom: New series refer to the United Kingdom. For 1992 to 1995, the levels are derived directly from the continuous Labour Force Survey. For 1984 to 1991, the trend in the data is taken from the annual Labour Force Survey. From 1970 to 1983, the trend corresponds to estimates by Professor Angus Maddison.
  United States: Data supplied by the Bureau of Labor Statistics and are based on the Current Population Survey. Series breaks at 1975/76 and 1989/90 are due to changes in population controls and at 1993/94 due to redesigned CPS questionnaire.

Table G. Incidence of long-term unemployment from survey-based data in selected OECD countries [a, b, c, d, e]
As a percentage of total unemployment

	1990 6 months and over	1990 12 months and over	1995 6 months and over	1995 12 months and over	1996 6 months and over	1996 12 months and over	1997 6 months and over	1997 12 months and over	1998 6 months and over	1998 12 months and over
Australia	41.0	21.6	51.3	30.8	48.5	28.4	51.4	30.7	52.2	33.6
Austria	..	..	42.8	25.6	42.5	25.6	47.7	28.7	45.3	30.2
Belgium	81.4	68.7		77.7	62.4	77.3	61.3	77.2	60.5	77.5	62.6
Canada	18.8	5.7	27.8	14.1	27.7	13.9		25.7	12.5	23.1	10.1
Czech Republic	..	..	52.5	30.6	52.3	31.3	53.2	30.5	54.6	31.2
Denmark	53.2	29.9		46.6	27.9	44.4	26.5	45.7	27.2	43.7	28.7
Finland [f]	32.6	9.2		56.6	37.6	55.5	34.5	48.6	29.8	42.2	27.5
France	55.5	38.0	64.0	42.3	61.5	39.5	63.7	41.2	64.2	44.1
Germany	64.7	46.8		65.9	48.7	65.3	47.8	68.5	50.1	69.2	52.2
Greece	71.9	49.8		72.7	51.4	74.7	56.7	76.5	55.7	..	..
Hungary	..	..	73.0	50.6	75.2	54.4	73.5	51.3	71.0	49.8
Iceland [f]	13.6	6.7	33.3	16.8	31.2	19.8	27.0	16.3	22.9	16.1
Ireland	81.0	66.0		77.9	61.4	75.7	59.5	73.6	57.0	..	..
Italy	85.2	69.8		80.2	63.6	80.8	65.6	81.8	66.3	81.6	66.7
Japan	39.0	19.1	37.7	18.1	40.4	20.2	41.3	21.8	39.0	20.3
Korea	13.9	2.6	16.9	3.4	15.1	3.0	15.3	2.1	14.5	1.6
Luxembourg [g]	(66.7)	(42.9)		(49.5)	(23.8)	(44.6)	(27.6)	(61.1)	(34.6)	(56.3)	(32.0)
Mexico	..	..	7.9	1.5	9.8	2.2	6.9	1.8	3.3	0.9
Netherlands	63.6	49.3		80.4	46.8	81.8	50.0	80.4	49.1	83.6	47.9
New Zealand	39.5	20.9	43.3	25.5	36.6	20.8	36.4	19.4	37.9	19.4
Norway	40.8	20.4	39.1	24.1		31.1	16.0	23.5	10.6	21.3	9.3
Poland	..	..	63.1	40.0	62.8	39.0	62.2	38.0	60.4	37.4
Portugal	62.4	44.8		65.1	50.9	66.7	53.1	66.7	55.6	64.6	44.6
Spain	70.2	54.0	72.8	56.9	72.2	55.7	71.8	55.5	70.4	54.1
Sweden	22.2	12.1		45.6	27.8	48.4	30.1	50.8	33.4	49.2	33.5
Switzerland [f]	26.2	16.4	50.4	33.6	52.1	25.0	49.4	28.5	48.9	34.8
Turkey	72.6	47.0	60.3	36.3	65.9	43.5	62.7	41.6	60.3	40.0
United Kingdom	50.3	34.4		60.8	43.6	58.1	39.8	54.8	38.6	48.0	33.1
United States	10.0	5.5		17.3	9.7	17.5	9.5		15.9	8.7	14.1	8.0
European Union [h]	65.3	48.6		68.3	50.2	67.4	49.3	68.2	50.1	67.1	50.1
OECD Europe [h]	65.7	48.1		66.9	47.9		66.6	47.6	67.0	48.0	65.5	47.6
Total OECD [h]	44.6	30.8		49.8	33.9		50.2	34.0		50.7	34.7	47.8	32.9

| Indicates break in series.

a) While data from labour force surveys make international comparisons easier, compared to a mixture of survey and registration data, they are not perfect. Questionnaire wording and design, survey timing, differences across countries in the age groups covered, and other reasons mean that care is required in interpreting cross-country differences in levels.
b) The duration of unemployment data base maintained by the Secretariat is composed of detailed duration categories disaggregated by age and sex. All totals are derived by adding each component. Thus, the total for men is derived by adding the number of unemployed men by each duration and age group category. Since published data are usually rounded to the nearest thousand, this method sometimes results in slight differences between the percentages shown here and those that would be obtained using the available published figures.
c) Data are averages of monthly figures for Canada, Sweden and the United States, averages of quarterly figures for Czech Republic, Hungary, Norway, New Zealand, Poland and Spain, and averages of semi annual figures for Turkey. The reference period for the remaining countries is as follows (among EU countries it occasionally varies from year to year): Australia, August; Austria, April; Belgium, April; Denmark, April-May; Finland, autumn; France, March; Germany, April; Greece, March-July; Iceland, April; Ireland, May; Italy, April; Japan, February; Luxembourg, April; Mexico, April; Netherlands, March-May; Portugal, February-April; Switzerland, second quarter; and the United Kingdom, March-May.
d) Data refer to persons aged 15 and over in Australia, Austria, Belgium, Canada, Czech Republic, Denmark, France, Germany, Greece, Ireland, in Italy, Japan, Luxembourg, Mexico, Netherlands, New Zealand, Poland, Portugal, Switzerland and Turkey; and aged 16 and over in Iceland, Spain, the United Kingdom and the United States. Data for Finland refer to persons aged 15-64 (excluding unemployment pensioners). Data for Hungary refer to persons aged 15-74, data for Norway refer to persons aged 16-74 and data for Sweden refer to persons aged 16-64.
e) Persons for whom no duration of unemployment was specified are excluded.
f) Data for 1990 refer to 1991.
g) Data in brackets are based on small sample sizes and, therefore, must be treated with care.
h) For above countries only.

Sources:
Data for *Austria, Belgium, Denmark, Germany, Greece, Ireland, Italy, Luxembourg, the Netherlands, Portugal and the United Kingdom* are based on the European Labour Force Survey and were supplied by Eurostat.
Australia: Australian Bureau of Statistics, *The Labour Force Australia*.
Canada: Unpublished data from the labour force survey supplied by Statistics Canada.
Czech Republic: Data from the Labour Force Sample Survey supplied by the Czech Statistical office.
Finland: Unpublished data from the Supplementary Labour Force Survey (biennial from 1989 until 1995, and annual from 1995 onwards) supplied by the Central Statistical Office.
France: Institut national de la statistique et des Études économiques, Enquête sur l'Emploi.
Hungary: Data from the Labour Force Survey supplied by the Central Statistical Office.
Iceland: Data from the Labour Force Survey supplied by Statistics Iceland.
Japan: Statistics Bureau, Managment and Coordination Agency, report on the Special survey of the Labour Force Survey.
Korea: Data from the Labour Force Survey supplied by the National Statistical Office (NSO).
Mexico: Data from the biennial Encuesta Nacional de Empleo (ENE) supplied by the Secretaría del Trabajo y Previsión Social (STPS).
New Zealand: Unpublished data from the household labour force survey supplied by the Department of Statistics.
Norway: Unpublished data from the labour force survey supplied by the Central Statistical Office.
Poland: Data from the Labour Force Survey supplied by the Central Statistical Office.
Spain: Unpublished data from the labour force survey supplied by the Ministry of Employment and Social Security.
Sweden: Statistics Sweden, AKU.
Switzerland: Data from the labour force survey supplied by the Swiss Federal Statistical Office.
Turkey: Data from the Household Labour Force Survey supplied by the State Institute of Statistics.
United States: Bureau of Labor Statistics, *Employment and Earnings*.

Table G. Incidence of long-term unemployment from survey-based data among men[a, b, c, d, e] (cont.)

As a percentage of male unemployment

	1990 6 months and over	1990 12 months and over	1995 6 months and over	1995 12 months and over	1996 6 months and over	1996 12 months and over	1997 6 months and over	1997 12 months and over	1998 6 months and over	1998 12 months and over
Australia	42.6	24.4	54.1	34.2	50.6	30.9	54.5	33.0	55.1	36.5
Austria	..	..	36.5	23.2	38.2	23.2	42.1	28.9	39.9	27.5
Belgium	79.5	66.1	76.4	61.4	75.2	58.9	76.6	59.4	75.9	60.3
Canada	19.1	6.6	29.1	15.9	28.4	15.3	27.2	14.5	24.5	11.5
Czech Republic	..	..	51.5	30.2	51.0	30.9	53.4	31.3	52.9	30.9
Denmark	48.9	27.8	51.9	31.9	44.2	28.1	44.5	26.3	43.7	25.8
Finland[f]	36.8	9.7	59.7	41.4	59.0	38.5	49.5	31.9	46.3	31.7
France	53.1	35.4	62.1	41.4	58.6	37.1	61.7	39.1	62.3	43.2
Germany	65.2	49.1	63.3	45.9	61.8	44.5	65.9	47.1	67.6	51.9
Greece	61.8	39.9	64.3	42.3	66.7	47.3	69.1	45.8	..	..
Hungary	..	..	74.0	52.0	76.8	57.0	74.2	52.6	71.5	50.2
Iceland[f]	5.1	1.3	31.4	16.5	34.4	23.7	27.2	20.1	21.4	13.6
Ireland	84.3	71.1	80.7	66.8	79.2	64.6	77.9	63.3	..	..
Italy	84.1	68.6	78.9	62.7	78.7	64.1	81.2	66.5	80.5	66.4
Japan	47.6	26.2	43.7	23.5	46.2	23.8	49.2	28.8	44.8	25.3
Korea	16.0	3.3	18.1	3.7	17.2	3.4	17.9	2.8	16.7	1.9
Luxembourg[g]	(80.0)	(60.0)	(50.6)	(26.0)	(49.0)	(30.1)	(65.7)	(32.7)	(57.3)	(38.0)
Mexico	..	..	7.4	1.3	9.7	2.1	8.6	1.2	4.2	1.2
Netherlands	65.6	55.2	78.7	51.6	81.4	54.3	76.6	49.9	81.1	51.4
New Zealand	44.1	24.5	48.3	29.7	40.4	24.0	40.4	22.2	41.2	22.6
Norway	37.9	19.0	43.4	28.3	32.7	18.2	28.3	13.0	22.5	10.0
Poland	..	..	59.4	36.2	59.3	35.2	57.8	33.5	55.2	32.5
Portugal	56.3	38.2	63.0	48.4	64.1	51.7	64.8	53.4	62.0	43.6
Spain	63.3	45.8	67.7	51.1	67.4	49.8	67.2	49.9	65.4	48.0
Sweden	22.2	12.3	49.3	31.4	51.6	33.6	53.1	36.1	52.2	36.3
Switzerland[f]	28.0	16.0	46.8	30.6	50.0	20.8	47.9	25.5	51.5	37.9
Turkey	71.2	44.9	56.1	32.2	63.7	39.9	59.3	38.1	58.1	37.5
United Kingdom	56.8	41.8	66.2	49.6	63.5	45.9	60.2	44.9	53.8	38.4
United States	12.1	7.0	18.7	11.0	18.5	10.3	16.7	9.4	15.2	8.8
European Union[h]	63.5	47.0	66.9	49.2	65.4	47.6	66.4	48.5	65.2	48.7
OECD Europe[h]	64.3	46.4	65.0	46.1	64.6	45.6	64.9	46.0	63.4	45.8
Total OECD[h]	43.6	29.7	48.5	32.9	49.0	32.8	49.9	33.8	46.6	31.7

| Indicates break in series.
Sources and notes: See total unemployment.

Table G. **Incidence of long-term unemployment from survey-based data among women** [a, b, c, d, e] *(cont.)*

As a percentage of female unemployment

	1990 6 months and over	1990 12 months and over	1995 6 months and over	1995 12 months and over	1996 6 months and over	1996 12 months and over	1997 6 months and over	1997 12 months and over	1998 6 months and over	1998 12 months and over
Australia	38.8	17.8	47.2	25.6	45.4	24.8	47.0	27.4	48.0	29.3
Austria	..	..	46.1	27.1	45.0	25.5	49.3	25.2	48.6	30.7
Belgium	82.5	70.0		78.7	63.2	79.1	63.3	77.8	61.5	78.9	64.7
Canada	18.4	4.5	26.1	11.9	26.8	12.2		23.9	10.2	21.3	8.3
Czech Republic	..	..	53.3	30.9	53.5	31.6	53.0	29.9	55.9	31.5
Denmark	57.7	32.0		42.5	24.9	44.6	25.3	46.7	27.9	43.7	30.7
Finland [f]	26.3	8.4		53.2	33.3	52.1	30.5	47.7	27.6	37.8	23.1
France	57.3	40.0	65.7	43.2	64.0	41.6	65.6	43.3	66.0	44.9
Germany	64.2	44.5		68.4	51.3	69.4	51.7	71.4	53.6	71.4	52.6
Greece	78.2	55.9		78.9	58.3	79.7	62.5	81.4	62.2	..	..
Hungary	..	..	71.3	48.3	72.7	50.4	72.3	49.2	70.1	49.2
Iceland [f]	21.1	11.5	35.5	17.2	27.8	15.9	26.8	12.6	24.1	18.1
Ireland	75.0	56.8	74.0	52.9	70.1	51.2	66.6	46.9	..	..
Italy	86.0	70.7		81.5	64.4	82.8	67.1	82.5	66.2	82.5	67.0
Japan	26.3	8.8	28.8	10.0	30.7	12.5	30.1	11.8	29.9	12.4
Korea	8.9	0.9	14.5	2.9	10.5	2.0	10.9	0.9	10.1	0.8
Luxembourg [g]	(55.6)	(33.3)		(48.0)	(21.0)	(40.6)	(25.3)	(57.3)	(36.1)	(55.6)	(27.2)
Mexico	..	..	9.0	1.7	10.0	2.4	4.9	2.4	2.2	0.4
Netherlands	62.0	44.6		82.1	42.0	82.1	46.1	83.4	48.5	85.6	45.2
New Zealand	32.7	15.5	36.7	20.1	31.9	16.8	31.4	16.0	33.8	15.3
Norway	45.0	22.5	26.5	14.7		29.4	13.7	17.9	7.7	20.0	8.6
Poland	..	..	66.6	43.7	66.1	42.5	66.0	41.9	65.1	41.8
Portugal	66.4	49.4		67.2	53.4	69.2	54.4	68.5	57.7	66.6	45.5
Spain	76.5	61.5	77.5	62.6	76.7	61.3	75.9	60.4	74.4	59.1
Sweden	22.2	11.8		40.8	22.9	44.5	25.8	48.1	30.1	45.6	30.1
Switzerland [f]	25.0	16.7	54.0	36.5	54.4	29.4	51.6	32.8	46.4	31.9
Turkey	75.6	51.2	71.1	46.9	72.3	53.6	69.7	49.0	65.8	46.1
United Kingdom	40.8	23.7		50.6	32.3	47.7	28.0	45.3	27.8	38.5	24.6
United States	7.3	3.7		15.6	8.1	16.2	8.4		14.9	8.0	12.8	7.1
European Union [h]	66.9	50.1		69.7	51.2	69.6	51.2	70.1	51.8	68.9	51.5
OECD Europe [h]	67.2	49.8	69.0	49.8		68.9	49.8	69.2	50.1	67.8	49.6
Total OECD [h]	45.6	32.1		51.2	35.1		51.5	35.4		51.6	35.7	49.2	34.2

| Indicates break in series.
Sources and notes: See total unemployment.

Table H. Public expenditure and participant inflows* in labour market programmes in OECD countries

Australia[a]

Programme categories	\multicolumn{4}{c}{Public expenditure as a percentage of GDP}	\multicolumn{4}{c}{Participant inflows as a percentage of the labour force}
	1994-95	1995-96	1996-97	1997-98	1994-95	1995-96	1996-97	1997-98
1. Public employment services and administration	0.20	0.24	0.24	0.21				
2. Labour market training	0.17	0.15	0.09	0.07	4.2	4.8	2.1	1.9
a) Training for unemployed adults and those at risk	0.16	0.14	0.08	0.06	3.7	4.2	1.8	1.6
b) Training for employed adults	0.01	0.01	0.01	–	0.5	0.6	0.4	0.2
3. Youth measures	0.07	0.06	0.06	0.06	1.2	1.3	1.2	1.9
a) Measures for unemployed and disadvantaged youth	0.04	0.03	0.01	–	0.5	0.4	0.2	0.3
b) Support of apprenticeship and related forms of general youth training	0.03	0.03	0.05	0.05	0.7	0.9	1.1	1.7
4. Subsidised employment	0.21	0.31	0.21	0.13	2.0	2.5	1.5	1.1
a) Subsidies to regular employment in the private sector	0.06	0.06	0.07	0.04	1.2	1.2	1.0	0.7
b) Support of unemployed persons starting enterprises	0.03	0.03	0.03	0.02	0.1	0.1	0.1	0.1
c) Direct job creation (public or non-profit)	0.12	0.22	0.11	0.07	0.7	1.1	0.4	0.3
5. Measures for the disabled	0.07	0.07	0.06	0.06	0.6	0.7	0.7	0.3
a) Vocational rehabilitation	0.03	0.03	0.02	0.02	0.3	0.3	0.3	0.3
b) Work for the disabled	0.04	0.04	0.04	0.04	0.3	0.4	0.4	–
6. Unemployment compensation	1.61	1.28	1.29	1.17				
7. Early retirement for labour market reasons	–	–	–	–				
TOTAL	**2.33**	**2.10**	**1.94**	**1.69**	**8.0**	**9.2**	**5.6**	**5.3**
Active measures (1-5)	0.72	0.83	0.66	0.52				
Passive measures (6 and 7)	1.61	1.28	1.29	1.17				
For reference:								
GDP (national currency, at current prices, 10⁹)	460.3	492.4	516.4	544.7				
Labour force (thousands)					8 917	9 113	9 222	9 295

a) Fiscal years starting on July 1.

Austria

Programme categories	\multicolumn{4}{c}{Public expenditure as a percentage of GDP}
	1995	1996	1997	1998
1. Public employment services and administration	0.13	0.14	0.14	0.13
2. Labour market training	0.12	0.15	0.17	0.15
a) Training for unemployed adults and those at risk	0.12	0.15	0.15	0.13
b) Training for employed adults	–	–	0.02	0.02
3. Youth measures	0.01	0.01	0.02	0.04
a) Measures for unemployed and disadvantaged youth	0.01	0.01	0.02	0.04
b) Support of apprenticeship and related forms of general youth training	–	–	–	0.01
4. Subsidised employment	0.05	0.05	0.07	0.07
a) Subsidies to regular employment in the private sector	0.02	0.02	0.03	0.03
b) Support of unemployed persons starting enterprises	–	–	–	0.01
c) Direct job creation (public or non-profit)	0.03	0.03	0.04	0.03
5. Measures for the disabled	0.06	0.05	0.05	0.05
a) Vocational rehabilitation	0.03	0.03	0.03	0.02
b) Work for the disabled	0.03	0.02	0.02	0.03
6. Unemployment compensation	1.30	1.29	1.21	1.16
7. Early retirement for labour market reasons	0.13	0.13	0.07	0.05
TOTAL	**1.80**	**1.81**	**1.73**	**1.66**
Active measures (1-5)	0.36	0.39	0.45	0.44
Passive measures (6 and 7)	1.43	1.41	1.28	1.22
For reference:				
GDP (national currency, at current prices, 10⁹)	2 334.4	2 421.6	2 516.9	2 630.9

Belgium

Programme categories	\multicolumn{4}{c}{Public expenditure as a percentage of GDP}	\multicolumn{4}{c}{Participant inflows as a percentage of the labour force}
	1994	1995	1996	1997	1994	1995	1996	1997
1. Public employment services and administration	0.23	0.22	0.20	0.19				
2. Labour market training	0.28	0.28	0.30	0.29	9.2	8.9	9.1	9.2
a) Training for unemployed adults and those at risk	0.18	0.17	0.18	0.17	3.1	2.7	2.9	3.0
b) Training for employed adults	0.11	0.12	0.12	0.12	6.1	6.2	6.2	6.2
3. Youth measures	0.08	0.07	0.03	0.01	0.8	0.7	0.5	0.2
a) Measures for unemployed and disadvantaged youth	0.08	0.07	0.03	0.01	0.8	0.7	0.5	0.2
b) Support of apprenticeship and related forms of general youth training	–	–	–	–	–	–	–	–
4. Subsidised employment	0.62	0.68	0.84	0.68	3.5	4.6	7.4	5.7
a) Subsidies to regular employment in the private sector	0.05	0.12	0.27	0.16	0.6	1.8	4.5	2.5
b) Support of unemployed persons starting enterprises	–	–	–	–	–	–	–	–
c) Direct job creation (public or non-profit)	0.57	0.56	0.56	0.51	2.9	2.9	2.8	3.2
5. Measures for the disabled	0.14	0.14	0.13	0.13	..	..	..	..
a) Vocational rehabilitation	0.04	0.04	0.03	0.03	..	..	..	..
b) Work for the disabled	0.10	0.10	0.10	0.10	..	..	..	..
6. Unemployment compensation	2.19	2.11	2.12	2.06				
7. Early retirement for labour market reasons	0.68	0.66	0.64	0.60				
TOTAL	**4.23**	**4.16**	**4.26**	**3.96**	**13.5**	**14.3**	**16.9**	**15.1**
Active measures (1-5)	1.35	1.40	1.50	1.29				
Passive measures (6 and 7)	2.88	2.76	2.77	2.67				
For reference:								
GDP (national currency, at current prices, 10⁹)	7 768.9	8 068.1	8 305.1	8 675.5				
Labour force (thousands)					4 280	4 301	4 306	4 310

Table H. **Public expenditure and participant inflows in labour market programmes in OECD countries** (cont.)

	Canada[a]							Czech Republic								Denmark							
	Public expenditure as a percentage of GDP			Participant inflows as a percentage of the labour force				Public expenditure as a percentage of GDP				Participant inflows as a percentage of the labour force				Public expenditure as a percentage of GDP				Participant inflows as a percentage of the labour force			
Programme categories	1994-95	1995-96	1996-97	1997-98	1994-95	1995-96	1996-97	1997-98	1995	1996	1997	1998	1995	1996	1997	1998	1995	1996	1997	1998	1995	1996	1997	1998
1. Public employment services and administration	0.21	0.21	0.19	0.18					0.10	0.09	0.08	0.08					0.12	0.12	0.13	0.14				
2. Labour market training	0.28	0.25	0.17	0.15	2.3	1.9	1.9	1.6	0.01	0.01	0.01	0.01	0.3	0.2	0.2	0.3	1.02	1.12	0.97	1.07	16.7	17.1	19.6	19.6
a) Training for unemployed adults and those at risk	0.27	0.24	0.16	0.15	2.3	1.9	1.9	1.6	0.01	0.01	0.01	0.01	0.3	0.2	0.2	0.3	0.71	0.82	0.68	0.73	8.6	8.2	9.2	9.8
b) Training for employed adults	0.01	0.01	–	–	–	–	–	–	–	–	–	–	–	–	–	–	0.31	0.30	0.30	0.34	8.0	8.9	10.4	9.8
3. Youth measures	0.02	0.02	0.02	0.03	0.5	0.5	0.5	..	0.01	0.01	0.01	0.01	0.1	0.1	0.1	0.2	0.15	0.09	0.10	0.08	1.8	1.7	1.5	1.6
a) Measures for unemployed and disadvantaged youth	0.01	0.01	0.01	0.02	–	0.2	0.2	..	0.01	0.01	0.01	0.01	0.1	0.1	0.1	0.2	0.15	0.09	0.10	0.08	1.8	1.7	1.5	1.6
b) Support of apprenticeship and related forms of general youth training	0.02	0.01	0.01	0.01	0.5	0.3	0.4	..	–	–	–	–	–	–	–	–	–	–	–	–	–	–	–	–
4. Subsidised employment	0.07	0.06	0.06	0.08	0.4	0.3	0.3	0.3	0.03	0.02	0.02	0.03	0.3	0.3	0.3	0.4	0.36	0.32	0.31	0.30	1.6	1.4	1.1	1.0
a) Subsidies to regular employment in the private sector	0.01	0.01	0.01	0.01	0.1	–	0.1	0.1	0.01	–	–	0.01	0.1	0.1	0.1	0.1	0.04	0.03	0.02	0.03	0.3	0.3	0.2	0.2
b) Support of unemployed persons starting enterprises	0.02	0.02	0.02	0.02	0.1	0.1	0.1	0.1	–	–	–	–	–	–	–	–	0.08	0.08	0.06	0.04	0.2	0.1	0.1	–
c) Direct job creation (public or non-profit)	0.04	0.03	0.02	0.05	0.2	0.2	0.1	0.1	0.01	0.01	0.01	0.02	0.2	0.2	0.2	0.2	0.24	0.21	0.23	0.23	1.1	1.0	0.8	0.8
5. Measures for the disabled	0.03	0.02	0.03	0.03	–	–	–	–	–	–	–	0.01	–	–	–	–	0.29	0.28	0.28	0.30	2.3	2.2	2.3	2.3
a) Vocational rehabilitation	0.03	0.02	0.03	0.03	–	–	–	–	–	–	–	–	–	–	–	–	0.29	0.28	0.28	0.30	2.3	2.2	2.3	2.3
b) Work for the disabled	–	–	–	–	–	–	–	–	–	–	–	0.01	–	–	–	–	–	–	–	–	–	–	–	–
6. Unemployment compensation	1.49	1.28	1.16	1.02					0.13	0.14	0.21	0.24					3.06	2.54	2.23	1.86				
7. Early retirement for labour market reasons	0.01	0.01	0.01	–					–	–	–	–					1.55	1.80	1.79	1.88				
TOTAL	2.11	1.85	1.64	1.49	3.2	2.7	2.7	..	0.27	0.26	0.32	0.37	0.7	0.6	0.6	0.9	6.55	6.27	5.81	5.63	22.3	22.4	24.5	24.5
Active measures (1-5)	0.61	0.56	0.47	0.46					0.14	0.13	0.12	0.13					1.95	1.92	1.80	1.89				
Passive measures (6 and 7)	1.51	1.29	1.17	1.02					0.13	0.14	0.21	0.24					4.61	4.35	4.02	3.74				
For reference:																								
GDP (national currency, at current prices, 10⁹)	780.2	811.0	838.2	873.8					1 348.7	1 532.6	1 649.5	1 776.7					969.1	1 013.9	1 064.2	1 053.5				
Labour force (thousands)	14 947	15 039	15 246	15 484									5 172	5 175	5 184	5 207					2 798	2 822	2 856	2 876

a) Fiscal years starting on April 1.

Table H. Public expenditure and participant inflows* in labour market programmes in OECD countries (cont.)

Finland

Programme categories	Public expenditure as a percentage of GDP 1995	1996	1997	1998	Participant inflows as a percentage of the labour force 1995	1996	1997	1998
1. Public employment services and administration	0.16	0.16	0.14	0.13				
2. Labour market training	0.45	0.57	0.54	0.41	3.7	4.7	5.2	4.4
a) Training for unemployed adults and those at risk	0.44	0.55	0.53	0.39	3.7	4.7	5.2	4.4
b) Training for employed adults	–	0.01	0.02	0.02	–	–	–	–
3. Youth measures	0.16	0.22	0.24	0.16	2.0	2.5	2.6	1.9
a) Measures for unemployed and disadvantaged youth	0.08	0.12	0.11	0.06	1.2	1.6	1.6	1.0
b) Support of apprenticeship and related forms of general youth training	0.08	0.10	0.13	0.11	0.8	0.9	1.0	0.9
4. Subsidised employment	0.68	0.66	0.53	0.42	5.1	4.8	4.4	3.8
a) Subsidies to regular employment in the private sector	0.11	0.09	0.09	0.10	1.2	1.2	1.3	1.5
b) Support of unemployed persons starting enterprises	0.04	0.03	0.03	0.03	0.3	0.2	0.2	0.2
c) Direct job creation (public or non-profit)	0.53	0.54	0.40	0.29	3.6	3.4	2.9	2.0
5. Measures for the disabled	0.14	0.13	0.12	0.11	0.7	0.8	0.8	0.8
a) Vocational rehabilitation	0.07	0.06	0.06	0.06	0.7	0.8	0.8	0.8
b) Work for the disabled	0.07	0.06	0.06	0.05	–	–	–	–
6. Unemployment compensation	3.57	3.27	2.78	2.35				
7. Early retirement for labour market reasons	0.44	0.42	0.43	0.45				
TOTAL	5.59	5.42	4.78	4.03	11.5	12.8	13.1	10.9
Active measures (1-5)	1.58	1.73	1.57	1.23				
Passive measures (6 and 7)	4.01	3.69	3.21	2.79				
For reference:								
GDP (national currency, at current prices, 10⁹)	549.9	574.0	622.1	666.9				
Labour force (thousands)					2522	2531	2562	2533

France

Programme categories	Public expenditure as a percentage of GDP 1994	1995	1996	1997	Participant inflows as a percentage of the labour force 1994	1995	1996	1997
1. Public employment services and administration	0.16	0.15	0.16	0.16				
2. Labour market training	0.42	0.38	0.36	0.35	3.9	3.5	3.3	2.8
a) Training for unemployed adults and those at risk	0.37	0.34	0.32	0.31	3.1	2.8	2.8	2.4
b) Training for employed adults	0.05	0.04	0.04	0.04	0.8	0.7	0.5	0.4
3. Youth measures	0.30	0.27	0.27	0.26	3.0	2.8	2.6	2.6
a) Measures for unemployed and disadvantaged youth	0.10	0.10	0.09	0.07	0.9	0.9	0.6	0.6
b) Support of apprenticeship and related forms of general youth training	0.20	0.17	0.18	0.19	2.2	2.0	2.0	2.0
4. Subsidised employment	0.33	0.40	0.49	0.52	4.2	4.5	4.3	4.5
a) Subsidies to regular employment in the private sector	0.12	0.16	0.25	0.32	2.0	2.3	2.4	2.8
b) Support of unemployed persons starting enterprises	0.03	0.04	0.02	–	0.3	0.3	0.2	0.1
c) Direct job creation (public or non-profit)	0.18	0.21	0.22	0.20	1.9	1.8	1.7	1.5
5. Measures for the disabled	0.09	0.10	0.08	0.08	0.3	0.3	0.3	0.3
a) Vocational rehabilitation	0.03	0.03	0.02	0.02	0.3	0.3	0.3	0.3
b) Work for the disabled	0.06	0.06	0.06	0.06	..	..	..	..
6. Unemployment compensation	1.57	1.43	1.44	1.50				
7. Early retirement for labour market reasons	0.38	0.36	0.36	0.35				
TOTAL	3.24	3.09	3.16	3.22	11.5	11.1	10.5	10.1
Active measures (1-5)	1.29	1.31	1.35	1.37				
Passive measures (6 and 7)	1.95	1.79	1.80	1.85				
For reference:								
GDP (national currency, at current prices, 10⁹)	7389.7	7662.4	7871.7	8137.1				
Labour force (thousands)					25324	25329	25592	25696

Germany

Programme categories	Public expenditure as a percentage of GDP 1995	1996	1997	1998	Participant inflows as a percentage of the labour force 1995	1996	1997	1998
1. Public employment services and administration	0.23	0.24	0.21	0.23				
2. Labour market training	0.38	0.45	0.36	0.34	2.0	1.9	1.3	1.5
a) Training for unemployed adults and those at risk	0.38	0.45	0.36	0.34	1.9	1.9	1.3	1.5
b) Training for employed adults	–	–	–	–	–	–	–	–
3. Youth measures	0.06	0.07	0.07	0.07	0.6	0.7	0.7	0.9
a) Measures for unemployed and disadvantaged youth	0.05	0.06	0.06	0.06	0.4	0.4	0.4	0.6
b) Support of apprenticeship and related forms of general youth training	0.01	0.01	0.01	0.01	0.2	0.3	0.3	0.3
4. Subsidised employment	0.44	0.42	0.33	0.39	1.4	1.4	1.2	2.1
a) Subsidies to regular employment in the private sector	0.07	0.07	0.05	0.03	0.3	0.2	0.2	0.2
b) Support of unemployed persons starting enterprises	0.02	0.03	0.03	0.03	0.2	0.2	0.2	0.3
c) Direct job creation (public or non-profit)	0.34	0.32	0.26	0.32	0.9	1.0	0.8	1.6
5. Measures for the disabled	0.26	0.27	0.28	0.25	0.3	0.3	0.3	0.3
a) Vocational rehabilitation	0.13	0.14	0.13	0.10	0.3	0.3	0.3	0.3
b) Work for the disabled	0.13	0.14	0.14	0.15	–	–	–	–
6. Unemployment compensation	2.09	2.38	2.50	2.29				
7. Early retirement for labour market reasons	0.29	0.15	0.05	–				
TOTAL	3.75	3.99	3.80	3.56	4.3	4.2	3.5	4.8
Active measures (1-5)	1.37	1.45	1.25	1.27				
Passive measures (6 and 7)	2.38	2.53	2.55	2.29				
For reference:								
GDP (national currency, at current prices, 10⁹)	3442.8	3523.5	3624.0	3758.1				
Labour force (thousands)					39507	39713	39602	39501

Table H. Public expenditure and participant inflows* in labour market programmes in OECD countries (cont.)

Programme categories	Greece 1995	Greece 1996	Greece 1997	Hungary Public expenditure as % of GDP 1994	Hungary 1995	Hungary 1996	Hungary 1997	Hungary Participant inflows as % of labour force 1994	Hungary 1995	Hungary 1996	Hungary 1997	Ireland Public expenditure as % of GDP 1994	Ireland 1995	Ireland 1996	Ireland Participant inflows as % of labour force 1994	Ireland 1995	Ireland 1996	Italy Public expenditure as % of GDP 1994	Italy 1995	Italy 1996
1. Public employment services and administration	0.14	0.14	0.12	0.15	0.13	0.11	0.13	–	–	–	–	0.28	0.27	0.24	–	–	–	–	–	–
2. Labour market training	0.13	0.09	0.06	0.19	0.13	0.08	0.09	1.2	0.8	1.2	1.2	0.23	0.22	0.21	4.7	4.8	4.1	0.04	0.04	0.04
a) Training for unemployed adults and those at risk	a	a	a	0.19	0.13	0.08	0.08	1.2	0.7	1.1	1.1	0.16	0.15	0.14	1.7	1.8	1.6	0.01	0.01	0.01
b) Training for employed adults	a	a	a	–	–	–	–	0.1	0.1	0.1	0.1	0.07	0.06	0.08	3.0	2.9	2.5	–	–	–
3. Youth measures	0.10	0.10	0.10	–	–	–	–	–	–	–	–	0.27	0.25	0.24	1.4	1.4	1.3	0.01	0.01	0.01
a) Measures for unemployed and disadvantaged youth	0.03	0.03	0.02	–	–	–	–	–	–	–	–	0.13	0.11	0.11	0.8	0.7	0.7	0.46	0.39	0.42
b) Support of apprenticeship and related forms of general youth training	0.07	0.07	0.07	–	–	–	–	–	–	–	–	0.15	0.14	0.13	0.7	0.6	0.6	0.06	0.03	0.04
4. Subsidised employment	0.08	0.10	0.06	0.27	0.17	0.18	0.23	3.0	2.7	4.4	3.6	0.68	0.86	0.88	5.2	5.6	5.7	0.40	0.36	0.38
a) Subsidies to regular employment in the private sector	0.05	0.07	0.04	0.12	0.06	0.06	0.08	1.6	0.8	1.1	1.3	0.11	0.17	0.24	1.4	1.8	1.9	0.86	0.69	0.61
b) Support of unemployed persons starting enterprises	0.02	0.02	0.02	0.02	–	–	–	0.2	0.1	0.1	0.1	0.02	0.01	0.02	0.1	0.1	0.1	0.86	0.68	0.56
c) Direct job creation (public or non-profit)	–	–	–	0.14	0.11	0.12	0.15	1.2	1.9	3.2	2.2	0.55	0.67	0.63	3.6	3.8	3.7	–	0.01	0.04
5. Measures for the disabled	–	0.03	0.01	–	–	–	–	–	–	–	–	0.12	0.09	0.08	0.2	0.1	0.1	–	–	–
a) Vocational rehabilitation	–	a	a	–	–	–	–	–	–	–	–	0.12	0.09	0.08	0.2	0.1	0.1	–	–	–
b) Work for the disabled	–	a	a	–	–	–	–	–	–	–	–	–	–	–	–	–	–	–	–	–
6. Unemployment compensation	0.43	0.44	0.50	1.07	0.71	0.60	0.46	–	–	–	–	2.77	2.57	2.29	–	–	–	0.92	0.68	0.68
7. Early retirement for labour market reasons	–	–	–	0.15	0.19	0.16	0.17	–	–	–	–	0.16	0.14	0.13	–	–	–	0.20	0.19	0.20
TOTAL	0.88	0.89	0.85	1.83	1.33	1.13	1.08	4.2	3.5	5.7	4.8	4.51	4.39	4.07	11.5	11.9	11.3	2.48	2.00	1.96
Active measures (1-5)	0.45	0.44	0.35	0.61	0.43	0.37	0.45					1.58	1.68	1.66				1.36	1.13	1.08
Passive measures (6 and 7)	0.43	0.44	0.50	1.22	0.91	0.76	0.63					2.93	2.71	2.42				1.12	0.87	0.88
For reference:																				
GDP (national currency, at current prices, 10⁹)	26 883.5	29 697.7	32 752.2	4 364.8	5 561.9	6 829.9	8 462.0					36.1	40.3	44.2				1 638 666	1 771 018	1 873 494
Labour force (thousands)								4 203	4 095	4 048	3 995				1 425	1 449	1 494			

a) No breakdown available for categories 2 "Labour market training" and 5 "Measures for the disabled".

Table H. Public expenditure and participant inflows* in labour market programmes in OECD countries (cont.)

Japan[a]

Programme categories	Public expenditure as a percentage of GDP 1995-96	1996-97	1997-98
1. Public employment services and administration	0.03	0.03	0.03
2. Labour market training	0.03	0.03	0.03
a) Training for unemployed adults and those at risk	0.03	0.03	0.03
b) Training for employed adults	–	–	–
3. Youth measures	–	–	–
a) Measures for unemployed and disadvantaged youth	–	–	–
b) Support of apprenticeship and related forms of general youth training	–	–	–
4. Subsidised employment	0.06	0.04	0.02
a) Subsidies to regular employment in the private sector	0.06	0.04	0.02
b) Support of unemployed persons starting enterprises	–	–	–
c) Direct job creation (public or non-profit)	–	–	–
5. Measures for the disabled	–	–	–
a) Vocational rehabilitation	–	–	–
b) Work for the disabled	–	–	–
6. Unemployment compensation	0.39	0.40	0.43
7. Early retirement for labour market reasons	–	–	–
TOTAL	0.51	0.50	0.52
Active measures (1-5)	0.13	0.10	0.09
Passive measures (6 and 7)	0.39	0.40	0.43
For reference:			
GDP (national currency, at current prices, 10⁹)	489 350.8	504 177.5	505 105.3

Korea

	Public expenditure as a percentage of GDP				Participant inflows as a percentage of the labour force			
	1994	1995	1996	1997	1994	1995	1996	1997
1.	0.03	0.03	0.04	0.04				
2.	0.01	0.02	0.03	0.04	0.4	0.3	0.4	2.0
a)	0.01	0.01	0.01	0.01	0.3	0.3	0.3	1.0
b)	0.01	0.01	0.02	0.02	–	–	0.1	1.1
3.	0.02	0.02	0.02	0.05	0.1	0.1	0.1	0.1
a)	0.02	0.02	0.02	0.05	0.1	0.1	0.1	0.1
b)	–	–	–	–	–	–	–	–
4.	–	–	–	–	–	0.1	0.4	0.5
a)	–	–	–	–	–	0.1	0.4	0.5
b)	–	–	–	–	–	–	–	–
c)	–	–	–	–	–	–	–	–
5.	0.01	–	–	0.02	0.1	0.1	0.1	0.2
a)	0.01	–	–	0.01	0.1	0.1	0.1	0.1
b)	–	–	–	0.01	0.1	0.1	0.1	0.1
6.	–	–	–	0.02				
7.	–	–	–	–				
TOTAL	0.06	0.08	0.09	0.16	0.6	0.6	1.0	2.7
Active	0.06	0.08	0.09	0.14				
Passive	–	–	–	0.02				
GDP	305 970.2	351 974.7	389 813.5	420 986.7				
Labour force (thousands)	20 326	20 796	21 188	21 604				

Luxembourg

	Public expenditure as a percentage of GDP				Participant inflows as a percentage of the labour force	
	1994	1995	1996	1997	1996	1997
1.	0.03	0.03	0.03	0.03	0.3	0.6
2.	0.02	0.02	0.01	0.01	0.2	0.5
a)	0.01	0.02	0.01	0.01	0.1	0.1
b)	–	–	–	–	–	–
3.	0.09	0.07	0.14	0.14	..	..
a)	0.05	0.05	0.06	0.09	0.6	0.7
b)	0.04	0.02	0.07	0.05	..	..
4.	0.01	0.03	0.06	0.07	0.3	0.4
a)	0.01	0.03	0.05	0.07	0.3	0.4
b)	–	–	–	–	–	–
c)	–	–	–	–	–	–
5.	0.04	0.05	0.04	0.04	..	..
a)	0.01	–	–	–	–	–
b)	0.03	0.04	0.04	0.04	..	..
6.	0.35	0.36	0.41	0.42		
7.	0.24	0.24	0.26	0.25		
TOTAL	0.78	0.80	0.95	0.97		
Active	0.19	0.20	0.28	0.30		
Passive	0.59	0.60	0.67	0.67		
GDP	487.7	509.7	525.4	563.8		
Labour force (thousands)			226	223		

Netherlands

	Public expenditure as a percentage of GDP				Participant inflows as a percentage of the labour force			
	1995	1996	1997	1998	1995	1996	1997	1998
1.	0.37	0.41	0.40	0.40				
2.	0.40	0.35	0.35	0.22	3.0	3.0	3.0	..
a)	0.39	0.33	0.32	0.22	2.7	2.4	2.3	
b)	0.01	0.02	0.03	–	0.2	0.7	0.7	
3.	0.09	0.10	0.11	0.05	0.8	0.8	0.8	..
a)	0.06	0.07	0.06	–	0.3	0.3	0.2	
b)	–	–	–	–	–	–	–	–
4.	0.02	0.04	0.04	0.05	0.5	0.5	0.5	
a)	0.10	0.15	0.26	0.50	0.4	1.3	1.8	..
b)	0.02	0.02	0.06	0.08	0.2	1.0	1.5	
c)	–	–	–	–	–	–	–	–
5.	0.08	0.12	0.20	0.42	0.2	0.2	0.2	0.3
a)	0.55	0.54	0.53	0.58	0.1	0.2	0.2	0.9
b)	0.55	0.54	0.53	0.58	0.1	0.2	0.2	0.9
6.	3.21	4.17	3.63	3.14				
7.	–	–	–	–				
TOTAL	4.72	5.72	5.28	4.90	4.3	5.3	5.8	..
Active	1.51	1.55	1.65	1.76				
Passive	3.21	4.17	3.63	3.14				
GDP	639.7	669.4	709.0	747.6				
Labour force (thousands)					7 410	7 517	7 673	7 784

a) Fiscal years starting on April 1.

250 – OECD Employment Outlook

Table H. Public expenditure and participant inflows* in labour market programmes in OECD countries (cont.)

New Zealand[a]

Programme categories	Public expenditure as a percentage of GDP				Participant inflows as a percentage of the labour force			
	1994-95	1995-96	1996-97	1997-98	1994-95	1995-96	1996-97	1997-98
1. Public employment services and administration	0.11	0.13	0.15	0.15	..	..	..	..
2. Labour market training	0.36	0.32	0.31	0.32	5.5	5.5	5.2	..
a) Training for unemployed adults and those at risk	0.36	0.32	0.31	0.32	5.5	5.5	5.2	..
b) Training for employed adults	–	–	–	–	–	–	–	–
3. Youth measures	0.08	0.09	0.10	0.08	..	2.0	1.9	2.6
a) Measures for unemployed and disadvantaged youth	0.01	0.02	0.02	0.01	0.2	0.2	0.1	0.1
b) Support of apprenticeship and related forms of general youth training	0.07	0.07	0.08	0.07	..	1.8	1.8	2.4
4. Subsidised employment	0.15	0.14	0.14	0.15	2.5	2.2	2.2	..
a) Subsidies to regular employment in the private sector	0.10	0.09	0.09	0.09	1.5	1.3	1.2	..
b) Support of unemployed persons starting enterprises	0.02	0.01	0.02	0.01	–	–	–	–
c) Direct job creation (public or non-profit)	0.04	0.03	0.04	0.04	0.9	0.9	0.9	..
5. Measures for the disabled	0.03	0.03	0.03	0.03	..	0.7	..	0.7
a) Vocational rehabilitation	0.01	0.01	0.02	0.02	..	0.7	..	0.4
b) Work for the disabled	0.01	0.01	0.02	0.02	–	–	–	0.3
6. Unemployment compensation	1.26	1.14	1.17	1.47	..	..	..	..
7. Early retirement for labour market reasons	–	–	–	–	–	–	–	–
TOTAL	2.00	1.85	1.91	2.20	..	..	..	..
Active measures (1-5)	0.74	0.71	0.73	0.74	..	10.4	..	..
Passive measures (6 and 7)	1.26	1.14	1.17	1.47	..	..	..	..
For reference:								
GDP (national currency, at current prices, 10⁹)	88.2	92.3	95.9	98.1				
Labour force (thousands)					1 728	1 782	1 839	1 873

Norway

Programme categories	Public expenditure as a percentage of GDP				Participant inflows as a percentage of the labour force			
	1995	1996	1997	1998	1995	1996	1997	1998
1. Public employment services and administration	0.18	0.16	0.16	0.16	..	..	..	..
2. Labour market training	0.23	0.18	0.13	0.10	2.8	2.1	1.6	1.3
a) Training for unemployed adults and those at risk	0.23	0.18	0.13	0.10	2.8	2.1	1.6	1.3
b) Training for employed adults	–	–	–	–	–	–	–	–
3. Youth measures	0.08	0.06	0.04	0.02	..	1.1	0.8	0.5
a) Measures for unemployed and disadvantaged youth	0.08	0.06	0.04	0.02	..	1.1	0.8	0.5
b) Support of apprenticeship and related forms of general youth training	–	–	–	–	–	–	–	–
4. Subsidised employment	0.22	0.16	0.07	0.04	..	1.0	0.5	0.4
a) Subsidies to regular employment in the private sector	0.08	0.06	0.04	0.03	..	0.3	0.3	0.3
b) Support of unemployed persons starting enterprises	0.01	0.01	0.01	–	–	0.4	0.1	0.1
c) Direct job creation (public or non-profit)	0.13	0.09	0.02	–	..	0.2	0.1	–
5. Measures for the disabled	0.63	0.60	0.57	0.59	..	..	..	1.8
a) Vocational rehabilitation	0.39	0.37	0.36	0.39	..	..	..	1.2
b) Work for the disabled	0.25	0.24	0.22	0.21	..	..	..	0.6
6. Unemployment compensation	1.10	0.90	0.70	0.49	..	..	..	..
7. Early retirement for labour market reasons	–	–	–	–	–	–	–	–
TOTAL	2.44	2.06	1.67	1.41	..	..	..	4.0
Active measures (1-5)	1.34	1.16	0.98	0.91				
Passive measures (6 and 7)	1.10	0.90	0.70	0.49				
GDP (national currency, at current prices, 10⁹)	928.7	1 020.1	1 084.8	1 100.8				
Labour force (thousands)					2 186	2 246	2 295	2 328

Poland

Programme categories	Public expenditure as a percentage of GDP			Participant inflows as a percentage of the labour force		
	1994	1995	1996	1994	1995	1996
1. Public employment services and administration	0.01	0.01	0.02	..	..	..
2. Labour market training	0.03	0.02	0.02	0.5	0.5	0.5
a) Training for unemployed adults and those at risk	0.03	0.02	0.02	0.5	0.5	0.5
b) Training for employed adults	–	–	–	–	–	–
3. Youth measures	0.07	0.08	0.10	1.5	1.9	1.9
a) Measures for unemployed and disadvantaged youth	0.01	0.02	0.03	–	0.1	0.2
b) Support of apprenticeship and related forms of general youth training	0.06	0.06	0.06	1.5	1.7	1.7
4. Subsidised employment	0.24	0.21	0.16	1.8	2.0	1.6
a) Subsidies to regular employment in the private sector	0.13	0.12	0.08	1.2	1.2	0.8
b) Support of unemployed persons starting enterprises	0.02	0.02	0.02	–	–	–
c) Direct job creation (public or non-profit)	0.10	0.08	0.07	0.6	0.7	0.7
5. Measures for the disabled	0.04	0.01	0.01	0.8	0.1	0.1
a) Vocational rehabilitation	0.01	–	–	0.3	–	–
b) Work for the disabled	0.04	0.01	0.01	0.4	0.1	0.1
6. Unemployment compensation	1.77	1.88	1.77	..	..	..
7. Early retirement for labour market reasons	0.10	0.05	0.05			
TOTAL	2.27	2.27	2.14	4.7	4.4	4.1
Active measures (1-5)	0.39	0.34	0.32			
Passive measures (6 and 7)	1.87	1.93	1.82			
GDP (national currency, at current prices, 10⁹)	210.4	286.0	362.2			
Labour force (thousands)				17 132	17 068	17 034

a) Fiscal years starting on July 1.

Table H. Public expenditure and participant inflows* in labour market programmes in OECD countries (cont.)

Portugal

Programme categories	Public expenditure as a percentage of GDP				Participant inflows as a percentage of the labour force			
	1994	1995	1996	1997	1994	1995	1996	1997
1. Public employment services and administration	0.11	0.10	0.11	0.11				
2. Labour market training	0.20	0.23	0.29	0.28	2.0	5.3	6.1	7.1
a) Training for unemployed adults and those at risk	0.05	0.05	0.05	0.08	0.4	0.2	0.3	0.6
b) Training for employed adults	0.15	0.19	0.24	0.20	1.5	5.1	5.7	6.5
3. Youth measures	0.27	0.34	0.31	..	2.0	2.0	2.6	..
a) Measures for unemployed and disadvantaged youth	0.14	0.16	0.15	..	1.1	1.1	1.3	..
b) Support of apprenticeship and related forms of general youth training	0.13	0.18	0.16	0.16	0.9	0.9	1.4	1.4
4. Subsidised employment	0.05	0.08	0.11	0.09	0.6	0.9	1.2	1.0
a) Subsidies to regular employment in the private sector	–	0.03	0.07	0.01	–	0.1	0.4	–
b) Support of unemployed persons starting enterprises	0.03	0.03	0.01	0.02	0.2	0.2	0.1	0.1
c) Direct job creation (public or non-profit)	0.01	0.03	0.03	0.06	0.5	0.6	0.7	0.8
5. Measures for the disabled	0.05	0.05	0.05	0.03	0.1	0.2	0.2	0.1
a) Vocational rehabilitation	0.04	0.04	0.04	0.02	0.1	0.1	0.1	0.1
b) Work for the disabled	0.01	0.01	0.01	0.01	–	0.1	–	–
6. Unemployment compensation	0.93	0.84	0.79	0.72				
7. Early retirement for labour market reasons	0.15	0.09	0.12	0.15				
TOTAL	**1.76**	**1.73**	**1.77**	..				
Active measures (1-5)	0.68	0.80	0.87	..	4.7	8.3	10.0	..
Passive measures (6 and 7)	1.08	0.93	0.91	0.87				

For reference:
GDP (national currency, at current prices, 10⁹): 14 628.8 15 817.7 16 785.3 17 756.8
Labour force (thousands): 4 820 4 802 4 887 4 967

Spain

	Public expenditure as a percentage of GDP				Participant inflows as a percentage of the labour force			
	1995	1996	1997	1998	1995	1996	1997	1998
1.	0.09	0.09	0.08	0.07				
2.	0.32	0.35	0.19	0.21	0.8	0.8	0.8	0.8
a)	0.24	0.26	0.11	0.10	0.5	0.5	0.6	0.5
b)	0.08	0.09	0.08	0.11	0.3	0.3	0.3	0.3
3.	0.09	0.08	0.07	0.07	0.1	0.1	1.9	4.1
a)	0.09	0.08	0.07	0.07	0.1	0.1	0.1	0.1
b)	–	–	–	–	–	–	1.8	3.9
4.	0.33	0.16	0.20	0.35	1.2	1.5	1.5	1.7
a)	0.24	0.08	0.11	0.24	–	–	–	–
b)	0.03	0.03	0.03	0.03	0.1	0.1	0.2	0.2
c)	0.05	0.05	0.06	0.07	1.0	1.3	1.3	1.4
5.	0.01	0.01	0.02	0.02	0.1	0.1	0.1	0.2
a)	–	–	–	–	–	–	–	–
b)	0.01	0.01	0.02	0.02	0.1	0.1	0.1	0.2
6.	2.41	2.11	1.88	1.64				
7.	a	a	a	a				
TOTAL	**3.25**	**2.79**	**2.43**	**2.36**				
Active (1-5)	0.84	0.69	0.56	0.72	2.2	2.5	4.4	6.7
Passive (6 and 7)	2.41	2.11	1.88	1.64				

GDP: 69 780.1 73 743.3 77 896.6 82 650.3
Labour force: 15 849 16 159 16 334 16 480

Sweden[b]

	Public expenditure as a percentage of GDP				Participant inflows as a percentage of the labour force			
	1994-95	1995-96	1997	1998	1994-95	1995-96	1997	1998
1.	0.27	0.26	0.30	0.30				
2.	0.77	0.55	0.43	0.48	4.4	4.6	4.2	4.7
a)	0.75	0.54	0.43	0.47	3.7	3.9	3.7	4.0
b)	0.02	0.02	0.01	0.01	0.7	0.6	0.5	0.6
3.	0.23	0.02	0.02	0.03	2.5	0.7	0.7	0.9
a)	0.23	0.02	0.02	0.03	2.5	0.7	0.7	0.9
b)	–	–	–	–	–	–	–	–
4.	0.90	0.82	0.70	0.58	6.1	7.7	7.5	5.4
a)	0.27	0.32	0.20	0.15	2.1	3.6	3.2	2.3
b)	0.09	0.07	0.08	0.09	0.5	0.4	0.5	0.4
c)	0.54	0.43	0.42	0.35	3.6	3.6	3.8	2.7
5.	0.82	0.70	0.62	0.62	1.4	0.9	1.0	1.1
a)	0.10	0.08	0.04	0.04	0.8	0.6	0.6	0.7
b)	0.72	0.62	0.59	0.58	0.6	0.3	0.4	0.5
6.	2.51	2.26	2.16	1.91				
7.	0.02	–	–	–				
TOTAL	**5.52**	**4.62**	**4.25**	**3.93**	14.4	13.8	13.4	12.1
Active (1-5)	2.99	2.36	2.09	2.01				
Passive (6 and 7)	2.53	2.26	2.16	1.91				

GDP: 1 592.9 2 517.4 1 738.9 1 803.7
Labour force: 4 296 4 325 4 264 4 256

Data for category 7 "Early retirement for labour market reasons" are included in category 6 "Unemployment compensation".

a) Data for category 7 "Early retirement for labour market reasons" are included in category 6 "Unemployment compensation".
b) Before 1995-96, fiscal years starting on July 1. From 1997, calendar years. 1995-96 includes 18 months, from July 1, 1995 to December 31, 1996.

Table H. Public expenditure and participant inflows* in labour market programmes in OECD countries

Programme categories	Switzerland Public expenditure as a percentage of GDP 1995	1996	1997	1998	Switzerland Public expenditure as a percentage of GDP 1994-95	1995-96	1996-97	1997-98	United Kingdom[a] Public expenditure as a percentage of GDP 1994-95	1995-96	1996-97	1997-98	United Kingdom[a] Participant inflows as a percentage of the labour force 1994-95	1995-96	1996-97	1997-98	United States[b] Public expenditure as a percentage of GDP 1994-95	1995-96	1996-97	1997-98	United States[b] Participant inflows as a percentage of the labour force 1995-96	1996-97	1997-98
1. Public employment services and administration	0.11	0.12	0.15	0.14	0.21	0.19	0.18	0.16									0.07	0.08	0.06	0.06			
2. Labour market training	0.09	0.06	0.23	0.19	0.14	0.10	0.09	0.07	1.3	1.0	1.0	0.9					0.04	0.04	0.04	0.04	0.7	0.8	0.8
a) Training for unemployed adults and those at risk	0.08	0.06	0.23	0.19	0.12	0.09	0.08	0.06	1.2	0.9	0.9	0.8					0.04	0.04	0.04	0.04	0.7	0.8	0.8
b) Training for employed adults	–	–	–	–	0.01	0.01	0.01	0.01	0.1	–	–	–					–	–	–	–	–	–	–
3. Youth measures	–	–	–	0.01	0.13	0.12	0.12	0.12	0.9	1.0	1.2	1.0					0.03	0.03	0.03	0.03	..	0.6	0.6
a) Measures for unemployed and disadvantaged youth	–	–	–	0.01	–	–	–	–	–	–	–	–					0.03	0.03	0.03	0.03	0.4	0.5	0.5
b) Support of apprenticeship and related forms of general youth training	–	–	–	–	0.13	0.12	0.12	0.12	0.8	1.0	1.1	1.0					–	–	–	–	..	..	..
4. Subsidised employment	0.09	0.16	0.23	0.21	0.03	0.02	–	–	0.3	0.1	–	–					0.01	0.01	0.01	0.01	..	..	..
a) Subsidies to regular employment in the private sector	0.01	0.01	0.01	0.01	–	–	–	–	–	–	–	–					0.01	–	–	–	–	–	–
b) Support of unemployed persons starting enterprises	–	–	–	0.01	0.01	0.01	–	–	0.1	–	–	–					–	–	–	–	–	–	–
c) Direct job creation (public or non-profit)	0.08	0.16	0.22	0.19	0.01	0.01	–	–	0.2	0.1	–	–					0.01	–	0.01	0.01	0.1	0.1	0.1
5. Measures for the disabled	0.20	0.20	0.15	0.15	0.03	0.03	0.02	0.02	0.2	0.2	0.2	0.2					0.04	0.04	0.03	0.04	..	..	..
a) Vocational rehabilitation	0.15	0.15	0.15	0.15	–	–	–	–	0.1	0.1	0.1	0.1					0.04	0.04	0.03	0.04	..	..	..
b) Work for the disabled	0.05	0.05	–	–	0.02	0.02	0.02	0.02	0.1	0.1	0.1	0.1					–	–	–	–	–	–	–
6. Unemployment compensation	1.15	1.27	1.41	1.07	1.39	1.24	1.03	0.82	–	–	–	–					0.35	0.34	0.26	0.25	–	–	–
7. Early retirement for labour market reasons	–	–	–	–	–	–	–	–	–	–	–	–					–	–	–	–	–	–	–
TOTAL	1.63	1.82	2.16	1.77	1.93	1.70	1.44	1.19	2.6	2.3	2.3	2.1					0.55	0.53	0.43	0.43			
Active measures (1-5)	0.48	0.54	0.76	0.70	0.53	0.45	0.41	0.37									0.20	0.19	0.17	0.18			
Passive measures (6 and 7)	1.15	1.27	1.41	1.07	1.39	1.24	1.03	0.82									0.35	0.34	0.26	0.25			

For reference:
GDP (national currency, at current prices, 10⁹): 363.5 364.8 370.5 382.3 670.3 706.4 747.6 793.6 | 7 195.6 7 555.0 8 001.9 8 404.3
Labour force (thousands): 27 416 27 352 27 475 27 593 | 134 652 137 075 138 725

* Data on annual inflows of participants have been collected only for categories 2 "Labour market training", 3 "Youth measures", 4 "Subsidised employment" and 5 "Measures for the disabled". The programmes have been classified into standardized categories and sub-categories. For their definitions, see OECD (1992), *Employment Outlook*, Paris. The total shown in the table must be interpreted with caution.
a) Excluding Northern Ireland. Fiscal years starting on April 1.
b) Fiscal years starting on October 1.

Source: OECD Database on labour market programmes. The data are compiled each year by the OECD on the basis of submissions from Member countries.

Labour market and social policy occasional papers

Already available, free of charge

Most recent releases are:

No. 25   MAKING THE PUBLIC EMPLOYMENT SERVICE MORE EFFECTIVE THROUGH THE INTRODUCTION OF MARKET SIGNALS (1997) Robert G. Fay

No. 26   THE CONCENTRATION OF WOMEN'S EMPLOYMENT AND RELATIVE OCCUPATIONAL PAY: A STATISTICAL FRAMEWORK FOR COMPARATIVE ANALYSIS (1997) Damian Grimshaw and Jill Rubery

No. 27   CHILDCARE AND ELDERLY CARE: WHAT OCCUPATIONAL OPPORTUNITIES FOR WOMEN? (1997) Susan Christopherson

No. 28   OECD SUBMISSION TO THE IRISH NATIONAL MINIMUM WAGE COMMISSION (1997)

No. 29   OECD SUBMISSION TO THE UK LOW PAY MISSION (1997)

No. 30   PRIVATE PENSIONS IN OECD COUNTRIES - FRANCE (1997) Emmanuel Reynaud *Available in French*

No. 31   KEY EMPLOYMENT POLICY CHALLENGES FACED BY OECD COUNTRIES (1998) OECD Submission to the G8 Growth, Employability and Inclusion Conference - London, 21-22 February 1998

No. 32   THE GROWING ROLE OF PRIVATE SOCIAL BENEFITS (1998) Willem Adema and Marcel Einerhand

No. 33   SOCIAL AND HEALTH POLICIES IN OECD COUNTRIES: A SURVEY OF CURRENT PROGRAMMES AND RECENT DEVELOPMENTS [text and Annex] (1998) D.W. Kalisch, T. Aman and L. A. Buchele *Available in French*

No. 34   MEASURES OF JOB SATISFACTION - WHAT MAKES A GOOD JOB? EVIDENCE FROM OECD COUNTRIES (1998) Andrew E. Clark *Available in French*

No. 35   WHAT WORKS AMONG ACTIVE LABOUR MARKET POLICIES: EVIDENCE FROM OECD COUNTRIES' EXPERIENCES (1998) John Martin

No. 36   HEALTH OUTCOMES IN OECD COUNTRIES: A FRAMEWORK OF HEALTH INDICATORS FOR OUTCOME-ORIENTED POLICYMAKING (1998) Melissa Jee and Zeynep Or

No. 37   THE HEALTH OF OLDER PERSONS IN OECD COUNTRIES: IS IT IMPROVING FAST ENOUGH TO COMPENSATE FOR POPULATION AGEING? (1998) S. Jacobzone, E. Cambois, E. Chaplain, J.M. Robine

No. 38   AGEING AND CARE FOR FRAIL ELDERLY PERSONS (1999) S. Jacobzone

Mailing List of Labour Market and Social Policy Occasional Papers

Please include the following name on the mailing list:
(write in capitals)

Name . . . .

Organisation . . . .

Address . . . .

Country . . . .

This form should be returned to:
    Labour Market and Social Policy Occasional Papers
    Directorate for Education, Employment, Labour and Social Affairs, Office 110
    OECD, 2 rue André Pascal, 75775 Paris Cedex 16, France

Information also available on Internet: http://www.oecd.org/els/papers/papers.htm

OCDE

Also available

The Public Employment Service in the United States (1999)
(81 19 99 021 P 1) ISBN 92-64-17011-1   FF 200   US$ 36   DM 60

Flexible Working Time: Collective Bargaining and Government Intervention (1995)
(81 19 95 011 P 1) ISBN 92-64-14316-5   FF 195   US$ 38   DM 59

Literacy Skills for the Knowledge Society: Further results from the International Adult Literacy survey (1997)
(81 19 97 071 P 1) ISBN 92-64-15624-0   FF 180   US$ 30   DM 53

Labour Market Policies: New Challenges Policies for Low-Paid Workers and Unskilled Job Seekers (1997)
General distribution document   Free of charge

The Battle Against Exclusion, Social assistance in Belgium, the Czech Republic, the Netherlands and Norway (1998)
(81 19 98 131 P 1) ISBN 92-64-16192-9   FF140   US$ 23   DM 42

Co-ordinating Services for Children and Youth at Risk: A World View (1998)
(96 19 98 011 E 1) ISBN 92-64-16319-0   FF 280   US$ 47   DM 83

Prices charged at the OECD Bookshop.
For further information, please consult the OECD online bookshop at: www.oecd.org.